LET ME SAY IT NOW

Rakesh Maria is one of the most distinguished police officers of our times. A recipient of the Police Medal for Meritorious Service in 1994 and the President's Medal for Distinguished Service in 2007, he held several important posts.

In his thirty-six long years in the Indian Police Service, he is credited with having built and led several Mumbai police teams which solved some of the most high-profile cases—the Mumbai serial blasts of 1993, the Indian Mujahideen module in 2008, the 26/11 terrorist attack on Mumbai, and the sensational Sheena Bora murder case which was brought to light when he was Commissioner of Police.

An avid sportsman, Maria enjoyed nothing better than a game of basketball with his constables and officers. He is also a taekwondo exponent, has an ear for music and is a voracious reader.

Rakesh Maria lives in Mumbai with his wife, Preeti, and has two sons, Kunal and Krish.

RAKESH MARIA

LET ME SAY IT NOW

WESTLAND
NON-FICTION

WESTLAND
NON·FICTION

First published by Westland Publications Private Limited in 2020

Published by Westland Non-Fiction, an imprint of Westland Books, a division of Nasadiya Technologies Private Limited, in 2022

No. 269/2B, First Floor, 'Irai Arul', Vimalraj Street, Nethaji Nagar, Allappakkam Main Road, Maduravoyal, Chennai 600095

ISBN: 9789395767200

10 9 8 7 6 5 4 3 2

Typeset by Ram Das Lal, New Delhi, NCR
Printed at Nutech Print Services Pvt. Ltd

Acknowledgements

Living an experience is easier than recreating it on paper years later for others to feel it. If I have succeeded in doing so even in a small measure, the credit goes to two people – my sister, Poonam Maria and a dear family friend, Kirti Samant Gupte.

The former being my sister, thanking her is just not done, for in true Indian tradition it would amount to an insult. However, I must note that I am indebted to Poonam for not missing a single of the innumerable sessions that went into the task, where she played the part of the much-needed sounding board. Combining her skills as an advocate and a ruthlessly doting sister, she put her heart and soul in seeing this book through. It was also Poonam who suggested that Kirti be taken on board for this project.

The latter, as Poonam's colleague and bestie, has had a ringside view of our family for the past three decades. Kirti brought with her an approach which was totally uncontrived and dispassionate. Brought up in a pure Marathi ethos and yet steeped in the generous Maharashtrian cosmopolitan culture of Mumbai, her versatility in Marathi, Hindi and even Gujarati made her keep me rooted in Mumbai's culture and reality which is the matrix of our police force. Moreover, as my contemporary, she has had first-hand experience of the period the book covers. And having worked as a junior to her father (the late Shamrao Samant, an eminent defence lawyer and a famous prosecutor the State relied on for conducting sensational cases of his times), she could easily relate to a police officer's life and predicament. It was the patient and insightful probing and interviewing by Poonam and Kirti that brought out the nuances that otherwise would have been lost. All those bits and pieces about my parents and my school for instance, would not have seen the light of day, had it not been for their insistence that without them my memoir would be incomplete. Long forgotten days appeared on the hazy canvas with surprising accuracy and when we came to the stressful and unpleasant bits, Kirti's humorous quips and banter with Poonam helped me see the lighter side and put things in perspective.

I cannot thank Kirti and Poonam enough for joining me on this cathartic journey and making it enjoyable too as we went along.

Nutan Bhurke and Nicholas D'Souza were my other unfailing support systems. They patiently bore with my lack of computer skills and old-fashioned ways of correcting drafts. I am grateful to both of them for the innumerable corrections they carried out and the printouts they took.

I must also thank Janardhan Naik, my batman who has worked with me for nearly two and a half decades. It is he who has meticulously maintained and filed my personal diaries, press cuttings, crime reports and records, case files, court case papers and judgements. The monumental task of filing, cataloguing and indexing these voluminous records for future reference would have simply not been possible but for his yeoman efforts.

Deeksha, my daughter-in-law, read the manuscript and I found her feedback most useful, coming as it did from a forthright youngster with no police background. As a late entrant into the Maria family, she had no preconceived notions and was unreservedly frank with her opinion.

And of course, words fail me when I come to my staunchest supports – my wife Preeti, and my sons, Kunal and Krish. Preeti's support and her endless love and admiration are the ingredients which have contributed and shaped my career immensely. She recognised my imperfections and stoically bore my mood swings and conniption fits. Life was always full of challenges. At every step one was expected to face failure as well as success; heartache as well as joy. On those dark and dreary days (of which there were many), the thought that there is somebody who is waiting for you at home with warm cuddles and the sweetest smile in the world acted as a therapeutic cure to all the maladies that life threw at you. It was Preeti's positive attitude, sense of humour and the ability to see the silver lining behind every dark cloud that helped me tide through crises. She kindled in me the feeling to look at life in a happier and positive way. A good wife is a man's most precious treasure. Preeti has been this and much more. She is the soul of the house, of the family, of the home. Preeti has been the backbone of the family providing us with nurturing care, love and oodles of happiness. To me she is like a lighthouse – shining a light across the dark sea, guiding me to become better; she is also the rock which keeps me steady and strong when the times are rough.

My sons, Kunal and Krish have been my pride and joy. There is a phrase about your kids' childhood – 'Don't blink. It goes by so fast!' In my case, the career took almost all my time and there was hardly any left to devote to or think about Preeti and the boys. Consequently, I missed the joy and euphoria of Kunal and Krish's transition from toddlers to adolescence to adulthood. In time which was less than the blinking of an eyelid, the fledglings were ready to fly. This is the price one pays in a uniformed service especially a time-consuming one like the police. Kunal and Krish have made me stronger by sharing their unconditional love, affection and admiration. They raise my spirits by sharing their cheerfulness and uninhibited laughter. They inspired me to make good choices, because I always think of what would make them happy and proud of me. The aim and goal to keep their world safe and be there to see them blossom and grow in their own unique ways was (and still is) the best feeling in the world. It is this feeling which has made me complete. Kunal and Krish still show me a reason to smile every day of my life. Their positivity and words of cheer are infectious. I feel blessed to have them in my life.

I must record my appreciation for the sincere and painstaking efforts by my editor Sudha Sadhanand and her team at Westland Publications. They were most patient with my style which they must have found a little old-fashioned and stiff. Yet they let me have my way or else I would not have been able to call this book my own. It was Sudha who steered the communication, exchanging drafts after drafts and seeking clarifications, and I cannot thank her enough for bridging the gap between me and her team.

A career in public service cannot be built individually. My seniors, constables and officers of the police force and hundreds of citizens from different walks of life have been instrumental in shaping whatever little success I have achieved. I salute their silent contribution which helped me reach a stage where I could even consider writing a memoir.

Contents

1

The Unkindest Cut

'Hearty Congratulations! Government has promoted you to the rank of DG with immediate effect and has posted you as DG HG Regards Bakshi.'

A text message had just popped up on the screen of my phone. It was 11:35 a.m. on 8 September 2015 and I was, or rather I thought I was, Commissioner of Police of Mumbai, this great city where I was born and brought up and so proud to belong to. This city of dreams that had given me so much and I was so happy and privileged to be of unconditional service to her.

I had several tasks on hand that day, or so I had thought. The most immediate was the meeting for the Ganapati festival bandobast scheduled at 2:30 in the afternoon in the North Region Office at Kandivali. The festival was to commence on 17 September and as usual, it was a huge challenge for my men. More than two lakh idols were expected to be immersed at the several beaches dotting our coastline and embracing enthusiastically within their arms, the city that never sleeps. Lakhs of devotees were to participate in the processions and queue up to bow down before the Lord so joyously welcomed and emplaced at pandals erected all over the city. All soft targets for terror attacks, needing our utmost vigilance. A constant laborious effort was being made to secure CCTV surveillance for all the major procession routes, complemented by drone cameras and special control rooms. Under the shadow of the recent hanging of the 1993 blast convict Yakub Memon and with the looming shadow of the punishment to be announced for the twelve convicts in the 2006 train blasts by the special Maharashtra Control of Organised Crime Act (MCOCA) court, an additional uncompromised degree of caution had to be exercised.

And here I was, reading my transfer order from no less an officer than the Additional Chief Secretary (ACS) of the Home department of the Government of Maharashtra, telling me that I had been promoted with immediate effect to the post of Director General of Home Guards!

To say that I was shocked would be an understatement. Gathering my wits, I immediately called the sender of the 'hearty congratulations' for further details. He told me that I was to hand over charge to Ahmed Javed immediately. Almost immediately, I got a call from Ahmed Javed. He said that he had in his hands written orders of his posting as Commissioner of Police, Mumbai. When should he come over to take charge? He asked. To that, I had no hesitation but to request him to give me an hour to pack my personal effects and bid goodbye to my office staff.

Ahmed Javed came to the CP's office around half past one and I handed over the charge to him with the media present in full strength to capture the moment.

Coming down the magnificent wooden staircase, its walls lined with portraits of stalwarts who had once adorned the prestigious and one of the most coveted offices that I had just vacated, I got a sense that they understood my feelings. Had I left this building just three weeks hence, on 30 September 2015, when my term as Commissioner of Police, Mumbai was to end, not much would have been lost, except that I would have been the beneficiary of the traditional farewell at the Naigaon Police Ground. My men, my well-wishers and friends would have made it a point to make the day memorable for me and my family. A day cemented into the labyrinth of memories carried forward by my family and I. Seldom expressed, but these 'trivial' things as one may perceive them to be, have an immeasurable bearing on the heart and soul of a man who has unquestionably and unwaveringly given his blood, sweat and tears to his work and who had settled for nothing less than giving all that was he was capable of giving, to the only job that he ever wanted and wished for.

And I would have been completely at peace with going out on 30 September. I wanted no extension. My still able shoulders wanted no big responsibilities thereafter. As a matter of fact, I had made a request to the Principal Secretary to the Chief Minister and to the Additional Chief Secretary (Home), that on completion of my term, I should be given a quieter non-executive posting. The rationale underlying this request was the wedding of my son, Kunal, which we had deliberately scheduled in November so that this one red-letter occasion in my life should not be scuttled by emergency duties.

It was another matter that I only got four days of leave for my own marriage. Back then I was, and, to this date I still am, in complete awe of the Service I had joined and nothing ever seemed to be even remotely as important as my uniform and the oath I had taken. This was different. I was creating happiness for my eldest child who had always let my work take precedence over all his needs. He had borne with courage and innocence all the ups and downs that he had to go through due to my work, including a terrorist threat to his own life as a schoolboy. He deserved nothing but uninterrupted happiness for this celebration. So when both the senior bureaucrats assured me that they would definitely consider my request, I was truly happy and prepared for my term ending on 30 September. Had they told me even a few days in advance that they were planning to kick me upstairs on this day, for whatever reasons, I would have understood it. Or at the least, would have made a bona fide effort to.

My car was waiting outside. My mind swimming in a sea of thoughts and emotions, I immediately proceeded to Kala Ghoda, to the office of the Director General, Home Guards and Civil Defence which was my new charge. It was whilst driving out of the familiar compound that a strange calm descended over me as I realised what an exciting journey it had been, despite this unkindest cut of all!

An ordinary boy from Bandra, a son of a Punjabi musician and a Pahadi housewife, from a family that had no links with the power-wielders or the elite of the city or the state, had not only dared to dream an unfathomable dream, but had also chased his dream of becoming a cop. Not only did he make it, but he had also reached one of the most coveted offices in the police hierarchy. Was it not a triumph of Indian democracy? A triumph of the inclusive and cosmopolitan spirit of Bombay, as we called her then, and of this great state of Maharashtra? Was it not a triumph of merit and a triumph of all those people who had recognised merit and given it a chance to prove itself? And most of all, was it not a great achievement for the simple and god-fearing couple who had brought up that boy in their crowded home in suburban Bombay, with other siblings, amidst love and warmth that was to last them forever?

Amidst the never-ending cacophony of phones ringing, the media frenzy and the formalities of taking charge of the new office, a film opened to a packed audience in the subconscious theatre of my mind, like a First Day, First Show, in Mumbai.

2

The Little World on St. Paul's Road

Home is always the leafy suburb that old Bandra was. We lived on the ground floor of Winnie Cottage, a quaint cottage on St. Paul's Road, the narrow lane connecting Hill Road with Perry Road in a predominantly Catholic neighbourhood. Our world was Dad, Mama, we the brood of siblings, our neighbours and Dad's Brobdingnagian circle of friends. Neighbours and friends could drop in at any time of the day in that small house with no questions asked. No one felt inconvenienced because there was no concept of privacy and personal space. Mama was shy and reserved, but Dad was a people's person and kept an open house. It was full of warmth and all the mad fun a growing group of children can create, supervised by a loving disciplinarian mother and an equally affectionate father who did not believe in disciplining anyone.

Behind us was the Chimbai village, a small fishing hamlet where everyone knew everyone else. It stretched from St. Andrew's Church to Carter Road and had a small sandy beach. The smell of drying fish did not bother you, once you got used to it. Beyond Chimbai roared the vast Arabian Sea, taken for granted like so many good things you do at that age, including your parents. You feel they will last forever and ever, unless it ends unexpectedly, as it happened with us when Dad died in 1983. He was just fifty-eight and Mama around forty-eight. Many things remained to be said and shared, including all those seemingly unimportant details about his childhood and growing up in Amritsar and Lahore, especially about his choice of a career in Hindi films and how he was drawn to Bombay for it.

I am speaking of the '50s when the Hindi film industry was not yet called 'Bollywood'. It had settled comfortably in its 'Golden Age', making not just good commercial films – mostly romantic musicals – but also 'Art' films which handled sensitive themes with considerable finesse. In the process, it produced some gems even in terms of the talent that went into their making. A heady mix of men and women, some in relentless pursuit of their creative dreams, some thrown by fate to eke out a living, some recklessly adventurous, passionate and dreaming, all struggling against insurmountable odds to be in control of their real destinies in a reel world full of charmed uncertainty.

They came to Bombay from different parts of the country, from towns and cities that had developed as cultural hubs in the pre-Partition era. Bombay, Calcutta and Lahore were major centres, producing films in local languages as well as Hindustani – the amalgamation of Hindi and Urdu. It was during this epoch that Bombay emerged as the most prominent centre for Hindustani films. It got closely linked with the Lahore film industry and attracted aspiring actors, musicians, singers and writers from Punjab. Some brilliant talent from the region, like K.L. Saigal, Prithviraj Kapoor and Kidar Sharma, first made their name in Calcutta and then migrated to Bombay. Soon even filmmakers and actors from the Bengali film world made it to Bombay. The arduously challenging, yet generous nature of this cosmopolitan city made it easy for the newcomers to make themselves at home. They became so one with her that they never looked back. Their success stories drew other young artists from their home regions to the City of Dreams.

Dad was one of them. Born and brought up in Amritsar, he

had attended the Hindu College in Lahore. He was the only son and had a sister. Their father worked in the Railways and the family was quite well off, with a bungalow on Lawrence Road in Amritsar, in the vicinity of 'Ghadiwali Kothi', as we were told.

Dad was tall, handsome, loved to dress well and had a command over English, Hindi and Urdu. He was not just well-read, he was quite versatile. He was passionate about music, had a beautiful voice and a flair for acting. He used to sing on the All India Radio (AIR) before coming to Bombay in his Twenties. This was in 1951 when music director Roshan, a fellow Punjabi, Roshan Nagrath – was making a mark for himself in Hindi cinema. Born in Gujranwala in Punjab, now part of Pakistan, Roshan was a trained classical musician and worked in the All India Radio in Delhi as a staff artist. He got a break when the great Kidar Sharma, who had a penchant for spotting talent, appointed him music director in his film *Neki Aur Badi* in 1949. The film was a commercial flop, but Kidar Sharma had such faith in Roshan's abilities that against the advice of his distributors, he retained Roshan to compose the music of his next film *Bawre Nain* (1950). His assessment proved right. The songs (penned by Kidar Sharma himself) were a hit and established Roshan as a music director to reckon with.

Dad got an opportunity to work with Roshan when Roshan had just commenced on his journey to reach his creative peak. Dad was hardworking and dedicated. He and Roshan developed a bond which culminated into a warm and lasting friendship. Dad settled into Hindi cinema, doing even small roles, besides his work in music. On the job, he picked up different skills and a sound understanding of the overall process of filmmaking. His versatility, coupled with his affability and adaptability, made him a good hands-on manager. Soon he got the opportunity to work as a production manager with none other than Kidar Sharma himself. A lyricist, script-writer, photographer and master of the art of film-making, Kidar Sharma was Dad's idol. Soon he began assisting Kidar Sharma in direction. Somewhere down the line, his real name Harikrishan Maria fell behind and the name assumed for the film industry – Vijay Maria – became his identity. But before that, he had got married in 1955 to a demure young woman from the beautiful and serene region of hilly Himachal.

Mama's name was Chandrakanta and her father was a reputed and wealthy lawyer in Dharamshala. He also owned shops and orchards. He had arranged her match with a young man from a large joint family and the groom had seven brothers. Mama's mother – our Nani – was most unhappy. Her studious and shy daughter would get smothered in the large joint family. Then came the proposal from Dad's family and Nani jumped at it because Dad was an only son. Even far-off Bombay and life with a filmwallah was preferred to sending her dear daughter to a house that was sure to dampen her spirits and cramp her style. So she convinced Grandfather – our Nana – to call off the engagement and get Mama married to Dad. As was the practice those days, Mama did not have much say in the matter. The first time she met Dad was on their marriage day. Can it be imagined in today's day and time of a couple entering the holy bonds of matrimony without even casting an eye on each other? Maybe those were the times when 'marriages were indeed made in Heaven'. In any case, she must have been happy to escape the ordeal of the earlier match.

From her peaceful and sheltered life in Himachal, Mama landed in bustling Bombay to take charge of a life that was surrounded by a medley of cultures never experienced before. When I try to visualise the darling of a prosperous, protective and deeply religious family, attending school and college (and even the RSS Mahila Shakha in Dharamshala as she told us) in salwar-kameez, studying Sanskrit and Hindi literature and pouring over her books, suddenly transported to St. Paul's Road, and communicating with the Patils and Pereiras, Desais and D'Souzas, D'Limas and D'Mellos and the Sheikhs and Khans and not to forget the film fraternity! How daunting it must have been for her!

And Dad and Mama were poles apart. Mama was deeply religious. She was a devout Ram bhakt. Her daily puja was a must for her. She observed rituals and fasts, but never imposed them on anyone. She visited temples, churches, and dargahs with equal faith, for she was deeply spiritual and pious.

Dad, on the other hand, was far from religious. Not much of a temple-goer and certainly not a rituals man, he let Mama pray to her heart's content and make up for both! On Mondays and Fridays she would be a vegetarian, fondly hoping for Dad to follow suit, but not he. You carry on, but let me have my meat, he would say. He would laugh and joke about her rituals, but never did be obstruct her beliefs and ways. She too stoically accepted that he would never change and did everything possible to let him have his lifestyle.

Mama never had to commute or travel long distances alone. Nor was she interested in shopping and having her own social life. Even if she was, she could not, so caught up was she in concentrating on us – managing us and our education – her topmost priority. Dad valued this contribution in his quiet way and to give her a well-deserved break from this monotony, he would insistently take her out on Friday nights to the movies, to catch the last show.

Nana-Nani never visited us. Dada-Dadi – my father's parents – often visited us. Dada moved in with us in his last days and breathed his last in our house.

Mama had studied in Hindi and Sanskrit. Though she understood English, she hadn't had much exposure to it and did not speak it. She was the serious sombre type and was not into gregarious socialising. Dad, on the other hand, was fond of music and Urdu *shayari* (poetry). He was happiest when listening to ghazals and poetry with friends. He loved his whiskey. Gold Flake was the brand he smoked. Evenings at home, when he was in, were typical of a filmi household. People gathered in our small sitting room and indulged enthusiastically in discussions on literature, music and the latest happenings in the industry. They enjoyed poetry and music sessions over good food and drink, and left feeling contended. Roshan, Shailendra, Raja Mehdi Ali Khan, Lekh Tandon, Rajendra Kumar, Bhappi Soni, O.P. Ralhan, Shetty, Ram Maheshwari and many more, were regular visitors to our house. On such days, and such days were often, the activity in the house would spill well over midnight and Mama had to be up early the next day to get us ready for our schools and daily routines. Even then her cramped kitchen ardently turned out meal after meal, wholesome and delicious, without much ado and enough to satiate the voracious appetites of growing athletic children, and a husband who expected her to keep provisions for extra food for at least half a dozen people at each meal!

However, on some core values, they were one. Both were absolutely down to earth. Dad worked hard and ensured that we never fell short of anything. There was no scarcity of food, basic clothing and educational facilities. He never thought of saving and spent liberally. He was not after money and never gave thought to acquiring assets, not even moving into a bigger house. He was generous to a fault. He diligently took care of his staff and junior colleagues, helped needy friends without keeping an account and never spoke about it. Mama never stopped him in this, nor did she grumble about it. She too was generous and helping in her own way, at times even more than Dad. Both never showed off nor did they brag about anything. They were respected in the neighbourhood and amongst their friends for their sincerity and genuineness.

In the midst of all the mayhem of a filmmaker's house, Mama strived to build a fortress without walls around her children;

just with the sheer strength and force of her personality and sincerity – to keep them focused on the straight and narrow path. For deep within her, she knew that if she did not, they could easily stray and lose themselves forever. And she did a brilliant job of it. She created a home that was as inclusive and cosmopolitan as Bombay itself, where she welcomed all of Dad's friends and neighbours, irrespective of caste, creed and status. She let him conduct his life the way he wanted but preserved an identity of her own that remained unshaken till the end. She was the presiding deity of the house whom all of us, including Dad, looked up to. Dad and Mama had arrived at a beautiful way of living in harmony, of living with each other's differences. What is more, they also understood that each child is different and created a world where every child was made to feel precious and allowed to pursue their own dreams provided he or she did their best.

3

The Making of a Bandra Boy

Dad used to be so busy with his erratic schedules that our studies and day-to-day routines were entirely left in Mama's hands. They had an unspoken division of labour in bringing us up. Spoiling us was Dad's domain and he did it happily. When it came to our studies and exams, it was Mama's territory and Dad dared not interfere. Dad signed all our report cards without a complaint. Mama was a toughie.

Even then, none of them forced us into a career. We were free to choose and decide. Dad would have been happy and supportive even if any of us had turned to the film industry. That is how I once acted as a child artist in a Punjabi film and Mama permitted me. I vividly remember that the shooting was near Alibaug. However, a sincere effort at formal education was an unwavering priority and Mama never compromised on that. However, those of us who did not take to academics were never humiliated or ill-treated.

After Mama's marriage, Nana-Nani were alone in Dharamshala. So Dad and Mama sent our eldest brother Rajesh (aka Raju), to Dharamshala to keep them company. For quite some time, till Raju was brought back after Nani's death in 1967, I was the eldest child in the house and perhaps developed a sense of responsibility.

Ironically though, the very start of my academic journey took a minor hit. It must have been quite a jolt to Mama when I was refused admission to St. Andrew's Kindergarten because I knew no English. The language spoken at home was either Hindi or Punjabi. St. Andrew's admitted me only the next year when they felt I had reached a sufficient proficiency in English. The same year, my younger sister, Poonam also got admission in the all-girls, Apostolic Carmel Convent School. Poonam and I began school and also completed our graduation in the same year. Therefore, many people often mistook us for twins.

We kids were more than a handful, but Mama was more than a match for us and could be severe if we tried her patience. She did not speak English, but she understood it and was a vigilant parent. It was she who attended all our PTA meetings.

Come monsoon and St. Paul's Road would brace itself for the annual rainwater flooding. At least twice each monsoon, the water would rise and get into our ground floor house. We got a feel of Venice without ever having visiting it – the children of the locality, spirited as we were, would get the small fishing boats from Chimbai and row them like the famed gondolas! Even otherwise, the road to our school would often get waterlogged. We would look forward to missing school, but Mama almost never gave us the pleasure. She would play spoilsport and drop us to school, wading through knee deep water, holding me and Manoj by hand with Pankaj on her hip. Missing school was a strict no-no.

During the long summer vacation in May, armed with small buckets and spades, Mama would take us to the sandy sea patch off Carter Road. I remember how euphoric it felt playing in the sand and collecting shells and little fishes. To quench the summer thirst, she would buy ice and make us lemonade or *kachhi lassi* – a cooling mix of milk and iced water and sugar. She would also take us to the Bandra Fair, a week-long fair held annually in September to mark the Feast of the Nativity of the Blessed Virgin Mary at the Basilica of Our Lady of the Mount.

Our neighbourhood looked like canvasses of cottages and bungalows with shrubs and fruit-bearing trees like mango, jackfruit, coconut, *jamb* (love apples), jamun, guava, tamarind and papaya. Hunger was many a times satiated by climbing the fruit trees and eating the fruit of our choice – most of the times this meant stealing a fruit! Can the children of today enjoy and experience this luxury? We were a bunch of several age-groups and such was the innocence of our childhood that we were content playing simple games which required no expensive equipment or fancy gear. Besides alley or street (gully) cricket and even gully football, Bandra also had a solid culture of sports, thanks to the schools which provided the infrastructure and opportunity for students. We made the most of it after school hours and keeping us bound to books for long was indeed a tough job for the elders.

However, 'Home at 7.00 p.m.' was an uncompromising rule in our home. We had no watches, but we made sure not to contravene it or else, there would be patterns resembling 'zebra crossings' on our palms. One of Mama's objectives in visiting the Bandra Fair was to replace her stock of canes which she kept at an easy reach, behind a large framed photograph which was hung at an incline on a string just as one entered the home. I remember a sari-clad Mama at the cane-stall, checking the tensile strength of canes like an expert, with an expression on her face that made it clear that she meant business. So we took utmost care to ensure that the canes remained unused and rested behind the photo frame. Once home, famished with the outdoor activity, she would give us a snack of boiled eggs or bananas and we had to then go find a corner and study till dinner.

I was obsessed with sports; cricket, football and basketball being my favourites. Our school, St. Andrew's, boasted of inter-school champion teams and was very sports-oriented, and I had the privilege to captain the school football, cricket and basketball teams. It was my sporting acumen which made me Dad's favourite.

Whenever he had the time, he would make it a point to come to the ground to watch me play the matches.

But I was something of a nerd too. So much so, that for Diwali when other kids wanted crackers, I preferred story books, which made me Mama's favourite. I was a good student and would practically scoop up all the prizes in all subjects. I remember Mama proudly attending every prize distribution ceremony; her inability to speak English never curtailed her enthusiasm whilst attending the functions. On Thursdays and Sundays (being holidays), I would accompany Mama to the Bandra bazaar to help her buy provisions. There was a sweetmeat shop next to the Kalidas Grocery Shop where she would buy me a big glass of sweet lassi. She couldn't help being partial to me, and I would always get extra helpings of sweets and goodies from her. If this was her way of incentivising others, it did not meet with much of a success. I recall once when I'd cried bitterly because I had stood second and not the regular first rank in class, my siblings were clearly not amused. They stood anywhere from the fifteenth to the last rank and yet could not manage a single tear!

Every Thursday, Dad would take me to his office. I was a clear favourite there as well mainly because of my academic and sporting achievements. Narayan and Damu, Dad's office assistants, would be deputed to take me to the nearby food joint (Gupta Lunch Home at Dadar) for chicken biryani or omelette-pav (bread).

When Dad was working with Kidar Sharma, their office used to be at Shree Sound Studios in Dadar. I remember one particular visit vividly. I must have been around ten and Kidar Sharma asked me about my school results. I had topped the class and when I told him, he said he must take me out for a movie. So we got into his car – a light green Triumph Mayflower. He first took me to the Strand Book Depot and bought me Jules Vernes' famous novel, *Twenty Thousand Leagues Under the Sea*. He then took me to the Strand Cinema to watch *20,000 Leagues Under the Sea*, a movie made on the classic, the first science fiction film shot in CinemaScope produced by Walt Disney. (I read and re-read the book, but unfortunately failed to preserve it.) Kidar Sharma would regularly enquire about my progress and Dad would share my achievements with him proudly.

After Dad's death, I lost touch with him. Years later, when I was posted as Commissioner of Police, Mumbai, there was a function in the Shanmukhananda Hall, Sion. The presenter was a lively and competent young lady who met me after the show and asked, 'Mr Maria, did you know Mr Kidar Sharma?'

'Yes, of course,' I said eagerly.

'I am his granddaughter,' she said. I was so happy to meet her and the spark in her reminded me of the kind man who had introduced me to a classic by showing me how it could be brought alive on celluloid. Looking back, I am amazed at the sensitivity that made a man of his stature spare thought and time for a schoolboy just to let him know that his accomplishment was not a small matter.

My father later worked with the Maheshwaris in their production house, Kalpanalok as a Production Manager. He also acted in the film *Kaajal* (1965). I remember accompanying him to the Apsara Theatre to watch *Kaajal* and assess the audience's reaction.

In *Neel Kamal* (1968) Dad not only acted, but also assisted Ram Maheshwari in direction. He also worked with director Bhappi Soni as Production Controller and even acted in his film, *Preetam* (1971).

I vividly remember being present on some days for the film shooting of *Hamari Yaad Aayegi* (1961), *Kaajal*, *Neel Kamal* – films Dad was associated with. Another fond memory is sitting on the lap of the famous actress Meena Kumari during the making of *Kaajal* and getting chocolates from her.

Dad was my undisputed hero and I used to love snatching moments with him, even if it meant just accompanying him to his office or when he went 'location hunting'. I also accompanied Dad to music sessions with well-known music composers. I remember sitting near a window on a long sofa in the renowned composer Ravi's house and observing the maestro intensely engaged in a music session with Dad, Ram and Pannalal Maheshwari for the film *Kaajal.* I did not have the talent to become a musician but, thanks to Dad, I developed an appreciation for good music which helped me combat stress and worries during my career, which unsurprisingly, were plentiful.

The most loathsome task, I found, was visiting stars and waiting patiently to get their dates for shooting schedules. I think it was Dad's agony during those visits that sub-consciously drove me to make up my mind not to venture into the film industry. The moods, whims and fancies of creative and artistic folk from the film world were clearly not my cup of tea.

Under Mama's watchful eye, Dad indulged us as much as he could. If he was shooting at R.K. Studios (which unfortunately now ceases to exist), he was sure to come via Jhama Sweets at Chembur and bring us gulab jamuns. Come the *patang*-flying (kite-flying) season – in the crisp and windy January weather around Makar Sankranti – and Dad would order the *badami, ghasleti manja* (specially made thread, coated with crushed glass, used for flying kites) and *phirkis* (wooden spools) all the way from Amritsar. The stock would be enough for all the children in the lane. The same was true for firecrackers and sweet delicacies during Diwali.

With Dad's immense composure and patience, we rarely ever saw him lose his temper with us. One such unforgettable instance was an indiscretion we were guilty of without realising its gravity. A starlet who performed bit roles as a vamp in films lived in the neighbourhood. She had starred in an Amitabh Bachchan film and in a particular scene is seen in the arms of a gangster mouthing the dialogue: 'I don't mind coke.' This dialogue became a mild sensation in the locality because the way she said in the film sounded funny and enough for us brats in the lane to say it aloud whenever she passed by. When she complained of this to one of the Catholic ladies in the neighbourhood, the latter retorted candidly that she should have thought twice before agreeing to essay such roles or utter those lines in the first place!

Ultimately, when the poor starlet could bear the irritation and ridicule no more, she came to see 'Uncle' – our Dad – and narrated her tale of woe, together with the neighbourhood lady's heartless comment. Dad was furious and none of us were spared his wrath, even me who was not party to the crime – my older brother, Raju and I received resounding slaps on the street itself. Dad made it more than clear that there would be 'zero tolerance' to any act which did not treat a woman, or for that matter any human being, with dignity.

We never had a family home – the 'back home' to speak of. We never went to Punjab or Himachal for vacations, nor did Mama and Dad go vacationing. In fact, the first time I went to Dharamshala and Amritsar was after my IPS training. If our school organised summer holiday and sports camps, which was a regular feature, that's where we went, for Mama made sure we didn't miss any school activity. Dad and Mama became such pucca Bombayites that we children never developed any regional identities. If anyone ever asked us where we came from, we would instinctively answer Bombay or Bambai or Mumbai, depending upon the language in which the question was being asked. It was only upon seeing their puzzled expressions, that we realised that they wanted to know about our roots. So it was with some effort that we learned the answer they were looking for – Punjabi. Yet we hardly felt Punjabi – we enjoyed our football and bombils (Bombay Duck), crossed our hearts when the teachers did not believe we were telling them the truth, spoke the Bandra lingo in which 'all of you' was 'you-all buggers' and in which even a woman could be hailed with, 'Hey Man! How are you, Man?' In fact we were quintessentially Mumbaikars, and within Mumbai – Bandra boys and girls.

4

Cop, Cop and Nothing But a Cop

Our first brush with the law was when Dad had stood surety for a man called Madan who used to work for him. He had committed some petty offence and Dad, the good Samaritan that he was, had bailed him out. One day we learned that Madan had jumped bail. Dad was called to the Bandra police station. It was raining cats and dogs and the damp and dark sky added to the sombre mood in the house, while we waited for Dad to return home. These visits to the Bandra police station accompanied by the tension-laden atmosphere at home stretched across a course of nearly three months till Madan was finally nabbed.

Otherwise, our contact with our police force was limited to the last scene in the movies when the khakhi-clad Inspector rushed in, accompanied by the lathi-wielding Bombay city constables in their old and prominent indigo blue uniform: Bermuda shorts, full-sleeved shirt, leather belt, brass buckle, cap, leather sandals and 'puttees' wound from the ankles to the knees. Their job was to do the mop-up operation after the hero had fixed the villains and rescued the heroine and the good people in the film.

Dad did not do any crime films, but by a strange coincidence, the plot of his last film revolved around a well-meaning chap who inadvertently keeps finding himself in conflict with the law and ending up in the lock-up, much to the despair of the local police inspector. To escape this jinx, he comes to Bombay and as luck would have it, falls foul of a notorious criminal. Then with a lot of complications and some song and dance sequences, he avoids jail time and lives happily ever after with the heroine. A regular Bollywood masala entertainer, it had a good cast and was released in November 1981 when I was undergoing the Civil Services Foundation Course training in Mussoorie. It was called *Jail Yatra* – *yatra* being the Hindi word for 'pilgrimage' or a 'trip'.

For as long as I can remember, crime, criminals, the underworld and law enforcers have always invoked an undeniable fascination within me. As a teenager, the first section I would go to in the daily *Times of India* was the crime page. Louis L'Amour, who wrote 'frontier westerns' was my favourite author. So was Oliver Strange. His *Sudden: The Marshal of Lawless* was a treasured book. The pages of the book weaved within their folds the tale of a town called Lawless in the Wild West with a seemingly never-ending band of criminals who ruled the roost. Nobody wants to be the Marshal of that town as the job is fraught with danger and the mission an impossibility. The hero called Sudden comes and takes up the 'suicidal' task. He cleans up the town and establishes order. Sudden is intelligent, quick, fearless, kind, strong, fair and law-abiding. Most importantly, the protagonist uses his gun only as a last resort.

Then there was this legendary lawman, Marshall Wyatt Earp of the Wild West. He becomes Marshal of a town called Tombstone, a regular den of criminals. I was fascinated by the way Earp cleaned up Tombstone. Such stories of brave and valiant policemen never failed to enthral me.

In school, I was always appointed the class monitor. I never did *dadagiri* – the Bombay word for bullying – as I was always trying to shepherd the flock and the teachers had great faith in me.

Our school, St. Andrew's at Bandra, was a great leveller. It had very rich children and also very poor. There were many who existed on the fringes of the law. For a major part of my school life, Father Rufus Pereira was our school principal. New Talkies was the nearest cinema hall, where now stands the Globus Mall. The theatre screened English movies from 2 to 4 in the afternoon. Concurrently, our noon session at school would begin at 2 p.m. and conclude at 4:30 p.m. This was very convenient for those who cut classes, as it matched perfectly with the cinema time. To keep a check on the students who would make it to the movies during this time, Father Rufus used to conduct occasional surprise checks in the theatre. His team included the Physical Training instructors and me. We would stand at the exit of the Lower Stalls as the boys could not afford higher tickets – the ticket to the Lower Stalls used to cost fifty-five paise; Upper Stalls seventy-five paise; while the well-to-do would go for Balcony which cost one rupee and five paise a ticket. My job was to stand next to Father Rufus and jot down, in a notebook, the names of the boys nabbed in the theatre. They were easily identifiable simply because they were dressed in the school uniform. The cleverer among them would duck behind the seats, trying to sneak out only after they were certain that it was safe to do so. But Father Rufus met their youthful wisdom with his own. Once all appeared to have left, he would have me look between the rows to ensure that all had indeed taken their leave. The manager of New Talkies was a Catholic gentleman, Tony Fernandes, and he could not say no to the Parish priest for the fear of inviting the wrath of God and Church! Once rounded up, all the truants were taken back to the school and given a caning. Not a single parent ever complained. They had tremendous respect for Father Rufus Pereira and had full faith in him. So, it was Father Rufus who gave me my first training in *nakabandi* – the term we use for setting up check-posts at exit and entry points in sensitive areas for surprise checking of criminals.

One day, Father Rufus took me to the school terrace and handed me a pair of binoculars. He asked me to train them at a building under construction named 'Samir Complex' opposite the Holy Family Hospital. I followed his direction and could see some of our students playing cards there. To my dismay, one of them was my younger brother Manoj! Father Rufus then asked me to jump over the school gate and bring the boys over. I obeyed and went up to the truant boys. They were surprised to see me. I told them that Father Rufus was watching them and showed them where he stood with his binoculars. They looked in his direction and I could barely suppress a smile as I saw Father Rufus waving out to them.

Father Rufus was a born teacher and he tried everything within his means to impart education that would be of practical use to the students. One such initiative was teaching us plumbing. The plumbing course began and Father Rufus was all excited about it, until one day all the taps in the school disappeared! Anyway, Father Rufus was not the one to give up and be ruffled by these small hiccups. He then introduced a bicycle repairs course. All of us learned to dismantle and reassemble bicycles. Needless to say, this time around, bicycle parts in the parking lot started vanishing. Whenever such unpleasant incidents occurred, I was used by the school as a bridge between the school and the pranksters. Instead of branding them as delinquents, Father Rufus tried to bring them back to the fold and I was one of his instruments.

Since I was very good at studies, I would also teach these laggards towards the end of the semester and help them pass through some last minute emergency coaching. Before every exam, the entire school would be called to the Assembly Hall. Father Rufus would address all the students with words that I do not think are possible for me to ever forget. 'I say don't copy. If you do, don't get caught. If you get caught, don't think that I will not punish you. I will definitely punish you.' Some would heed the advice, but some just ignored it. For the latter, preparation for exams was called preparing *chivda*– small notes written in very small handwriting which could be hidden in the folds and tucks of clothing to be used as exam-hall aide-memoires.

Copying was developed into a fine art by some of the boys at St. Andrew's. Michael would invariably have a fall and a plaster put around his left wrist just before the exams. A convenient ruse to hide the chivda so painstakingly prepared by him. In those times, the school had a big brass gong which would be rung every half hour to mark the time elapsed. The task of banging the gong was entrusted to a back-bencher, Teddy. Prior to the Geometry exam, Teddy had written some of the important theorems very meticulously on the huge brass gong. As soon as the question paper was received, Teddy anxiously waited for the half hour gong to be sounded so that he could go and read the theorems written on the gong. But unfortunately, Teddy still failed because every time (half hour) that Teddy read the theorem from the gong, he forgot it by the time he reached his examination seat! Poor guy!

Our friend Francis (name changed to protect him from answering embarrassing questions by his children) was another expert at preparing chivda. At a History exam, Francis started copying from his chivda and the teacher – a lady – got suspicious. She checked his shirt pocket and found a note. He was so meticulous that the note in the shirt pocket bore the legend to the chivda hidden all over his body. The teacher had simply to read the legend and ask Francis to fetch either 'Akbar' from the trouser's right side pocket or 'Aurangzeb' from the left side pocket or 'Shivaji' from the back pocket! So Francis got caught and was punished. Instead of mending his ways and preparing for his next exam, Francis spent the entire term on devising a plan to make sure that the teacher would never frisk him again. Before the next exam, Francis boasted to everyone that it would be the last exam she checked him and all of us waited with bated breath to see what devious scheme Francis had plotted.

The exam began and the teacher began her rounds, naturally

keeping an eye on Francis who now had a reputation. She saw Francis fidgeting with his pant pocket and decided to act. Like a drone towards the intended target, she honed in on Francis. She put her hand inside Francis's pant pocket. Just as everyone thought that Francis's goose was cooked once again, the teacher recoiled and pulled back as if she had had an electric shock. She left the classroom in a hurry and never came back! Francis, calm and composed as ever, continued as if nothing had happened. After the exam, everyone gathered around Francis with just one query, 'What happened? Why did she leave like that?'

'Put your hand inside my pocket,' said Francis with victory writ large on his face. We did and what horror! He had slit his trousers' pocket and was not wearing his underwear!

Boys of St. Andrew's always looked forward to the Bandra Fair. St. Aloysius had a little garden where they used to hold a discotheque called 'September Garden', during the fair. Girls from Carmel Convent and St. Joseph would be at the disco and boys from St. Andrew's, St. Stanislaus and other schools would do their best to attend in their best attire. Very much akin to peacocks strutting around to impress the peahens! We were mostly from the middle class and poor backgrounds and new clothes were a rarity, generally made only for a festival or some special occasion.

That year our school assembly hall had new curtains, a kind of dark bottle green. The new curtains suddenly disappeared when the Bandra Fair was round the corner. Their disappearance was a big mystery until we had our friends Brian, Sheldon and my brother Manoj and some other boys turning out at the September Garden in identical dark bottle green bell-bottoms with forty-inch flares as was the fashion. All were caught and were penalised and chastised. Had they had the money to dye the pants, it would have been a different story altogether. It was all clean fun and is still a story to enliven our get-togethers and reunions.

I think if genetics is a factor, the cop in me comes entirely from Mama. Poor Dad had no inclination whatsoever to police anyone. The *satyashodhaks* – 'truth-finders' – that is what the canes or batons at the police stations are called in Mumbai – always reminded me of Mama and the fresh stock of canes she used to buy at the Bandra Fair each year. Credit must also go to St. Andrew's, Father Rufus and the band of Andrean 'delinquents' for strengthening the latent policing abilities in me.

I passed the Secondary School Certificate (SSC) exam in 1974. Being a good student, I managed to do well in Science and Maths, but I did not particularly enjoy them. Humanities was the stream for me. I was crazy about cricket and basketball. So I needed a college that would give me an opportunity to continue with my sporting endeavours. Luckily, St. Xavier's College fit the bill. Not only was it the best college for Arts, but it also had a good record for sports.

Poonam and I cleared SSC the same year, but we went our own ways. It was a pleasant surprise when we found that, by sheer coincidence, both of us had taken admission to St. Xavier's. She had gone independently with some of her friends and secured her admission. Like I said earlier, for most part of our growing-up, we were mistaken to be twins.

My schedule at St. Xavier's was quite rigorous. The basketball practice was at 7 o'clock in the morning and I made it a point to never miss it. Then one would go to the hostel and have a bath before attending lectures. Later, lunch would be at the college canteen or at Cafe Metro nearby. The cricket team practice would be from 4 to 6.30 p.m. at the Azad Maidan ground just across the college. I also enrolled myself into karate classes at the Wankhede Stadium, when I decided to aim for the Indian Police Service (IPS). Thus, after an exhausting action-packed day, I would board the train for the ride back to Bandra.

I was always shy with girls and could never find words when they were around, much to the exasperation of Poonam. So much so that her friends would laugh and joke about this and ask her if I had a speech problem. With Mama's discipline and the unwavering rule of having to be home by 7 in the evening, socialising did not make it to our agenda anyway. I remember a lone birthday party of her friend that Poonam attended one evening. She and another friend teamed up to buy a gift for the birthday girl and went to the party. Shortly after, when it grew dark, Mama deputed me to go to the house and escort Poonam back. I promptly followed Mama's orders and went to the house and rang the bell. I still remember the shock and dismay on the faces of the girls who had just made a fruit punch and were about to ladle it around. The party had only just begun and poor Poonam had to make her excuses and say goodbye.

It was in the third year of college that I decided I would take the Civil Services exam because my heart was set on the Indian Police Service. Though Mama was very particular about our studies, she never interfered in our choice of a career beyond a point. Left to herself she would have loved to have her son either in the Indian Army, Navy, Air Force or the Police. So when I decided to aim for the Police Service, she was more than happy and supported me to the hilt. Dad, on the other hand, did not have such idealistic dreams for us and used to be a little worried about my ambition, for he wanted us to achieve our goals in an easy-going way, enjoying life and without setbacks and disappointments. Nevertheless, he was no less of a support system to me at every step of the way.

With my sights set on the Civil Services exam, for my Bachelor of Arts, I chose History, Political Science and International Relations. In the final year of college, I toiled arduously to secure my B.A. degree with Honours. I had set a target for myself. I must clear the Civil Services examination in the very first attempt. Therefore, upon completion of my B.A., I devoted an entire year to the preparations for the challenging exams ahead.

Now I had no background in the Civil Services in the family, nor did we have any friends in the Service. So other than my dreams, I had no mentors around to tell me anything about Civil Services in general or the police force in particular. Moreover, the Civil Services was not a coveted career for Bombay students then and the city did not have many facilities for guiding aspiring students. I found out that S.N. Das Gupta College in Delhi could help me understand the format of the exam. So I joined their Study Circle for the IAS entrance exam for one month. I stayed with family friends at Vasant Vihar in Delhi, and completed the course. On coming back, I appeared for the entrance exam and cleared it in the first shot! Subsequently, I passed even the main exam in the very first attempt.

Then came the interview. The Chairman of the Interview panel was Air Chief Marshal Pratap Chandra Lal. Prior to the interview, we were required to fill a form and write our respective career options. Generally, the aspirants wrote Indian Foreign Service (IFS) as the first option, thereafter the Indian Administrative Service (IAS), followed by the Indian Police Service and then the Indian Revenue Service (IRS). I looked at the form. The Indian Police Service was my dream. It was the only dream that I had ever dreamed for myself. It was all I wanted. I just could not get myself to writing anything other than IPS on the form. So, I did what my heart prompted me. I wrote IPS five times, for all the options and went in for the interview.

'Son, I think you have made a mistake. You have written IPS five times,' said Mr Lal to me, looking at me with concern.

'No, sir, it's not a mistake,' I said. 'It is deliberate. Sir, give me IPS or nothing.'

The rest of the interview went well. I got 235 marks out of 250 and got into the IPS....a dream fulfilled!

We also had to give preference for cadres. My first preference was Maharashtra because I belonged to Maharashtra and it is a prime cadre, so there was no issue there. For the second preference, I wrote Punjab. Why? Because my father was from Punjab. For the third preference, I wrote Jammu and Kashmir. The reason being that mother was from the hills of the Himalayas. Looking back I feel how naive was I!

Anyway, I got Maharashtra and I was thrilled. I was the only insider – Maharashtrian – to get into the IPS that year.

My entry into the IPS was, of course, a matter of great pride for my family. However, during those times hardly anyone around us knew what IPS was. None of them had had any occasion to give much thought to something called the IPS. So when my father told one of his friends that I had got into the IPS, he'd said, 'Congratulations! But what does the company do?'

The first IPS officers I met were the ones who came to lecture us at Mussoorie when we were doing the three months Foundation Course. One month was spent at the National Civil Defence College in Nagpur and one year of very intense physical and classroom training at the Sardar Vallabhbhai Patel National Police Academy in Hyderabad. We also had to do a fifteen day Army Attachment. Then we spent the next three months at the Police Training School at Nashik where the distinctive emphasis of the training was on Maharashtra specific laws, procedures and rules. A. S. Samra was the Director of the Police Training School, Nashik, but within a short time, he completed his posting and another icon Arvind Inamdar, subsequently, took his place.

Everything looked well. I was training. I was upbeat. I had already started to breathe in the reality of my dream. But this unparalleled jubilation was not to last. Towards the end of my Nashik training, Dad suddenly took ill. The message came that he was not keeping well and the Director, Arvind Inamdar granted me leave to go to Bombay.

Till then, none of us in the family had to tackle major medical issues and the world of specialist doctors and second opinions. We struggled to get a proper diagnosis. The doctor who was treating him thought it was a heart issue. When things did not improve, further investigations were carried out at a bigger hospital. The final diagnosis was a brain tumour. Mama, our pillar of strength, was devastated. We did not how to take care of Mama – the one who had devoted her life to caring and looking after us.

When I visited Dad at the Bombay Hospital, he was in a comatose state, unable to recognise me. My heart ached to see him in that condition. My hero who had catered to every single wish of mine; the man who supported me and gave wings to my dreams; the man who had taken pride in all of my achievements, big and small, lay before me, so close yet so far and I was absolutely helpless. I died a thousand deaths – just holding his limp hand and watching him float away from us. Fortunately, he did not suffer for too long. In March 1983 he passed away. As soon as the funeral rites were completed, I went back to training with a part of me gone forever. Life would never be the same anymore.

In April 1983, I received orders for my first posting as Supernumerary Assistant Superintendent of Police and a little before Ambedkar Jayanti, 14 April that year, I reported in Akola to begin work. With a regret, that my Dad, my hero, was not there to savour the moment and my Mama, my inspiration, was hardly her own self, struggling to come to terms with her bereavement. Her health deteriorated. The little world on St. Paul's Road was now quiet and forlorn. With me away – the responsibility of looking after Mama precipitously fell all of a sudden on the slender shoulders of our sister Poonam. She understood her responsibilities, said nothing and with newfound strength and determination, simply rose to the occasion and took charge.

5

Son of the Soil

A supernumerary post is an add-on to the prescribed number of posts. So as a supernumerary officer, you are associated with the regular manpower or substitute them in case of a need.

As a newbie Supernumerary Assistant Superintendent of Police (ASP), an IPS entrant has to do one city police station and one rural police station, as if he or she were the Inspector-in-Charge of that police station. This is the sure shot way of getting the rookie officer direct experience of grass roots policing before he or she gets ensconced in the elite rank of the Service, distanced from the hurly-burly of police stations.

This is one's first posting. After all the heady excitement of your selection into the much-coveted Service, of donning the uniform and attending the prestigious National Police Academy, you finally step into 'Reality' with a capital 'R'. The training has insulated you from local biases, showed you the larger picture and launched you on to the path of ideals and integrity to take up your national duty. At the same time, the Police Academy has tried its best to recreate real-life situations that you are likely to face during the course of the duty. They gave you real-life examples and showed you the pitfalls, making you prepare mentally to be a decision maker. You were given options and you made your choices, looking at your instructors who guided and corrected you, for nods of approval or frowns of disapproval. Still, it all remained bookish.

Now, it is you and you alone who has to choose your options and face the consequences thereof. You have real subordinate officers with tons of work experience. Now they are looking up to you for decisions. They are going to deliberately ask you, *kya karenge, sir?* (What shall we do, sir?) They will test your mettle and assess your professional competence and calibre. They consider themselves good at gauging: '*Kaun kitne paani mein?*' Literally meaning, who is in the waters and how deep are they. And of course, how well can they manage! Some may even have little disdain—'New IPS officer, huh! Seen them before. Been there, done that!'

At one level, you are like a spectator of a boxing match now thrust into the ring to fend for himself. Punch or parry is your decision alone. At another level, you are entering a team sport, certainly not in a friendly benefit match. You are a rookie, called upon to enter the field straight as the captain, in a game that is already on! Thrust into the thick of things, where you have to build your reputation and make decisive calls all the time; you are called upon to rein in foxy, pernicious and tricky subordinates who have been doing their own thing for quite some time.

What is more, the IPS makes its officer an enigma wrapped in a certain aura, both for the public as well for its subordinate officers. The Service makes them expect something of an extraordinary calibre from you – heroic and magical – and prompts them to watch you with great and sustained interest to test if you can acquit yourself well.

So when you arrive on the scene, it is as if the State has sent a gladiator into a war! Deliver, not just entertain, but deliver with elan!

As Supernumerary ASP, I was first posted at the City Kotwali police station in Akola city. Akola city is about 300 miles east of the state capital, Bombay and 140 miles west of the second capital Nagpur. It is the administrative headquarters of District

Akola, located in the north central part of Maharashtra in the Vidarbha region. It is the third largest city in Vidarbha after Nagpur and Amravati. A prominent road and rail junction, it is an important commercial trading centre. At that time, Shivajirao Baraokar was the Deputy Inspector General (DIG) of the Amravati Range and Datta Chaudhary was the Superintendent of Police (SP), Akola district.

Even if you are itching to know how your superiors are, you cannot risk asking your subordinates for you never know what they may report. It came as a great relief, however, to find in Datta Chaudhary a soft-spoken and courteous boss, willing to go out of his way to educate and show me the ropes, as also to sort out my difficulties. He began taking me along for important official meetings and for visits to police stations to put me through the grind.

At the back of your mind, there is always the unexpressed fear: what if you go wrong? Fortunately, Baraokar and Chaudhary, both IPS officers themselves, were very supportive and receptive. If you go wrong, do not worry; we are there, that is the kind of confidence they instilled in me, treating me as if they understood, having gone through the travails and tribulations themselves.

The first time I met Shivajirao Baraokar was when he came to Akola when I was just two or three days old as a supernumerary. He was reviewing the Ambedkar Jayanti bandobast and was on his way to Buldhana. SP Datta Chaudhary, Additional SP P.P.P. Sharma and I received him at Balapur police station which is on the highway. He came in, took off his cap and sat down in the Inspector's chair. The Vidarbha area is like a furnace in the summers. It was a peak summer afternoon and I found it odd that the fan should be switched off. As I moved towards the switch to put it on, I saw Datta Chaudhary jerking his head in a weird manner and staring at me with eyebrows raised. I had just joined and did not know much about any of them. Though I was a little worried, I thought that he had a stiff neck or a nervous twitch. I went ahead and put on the switch. To my astonishment, Datta Chaudhary lunged forward in a flash of a second and switched it off! Then I noticed that DIG Baraokar was clutching his head tightly. Only then did it dawn on me that he was sporting a wig. Datta Chaudhary had saved all of us, and especially me, from a major embarrassment!

After this near goof-up, I was a little worried about facing Baraokar again. But, at the next meeting, I found him very affable and gracious. He told me that he was keen on exercise and his favourite form of exercise was going for long walks. I said that I, too, was keen on fitness and informed him about the sports I played. He said he would take me for my word and asked me to accompany him on a long walk. I said I would gladly do so. So he asked me to be at the Akola Circuit House at 4:30 in the evening, equipped for a walk.

At 4:30 sharp, I was at the Circuit House, dressed in my sports kit and sneakers. He came out immediately and said, '*Chalo,* let's go!' From the Circuit House, we started walking what seemed like an endless walk. We soon reached the highway and walked along it right up to the Balapur police station! This must have been a distance of approximately twenty-five km! I felt that he was waiting for me to say, 'Sir! Shall we turn back!' But, I did not let him savour that joy. When we reached Balapur police station, he said, 'Now let's turn back!' He called for his vehicle and we returned to the Circuit House. I think he had been assessing me all the time and testing my stamina and resolve. Trying to see if my talk about my sports and fitness was just bragging. He found that I was not grandstanding and could walk the talk!

Blessed with the 'Maria' in my surname, many thought I was a Christian from some coastal town down South. Those who had learned that I was a Punjabi, took me to be straight from up North somewhere. Little did they know that I was from a

Maharashtrian village called 'Vandre' which had become 'Bandra' because the Portuguese and the British could not handle the pronunciation. I never tried to change people's perceptions as I believed that ultimately it was me as a person and as a police officer that would matter to them, rather than my origin, language, caste, creed or religion. Most of the time I was proven right and it reinforced my faith.

I cannot claim literary proficiency in Marathi, but it was part of my school curriculum right up to SSC. I had also opted for Marathi in the First Year and Intermediate Arts at College. Having rubbed shoulders with Marathi friends on and off sports grounds, I could communicate with ease in what could be called 'Bambaiya Marathi'. Even then, the Marathi of the interiors of Maharashtra was quite another matter. Therefore, though I was exempted from the Marathi language proficiency course in the Nashik Police Training School, a rural posting in Maharashtra meant, to some extent, an acid test to prove that I was a born Maharashtrian like any other Bombay kid.

As I could not live without sports, I joined the constables and junior officers on the playground almost immediately after taking charge. I got along so well with them that they realised that I really did not differentiate between a constable and a senior officer beyond the bare requisites of our hierarchy. When we went to Yavatmal for the Range Police Sports, I even stayed with the constabulary in the barracks for all the four days of the Games.

The Inspector-in-Charge of the City Kotwali police station, P.G. Patil, was a seasoned and battle-scarred veteran. I was all excited to get cracking and naturally, poor Patil was a little wary of my enthusiasm. Every night, I would go foot patrolling with the Beat Constables and join them in surveillance, returning home around 4 a.m. in the morning. I remember, I'd once invited Poonam to visit me and when she did, she'd got thoroughly bored. She would be alone in the house the whole day. To keep her company was just an old maid, 'regaling' her with the tales of all the past incumbents to the minutest detail!

Working at the City Kotwali police station, I found that their recent detection record was very poor. What could be the reason? I asked the officers. They told me that the local Magistrate was inordinately strict and would not easily give the accused into their custody. When the arrested accused were produced before him, the first question he would ask them was, 'Did the police beat you?' They would invariably say yes, even if we hadn't. He would then immediately pass the order of judicial custody.

How would he change his perspective?

Then it so happened that one night, there was a burglary in the house of the Magistrate's close relative. A 'Two-in-One' (cassette player-cum-radio, quite a precious possession those days), two watches and a purse were stolen in the night. At 8:30 a.m., I received a call from the SP. The Magistrate wanted to see us in his chamber at 10:30 a.m. We went there to find His Honour livid and fuming. How on earth could we have let this happen? Where was prevention! How useless! So on and so forth. The SP was most uncomfortable. I assured His Honour and the SP that a specially dedicated team would be put on the job to concentrate on the detection of the case and we would leave no stone unturned to do our best.

In the evening, the Magistrate's orderly came to the police station and said that His Honour wanted me to see him in his chamber. I promptly obeyed the summons.

'What is the progress?' His Honour asked.

'I am trying my best, sir. I am doing everything possible.' I reassured him albeit not very convincingly.

The next day, the SP gave me a call. The Magistrate had telephoned him to ask about the progress in the investigation. Datta Chaudhary told me that never in his life had he faced the ire of a Magistrate, the way he had to now. I apologised profusely and assured him that I was on the job. Two more days passed during which the Magistrate kept phoning the SP regularly and the SP, in turn, kept calling me. Finally, a thief was arrested on suspicion. He was a reputed expert in his field, a specialist in the very same modus operandi employed by the burglar in our case! He was sent to the Magistrate for remand, and lo and behold! We got ten days' police custody! Quite a record! So we had enough time to carry out our investigation. Yet the very next day, the Magistrate sent for me again.

'Has he given any clues?' He asked.

'No, sir, not yet,' I confessed. 'But we are trying our utmost to get the truth out of him, sir. We are interrogating him.' I could see that His Honour was quite disappointed.

The next day the Magistrate's orderly dropped in at the police station. 'Has the thief opened up? Is he not talking?' He wanted to know.

'No, he has not,' the officers answered, to his disappointment.

'Oh, come on! You people know how to get things out of him!' He winked like a knowledgeable man.

'We cannot touch him or we will be in trouble! You do understand, don't you?' My chaps explained to him and he left, only to return the next day to find out if we had made any progress.

'No, not yet. But our questioning is on, don't worry,' he was told.

'Haven't you *given* him *anything*?' He asked, making an action with his palm as if slapping somebody with it.

'Oh no! How could we! You know how His Honour does not take kindly to such methods,' said my chaps, expressing horror at the very thought.

'Oh, go on! Please feel free! *I* am there, why are you worried?' He began coaxing the officers with a sly smile.

'No, no! Please, we *cannot*!' the embarrassed officers begged him.

Simultaneously, we now noticed a sea-change in His Honour's approach to the accused who were being produced before him. Instead of probing deeply to find out if the police had assaulted them, he began observing how detection and convictions rates had fallen and how people needed to co-operate with the police!

It was just then that the Control Room received an anonymous call that there was a suspicious bundle lying in a field that needed to be looked into. We immediately made a Station Diary entry and a team was dispatched to the spot. What luck! The bundle contained the goods stolen from His Honour's relative's house. The thief we had arrested on suspicion had to be discharged and, from that day, His Honour never refused us police custody of the accused.

The rural police station I had to work at as a supernumerary ASP was Murtizapur, which was a taluka place. The adjoining highway had heavy truck traffic. There was a high incidence of prostitution on the highway and it used to spark unruly behaviour and drunkenness among the truckers who would halt there at the behest of the prostitutes. It was a headache for the law-abiding and I had to intensify our night patrol and round up the prostitutes. I would produce them in court the next day and they would immediately get released on bail. The same night they would be back soliciting on the highway with the pimps to mock at us. I kept racking my brains for a solution. It did come to me all of a sudden, an idea that I decided I must try out.

The next morning, I sat with six pairs of scissors on my desk and issued orders that all the pimps be rounded up and brought before me. The order made quite a stir and soon a motley group of pimps stood before me, quite surprised to be disturbed at that unearthly hour.

I pointed at the scissors and said, 'You see what I have here?' They nodded.

'If I find any of you, or your lady friends, soliciting on the highway under my jurisdiction, I am going to chop their hair off and even yours with these,' I said each of these words slowly, menacingly and carefully as I lifted the scissors and held them up.

They gaped at me and so did the officers and constables present. No one had expected something like this. They did not know what to make of it, but knew that what I said was do-able. From my tone and my body language, they must have also assessed and reckoned that I was perfectly capable of doing it. From that night onwards, the prostitution on the highway came to an abrupt end and did not raise its head, at least till I was in the district. We were no longer the laughing stock that the pimps and prostitutes had reduced us to.

Akola also had a proliferation of *matka* dens. Matka is a form of gambling – illegal lottery. Originally the lucky numbers were based on the opening and closing rates of the New York Cotton Exchange, but later they were drawn from chits kept in a 'notional pot' – matka. Like with all things underground, a lot of criminal activity flourished under the umbrellas of the matka dons and also around their dens. But more about matka later.

In Akola, the biggest matka kingpin was a former wrestler called Shravan Bhirad Pehalwan (pehelwan meaning wrestler). Bhirad had, under his command, a large gang of goondas. People of Akola were mortally afraid of him and even policemen were wary of crossing swords with him. He had, I was told, considerable political backing.

I decided that I would destroy the aura of fear that Bhirad had acquired. In order to maintain secrecy, I chose the boys from my football team and planned a raid on Bhirad's matka den. Bhirad was a tall, well-built man in his Forties and had a thick handlebar moustache that he was very proud of. I was thin, tall and lanky, but I had proficiency in karate and my gurus were none other than Sensei Parvez Mistry and Burge Cooper. I had been part of the Maharashtra Karate squad that had participated in the

Nationals in Bangalore in 1979. So I was quite confident that Bhirad would not have it easy if I met him.

We struck as planned. Bhirad was quite taken aback to see us in his den. Without losing a second, I gave him a well-timed *chudan mae-geri* kick to his stomach and he fell. Even in that melee, his moustache was most tempting. Without further ado, I held the handlebars with both my hands and pulled him up from the floor. He did not know what had hit him. We rounded up all the gang members present in the den and took them to the police station. The procession made quite a grand spectacle and, as expected, this one act sent a powerful message to all the bad elements in Akola city, bringing the lawlessness under control. Our image was definitely restored.

Thereafter, every morning when I came to the police station, I found people gathered outside in large numbers. I thought they were there to lodge complaints or make representations, but that was not the case. Bhirad's arrest had made such a sensation that people used to gather there just to see me! They wanted to catch a glimpse of the new brave police officer who had the temerity to pull Bhirad's moustache! This also made it to the local newspapers and I was most embarrassed when one day Datta Chaudhary told me that his wife wanted to invite me to tea to their house as her friends wanted to meet me. I could think of no excuse to fob off the invite and one afternoon I put on my best clothes and landed at the Chaudharys' where all the good ladies met me and told me to keep up the good work. Given my track record of conversation with the fairer sex, I had very few words at my command to respond adequately. I compensated the deficiency with as many smiles as I could garner and knowing how gawky they must have made me look, I had no appetite for the delectable spread Mrs Chaudhary had laid out on the table.

Pleased with my good work, the DIG asked for my posting as ASP of Khamgaon which is part of district Buldhana within the Amravati Range. The government acceded to his request and issued the necessary orders. Both Shivajirao Baraokar and Datta Chaudhary had given me a free hand. They had let me experiment and gather invaluable experience which helped me build my confidence.

I could only go back to Akola again, many years later when I became Inspector General (Training and Special Units), Maharashtra and had to visit the Police Training School in Akola. Word went around that I was in town and many old-timers dropped in to see me, many of them the juniors I had worked with. Old constables who were now Assistant Sub Inspectors on the verge of retirement, my erstwhile teammates who were in my squad that hit Bhirad's den. They brought back fond memories of the love that I had received in the city and its surroundings, both from the public as well as my juniors.

They reminded me of the Ganapati festival shortly after my 'victory' over Bhirad Pehelwan. The entire police force of the city was geared up for the bandobast and I too was on my toes. Immersion processions were proceeding along the designated routes and the usual slogans were being raised. Suddenly, I found the slogans a little strange. Was I hearing right? Ganapati Bappa *Maria*! Not 'Ganapati Bappa *Morya*?' And I looked around in disbelief to see if the others too had heard what I had. Or were my ears playing a trick on me? But, my officers and men were grinning from ear to ear and enjoying my discomfiture. Just a little bit of fun at the expense of the new ASP. The disarming humour did not fail to blur my vision, momentarily, with a film of moisture it brought to my eyes. Yes, the crowds were acknowledging me in a warm way! What more could you want at that young age when you had just begun your journey in their service!

6

Bombay Beckons

It was on 1 February 1984 when I took charge of my post as a full-fledged Assistant Superintendent of Police of Khamgaon Sub-division.

Hasan Gafoor, an eminent IPS officer, was the Superintendent of Police of Buldhana district under which came Khamgaon. Gafoor and his wife, Saman took to me instantly and looked after me like family. Saman Gafoor would frequently invite me to their house for home-cooked meals and if they could not meet me for a long time for some reason, there would be phone calls to ask after me, which showed their genuine concern. Soft-spoken, polished and suave, Gafoor came from a distinguished aristocratic family. He was particularly fond of Urdu poetry and had excellent taste in literature and music, from Habib Wali Mohammad's ghazals to Habib Painter's qawwalis. Needless to say, Gafoor became a father figure to me. As regards work, he was a thorough professional, though a man of a few words and completely unassuming. He took a keen interest in my work and progress.

I realised that taking a cue from my work in Akola, people in Khamgaon had high expectations of me. Like Akola, Khamgaon had its own share of criminal gangs, goondas, liquor dens and gambling dens, with the usual pattern of criminals entering politics to strengthen their clout. The local political heavyweight was Dilip Sananda. The Sanandas were a powerful and wealthy family whose prosperity and clout was linked to dubious activities. They were moneylenders, ran gambling dens and to garner popular support they organised Ganapati and Navaratri festivals through 'mandals' (associations) which attracted the local youth and groomed them into 'cadres'. People were harassed and afraid of the gangs. They wanted strict action, as did my bosses. So, the first thing that I probably did was to raid the gambling dens and smashed them, inviting the ire of the gangs. It was also the first time in my career that private criminal cases were deliberately registered against me and my juniors to put spokes in the wheels and stop us in our tracks. But, the truth was on our side and they did not succeed. Our bold action earned us the love and respect from the public and the media also lauded our work.

Every ASP has to personally investigate six important cases in a year. In the jurisdiction of Borakhedi police station in Buldhana district, there was a heinous rape and dacoity reported in a secluded farmhouse. The dacoits had raped both the lady of the house and her daughter who had just delivered a baby girl. The young mother had put up a spirited resistance, but the barbaric culprits had taken the newborn to the well and threatened to drown it if the young mother did not submit to their lust.

The SP asked me to take up this case for personal investigation. The Dog Squad was called in and our investigations commenced. All indications pointed to the role of some Pardhis. The 'Pardhi' is a tribe notified as a 'criminal tribe' by the British who had classified almost 150 tribes as such, under the infamous Criminal Tribes Act of 1871. In 1952, the tribe was de-notified. Yet they continued to face social discrimination as the stigma of years of branding was hard to get rid of. Poverty, lack of education and exclusion kept them bound to their old ways.

We learned that some of the suspects were hiding among the pavement dwellers on P. D'Mello Road in Bombay. So, I came down to Bombay with a team of officers and men. We arrested three suspects and took them back to Borakhedi. Fresh out of the Police Academy, it was fully ingrained in my mind that third-degree method was wrong, a strict no-no and to be avoided at all costs. Then, these were poor tribals, unfairly blacklisted and ostracised. You had to be sensitive to their plight. So I began interrogating the three Pardhis with all the emotions and goodness at my command, interspersing the interrogation with *chahaa* (tea), *paan* (betel leaf) and snacks. I ordered the old police Inspector-in-Charge and other officers to wait outside. Each time when I left the room, I made it explicitly clear that nobody was to interrogate the suspects till I got back. On return, I would resume my questioning, ordering refreshments as we went along. The Pardhis took my hospitality in their stride and gave away nothing. The local officers, frustrated to the hilt, waited patiently for my 'textbook interrogation' to work wonders. With things obviously progressing at a snail's pace, even my own frustration was mounting, but I could not show it. I had no clue how to achieve a breakthrough. The police custody remand of these rapists/dacoits was fast running out.

One afternoon, as my 'textbook' interrogation continued, there was a knock on the door. 'Come in!' I said, watching the Pardhis help themselves to paan after wiping the tea off their moustaches.

It was the Inspector. 'Sir, you are tired! Please take a short break,' he said. I was grateful for the diversion and came out of the room. I splashed some water on my face, stretched my tired and stressed limbs and strolled to the peepul tree in the police station compound. I sat on its *paar*, the round platform seat that they build around tree trunks. I sat there deep in thought as to what I should do next, how I should frame my questions and how to get the police remand extended. Suddenly, I heard screams. Before I could get up and comprehend where they emanated from, the Inspector emerged and came towards me. 'Sir, the case is detected. Let us go and do the recovery,' he said. He meant the recovery of stolen goods, the evidentiary link to connect the crime with the culprits. The look on his face said, '*Young man, with this type of hardened criminals, only these things work! They are seasoned and you too have to be.*'

I quietly followed the old greyhound. The necessary paperwork done, he piled up the Pardhis – well secured by hefty guards – into a van. We followed their directions and drove to the spot they indicated. We dug at the spot they showed us and secured the loot. An important lesson had been learned. Different things work with different criminals.

Khamgaon was a sensitive posting as it had a history of communal tension. I was in Khamgaon for two years and toiled incessantly, keeping my nose to the grindstone. I firmly believed that the worst scourge of criminality is to drive a schism between communities. The hard work paid off, because during my posting, there was no communal riot in Khamgaon, crime was under control and my work was appreciated by my seniors. What is more, I got married while posted in Khamgaon.

It was an arranged match, decided while Dad was alive and had met the bride-to-be – a pucca Delhi girl. A Miss Chopra schooled in Delhi and with a History Major from Lady Shri Ram College, Preeti was the middle one of a triumvirate of doting daughters. She had just returned from Hanover, Germany after completing an educational stint in History. Their father, a no-nonsense disciplinarian, was a government servant. From this formidable combination, my saviour was the bride's mother, Promilla Chopra, who had close links with Maharashtra. Being born and raised in Nashik, she could even speak fluent Marathi. She came from a prosperous business family of Nashik. Her father had been a wealthy construction contractor and had a sprawling bungalow in Nashik.

The bungalow of the ASP in Khamgaon was on a hill. I was so busy with the hurly-burly of police work that I had not bothered to give any thought to furnishing it. It was sparse and spartan with just a bed, a desk and a chair. The bed was just one of those provided to the constabulary recruits which they got me from the headquarters. I was more than happy with the comfort it offered. After a hard day's slog, sleep descended the minute you lay on it and then as soon as your eyes opened, you were out of it in a jiffy to get back at the gamblers, liquor barons and all other vile species from the netherworld!

All this happy harmony was rudely disturbed one day by a single phone call and that too not from any gangster, superior or politician. It was Mr Chopra, out of the blue. He said that he was on an official visit to Nagpur and had finished his work earlier than expected. 'My meeting is over and I have some time on hand. My return ticket is booked on the train from Bhusawal. I thought I can come and spend a day with you tomorrow?' he asked.

I was quite surprised. Preeti was in Germany, but she could have informed me that her father would be in my vicinity! Neither was there an advance intimation from him after reaching Nagpur. Nor did he have any relations or friends in Bhusawal that I knew of, that he should book the return ticket from Bhusawal! I immediately sensed that I was speaking to a one-man fact-finding commission, a special branch officer who had arrived from another state for character verification of the target that was me!

I had just one bed. No TV. A bare house. What would he think of me to find me living like this! The driver deputed on my police jeep was one Eknath Rinde. He saw me in my gloom on the return journey home and sensed that something was seriously wrong. *'Saab, kya hua? Kuchh problem hai kya?'* (Sir, what happened? Any problem?) he couldn't resist asking.

'Kal hone wale sasur aa rahen hain, Rinde!' (My father-in-law-to-be is coming to see me tomorrow, Rinde!) I was grateful to have someone to talk to.

'Koi problem nahin, sir. Khana peena laga denge. Poora intezam

ho jayega,' Rinde assured me (No problem, sir. We will get the food and the beverages. All arrangements will be taken care of).

'That is not enough, Rinde. Look at the way I am living! As if in a barrack! There is not even a decent bed for him in the house.' I expressed my anxiety.

'Don't worry, *saab. Apne rishtedar ki furniture ki dukaan hai. Poori dukaan idhar laga denge kaam hone tak!'* I couldn't believe my ears. He was saying that one of his relatives had a furniture shop and he would press all the furniture into my service till 'the job was done'.

In Akola, I had arranged a foldable bed for Poonam and she had purchased all the basic kitchen utensils for me. Now this was not my sister who was visiting me. It was my father-in-law and the honour of the Marias was at stake. In such circumstances, Rinde was like a blessing and I thanked god for His foresight in providing me with such a resourceful charioteer like Lord Krishna to Arjuna.

Rinde stood by his word and overnight my 'shell flat' was converted into a 'show flat', as they say in builders' terminology when a bare flat is furnished for display to prospective customers.

The visit went off very well and my family and I – Rinde, my orderlies, constables, officers and men – waved goodbye to Mr Chopra as he left for Bhusawal.

'Sir, shall we send the furniture off?' Rinde came rubbing his hands with the satisfaction of a job done well and a mischievous smile on his face. I was about to say yes when a thought struck me. 'No, Rinde! *Tyanna train madhe basu dya. Parat aale tar...!'* (Wait till he is on the train. What if he comes back!) The vision of the train getting cancelled and Mr Chopra returning to a bare barrack flashed before my eyes.

I knew that Mr Chopra was not interested in the furniture. He wanted to see and know me as a person and had enough savoir-faire and worldly experience not to go by the furniture to assess a young man's worth. Yet I did not dare take any chances, because I felt any man would want to see his daughter in a reasonably well-appointed house, especially in a match that he has arranged. So it was a pleasure to hear Preeti on the phone when she said that her Dad was impressed. I probed a little and she said: 'By you and your house.' So all the trouble that we took had been worth it.

The marriage was to be solemnised in Delhi and the date was fixed after Hasan Gafoor granted me the necessary leave. The invitation cards were printed and I, as per protocol, went to the Range Police Headquarters at Amravati to meet DIG Shivajirao Baraokar to invite him. With a smart salute, I handed over the wedding card and was digging out the sentences I had thought of to ask him to attend it, knowing full well that he would not bother to come all the way to Delhi and quite happy about it, for imagine the stress of looking after him when you have sufficient stress already of being the groom. He began reading the card and looked up at me with an incredulous expression. Something was not right. But what?

'How can you get married on this date?' He asked.

'Sir?' I managed to say.

'There is the important Sharda Devi bandobast to be deployed on these dates! How did the SP grant you leave?' He said and I was speechless. He immediately dialled Hasan Gafoor and told him point blank that he could not spare me during the Sharda Devi festival. Crestfallen, I exited, searched for a PCO (Public Call Office) and called up Preeti. When I broke the news to her, she just went silent. Then Mr Chopra came on the line and I explained to him what had happened. Luckily for me, being in the government service, he understood my predicament. He asked me to go back to the DIG and get alternate dates so that fresh cards could be printed. Relieved that somebody could understand my situation, I went back to DIG Baraokar and asked him when I could get married. People go to pundits (priests) for *muhurats* (auspicious date and time). I got them from my DIG. He called for the police bandobast calendar and after a lot of deliberation gave me four days leave in October: 9, 10, 11 and 12. I went back to the PCO and dialled Mr Chopra. He calmly jotted the dates down. Without any complaint, he rehashed all the arrangements to accommodate the bandobast calendar of Maharashtra Police and had fresh cards printed.

I took the early morning train from Bhusawal on 9 October and reached Delhi late in the evening. My family had already reached Delhi from Bombay, thoroughly disappointed at not having the groom in the marriage party.

We got married on 10 October. The next day, I left Delhi by the Rajdhani Express with Preeti and my family. We reached Bombay on the morning of 12 October. It was Karwa Chauth, the day married women from the north keep a day-long fast for the well-being of their husbands. They break it only after the sighting of the moon. Bollywood has impressed me thoroughly with the importance of Karwa Chauth now. Then, I had not bothered to apply my mind to it, till my mother made sure that it was followed sufficiently to fit the stipulations of the DIG who had made it abundantly clear that come what may, Preeti and I had to be on the Howrah Mail to Khamgaon on the night of 12 October.

En route, the first railway station in my jurisdiction was Malkapur. Thereafter came Nandura, then Jalamb and lastly Shegaon. Preeti and I were flabbergasted when at each of these stations, there were hundreds of people waiting on the platform with garlands to greet us, having learned that we were returning almost straight from our marriage pandal. We did not know how to respond to the love and affection that they showered upon us. It was, indeed, overwhelming and touching.

I was in my office on 13 October. With just four days of leave and all of it over already, there was no way we could have planned a honeymoon. So I arranged an inspection at Tamgaon,

Sangrampur police station – a small town nestling at the foothills of the picturesque Satpura range. On reaching there, I dropped Preeti at the guest house and went to the police station for inspection. It was a beautiful quaint guest house, with old wooden flooring, two rooms and a veranda. Hardly had I commenced the inspection when a constable came running to me to say that 'madam' had summoned me back immediately. I was alarmed and rushed to the guest house to find Preeti waiting for me in the porch, surrounded with unopened bags.

'I am not staying here a minute longer. It is a haunted house,' she declared and there was no way I could make her change her mind, so petrified was she.

After I had left her at the guest house, the *khansama* (cook-cum-caretaker) and his wife had come to take the food order from her and began chatting with her.

'What a lovely old place! Do many visitors come here?' asked Preeti.

'Yes, M'aam, it is very nice and quiet, but nobody comes here.' They said matter-of-factly.

'Why is that so?' asked Preeti. And then they narrated the grisly story to her. A British officer living there had had an affair with the then khansama's daughter. The discovery of the affair had infuriated the khansama so much that he had chopped off the officer's head while he was asleep and the officer's headless ghost now walked the place with its boots on!

I tried to reason with Preeti. Firstly, there is no such thing as ghosts. It did not work. Secondly, the story was just a ruse to ensure that no senior officer visited the guest house. This did not work either. She just refused to listen. So that was the end of our brief honeymoon in the lovely old place.

We thoroughly enjoyed our stint at Khamgaon. It helped us bond which has lasted us throughout. Uninitiated in the Marathi language, Preeti totally depended on me for communicating with the people around us. One day she asked the house-help to get her a kilogram of meat from the market. When he returned with one kilo of salt, she just could not understand what had gone wrong. This is how she learned that the Marathi word for salt was *meeth*. On another occasion, she sent him to buy one kilo of *seb*, which is the Hindi word for apples. He returned with the savoury snack *sev gathya*!

On 31 October, I took Preeti to Shegaon to the shrine of the great saint Shri Gajanan Maharaj. The local police station had organised tea for us after the darshan, where the families of policemen were to meet us. While we were at the guest house and about to leave for tea, news came in that Prime Minister Indira Gandhi had been assassinated. The assassins were her Sikh bodyguards. Anti-Sikh riots were a distinct possibility and we had to ensure utmost protection to the Sikhs in the jurisdiction. I sent Preeti back to Khamgaon, holstered my revolver and immediately proceeded to the highway to prevent attacks on Sikh truckers. Simultaneously, I issued instructions to tighten security at all sensitive points. I immediately deployed pickets at the points where the highway entered and exited my jurisdiction and provided armed escorts to Sikh truckers by forming convoys. This ensured that on the highway stretch, under my jurisdiction, no untoward incident occurred. I returned home to Khamgaon after nearly a week. If mobile phones were a distant dream, to get to a fixed line phone was also a luxury those days as it was in many Indian hinterlands. Left in the interiors of unfamiliar rural surroundings, for an anxious week to fend for herself, was quite a daunting experience for poor Preeti. Coming as it did, after a whirlwind marriage, followed by hectic journeys on the Rajdhani and the Howrah Mail, and that too immediately after her return from a happy student life in Hanover! But she managed well and braced herself to prepare for what promised to be a life full of such uncertainties.

The story of how I had put up the curtains in my bachelor's

pad at Khamgaon is something Preeti loves recounting with glee even now. I still remember the expression on Preeti's face when she had stepped into the living room. 'What is this? How come...? I think the poor chaps don't know that the right side must face us!' she had said, alluding to my house-helps, as she set her eyes on the drab curtain lining facing us. I realised that a confession was due. When she learned that it was done at my directions, she'd almost died laughing. I had sincerely thought that the beautiful right side must be seen from outside the house! The poor orderlies had tried to reason with me, but I would not budge. No way could the ASP's orders be flouted and they resigned themselves to my logic. Now, with the wife in charge of the house, things naturally improved. With her touch, within the meagre budget at our disposal, she managed to put life in the bureaucratised atmosphere of the official residence provided to us. With her help, I began discovering that the curtain episode did not mean that I was hopeless at living space designing.

After Khamgaon, I was posted to Osmanabad as the Superintendent of Police. I took charge of the post on 7 September 1985. As I was awaiting my promotion orders, the police grapevine had it that DIG Baraokar was impressed with my performance and was trying for my posting to Yavatmal as the District SP. However, when the actual orders were issued, I was instead appointed as SP, Osmanabad. I was wondering how this change could have taken place. It was then that I learned the reason.

The then Chief Minister of Maharashtra was Shivajirao Patil Nilangekar who was from Latur which has been carved out of Osmanabad. There were two groups in Osmanabad district. One owing allegiance to the chief minister and the other to another heavyweight – Padamsinh Patil, an influential Maratha leader from the district. He controlled Terna Sugar factory in Dhoki which is in Osmanabad, but close to Latur city. In the general body meeting of the cooperative society controlling the Terna Sugar Factory, the chief minister's group had created a ruckus leading to assault and affray when Padamsinh Patil was alleged to have taken out his licensed revolver and fired in the air. After great difficulty, the rival group had managed to get an FIR registered, despite their allegiance to the chief minister's group.

Even though the offence was registered, the local police could not muster the courage to arrest Padamsinh Patil and there was considerable media uproar. The chief minister was reported to be in search of an SP who could control the Padamsinh group and arrest him. I was selected to go to Osmanabad and complete this incommodious task. I had to go to a district to arrest one of its most puissant leaders.

Preeti and I had one small truckload of household goods to be carted to our next destination. We hired a private taxi and left for Osmanabad, with the truck following. I was not sure if I would last in Osmanabad for more than a week given my impending showdown with the influential Padamsinh Patil. I had told Preeti that we would check into the Government Guest House and not unload the truck until we were sure about our next posting! So we checked in at the guest house, accommodated the truck driver in the headquarters and told him that he would have to stay there for a week or ten days.

I immediately took charge as SP, Osmanabad and called the Inspector of the District Special Branch, one Police Inspector Vasantrao Deshmukh. 'We have to arrest Padamsinh Patil,' I said to him. 'Sir, it will definitely cause a major law and order problem,' he said. '*Karyakartey rastyaavar yetil.*' He meant that the workers or associates of the Padamsinh faction would take to the streets.

'In that case, go to his house and ask him to talk to me on the phone,' I said. Deshmukh followed my orders and, soon, I received a telephone call at the office from Padamsinh Patil.

The gist of the conversation with Padamsinh Patil was this: I am posted as SP of the district. I was not interested to be here. I was preparing to go to Yavatmal. But now I am reluctantly here and there are clear instructions that I should arrest you.

He said, 'If you try to arrest me, there will be a law and order problem.'

I again said that I was not interested in being in Osmanabad and would be perfectly happy elsewhere. A transfer would be most welcome and I am ready to take the risk. My truck with my household articles is still unpacked. I am ready and itching for a transfer. But for you, it will be a problem. Your image will take a huge beating. But you have a way out and can save face. Just say you don't want to create violence in the district and inconvenience the inhabitants. So you will go to the SP and surrender. That will be like a true leader.

There was a small pause before he asked, 'Where are you?'

'I am in my office, waiting for you,' I answered.

He came to my office with his supporters and surrendered with great fanfare. Soon our truck was unpacked and no law and order problem was reported in the district for the nearly two years of my tenure in Osmanabad.

Even in the midst of an exciting and challenging professional life, sports took centre stage and I must thank my stars for such a wonderful deviation. The Maharashtra State Police Games (MSPG) are akin to the Olympics for the Force as teams from various Ranges and Commissionerates compete to show off their skills in various team sports, individual sports and athletics. I made it a point to play with the men and being reasonably good at basketball, I had taken the lead to form a good team for the Aurangabad Range with the constables. Our team was to leave in a few days for Aurangabad. I was eager and very keen to be part of the team and enter the fray. I needed the permission of the DIG Aurangabad, Sampath Kumar Iyengar, who was known to be a hot-headed officer with a short fuse. He did not know that his subordinates called him *'angaar'* which means burning ember. I mustered the courage and picked up the hotline.

'Sir, this is Rakesh Maria, SP, Osmanabad,' I said as he came on the line.

'Yes, Mr Maria! What can I do for you?' He said. He was known for his fluent English and an impeccable accent.

'Sir, the Police Games are starting in Aurangabad.' I took a little pause.

'Oh! That's news to me!' He was at his sardonic best. He was the Organising Secretary of the Games and here I was, informing him that the games were starting in Aurangabad. How stupid of me! Still I managed to proceed.

'My request, sir. Our basketball team is going to participate. Even I play basketball.' I began preparing the foundation.

'So?' came the defying interruption.

'Sir, I am requesting permission to come to Aurangabad to play in the team. I play basketball reasonably well, sir,' I completed, trying best not to sound as if I was bragging.

'Even I play hockey reasonably well. But that does not mean I will accompany the Indian team for the Olympics!' came the crushing reply and I could feel my ears going hot.

'Sorry, sir, for having wasted your time,' I said and he banged the phone down.

My team went to Aurangabad without me. The Games started and we barely won the first round to make it to the next.

Late in the night, I got a wireless message that I should speak to S. Iyengar. I was petrified. Now, what have I done? Had an incident occurred in my district about which I wasn't aware? So I called the Control Room and asked. *'Kidhar kuchh lafda hua hai kya?'* (Has some serious incident been reported from anywhere?) The answer was in the negative. Then I spoke to Iyengar.

'I went to watch the basketball match. The boys tell me that they need you. Seeing them play, I don't think you can make any further difference to the team, but I will accede to your request and permit you to join them.'

I could not believe my ears. 'When can I come down, sir?' I asked.

'Tomorrow morning,' I could feel the reluctance in the voice.

The next morning, Preeti and I left for Aurangabad. Luck was with us and the team got galvanised. We reached the finals and lost to the much superior State Reserve Police Force (SRPF) team who were the defending champions for the last decade or so! But, it was the first time that Aurangabad Range had earned a medal in basketball and that too a silver.

Later I got to know that as the Range DIG, after the first win with the slim margin, Iyengar had gone to meet the boys to boost their spirit. *'Baal-baal bach gaye aap log!'* he said to the team. It meant that it was a close shave! The team could not contain their feelings and told him that they needed me to boost the strength of the team. 'Sir, please call Maria *Saab*. We need him,' some had ventured to say. That had turned the scales in my favour and I was permitted to join the team.

With trial and error, Preeti had begun picking up Marathi and she was doing an admirable job of it.I was enjoying my work. Even Preeti was getting used to a quieter life in a rural environment. We least expected to be transferred to a big city, until one morning in the last week of January 1987, when Poonam called to say that according to the papers, I was to be transferred to Bombay. How was that possible? Normally, only a Deputy Commissioner rank officer with a minimum of eight to ten years of experience is posted to Bombay. Yet it got me thinking. Could such rumours be baseless?

The next day, I got a call from Suryakant Jog, the venerable Inspector General, at the State Police Headquarters. 'You are coming to Bombay, so get ready!' he announced. Then I got a call from D.S. Soman, the Commissioner of Police, Bombay. 'Hand over charge and come to Bombay,' he said.

'Sir, it will be very difficult for me to work in Bombay because

I am from Bombay and know people there,' I began making my excuses. I was not at all keen to be back in Bombay. I liked the work in the districts and the friendly, warm atmosphere. But I knew I was not doing a good job of it and it did not work. The transfer orders were issued and we again began packing up.

I was the first from my batch to be posted to Bombay and the reason for my transfer was far from ordinary. I was to replace Y.C. Pawar, a brave and experienced senior officer who was Deputy Commissioner of Police of Zone-IV. In 1987, Zone-IV covered a sprawling area and comprised Dadar, Mahim, Matunga, Dharavi, Antop Hill, Chembur, RCF, Trombay and Deonar police stations. They had large South Indian pockets which were strongholds of Varda Dada – Varadarajan Mudaliar – a don of South Indian origin. Varadarajan's career in crime had begun as a cargo thief in the Bombay docks. He had developed a mass base by helping the impoverished South Indian residents in slums like Dharavi and Antop Hill and had expanded his activities into the manufacture of illicit liquor, bootlegging, extortion, kidnappings, contract killings, land grabbing and gambling. He is credited with having started a monthly kickback system to the police and other government officers, to ensure that they turned a blind eye to his nefarious activities. And he also had the dubious distinction of running a parallel judicial system to dispense speedy 'justice' in his strongholds.

It was Julio Ribeiro and Y.C. Pawar who took up the challenge to curb Varda's activities and targeted him systematically. They succeeded. With quite a few gang members behind bars, and with many of his operations closed down or curbed, Varda had fled to Tamil Nadu. Now Y.C. Pawar's tenure was about to end and the senior police hierarchy had chosen me as his replacement. It was a huge challenge. If it was my fame with Bhirad Pehelwan in Akola and the Sanandas in Khamgaon that had landed me in Bombay so soon, I knew that a Bombay don and his cohorts were quite another cup of tea.

I came to Bombay and called on the Commissioner of Police, D.S. Soman, a highly respected officer that we all stood in awe of. Soman told me that I had to continue YC's work. It meant that the pressure on Varda had to be maintained at any cost.

I took charge from Y.C. Pawar on 1 February 1987. He gave me a thorough briefing on Varda and the action he had taken so far – how he had built up the pressure. I decided to lose no time in showing Varda and his men, as well as my own policemen, that YC's successor was as determined as he, if not more. The same evening, I told my officers that I wanted to go to Antop Hill. Varda was in Chennai and was unwell, but his close right-hand man operated from Antop Hill. He was a Sikh, one Sardar Mohinder Singh Vij aka Soma bhai. Another trusted aide was a man called Thomas Kurien aka Khaja bhai, but it was the Sikh who had gained disrepute for his ruthlessness and violence.

I straightaway went to Mohinder Singh aka Soma's house. Though I went unannounced, he managed to escape from the back door. Nevertheless, the desired signal went out that the guy they might take to be a kid, only five years old in khakhi, was not to be taken lightly. Even the Senior Inspectors in my jurisdiction, all with thirty years and more of experience, realised that I meant business. If I kept Varda's henchmen on the run, they would be unavailable to Varda for running his empire. So we kept up the intense pressure on them and the strategy paid off. Varda never came back and ultimately died in Chennai in January 1988.

The official accommodation allotted to us was in Dadar, a typical Maharashtrian area, vibrant and in the thick of things, be it politics, culture, commerce or anything. As Bombay was again seeping into my spirit, one of the happiest moments made it into our lives. Preeti and I were blessed with our firstborn, Kunal. Mama was thrilled to hold her first grandchild in her arms. How she must have missed Dad who adored children. With his own grandchild, his joy would have known no bounds.

7

Mukkam Raigad

It was 10 October 1988, and a Monday. Kunal was barely four and a half months old. We were beginning to have or just about acquiring a general sense of parenting with all its anxious moments when the baby refuses to go as per your plans and your frequently peaking anxiety can only be addressed by paediatric or grandma consultations. Even then, a small family celebration was slated for the evening at our Dadar home because it was our wedding anniversary.

Around 8 o'clock in the morning, as I was getting ready to commence a hectic Bombay week, I got a call from S.P. Singh, the Director General of Police. 'Are you ready for a change?' he asked me. I was puzzled but thought he was offering me a different Police Zone. So I said, 'Yes, sir, I am ready.'

'Oh good! Then go and take charge in Alibaug,' he said.

'Sir!' I was flabbergasted. My sincerest worry found words and I said, 'Sir! My son is barely four months old and it will be very hard for my wife, sir! Also, I have just completed twenty months as DCP in Bombay!'

'You keep this house for the family, but go immediately to Alibaug, and take charge this very afternoon.' He was very clear and firm in his resolve and there was little scope for anything else.

I tried to break the news to Preeti as gently as possible but failed miserably. Then I called up Mama. She too was upset. There is a ferry service available! I can make it to Bombay in an hour and a half! I tried to reason with them, but failed miserably and by three in the afternoon that day, I had taken charge in Alibaug as the Superintendent of Police, Raigad district.

My unexpected transfer to Alibaug was caused by the sudden transfer of my predecessor S.S. Wagal. Sharad Pawar was the Chief Minister of the state. An industrialist and mill-owner had a plant called Sadhna Nitrochem at Dhatav in Roha and he was facing serious trouble with the labour union. He needed police help and the chief minister had spoken to Wagal to personally look into the matter. Wagal instructed the Special Branch at Raigad to keep a watch and be alert. However, somewhere at the lower levels, the issue was lost sight of and things went horribly wrong. The officers seemed not to have paid adequate attention to Wagal's orders. On 1 October 1988, the workers set fire to the factory and grievously assaulted the manager. He had to be shifted to the Hinduja Hospital in Bombay. Matters came to a head and as it happens often, the boss had to take the blame.

Soon Preeti and Kunal joined me in Alibaug and we slowly settled down in the beautiful old bungalow of the SP on Alibaug beach. I was SP, Raigad for about three and a half years. Raigad was communally sensitive and politically highly volatile. The Peasants and Workers Party (PWP) of India, called the Shetkari Kamgar Paksh in Marathi, was the prominent political party in the district. In fact, the leader of the Opposition in the Maharashtra Legislative Assembly was Datta Patil of the PWP who was also the MLA from Alibaug. For the Congress party, Abdul Rahman Antulay was a big leader from the area. The Shiv Sena was also making inroads into the political stage of the district.

On the other hand, there was a pan-Indian phenomenon which was unfolding. The BJP's Shri Ram Jyot Yatra was passing through communally sensitive areas of Raigad, posing a big challenge to the police. On 5 October 1990, a serious incident occurred at Morba when the Ram Jyot Yatra was passing from Mangaon to Shrivardhan. Some Muslims threw stones at the yatra. This was followed by incidents of arson and attacks on the police personnel. The Sub-Divisional Magistrate and the Sub-Divisional Police Officer of Mahad had to open fire to quell the riot and confront the mobs. The chariot was abandoned and there was serious communal tension. I rushed to the spot and found a big standoff, with the police arraigned on one side and the Muslims on the other, at some distance. The tension was palpable and the slightest wrong move on either side could have led to disastrous consequences. My officers said, 'Sir, we cannot proceed. If we do, we will be attacked and we will have to open fire again!' That was obviously the last thing the administration wanted.

'Let me see what I can do,' I said. I then left the vehicles and my staff behind, asking them not to follow me, come what may. I began walking alone towards the Muslims. As I advanced, a few stones came hurtling towards me. Luckily they did not reach me, but my men were naturally concerned and urged me to return. However, I did not stop and ordered them not to advance. Fortunately, they did not panic and obeyed me. I could see that some elders from the mob were asking the boys not to pelt stones. This was reassuring. It meant that all sense was not lost yet. I continued to walk and reached them in a few agonising minutes which seemed to stretch forever. Some of them then came forward and said that they had not done anything wrong, but the Hindus had provoked them and they had only retaliated. Now the main task was not to waste time in arguments, but quickly disperse the mob and ensure that no further violence occurred. So I told them firmly that if the chariot was not allowed to pass, I would be compelled to take action and open fire which could lead to unnecessary loss of lives and limbs. The stoppage of the chariot had the potential to fuel rumour-mongering and exacerbate communal tensions, not only in Raigad district but the entire country. They understood what I said and agreed to let the chariot pass. Thus, we avoided confrontation and a major communal conflagration was averted. At such times, besides luck, a lot depends on the officers' presence of mind and their ability to control their own and their juniors' panic reactions.

I camped in Mangaon that day. The District Magistrate/ Collector was Ganesh Walavalkar, IAS, a reputed officer. He, too, had rushed to Morba. The next day, a peace committee meeting was held at the Irrigation Department Guest House at Kolad in Roha. It was attended by important leaders including veterans like Shiv Sena leader Manohar Joshi and Congress leader A.R. Antulay. Antulay was fretting and fuming. He was all praise for me but vented his ire on the Collector. He announced that he would seek the Collector's transfer. Walavalkar was a true gentleman and a dedicated officer. He had done nothing wrong to deserve a transfer. When Antulay kept talking about Walavalkar's transfer, I could not bear it and said that if that was the case, even I, as the Superintendent of Police, deserved to be transferred. 'No, no, we are not seeking *your* transfer!' said Antulay, but I strongly defended the Collector. Antulay was taken aback and fortunately the situation was swiftly defused. Had Walavalkar been transferred, it would have been grave injustice. I felt happy at the thought that my interjection must have played some role in averting an innocent civil servant from getting sacrificed.

It was the summer of 1992 and I had completed three and a half years in Raigad. It was a record of sorts. My transfer orders had been issued twice, once for posting as DCP, Kalyan and then for posting as SP, Thane (Rural). These transfers were called off because the locals and the politicians, led by Datta Patil of the PWP, wanted me to continue. However, I badly needed a change and wanted to move on.

The Mumbai-Pune Expressway was yet to be constructed and there was a recurring problem of huge traffic jams on the old and winding Bombay-Poona highway. Dr Parvinder Singh Pasricha was posted in Bombay as the Additional Commissioner of Police, Traffic. He was an acclaimed expert on traffic control, having done his doctorate in Traffic Management and had introduced a slew of changes to improve the traffic situation in Bombay.

One day, the Bombay-Poona highway was blocked with the mother of all snarls. Cars were stuck for almost twenty-four hours. I received a call from Dr Pasricha who was desperately looking for a solution. He asked me to ascertain the reason and see if I could clear it. Khopoli was one of my police stations and parts of Borghat too came under my jurisdiction. I rushed to Khopoli via Nagothane. Along the Khopoli-Lonavala stretch, there were numerous dhabas (inexpensive roadside refreshment joints) thronged and patronised by truckers. These dhabas were notorious for prostitution and other dubious activities. As expected, I found many trucks and vehicles parked in a haphazard manner and realised that some harsh policing was needed if we had to restore some order. I simply got out of my vehicle, took out a lathi and started hitting the truck drivers. In the process, a few windscreens also took hits, but it had the desired effect. All of them scurried back into their trucks, tempos and taxis, and, in the space of one hour, the whole traffic jam was cleared!

This probably created an impression in the corridors of power in Bombay that I had a good sense of traffic control! Coincidentally, it so happened that at that very moment, Dr Pasricha was looking for some junior IPS officer who could be trained in traffic control under his guidance. I think it was my 'great prowess' at traffic clearance on the Bombay-Poona Highway that convinced Dr Pasricha and S. Ramamurthy, the Director General of Police, Maharashtra, that they had found the man they were looking for. So I was sounded that the state government felt that I should be posted as Deputy Commissioner of Police, Traffic, in Bombay. Glad to get to move on, I said yes and, in May 1992, I was posted in the Bombay Commissionerate as DCP (Traffic).

8

God Disposes

I worked for a couple of months under the tutelage of Dr P.S. Pasricha and zealously tried to imbibe the skills needed to tackle the growing traffic needs of the city. Impressed by my enthusiasm and sincerity, Commissioner Shrikant Bapat and Dr Pasricha selected me for traffic training in Japan in October 1992 under a Government of India initiative.

My training in Tokyo was for three months, October, November and December 1992. The Ganapati bandobast is a huge challenge for the Bombay police, especially for the traffic branch. Despite being DCP (Traffic), Bombay, the senior echelons selected me to be at the main immersion spot in the city i.e., Girgaum Chowpatty. I completed the Ganapati bandobast to satisfaction and flew out to Japan. The training in Tokyo was excellent and as it progressed, I began to believe that specialisation in 'Traffic Control' could be my forte.

On 6 December 1992, I was in Tokyo, entirely clueless about the events unfolding in Ayodhya. It was my old Japanese professor who told me that there were riots in India because a mosque had been demolished. It was subsequently on television that I saw news reports of the Babri demolition and the riots that had erupted in different parts of the country including Bombay.

On completion of the training, I left Tokyo on 4 January 1993 and reached Bombay the next night. The first phase of the riots –

the December phase – had come to an end and the city seemed to be limping back to normalcy. As my flight was beginning its descent into Bombay that night, a group of knifers was giving effect to their sinister design in a dark lane of the area known as Dongri. A few *mathadi* loaders were sleeping in the godown of Vijay Transport Company. One of them stepped out to relieve himself and he was attacked by the group. The others heard his screams and rushed to his help. They too were stabbed and the attackers disappeared in the cloak of darkness. Four mathadis were admitted to J.J. Hospital. Of them, Laxman Kadam and Rajaram Kadam were declared dead on admission.

These loaders were not the sundry migrant labour easily available in the city. They were mathadis; mathadi is the word for a loader who carries goods on his head (*matha)* or lugs them on his back. Predominantly Maratha Hindus, they originally have their roots in *Paschim* (Western) Maharashtra which comprises five districts: Pune, Solapur, Satara, Sangli and Kolhapur. They load and unload tonnes of goods in the markets and yards all over the city. For long they worked under extreme exploitative conditions. In the late sixties, the mathadis were organised under strong leadership. Special legislation was enacted and welfare boards were set up to ensure that they got minimum monthly wages and job security. The mathadi unions then emerged as a formidable force. Therefore, any act of violence against mathadi workers is a potential threat to law and order, particularly in the port city of Bombay. When the mathadis strike work, the commercial nerve centre of the country gets paralysed. Could the criminals targeting these workers have factored all this in? Or was it just a mindless act in the chain reaction of communal retaliation?

I was not aware of these happenings when, as per protocol, on the morning of 6 January I went to call on the Commissioner of Police, Shrikant Bapat. He was in the midst of several meetings and my turn came at only around 3 p.m. Shrikant Bapat was an officer who was known for his sterling integrity and undoubted professional competence. All of us looked up to him with great reverence. An effusive welcome was the last thing one expected from him, for he was a man of few words. His extensive work in the Intelligence Bureau (IB) had added quiet steel to his persona. Even then, in normal times, a twinkle in his light eyes would have surely greeted me. Not today, for his plate was full. Before we could say much to each other, the Control Room reported that communal trouble had flared up again! It was a grim Commissioner of Police who ordered me to go straight to Mahim and take charge of the Traffic Police chowki there. My immediate task was to ensure safe passage for all the VIPs en route from the airport to the city. The winter session of the Assembly was on in Nagpur and there was a lot of VIP movement on that count as well.

The murders of the mathadis had created tremendous tension in Masjid Bunder, Pydhonie, Dongri and the surrounding areas. The mathadi unions had called for a bandh in the wholesale markets. Meetings were addressed by leaders who condemned the police and the government for their failure in protecting citizens. Fears were expressed that if such a situation persisted, Hindus would have to arm themselves.

In an atmosphere charged with communal tension, the mathadi murders were bound to send communal signals. The riots had ended, but sporadic violent incidents continued to be reported from different parts of the city. The mathadi murders had followed a series of stabbings particularly between 1-5 January 1993. Large number of stabbings had taken place in the Muslim-dominated areas of south Bombay and a majority of victims were Hindus. Was this part of a bigger game plan with the intention of whipping up communal frenzy?

When I saluted the CP to take his leave, something tugged at my heartstrings. A highly distinguished and decorated IPS officer with impeccable credentials, a man with a confident but quiet style of work, had been placed by destiny into the limelight: to head an under-remunerated, outnumbered, overburdened and ill-equipped force, manned by men who had not had a good night's sleep for days together; to control a conflict in a city bursting at its seams and weighed by a myriad problems, long unaddressed and festering like unattended sores.

And I was one of his *lieutenants. He* depended on me to see my beloved city through this ordeal. Times were abnormal and all senior officers, whatever their posts, were doing their utmost to maintain law and order. Unlike other colleagues who had faced the riots and slogged nonstop, I was better rested. I had better deliver.

The situation began sinking in with its full import as I ordered my driver to head for the Mahim Traffic chowki. There was no time to stop at my own office of DCP (Traffic) at the Pochkanwalla Road in Worli.

There was no Bandra-Worli Sea Link then and the Lady Jamshetji Road and Veer Savarkar Marg were the most crucial connections linking the suburbs to south Bombay. It was like a chicken's neck and a communally sensitive spot through which all VIP movement would pass. The word chowki means a small sub-station. The Mahim Traffic Police chowki is a small structure where the Lady Jamshetji Road, Veer Savarkar Marg and the narrow Balamiya road from the Kapad Bazar meet. It is amidst a ghetto where temples, mosques, churches and dargahs sit cheek by jowl. I took charge of the chowki and tightened the patrolling at the sensitive spots. The situation worsened progressively from the evening of that day. Stabbings and mob violence spread to several parts of the city. In the early hours of 8 January 1993, the Radhabai Chawl incident occurred. Six residents of a chawl in Jogeshwari were locked from outside and set on fire by miscreants. This news spread like wildfire providing a flashpoint for the Hindu backlash to commence. Defiant mobs challenged the police authority as never before. In one shocking incident at Pydhonie, a crude bomb was hurled at the Police Commissioner's car, something which was unheard of and a thing Bombay would never do. A curfew was imposed and ultimately the Army had to be called in.

Hasan Gafoor, who was my boss when I was the Assistant Superintendent of Police, Khamgaon in Buldhana district, was now the Additional Commissioner of Crime Branch. He was in charge of the Dadar-Mahim areas for riot control. He used to enlist my help to assist the local police for riot control and as did Dr P. S. Pasricha who was looking after Dharavi and the eastern suburbs. On 10 January 1993, even I had to order firing and had to open fire myself to quell a riot at Reti Bunder in Mahim. The miscreants had set fire to the bamboo and wood market there. Despite our repeated pleas and warnings, the mob continued to pelt stones and fireballs. As a result of the police firing, the mob at Reti Bunder dispersed. Along with my Traffic Branch staff and the fire brigade I then went about the task of extinguishing the fire which was spreading with rapid intensity. Whilst this operation was on, I received information on the wireless network about the assemblage of riotous mobs inside the Fishermen Colony area. I rushed inside the Fishermen Colony and noticed a mob of Hindus near the St. Xavier's Institute hurling stones, bricks, soda water bottles and fireballs towards Hari Zendi. Another huge mob of Muslims had assembled on the Hari Zendi side and they too were reciprocating in kind at their Hindu adversaries. The small police force present there was caught in the centre of this mindless mini war. The situation was extremely violent and surcharged. There was no other option before me, but to take stern action. I opened fire along with the State Reserve Police Force (SRPF) contingent. In both the firing incidents at Reti Bunder and the Fishermen Colony, the police action resulted in two deaths – one Hindu and one Muslim. The situation was soon brought under control. It seemed as if all the latent animosities, personal grudges and hatred had welled up to fuel violence; real and imaginary scores were being settled with a vengeance. Suddenly the warmth and friendliness of the city seemed a thing of the past.

Rumours were rife. Even the law-abiding citizens were inadvertently mongering rumours by dialling their near and dear ones to give unverified alerts. Just in case!

The administration permitting Muslims to spill over on to the streets to offer Friday namaaz and thereby obstruct traffic and use loudspeakers to announce the daily azaans, have long been contentious civic issues in Bombay. In the tense communal atmosphere, these issues surfaced and as a retaliatory measure, Hindus began holding *mahaaratis* – large hymn-singing gatherings – in temples on different days. The congregations would spill over into the streets and bring traffic to halt. It added to the overflowing cup of police woes, but we had to tread carefully. What is good for the goose is good for the gander was the argument which was difficult to fault, especially in the current scenario. We had to arrange safe passage for ambulances, funeral processions, essential commodities and manpower that rendered essential services. When everything else was failing, the police were the only ones left holding the baby. Restoring discipline was a priority for which we had to be harsh; assuaging victims' grief also became our job where we had to shed our harshness. It was all easier said than done, but the police are and were even then expected to be perfect humans.

The riots raged on till mid-January. Thereafter, the situation improved slowly, but not before taking its toll on the police force which came under severe criticism for failing to control the situation, being biased and siding with the Hindus. The Congress was ruling both at the Centre and in the state. The failure to protect the Babri mosque was already a huge embarrassment for the government. Coupled with the unprecedented riots in Bombay in which even the state's chief minister was seen as a complete failure, the expected remedial measures were bound to begin with Bombay and that too with its police. In the unprecedented upheavals that followed, the police force was the worst hit. The Commissioner of Police, Shrikant Bapat was replaced by his good friend and batchmate Amarjit Singh Samra, the Commissioner of Police of the adjoining Thane city. The removal of the Commissioner of Police was not enough to satisfy the critics and in February, Chief Minister Sudhakarrao Naik too had to make an exit. He was replaced by the then Union Defence Minister, Sharad Pawar. A Commission of Inquiry into the causes of the riots was appointed, headed by a High Court Judge. All the sixty-seven police stations of the city now had to make preparations to appear before the Commission. The rank and file of the once-revered Bombay police were not only thoroughly exhausted, but they were also completely demoralised. 'Sir, if this is how we are going to be treated, it is better not to open fire again, whatever the situation,' they would say sharing their feelings. Keeping their spirits up and motivating them to go on with their usual nonstop thankless work was a challenge in itself.

As I was toiling away as the 'chowkidar' at the 'chicken's neck', my Japanese training in traffic management seemed all but forgotten, even by my superiors. Man proposes and God disposes is not something you believe in when you are in your Thirties – the halcyon days when you feel that hard work and perseverance are enough for shaping your life the way you want. So amidst all the mayhem, I was waiting to get back to my new found specialisation in traffic management, when a bomb went off at the Lucky Petrol Pump next to the Shiv Sena Bhavan on the afternoon of 12 March, a Friday, when the devout had assembled for their Asr namaaz.

The Shiv Sena Bhavan, the headquarters of the Shiv Sena, is not far from the Mahim Traffic Police chowki where I was that day. As I rushed to the bomb blast site with my traffic team, little did I know that a dream-come-true challenge was waiting for me in the tragedy that was playing itself out. A challenge fit to be tackled by both, the fictional Marshal of Lawless and the real Marshall of Tombstone, and bring out the best in them.

9

The Mother of All Serial Blasts

The Sena Bhavan blast was the third explosion of that day. The first to go off was the one at the Stock Exchange Building at Fort at 1:30 in the afternoon and the second at Katha Bazar at 2:15. I was at the Mahim Traffic chowki when we received the alerts of these blasts.

I was gearing up to intensify patrolling when the bomb went off at 2:30 p.m. at the Lucky Petrol Pump adjoining the Sena Bhavan. I immediately jumped into my car and with my team following, took the Lady Jamshetji Road to reach the spot. It must have taken us barely seven to eight minutes, but already a huge crowd had gathered at the Ram Ganesh Gadkari Chowk where the Sena Bhavan stands. We had to park our vehicles near the Kohinoor Mill and cross the large junction on foot to reach the bomb site. Good Samaritans and the nearby police pickets were already at work. The injured had been moved to hospitals. The petrol pump building was completely destroyed. Remains of mangled cars were strewn around the petrol pump with blood splattered all over. The final toll of this blast was four dead and fifty injured.

Even the most trivial incident could set afire the tinderbox that Bombay was those days, and this was no trivial incident. Had the explosion reached the petrol tank underneath, the toll would have been much higher. The intended target appeared to be the Sena Bhavan which had round the clock security. Vehicles cannot be parked near the building as it stands squarely at the busy junction. The only way to target it with a car bomb was to park the explosives-laden car near the wall separating it from the petrol pump. That is what the culprits had done.

It definitely looked like a larger conspiracy. I informed the Control Room to issue alerts to the railway stations and airports to be on the lookout for suspicious movement of people to prevent the culprits from leaving the city.

Some senior Shiv Sena leaders were already present on the spot, including Manohar Joshi and Diwakar Raote. I told them that this appeared to be a chain of explosions and a larger conspiracy. They were anxious that there could be bombs planted inside the Sena Bhavan. The crowd was swelling. More and more party supporters were arriving to lend a helping hand. They were agitated and restless. I was the first DCP-level officer to reach the spot and they naturally looked up to me for solution and action. I had to allay their fears and act fast. All I could do for the moment to placate them was to enter the Sena Bhavan with the Traffic Division personnel and check if there were bombs. So we entered the building, performed 'bomb detection and disposal' duties by poking at things with our lathis and emerged to report that there were no bombs or rather we had not found any. Just as I was announcing this to the crowd, my wireless operator, Todkar, whispered in my ear that there had been a massive blast at Century Bazar in Worli.

My worst fears confirmed, I began explaining to the crowd the grave emergency we were facing, requesting them to disperse. 'Allow us to perform our duties. Your presence will only hamper our movements! Please ask all your followers to be calm. There is a chain of explosions in different parts of the city. This looks like a deliberate attempt to incite communal riots. We must do everything to stop riots from erupting....'

Fortunately, they appreciated the gravity of the situation. As they began dispersing quietly, I got a wireless call that there was communal tension in the Fishermen's Colony at Mahim. This was the very location where I had opened fire to quell a riot in January early that year. I knew how sensitive that location was. I had to handle the mobs immediately or riots would definitely erupt!

As I began leaving for Mahim, we heard a deafening sound from the direction of the Tilak Bridge. An explosion had ripped through Plaza Cinema which is at a short distance east of Sena Bhavan. But I had to rush to Mahim. So I again requested the crowd that they must keep calm and help us tackle the situation and I, along with my team sped towards Mahim. As my vehicle crossed Raja Badhe Chowk, I saw a man lying on the road in front of Citylight Cinema. A group of hoodlums was kicking and assaulting the poor soul, while a couple of men were attempting to lift a big boulder as if to smash his skull. I yelled at my driver to speed up our Ambassador car and thrust my arm and head out of the window, aiming my revolver at the miscreants. Seeing us approach, with a revolver aimed at them and the siren blaring, the assailants took to their heels.

The victim was a gentleman called Huzeifa Kachwala, an old Bohri Muslim glass merchant. It was because he was wearing the traditional Bohri skull cap that some miscreants had pulled him out of a BEST bus. It was sheer providence that I happened to be close by and could rush to his aid. Otherwise, he would have surely been killed.

Huzeifa Kachwala, however, feels grateful to me, which is really touching. Every 12 March he comes to visit me without fail, with a single red rose. When I see him, the memories of that horrific day come alive in my mind, as if it were just yesterday.

I reached the Mahim Causeway and found that shops and cars had been set ablaze and groups of Hindus and Muslims had gathered to confront each other. The fishermen were fuming with anger because some miscreants had lobbed hand grenades at their homes from a passing vehicle. This had happened around 2:45 p.m. The Additional Commissioner Y. C. Pawar had also reached there and for the next hour or so, we talked to both the groups and explained to them what was happening across the city. We managed to put sense into them that a deliberate attempt was being made to foment trouble, just to make the two communities fight. Good sense prevailed, they listened to us and a major conflagration was averted. Real wisdom is seeing through things, not just see things, as the saying goes. At last Bombayites were regaining their wisdom.

The Plaza Theatre bomb had gone off some forty-five minutes later than the blast at the Sena Bhavan. From 1:30 p.m. to 3:40 p.m. on that fateful day, in a span of just a hundred minutes, twelve bomb explosions had occurred throughout Bombay, most of them at intervals of just ten to fifteen minutes. And we did not know what more lay in store.

Hospitals were flooded with the injured. Phone lines were jammed and panic-stricken citizens were fleeing the blast sites and the surrounding areas, many rushing home to safety, some to schools to pick up children and some to look for their near and dear ones likely to be caught in the blasts. For the past some months, major roadwork was going on in the city for concretisation. Dug up roads obstructed movement of emergency vehicles like ambulances and fire brigade vans. The police had to secure and sanitise the scenes of crime, provide bandobast to all the hospitals looking after the injured, enhance security at sensitive locations, increase surveillance at checkposts, exit and entry points, instil confidence in the panic-stricken people, and most importantly, ensure that riots did not erupt in the city again. A tall order indeed, given the prevailing circumstances!

I was patrolling the streets with my traffic squad when around 9 p.m. I got a message that the CP Amarjit Singh Samra, who was visiting the blast sites, was now on his way to Plaza Cinema. I received him at Plaza. After inspecting the site, he visited the Sena Bhavan. I briefed him about the incident and he also spoke to the other officers present there. Then I sat in his car and we made our way to the Fishermen's Colony at Mahim. He was gazing out of the window and appeared to be in deep thought. *What could be passing through the mind of this man who was responsible for the security of a city where nothing was going right? What could be his feelings right now?* As I wondered, he suddenly turned towards me and said gently, 'Rakesh, I hope you have had something to eat? You have a long night ahead.'

The genuine concern in his tone reminded me that none of us had eaten anything since the afternoon. I looked in amazement at his composed demeanour, the mark of a great leader. He was waiting for my answer. 'I will eat something, sir, not to worry!' I mumbled as we reached the Fishermen's Colony. It was a very important lesson learnt and ingrained in my mind. No matter how serious the crisis, how stressed you are, to build the morale of your juniors is a leader's foremost duty.

After visiting the Fishermen's Colony, the CP left for Hotel Searock in Bandra, another blast site. I returned to my Traffic chowki to spend the whole night there, which had become a habit since the riots. The most important task was to ensure that both the communities kept their cool and we nip communal trouble in the bud. But how was the city going to react? Would they be at each other's throats again? That was the moot question.

The next morning we had our answer. Our city behaved most responsibly as if she had seen through the plot. Her inherent resilience shone through. Medical and paramedical staff worked on a war footing. Attendance in offices was almost 100 per cent. After queuing up in the night to donate blood, people had reported at work with their chins up to send a message across the border: 'We will not let you scare us!' They went about their daily chores like any other day. Our instructions were to exhibit a strong police presence on the streets. We followed the instructions with full might, each one of us working relentlessly, without a break. That we did not have to requisition the Army back proved that we had succeeded.

On the morning of 14 March, an alert citizen, Dr Jaychand Mandot, did a great job. He dialled number 100 and reported to the Police Control Room that there was a Bajaj scooter lying unattended outside his dispensary on Naigaon Cross Road in Dadar and no one knew whom it belonged to. By this time everybody in Bombay knew that explosives-laden scooters and cars were used as bombs. The doctor had not opened his dispensary on 13 March. That day when he did, he saw the scooter which was probably lying there since 12 March. The Control Room informed Matunga police station. The Matunga police team rushed to the spot and on preliminary inspection found a black sticky substance in the scooter's trunk. The nearest Bomb Detection and Disposal Squad (BDDS), which was at the airport, was summoned. As DCP (Traffic), I too reached there with my men, to divert traffic and erect barricades. The operation lasted the entire afternoon. Major Jadhav of the BDDS defused the bomb and informed me that the black sticky substance appeared to be RDX or PETN/SYMTEX mixed with grease. The scooter had around one-and-a-half kg of explosives stuffed into its trunk with a timer embedded in it. For some inexplicable reason, maybe the will of the Almighty, the scooter bomb had not exploded. In that congested locality and with the old buildings around, the impact and the likely casualties would have been catastrophic. The Traffic branch arranged for the scooter to be towed to the compound of Matunga police station, removed the barricades and normalised traffic by 6 in the evening.

Just then I received a call on the wireless that 'King' wanted me to meet him in his chamber. (King was the wireless call sign for the CP.) I reached Crawford Market around 6:30 p.m. and found the CP with Mahesh Narayan Singh, the Joint CP (Crime). This was the first time since my posting in the city that the CP and the Joint CP had summoned me.

'Sit down, Rakesh! How are you? Have you had any rest?' Samra began.

'Yes, sir.... I am fine, sir..... Oh yes, sir!' were the typical answers of a junior officer that I delivered.

'You know how serious these blasts are, Rakesh. We have no clue who is responsible and if not nabbed soon, the perpetrators could strike again,' he said and continued with all the details of the explosions that highlighted how deadly the conspiracy was: the powerful explosives, the targets selected, the extensive damage to life and property, the timing, the sinister design to cause riots, all of it. And my mind went into a whirl. *This had absolutely no connection whatsoever with the cordoning off of the scooter at Dadar or defusing the tension at the Fishermen's Colony, situations that I had handled. Why is the CP telling me all this? Why am I here?* I looked at both the gentlemen for clues but their faces were impassive.

'The prestige of Bombay police is at stake. The most worrying part is that they may strike again. Before they do it, we need to nab them,' Samra continued and then he said something totally unexpected, 'We have decided that you will take up the investigation and detect this case.'

I went totally numb. This was huge. Till then, I had not done any great detection work in Bombay, except for the short stint as DCP, Zone-IV. What has made them pick me – one of the most junior IPS officers in the city? What made them repose faith in me? My contact with Samra was limited to my training at Nashik Police Training School when he headed it for a short time before Arvind Inamdar took over. As regards M. N. Singh, I had worked under him when I was SP, Osmanabad, and he was DIG of Aurangabad Range. But to entrust me with an investigation of this magnitude and importance, when I was only twelve years old in Service! And although a Bombay guy, I had spent just a little over two years in the city as a policeman, as DCP, Zone-IV for twenty months and DCP (Traffic) for ten months.

The feeling of numbness was soon overtaken by fear. Fear of failure. The reputation of the Force was at stake. Already being made to face a Commission of Inquiry for the failure to deal with unprecedented riots, our competence was being disputed. We were being scorned and the morale of our officers and men was pretty low. The world was watching us now. How is India going to deal with this challenge? Imagine the Bombay police becoming a laughing stock and that too with me leading the investigation? Will I be able to deliver?

History bears testimony, and time and again it had been proven, how easy it is to brand a policeman a failure and make a scapegoat out of him. *Is that where destiny was taking me? Towards an assured failure? But then, opportunities often come disguised, sometimes as crises. I have always dreamt of being a good detective. And when I am picked to solve a really challenging case, here I am, developing cold feet. Should I not be excited! What's wrong with me! Is this not a god-sent?*

I was talking myself out of the fear as Samra summarised: 'You pick the team of your choice and start immediately.'

An opportunity not just to prove myself, but to serve my Commissioner, my Force and my nation. Which Bombay officer worth his salt would have said no?

'I will do my best, sir. I will. I will not let you down,' I heard myself say.

'Take any men of your choice. We want results. Give me the names and I will issue orders to make them available to you,' M.N. Singh added.

Both the gentlemen wished me luck as I took their leave. As my vehicle headed toward the Mahim Traffic chowki, I wondered if it was all a dream. I was not the same man who had entered the CP's chamber earlier in the evening.

From the Traffic chowki at Mahim, I made a call to Preeti. 'I will not be able to come home tonight, Preeti,' I began telling her.

'Yes, I know that,' she said. With the abnormal situation in the city, she was expecting it. Then I told her what had happened. 'I cannot believe that they have given this task to me, Preeti,' I confessed.

'Why? You work so hard and so sincerely. They know it! That's why they have given it to you,' she had a simple explanation. She must have detected some anxiety in my tone for she immediately added reassuringly, 'Don't worry! You will solve it! Have faith.' And she rung off with, 'It only means that I won't see you at home in the near future. That's fine and all the best!'

I then called the officers and men of the Traffic Department who had been my team for riot control and for all that that had been coming my way since 6 January. They were ACP Bhaskar Dangle, Inspectors Deedar Singh, Nawal Driver, Assistant Police Inspectors G.D. Kirdant and Senior Inspectors V. V. Vani and Shrirang Nadgauda. They simply gaped at me when I told them what had come to us. 'All of you are part of it. We have no clues and we have to start from scratch.' As my words sank in, I could see excitement light up their tired eyes.

My first orders were to get in touch with the Control Room and let them inform us if anything out of the ordinary had been reported on 12 March.

It must have been around 8:00 p.m. that I had returned to Mahim. Around 9:30 p.m., the Control Room came up with information about three unusual incidents. One was a suspicious looking vehicle with people in Bhandup. The occupants of the vehicle had left in a hurry once the blasts had started. One more near a hotel in Juhu where the occupants in two cars had exchanged a bag and left in a hurry. And the third in Worli where a

Maruti van with a cache of weapons was found abandoned outside the Siemens factory and was towed away to the police station.

'Come, let's go to Worli!' I told the team. We hopped into our vehicles and zoomed to Worli police station, reaching it around 10:30 p.m. Two young officers began giving me the details. They had just finished their probation period and this was their first posting. One was Detection Officer Dinesh Kadam and the other was Dhananjay Daund, Beat Officer. What I learnt was shocking. The weapons found in the Maruti van were no ordinary country-made *kattas* and choppers. There were seven AK-56 assault rifles, fourteen magazines, pistols, four hand grenades and a timer detonator pencil. Also seized were a *tasbih* or *misbah* which is a rosary used by Muslims and also some Zamzam holy water. The surmise was that some underworld goons must have abandoned their car, fearing nakabandis that we had erected all over the city post the blasts.

I immediately issued instructions to ascertain the name in which the car was registered. Being in the Traffic Department did help, for despite the hour, the name could be traced and it turned out to be one Rubina Suleiman Memon from Al Husseini building in Mahim.

'Let's go! Back to Mahim!' I said to my team and asked both, Dinesh Kadam and Dhananjay Daund, to accompany us. Their enthusiasm and desire to do something was infectious. I needed these qualities in my team. By the time all of us reached Mahim Traffic chowki, it was midnight. Mahim had been one of the police stations under me when I was DCP, Zone-IV. During the riots, I had to do a lot of legwork in Mahim when a number of old contacts had got revived and some new ones were developed. So when I got to know the name of the owner of the Maruti van, I sent for one of the informants.

'Who is this Memon from Al Husseini building?' I asked him when he came to the chowki.

'Tiger Memon, sir. He has a flat there.'

'Tiger Memon?' I had heard this name for the first time. 'Who is he?'

'He is a smuggler, sir. Underworld, sir.'

I instinctively decided to go to Tiger Memon's flat for questioning. When we reached the flat we found it locked. We made enquiries in the building, but no information was forthcoming. So I called *panchas* (independent witnesses) and broke open the flat in their presence. We entered the flat and began our search. Overseeing the procedure, I was standing in the passage, where stood a refrigerator. Tired, I rested my arm on it and something metallic clanked under my elbow. I picked it up and it turned out to be a Bajaj scooter key. The number on the key was 449.

Bajaj scooter? One more! A lock clicked open in my brain as I inspected the key. I called out to Dangle and instructed him, 'Take this key to Matunga police station and see if it is of the scooter that was towed from Naigaon Cross Road.'

The panchanama was underway in Tiger Memon's house, but I had many things to do, like drawing more officers and men to form my detection squad. So I came to the Senior Inspector's chamber at Mahim police station. In about forty minutes, I received a call. It was an excited Dangle at the other end and he was almost screaming. 'Sir, the key has matched! The key has matched!'

The first two pieces of the jigsaw had locked neatly!

I rushed back to the Mahim Traffic chowki and again sent for the informant. The reason for this was to protect the identity of the 'source'. His coming to the police station would have exposed his identity and compromised his position. 'Give me more details of this Tiger,' I said. He obliged. He told me that Tiger Memon was an extremely dangerous man. 'He assaults even Customs officers, sir!' he said. He could not give me Tiger's whereabouts but instead gave me details of his manager. He was one Asgar Yusuf Mukadam. A few further enquiries and

I managed to get his address which was in an area known as Seven Bungalows in Andheri.

I immediately despatched Nadgauda and Kirdant to get Mukadam. In the meantime, I got to know that the search in Tiger's flat had yielded substantial cash and valuables from the *tijori* (safe), like gold ornaments, diamonds and high-end watches.

Around 3 or 3:30 in the morning, Asgar Mukadam was brought before me. Two elderly couples were with him. One was his parents and the other his aunt and uncle. I began questioning him in their presence.

'Bahut kamina insan hai,' he said describing Tiger Memon as an extremely mean person. 'Doesn't pay salary and gives filthy abuses. I left his job because of that.'

As I searched his face for signs of deceit, he began avoiding eye contact. The fellow was obviously lying. I gave Dinesh Kadam a signal. Dinesh put a hand on Mukadam's shoulder with a firm grip. The first to wince were the aunt and the uncle. *'Saab, yeh bahut masoom hai. Isne kuchh nahin kiya,'* the couple was pleading that Mukadam was innocent and he had done nothing. The look he exchanged with them made it obvious that he was very close to them. Closer than he was to his parents. Later on, I got to know that the uncle and aunt had adopted him.

'The very fact that I reached you means I know something. If you don't tell me the truth, I will take action against your uncle and aunt for harbouring a criminal like you,' I told him and it worked. His immediate response was, 'Sir, I want to talk to you alone.'

I ordered everyone to leave. Only Asgar Mukadam and I were left in the room. He sat down and started singing like a canary. He gave me the entire story, the conspiracy, the training abroad, the selection of targets and the filling of vehicles with explosives. He further told me that Tiger Memon was sure that riots would erupt after the blasts. He had given 5,000 rupees to each one of the saboteurs with specific instructions to leave the city and go to Nepal by different routes. From Nepal they would be taken to Dubai, he had promised. So, all had fled Bombay except Asgar Mukadam because someone in his family was unwell.

It was now around 5 in the morning. I thought I should wait till 6 a.m. to break the news to the CP and the Joint CP. They must be tired with the recent happenings and deservedly could do with an extra hour of sleep, I thought.

All those saboteurs heading towards the Indo-Nepal border had to be hunted out and arrested, and that could not wait. I called in my team and said, 'The case is detected. Now our immediate priority is to pick up all the accused involved in this dastardly act.'

The happiness on their faces was a pleasure to behold. All the fatigue of more than forty hours of intensely stressful and nonstop duty evaporated instantly and we got cracking. I briefed them and dispatched them to get some of the suspects on my radar, but not before asking them to recommend officers and constables to join the team at once. They suggested some names and I immediately, despite the unearthly hour, began contacting them and their superiors so that they could join me, without any delay, to help me complete the mission.

Dawns at police stations are peculiarly uneasy like dawns in hospitals. Daybreak takes away merely the darkness, but not the gloom or disease or evil, nor the unpleasantness of the measures to be taken to combat the disease or the evil. The uncertainty of the outcome hangs in the atmosphere like an invisible smog.

The first call I made was to Preeti. 'I have detected the biggest case of my life!' I declared. There was no response from the other end. She must be sleepy, I thought and repeated myself. 'Yes, I am listening,' she said. 'I said you will crack it, didn't I? Congratulations! My prayers are with you. Please phone Mama and seek her blessings.' And she did not ask when I would be back home.

As I became aware of the aartis, bells and azaans of that daybreak, I could not wait to tell my mother about my new responsibility. I needed her blessings for the tough job that lay ahead. I dialled her number and told her how the CP had assigned me the task and how fortunate I was to have detected the case before daybreak.

She was so proud. I warned her that she had to work overtime now, for the difficult part of the job was still to start and I needed her prayers. 'The more sugar you put in the tea, the sweeter it will be; the more the *mehnat* (hard work), the better the results,' she answered. Just like what she used to tell me when I was preparing for my Civil Services exam, handing me my favourite chocolate biscuits to see me through the boredom of cramming. She also added a blessing which she had adopted after I joined the IPS: 'God will be with you since you are on the path of truth.'

By then the new day had arrived for good, and with it, a new life.

10

Enter the World of International Terror

'Sir, case detected!' I announced.

It was six in the morning of 15 March 1993 and I was speaking to M.N. Singh, the Joint Commissioner of Police (Crime), a little less than twelve hours since he and the Commissioner of Police, A. S. Samra had ordered me to detect the case. There was a small pause and then he said, 'Tell me what you have found.'

With a racing heart, I narrated to him all that I had learned.

'I want utmost secrecy for this, Rakesh!' he said. 'Otherwise these fellows will be out of the country and we will never be able to lay our hands on them. I want each and every one of them behind bars.'

I updated him as to how I was gearing up for it, how I had already dispatched some officers out in the field and how I had started drawing more officers for the mission. He listened intently, gave me some concrete suggestions and asked me to inform the CP immediately.

The CP was overjoyed when I broke the news to him. I could sense the relief in his voice and felt happy that I was instrumental in having eased his burden a little. He, too, expressed his anxiety about not getting our hands on the culprits and the need to maintain secrecy. I promised him that I would leave no stone unturned. He assured me of complete support in terms of material and manpower and asked me to keep him posted on every important development.

The saboteurs had a head start of almost forty-eight hours over us. I was racing against time and needed officers and men of high energy levels who would enjoy a good chase – and possess a temperament full of *'karna hai'* (must do) attitude. I had seen the enthusiasm and zeal in the officers that I had picked from the Worli and Mahim police stations. I needed more of them. So I deliberately looked for younger men, some of them just in their very first posting at a police station, and went on adding them to the squad. I was meeting most of them for the first time, but that did not come in the way of building a team. They were unaffected, enthusiastic, idealistic and raring to go. Each one of them regarded it as an honour to be selected for this investigation which they viewed as a work of immense national importance.

So I managed to zero in on good detection talent from different police stations. Sincere and bright officers like Sukhlal Warpe, P. D. Hadap and Nirlekar from Dadar, Angadi from Byculla, S. D. Bhandalkar from Dharavi, S. T. Kolekar, A. R. Shastri and V.A. Vast from Mahim, P. D. Khanwilkar and P. R. Ghate from N.M. Joshi Marg, N. Bhosale Patil from R.A.K. Marg, V. R. Shinde, R. D. Farande and H. B. Pawar from Worli, became an integral part of the squad. This is how in the next two to three days, the core detection team was formed. As we went along, our numbers rose to 162, counting both officers and men.

Travelling by train and road, and only on the rare occasion by air, these officers and men fanned out to seventy-nine towns and cities located in twenty-one States and two Union Territories of India. There were no cell phones then, nor were we technology savvy. The only computers we had were the hard discs of our brains and the software was our hard resolve. We arrested in all 189 accused.

What caught my attention was the fact that most of the foot-soldiers arrested were the sole breadwinners of their families. Aggrieved and angered by the riots, they had easily fallen prey to

Pakistan's Inter-Services Intelligence (ISI) and the Muslim dons of the underworld and ended up doing all the legwork to execute the conspiracy. They were car mechanics, men doing menial jobs, daily wage earners, brainwashed and radicalised. Poor, illiterate youth manipulated by Dawood and Anees Ibrahim, Mohammad Dosa and Tiger Memon through their lieutenants who had played upon their emotions. And Dawood, Anees, Dosa and Tiger were all themselves tucked away safely with their families in the comforts of Dubai, Islamabad, Lahore and Karachi.

Post the Bangladesh debacle, the ISI had been trying hard to gain a foothold amongst the Indian Muslims to destabilise India, but without much success. It was only in the late eighties that their sustained efforts reaped some success as the 'Students Islamic Movement of India' (SIMI) began making headway in influencing young impressionable Muslim youth. Dr Jalees Ansari was originally a SIMI member. Later, he formed his own outfit, Tanzeem–Islahul-Musalmeen in 1988 and began engineering explosions to avenge the alleged atrocities reported against Muslims. He was arrested only in January 1994.

With the demolition of the Babri mosque and the consequent countrywide riots, the ISI's task became easier. They could now use the Muslim dons of the Bombay underworld. A ready network for clandestine movement and distribution of arms, ammunition and funds, with enough cheap manpower to commit the deadliest of crimes at the shortest notice, was now available on a platter. All that the ISI had to do was to give these lumpen elements a 'higher purpose' through indoctrination, make them feel important and valued enough to get committed to foreign masters, and then train and equip them in the use of sophisticated arms and explosives to wreak havoc on India's integrity and stability.

The underworld grapevine has it that after the first phase of the December 1992 riots, some of the aggrieved Bombay Muslims had sent a message to Dawood Ibrahim for help; but he could not oblige. To provoke and instigate him into action goes the story, some Muslim women sent him bangles, the ultimate Indian way of humiliating a man, by questioning his masculinity. Now whether the bangles were really sent or not, and if they were, whether the ISI was behind the dispatch itself, Dawood threw in his lot with the ISI to avenge the fall of the Babri mosque and the December riots. It must have truly warmed the ISI's cockles.

In any case, in December 1992, Dawood, Tiger Memon, and Mohammad Dosa got together along with the ISI to hatch the conspiracy and began planning it meticulously, taking care and exercising caution to keep their Hindu henchmen completely in the dark.

The object of the conspiracy was nothing less than waging war against the Government of India and engineering violence in different parts of the country to overawe the Indian State by exploiting the communal sentiments of the Muslims and provoke them to resort to terrorist acts in the name of religion, by creating instability through fomenting Hindu-Muslim riots and causing acts of wanton killing to terrorise the Indian people through the use of firearms and bomb explosions.

The original plan was to cause Hindu-Muslim riots all over the country in April 1993 on Shiv Jayanti – the birth anniversary of the founder of the Maratha Empire, Chhatrapati Shivaji Maharaj. The riots were to be triggered by causing massive explosions at carefully selected strategic targets which would unmistakably point towards a Muslim hand and invite the Hindu ire. To enable the Muslims to defend themselves and attack the Hindus and the security forces, the former were to be equipped, well in advance, with sophisticated arms and ammunition enough for waging a war. The cities on the bomb blasts list included the metro cities of Mumbai, Chennai, Kolkata, Delhi, Bengaluru, Surat and Ahmedabad.

Between December 1992 and January 1993, Dawood and

Anees Ibrahim, through Tiger Memon, summoned eight other conspirators to Dubai. They included Mohammad Dosa and Tiger's two brothers Yakub and Ayub. Yakub was a chartered accountant and his office premises in Mahim, 'Tejarath International', was heavily damaged in the communal riots. The brothers were deeply disturbed, seething with anger and desperate to wreak revenge.

The conspirators held meetings to chalk out detailed plans and some Pakistanis actively participated in the meetings. Tiger and Mohammad Dosa took up the responsibility of securing landings of the ISI supplied arms, ammunition and explosives on the Indian coast, of transporting them to Bombay and also of deploying men to assemble the car and scooter bombs and set off explosions.

Training saboteurs to handle weapons and explosives was another crucial step for which Dawood and Anees Ibrahim, Mohammad Dosa, and the Memon brothers selected Muslim youth through their trusted lieutenants. Between January and March 1993, at least twenty-three such boys were sent to Islamabad via Dubai. Their families were informed that they were going abroad ostensibly for jobs and had no inkling whatsoever that they were recruits for terror operations to wage a war against India. The training was supervised and controlled by Pakistani agents and army officers who taught them to use grenades, rocket launchers and automatic weapons and also to assemble bombs with timer devices and detonators.

After the terror training, the newly trained recruits were flown back to Dubai. The journey from Dubai to Islamabad and back was by Pakistan International Airlines (PIA), Pakistan's national carrier. On the few passports that were seized, we found stamps of exit from Dubai, but no corresponding landing or disembarkation entries to give away the destinations. Again, there were stamps of re-entry into Dubai after forty-five days, but no corresponding exit stamps from another country. This was obviously because they were not subjected to any immigration or emigration formalities at

Islamabad. After landing back in Dubai, they were administered an oath of secrecy and made to take vows that they would lay down their lives to achieve their objective. Those who could not be taken to Pakistan were instead trained in the forests of Sandheri and Bhorghat which come under the jurisdiction of Goregaon police station in Raigad district of Maharashtra.

Simultaneously, arrangements were on to smuggle in, through the Western coast, huge quantities of explosives, arms and ammunition supplied by the ISI. The first landing was organised by Mohammad Dosa on the coast of Village Dighi in Raigad district on 9 January through his landing agents, Mechanic Chacha and Uttam Potdar. To ensure a smooth landing, on 6 January, Mohammad Dosa and Mechanic Chacha met Customs officials at Hotel Persian Darbar in Panvel and secured their connivance. Twenty-three men participated in the landing and they also included subverted Customs officers and policemen.

Two more landings took place at the Shekhadi coast in Shrivardhan Taluka in Raigad between 2-8 February 1993. These were organised by Dawood and Tiger Memon through their landing agents, Dawood Taklya, Dadabhai Parkar and Rahim Laundrywala. For these landings, Tiger met Customs officials on 2 February at Hotel Big Splash in Alibaug to secure their connivance. In all fifty men participated in the landing, loading, unloading, transportation and storage of the contraband. For planting RDX, vehicles worth lakhs of rupees were bought by the gang in bogus names and addresses.

On 4 March, Tiger Memon held important preparatory meetings at Hotel Taj Mahal. It was attended by some of his most trusted lieutenants including Badshah Khan, who later turned approver. At this meeting, Tiger disclosed the detailed plan of causing blasts in Bombay at select Hindu localities, important iconic buildings and installations, and the mass massacre of Shiv Sena and BJP corporators by storming the Bombay Municipal Corporation building. The targets selected were the Shiv Sena Bhavan, the Bombay Municipal Corporation building, the Bombay Stock Exchange building, the Air India building, the Sahar International Airport, Plaza Theatre, Century Bazar at Worli, Hotel Searock at Bandra, Hotel Centaur at Juhu, Hotel Centaur at Santacruz and the oil dumps at Chembur.

Then taking the henchmen along, Tiger personally carried out reconnaissance of the Bombay Municipal Corporation and the Stock Exchange buildings. More such meetings were held to form groups and assign the specific tasks of planting RDX-laden vehicles and suitcases, lobbing hand grenades and opening fire through AK-56 rifles.

On Tiger's directives, each group began reconnaissance of its allotted target, carefully surveying the approach and escape routes. They were compelled to drop the idea of targeting the Chembur oil dumps since parking a car bomb near the dump did not look feasible in view of the high level of security deployed at the dumps. The height of the protective wall also made it well-nigh impossible to lob grenades. So instead, newer targets were now added, such as the bustling market streets of Zaveri Bazar, Dhanji Street and Katha Bazar.

Tiger saw to it that his entire family was moved to the safe haven of Dubai between 3-11 March. While the Memon family were all safely ensconced abroad, the saboteurs were preparing car and scooter bombs in the garage and open spaces in the Al Husseini building to cause mayhem and destruction in Bombay.

On the night between 11 and 12 March, Tiger conducted the final meeting at Al Husseini building to ensure perfect and flawless execution of the blasts. Satisfied that everything was lined up with clockwork precision, he handed a lakh of rupees to Javed Chikna and gave each of the saboteurs 5,000 rupees to see them through to Nepal. Then he hugged each one of them, promised to see them in Dubai and left for the Sahar Airport to catch the 5:30 a.m. Emirates flight to Dubai. Within a couple of hours, he was with the main co-conspirators and his family, eagerly awaiting the fruition of the unholy conspiracy which was scheduled to commence during the Friday afternoon prayers in the holy month of Ramzan.

As per the diabolical design, well before noon, the 'harbingers of death' began driving out of the Al Husseini building, one by one, on journeys of annihilation and destruction. Out rolled five scooter bombs, five car bombs, two motorcycles bearing men armed with hand grenades, one Maruti van that carried men with hand grenades and guns, and three men carrying suitcase bombs.

At 1:30 p.m., a car bomb exploded at the underground parking lot of the Stock Exchange building, killing eighty-four and injuring 218.

At 2:15 p.m., a scooter bomb exploded in Katha Bazar, killing five and injuring sixteen.

At 2:30 p.m., a car bomb exploded at the Lucky Petrol Pump next to the Shiv Sena Bhavan killing four and injuring fifty.

At 2:45 p.m., a car bomb went off at Century Bazar in Worli, killing 113 and injuring 227. Laden with five kg of RDX, the Century Bazar car bomb was a Commander jeep and the largest bomb of the day to explode. It accounted for the highest toll destroying in its wake, an entire BEST bus packed with passengers!

At 2:45 p.m., a Maruti van with five men had just crossed the Passport Office in Worli. The massive explosion at Century Bazar lifted the Maruti van up in the air and brought it down with such an impact that it shattered the nerves of the men within. In the panic and anticipating the police to set up nakabandis or checkposts all over the city, the trained terrorists abandoned the van near the Siemens Factory and fled. They were on their way to the BMC Headquarters in Fort to gun down Shiv Sena and BJP corporators and carried automatic weapons and hand grenades.

At 2:45 p.m., another car bomb exploded, this time in the

> tunnel road of the Air India building and killed twenty persons and injured eighty-seven.
>
> Around the same time, at 2:45 p.m., six saboteurs passed the Mahim slope hutments in a Maruti van and lobbed hand grenades at the fishermen's houses, causing three deaths, injuring six persons and sparking off a communal riot in which several cars and shops were gutted.
>
> At 3:05 p.m., a scooter bomb exploded in Zaveri Bazar, at the junction of Shaikh Memon Street and Mirza Street, killing seventeen and injuring fifty-seven.
>
> At 3:10 p.m., in Hotel Sea Rock, a five-star hotel at Bandra Land's End, a suitcase bomb exploded. It damaged property, but fortuitously there were no casualties.
>
> At 3:15 p.m., a car bomb exploded in the compound of the Plaza Cinema in Dadar, killing ten and injuring thirty-six persons.
>
> At 3:15 p.m., two saboteurs on a motorcycle reached the flyover near the Sahar International Airport, lobbed a hand grenade at Bay No. 54 and fled. Luckily no life was lost.
>
> At 3:20 p.m., a suitcase bomb exploded, this time in another five-star hotel, Hotel Centaur at Juhu, injuring three persons. Fortunately, no life was lost.
>
> At 3:40 p.m., a suitcase bomb went off in a room at Hotel Airport Centaur, a five-star hotel near the Bombay airport, leaving two dead and eight injured.
>
> And then there were the three bombs which failed to explode: at Naigaum Cross Road, at Dhanji Street and at Shaikh Memon Street in Zaveri Bazar.

And now all those monsters were at large, on their way out of the city and the country, or ensconced in safe houses, well out of the reach of the Bombay police. It was my duty to ensure that each one of them was tracked and brought to face trial. There was so much suspicion and hostility in the air, during and after the riots, that informants had all but disappeared. Society was totally polarised and the police were flooded with vague information which was mostly rumours. It was in such a difficult and uncooperative atmosphere that the police had to track down the culprits who had the benefit and support of a strong network of underworld connections to harbour them and help them escape.

An example of such support was an accused, Salim Durrani aka Salim Tonk who was arrested from Bombay on charges of aiding and abetting the terrorist conspiracy. A well-read and educated man from the erstwhile royal family of Tonk in Rajasthan, he had also participated in some of the earliest conspiracy meetings. Badshah Khan, a key operative whom we arrested from Rampur in UP, divulged that a large group of the saboteurs were holed up in Tonk under Salim Tonk's patronage. I immediately rushed a team to Tonk, headed by Dinesh Kadam, along with Badshah Khan to identify and nab them. For two days, Dinesh Kadam toiled hard in Tonk, but with no success. So, I had no alternative but to send Tonk to Tonk. Another team headed by Inspector H.B. Pawar immediately rushed with him to Jaipur by air. They met Dinesh Kadam and his team outside Tonk. Salim Tonk cautioned the officers that if the residents of Tonk found him with handcuffs, there would be commotion leading to a major law and order issue. The team then took off his handcuffs and held him by his hand. No one knew that Salim Tonk was under arrest and neither did Salim attempt to announce the same to the world. And indeed, the residents of Tonk would bow before Salim and even prostrate on the ground and touch his feet! This was highly embarrassing for Mssrs. Pawar, Kadam and company hovering around Salim.

They were received at the palatial family home by Salim's brother who informed them that Salim's earlier 'guests' had left the house a couple of days back. Then a manservant arrived to deliver a message that Her Highness, Salim's mother, desired to meet him and his friends. So Salim and 'friends' presented themselves before the Grand Old Lady in her opulently furnished Darbar Hall to pay their respects. They must have put their best foot forward, for they all received from the Queen Mother Rs.100 each, the customary token of royal munificence! They accepted it solemnly, but not without feeling a tinge of sadness to keep the good old lady in the dark about the real state of affairs. Then Salim Tonk returned to Bombay with his 'new friends' who had more pressing things to accomplish with his help.

Badshah Khan, who later turned approver, had to accompany the team to Delhi to look for his illustrious colleagues. From Delhi, he was made to speak to Tiger Memon in Dubai. Tiger was totally unaware that Badshah was in police custody and was helping the police.

'*Mein Rampur se Dilli ayah hoon!*' (I have come to Delhi from Rampur!) Badshah announced to Tiger on the phone. '*Ab mujhe kya karna hai? Yahan koi nahi hai,*' (What do I do next? No one is here), he asked.

'*Nikal, aur Calcutta jaa. Wahaan se call kar,*' (Leave, and go to Calcutta. Call me from there), directed Tiger and then added, '*Apne lodge ka naam bataana, phir hum dekhenge.*' (Let me know the name of your lodge and then we will see.)

The team promptly informed me of this development. I asked them to proceed to Calcutta, check in at a lodge and call Tiger. Now should Badshah be allowed to have a separate room? If someone shared a room with him, it could raise suspicion, in case the gang kept a watch on him. Could Badshah be trusted to stay alone? Many a time, at crucial stages of the investigation, as a lead investigator one reaches such crossroads. Does one take the chance and jeopardise the operation? Or do you gamble and do something that involves risks, but may result in benefits if things pan out as you hope they will. It is the investigator's call and it is his neck on the chopping block! I decided to take the risk. Immediately from Delhi, the team took Badshah by air to Calcutta. This would give them vital additional time to familiarise themselves with the terrain and topography of Calcutta. They found a suitable Delhi-Calcutta train that Badshah could have boarded, had he indeed taken a train to Calcutta. After its arrival in Calcutta, they checked in at a lodge. Then Badshah was made to call Tiger again and give him the details of his lodge. Tiger asked him to stand outside the lodge and said that one Hidaytullah would fetch him from there.

Now the question arose that if they leave Badshah standing on the road all by himself, would he run away and escape? My officers asked me for my decision. Again, I decided to take a calculated risk. So Badshah was allowed to stand on the road and the team discreetly watched him from a distance. Shortly, an Ambassador car appeared on the street, slowed down and then halted a short distance away. Badshah did not know what he should do and glanced at my officers for an instructional signal. The officers, too, had not anticipated this scenario and Badshah was asked to stay put. The car waited for a little while more and then drove away. On our instructions, an hour later, Badshah again called up Tiger and said that no one had turned up. Tiger asked him to go out and wait again. Badshah again stood on the road. Soon the same car returned and parked there. No one got out, neither did Badshah approach it and the car left after a while. Badshah again phoned Tiger to report this, but Tiger did not pick up his call. The team could not undertake any more risks and I had to call them back. However, it confirmed that Badshah Khan was indeed remorseful now and would not attempt to escape.

Dawood, Anees, Tiger Memon and Mohammad Dosa had masterminded the storage and distribution of the smuggled weapons among a large number of operatives through their lieutenants who included Baba Musa Chauhan, Samir Hingora, Hanif Kadawala, Salim Kurla, Abu Salem and Manzoor Ahmed Sayed Ahmed. When such suspects were pulled in for questioning, they would not easily part with the truth. They would try as much as possible to obfuscate matters or extricate themselves by putting the blame on others. The attempt would be to get to any extent to avoid admitting culpability. To trace each transaction with facts and to establish links, meticulous interrogation and investigation were necessary, that too in the shortest possible time. This was the case with the role of Baba Musa Chauhan and the manner it led to some shocking discoveries.

During the course of the investigation, it transpired that Baba Musa Chauhan of Chauhan Motor Training School had stored and distributed the smuggled weapons for Anees Ibrahim. When Baba Chauhan was questioned, he stated that he was a peripheral participant, but Hanif and Sameer know more about it. And who were Hanif and Samir? None other than Hanif Kadawala, the owner of 'Tawaa' – a famous eatery in Bandra, and Samir Hingora, the President of the Indian Motion Pictures Producers' Association (IMPPA). Together they ran a company called Magnum Videos and produced films. 'They are Anees' men,' disclosed Baba Chauhan.

So Hanif and Samir were called in for questioning. They were wealthy businessmen with a battery of good lawyers at their disposal and not easy nuts to crack. They were street-smart and as shifty as alley rats! Initially, they totally denied all insinuations. Skilful interrogation brought out details which made it amply clear that the duo knew much more than they pretended to. The greasy and slippery partners were arrested for their role in the chain of supply and distribution of dangerous arms and ammunition in a notified area. Then for some inexplicable reason, Hanif and Samir decided to squeal on a friend. One day, one of the lock-up guards at Mahim police station came to me and reported that Hanif and Samir desired to speak with me as they had something important to tell me. So I sent for them.

'Aap bade logon ko pakadtey nahi kya?' (You don't catch the high and mighty, do you?) they taunted me.

'Who is that?'

'Sanju Baba,' came the answer.

'Sanju who?'

'Sanjay Dutt, the hero.'

'Sanjay Dutt? How is he involved?' I couldn't believe what I had heard.

And a new angle emerged. They said that it was Baba Chauhan who had brought the car with the weapons to them at Anees Ibrahim's bidding. Samir had merely piloted it to Sanjay Dutt's bungalow where the weapons were offloaded. After a few days, Baba Chauhan had sent another vehicle, a Maruti 1000. This time it was Hanif who had piloted it to the Dutt bungalow. Sanjay Dutt had retained some weapons and returned the rest. And what was the destination of the weapons from there? They said they did not know.

This meant that Baba Chauhan knew much more than what he had divulged! So I accosted him again. Confronted with irrefutable details and facts, he had no other option but to admit his part and said that the car used for the second trip belonged to one Manzoor Ahmed. His address was traced and Manzoor Ahmed was hauled in. Where did he transport the weapons from Sanjay Dutt's house? Manzoor provided the name and address of one Zaibunnisa Qazi residing near the Mount Mary Church in Bandra.

So I immediately sent a team to bring in Zaibunnisa. No sooner did I begin questioning her that tears welled up in her eyes and she wept inconsolably. Her tale of woe was about her three young daughters, the tough times they were facing and how she knew nothing. The dramatic performance tugged at my heartstrings and was rich in pathos. I felt sorry for her. The last thing I wanted to do was to harass the innocent and more so a woman. So I asked her to leave. Then I got pre-occupied with other pending matters like remand and bail applications, and could find the time to question Manzoor Ahmed only in the late afternoon 'You think you can fool me?' I began and told him how Zaibunnisa had pleaded her innocence.

'Sir, that woman is lying blatantly. She knows everything. If you do not believe me, please call her and let me speak with her. I am telling you the truth,' Manzoor pleaded.

Manzoor disclosed further details of the Zaibunnisa Qazi home visit and gave me a name I had never heard before. Abu Salem Abdul Qayyum Ansari, a youth just around twenty-five years old. Manzoor said that it was this Abu Salem who had called him in his car. Both of them belonged to Azamgarh in UP. 'Abu Salem told me that we had to go to Hero's house and take some *samaan* (stuff) to another place....'

So I immediately sent a team for Zaibunnisa again. This time I was seething with anger and furious with her lies and the theatrics she had enacted to mislead me. The moment she came before me, I got up in fury and would have given her a resounding slap, had she not immediately begged my forgiveness and confessed that Abu Salem had indeed left the weapons with her. She gave me his address in Andheri.

'If I don't get him, you had better watch out,' I threatened her.

'Sir, the minute you permitted me to leave, I phoned Abu Salem right from the PCO outside the police station,' she confessed, holding her ears. 'I told him that because of him, the police had come to my house. He said he was going to make a run for it and also asked me to make a quick exit.'

What a terrible mistake I had committed! I had believed this woman who was adept at lying and let her pull a fast one on me! Instead of sympathising and commiserating with her, if only I had initially slapped her, the saga of the Bombay underworld would have been so different. Immediately on receiving Zaibunnisa's alert call, Abu Salem had taken to his heels. He took the first available flight to Delhi and thereafter escaped to Nepal and from there to Dubai to evolve into and emerge as Anees Ibrahim's chief extortionist. Had I seen through Zaibunnisa's crocodile tears, Abu Salem would have been cooling his heels in prison and not be the menace he proved to be for Bombay businessmen, filmwallahs and builders right through the mid-90s till his arrest in Lisbon, Portugal by the Interpol on 20 September 2002. Such are the twists and turns of fate!

On connecting all the dots, through sustained interrogation, what we found was that on Anees Ibrahim's directions, Baba Chauhan had sent Abu Salem in a Maruti van fitted with a hidden cavity to Gujarat, to transport weapons from Bharuch to Bombay. Once the weapons were brought into the city, they needed a quiet, secluded nook to open the cavity and unload the weapons. Baba Chauhan dialled Anees and sought his directions. Anees thought that Hanif and Samir's office on Linking Road would be the perfect spot. So he phoned them; but, they said that it was unsafe to use their office as they had an ongoing dispute with the landlord who used to frequently summon the police at the slightest excuse. So they suggested to Anees, 'Why not use Hero's house?' 'Hero' was none other than Sanjay Dutt who was known to Anees Ibrahim. Anees jumped at the idea and promptly phoned Sanjay Dutt, who too was game for it.

Sanjay's father Sunil Dutt, the sitting MP from Bombay north west, was perceived as pro-Muslim and anti-Hindu by the Hindu Right-wing. They held him responsible for the sprawling Muslim slums that had come up at the Bandra Reclamation and accused him of minority vote bank politics. Sunil Dutt was among the activists who saw the State and police as failures in their duty to protect the Muslims during the riots. In protest, he had even tendered his resignation which was not accepted. He had also done a lot of relief work for the riot-affected and had been receiving threats for his work. Therefore, a police guard had been stationed at his house since the riots.

On 16 January 1993, Anees directed Hanif and Samir to take

the arms-laden car to Hero's house. Driving his own vehicle, Samir piloted the Maruti van driven by Abu Salem to the Dutt bungalow. Baba Chauhan also went along. The Hero was expecting them and asked the constable on guard duty to stand away so that the illegal activity in the garage would not come in the constable's line of sight. From the garage, Sanjay Dutt procured tools to open the hidden cavity. He kept 3 AK-56 rifles, twenty-five hand grenades, one 9mm pistol and some cartridges for himself, put them in a duffle bag and carried them inside the house. Their task accomplished, Samir and Baba Chauhan left the bungalow in their vehicles.

A couple of days later, Hero began feeling uneasy with the 'baggage' he had in his possession. He phoned Anees and requested him to take away some weapons. So Anees entrusted the task to Baba Chauhan. Baba Chauhan, in turn, asked Abu Salem to go to the Dutt bungalow to collect the weapons, but Salem feared that he may not be allowed entry. So Anees asked him to go to Hanif and Samir and take them along. Abu Salem needed a vehicle to ferry the weapons. So he summoned his friend, Manzoor Ahmed, with his car. Manzoor drove Abu Salem to Hanif and Samir. Hanif in his own car then piloted Manzoor's car. The Hero was again present. He returned two AK-56 rifles, hand grenades and some cartridges. Hanif returned to his office and Abu Salem took the weapons in Manzoor Ahmed's car to Zaibunnisa Qazi's house in Bandra. He left the bag with her for safekeeping, explaining to her what it contained. After a few days, he returned to fetch and take the deadly consignment away.

The discovery of Sanjay Dutt's involvement in the blast conspiracy was a real shocker and a revelation. I immediately called up M.N. Singh and shared this epiphany with him.

'Are you sure?' He asked me.

'Yes, sir, quite sure. And I have the entire chain, but Dutt.'

'Where is the bag?' M.N. Singh asked.

'Lying in his house, in his bedroom, I think. If I go, I will be able to recover it.'

'OK, but you will have to take care to follow proper procedure,' he warned me. 'His father is a Member of Parliament. You will be entering an MP's house. So let's keep the CP informed.' Then M.N. Singh and I met the CP and briefed him.

Samra was thoughtful. There was massive tension between the Shiv Sena and Sunil Dutt. Post the riots, Sunil Dutt had taken part in a dharna and also led a peace march with his daughter, Priya Dutt. He was taking a strong position against the government. Samra wanted us to be very careful or we would unnecessarily invite flak which would derail the investigation and only benefit the accused. We were already aware that Sanjay Dutt was in Mauritius, shooting for his film *Aatish*. Samra advised us to wait until he came back.

'If we act before his return, he will get alerted and may abscond. The moment he is back, we shall pick him up. Let's maintain secrecy. No one should know. Do you know when he is coming back?'

I said I would ascertain it discreetly. Armed with this advice, I returned to plan about how to go about it. However, the very next day, much to our dismay, the front page of *The Daily* screamed: 'Sanjay has an AK-56'. The reporter was Baljeet Parmar. How did he get wind of this news? It was impossible! I was exasperated, as were Samra and M.N. Singh. Immediately, there was speculation all over that Sanjay Dutt was being framed because of the undercurrent of rivalry between Sunil Dutt and Chief Minister Sharad Pawar, both leaders of the Congress party. This was baseless and unfounded. Samra, Singh and I were aware that there was not an iota of truth in it.

None of us could fathom how reporter Baljeet Parmar had uncovered or caught on to this shard of information. Much later did the reporter disclose, in a press interview, that it was a cursory remark by our senior colleague Y.C. Pawar that had led him on the scent. At that time, however, all of us were totally clueless about how it had leaked.

Then Samra called me at Mahim police station. He had received a call from Sanjay Dutt from Mauritius, who had been alerted by the news in *The Daily*. The Hero was trying to assure Samra that he was not involved. The seeds of suspicion sowed in his mind by 'the boy' himself, Samra wanted to be absolutely sure. I reassured Samra that my mind was definitely free from doubt and I had enough evidence to arrest Sanjay and to justify further investigation. A few days later, Sanjay Dutt called up Samra to inform that he was returning to India. Samra promptly conveyed the same to M.N. Singh and me.

As per the directions of my superiors, I waited patiently for Sanjay Dutt to return. We got the details of his return flight. I was to go to the airport to arrest him. I was under severe stress. Sanjay Dutt was not going to be like ordinary criminals. He was the son of a Hindi film hero-turned-Congress leader who had impeccable secular credentials. He was the son of a Muslim actress who was synonymous with 'Mother India' – her role as a dedicated and just mother in her epic film by the same name. She had died of cancer when this child was in his teens and the 'boy-child' was reported to have had a lot of ups and downs in his personal life. The couple stood for secular values of India and its famous film industry. And the 'poor boy' could have run away from Mauritius, but he was returning to India. The Bombay police had already been called upon to prove before a judicial commission that they were not anti-Muslim, was going to have to deal with this 'poor boy'. The party supporters and the activists were all getting ready to roll up their sleeves for a good fight. The entire world's attention was now on Bombay police arresting a well-connected secular celebrity who was involved in the serial blasts.

I was assuredly confident of Sanjay Dutt's involvement in the weapon supply chain, but I had to get him to admit it. What strategy should I adopt? I cannot treat him with kid gloves. How am I going to get him out of the aura and protective umbrella of his high-powered and respected family to stand on his own merit and accept the truth? He is used to the canopy of his family's name and respectability. As long as he is under its shade, he will not come out with the truth. He will have the whole shebang of legal eagles who will do their best to strategise and prove the police theory wrong and packed with falsehood. We had already lost the element of surprise, thanks to the blasted report in *The Daily*. Now, he will be prepared and sufficiently well-tutored with his defence. And he is good at histrionics. I was a policeman and not an actor. Barring my brief child actor stint in the Punjabi movie, I had no experience in play-acting. Most importantly and crucially, it was my team's investigation that had caused the CP and the Joint CP to take on the world to arrest Sanjay Dutt. Their reputation and the reputation of the Bombay police were at stake. And it was all under my stewardship. The stress was tremendous, and the pressure was building up, the like of which I had never experienced before. How was I to manage it? And then I had this 'Eureka, Eureka' moment! The fog of doubt lifted, adrenaline rushed through my whole system, clearing the mist in my mind. I had the broad outlines of the strategy clearly chalked out.

That day not more than eight-ten police personnel went to the airport. I had handpicked even the constables who would accompany Sanjay and watch over him every single moment in the lock-up. I had discussed and brainstormed with them each and every possibility we would face. 'Please don't be star-struck! I depend on you. You have to be like stone statues,' I warned and drilled into them that they had to scrupulously follow my instructions or else the entire plan or strategy would come to naught.

On 19 April 1993, the flight was to arrive around 2 a.m. People had gathered in hundreds outside the Sahar Airport, International terminal. Sanjay's family was there accompanied by their film fraternity, as were hundreds of political supporters of Sunil Dutt all set to show solidarity, and of course, the media. My strategy hinged on the arrest to be swift and quick and without providing the hordes gathered outside an opportunity to dramatise it. I was in my civvies, waiting with the team on the aerobridge where it meets the aircraft. Sanjay Dutt, a first class passenger, was the first to disembark out of the aircraft door. As he did, I put my hand round his shoulder and drew him aside. I did not know him. So I introduced myself, 'I am DCP Rakesh Maria. Where are your boarding pass and passport? Give them to me.'

He looked at me dazed and in a state of shock and meekly handed over the passport and boarding pass without a word. I gave them to one of my officers who left to collect his bags. I walked Sanjay Dutt down the steps, from the aerobridge ladder near the aircraft door, on to the tarmac. As per the plan, two vehicles were waiting for us there: my official Ambassador car and a Crime Branch jeep. I sat in my car, next to the driver and Sanjay Dutt was made to sit behind between two constables.

The Domestic terminal at Santacruz and the International terminal at Sahar share the same airstrips. With the jeep closely following us, we drove on the tarmac to Santacruz – the Domestic terminal. No one spoke a word to Sanjay Dutt during the entire journey. I had categorically instructed the constables that whatever he said or asked, they must not respond, nor utter a single word. Sanjay repeatedly kept enquiring as to where we were taking him. He kept moaning that his father, his family were waiting for him. 'You cannot do this. Let me meet them once. Let me meet my father!' he kept saying, but none of us uttered even a word. The constables sat totally expressionless, without even turning their faces to look at Sanjay. Like stone statues!

Coming out of the Santacruz Domestic Airport, we brought

Sanjay straight to the Crime Branch in the CP's office at Crawford Market. He was taken to a room with an attached toilet that I had already identified earlier in the day. It was manned by carefully selected handpicked guards. Nobody except me was to speak to him; nobody was allowed to enter the room without my permission. If he wanted to use the toilet, he was to keep its door ajar. Smoking too was prohibited.

In the meanwhile, my officers had collected his baggage and handed it over to his family waiting outside the Sahar International terminal. M.N. Singh had instructed me that he would come to his office at 9:30 a.m. and I was to produce Sanjay before him. At 8:00 a.m. sharp, I went to the room housing Sanjay Dutt with handpicked officers. Nobody had uttered a word to him or responded to his queries right through the night. Bereft of family support and with not a soul to extend him any sympathy, Sanjay Dutt looked completely forlorn and broken. Had I allowed him to meet his family, he would have been another man altogether.

'Will *you* tell me the truth or do you want *me* to tell you your story?' I asked him.

'Sir, maine kuchch nahi kiya!' He was sitting on a chair, looking at me with soulful eyes and whining: Sir, I have not done anything!

The tension and stress of the last few days caught up with me. I could not bear the lie and couldn't help but plant a tight slap on his cheek. He tilted backwards, his legs going up in mid-air and I swiftly held him by his mane of long, gold-tinted hair. Looking literally down upon him into his horrified and scared eyes I said, 'I am asking you like a gentleman, you answer like one.'

'Sir, can I talk to you in private?' He asked in a quavering voice, looking up at me in a frozen stare, broken and shaken. This was much shorter and quicker than I had expected! I sent the officers out and, then Sanjay Dutt told me everything, crying like a child. He corroborated all that Hanif, Samir and the others had said.

'So, the weapons are in your house?' I asked him. 'Come and show me where they are.'

He fell sobbing at my feet and said, 'Sir, I have destroyed them.' Then he catalogued in detail how, after the news report had appeared in *The Daily*, he had tasked his friends to go to his house, take out the weapons and destroy them. I immediately sent teams to pick up his friends Yusuf Nullwala, Ajay Marwah, Kersi Adjania and Rusi Mulla who had aided and abetted Sanjay in destroying the weapons.

After he had finished, he fervently pleaded, 'Please don't tell my father any of this.'

'I cannot hide anything. I must tell the truth. It's time you stood up to face the consequences of the mistakes that you have made. Grow up and own up! Tell your father what you have done,' I said to him as he still kept pleading with me not to tell his father.

By then it was 9:30 a.m. and I was informed that M.N. Singh had arrived in his office. I produced Sanjay before him and let Sanjay speak for himself. He reiterated the entire sequence of events. M.N. Singh was satisfied and relieved that we had not been led up the garden path.

That very afternoon, Sanjay Dutt was produced before the court which remanded him to our custody. He was kept in the Crime Branch lock-up. Sometime late in the afternoon, Samra called on the police hotline and said that Sunil Dutt and some of the film fraternity were still sceptical about our investigation into Sanjay's role and wanted to meet me. Would I see him? He asked. I said, of course, I had no problem meeting them. Then, M. N. Singh also called me to say that Sunil Dutt and some of his associates were coming to the Crime Branch and I should meet them to address their apprehensions and doubts.

Giving patient hearings to the families of the serial blasts accused, especially parents, was a routine thing for me. The parents used to be in utter disbelief that their offspring could do such a terrible act against the State. When I informed them that I had no reason to implicate anyone falsely, they would agree, but still not believe that their sons had committed such a heinous crime. Ultimately, I would let the accused speak to them to ascertain if I was lying. Invariably, the accused would confess and the crestfallen family would leave shaken and shocked. Today, the same predicament awaited a celebrity father who treasured his family's patriotism and could never conceive that his son hobnobbed with anti-nationals or had a hand in nefarious activities.

Later that evening, Sunil Dutt accompanied by Rajendra Kumar, Mahesh Bhatt, Yash Johar and Baldev Khosa came to see me. I did not know any of them, despite my Bollywood lineage.

Sunil Dutt spoke first. 'You know me,' he said. 'Nationalism is in my blood. It runs in our veins. How can *my* son do this! It is impossible,' he said.

I replied that it was indeed unfortunate, but it had happened. That was the truth. Why would the police implicate anyone like this? Go after someone without a valid cause? I would never do it! Sunil Dutt still kept expressing his disbelief. I then said that I would call Sanjay right there. Let him answer for himself.

Sanjay was called in. No sooner he entered, he saw his father and immediately burst into tears. He touched his father's feet and said, 'Sorry! Please forgive me. *Merese galti ho gayi.*' I have made a mistake, he confessed. He then proceeded to narrate his follies.

Sunil Dutt was stunned with this admission of guilt. During this entire engagement, my eyes were transfixed on Sunil Dutt. The expression on his face is hard to describe. The blood just drained from his face. It was as if the impact of the confession had knocked every wisp of air from his lungs. The incredulity of what he had just heard rendered him speechless and totally stunned. The magnitude and gravity of Sanjay's actions shook the foundations of his belief and confidence. He was a broken man – his reputation, stature and standing punctured and deflated.

The first image that flashed in my mind was that of my own son, though barely five then. It was accompanied by the realisation that never should there be such a communication gap between a father and his son! The hurt, grief and pain in Sunil Dutt's eyes are forever etched in my mind. He never expected Sanjay to have done anything so serious and far-reaching. A small stupidity, idiocy or imprudence he could have easily handled. Even there, he was fervently hoping to be proved wrong and now all those hopes were dashed. As regards Sanjay, he had hoped and pleaded that I would shield him, not tell his father what he had done. And then he could still carry on being the unfortunate and misunderstood victim of an unfair destiny! Devastated, Sunil Dutt did not utter a single word thereafter and we led Sanjay away.

I had not been home since the eventful day of 12 March 1993. However, that night, I made it a point to go home. The first thing I did on reaching home was to go and hug my son, Kunal. I felt so miserable. I was not in a position to give him much time. I hoped he would understand me and pardon me as he grew up.

During the period that Sanjay Dutt was in our custody, he was an emotional wreck. I had instructed the guards to be watchful that he did not harm himself. He would keep asking the guards to let him speak to me. Whenever I got the time, I would ask him to be brought to me. My hectic and overloaded work schedule had no time to listen to his outpourings about his trials and tribulations. However, given his emotional state of mind, I did not want him to cause himself bodily harm. Imagine the hue and cry raised about police brutality and their usage of third-degree on an 'innocent' filmi hero, if that had happened. So, I would ask him to be brought to me late in the night after all my important work was done. Then it would all be about his troubled past, addictions, attachment to his mother, how her death had affected him and how he used to miss her, and also his affairs of the heart! He would cry incessantly and I would console and advise him to have courage, learn from his mistakes, face life and take consequences of his actions. Some of the things he narrated to me, however, gave me an understanding of the Bollywood-underworld nexus, especially the inroads that the organised crime syndicates had made into the tinsel world. On completion of his police custody remand, Sanjay Dutt was transferred to judicial custody in the Arthur Road Jail and I heaved a sigh of relief.

In the last week of April 1993, we had moved to the Crime Branch in the CP's office as space at Mahim police station was no longer sufficient to meet our growing requirements. The Joint CP, Crime, issued orders that I would continue to be in charge of the investigation under his overall supervision until further orders and to retain officers and men associated with the investigation. ACP S. K. Babar had been appointed as the Investigation Officer (IO) under the Terrorists and Disruptive Activities (Prevention) Act or TADA which was applicable to the conspiracy.

Our task of tracing the saboteurs extended beyond May. On 1 June 1993, we arrested four young Pakistani trained recruits from a room in Hotel Tulsi in Baroda. They were Mohammad Sayyed, Shaikh Usman Man Khan, Mohammad Hanif Driver and Shaikh Ibrahim. They had been indoctrinated and recruited by Anees Ibrahim through his lieutenant Salim Kurla and trained in Pakistan where Shaikh Ibrahim had even been injured while handling a rocket launcher and hospitalised. On 30 May, a credible source requested for an 'audience' in Dharavi. He was a dependable informant with a good track record to reckon with. I went incognito to meet him. He provided information about the four holed up in the hotel awaiting instructions to strike and be launched for future terror attacks. I, soon, put together a team headed by Dinesh Kadam and comprising Sukhlal Varpe, Dhananjay Daund, Srirang Nadgauda, Vani, Kirdant and Ram Kadam and despatched them to Baroda.

The targeted suspects were in room number 204 which was

on the second floor of the hotel. How could the mission be accomplished without any exchange of gunfire or endangering the lives of the team members and not to mention the genuine patrons inside the hotel? An operation was quickly planned and put into effect. All of a sudden, the electricity in room 204 failed and the inconvenienced guests dialled the reception to complain about the same. The portly and courteous receptionist assured them that the electrician would visit their room immediately and rectify the defect. Promptly, there was a knock on the door and the electricians walked in, announcing to the guests that their time was up! Mohammad Saiyyad, who was seated on the windowsill, thought it best to jump straight out of the window, only to be neatly collected with a fractured leg by a couple of gentlemen who were only too happy to receive him on the ground. They were my constables Arun Adam and Asam Farooqui of the Bombay Crime Branch. The 'highly qualified' electricians were Sub-Inspectors Sukhlal Warpe and Dinesh Kadam. The receptionist was our very own Ram Kadam, whose portly stature made him best suited for somewhat static jobs. Other officers who were placed at strategic positions in the hotel were Daund, Nadgauda, Vani and Kirdant. The team communicated to me of their success and, as usual, I heaved a big sigh of relief and waited for their return to Bombay with their troublesome charges to make them stand trial. The man who had recruited them – Salim Kurla – was subsequently arrested in Hyderabad by the Central Bureau of Investigation (CBI). He secured bail and was admitted to the Belle Vue Nursing Home in the suburb of Andheri where gangster Chhota Rajan's men shot him dead in April 1998.

My job was to give the detection and investigation team headed by ACP Babar the '*aagey ki chaal*' (the way forward) like the lead artisan does when executing a project of masonry or carpentry. It meant conducting and guiding interrogations, preparing remand applications, sending teams for arrests and recoveries, being at the other end of the receiver 24 by 7 to talk to the teams out in the field, meeting the families, and a myriad of such activities that are needed to coordinate such a big team. The press was totally being handled by M.N. Singh and Samra. That was their domain. Luckily, we did not have so many TV channels and the media those days understood and acknowledged its responsibility much better than today. Editors deployed senior and responsible reporters on crime beats. The report in *The Daily* about Sanjay Dutt was an exception. Otherwise, if this was not so, the fugitives on the run would have got alerted and we would never have been able to nab the number of accused that we ultimately did.

As the investigation gathered speed, we succeeded in seizing a total of 2,313 kgs of RDX, 1,132 kgs of gelatine, sixty-three AK-56 rifles, 496 hand grenades, and 39,000 live rounds of AK-56, and 9mm pistols in thirty-three different cases in Mumbai, Thane, and Raigad districts. The biggest seizure was affected when divers pulled out gunny bags with 1,250 kg of *kala sabun* (black soap, the term for RDX used by the accused) and 558 kg of gelatine from the bed of Nagla Bunder Creek in Thane and another twenty-nine kg of RDX from China Creek.

It was very evident and obvious that the conspirators were preparing for an act of retribution much more dire and sinister than just delivering a small lesson to the rival community to vent their anger and satiate their urge to wreak revenge. They were waging a war, not just on their own steam, but hand-in-glove with and under the command of the enemy of the Nation. They were part of an international network of terror that was waging war for a religious and radical ideology. They had altered, forever, the rules of policing in Bombay. They had introduced Bombay police to the world of international terror. For these were the first serial blasts of its kind in the world and demanded different strategies, tactics and measures.

Why did the conspirators advance the date of the blasts from

Shiv Jayanti in April to 12 March? As per one conjecture, it was because they feared that one of the operatives, unexpectedly arrested in another case on 9 March, would spill the beans. That operative was one Gul Mohammed aka Gullu, a resident of Behrampada in Bandra (East) and was wanted in an assault and extortion case at Kherwadi police station. He was one of the recruits sent to Pakistan for explosives handling and arms training to carry out the blasts. But this theory does not hold water. Tiger Memon had been holding meetings prior to 9 March to give final touches to the 12 March plan. He had also dispatched his family to Dubai between 3-11 March. Then why was the date advanced?

Our investigation revealed that it was advanced by Tiger Memon to 12 March so that it would coincide with the anniversary of a major battle which was the turning point in the early history of Islam. That battle was the famous 'Battle of Badr' which took place between the Meccans and the Muslims led by Prophet Muhammad. A raiding party of about 300 Muslims lured the enemy caravan to battle. Despite the superior numbers of the Meccan forces which were about 1,000 men, Prophet Muhammad's army scored a resounding and decisive victory. The holy Quran speaks of angels descending from heaven to kill the Meccans who included, in their ranks, Prophet Muhammad's main rival. The victory is seen as a divine sanction for Islam. Seen as the first military victory of the Prophet, it dealt a severe and fatal blow to the prestige of the Meccan tribes, strengthened the political position of Muslims and established Islam as a force in the Arabian Peninsula.

The actual date of the Battle of Badr was 13 March 624 CE, which was the seventeenth day of the month of Ramzan. In 1993, the seventeenth day of Ramzan fell on 11 March when the countdown to the serial blasts to be staged the next day, a Friday, began. This categorically disproves that the timing of the blasts had anything to do with the arrest of Gul Mohammad aka Gullu.

On 29 March 1993, Gullu was arrested on a transfer warrant in the blasts case. He disclosed that he could never hide anything from his mother and had ultimately divulged to her the diabolical designs of the conspirators and his close-knit trainees. The wily and wise matriarch forbade him from participating any further in the plot. She would rather have him locked away, safely behind bars, so that even his ruthless bosses would not suspect that he had developed cold feet. So Gullu felt that the best option out of the impending satanical machinations was to get himself arrested in the other case, which he did on 9 March. He was sitting pretty in the lock-up, quiet about his role in the impending havoc.

I had not gone home from the day of the blasts till almost the end of April, except that one day when I had rushed home to hug Kunal after witnessing Sunil Dutt's predicament. My residence was in the Haji Ali Government Quarters. In the months preceding the blasts, Kunal had developed the habit of waiting up for me, even if I got home very late. We had a little ritual. I would tell him a story and he would fall asleep listening to it. I would have my dinner thereafter. Now with my long absence from home, Kunal had got crankier and more irritable by the day. His tantrums and moods were creating hell for Preeti. On certain nights, things reached such a pass that he had to be brought to the Mahim police station after midnight. I would leave interrogation and meet him in my car parked in the open dark space between the ACP office and the Mahim police station. He would cling to me and I would tell him stories till he drifted off to sleep. Then I would slip off quietly back to work and the car would ferry him back home.

I was stationary in Bombay and had the advantage of my rank and better facilities to help me bring my child in a car to meet and see me. My officers and men were going all over the country. Their children must have missed them equally! Some had problems much graver than mine. Ailing parents, children preparing for exams, nervous wives running the households single-handedly on shoestring budgets. But there is an unwritten rule in the police: no whining about your personal problems. It is seen as a sign of weakness if you do. We all follow it strictly and pretend such problems do not exist. We know that our seniors are aware of all these problems. We also know that if they start heeding them, neither they nor we will be able to do any work.

It is a daily struggle, a hurdles race, with sacks on, just to maintain an ordinary existence in Bombay. And the lower down the rungs of the social ladder, the worse is your race. It is a miracle that the participant is happy that he has qualified for this race! He continues in his marathon effort, ungrudgingly, and gives his best to his work, keeping the smile on his face intact even in the worst of circumstances. And when it comes to facing a disaster, you cannot beat a Bombay resident. The lower down the social ladder, the more you rise to the occasion. This was amply proved on 12 March when the bombs tried to destroy Bombay's soul. The policeman of Bombay, howsoever maligned, is of the same timbre. Not a single officer or constable from my detection team did ever come up to me with his or her personal problems to ask for time off. They ate street food on the go, popped pills for headaches, acidity, hypertension and indigestion, barked at their families for fussy calls, did not ask for any special facilities and just went on dauntless and determined. They grittily stuck their necks out on the line, fearlessly took grave risks to their lives and limbs and never said no to me. Behind each of them stood families and friends whose support and sacrifice has gone unrecorded and unrewarded. And the police wives went on playing both father and mother, spiritedly and stout heartedly!

Each member of the detection squad was now an enemy of the conspirators, but I was more so. I had become the face of the investigation, so the brunt fell on me. My family was receiving threat calls, both at my house in the Haji Ali Government quarters and at my mother's home in Bandra. I was the recipient of umpteen number of threat letters. I was now being branded as anti-Muslim. Once, a delegation of burqa-clad women went to my mother to protest against me. She received them with patience and did her best to calm them down. They left, asking her to counsel me. Another time, in the middle of the night, an ambulance arrived at my mother's house. My sister Poonam would not open the door to anyone without ascertaining who they were. *'Rakesh Maria ke liye ambulance bheja hai,'* the ambulance man said. They had received a call asking for an ambulance urgently for Rakesh Maria at his Bandra house. Preeti and Poonam kept on receiving calls that showered them with the choicest of abuses. Sometimes the callers would leave dates on which I was to be bumped off. Twice, Kunal's school had to be evacuated because of bomb threats. Soon, my superiors decided to extend protection to me, my mother and Kunal. Friends stopped travelling in the same car with me and parents stopped sending their wards to play with Kunal. Why unnecessarily come in the line of fire or court danger with the Marias! This was the price we had to pay for doing national duty. On the one hand, you are fighting the underworld and the terrorists. On the other, you need to keep boosting the morale of your family, your officers and men. No one can comprehend or discern what you go through within yourself, because you do not let it show through. 'None knows where the shoe pinches, but them that wear it!'

The police team that came with me on this exciting mission stayed with me throughout, even when they had to go their different ways. Of them, we lost Senior Inspector Vani (from the Traffic Division) to a cruel quirk of fate. He was a tough boxer and fit as a fiddle. He was travelling during the monsoons to his village in the Konkan when his car skidded and got stuck in the slush on the shoulder of the road. He tried to pull it out, but, in a bizarre twist of fate, it fell on him, killing him in the freak accident. We lost an excellent officer whom I sorely missed, especially whenever some important tasks came up where his talents would have been immensely useful.

The bomb blasts case gave me a lot. For my work, I was awarded the Police Medal for Meritorious Service in 1994 after completing barely thirteen years of service, when it is mandatorily considered only for officers after a minimum of fifteen years of service. On Amarjit Singh Samra's promotion and transfer, another distinguished officer Satish Sahney took over as the Commissioner of Police, Bombay. He and M.N. Singh recommended my name for an out-of-turn medal which is an All India award conferred by the Union Government. The only other IPS officer to have got the award before completing the stipulated fifteen years in service is K. Vijaya Rama Rao, former Director of the CBI.

I read somewhere about senior officers always being on the lookout for good juniors and entrusting them with responsibilities when suitable opportunities emerge. If that is how I got selected for this job, I am eternally grateful to A.S. Samra and M.N. Singh. They already had a full-fledged Crime Branch in existence. Despite this, they should tell me, just two days after the blasts, that I have to detect the case! What did they see in me? I really have no clue. It was a bold decision to entrust the detection of such a sensitive case to a raw junior like me. And it makes me wonder at the Hidden Hand that ensured that I would be at the right place at the right time to take up the responsibility. It had ensured that Dr P. S. Pasricha and S. Ramamurthy make me DCP (Traffic) and it had ensured that Shrikant Bapat sends me first to Tokyo for a 'break' and then to the arduous task at the Mahim Police chowki for manning the 'chicken's neck'. And then it made A. S. Samra and M.N. Singh think of me on 14 March 1993, to detect the case.

When I say that with the bomb blast case my life changed forever, I also mean that it sort of took me into the 'big league', where I got to learn a lot from inspirational and iconic senior officers. A lot was expected from Shrikant Bapat when he took charge, but before he could really settle down, the overwhelming events turned everything topsy-turvy. Unfortunately for the city, he had had a very short stint. But I do remember his meetings, which I feel were some of the best that I have had the good fortune to attend. His precise questions did not allow officers to ramble on endlessly and they had to speak sense and facts or not at all. He could not be fooled.

From A. S. Samra, Satish Sahney and M.N. Singh, there was so much to learn and absorb – the way, in their own quite distinct styles, they inspired their juniors; the way they carried themselves in the most stressful of circumstances; the dignity and aura they brought to the office; their professionalism and the way they protected their junior officers and delegated work.

How I was to arrest Sanjay Dutt, had been left entirely to me. Nobody had exerted any pressure whatsoever on me. I had received the total and complete support from Samra and Singh. In them, I was fortunate to have great superiors to guide, protect and support me. They were the banyan tree whose protective shade shielded me from all the vagaries of external influence and pressures. If anyone had tried to pressurise them, I do not know. They shielded me and let me do my job unhindered and undisturbed. I did not receive a single phone call from anyone after I had picked up Sanjay Dutt and brought him to the Crime Branch for arrest and questioning. I was allowed to do my duty without hindrance, only because I was blessed to work under such dynamic and supportive seniors.

But I had, even more, to learn from my juniors. The way they placed their trust, faith and life at my disposal, put in without fuss the man-hours I demanded of them – it is from them that I learned how to place work before everything else. When you see them putting in such hard work and toil, you cannot back out or shirk. When they do not go home, neither do you. This is how mutual trust and rapport developed between constables and officers, and the walls of hierarchy melted away.

For the excellent and yeoman work done by the team for the detection and investigation of the 1993 serial blasts, we recommended them for rewards. The rewards took long to come. When they ultimately did, nearly a decade and a half later, the list came to me and one of the officers who happened to meet me on that day remarked, 'Finally something received, sir! Now at least Dinesh Kadam and Nitin Bhosale Patil will be able to recover the money they lost when they sold off their watch and gold chain!'

'What? Come again!' I said to him, flabbergasted.

It was then that I learnt that when the team was in Calcutta with Badshah Khan, at one point all their money had got exhausted. Dinesh Kadam sold his watch and Nitin Bhosale Patil his gold chain to get a princely sum of 2,500 rupees in those times to finance the rest of the stay. That was their commitment, dedication and fidelity for duty!

It was, indeed, their greatness not to bother me with such problems when I was in the thick of battle. This was just one instance of the immense sacrifice and the indefatigable industry exhibited by a couple of my lieutenants, that had come to my notice with the chance remark of a fellow officer! I am sure there are hundreds of similar incidents, of all the other members of the team, which I will never come to know, and therefore, will never be able to acknowledge or appreciate!

11

When Your Calling Comes Calling

My detection work for the 1993 Bombay serial blasts was a watershed in my career. I was thrust into it by unforeseen circumstances, catapulted on to the centre stage of hardcore detection, which gave me the opportunity to work with a group of officers and men who rose to the challenge that brought out the best in them. I was able to develop informants and understand the working of the underworld. People would come on their own to me and share information. I came across hundreds of people from different strata. These interactions gave me deep insight into the human nature. I spent hours poring over crime records and studying old cases.

I had to get in touch with retired officers and constables who had handled gangsters, history-sheeters and sensitive cases, and could give me important insights. I began getting the hang of who exactly should be contacted for information and how. Naturally, my network spread and with it grew my experience and skills as a detection officer. I began to learn the art of interrogation and Intelligence gathering, and analysing, developing and acting on information. I learned the value of thorough paperwork to achieve a foolproof investigation that would withstand judicial scrutiny.

Most importantly, I began to fathom how to spot talent in my colleagues and use them for the right purpose to build good detection teams. Some would be good for surveillance and long follow-ups. Some were excellent at interrogation, but hopeless at paperwork. Some had very good legal acumen, but could not communicate with people. Some had excellent common sense and could improvise and adapt to changing situations without causing any mess-ups and could take surprises in their stride. To understand their plus and minus points, their strengths and weaknesses and then deploy them appropriately was the key. This happens only when you work with officers and men continuously, under stress and in challenges which we had aplenty.

In the aftermath of the Babri masjid demolition and the 1993 riots, the Bombay underworld got divided on religious lines. Till then it was by and large 'secular'. Mastan Mirza aka Haji Mastan, Yusuf Patel and Abdul Karim Sher Khan aka Karim Lala had Hindu as well as Muslim henchmen, with some Christians thrown into the mix. So had Dawood Ibrahim. Only post the December 1992 riots did the 'secularism' of the underworld begin showing real cracks. The serial blasts of 1993 completed the divide. While planning the blasts, Dawood took care to keep his Hindu ally, Chhota Rajan in the dark. Chhota Rajan was in Dubai at that time but had no clue what was in the offing. Shocked to learn that Dawood had engineered the blasts, he split from the gang and escaped from Dubai. Then, through his henchmen D.K. Rao alias Dilip Bora, Rohit Varma, Ravi Pujari and Hemant Pujari, he began masterminding killings of the blast accused released on bail. He also targeted businessmen suspected to be close to Dawood.

In retaliation, Dawood began killing Shiv Sena and BJP leaders who were under the scanner for their role in the riots. They included those whose names had cropped up in the Srikrishna Commission of Inquiry. Some Shiv Sena and BJP corporators began receiving threats and the state had to provide them with police protection. After the split, Sunil Sawant alias Sautya and Sharad Shetty alias Anna, though Hindus, continued to remain with Dawood. Chhota Rajan killed them later in Dubai.

While I was completing the blasts' investigation and running against time to beat the deadline for filing the monumental charge sheet, there were sensational shoot-outs in the city in which some prominent legislators were killed. On 21 April 1993, just over a month after the blasts, Ziauddin Bukhari, Muslim League member and ex-Member of the Legislative Assembly, was shot down at point blank range while sitting in his office-cum-shop 'God's Gift' in Byculla. On 29 May 1993, Ramesh More, trade union leader and Shiv Sena Member of the Legislative Council, was gunned down as he walked to his house in Andheri. On 1 June 1993, Prem Kumar Sharma, BJP Member of the Legislative Assembly, was shot dead when on his way to a dinner at a restaurant to celebrate his daughter's academic success. The local police and the Crime Branch were working on the cases. There were several conjectures about the motive behind the killings, the obvious one being the communal angle.

Though I was not in the Crime Branch, CP Amarjit Singh Samra and Joint CP (Crime) M.N. Singh directed me to assist in the detection of the shoot-outs. My newly formed team started a parallel investigation along with the Sectional Police and the Crime Branch. Through my network, I was able to gather reliable information on the identity of Ziauddin Bukhari's shooters. The finger pointed towards gangster Arun Gulab Gawli's men; the motive was a land dispute. The shooters were Baban Ramchandra Raghav, Rahul Sakharam Pol, Rajesh Mahadev Bhange alias Raju Batata and Vijay Bapu Salve alias Narsale. They were holed up in places like Mangaon, Mahad and Shrivardhan, which were in the Raigad district.

The chase began, but something unusual kept happening. Our informant would tip us off about the locations, but every time the team reached, they would find to their dismay that the suspects had just fled. I got highly suspicious. Was there a mole in my team? Was their integrity doubtful?

So when Sub Inspector Dinesh Kadam came to me with a fresh tip-off that two of the shooters were holed up at Wai in Satara district, I was in a dilemma. Should I entrust the job to this team or should I give it to another set of officers? Do I waste one more precious opportunity just to test their loyalty?

I would be the last person to go quiet on receipt of such information. Finding me unenthused, Dinesh Kadam sensed that I was not my usual self.

'*Kya baat hai, sir?* Is there a problem?' he asked me anxiously.

I decided to be frank with him. 'Dinesh, I am wondering if someone in our team is not loyal any longer,' I confessed. The expression on his face was enough to tell me that I had hurt him deeply.

'Sir, how can you think like this? I can vouch for each and every one of them! We will never be disloyal to the department and to you, sir.'

'Believe me, it is as much a shock to me that I should think this way, Dinesh. I am sorry to hurt you, but I have to be transparent. Otherwise, we will never be able to do our job,' I told him.

He then appreciated my torment, but still would have none of my doubts. I told him that I wanted to be proved wrong, but as a matter of abundant precaution, this time nobody else should be made aware of the location and the forthcoming raid. And most importantly, this time we should not requisition any police vehicle for the raid. It is a normal practice that whenever a police team leaves for a raid and search operation outside Mumbai city, the vehicles with drivers, are requisitioned from the Motor Transport (MT) Division located at Nagpada. I had a gut feeling that if not in my team, then the mole must be in the MT Division. Dinesh Kadam agreed to this and we began planning the operation.

I telephoned a friend and requested for his Maruti van with a driver. Without any advance intimation, I called the team to the parking lot in the Mahalaxmi Race Course where I briefed them, gave them a pep talk and wished them good luck. They left in the Maruti van and, as per plan, reached Wai where they arrested Baban Ramchandra Raghav. Based on the information he gave, the team then arrested Rahul Sakharam Pol from Chaturshringhi in Pune. In a space of a few days, Raju Batata and Vijay Bapu Salve alias Narsale were also arrested from Vikhroli and Byculla respectively.

My suspicion about loyalty rankled in Dinesh Kadam's mind and probably the first question he posed to Baban Raghav was, how did they manage to evade us or to get the wind of our movements. His answer proved that I had been right. The Arun Gawli gang had developed moles in our Motor Transport division. What he said further, pulled the carpet from under our feet. A police driver of a DCP rank officer had provided him shelter at Wai! Later the driver was arrested and dismissed from service.

Building faith and loyalty in your detection teams go through such tough trials and tribulations. Often criminals deliberately create misunderstandings and it is very difficult for the leader not to get swayed and cause injustice. It is a very painful process and when you manage to forge cohesion, it is a reward in itself.

The breakthrough in the Ziauddin Bukhari murder case came as a great relief as it confirmed that all the killings did not have a communal angle merely because the related issues or the killers represented any community. Thereafter, I also got leads on the killers of Prem Kumar Sharma and Ramesh More. My team and I were instrumental in detecting these cases too and in nabbing the culprits. Even then, by the time we reached the end of 1993, the underworld gangs had begun wreaking revenge on each other with full gusto.

On 4 November 1993, we filed the primary charge sheet (running into a whopping 9,392 pages) in the Designated Terrorist

And Disruptive Activities (Prevention) Act (TADA) court against 189 accused in the serial bomb blasts case. With this Herculean task achieved within the stipulated period, my primary work in the Crime Branch was over. The office of the Deputy Commissioner of Police (Traffic) that I had not entered since the day I had left for the Traffic Training to Japan was waiting for me. It was time to go back.

Something tugged at my heart. Frankly speaking, I was sad. Just ten months back my spirits were sort of on top of the world with my new found specialisation in traffic control and the training in Japan. And here I was now, the same policeman, trying hard to convince himself that traffic control was indeed his specialisation! Or was it? I loved the challenge of undetected crime. The thrill of ferreting out clues, the adrenalin rush during the chase for the culprits, the battle of wits during the interrogation, and the ultimate high of detection – were emotions that were latent in my subconscious since childhood and had just found vent and recently surfaced during the last few months doing pure crime detection work. Miserable at the thought of not chasing the baddies any more, I was mentally preparing myself to bid goodbye to the Crime Branch and move out, when on 1 December, late in the afternoon, I was called by the new Police Commissioner Satish Sahney to the CP's chamber. Joint CP (Crime) M.N. Singh was sitting with him when I entered. I saluted them and Sahney asked me to sit down.

'We want you to work in the Crime Branch,' said Sahney simply. I could not believe my ears. As the sentence sunk in, there also loomed the guilt in me. The government had spent on my training in Japan. I was being groomed for that important portfolio. So I began anxiously, 'But, sir, I have been brought to Bombay for traffic....I was sent to Japan for training....'

Satish Sahney, the pucca gentleman, managed to conceal his boredom at my mumbling and said, 'Have you finished what you had to say? I have heard your case. I am your superior officer and it is for me to assess your capabilities. What is good for the department and what is beneficial for your career is for me to decide. That decision is mine. You are suited for crime work and that is your calling. Your orders are being issued. You will be DCP (Detection) in the Crime Branch.'

Until then there was no post of DCP in the Crime Branch. Under the CP came the Joint CP (Crime) and then the Additional CP (Crime) to whom all the Crime Branch units reported. Now a post of DCP (Detection) was created and I was its first incumbent. It was my work in the blasts' case and the three quick detections of murders of political personages my team and I had made, that had convinced the CP and Joint CP (Crime) that my experience and talent had to be used and nurtured to tackle the underworld and the crime in the city.

I was honoured, to say the least. It was the greatness and foresight of Satish Sahney and M.N. Singh that they should acknowledge the work of a junior officer not just by recommending him for an out-of-turn Police Medal for Meritorious Service, but by getting him into the prestigious Bombay Crime Branch when he had completed just twelve years of police service.

I took up the new post on 13 December 1993. For someone who had grown up reading about ace Mumbai Crime Branch sleuths like Suresh Pendse and Vinayak Vakatkar, this was pure happiness and unadulterated bliss. But with it came a huge responsibility and I began my work passionately, building teams and eager to prove that those who had reposed their faith in me were not mistaken.

But the Bombay Dons and their gangs were determined not to give me any time to savour this joy and elation. Their bitter turf wars were on and I straightaway plunged into the job of gathering my men, inspiring them, motivating them, strategising, and guiding them. Much like a captain going into a huddle with his team at every strategic moment. At the beginning of every match, every inning, every break and after every setback! The only difference was that this was no sport. It was a deadly game bitterly fought against a whole lot of unscrupulous teams, all at the same time. Unlike your team, the opposite teams were not bound by any law, nor did they have any qualms about dealing in death.

12

Gang War in Girangaon

The sun blazed mercilessly on the Mahalaxmi bridge. It was close to twelve noon and the traffic signal atop the bridge was trying to put some sense into the busy junction. It was a sweltering summer day and a harried Abdul Yusuf Shaikh, the traffic constable in charge, was at his athletic best. He had just sprinted towards the pavement where the railway station entrance opens onto the bridge, screaming himself hoarse at the cheeky taxis halting to drop off passengers and lingering on for customers. Little did he know that he was about to witness a high profile murder which was unfolding at that very minute, just a few feet away.

At the signal had halted a cream-coloured Mercedes, its owner sitting next to the chauffeur, as was his practice. He was on his way to his office in Byculla, probably thinking of the various tasks on his agenda for the multi-crore deal that he was hoping to close soon. A lot of planning had gone into it and he was tackling different types of people – some politicians, some activists, some union leaders, and some others of a rather dubious vocation and disposition. He was raring to go, quite confident that he would pull it off, ultimately, though things were far from easy. Yet the last thing he expected was someone to just smash the window of his beautiful car with a hammer and pump bullets into him. But that is exactly what happened. Neither he nor his loyal chauffeur had noticed that some two-wheelers and a car had kept them close company right from the moment they had left his tony Malabar Hill bungalow.

A Yamaha motorcycle pulled up alongside his window and the two riders jumped off. The Mercedes could be bulletproof and the assailants did not want to leave anything to chance. Within a split second, they had smashed the car window to smithereens with a hammer and pumped bullets into their target. He was Sunit Khatau, the fifty-five-year-old Chairman and Managing Director of Khatau Makenji Spinning and Weaving Mills which had turned 125 that very year.

Hearing the gunshots and the wild honking of panic-stricken motorists, Constable Shaikh turned back and just as he was trying to comprehend what had happened, the killers were speeding away towards Worli abusing the motorists in Hindi to get out of the way. There were two two-wheelers with pillion riders brandishing revolvers and also a blue Maruti car escorted by two more two-wheelers. One of the men sitting in the Maruti car was shouting at the men on the two-wheelers in Marathi. Two *dhobis* (washermen) working at the nearby *dhobi ghat* (lavoirs) also witnessed the attack and the assailants fleeing away.

In the avalanche of bullets directed towards Sunit Khatau, one of the bullets had struck his chauffeur, Anand Ghorpade; but despite the injury, he displayed a great presence of mind. Unmindful of his own injury, he whisked his master away straight to the B.Y.L. Nair Charitable Hospital which was close by. But it was too late. Sunit Khatau was declared dead on arrival. The Tardeo police, under whose jurisdiction the scene of offence fell, rushed to the spot and investigations began.

The day was 7 May 1994 and I was barely five months old in my office of DCP (Detection), Crime Branch, Bombay. The cold-blooded murder in broad daylight sent shockwaves across the city. It was the first time that an industrialist had been murdered in Bombay. And he was no ordinary industrialist. Sunit Khatau represented one of the most distinguished merchant and trading families who were pioneers in the cotton textile industry in the city, several of whom came from diverse backgrounds: Parsis, Gujarati Hindus, Jews, and even Ismailis. Their saga of success had begun with Nanabhoy Davar of Bombay Spinning and Weaving Company and Maneckji Petit who set up the Oriental Spinning and Weaving Company in 1855. The Davars and the Petits were followed by the Tatas, Wadias, Sassoons, Morarjees, Thackerseys, and the Khataus. The Khatau mill was set up in 1874 and grew to be one of the largest in the industry. In 1875, the textile mill-owners formed the Bombay Mill Owners Association, a prestigious industry association in the country and the textile industry soon became the backbone of India's economy. The mill-owners stood for the success of indigenous entrepreneurship. As the freedom struggle took shape, they were genuinely drawn to its dynamic leaders and gave valuable support to the nationalist movement.

However, in 1994, the textile mills were an ailing conglomerate of sick units, no longer the thriving industry and pride of Bombay. Even then, the mill-owners, particularly the scions of the distinguished pioneers, were still looked up to. That one of them could be murdered so casually, was unthinkable and hard to accept, even for their severest of critics. The murderers had, therefore, thrown an open challenge at the Bombay police which could not be taken lightly. The process of transferring this high-profile case to the Crime Branch had already begun when I sat in my office the next day, mulling over strategies for quick detection. As I was conferring with my colleagues, Umesh Prabhale, my Personal Assistant, sent in a visitor's slip. The name and the purpose of the visit were entered in a neat hand in English: Meherunnisa. Official.

I could not place the name and, as soon as I had finished

my meeting, I sent for her. In came a woman fully covered in a burqa and wearing a very pleasing fragrance. No sooner had she taken a seat than she shot a question at me, *'Sir, aap par kitna bharosa kar sakti hoon?'*

I was taken aback. This woman was actually asking me how much she could trust me. I regained my composure and said, 'I am a police officer. I am here to help people. You have to repose faith in me if you want me to help you.'

'Lekin sir, yeh toh mere zindagi aur maut ka sawal hai!' she said. It meant that it was a question of life and death for her. She was scared of her identity being exposed and I could sense the anxiety in her tone. I thought for a while and looked at the visitor's slip.

'First of all, I have not seen your face. Then I am also pretty certain that this name that you have written here, is not your real name,' I said. 'So there is no question of me knowing who you are. But I assure you that whatever you tell me will remain with me. It will not go beyond the confines of this room. And you have to take my word for it. Beyond this, there is nothing I can say to make you trust me.'

About ten seconds of silence followed and then she said in fluent English, sounding quite polished, 'Sir, I can help you with the Sunit Khatau murder case.'

I was astounded. *Here I had just started activating my informants to get leads and in walks someone, the very next day of the murder, to nonchalantly tell me who the murderers are? Was I dreaming? Was someone trying to throw us off their scent? How could she help?* As I was lost in these thoughts, she asked me again if she could trust me. *'Sir, aap par bharosa kar sakti hoon na?'* The tone was pleading.

'I am giving you my word that whatever you tell me will remain with me,' I assured her earnestly.

'Sir, yeh kaam Amar Naik gang ke Omprakash Bharadwaj – Omi ne kiya hai, apne ladkon ke saath,' (The killing was executed by

Omprakash Bharadwaj aka Omi and his boys. They belong to the Amar Naik gang) she said.

'Who is he? And how can you be so sure? How do you know?' I asked.

'Sir, I am a bar dancer,' She said and lifted her veil with a swoosh. She was an exceptionally beautiful girl and barely nineteen or twenty years of age. Not only was she well-groomed, she was endowed with natural beauty. 'I have now put my life in your hands and I trust you with it, sir,' she added and I could see fear clouding her eyes.

After I had reassured her again that I would keep her identity a secret, she began narrating her story. She gave me the name of the bar where she was working and said that she was earning almost a couple of lakh of rupees a month. I looked at her with shock and disbelief, as a couple of lakhs a month was a lot of money in 1994. I could trace a hint of a smile on her face. She realised that I was a little sceptical about her earnings.

'Sir, I also entertain clients outside. I have a permanent room booked in my name in a hotel for the whole year,' she explained without an iota of shyness or any qualms of morality whatsoever. She also provided me with the name of a very well-known hotel in the western suburbs where she conducted her 'extra-curricular' activities.

I asked her about her family. She said that she hailed from Uttar Pradesh and was the sole breadwinner for her family. She added that she had a widowed mother and she was educating her younger siblings in boarding schools. The family stayed in a posh apartment in the suburbs. Everything was going well until a customer watched her dance and asked her out for the night, a couple of months ago.

She took him to her hotel room and he paid her well. The patron seemed smitten with her, but she was quite used to men taking a fancy for her. What she was totally unprepared for was what transpired thereafter. The man not only started coming almost every evening to the bar but began monopolising her. No other customer could shower money on her, leave alone take her out for a single night. Her protests were met with him taking out a revolver and threatening to shoot her or anybody else who dared come between them. She had no choice but to bow to his unrequited 'love' and wishes.

By this time she had learned that he was Omi Bharadwaj, a sharpshooter from Amar Naik's gang and an important lieutenant in his drug business. He began confiding in her and boasting about his exploits. Then instead of her hotel room, he started taking her to a flat in Thane on a motorbike. Her entire 'career' came to a standstill and life became one big hell. Her earnings plummeted. The flat he took her to was not his residence. He lived in another flat in Thane with his wife and children.

She gave me the addresses of both the flats and also the number of his motorbike which was MH 06 A 3650. It was a Yamaha and she had got to know during her last night's tryst with him, that this was the motorbike he had used for killing Sunit Khatau.

The story ended and she looked relieved. 'Sir, now my life is in your hands,' she repeated. 'Henceforth I will not come to meet you. Please tell me how I should contact you in case I need help or if I have to give you more information. I will phone you as Meherunnisa,' she said.

I gave her my office and residential numbers and told her that she could call me whenever she wanted. I also assured her that I would do everything possible to ensure her safety. Her eyes no longer held the fear with which she had entered and she then left my cabin, taking care to cover her face before stepping out.

I immediately called the Crime Branch team I had put together for this investigation. Senior Inspector Nikam was being assisted by Inspector Johri and other officers. I shared with them the information that I had received without divulging anything about Meherunnisa. The Crime Branch immediately flashed the motorcycle number on all the police wireless networks with instructions to pick up the bike along with the occupant the minute it was spotted. I also deputed men to keep vigil on both the apartments in Thane.

The breakthrough came on 11 May. A traffic constable on duty at the Ratan Tata Institute junction at Babulnath spotted a Yamaha bike with the number we had flashed on the wireless. He stopped the bike and immediately took it and its rider to the Tardeo police station. The Tardeo police discovered that the rider was not carrying the mandatory motor vehicle papers. He gave his name as Rajinder Singh Negi. The Tardeo police detained the motorcycle and asked Negi to go and fetch the papers which he promised to do the next day.

In the meanwhile, the Police Control Room was informed about the motorbike being detained by the Traffic police. This was also communicated to the Crime Branch at whose instance the message had been flashed. The Crime Branch team rushed to the Tardeo police station and when they found that Negi had been allowed to go home, apart from pulling their hair and phoning me about what had happened, they could do little else. I, too, could do nothing but rant in consternation at the lackadaisical approach of the Tardeo police station officers. All of us waited with prayers on our lips and hope in our hearts for the next day to arrive and fetch Negi to the police station. The individual who must have prayed the most that day would have been was the Duty Officer in-charge who had permitted Negi to leave the police station in the first place. He knew that his job was at stake. God must have had a special place in His heart for this officer, for the next day Negi returned to the police station with the papers. I am very sure that the Duty Officer must have embraced him hard! Negi's interrogation revealed that he was a close friend of Omi

Bharadwaj. Omi often borrowed his bike and his men collected it from Negi from different spots. On the day of the murder, he had dropped the bike at Tardeo Road at Omi's instance at 9:30 a.m. and handed over the keys to an acolyte called Santosh Pangerkar. At 6:30 in the evening, the bike was duly delivered back to Negi.

On 14 May, one of Omi's boys came on a motorbike to Poladia Apartments, the building where Omi lived in Thane with his wife and family. The man went up to his flat and came down with a suitcase. He was detained by the waiting Crime Branch team. This gang member's name was Sunil Shelar. The suitcase contained Omi's clothes and some documents including his bank passbook. Shelar was also found in possession of a .38 revolver. Apparently, he was collecting things that Omi needed whilst on the run.

With leads provided by Shelar and Negi, Inspectors Tejale, Patkar and their team picked up Santosh Pangerkar and another accused called Pramod Shinde from Nerul. Pangerkar had an entry-exit wound above his left knee and the explanation offered was that he had sustained it accidentally at the time of the Sunit Khatau killing from the gun of Raju Vikhroli, another shooter.

We also discovered Omi's pager number, but he and Amar Naik had simply vanished without a trace. The Crime Branch was making relentless efforts and moving heaven and earth to locate them, when one day in June, late in the night, the team picked up a boy suspected to be in close contact with Amar Naik and brought him straight to me for questioning. I began probing him and within half an hour he broke down and admitted to his close association with Amar Naik. I promised him immunity from police action if he assisted us in nabbing Amar Naik. To our utter surprise, he put his hand inside his trouser pocket and pulled out a door key. We could not believe our luck when, in a matter-of-fact way, he told us that the keys were of a flat that Amar Naik visited maybe twice or thrice in a fortnight and that he was the caretaker of the flat. Amar Naik possessed another set of keys and used it to let himself in! Now, who was available at that hour in the Crime Branch compound to go camp in the flat with the caretaker and nab Amar Naik?

I called them to my cabin to brief them. They were to go to the flat with some dry rations, hide inside the flat and nab Amar Naik as soon as he came there. The only other key was with Amar Naik and only he could enter the flat. So they had to keep vigil and be absolutely alert. They would get only one opportunity to nab a most wanted gangster and if they availed it, it would be a feather in the Crime Branch and Bombay police's cap. I motivated them thus and they appeared quite charged as they left on the mission with the caretaker.

They reached the flat well after midnight and telephoned me at home to inform me that they had reached. They assured me that they would take all the possible care and keep me posted of the developments. It was around 7:30 in the morning when my bedside phone rang. I picked up the phone. 'Sir, bad luck. *Toh palala,*' said the voice from the other end; why for a second, my head went into a spin. It was the officer from Amar Naik's flat. Amar Naik had escaped! How did this happen? I almost screamed.

What they told me was so unprofessional and shameful that the moment I heard it, cold anger took over and replaced all the anxiety associated with the operation. After entering the flat, the two officers had changed their clothes and had comfortably settled down for the night. In the morning after waking up at around 6:30 a.m., they asked the caretaker to prepare tea for them. Whilst waiting for the tea to be served, one of them heard the sound of a key being inserted into the main door. So he tiptoed to the entrance and stood next to the door. The door opened and there stood Amar Naik staring straight into his eyes. Amar Naik immediately realised that something was amiss and his hand instinctively went to his trouser pocket. Suspecting that he was whipping out a gun, the officer grabbed his hand. They struggled for a few seconds, at the end of which all that the officer got was a napkin that Amar Naik had let go before fleeing at top speed down the staircase. The officer would have followed him immediately, had his lungi not given way during the scuffle! He desperately called out to the other officer who was in the other room. He too was in his lungi and by the time they changed into their trousers to give a chase, Amar Naik had vanished into thin air and we had lost a golden opportunity to bring him to trial.

I blamed only myself for what had happened. I should have paid meticulous attention to the planning and execution of this operation. It was a valuable lesson learnt albeit at a heavy price. Proper selection of the team and issuing detailed instructions to them, after considering each and every possibility, was imperative if success was to be achieved in such a delicate operation. Common sense is indeed a rare commodity. Even to this day, I still cannot imagine or fathom how the two officers could have chosen lungis (an unstitched wraparound, which is just wound around your waist) to sleep in when they were supposed to be totally alert and geared for action every minute! The only consolation was that they had confessed to what had actually happened, instead of hushing up their failure, or cooking up stories to cover their stupidity.

Trying to make light of the spirits dampened by this big boo-boo, we continued to chase Amar Naik and Omi with all the ingenuity and ability in our command. I was in touch with several informants including Meherunnisa. Ultimately on 14 July, on receiving credible information, our team comprising Senior Police Inspector Shamrao Jedhe, Inspector Fattesingh Gaikwad, Assistant Police Inspectors Mangesh Pote and Pramod Khade, Sub Inspectors Bajirao Patil and Yashwant Desai lay in wait for Omi. On seeing them, the dangerous desperado that he was, Omi opened fire which was retaliated to by the team which led to his death in the encounter.

But why did Amar Naik, Omi and gang murder Sunit Khatau? Who had set them upon him? There were already a number of theories floating around and as investigators, we had to look at all the possible angles.

The arrow of suspicion first pointed towards the 18 April 1994 shoot-out in the compound of the Bombay Sessions Court. Ashwin Naik, an under trial, ganglord Amar Naik's brother and an Electronics engineer, was shot at by a shooter from the rival Arun Gawli gang who came donning a lawyer's gown. Although he had providentially survived, it had left Ashwin Naik paralysed from the waist down. Amar Naik's anger knew no bounds and he swore revenge on the killers. He suspected that it was Sunit Khatau who was financing Gawli.

Why would Sunit Khatau, the amiable mill-owner whose only known passion was horse racing, who loved his Sunday morning visits to the Mahalaxmi race course to watch his horses exercise and prided himself as the most successful horse-owner in the country, team up with Arun Gawli of all the people?

The answer probably lay in one more failed shoot-out that had taken place just a fortnight before the Sunit Khatau murder. Gunmen, who had yet again come riding on bikes, had fired at the car of Shankarrao Jadhav, the newly-elected President of the Congress-affiliated Rashtriya Mill Mazdoor Sangh (RMMS), which represented over 1,00,000 textile mill workers of Bombay. The shots had narrowly missed Jadhav, but not without highlighting the underworld's growing involvement in the city's textile industry.

There were fifty-four mills in the city and thirty-two of them were still under the private sector. They were spread over around 500 acres of prime land in south-central Bombay where land prices had skyrocketed exponentially per square foot. The gangs had been muscling their way into the textile mills to appropriate their share in this prime land worth thousands of crores of rupees. And how could they get a role in the sale of the lands that belonged to the mills? The answer lay in the history of the 'Village of Mills' – Girangaon. A 'village' that very few Mumbaikars now know about or care to find out about, even as they zip across from one end of the city to the other, over the newly constructed freeways, sea link and flyovers, completely oblivious that they are bypassing what was once the throbbing heart of the city. Or when they vie to buy swanky flats in what was once a place where people set their watches and clocks by the wails of the mill sirens.

To promote industrialisation and urban development, the Colonial government had earmarked large tracts of vacant or reclaimed land in Tardeo, Byculla, Chinchpokli, Sewri, Mazgaon, Parel, Lalbaug, Saat Rasta, Elphinstone Road, Prabhadevi, Worli and Dadar. The mill-owners set up their plants and built housing colonies (called *chawls*) for workers on these lands which were allotted to them at concessional rates and reserved for industrial use under the Municipal Development rules. Soon the tracts developed into a densely populated area and came to be known as 'Girangaon' – the 'Village of Mills'. *Giran* means 'mill' and *gaon* means 'village' in Marathi, the language of its simple and hardworking folk who were mostly from the coastal belt of Western Maharashtra, driven out of their villages by famines and Colonial policies that extracted revenue from the hinterland without contributing to its development. It was in Girangaon that India's first 'working class' took shape and gave the city a culture quite different from that of the middle class that had reigned here until then. The area south of Girangaon remained the elite quarters of the city, whereas towards the north and the west came up the new suburbs. Nestling among them, Girangaon retained its distinct identity.

Initially, the workers' protests and demands were spontaneous and lacking in leadership. The late twenties saw the birth of the Girni Kamgar Union and the beginning of the trade union movement in India, which was dominated by the Left until the forties. Both the Left and the Congress were vying for the mill workers' attention. To secure a foothold in Girangaon, the Congress started its own trade unions which they wanted to run on Gandhian principles as opposed to the communist ideology of the Left. The mill workers though increasingly aware of their rights, proved that not only did they have an independent mind but were, above all, fierce nationalists. The communist support to the Allied war effort alienated them and the workers began leaning towards the Congress. The mill-owners, too, supported the freedom movement but naturally preferred the Congress over the communists.

In 1947 after the Congress assumed power, all their textile workers' unions were consolidated into the Rashtriya Mill Mazdoor Sangh. Several legislations were enacted to provide for workers' welfare and job security, but the Bombay Industrial Relations Act (BIRA) 1948 came as a controversial enactment under which the RMMS was made the sole legal representative of the textile workers. The object was to contain the menace of frequent strikes and also force the recalcitrant management and owners to deal with workers through arbitration binding on both parties. However, gradually the workers began to perceive the RMMS as a tool of the mill-owners and the government, and the Left parties started regaining their foothold.

In the meanwhile, the Samyukta Maharashtra movement for a united Maharashtra and the inclusion of Bombay in the Marathi State caught the imagination of the mill workers who were predominantly Marathi-speaking. A large number of the 105 martyrs who laid their lives for the cause, came from the mill areas. The communists took part in the movement but, subsequently, could not match up to the workers' expectations. The sixties saw the emergence of a new party which would vie for their attention: the Shiv Sena which could articulate the interests of the Marathi-speaking working class in their own language and through a grassroots organisation easily access and identify with an outfit that would align with different forces to see the communists out. If that was not enough, another prominent leader emerged on his own merit: Dr Datta Samant, a popular general medical practitioner, who was moved by the struggle of his patients, most of whom were working class people. He began work by joining the Congress and emerged as a militant labour leader who never compromised on the workers' interests under any circumstances. He outshone the established leaders and, in him, the workers began seeing their Messiah and the industrialists, their Nemesis. Although a Congress Member of the Legislative Council, Datta Samant was placed under preventive detention by the Congress government during the Emergency and it only strengthened his stature as a leader who put the workers' interests before politics. In 1981, he led some of the workers who were in conflict with the Bombay Mill Owners Association by rejecting the RMMS. The workers wanted the strongest action possible and rejected his suggestion that they wait for the outcome of the initial strike. Ultimately, Dr Samant led them into a massive strike and an estimated three lakh mill workers walked out and the textile mills of the city were shut down for over a year. One of the demands was the abolition of BIRA and de-recognition of the RMMS as their only official union. Had the strike succeeded, it would have tarnished the city's reputation as a commercial and industrial centre and damaged the economy. Despite severe losses, the government and the mill-owners refused to budge. The mill-owners began shutting down their plants or relocated them outside the city. Those that remained in business began subcontracting textile production to cheap power looms outside the city that employed unprotected labour. As days and months passed without any resolution of the conflict, and with other parties cashing in on the opportunity to make inroads, the workers' unity began to show cracks and the strike collapsed without securing any concessions.

What followed thereafter was truly tragic. Dr Samant remained popular, but his clout declined and the closure of the textile mills left thousands of workers unemployed, bringing misery to their households. Girangaon was overcast by despair and discontent. Suddenly housewives and children had to find work to make ends meet and their pride and self-esteem were shattered. The youth was agitated and felt let down.

The mill-owners then began claiming that the mills could not be made profitable and viable unless they were allowed to sell the prime property they occupied in south-central Bombay. The workers eyed these claims with suspicion and felt that sickness of the mills came from the steep rise in the price of real estate in the island city in the seventies due to the hoarding of urban land and the non-implementation of the Urban Land Ceiling Act, 1976. They felt that the mills were deliberately being rendered sick by their owners who were siphoning off funds to other businesses rather than putting them into the mills. Sale of mill land was definitely more profitable than running businesses and industries on the land. But the mill lands were reserved for industrial use and no one dared disturb the reservation for the fear of the agitation it would definitely set off. So in the early nineties, coinciding with the liberalisation of the economy, as the market value of the mill lands in Bombay peaked, so did the applications to the Board for Industrial and Financial Reconstruction (BIFR) by the 'sick' and 'ailing' textile mills.

The Khatau Mill was one such sick mill and had around 5,000 workers. It occupied close to 50,000 square meters of prime land in Byculla and had accumulated huge losses. The management went to the BIFR for a rehabilitation package which included the sale of the Byculla land. Sunit Khatau wanted to shift the mill either to a larger plot of much lesser value in the suburb of Borivali or to distant Mahad in Raigad district, where the mill had established a weaving unit in 1985. The government was ready to give its approval provided the recognised union, RMMS gave its consent. According to Sunit Khatau, the land was only worth eighty crores. Going by the property rates in the adjacent areas, some estimated that it was closer to three hundred crores.

The then President of the RMMS, Haribhau Naik, refused to allow the sale to go through unless there was a clear proposal to rehabilitate the workers who would lose their jobs. Surprisingly, he was defeated in the RMMS elections by Shankarrao Jadhav. Rumours were rife that it was Sunit Khatau who had engineered the defeat and that too with the help of the gangster Arun Gawli, once a worker at Khatau Mills. Gawli's kith and kin were working as Khatau's personal assistants and bodyguards. There were rumours that Shankarrao Jadhav had promised to 'persuade' the workers to shift to Borivali, supported and protected by the Arun Gawli gang, and that Sunit Khatau had promised Gawli five per cent of the sale value. It was said that Gawli's men had gone on a rampage inside the mill and coerced the workers to sign a declaration agreeing to relocate the mill to Borivali. With the declaration, Sunit Khatau had gone to the state government to seek permission to sell the land and had almost finalised a contract with a construction company for four hundred crores. Had the Khatau Mill land deal gone through, Gawli's position in the gang world would have no doubt strengthened manifold, and that was certainly not what Amar Naik wanted. This was the reason for the failed assassination attempt by the Amar Naik gang on Shankarrao Jadhav.

The Crime Branch investigations soon revealed that it was indeed Amar Naik who had engineered the killing of Sunit Khatau. It was after the attempt on Ashwin Naik in April that Amar Naik decided to wreak revenge on Gawli. Gawli definitely drew his strength from his proximity to Sunit Khatau and finishing Khatau was a sure-shot way of hitting at Gawli's financial clout. The Amar Naik gang kept a close watch on Khatau's movements. Prior to the murder, the assailants had tracked Sunit Khatau's movements and carried out reconnaissance. On the day of the murder, the hitmen gathered near Khatau's sprawling bungalow on Manav Mandir Marg in Walkeshwar. Amar Naik and Omi Bharadwaj arrived in a blue Maruti car. Dinesh Mithbaokar and Raosaheb Killedar rode a Kinetic Honda and Raju Vikhroli and Santosh Pangerkar came on a Yamaha motorcycle. They tailed Khatau's car. At the Mahalaxmi signal, on the signal turning red, Mithbaokar smashed the car window with a hammer and Pangerkar, Raju Vikhroli and Raosaheb Killedar fired on Sunit Khatau from their pistols.

The investigation was completed and we filed the charge sheet in the Designated Court under the Terrorist and Disruptive Activities (Prevention) Act or TADA against the twelve men who were arrested and also those who were absconding like, Amar Naik, Raju Vikhroli and Raosaheb Killedar. Amar Naik was killed in a police encounter almost two years later in August 1996. Subsequently, Raju Vikhroli and Raosaheb Killedar were also killed in police encounters, the former on 23 June 1995 and the latter on 10 January 1996. During the trial which concluded in March 1999, many crucial witnesses including two vital eyewitnesses turned hostile in court. Although the murder was committed in broad daylight at a busy junction where many motorists had witnessed it, none came forward to depose as witnesses or help the police with numbers and descriptions of the car and two-wheelers used by the killers. The two washermen who had come forward initially and identified some of the accused then did a volte-face and did not support the prosecution in court. Unfortunately, the court also arrived at the decision that the investigation had not met some of the requirements such as the procedure for the test identification parade and the care which was required to be taken while recording the confessional statements under the stringent TADA Act. The trial resulted in acquittal and it has been a matter of regret and a deep sense of failure in my career. It was in the early days of my career in crime detection and investigation and the beginning of getting to understand how difficult it is to get convictions despite receiving credible leads if you were not in a position to carry out flawless investigation backed by good documentation and paperwork. And not to mention the shepherding of eyewitnesses from the pulls and pressures exerted by organised crime syndicates!

Both Gawli and Amar Naik came from a working class background – from mill workers' families. Their dramatic rise in the underworld which enabled them to rub shoulders with the mill-owners and political leaders, and call the shots, both literally and figuratively, was a fascinating reality. For the first time, the Sunit Khatau murder case brought me close to the saga of the breakdown of the old community in Girangaon. It gave me a better understanding of a bygone era, throwing light on the plight of the rudderless working class youth from the Village of Mills – how they felt betrayed and victimised, how they drifted into political camps or strayed into crime and how they fell prey to dangerous temptations and easy money in this 'Maya Nagri' (City of Illusions) called Bombay.

13

The Deadly Darling

On 25 August 1994, at about 10 a.m., a white Ambassador car emerged from a residential building, J.D. Alves Co-operative Housing Society in Bandra on the busy Hill Road. Suddenly two men appeared from nowhere and riddled the car with their AK-56 assault rifles. The chauffeur came out of the car. One of the assailants opened fire on him and he was injured. Constable Bhikru Tadvi, the police guard in the front seat next to the driver, came out with his Sten gun and returned the fire. The assailant pumped him with several bullets to ensure that he did not survive. The passenger in the back seat was killed on the spot. Two passers-by were also injured in the firing. There was a big commotion and people started running helter-skelter. In the mayhem, the assailants disappeared into thin air.

All this had happened in broad daylight in a busy Bombay street. The shopkeepers downed their shutters and news spread across the city in no time. The Opposition proclaimed a bandh for the next day when the funeral was to be held. The spectre of communal clashes raised its ugly head over the city, for the victim was no ordinary target. He was Ramdas Shriniwas Nayak, the City President of the BJP.

An alumnus of the Jesuit St Stanislaus' High School in Bandra, Ramdas Nayak was a popular Municipal corporator and also a member of the Legislative Assembly. But what he was most famous for was his private criminal complaint filed against Chief Minister A.R.Antulay that had led to Antulay's resignation. Antulay was Maharashtra's first Muslim Chief Minister (1980-1982). A staunch Indira Gandhi follower, he had floated a trust called 'Indira Gandhi Pratibha Pratishthan'. Cement was a controlled commodity then and Antulay was accused of favouring trust donors while allotting cement quotas. It was perhaps the first time that a Chief Minister had to quit office for his alleged role in a scam. Antulay fought a long legal battle which would ultimately go in his favour in 2013, but, in 1994, Nayak was the dynamic Opposition leader who had made a chief minister accountable.

I was DCP (Detection) and was in my office when the news of Ramdas Nayak's assassination came in. All top officers, including the Commissioner of Police Satish Sahney and Joint Commissioner of Police M. N. Singh, rushed to the spot. Later we were summoned to Varsha, the Chief Minister's official residence, to receive a talking to from Sharad Pawar. Thereafter, it was the turn of M. N. Singh and me to get a dressing down from the Commissioner of Police in his office. A thorough gentleman, Sahney was at his curtest best. Since we had not prevented it, we better detect it in a short time. From there I came to M.N. Singh's chamber where I had summoned all the ACPs and Senior Police Inspectors of my Crime Branch team. There M. N. Singh let fly at us. Hanging our heads in shame, my team and I headed to my cabin. There it was my turn to lose my cool.

This may sound funny in hindsight, but this is probably the 'Top Down' stuff that management gurus talk about. Instead of some carefully worked out strategy, it is just the most natural thing to happen in a crisis, especially in a uniformed service. Therefore, I am sure that after leaving my cabin, the ACPs and the Senior Police Inspectors must have given a similar verbal lashing to their juniors and it would have trickled down all the way to the constables.

The police had their hands full. Bombay was sitting on a powder keg. The air of suspicion amongst the communities was further vitiated and complicated by the feud between Dawood Ibrahim, now the self-styled Muslim don and Chhota Rajan, the self-styled Hindu don. So fragile was the social fabric of the city that even a tiny spark was enough to ignite a communal conflagration. That included attempts on the lives of the leaders of the communities. To ensure that there was no incident that would spark communal violence, we had to protect the likely targets. It was under these circumstances that police protection was being provided to a large number of BJP leaders, Shiv Sena Shakha Pramukhs and Bajrang Dal and Vishwa Hindu Parishad (VHP) leaders.

'It was a determined attack with a weapon of tremendous firepower,' the Commissioner of Police had said to the press. The last time the underworld had used such powerful weapons was in the infamous J.J. Hospital shoot-out of September 1992, when an AK-47 was used by Dawood's henchmen to shoot at Arun Gawli's men, Shailesh Haldankar and Bipin Shere. They had killed Dawood's brother-in-law Ibrahim Parkar (aka Ankur Bhatia), his sister Hasina's husband. The murderers had been admitted to the prisoners' ward at the hospital. Two police constables had lost their lives in the shoot-out and six others had been injured, including a nurse. Whoever had killed Ramdas Nayak had reminded us of the J.J. Hospital shoot-out and sent a clear message out that they had no fear of cops. The protection we had provided to their target was no deterrent. Our constable who had tried to crawl to safety was killed in cold blood.

We had to pursue various angles – the financial angle including land or property disputes, the political angle since it was a politician who was murdered, and also the religious rivalry within the underworld. It was around 5 p.m. when the team and I met in my office. I told them that I wanted information by 10 o' clock that very night and they all trooped out of my cabin with grim determined faces. Around 8 p.m., an old and experienced hand entered my cabin.

'*Sir, humne section garam kiya hai*,' he said. Literally translated, it meant, 'We have heated up the section.' This is Bombay police lingo for creating a stir in the jurisdiction by actions like picking up bad characters from known gangs for enquiry and raiding their dens and hideouts to send out a strong message that the police meant business.

'So? What is the outcome?' I asked. I could see that he had something important to say.

'Sir, we have received a message. They are ready to give you the original weapons, but dummy accused. You will be able to detect the case.'

For a few seconds, I couldn't understand what he meant. Then I realised that the gang was trying to cut a deal with the police in order to placate us and take the pressure off them. To protect their priceless prime shooters, they would surrender some lesser members, and they would give us the weapons used so that the scientific forensic investigation would authenticate the so-called detection.

'Detect! This way! I cannot do it. You are way too senior to me, with more than twenty-five years of experience and I am just twelve years old in the Service. But you know that once I do such things, I will lose my credibility and we will become pawns in their hands. No. Let us do our job. No deals,' I said.

'Sir, it was my duty to convey the message to you, but I agree with you. Let us not bother about the pressure, sir. We are used to it. We will do our best,' the officer agreed.

Next day was the funeral and the bandh. Speculation was rife and included a theory that the killers could be Afghan mercenaries from Kashmir who had retaliated for Nayak's help towards fighting terrorism in Doda. The slogans raised at Nayak's funeral included, 'Sharad Pawar is a killer.' The political parties started playing up the rivalry angle and the politician-underworld nexus. The then BJP President L.K. Advani commented: 'It can't be an occupational hazard of public service that you get killed. If the culprits cannot be arrested, this Government can't stay even one day.'

Now our ordeal began. As usual, the police were at the receiving end. The ruling party was upset. The Opposition was all out to draw every bit of mileage they could. The press was critical. We were being ridiculed for incompetence and Intelligence failure. People think that the police ought to know everything before it happens. They forget that crime has been happening since time immemorial and all crimes cannot be prevented. If that was possible, we would have no courts across the world.

We were trying hard to get information on the killers. We had some hard evidence to work on. The assailants had sprinted towards Bandra station. A stolen motorcycle used in the escape was found abandoned at a junction. A rickshaw was also found abandoned near the station with firearms in it. The assailants had forced the driver at gunpoint to hand over the auto rickshaw and had driven off in it. An abandoned Fiat Premier Padmini car with a changed number plate was also found. We were working hard on these facts to establish links. Yet, it was mid-September and we still had no information on the identity of the killers.

One afternoon, as I sat in my office riffling through some old crime records, the phone rang. There were no mobile phones then. It was the landline and it was Prabhale, my personal assistant. He said that there was a man on the line who wanted to give some important information only to me. I immediately took the phone.

'*Saab*, do you want information on the Ramdas Nayak case?' said a male voice from the other end in chaste Hindi.

'Yes, tell me!' I said eagerly, although I could not believe my ears.

'*Saab*, but to get the information, you will have to come out to meet me,' said the man.

'Come out and meet you?' I was a bit cautious. 'OK. Tell me where?'

'*Saab*, I will send a car to fetch you.'

Car to fetch me! It could be a trap. But I was desperate for information and decided to play along. So desperate that even if he had told me to perform a classical dance at the Hutatma Chowk, I would have attempted it! That was my level of despair. I was willing to undergo any ordeal or risk. 'Agreed. Tell me when and where?'

'Within a short time from now. At 2 o' clock, outside Badshah Cold Drink House, opposite your office?'

'Will do! I will be there,' I said.

'Khuda Hafiz, *saab*,' he said and rung off.

I too shot up a prayer. I needed His help badly. There was not much time left for 2 o'clock. Thanks to my work on the serial blasts, I was myself a target of terrorists and the underworld. I had a large posse of armed commandos guarding me. Convincing them not to follow me whenever I went incognito to meet informants was always a difficult and delicate operation, but I used to manage it at such times. As is the Crime Branch practice, I was in civvies, so there was no need to change my clothes.

I crossed the busy Lokmanya Tilak Marg and stood outside Badshah Cold Drink House which is famous for its *falooda,* a rich milkshake. It was ages since I had the privilege to walk the crowded streets like a common citizen, but I was too preoccupied to enjoy the hustle and bustle of the Crawford Market area, leave alone pick up a falooda from Badshah.

Within a short while, a white-coloured Maruti van with tinted glasses pulled up near me. The number plate was mud-splattered so I could not note down the number. In any case, it must have been a stolen vehicle, I thought to myself. The door slid open. There were two young men inside and they beckoned me in. The moment I sat inside, they slid the door shut and before I knew what was happening, they had blindfolded me. Immediately in my mind, the thought flashed: *I was DCP (Detection) of Bombay, of its legendary Crime Branch, one of the most important and powerful posts and here I was, blindfolded and at the total mercy of these unknown individuals! What am I doing?* But then, desperate situations demand desperate measures. If I had to detect this case, even if it meant clutching at straws, I would do it. The van started and we drove for about fifteen minutes. From the sounds, I could sense that I was still in a crowded area of south Bombay. Then the van stopped and the door opened. The boys held my hands and led me up a staircase. We entered a room and I could feel that it was air-conditioned. They sat me on a chair and, in less than thirty seconds, I heard the voice of the man who had spoken to me on the phone.

'*Saab, aapse maafi chaahata hoon*,' he said asking for my forgiveness. 'There was no other way I could have done this.'

'It's all right. Tell me what you know?' I said.

'Have you heard of Feroz Kokani?' He asked me.

'Feroz Kokani? No, who is he?' I asked.

'*Young daring ladka hai. Isne yeh kaam bajaya hai*,' he said. He meant that he was a gutsy young boy who had carried out the job.

'Any other information?' I asked him.

'*Jaise aati rahegi, bataata rahoonga*,' he said, meaning that he would pass on the information to me as and when he received it.

That was it and I was driven back to Badshah Cold Drink House just the way I had been brought from there. My blindfold was untied and I got off the vehicle. I came back to my office, immediately called my team, gave them the name and the chase began.

I activated all my sources to find out more about him. We began getting little bits and pieces to complete the jigsaw. Feroz Abdullah Sarguru alias Kokani was only in his early Twenties. From his looks, it was difficult to believe that he could hurt even a fly.

He lived behind the Sheikh Misri Dargah in the Antop Hill area. He was called Kokani because he hailed from Konkan, from a village called Panhalje in Taluka Chiplun in Ratnagiri district. In 1989, while studying at Maharashtra College in Nagpada, he had got friendly with a girl and some boys had begun bullying him over it. He had stabbed one of them outside Siddharth College in the Fort area, and was arrested. The next murder he was involved in was of one Sanjay Yadav at Wadi Bunder, Dockyard. After that, there was no looking back and his career in crime took off.

We intensified our chase, but no sooner had I come close to netting him than he killed the informant who had given me the lead – Juber Parveen who was shot down on 26 September 1994 outside the Jumma Masjid. A huge crowd had gathered for namaaz when Kokani had opened fire on Juber who was washing his feet. Juber died on the spot. This was a great setback for me personally as DCP (Detection). Earlier in the year, Dawood and Chhota Shakeel had embarked upon the identification and elimination of my informants. This was done with the express objective of putting a spoke in the Bombay Crime Branch's planned offensive against the Dawood syndicate. The first informant to be fired upon was one Abdul Mannan Shaikh on 20 January 1994 and the spot was in Pydhoni. Although both the rounds had hit him, Mannan had survived to tell the tale. On 26 March 1994 at 21:15 hours, a reliable and trustworthy informant of mine, Haji Bidar alias Sayyed Amir Haider, a resident of Tantanpura Street, had been shot dead in cold blood at the Nishanpada Cross Road in front of the Rehmania Bread and Provision Store in Dongri.

The assailants of both the informants remained unknown and elusive. I was trying to grapple with the loss of Haji Bidar when this new onslaught on my informants by Feroz Kokani pushed my back to the wall. Death had cast its ugly shadow on my informants. Feroz Kokani was putting the fear of death in my informants. At this rate, my sources would dry up! It was now a matter of my survival as an Intelligence gatherer. Working in the Crime Branch without informants is impossible. If my informants were going to be killed like this, very soon all of them would desert me. I had to get Feroz Kokani. And quickly.

On 19 October 1994, I was in my office and the same person who had given me Kokani's name phoned me again.

'*Saab, aapko Feroz Kokani chahiye kya*?' (Sir, do you want Feroz Kokani?) He asked me.

'Yes, of course!' He knew what I wanted very well. Need he ask?

'He is in Bangalore,' he said. '*Aapko khud jana padega*,' meaning that I would have to go myself to get him. These words were music to my ears. I was also a little surprised that he had given this information without asking me to meet him in person as he had done the last time. Probably he was more confident about me now or because he cared even less about his own safety, so bad was his own equation with Feroz Kokani now.

'Call me in fifteen minutes,' I told him and disconnected the line. I enquired where M.N. Singh was. He was with the Commissioner of Police. I told Prabhale that the informant would be calling me again and that he should be given the CP's office number to speak to me. I then strode across to the CP's office and told Satish Sahney and M.N. Singh that I needed to go to Bangalore, after explaining the reason. To my dismay, they flatly refused permission because they felt that it could be a trap. As it is I was receiving threats and they did not want to put my life in danger.

'But, sir, he has killed my informants. I cannot miss this chance and I should be there to arrest him!' I said in desperation.

'No. You will send your team,' said Sahney and from his face, I could sense that he was not going to budge.

Just then the phone rang. Sahney answered it and handed over the receiver to me. It was 'The Voice'. I told him that it would not be possible for me to travel to Bangalore, but I would send a team instead. There was a short pause and my anxiety peaked. What if he withdrew?

'OK, *saab*. But then how do we do it? How will I convey the information to them?' He asked and I was relieved.

'Don't worry. You will be in touch with me and I will pass on the information to them. I will coordinate,' I assured him and he agreed.

Now I needed unmarked vehicles, safe accommodation and telephone connections in Bangalore. M.N. Singh spoke to H.T. Sangliana, his batch-mate and counterpart in Bangalore. Sangliana assured all the support and I got my team ready. Police Inspector Narendra Singh and Sub Inspectors Suhail Buddha, Sukhlal Warpe and Dinesh Kadam were the men I zeroed in on. The same afternoon they flew by Air India, reaching Bangalore around 4-4:30 in the evening. They were met by Sangliana's team, and were set up in a safe house with a phone and two unmarked vehicles.

As soon as they informed me that they were all set, my informant phoned me and said that Feroz Kokani had decided to go watch a film and we could arrest him there. So I contacted my team and they began preparing to go to the cinema hall. But shortly thereafter, I got a call from the informant again to say that Feroz had dropped the cinema plan. Instead, he was going to stay in the hotel and have a beer party with his mates. The hotel was Blue Diamond on Platform Road in Sheshadri Puram, and he was in room number 206.

I conferred with the team and we then chalked out a plan. The first step was to take the hotel manager into confidence. The team went in two groups and booked two rooms, acting like businessmen. Then they got in touch with the manager and disclosed their identities. The manager agreed to cooperate. As if he had a choice in the matter! Around 7:00 p.m., the room service received an order from room 206 for chicken lollipops. The team decided to use a trolley to carry the food to the room. Sub Inspector Warpe acted as the waiter, hid his revolver in the food trolley and trundled it to the room. He kept the door open under the pretext of taking the trolley inside and the rest of the team hid outside. Feroz Kokani and the two boys were in the room. Warpe bent as if to take out the plates, but took out the revolver instead and aimed at them. Immediately the others rushed in and arrested the occupants who were taken completely by surprise.

So much was my anger directed at Kokani for the loss of my informants that I had told my officers that they should make him speak to me as soon as he was arrested. So they made him speak to me on the phone. Very rarely do I abuse, but this time I could not control myself. After I had given vent to my fury, I said to him, 'This is going to be the last day of your life. Make your last wish. Eat or drink whatever you want, my men will give it to you.'

To which he answered, '*Sir, mujhko jo karna thaa, woh maine kiya. Aapko jo karna hai, aap karo*,' (Sir, I have done what I had wanted to; you do whatever you want to). Despite this bravado, he was quite shaken, said, my officers. Right through the journey, he was morose and gloomy. My team took the earliest flight and brought him to Bombay. I was waiting in a car outside the airport to interrogate him. I knew he was very young, but when I saw him I was quite taken aback by his callow look. Then I remembered all the heinous things he had done and his impudence. I couldn't help but plant a tight slap on his cheek.

'It will take almost an hour to reach my office. Will you tell me all that you have done in that one hour, or would you rather do it after reaching?' I asked him. He got the message. From there to my office, he confessed to twenty-one murders and attempted murders, including the stabbings of mathadi workers (Hindu loaders who worked in the docks and markets) that had ignited the January 1993 phase of the riots in Bombay. These were followed by a spate of stabbings of Hindus in the lanes and by-lanes. He told me that they had carried out those stabbings with *khanjars* (daggers). He confessed that it was he who had fired on Ashok Traders in the Masjid area at that time. He had also murdered Shiv Sena leader, R.T. Sagwekar in 1994. Most importantly, Feroz Kokani confessed to the murders of my informants Haji Bidar in Dongri in March 1994, Juber Parveen outside the Jumma Masjid on 26 September 1994 and firing on my informant, Abdul Mannan in January 1994.

I interrogated Feroz the whole night, checking and cross-checking various facts. He said that the conspiracy to kill Ramdas Nayak was hatched in the Seven Bungalows area in Andheri and he had himself planned the entire killing. Dawood and Chhota Shakeel had arranged for the weapons through gangster Majid Bharuchi, and to collect them they had travelled to Bharuch in Gujarat. He also told me that they were planning to kill film star Shatrughan Sinha after the murder of Ramdas Nayak.

Within twenty-four hours of his arrest, Feroz Kokani was produced before the court and then remanded to our custody. At that time even Arun Gawli was in the custody of Crime Branch. On the one hand, these gangs were putting Bombay police through tremendous hassles and on the other hand, we had two of them as our guests. Two sworn rivals and major troublemakers at that, sitting peacefully and cushy in our lock-up with just a wall separating them! On top of it all, we were supposed to guard them! So a bright idea struck me. Let us see what happens if they come face to face. When I shared this thought with my officers and men, I could see that they too looked on the prospect with glee. So we did it. But to our shock, instead of sparks flying, they started bonding and began chatting and gossiping happily, like long-lost friends!

From 1994 to 1998 Kokani was in custody. Later, a few more accused were arrested for the conspiracy. I was out of the Crime Branch in July 1996, but I got to know from my sources that Kokani had been sending messages to Dawood and Chhota Shakeel asking for help to escape or at least get him bail. Then when Kokani felt that they were not responding, he began ranting against them, threatening to join either Gawli's or Chhota Rajan's gang. Maybe the bond forged in our lock-up had made him seriously consider the option of joining Gawli! Dawood and Chhota Shakeel came to know of this. They must have decided that they could not afford this defection and impudence. So they planned his escape from J.J. Hospital. My informants told me about the plan and I immediately passed on the information to the concerned officers.

However, on 6 May 1998 at 15:45 hours, while the murder trial was on, Kokani succeeded in escaping from custody and absconded. He had been brought to the Radiology Department of J.J. Hospital for some investigation when two men on a bike had barged into the hospital and opened fire at his police escort, injuring two of the policemen seriously. A Head Constable, B.D. Kardile, had succumbed to his injuries in the attack. Kokani fled to Karachi via Nepal. He never stood trial. His brother was later arrested for helping him escape.

After some years, we began receiving reports that Kokani had been killed by the Dawood gang sometime in 2003. It seems they had taken him to Karachi via the land route. He was then taken on a barge and they had beaten the hell out of him. His hands and feet were tied and he was drowned with a big heavy stone tied around his neck.

Had it not been for my gutsy team who risked their lives in Bangalore that evening, I would not have been able to arrest Feroz Kokani. Inspector Narendra Singh and Sub Inspectors Warpe, Buddha and Dinesh Kadam did a remarkable job, right from planning to execution. It is such officers, who put their lives at peril in the line of duty every single moment, who make a police Force proud. But instead if they make a single mistake, they are hauled over the coals for the rest of their lives. Their exemplary work is taken for granted. For instance, the arrest they made in Bangalore. One slip or a second's delay in action could have been a matter of life and death. Had it gone wrong, they would have never been forgiven.

I have often been criticised that I have only worked with certain officers and select teams. But it must be appreciated that to carry out jobs to this level of finesse and perfection, you need to develop a rapport, trust, and tuning. You need to understand each other's style of working and communication. So one prefers to work with tried and trusted officers and men when one has just one opportunity to do a major operation. This could be the thin line which demarcates success from failure.

Coming back to Feroz Kokani, how did such a baby-faced young man commit such cold-blooded killings? I was told that Feroz Kokani's pet name in the netherworld was 'Darling'.

And then there was this weird thing that the lock-up guards had told me about him, which is quite unforgettable. It was about the big black ants that made their way into his lock-up cell. Feroz Kokani loved to pick them up with his fingers. He would hold them up, break their legs one by one, and watch the legless bodies wriggle.

Perhaps he couldn't help himself.

14

Tracking the Dispatch to Death

25 September 1994 was a Sunday. It was one of those rare days when one got to avail the luxury of spending a Sunday with the family. I was at home when, shortly after eight in the evening came the report that some unknown assailants had shot dead a man in Charkop in the western suburb of Kandivali. Since it was a case of firing, as per mandatory procedure, not just the local police, even the local Crime Branch team rushed to the spot. The victim was a twenty-eight-year-old young man called Santosh Pandurang Patole. He was standing outside the Navnirman Cooperative Housing Society in Sector 3 when suddenly the assailants had opened fire on him, hitting him on the chest.

'What was he? A businessman? Builder? Hotelier?' I asked my officers.

'No, sir! He was a postman,' came the reply.

'What? A postman!'

For me the word postman conjured up a benignly familiar figure, deputed on the rounds of your street for years together, dressed in khakhi, going from door to door, walking up five-storied buildings without a frown in scorching summers and in monsoon deluge. All without any expectations, save during the festival of Diwali when he would be entitled to a bakhshish and a packet of sweets to suit the householder's pocket. He was witness to our joys and sorrows written on the palm-sized postcards or inland letters that, unfortunately, no one writes any more. Occasionally, he brought envelopes with interesting stamps 'from foreign' which would be pasted in albums or exchanged for better and rarer ones. He knew your loved ones abroad and would even ask if all was OK with them, for he was almost family. The only time he was dreaded was when schools broke for summer vacations and the academic results were awaited by post. Otherwise, he was a friendly character for the neighbourhood who could be attacked only by untrained dogs or an occasional demented person or a drunk. That he or any of his ilk could be murdered was just unthinkable. Why in damnation would anyone dispatch a postman to death, and that too by ruthlessly gunning him down?

But then as the investigation progressed, it turned out that Santosh Patole might not exactly be the run of the mill postman that I had in my mind, romanticised by Bollywood in some of its hits. Attached to the foreign post office at the Sahar International Airport in its sorting department, Patole had quite a colourful and debonair personality. He was unmarried but lived in Charkop with his girlfriend who was a bar dancer, whereas his mother and brother lived in the Post and Telegraph Colony quarters at Santacruz. His girlfriend was pregnant and they seemed to be doing well together. He also owned a Maruti 800 car which he had rented out as a tourist vehicle. Quite an achievement for a young man who was just twenty-eight and from a simple and humble background!

Patole had spent the last Sunday of his life at his house in Charkop, apparently drinking since the morning, until he stepped out to rendezvous with his death on the street just outside the building. Was he disturbed over something? A property dispute? Was there a love triangle? Some enmity over the bar girl? An 'ex' lurking behind the scenes and waiting for an opportunity to wreak revenge? No, said the bar girl. No, said even other acquaintances who could throw some light on Patole, including the mother and the brother who lived in his Santacruz quarters. Was this then a case of mistaken identity?

No one could give us any clue as to why a postman, who had no axe to grind with anyone, should be killed underworld style, by vehicle-borne assailants firing shots and disappearing into thin air. Despite our best efforts, the investigation reached a dead end.

Then towards the end of the year 1994, I received some shocking information from a *khabri*: '*Saab*, it is Abu Salem who had the postman killed.' I immediately summoned Assistant Police Inspector Abhay Shastri and his team from Unit X of the Crime Branch and put them on the job to explore the new angle. Skilful enquiries and a sustained watch over the foreign post office threw up striking revelations: Postman Patole used to hobnob with members of the Dawood Ibrahim gang who were working under Anees Ibrahim, Aftab Batki and Abu Salem in their currency smuggling racket!

The gang was smuggling Indian and foreign currency for *hawala* transactions through parcels sent by airmail. At the International Airport, the parcels that need Customs scrutiny are segregated and taken to the General Post Office (GPO) located near the Chhatrapati Shivaji Terminal (old Victoria Terminus) in south Mumbai. Only after the Customs checking at the GPO are the parcels dispatched to their destinations. Therefore, evading Customs check was possible only if some postal staff cooperated and connived with the gang en route.

The modus operandi of the gang was efficaciously simple. They would corrupt postal staff and rope them in to tamper with the parcels. Parcels of foreign currency would be airmailed from cities abroad to Bombay. The details of their weight, description and address would be intimated in advance to the gang members in Bombay who in turn would relay this information on to their 'friendly' postmen who would be on duty when the parcels arrived. Our investigation and probe revealed that Santosh Patole was one such 'cooperative' postman. In the house at the Post and Telegraph Colony at Santacruz, with the help of his mother and brother, Patole would prepare identical parcels filled with innocuous things. He would then take them to the postal van carrying the currency parcels on its way to the GPO, identify the currency parcel and replace them with fake parcels which would then go to the GPO for the mandatory Customs check. The original parcels with foreign currency would be handed over to the gang. The same was done albeit in the reverse order, for posting currency from Bombay to foreign countries. Parcels of foreign currency would be handed over to Patole. He would replace the identical Custom-checked parcels with the currency parcels so that they could go out of the country undetected.

Patole's time on Planet Earth was up when a parcel of foreign currency went missing and could not be delivered to the gang. When high denomination notes are used, even slim wads can make huge amounts and just one such missing parcel entails a huge loss. The gang suspected that Patole had misappropriated the money. The henchmen questioned him rigorously, but he insisted that he had no clue whatsoever as to where it had gone. The bosses were firm. They were ruthless in these matters and misappropriation or cheating of any kind was totally unacceptable and not forgiven! Patole was not irreplaceable and that was the message they wanted to drive home to all those who dared to stray.

Four gang members were entrusted with the task of eliminating Patole. They were Nabi Allauddin Sheikh, Abid, Aziz, and Mohammed Isaque Sheikh. These were the very men who used to visit Patole's mother's house in Santacruz to drop and fetch contraband currency parcels. It was no wonder that Patole's mother and brother were keeping mum about the whole business. They were very much in on it and, in fact, were an integral and core part of this well-oiled racket!

Now we had to trace Nabi and his associates. We were

searching for them for months, but they continued to elude us. They seemed to have just vanished. Then we learned that Nabi was having an affair with a married woman whose husband was working in the Gulf. It was just a matter of time and some robust police leg-work before crucial information was gleaned about the exact location of their illicit sojourns. A trap was laid and Lothario Nabi walked right into it!

Nabi soon began chirping and gave us the details of the racket which confirmed that the whole operation was being carried out under the aegis of Anees Ibrahim, Aftab Batki and Abu Salem from Dubai. The gun used to kill Patole was provided to Nabi near the Persian Darbar restaurant in Bandra. The four assailants had then gone to Patole's house in a car and despatched him to the netherworld. Nabi squealed on the whereabouts of the co-accused and soon they were also cooling their heels in the Crime Branch lock-up. In their interrogation, they accepted that they were party to the murder.

What came next, we were totally unprepared for. Santosh Patole was not their only victim! They had dispatched another postman to death! They had dumped his body on the service road near the Nirlon Company at Goregaon (East). He was Ravi Narayan Padhi, from the State of Orissa, now Odisha. He too worked in the sorting section of the foreign post office at Sahar and he too was their accomplice in the currency smuggling racket. They had killed him on 28 January 1994.

We immediately made enquiries with the Goregaon police station under whose jurisdiction the spot fell. Indeed, on 28 January 1994, a traffic constable had reported a body lying on the service road near the Nirlon Company. He was on beat duty when he had noticed a crowd gathered on the road around a male body lying on the service road. He had immediately reported the discovery to the Police Control Room and the Goregaon police had arrived on the scene. The body was so mutilated that it couldn't be identified. The deceased had not just been strangled and stabbed, but acid had also been thrown on his face to disfigure it beyond recognition. A bottle of acid was found lying nearby and fumes were emanating from the corpse.

The only piece of evidence found on the corpse was the shirt that had a tailor mark 'A1 Menswear Tailor, Ramabai Colony, Ghatkopar East.' Officers of the Goregaon police station wasted no time in rushing to the Ramabai Colony but found the shop shut. They traced the tailor who used to stitch clothes there, a young man called Mohammad Ismail Saiyad. He informed them that the shop had closed down one and a half years back and the owner, Barndas Nadar had returned to his village in Tamil Nadu. The officers showed him the shirt and asked him if he could shed any light about the person who had got it stitched. Mohammad Saiyad said he only stitched clothes in the shop and had nothing to do with the customers. He, however, provided the address of the owner and the Goregaon police were soon on their way to Kanyakumari to check with Barndas Nadar. He, too, could not recall anything about the client for whom he had got the shirt stitched. Unfortunately, that was the end of the enquiry. As per standard police procedure, the Goregaon police sent the photographs of the body to all the police stations in Maharashtra and cremated it. So the body remained unidentified in the police records till April 1995 when we arrested Nabi and he began to sing.

But had no one missed a postman working at the sorting office at the Sahar International Airport? Well, yes. Not only had a father been crying hoarse in Orissa about his son's disappearance, but he had also written several letters to the authorities complaining about it and even giving names of people he suspected to be involved. The Matunga police station confirmed that a missing person's complaint had been lodged for postman Ravi Narayan Padhi. He was thirty years of age and resided with his sister and her husband in the Central Government Staff Colony at Antop Hill in Bombay. His brother-in-law, Simanchand Chaudhary, worked in the Naval Stores as a labourer. On 27 January 1994, Ravi Padhi had left the house at 9 a.m. and never returned. The brother-in-law had lodged a missing complaint at the Matunga police station and even written to the postal authorities about his disappearance. When Ravi Padhi did not show up for a long time, the brother-in-law wrote a letter to Padhi's father in Orissa and enquired if Ravi Padhi had come home. He had not. The father then wrote to the postal authorities, besides also writing a letter to the Deputy Commissioner of Police, Zone-IV on 1 March 1994. In that letter, he had stated that it had been brought to his knowledge that his son was involved in criminal activities with some office colleagues, but did not know the exact nature of these activities. He said that though he himself had not received any extra money from his son, he had come to know that some of his son's colleagues had in a short span of time, amassed unaccounted wealth and become quite prosperous. He gave their names in the letter and also said that the criminal activity was carried out under the directions of 'an outsider' called Tamhanekar – a man who was not from the postal staff.

Nabi and his associates confirmed that even Padhi was involved in their currency smuggling racket and was suspected to have misappropriated currency. So, as per the directives of their masters in the Gulf Kingdom of Dubai, they had picked him up and taken him to a flower shop near the Makhdoom Shah Baba Dargah at Mahim. There they had questioned and tortured him to make him come clean, but he could provide no details. So they had contacted and updated their bosses in Dubai and got the green signal to stamp Postman Padhi out of this world. Following the diktat, they first strangled and stabbed him to death. They then put the body in a Maruti van and took it to Goregaon where they threw it on the service road near the Nirlon Company. To ensure that he would not be identified, they disfigured his face with acid. In further investigation, Padhi's Identity Card was found in Nabi's house. Despite a lot of effort, Tamhanekar, under whose directions Padhi was suspected to be operating, could not be traced till the end. The informant grapevine was abuzz that he had fled to Dubai no sooner than Nabi and gang were arrested.

The Crime Branch completed the investigation of Patole's murder and filed the requisite charge sheet in the court of law. Unfortunately, witnesses turned hostile and all the accused were acquitted by Judge J.W. Singh (who was incidentally later tried under MCOCA on the charge of proximity with the Dawood Ibrahim gang. The judge was subsequently acquitted as the then Additional Chief Secretary {Home} who had authorised interception of the alleged telephonic conversations between the Judge and Chhota Shakeel, never placed the order before any Review Committee as mandated under the law, which constituted a serious breach of the safeguards provided by the Act). The murder of Padhi was investigated by the Goregaon police station and even this trial ended in an acquittal as the witnesses turned hostile.

These two acquittals were disturbing, to say the least. There was absolutely no doubt in our minds about the guilt of the accused, but we could not prevent witnesses from turning hostile, such was the underworld's clout and the fear they evoked. As a Deputy Commissioner of Police who had barely completed nine months of incubation period in the Crime Branch, it was just the beginning of a learning process: the tough process of securing justice for the State and the victims of crimes, when the accused are backed and protected by the underworld.

Detecting a case is only a quarter of the job of a policeman. The remaining three quarters are the most crucial: preparing a watertight case; securing good and able prosecutors from those available on the panels to match the skills and acumen of the legal eagles engaged by the rich and powerful dons; motivating the overburdened investigating officers who have moved on to different postings and ensuring that they continue to evince a keen interest in the trial, ascertaining that they are made available by their new bosses to brief the prosecutors and keep the morale of the witnesses high, ensuring that the witnesses do not lose their nerve!

Cases come up for trial agonisingly late unless they are fast-tracked by the higher courts. Gone are the days when trials were conducted continuously, on a day-to-day basis. The cases in which the accused are not on bail are given precedence, whereas those where the accused are on bail can take aeons to come up. By the time they do, all the police officers who have dealt with the investigation are transferred. Memories fade. Witnesses get scattered and are tampered with through intimidation or allurements. The State fees for the Panel Prosecutors are abysmally low. Reputed and experienced lawyers are not willing to take up cudgels for the prosecution unless they get specially appointed at high fees. The State is rarely ready to make such special appointments unless the cases are sensational and there is a huge public outcry. And if you get adverse judgements and orders, you need to go into appeal to higher courts, and again get seasoned Government Pleaders to present your case. The entire process is so frustrating that it is a wonder that we get convictions at all.

Even then, failure to secure convictions as happened in the murder of the two postmen, remains perpetually etched in my memory as low points of my career. For a keen detection officer, it can never be compensated by praise and convictions in other cases.

15

Ticket Checkers on the Punjab Mail

It was past midnight and I was tossing and turning in my bed, waiting for that one phone call which would lift a huge burden off my shoulders. The call that would announce that we had the killers in our dragnet.

At most times, despite being conditioned by my mother's intense faith in Him, I do not believe that God easily favours the good. Experience shows that fortune smiles first on the bad and the sinners and quite, quite late on the good and the god-fearing. And when it does smile on the latter, it is often not in their lifetime. Mama would attribute this to our 'Kaliyug,' but that was no consolation. Such gloomy thoughts persisted to bother me as the night wore on, making me forget the humorous side of god. Of all the days, He had chosen last evening to play the fool with the prestigious Crime Branch of Mumbai city. Probably because it was All Fools' Day and He wanted to tell us that we were like all ordinary people.

It was the 1 of April 1995. Early in the morning, one of my informants asked me for an immediate meeting, at 11:00 a.m. I did not waste a moment and rushed for the rendezvous which he had fixed near the godowns located at Reay Road. It was a spot where just a few trucks were parked near the freight wagons and hardly a soul was around. The man was there as promised. He told me that Sautya aka Sunil Sawant had instructed his shooters to leave Mumbai city limits, go to Nepal via Delhi from where they would be flown out to Dubai. Because we – the police – had made *'the section garam'*. So it was no longer safe for them to remain in India.

There had been seven gangland shoot-outs in the city in a span of one year and two of them just in the preceding one week. On 23 March 1995, one Pravin Gavand was killed at Bhoiwada. He used to collect 'protection money' on behalf of Sautya, a Dawood Ibrahim ally. On 30 March 1995, one Syed Asif Manan was gunned down. He was suspected to be laundering money for Chhota Rajan.

The Crime Branch was expected to nip gangland activities in the bud. These shoot-outs were proving us as failures. Media barbs and the ignominy of the political bosses questioning our professional competence was a daily feature of our existence. We had information that it was Sautya who was behind these shoot-outs, but we had no tangible information on the identity of the shooters. We were rounding up known acolytes to get more details. Raiding their hideouts, making things 'hot' for the gangs. That is what *'section garam'* meant. Goading our informants to come up with timely and actionable Intelligence on the designs of the dons was giving all of us sleepless nights.

Now, this khabri was telling me that two of Sautya's ace shooters known as Jeetu and Ramya were to leave by the Punjab Mail for Delhi that very evening. The word khabri comes from the word *khabar* which means information. But who were these men? Where did they live? What was their background? How did they look? Any photographs to help us identify them? Who would know them? Past records? Nothing more was forthcoming.

I returned to my office, thinking of the men I would pit against Sautya's – who would put their heart and soul in the operation and not be indifferent to the outcome. When I reached my office it was already lunchtime. I immediately contacted Sub Inspector

Sohail Buddha who was attached to the Bandra Unit of the Crime Branch. I gave him the names of the five officers I needed to take the Punjab Mail to Delhi that very evening, including himself. I expected them to be at my office at three p.m. The other four officers were Dinesh Kadam, Abhay Shastri, Shivaji Kolekar and Narendra Singh.

It was three already, but there was no sign of them. I contacted Sohail Buddha. 'What happened? Why are you guys not here, Sohail?'

'Sir, I had called all of them to Bandra at 2 p.m. so that we could reach your office at 3 p.m. I told them we had to go to Delhi,' he said sounding nervous.

'Then what happened?' I was impatient.

'Sir, they all thought it was an "April Fool" prank. So none of them turned up at 2 p.m. So I called them again, sir. I really abused them, sir. Now they are all on their way. We will reach by 4 p.m., sir. Sorry, sir.'

I was aghast. A prank! Do Crime Branch officers play pranks? Whom am I entrusting this crucial task to? I was furious.

At quarter past four they all trooped in, looking sheepish like a pack of schoolboys. I was still seething with anger and they had guilt written all over their faces. The Mumbai-Firozpur Punjab Mail was to leave Victoria Terminus around 7:30 in the evening. So we had no time to do the post-mortem of the one hour we had lost to 'All Fools' Day'. That could wait. Now we had to just get on with the job and decide how we were going to look for Jeetu and Ramya on that train.

Over the last two years, these officers had come to understand my style of functioning and I theirs. I felt I could trust them with my life. I had never felt the need to throw my seniority around. All those who worked with me right up to the constables, had the liberty to speak and discuss about investigations directly with me, any time of the day or night. When we gathered to plan an operation, everyone was free to speak up, contribute and dissent. And once the strategy discussions began, all else was forgotten. This is what happened now. The atmosphere eased and they all began pointing out the hurdles and suggesting ways we could overcome them.

It was the summer holiday season. And today was Saturday. Trains would be packed with people travelling to various destinations, Bombay-Delhi being no exception. How were they to search an entire train without the full names or descriptions of the men? Men whose names did not figure on the reservation charts? Men who could be travelling under false identities? The train had twenty-four bogeys with a total capacity of 1,550 passengers. In the peak summer holiday season, the number would definitely go above 2,000. The General Class had two unreserved bogeys with 108 passengers per bogey, but in summer it would be crammed with many more. When this proverbial needle in the haystack was brought to my notice, commanding all the authority and ingenuity at my disposal, I delivered a little pep talk: they were born to take on such challenges or they would not be in the famed Mumbai Crime Branch. Great moments are born from great opportunities. The smiles on their faces made me feel that they were thinking to themselves, 'He is sending us on a "Mission Impossible" and coating the bitter pill with sugar!' But when they assured me that they were ready to undertake the mission, I knew that they would leave no stone unturned.

After some quick brainstorming, I got in touch with my batch-mate C.P. Sharma in the Indian Railways Traffic Service. I explained to him the importance and urgency of our mission and requested his assistance. Together we decided that my officers would wear black coats and pose as Train Ticket Examiners (TTEs) so that they could fine-comb all the compartments. They would ask the passengers for their tickets, ascertain their names and chat a little with them. It would give them time to observe the passengers closely and see if anything was amiss. We also had to keep in mind that the shooters could be travelling with women and children as a cover, to evade us. Such sharpshooters are quite a pampered lot. Every need of theirs is taken care of. Ganglords are ready to surrender dummy accused to the police to protect them from courts and prisons. The reason being that finding equally hardened killing-machines for gang work is very difficult. So these men could be travelling in first-class comfort. Moreover, they could board from anywhere. Even from Nashik as the informant had warned us, though the most probable place for boarding was Mumbai. So every passenger had to be checked. No exception whatsoever. We could take no chances. And our team had to keep me updated. For this, they would have to contact me after reaching a railway station en route as there were no cell phones then.

C.P. Sharma assured me that he would immediately brief his key men in the railway administration to give us complete support. Now how about the black coats for the five officers? Obviously, Sharma would have to help us there. We had no time to go looking for black coats as it was already close to departure time.

In the late evening, five of my crime branch officers struggled into used black coats of five TTEs of Central Railways, enjoying the 'rich fragrance' of their summer sweat! Luckily nature helps you survive such ordeals by switching off your sense of smell; so they must have stopped smelling their coats after a while. They then boarded the Punjab Mail at the Victoria Terminus to look for Ramya and Jeetu from among 2,000 odd, tired and sleepy passengers who must not suspect that the TTEs were fresh untrained recruits to the job.

As expected, it was a long and arduous task. They commenced the combing operation, compartment by compartment. Beyond a point, they could not disturb the passengers who were getting ready to sleep. They had to be polite and not ruffle feathers. Time flew by and with it grew my despondency. As I reached the point of questioning the gods about their competence, the phone rang. It was Sohail Buddha from the Bhusawal station and he had nothing positive to report.

I tried getting some sleep, failed miserably and braced myself for a nail-biting day ahead. It was. When in such extreme difficulties, I would invoke my mother's jurisdiction. I would ring her up and say, 'Mama, I have an important investigation going on. I need you to pray for me. It is very, very important.' Just that, without giving her any details, and she would immediately oblige, go to her little temple in the house, take her prayer beads, light a lamp and chant her prayers. As my desperation grew, I made the SOS call to Mama.

The exception to the Divine Policy for Kaliyug happened only when the train neared Nizamuddin Railway Station – a destination just twenty to thirty minutes from New Delhi Railway Station. This was the evening of 2 April. The officers had started checking the last remaining unreserved compartment. Dinesh Kadam reached one young man dressed in jeans, took his ticket in hand and asked him his name.

'Jitendra Rane,' answered the youth. The name rang a bell. Jeetu? *'Kay, Marathi ka,'* Kadam struck a friendly conversation with the youth in Marathi asking him if he was a Maharashtrian.

'Hoy, Marathi,' he got the answer in the affirmative.

Sitting separately some distance away from Jitendra Rane was another denim-clad youth.

'Ramchandra Gurav,' said the young man when Dinesh Kadam asked him his name. Now Dinesh Kadam couldn't help but stiffen, but he managed to hide it under his black coat. Ramya! And Jeetu? Both the tickets were up to New Delhi. Have we found them! In Punjab, a Rakesh could be a Bobby and in Bengal, a Sharmila could be Moon Moon. But amongst the Marathi people, pet names are generally derived from their given names. So Jitendra Rane could be Jeetu and Ramchandra Gurav could be Ramu or Ramya.

Dinesh Kadam discreetly signalled to Narendra Singh who got the message. The two went about the task of checking the details of other passengers but kept a watch on the two boys, two Marathi youths, sitting separately in the same compartment and not communicating with each other.

Narendra Singh then left the compartment and alerted the other team members. As soon as the train pulled into New Delhi Railway Station, our five ticket checkers followed the two suspects discreetly. Alighting separately, the young men left the railway station and were met by a third youth outside. The trio then hailed an auto rickshaw and left together. The team followed them in two separate auto rickshaws.

The suspects reached the Kashmiri Gate area and booked themselves into a lodge. Sohail Buddha immediately phoned me and narrated the developments. I instructed him that without any loss of time and after taking all due precautions, as the suspects could be armed, they should enter the room and nab them for questioning. The team managed it perfectly and the three youths were picked up. The third youth was identified as Parshuram Chavan. Their interrogation disclosed that they were contract killers working for the Sunil Sawant faction of the Dawood Ibrahim gang.

They were flown down to Mumbai and they disclosed their complicity in seven gangland shoot-outs: Vijay Thorat's murder of March 1994; Vinod Shetty's murder and Jitendra Raut's murder of April 1994; Vijay Makkad's murder of May 1994; Murli Lakhani's kidnapping of November 1994; and the March 1995 murders of Pravin Gavand and Syed Asif Manan. Of these, the Jitendra Raut murder was a case of mistaken identity. The poor victim was the chauffeur of Anandrao Adsul, the Shiv Sena union leader. They had killed him mistaking him for his master. Getting leads from these arrests, we made ten more arrests and the city received a much-needed respite from gangland shoot-outs.

Every operation is followed by a debriefing session. When we sat down to dissect this operation, I learnt an important lesson. A stray comment that someone had made, had made me halt and probe further. After a lot of coaxing, the team finally told me that by the time the operation was over, they had only twenty rupees left on them. They'd spent seven rupees on the last call they made to me from Delhi. Out of the remaining thirteen rupees, they had bought a chocolate bar and shared it before boarding the flight. I felt terribly guilty as a leader, for my failure to ensure that they had enough money on them while leaving. Time was so short! And they had first mistaken it to be a prank. Then when they realised that it was not, they rushed to me 'as is where is!' In Marathi, we tell our men, *'Jasey asal tasey nighoon ya,'* (Come immediately the way you are). And they do. So they did not have much cash nor any provisions or clothes.

But why did they not tell me? Because I was so angry, worried and disturbed by the one hour delay due to 'April Fool' that they did not have the heart and courage to tell me that they were ill prepared to take the journey.

This episode proved that for any Intelligence input to fructify, it needs to be complemented by diligent, efficacious and painstaking police leg work. The officers and men involved have to be trusted to take the information received to its logical conclusion. The police gets but only a single chance to nab the suspect after days, weeks, months and sometimes even years of a hard, painstaking investigation. That is why the team has to be absolutely trustworthy, dedicated and ready to put in long tedious man-hours. It is at times like these that one needs a team that one can depend on to take up sensitive and high-risk tasks.

It was nothing but the never say die attitude of my team, their sheer grit and passion for their work that got us this breakthrough. I was conscious of the fact that it was their faith in my judgement and their readiness to follow my directions without demur that made me a leader, not vice-versa.

16

Another Tryst with the Underworld

It was October 1998 and Mumbai was on edge. The city's worst phase of extortions and shoot-outs was at its peak. Abu Salem and Chhota Shakeel, on behalf of Anees and Dawood Ibrahim, were threatening the film industry, builders and businessmen. Chhota Rajan, Arun Gawli and Ashwin Naik were equally relentless in browbeating builders and the merchant community.

The BJP-Shiv Sena government was in power in Maharashtra and the state police force was led by the legendary Arvind Inamdar, the Director General of Police, Maharashtra. R.H. Mendonca, popularly known as Ronnie Mendonca, another Maharashtra police icon, was the Commissioner of Police, Mumbai. He had taken charge on 21 August 1997, almost a year ago.

The pressure on the government and on Mumbai police was mounting by the day. An interview of the Commissioner of Police dated 26 May 1998 on *Rediff* Internet was prefaced by these words which caught the mood of the city:

> Ronald Hyacinth Mendonca has been a popular cop. A tough, incorruptible, no-nonsense cop who does his job without fear or favour. But why has he failed to stop Bombay's frightening downslide into crime? Why is India's most happening city suddenly running scared? Why are the cops looking like losers in their battle against the underworld? Is it political patronage? Or is it

corruption? Or plain inefficiency? Or have the courts taken the mickey out of what was once the nation's finest police force? Pritish Nandy speaks to the City's Police Commissioner....

On 8 October, late in the evening, Bharat Shah, a wealthy city businessman, was shot dead close to his well-known apparel showrooms 'Roopam' and 'Roopmilan'. The city Police Commissioner's office is just across the road but it did not deter the gunmen from imperturbably pumping bullets into Shah. Their job done, they unflappably melted away in the crowd in the bustling Crawford Market area.

On the afternoon of 13 October in the eastern suburb of Bhandup, Krishnadas and Haridas Kurup, owners of Madras Café, were shot dead at the cash counter of their restaurant. The gunmen also fired indiscriminately at the stunned customers before taking off on a motorcycle. Such temerarious shoot-outs were almost a daily feature and had cast a pall of gloom on the city's businessmen who lived in the constant dread of receiving extortion calls. From which gang and when – that was the only uncertainty. A wedding in a wealthy family was the surest way to invite such blood-curdling attention from these uninvited guests who considered it to be their right to have a fair share of the wedding budget earmarked for them. Obviously, the terrified families dared not lodge complaints. Scandal and bloodshed were the last things they wanted, especially in the weddings of their precious offspring. So the facts of such calls and the resultant transactions could be gleaned only from the whispers doing the rounds in the commercial markets.

Media reports constantly highlighted the spurt in the extortion calls in the busy festival season. There had been no less than twelve shoot-outs in the fifteen days since the Dussehra festival. Cognisance of the downslide had prompted, as per news reports, the then Union Home Secretary, Anil Baijal, to have flown down from Delhi to take a review of the situation. However, crime observers like Smriti Koppikar of *India Today* found the police listless and attributed it to the Justice Aloysius Stanislaus Aguiar report released on 28 September.

There had been nearly eighty police encounters the previous year and petitions were filed in the Bombay High Court challenging the veracity of some of the encounters. The petitioners claimed that the encounters were stage-managed and the Bombay High Court had appointed Justice Aguiar to inquire into the allegations. The Aguiar Report observed that the three encounter cases, which were subjected to scrutiny, were staged by the police to get rid of certain criminals. The next hearing of the petitions against the encounters was scheduled for mid-November when the High Court would be examining these serious observations. It was perceived that not only had the probe and the Report lowered the morale of the police, but they had also equivalently emboldened the gangsters to go on a rampage.

Smriti Koppikar rounded off her article in *India Today* (dated 26 October 1998) with a conclusion that was hardly flattering for the best police force east of Suez:

> Officials involved in the encounters last year may or may not be prosecuted, but the fear of judicial scrutiny has immobilised the Mumbai Police. Stuck in a no-win situation, the force is at a loss for solutions. Insecurity, it seems, is as deep in the police as in the citizens.

I was Assistant Inspector General (Law and Order, and Crime) as a Staff Officer to the DGP, Maharashtra. My office was a cabin on the first floor of the DGP's office housed in the spacious heritage building at Kala Ghoda originally built for the Royal Alfred Sailors Home in the 1870s. One afternoon, as I sat handling some routine work, who should walk in but Ronnie Mendonca! Startled, I sprang to my feet to salute him.

'What are you doing here, Rakesh?' He said, with a pleasant smile that was his hallmark. 'And when I need you in the city! A war is on!' He added. By war, he obviously meant the war against the underworld.

'Whatever you deem fit, sir!' I replied, searching his face for a clue. He said he had come to meet the DGP and was in a hurry on his way back to return to his office. He left immediately, but not without leaving me with a feeling that he meant what he had said.

I did not have to wait too long for a confirmation. The very next day, I received a call from Gopinath Munde, the Deputy Chief Minister who also held the Home portfolio. He wanted me to see him in his chamber.

I immediately apprised DGP Inamdar that Gopinath Munde had summoned me. To my surprise, Inamdar said that he had been expecting it. Munde had held a meeting with him and Ronnie Mendonca to discuss the alarming situation and one measure under consideration was to bring me back into the city police to utilise my informant network.

The dark, cryptic and enigmatic world of informants always fascinated me. I had developed a vast network of informants while working on the blast cases and as DCP (Detection) in the Crime Branch. The informants are quite a peculiar and distinctive ilk. Once they develop confidence and trust in you, they are bound to you forever. Within their own set of constraints, they develop some sort of loyalty and fealty towards you. Even if you are not in *the* saddle any more, and are cooling your heels in some hackneyed and non-descript posting, they continue to pass on information to you because they feel confident that you will ensure that it is taken seriously and acted upon. So even after my transfer to the DGP office, I had continued to receive important bits of information from my sources which I would promptly pass on to the Crime Branch. One such instance was the unforgettably chilling call that

I had received well past midnight and in the early hours of 22 April 1997. As the bedside phone began quivering with its shrill bell, as usual, poor Preeti also sat up in bed, bleary-eyed.

'Sir, Gulshan Kumar ka wicket girnewala hai,' it was the voice of a reliable source from the other end, telling me in a tone of great urgency that the 'wicket' of Gulshan Kumar was slated to fall!

Gulshan Kumar was the famous and contentious 'Cassette King' whose rags to riches story was fraught with recriminations and speculations about the legality of the means he employed to get there. They ranged from charges of sheer piracy to smart tapping of the loopholes of the Indian Copyright Act that proved to be a game changer. The son of a fruit juice seller, his career in the music industry had begun as an ordinary shopkeeper selling records and audio cassettes in Delhi. Then he had graduated to producing cheap audio cassettes himself, starting his own ventures 'Super Cassette Industries' and 'T-Series'. He made a fortune out of the sale and export of audio cassettes. Within a decade, he was running a multi-crore business empire and posing a serious threat to the established brands in the industry.

He then moved to Mumbai and made his foray into Bollywood as a producer. The success of his early hits made him a force to reckon with and with the confidence garnered from the rapid rise, he began giving breaks to newcomers and lesser-known talent. He was quick to pick up market trends and then diversified into different businesses. For instance, he flooded the market with devotional songs, tapping a need in his characteristic style and fulfilling it with a gusto that his established rivals found hard to match. As a result, to many, he came across as audacious and ruthless. They saw and resented him as an upstart least concerned about the established names and norms of the industry.

'*Kaun giraanewala hai wicket*?'(Who is going to take the wicket?) I asked.

'Abu Salem, saab. Usne apne shooters ke saath sab plan nakki kiya

hai. Gulshan Kumar roz subah gharse nikalke pahle ek Shiv mandir jata hai. Vahin pe kaam khatam karne wale hain,' the informant was very clear: Abu Salem was the one who was planning to kill Gulshan Kumar. He had finalised the plan with his shooters. The first thing that Gulshan Kumar did in the morning after leaving his house each day was to go to a nearby Shiva temple. That is where they were going to bump him off.

Gulshan Kumar was deeply religious. He was a devout Shiva and Devi bhakt.

'Khabar pakki hai kya?' (Is the information confirmed?) I asked.

'Ekdum pakki, saab, nahin toh aapko kaise bataataa?' (Absolutely confirmed, otherwise, why would I tell you?) he said.

'Theek hai. Kuchh aur khabar milee toh bataanaa,' (OK. Let me know if you get more information) I said before hanging up.

Preeti saw me deep in thought. 'Everything OK?' She asked, knowing full well that it was not.

'I have info that someone is going to be shot dead,' I said.

'Alert someone!' she said.

'Yes, I know, but before I do that, I have to get something confirmed,' I said.

Needless to say that both of us could hardly sleep thereafter. The first thing I did after daybreak was call Mahesh Bhatt, film director and producer. He sounded surprised at the early morning call, but I straightaway shot the question. 'Do you know Gulshan Kumar?'

'Yes, of course, I am directing a film for him,' he answered.

'Please find out if he goes to a nearby Shiva temple every morning. Will you? It is urgent,' I said and then realised that an explanation was due for such a peculiar request. I explained to him the reason.

After a while, Mahesh Bhatt called and confirmed that Gulshan Kumar never missed his morning visit to the Shiva temple. Bhatt had shared my information with him and warned him about the impending danger. Then I told Bhatt that I would be briefing the Crime Branch and he must tell Gulshan Kumar not to stir out of the house till the Crime Branch had got in touch with him and made arrangements for his safety. I then called up the Crime Branch and gave them the details furnished by my informant. The Crime Branch then extended the requisite protection to Gulshan Kumar.

Therefore, it came as a big shock to me when on 12 August 1997, I received a call that conveyed the news of Gulshan Kumar's murder. 'Where?' I asked.

'As he was coming out of the Shiva temple!' was the answer.

'But how? Didn't he have the Mumbai police's protection?' I asked.

Post a few enquiries, I learned that after some time, a contingent of UP police commandos had begun providing protection to Gulshan Kumar, as he had a cassette factory in NOIDA in Uttar Pradesh. The protection provided by the Mumbai police was therefore withdrawn. Somewhere down the line, routine and apathy could have set in, as it often happens in prolonged watch and ward duties. The guard is lowered and when you least expect it, the enemy takes his chance. After months of alertness and vigil, the mind starts inferring or deducing that the danger has passed. This is what happened with the protective security detail with Gulshan Kumar. Both, the protectors and the protectee, relaxed. Their sloth and complacency were punished by the patient underworld biding its time phlegmatically. Gulshan Kumar was shot down just the way his enemies had planned, at the temple he visited daily, without fail, when in Mumbai.

Another information that I had passed on to the Crime Branch in late 1996 was the plan to kill trade union leader, Dr Datta Samant. A couple of months thereafter, I had gone from the DGP office to Aurangabad for some official work. Whilst there, on 16 January 1997, I received news that Datta Samant had been shot dead. Then I got a call from R.S. Sharma, the Joint CP (Crime) to get in touch with the investigating team to see if I could throw more light on the matter and assist them in the investigation.

My junior officers, therefore, used to joke that I was a foreteller of doom! It was this track record that was now taking me back to the city police.

* * *

I immediately met Gopinath Munde. He briefed me on the government's concern and anxiety about the growing underworld threat. They were distressed that it was taking a toll on the morale of the entrepreneurs and damaging Mumbai's reputation in the business world. He said that the government had decided to appoint me as Additional Commissioner of Police in Mumbai city and expected me to help them get a firm grip on the situation. I said I would undoubtedly do my best. I was holding the rank of Deputy Commissioner and was due for a DIG promotion which was equivalent to that of the Additional Commissioner. I was second or third on the list. Munde said that it would all be taken care of.

In three or four days, orders were issued for posting me as Additional Commissioner of Police, Mumbai. It was now the prerogative of the CP to post me wherever he deemed fit. When I reported to him on 23 November 1998, Mendonca asked me how I would like to go about my new assignment. I said that if he could post me as Additional Commissioner in the Crime Branch, I would be able to utilise its infrastructure and manpower to effectively tackle the underworld menace. He thought for a while and then said, 'No. I will post you as Additional Commissioner of the Northwest Region.'

That was indeed a new way to look at the problem! Northwest Mumbai was 'ground zero' of the underworld menace. Most of the film industry was located there, as also a majority of builders and their construction projects. Bandra to Dahisar was the stretch most affected when it came to extortions and gangland shoot-outs. Thus, was issued my order for posting as Additional Commissioner of Police for the Northwest Region. The promotion that was due in about three to four months, happened earlier, and all the other promotions were carried out expeditiously to give effect to this decision.

There were high expectations of me which brought tremendous pressure. But there was a silver lining, or so I thought. My office was on Carter Road in Bandra, a beautiful stretch along the seafront. For the Bandra boy in me, it was a homecoming. The Additional CP's office was at Carter Road and Mama and Poonam were at a stone's throw away on St. Paul's Road. I could keep dropping in regularly to see them!

I took charge on the same day and the schedule was packed with long meetings with my new teammates to discuss strategy and tactics. I could leave the office only around midnight and I went straight to meet Mama who was eagerly waiting for me. Preeti had already reached there. We needed Mama's blessings for my new challenging task.

'Now you will keep coming more often to see me!' Mama said as I touched her feet.

'Yes, Mama, of course!' I said and I meant it.

'God has given you this position to help people. Never be afraid because the truth will be your shield. Truth shall always prevail,' she said. It was what she always told me. Yet each time she said it, I could feel a tug at my heartstrings. A reminder of why I was doing what I was. I went home that night with my head full of information and ideas, planning for more brainstorming sessions the next day. I was raring to go.

There was not much time to sit and ideate. Within a fortnight of my taking over, there was a big shoot-out in Andheri. On 8 December 1998, in the jurisdiction of D.N. Nagar police station, two people were shot dead: Iqbal Jumma Chunawala, a twenty-eight-year-old businessman along with his servant, Mani alias Munni Subramaniam Swamy. The killings were executed, gangland style, in the afternoon in the victim's office.

'The underworld has sent you a salaam, *saab*!' My officers tried putting it in a nice way. I knew it was no salutation. Rather they were cocking a snook at me. I was being tested.

'Dey daan chhootey grahan.' That was the tagline Chhota Shakil loved throwing at the hexed victim in his extortion calls. *Daan* means alms or donation. *Grahan* means eclipse. By tradition, a grahan is regarded as an inauspicious event – when the sun or the moon is seen as besieged. For the release of the sun and the moon from the evil, people are exhorted to give alms. Donate and the eclipse shall recede! That's the cry of the beggars when an eclipse is on. And people do make it a point to give clothes and other things as alms to mitigate the ill effects of the eclipse. Donate to us and we will release you! The veiled threat in the dark humour could not be missed.

There were 341 extortions reported in Mumbai city during the calendar year 1998 and my first priority was to build confidence in the victims – in the business community and Bollywood – to come forward and report the threats. I began work in right earnest to be accessible to all, day and night. We began making concerted efforts to use the Maharashtra Prevention of Dangerous Activities of Slumlords, Bootleggers, Drug-Offenders and Dangerous Persons Act (MPDA) to curb the activities of the gangsters. There were 638 detentions under the MPDA for the whole city in 1998-99 and out of these, 276 were from the Northwest region alone – the region under me. Such preventive detentions along with the policy of 'zero tolerance' for gangland activities began paying some dividends and we slowly began to see the tide turn.

Sometimes one got a feeling that the underworld enjoyed playing cat and mouse with the *filmies*. They enjoyed the kick they got out of calling the shots to make the 'Bollywood Badshahs' bow to their bidding and dance to their tunes. The dons would force the producers to give roles to particular actors and actresses of their choice. They would intimidate the producers to sell the worldwide distribution rights for the overseas distribution of films to their fronts or cronies as Bollywood films had now become a lucrative business in overseas markets. They would command the presence of actresses and models in their boudoirs in overseas locations and make actors give performances at their birthday bashes. The 1994 murder of producer Javed Riaz Siddiqui, a small-time producer trying to climb a notch up, was a classic example of how they pressurised Bollywood to kowtow to them. Javed Siddiqui had announced a film with Mithun Chakraborty, Vinod Khanna and Raj Babbar under his banner, Farah Arts. Abu Salem had already exerted pressure on him to cast the Pakistani actress Anita Ayub as the leading lady in the film. However, Javed Siddiqui soon realised that it was not commercially viable to cast Anita Ayub. She added no value to the film project. So he began the quest for a 'saleable' leading lady. His crime was that he wanted to dump Anita Ayub from the film and asked for the signing amount of one lakh rupees to be returned. This infuriated the Dubai dons and an incensed Abu Salem threatened Javed Siddiqui with dire consequences. 'Why don't you ask Magnum Films as they are much bigger than me,' pleaded Javed Siddiqui. But Abu Salem would brook no questioning of his *firman* (edict). On 7 June 1994, Javed Siddiqui was shot dead in broad daylight on a busy street in full view of his hapless wife.

Not only were property, financial and civil disputes being settled by the underworld, but Dawood Ibrahim's hegemony was also such that Bollywood squabbles and dissonance were being taken to his 'court' for 'justice'. There was a disagreement between two film production houses as regards the date of release of their films. Producers are very cagey and superstitious about the release date of their films. Also, if the weekend of the release was followed by a holiday on Monday, it would ensure bumper box-office collections. Further, two big budget films releasing on the same day would surely entail a financial debacle. So, this dispute between the two well-known film moguls was decided in Dubai by Dawood Ibrahim. Once the decision was made, it was binding on all concerned and there was no court of appeal!

On another occasion, a top Bollywood hero had gone to Dubai to perform a dance on Dawood's birthday. After his return to Mumbai, one day he was whisked away at gunpoint from Film City by the Arun Gawli gang and brought to the Dagdi Chawl at Saat Rasta. Gawli's ostentatious Navaratri celebrations were on and the hero was made to dance for the benefit of the revellers! This was one-upmanship or assertion of dominance that was a regular feature in the underworld of the eighties and nineties.

I distinctly remember the visit of a very senior and respected producer-director to my office, accompanied by a lady in a burqa.

'I have come to you to seek help for this young lady, Mr Maria!' He said and the look on his face made it clear that the matter was serious. The visitor slip was silent on the identity of the woman.

'Yes tell me, what can I do for you?' I asked.

'She is a well-known actress in films and television, and of late she has been receiving threatening calls from Anees Ibrahim. She has been warned that if she complains she will be killed. She was not ready to come to you but I have assured her that I will see to it that her identity is not revealed, that I will persuade you to maintain strict confidentiality about her name.'

'Certainly, we will take utmost precaution to keep the information confidential, but I cannot help you if you don't divulge what exactly is the matter,' I assured him. 'How much is he asking for?'

There was a pause, at the end of which it was the lady who spoke.

'He is not asking for money. He wants me to go to Dubai,' she said, without taking off her veil.

'Wants you to go to Dubai....?' I repeated her answer with a hint of a question in my tone, trying to deduce if what I understood by it was the same as what she had meant.

'He wants to sleep with me,' she said in a voice choked with anguish. Then she lifted her veil. She was a respected name in the entertainment world. Tears began streaming down her cheeks.

'She is pestered with calls. He seems to be obsessed with her. She was contemplating suicide and luckily she confided in me. Tell me, how we can save her?' said the gentleman who had persuaded the woman to seek my help. They had placed their lives in my hands and the slightest mishandling on our part would mean sure death or grievous bodily harm for both.

'I salute your wisdom and courage, sir. I will do my utmost to live up to your expectations,' I promised him.

'But if you register any complaint, Mr Maria, I will not be able to sustain it. I am sinking deeper into depression day by day. I can think of nothing but suicide. I would rather die than go into his hands,' the woman pleaded with me.

I called some of my most experienced and seasoned officers and explained the delicate nature of the problem. They handled it with great care and we provided protection to the defenceless victim for months on end, maintaining strict confidentiality. Luckily, it worked. She gathered the courage to face the ordeal. Ultimately, with our help and support, she could withstand the pressure to survive without compromising her pride and honour. The stress it caused to us was tremendous. And the success when it came, was one of the several such stories that we had to keep mum about.

So the underworld had their tentacles already spread and embedded deep in Bollywood and they knew exactly how to hit the producers, directors and actors where it would hurt them the most. I had to be in constant touch with most of the film industry stalwarts and even small-time producers and starlets to boost their confidence and provide protection. 'Do not give in to their demands. We will stand with you and provide protection.' This was my ceaseless plea to all those subjected to extortion calls and intimidation. But, this is easier said than done. People in the entertainment or those in the real estate industry were simply not mentally prepared or psychologically equipped to deal with threats to their lives or to the lives of their kith and kin. However, in all fairness, the truth and reality were that the late Yash Chopra, Ramesh Sippy, Mahesh Bhatt, Vidhu Vinod Chopra, Manmohan Shetty and others firmly stood their ground and refused to be cowed down. They proved to be the real 'reel' heroes, leading the way to show the film industry how to take on the organised crime syndicates.

With the concerted action of the sectional police and the Crime Branch, the tide finally began turning and despite the Justice Aguiar Report we managed to tighten the noose on the gang activities. The real war had just begun and though under severe and perpetual stress, I was enjoying the hard-earned success. But then, something else was in store for me.

The Maharashtra Assembly elections were held in September 1999 and the Congress-NCP alliance came to power and I was thrown out. Why? Because one day an acquaintance phoned me and asked, 'Have you heard of what happened in Bandra last night?'

No, I hadn't. I had not heard that some men had wined and dined in a restaurant in Bandra and when handed their bill, they had felt insulted and offended that they should be asked to pay. They had an altercation with the staff who had insisted on payment. The men had paid and left, only to return with some more of their colleagues. Then they had smashed the glass on the counter. They had pushed, slapped and abused the staff. The management had attempted to lodge a complaint at the police station, but the officer had dilly-dallied and finally asked them to come the next day.

I immediately made enquiries with the police station and was told that nobody had come to lodge such a complaint. I told them that the complainant would be coming to the police station and they must lodge the FIR, investigate the matter and bring the culprits to book. Within half an hour, I received a call from the office of the Deputy Chief Minister, saying that a false complaint was being lodged and the police should not entertain it. I was firm and said that the police would follow the due process, conduct a fair and impartial investigation and take the offence to its logical conclusion. Knowing that I was closely monitoring the case, the investigation was impartially conducted and the accused were arrested sometime in November.

With the arrests, the bells tolled for me. There was a murmur that the arrested accused had good connections with the office of the Home Minister and that I would be transferred.

The nature of our work dictates that holidays are always uncertain and frequent leave just not possible. Yet I had made a rule for myself that every year I would try to take a few days off in December, to coincide with the school holidays. That year too I had put up my leave application in September itself and it was duly sanctioned. When the news of my impending transfer began doing the rounds, the CP Ronnie Mendonca said to me, 'Rakesh, please don't go on leave now, when they want to transfer you. Go later.'

It was during his tenure that I had come in and it was during his tenure that I would be out. He was clearly not happy with it. I said 'Sir, whether I go on leave or not, they will definitely transfer me. So let me go. My wife and children are looking forward to the vacation. I have given my word to my family. Let me keep it.' Kunal was twelve and excited about the holidays. Krish was only four and I wanted some quality time with him. As expected, my transfer order arrived when I was on leave. As per norms and practices, I was to be in the Northwest Region for at least two years and I had completed only thirteen months!

Did I see Mama as often as I had thought I would? On the contrary. Probably, I saw her even less. Those days St. Paul's Road was a two-way street, unlike the one-way street that it is now. I would pass the house frequently on my way to the office or back. To keep important appointments. To chase information! And to visit 'spots'. One day – I clearly remember – I'd attended four gangland shoot-outs in my region! One in Borivali, one in Kandivali, one in D.N. Nagar and one near the Gaiety-Galaxy Cinema theatres in Khar. And I could not afford the luxury of stopping even for a few moments at Mama's, for I was always running against time. Sometimes I would see her sitting in her favourite rocking chair in the balcony just to catch a glimpse of me zipping past her. She would sigh and complain to Poonam, 'He is so near! And his visits are even rarer now.'

I know that even in that complaint there was a tinge of pride. For in the heart of her hearts, she knew that her son may not see her as much as she wanted him to, but he was doing exactly what she wanted him to do.

17

Policing the Lifeline

As prognosticated, my transfer orders were issued when I was away on holiday and it was clear that I had been singled out for transfer. I had barely completed thirteen months as Additional CP (Northwest Region). I took charge of my new posting on 21 January 2000.

Though I was now Commissioner of Police, Railways, in the city of Mumbai, in the police hierarchy it was regarded as a demotion, as if it were an office not of much consequence. The post was regarded as frivolous and insignificant, as if from the spotlight while tackling dangerous extortionists and terrorists, now my job had shifted to the shadows in the wings, reduced to the run-of-the-mill looking out for petty thieves – pickpockets, bag-lifters and chain-snatchers.

However, what begged the question was, could the importance of Mumbai's railway network be doubted even for a moment? For the benefit of the stranger to Mumbai, I must point out that her suburban railway network is indeed a vital lifeline for this commercial nerve centre of the country. It is the busiest commuter train system in the world and daily operates more than 2,000 services. Close to seven and a half million people use it for their daily commute and severe overcrowding is endemic on all its sectors. The lines fall silent only late in the night, for a brief interval of just a couple of hours. To quote the travel portal

Cleartrip.com, Mumbai's local trains are in many ways a defining feature of the city.

And if you looked at its raison d'etre, by no stretch of imagination can the post of Mumbai's Railway Police Commissioner be regarded as an innocuous office. Here is what the Railway Police Commissionerate website has to say about it:

> The need to create Railway Police Commissionerate and to give executive magisterial power to the Railway Police was emphasized due to the increased number of body and property offences, incidents of stone pelting on the running trains, rail-roko agitations by the commuters, as well as for safeguarding the interest of passengers which increased manifold.
>
> The Mumbai Railway Police Commissionerate came into existence w.e.f. 2.10.1999 by augmentation of jurisdiction carved out from Pune Railway District in erstwhile Mumbai Railway District by extending the jurisdiction up to Kasara and Khopoli and creation of five new police stations and creating the new posts of Commissioner of Police, Dy Commissioner of Police and Asstt. Commissioner of Police to supervise the jurisdiction of Mumbai railway police Commissionerate.
>
> After formation of Railway Police Commissionerate in the year 1999, the post of Commissioner of Police was upgraded to the rank of Spl. Inspector General of Police in the year 2007.
>
> The Railway police are entrusted with the responsibility of registration, Investigation and prosecution of crime along with keeping law and order in the jurisdiction.

The creation of a separate Railway Police Commissionerate was precipitated by a very disturbing and galling incident which had occurred on the Western Line, early in the morning of 28 October 1998. A twenty-three-year-old college girl from an unpretentious background had boarded the 5:45 a.m. Churchgate-bound local at Borivali station. She had only eighty rupees in her purse and was on her way to college to take a Maths exam. A drug addict entered the near-empty compartment and accosted her for money. The spirited girl did not oblige and the drug addict attacked her. She stiffly resisted the assault, but he dragged her and pushed her out of the moving train. She fell on the tracks and the train ran over both her legs. She lay bleeding on the tracks for some forty-five minutes before being shifted to the nearest railway station. It took another agonising forty-five minutes to shift her to the hospital. Luckily, she did not bleed to death and though she lost both her legs, she survived to shake Mumbai to her core. The name of the girl is Jayabala Ashar and she stands for the never say die spirit of the women of Mumbai who run the city shoulder to shoulder with the men. The railway network ferries women commuters like students and teachers, ayahs, nurses and other healthcare professionals, policewomen and guards, reporters and telephone operators, and a host of other shift workers who use the transport services even at odd hours.

A dedicated team was formed to trace the culprit but in vain. Help poured in for the brave young lady and the incident brought into sharp focus the serious issue of the security of passengers using Mumbai's suburban rail network. It paved the way for a separate Railway Police Commissionerate which took shape a year later in October 1999.

I was just the second Commissioner to occupy the post and my predecessor, S. M. Mushrif had held the charge only for a couple of months before his transfer to Pune. So a lot of groundwork had to be done to establish the Railway Police Commissionerate on a solid foundation. I enjoyed my work to the hilt because along with the organisational work, I really got to do what I love doing the most – hardcore grass roots policing. The time spent as Railway Police Commissioner was, in fact, a blessing in disguise. It was a crash course to help me brush up on my knowledge of textbook policing practices and skills of community policing.

I put in place a well-chalked out system of armed police

escorts in ladies' compartments between 6:00 p.m. to 6:00 a.m. To ensure the presence of police escorts, I would personally travel on trains after 9:00 p.m. This, in turn, made sure that the other senior officers and police station in-charges remained vigilant and alert. The measures had just about begun restoring people's confidence in us when I received complaints from groups of lady passengers travelling on local trains about acute harassment from eunuchs. They would enter the ladies' compartments to collect alms. If the ladies did not part with cash readily, the eunuchs would frighten them with lewd gestures, curses and predictions of doom. Some would even touch them inappropriately. It was nothing but extortion. I immediately instructed my staff to keep vigil and they rounded up some eunuchs found indulging in such blatant extortion. Now the arrested eunuchs had to be locked up.

'Sir, tyanna male lock-up madhye taku ki female lock-up madhye?' one of the Senior Inspectors phoned me and asked for my decision. They wanted to know whether the rounded up eunuchs should be kept in the male lock-up or in the female lock-up. I had not thought of this! After a quick think, I instructed that they be kept in the male lock-ups. Bad characters, rounded up for harassing women, could not be housed in female lock-ups!

A couple of days later, as I was sitting in my office, my Personal Assistant Narendra Khopkar called me on the intercom and said that I had visitors. A delegation.

'Who are they, and what do they want?' I asked.

'Sir, it is a *Trutiya Panthi* delegation,' said Khopkar in Marathi. For a moment I was clueless. Then it dawned on me. Trutiya Panthi meant eunuchs; a literal translation meaning 'those of the third path'.

'OK!' I said. 'Send them in!'

'Sir, should we send *in mahila* constables or *purush* constables with them?' My chaps were clearly worried. They wanted to know if they should send in male constables or female constables for my protection.

'Send both,' I said. You never know! Imagine the headlines the next day! 'Rakesh Maria held hostage by eunuchs in his own office!'

The delegation walked in. It was led by Lakshmi Narayan Tripathi who is a well-known transgender leader and an activist of the eunuchs. She told me that the eunuchs we had accommodated in the male lock-ups were being molested by the inmates. Now, this was a new problem, an altogether different angle. Lakshmi was armed with books and case law to show me that they should have been treated like women. This frankly was news to me. We had a long and fruitful discussion on the issue. I explained to the delegates the seriousness of the complaints we were receiving. I told Lakshmi Tripathi to send a word out in their community that they must forthwith stop the extortion in railway compartments and there would be no arrests. To this, her reply was that there was a cartel or ring of bogus eunuchs and they were the ones who indulged in such extortion. They were males dressed and posing as eunuchs to extort money and they brought the whole community into disrepute. It was then proposed that a joint drive be undertaken to ferret out and initiate legal action against the 'imposters'. So, we launched a special joint drive of the eunuchs and Government Railway Police. We succeeded in sorting out the problem by taking steps in consultation with the eunuch leaders and as long as I was there, no more complaints were received from the lady passengers against eunuchs.

I found the delegation of eunuchs to be one of the most courteous, well-behaved and reasonable that I had ever received, and they worked with us with utmost sincerity.

There was yet another menace which warranted our immediate attention: stone-pelting at trains. Miscreants would take positions near the tracks and pelt stones at running trains. A stone thrown at a speeding train, even from a long distance, can cause calamitous and debilitating damage. The victims would be the hapless commuters who, with great difficulty, would have managed to grab a window seat or who barely would have secured a foothold or even a toehold in the doorway. They would sustain serious injuries, often on the face and in the eye. There are congested slums along the tracks and the needle of suspicion naturally pointed towards the lumpen elements, urchins and pranksters from amongst the slum dwellers. The Railway Police had tried various measures like foot-patrolling the tracks but had been unable to make any headway. The peril and vulnerability of the unfortunate commuters continued to loom large.

I decided to form committees of slum dwellers to help us maintain vigil on the tracks. My men worked jointly with the slum dwellers and gleaned information that outsiders would come in, pelt stones on speeding trains and disappear. We suspected that this was part of a larger conspiracy of destabilising the city to create doubt about the safety of its transport system, but did not get any hard evidentiary support. Today, investigations into train derailment cases have proved that this is part of the grand design of Pakistan's ISI to create fear, panic and chaos in the entire country. Removing fishplates, placing cement blocks or boulders across railway tracks to cause fractures, are part of this game plan. So in hindsight, I suspect that pelting of stones by 'outsiders' from slums along the railway tracks could have been a part of the ISI's devious tactics to create fear and panic in the metropolis. The Railway Police, in partnership with Mohalla Committees in the settlements along the railway tracks, commenced patrolling and maintaining surveillance. Soon we had considerable success in deterring the miscreants. The incidents of stone-pelting reduced drastically and the city could heave a sigh of relief.

I found the senior echelons of the Railway administration most receptive to my suggestions. I had one DCP in charge of the Western Railway and one of the Central Railway and we began inspecting each and every aspect of security on the stations and the tracks. It was observed that the illumination at the stations was an important component in the security algorithm. Strangely enough, some areas used to be invariably ill-lit, for instance, those near the public toilets at the far ends of the stations. All forms of perversions including drug addiction were rampant there. We conveyed our concerns to the Railway administration and they took immediate steps to cure the deficiency.

Then there was the vexatious issue of owners of the stalls on the platforms, who used to let outsiders sleep on the roofs of their stalls by charging them 'fees'. All manner of riff-raff and undesirables would converge on the platforms and stations after their malefactions and transgressions in the city. This added to the general sense of insecurity at the stations and was pointed out to the Railway officials who started a drive against such practices.

The issues that we were grappling with concerned the security of the common man, small things that the affluent Mumbaikar had no clue of. Several rounds of meetings were held with the officers of the Railway administration. Special drives were launched to tighten the process of entry and access, and other safety issues. I found that until then the different branches worked in silos. We had the Government Railway Police (GRP) and the Railway Protection Force (RPF). RPF worked under the General Manager, Railways and the Divisional railway officers. I found the officers of the RPF and the Indian Railway Traffic Services most competent and receptive even to the basic suggestions we made, based on our experience of the ground situation. As we began working in close consultation and coordination with them on safety and security issues, I succeeded in bringing all of them together on the same platform and found them genuinely happy and relieved at the prospect of finding answers to the problems facing the railways. Towards the end of my tenure, orders were issued for my posting as Inspector General in the RPF on deputation. However, the Maharashtra government wrote to the Ministry of Home Affairs (MHA) in New Delhi to say that my services for Central deputation could not be spared. Thus, my order for deputation was cancelled.

I also began the system of making applications to the court for permission to return the stolen valuables recovered from the arrested accused to the rightful owners. I realised that the victims of pickpockets and chain-snatchers were generally the poor and middle-class commuters who firstly could not afford the luxury of commuting in the city by cars and, secondly, had no money to engage lawyers to make applications for return of their stolen property. The pickpockets would generally target the victims around salary time. The poor man who had lost his entire month's wages was already in debt. The gold *mangalsutra* snatched from a poor working-class woman would invariably be her only ornament of real gold, pawned a number of times for a quick emergency loan and recovered from the moneylender by paying interest at astronomical rates for future emergencies. It was pure joy to see their faces light up when we handed the mangalsutras to them on our own, without their having to grovel before the police or the courts. I made it a point to click pictures of the handing over and have them published in newspapers so that the general public got to know that the Railway Police were indeed working for them. We needed their faith in us to be restored.

The office of the Railway Police Commissioner was located just outside the Byculla Railway station. Once upon a time a prominent part of the city, Byculla now is a congested area with most structures dilapidated and gone to seed. The building which housed my office hardly befitted the stature of the Railway Police Commissioner. It was very cramped and some staff had to be accommodated elsewhere. So I took it up with the Railway administration and requested that they should give us a bigger and better building. They were gracious and amiable and asked me to identify a suitable property. Soon a spacious building at Carnac Bunder on P. D'Mello Road was identified. I confabulated with the railway engineers to design the Commissioner's Offices, the Control Room, Conference Hall and other facilities. The work started in my tenure but was completed only after my departure.

Then there was the Railway Police Headquarters at Ghatkopar, just opposite Ramabai Nagar – a slum which had shot into limelight with the serious riot that had erupted there in 1997. It had police lines (residential quarters for policemen) on a large campus which was mostly marshy with open spaces encroached and arrogated by trespassers. I initiated measures to stop further encroachment and to protect the property. I would visit the police lines, interact with the men and fresh recruits and inspect the recruits' barracks. The campus had a large parade ground and my love for sports and the outdoors drew me to the place. The Maharashtra State Police Games (MSPG) were around the corner and the Railway Police team was to participate. It occurred to me that the place had great potential for sports. Right through my career, I have enjoyed roughing it out on the sports fields with my men, just as I have not hesitated to stand shoulder to shoulder with them in bandobasts. That is where all barriers are broken down and all ranks become one. I have been a teammate in district teams and I have stayed in barracks with the constables and subordinate officers when we went for Range level games.

I discussed my thoughts with the DGP S.C. Malhotra. He wholeheartedly approved of the idea and gave me the go-ahead. I got cracking and we created at the ground an all-weather athletic track, a football turf field and a floodlit terrain that could be used for volley ball, basketball and kabaddi. We also added a turf hockey stadium with stands for spectators with funds provided by the DGP's office. The hockey ground was of such a high standard and quality that the Maharashtra Police hosted the All India Police Hockey Championships there which the late K.P.S. Gill, who was then the Indian Hockey Federation Chief, attended. This sports complex subsequently got designated as the Maharashtra State Police Sports Headquarters.

In 2000 and 2001, I recruited a large number of sportsmen as constables in the Railway Police. It was the first time that such large recruitment of sportsmen had taken place in the Railway Police. Till then, the Railway Police were laggards in sports. For the march-past at the opening ceremony at the State Police Games, the teams stand in as per their performance standings at the previous Games. The Railway Police Range team would invariably be at the tail-end. My initiative changed it all. Our team got so enthused that in 2002 at the Kolhapur Games, the Railway Police were declared the overall champions and my dream came true. The joy of my contingent as I walked up the dais to collect the trophy from the chief minister is still fresh in my memory. It was the first time ever that the railway team had attracted eyeballs and plaudits at the Games. On the return, a bada khana was arranged to celebrate this Herculean feat. A bada khana is organised on special occasions when all ranks – officers and men – dine together and make merry, mingling freely in a celebratory atmosphere. Ranks disappear and the Force unites to celebrate a victory.

Making the railway policemen take pride in their organisation, restoring to the commuters their stolen belongings bought out of their hard-earned income, deterring pickpockets and bag-lifters, creating community-police partnership to ward off stone-pelters, all these may not be considered extraordinary jobs, but they were immensely satisfying to the policeman in me. It was the office of Mumbai's Railway Police Commissioner that gave me the maximum job satisfaction. I wanted to go on in it, and create a policing system that would rival the best in the world. I was thoroughly enjoying this assignment which gave me the unbridled joy of creating something truly worthwhile and lasting.

Little did I know that the life which I thought I had left behind, had hitched a ride on the city's lifeline and had been quietly and surreptitiously following me. It was beckoning out to me yet again.

18

Battling a Thousand Cuts

The deafening sound of a powerful explosion brought our basketball game to an abrupt end. It was around 6:45 in the evening of 2 December 2002, and I was in the Ghatkopar Railway Sports Complex, practising with my Railway Police team. The sound had emanated from the direction of the Ghatkopar railway station. All of us rushed to the station to find a horrific site staring at us. Outside the station, an explosion had ripped through a BEST bus, throwing the entire area into a state of panic and confusion. The local police were already on the spot, rushing the injured to hospitals. Luckily, Ghatkopar being the last stop, all the passengers had disembarked and those for the return trip had not yet boarded when the bomb went off. Even then, the final toll of the blast was to reach two dead and over fifty injured.

The first instinct, as a police officer, was the sigh of relief that comes from knowing that the serious incident has not occurred in your jurisdiction. To the Railway Police, jurisdiction means inside the station or on the tracks. However, the very next instinct was that of the law enforcer and investigator, fully aware of the meaninglessness and futility of jurisdiction and boundaries, when it comes to prevention and detection.

Whoever had perpetrated this was specifically targeting the mass transportation system of the city and the railways would not be too far off their radar. I immediately issued alerts to my own Railway Police stations and specialised branches. The main difficulty in policing the railways in Mumbai lies in securing control over access to the stations and the tracks. Our stations are so porous that all and sundry can access them without having to pass through the entrances. Next is the sheer volume of commuters. It is well-nigh impossible to implement frisking or use devices like metal detectors for such volumes, especially during peak hours. Still, we had to do our utmost to keep vigil.

Before the day ended, more disturbing news was received. At 9:30 p.m., the MIDC police station in Andheri (East) received information that a suspicious bag was lying underneath the rear seat in a BEST bus plying on route number 336 near the SEEPZ bus depot. The Bomb Detection and Disposal Squad (BDDS) was summoned and they announced that the bag contained an unexploded time bomb. It was defused the next day by a team of the National Security Guards (NSG) summoned from New Delhi.

My fears were not unfounded. Just four days later, the next blast went off in the McDonald's outlet at the Bombay Central Railway Station, a major railway station on the Western Line. The station was crowded as usual. Luckily, there was no loss of life, but twenty-seven persons were injured. The day was the anniversary of the Babri mosque demolition, 6 December.

As the investigations proceeded, on 27 January 2003, three weeks after the Bombay Central Station blast, a day after Republic Day and just a day ahead of Prime Minister Atal Bihari Vajpayee's visit to the metropolis, a powerful bomb exploded in a crowded market area in the eastern part of the suburb Vile Parle, killing one and injuring twenty-eight. The spot was near the Dinanath Mangeshkar Auditorium and again just outside the railway station. The time was around 8:30 p.m. There was tremendous unease in the air. City Police Commissioner R.S. Sharma assured the reporters that tight security was deployed for the Prime Minister's visit. The BJP ruling at the Centre was in the Opposition in the state. They blamed the Congress-NCP government in the state for laxity in preventing the series of explosions – now three in two months.

Then, on Thursday, 13 March 2003, around 8:30 p.m. there was a powerful explosion at the Mulund railway station on a local train. This blast blew apart the first class ladies' compartment of a Karjat-bound local train. The bomb had apparently been placed on an overhead rack and left the roof of the compartment severely mangled. It killed twelve and injured seventy-one. Among the dead were two lady police constables. The blast had occurred a day after the tenth anniversary of the serial bomb blasts of 1993.

My Railway Police teams were toiling hard to detect the cases but without much success. Other agencies such as the Crime Branch, too, were on the job and on 15 March 2003, the Director General of Police, Maharashtra issued orders transferring the blast cases in our jurisdiction to the Mumbai police. In April 2003, the Crime Branch succeeded in detecting the blasts by busting a module led by Saquib Nachan. All of us heaved a huge sigh of relief, in the comfort of the belief that there would be some respite now.

However, our comfort was short-lived and it came as a big jolt when on 28 July 2003, at 9:10 p.m., a powerful explosion ripped apart a BEST bus, again in Ghatkopar, killing two persons and injuring sixty. The bus was on route number 340 and had originated from Andheri. The bomb had gone off when the bus was nearing its last stop on the busy Lal Bahadur Shastri Marg. Luckily, several of the passengers had alighted earlier, fortuitously reducing the number of casualties. Even then, another bus nearby, two motorbikes and some shops and buildings in the vicinity, were affected by the impact.

This was the fifth bomb blast in the city in a span of eight months. At the Rajawadi Hospital where the injured were rushed, Shiv Sainiks gheraoed Minister of State for Home Kripashankar

Singh, blaming the government for failing to tackle the terrorist threat. The then Deputy Chief Minister Chhagan Bhujbal claimed to have warned the police about terrorist groups being active in Ghatkopar. He also said that the state government had taken this blast as a challenge. The press reported that the then Joint Commissioner of Police (Crime) had said that the explosion was similar to the one that had taken place in a BEST bus in Ghatkopar in December 2002. The Sena and the BJP, in protest, were reported to be planning a bandh on 30 July, with the support of the Vishwa Hindu Parishad or VHP.

The occurrence of this powerful blast, despite the detection of the earlier ones, suggested that there were other terror modules active, determined to bleed India with a thousand cuts, in the words of the ex-ISI Chief, Lt. Gen. (retd.) Hamid Gul. In a conventional war, Pakistan cannot simply hope to match India. The only way they could hurt India was by terrorising our common man, hitting at our economy, destabilising our commercial capital, hurting our tourism and deterring our foreign investors. And Pakistan made no bones about it.

To discuss the ongoing terrorist assaults and to chalk out a strategy to combat them, the Deputy Chief Minister who was also the Home Minister, convened a meeting in his chamber. The DGP, CP, Mumbai, senior officers from the Intelligence Bureau (IB) and other senior officers including me attended the meeting. After the meeting, as I was leaving, the DGP asked me to stay back. I went out and waited. After a while, I was summoned in. The Home Minister, the DGP and the CP (Mumbai) were present.

'We want you to take up detection of this case, Rakesh,' said Subhash Malhotra, the DGP. 'You will need to utilise the Mumbai police resources. So we are posting you in Mumbai police.'

I was taken aback. This was quite a surprise. I did not know how to react, because I felt quite sad. I was enjoying my work with the Railway Police. So I tried to assure them that, even as

CP, Railways, I was on the job, as were all the senior officers of the city. We were keeping our eyes and ears open. I could enlist the help of the city police, as and when necessary, and there was no need to post me in Mumbai police. Yet they were firm in their decision. 'You form a team and take whomsoever you want; your orders are being issued,' said the DGP with finality.

The order was issued immediately and I was made Additional Commissioner of Police (Crime), even though my promotion to the rank of Inspector General/Joint Commissioner was due in a few months' time. Leaving my Railway Police colleagues all of a sudden was truly a sad moment. We had commenced a slew of innovative policing schemes and were awaiting their fruition. As I completed the formalities of handing over charge, I could see that all of them were equally affected.

On 19 March 2003, I reported at the office of the Commissioner of Police, Mumbai, near Crawford Market. It was my second stint there. For the first stint, the post was DCP (Detection), specially created by the then CP Satish Sahney and Joint CP M.N. Singh, to fulfil an urgent need. Now again a unique mandate was given to me to handle a serious threat. It was specified in the transfer order that I was to be responsible for the prevention and detection of all bomb-related cases.

The blasts were a well thought out strategy to throttle the pulse of the city's commerce, coming as they did when the financial sector was showing noticeable improvement. The Ganapati festival was around the corner to flag off the season of festivals. People were gearing up for a good season of celebrations which meant brisk commercial activity. Hotels were filling up with tourists. Even the Kumbh Mela was approaching. This provided ample opportunity for the terrorists and their handlers ensconced abroad to cause devastation. Besides BEST buses and local trains, they could simply target bazars, congregations and processions – all soft targets for easy pickings!

Activating informants was the most important priority if we stood any chance of busting the module. I immediately began working on several leads, coordinating the hunt day and night, and dispatching teams to different places like Assam, Bangalore and Ahmedabad. The exhilarating team sports at the Ghatkopar Railway Police grounds began receding into fond memories. They were replaced by the sinister and sapping cat and mouse games to counter masterminds of terror.

Just then a source provided me with information on one Shaikh Mohammad Ali Alam Shaikh aka Aziz aka Mansoor Bhai from Deonar near Ghatkopar, a *zari* worker (an artisan who specialises in gold/silver embroidery) in his Thirties, who had received terror training in Pakistan. Hailing from a very poor family from Amethi in Uttar Pradesh, Mansoor had come to Mumbai after passing his Secondary School Certificate (SSC) examination. He had joined the Students' Islamic Movement of India (SIMI) in December 1992 at their conference held at the Bandra Reclamation which had even been addressed by some Pakistani delegates. The man who had indoctrinated him and sent him to Pakistan for terror training was someone called Riyaz Bhatkal whom he had first met at the SIMI office in Kurla. After returning from training in Pakistan, around the end of March 2003, Mansoor had met Riyaz Bhatkal at the Kurla mosque. Riaz also had a brother called Iqbal aka Asad who too was involved in brainwashing Mansoor.

The moment we began pursuing Mansoor, Riyaz and Iqbal Bhatkal vanished. What were the brothers up to? How many more gullible youth had they succeeded in indoctrinating?

And who were these sleeper cells sharpening their skills, with every passing moment, to plant a thousand cuts to bleed our dear Mumbai? We were already nearing the end of August and still, there was no breakthrough in sight. Answers to all these pertinent and grave questions continued to elude us and gave us all sleepless nights.

19

Hear the Big Bang!

I was in my office on 25 August 2003, a Monday, when we received the next laceration from the terrorists. Around lunchtime, two massive explosions rocked south Mumbai within minutes of each other and this time it was reminiscent of the 1993 serial blasts, such was the magnitude of the destruction caused. The reason was revealed later by the Chemical Analyser's report: the explosive used in both the bombs was RDX.

The first bomb went off at 12:40 p.m. at Dhanji Street in the landmark district of Zaveri Bazar, near Mumba Devi – the temple of the presiding deity of Mumbai. It is Mumbai's old jewellery market where dilapidated buildings house sparkling showrooms of precious metal and gems. The shops are backed by cubbyhole workshops manned by poor artisans, often migrant labour, slogging hard to craft exquisite jewellery. One of the busiest areas of the city and hard to navigate during the daytime, its narrow streets are packed with honking vehicles. Diamond brokers transact business worth crores of rupees on the sidewalks. Debris sent flying by the deafening blast ripped through the workshops and showrooms. The explosion silenced the din only for a few deadly seconds and then, all hell broke loose. The toll it took was thirty-six killed and 138 injured, all innocent ordinary people who had no clue that they could be on someone's hit list.

The other bomb went off at 13:07, in the paid parking at

the Gateway of India. Constructed on the waterfront of Apollo Bunder, 'the Gateway' – as it is popularly called – is a landmark erected in 1924 to commemorate the landing of King George V and Queen Mary on their visit to India which took place in 1911. It is a must-do tourist destination. Next to it is the iconic Taj Mahal Palace hotel built in 1903, twenty-one years before the Gateway. Seen as an immensely successful step in the revival of indigenous entrepreneurship, the hotel holds pride of place in the Indian psyche as a mark of national awakening and self-respect. For the Mumbaikar, it is 'The Taj!' At lunchtime, the piazza in front of the Taj hotel is buzzing with activity and the surrounding area is quite crowded, not just with tourists, photographers, hawkers and beggars, but also by the business community attending meetings and conferences. It is a big leveller, this area, where the poor, the rich and the middle class, from India and abroad, all converge with their own kind of zest for life that adds to the famed spirit of Mumbai.

The taxi in which the bomb was planted at the Gateway flew some thirty feet up in the air before landing in a heap of twisted metal. It left a deep crater where it had been parked. Part of its Compressed Natural Gas (CNG) cylinder flew over several buildings to land about 400 metres away, near the office of the Director General of Police of Maharashtra at Kala Ghoda. Glass panes of the Taj shuddered. People on the street outside saw body parts flying around. The toll of this blast was to reach sixteen killed and forty-six injured.

There was another worrying factor. At 12:15, about twenty-five minutes before the blasts, someone claiming to be from the 'Gujarat Muslim Revenge Force' (GMRF) had made a call to the cable network In-Mumbai and said, 'Hear the Big Bang!' That was it and no further details. This was chillingly reminiscent of the email received by NDTV on 27 July, a day before the blast on bus number 340 in Ghatkopar. Even in that mail, it was the

'Gujarat Muslim Revenge Force' that had claimed responsibility for all the blasts and left an ominous warning: 'Hear a Big Bang tomorrow.' NDTV had informed the police of this mail a day after the blast. These two audacious intimations, not just promising destruction but keeping the promise, indicated that the module was getting increasingly emboldened. Their sinister authors must be gloating over their diabolical success that very minute, glued to their TV sets and phones.

The bomb that exploded at Dhanji Street was also planted in a taxi. From whatever was discernible from the damaged number plate, the investigators checked all the likely permutations and combinations to zero in on the identity of the unfortunate driver, thirty-one-year-old Umeshchandra Upadhyay who was killed in the explosion, precisely the way the terrorists had intended him to.

What they had not bargained for, however, was the miraculous escape of Shivnarayan Vasudeo Pandey, the driver of the taxi-bomb planted at the Gateway. He had missed death by the skin of his teeth and lived to walk up to the police to tell his tale. Was he going to be the Nemesis of the terrorists? As investigators, it is ingrained in us that no crime is perfect. Pandey's survival proved this maxim.

Pandey was brought to me in the Crime Branch late in the evening. I looked in wonder at the simple soul sitting across my desk. The man with a birth-chart that astrologers would love to pore over and a palm that palmists would love to gaze at! Was he cognizant of how important he was for me if I had to crack this case? He was wholly oblivious to the significance of the role that destiny had cast him in. He was thoroughly exhausted and still in a state of daze and shock. It took me quite some time to make him relax and restore his confidence. I could empathise with him and that gave him some comfort. Slowly, he could narrate the facts in clearer detail.

Pandey's story began on the morning of the previous day when he had parked his taxi opposite the Amber Oscar Cinema in the western suburb of Andheri and a man had approached him, enquiring if he could be hired for daylong sightseeing. After some haggling, the fare was fixed and the man got into the taxi. He directed Pandey to drive to the end of Azad Galli (a *galli* meaning a lane) where one bearded man, two women and a little girl boarded the taxi. They appeared to be a family – parents and two daughters. Then the entourage drove to Colaba. The man in the front seat asked Pandey if he could park the taxi in the compound of Hotel Taj Mahal and Pandey replied in the negative. When they reached the Gateway, the man paid Pandey some advance and asked him to park the taxi in the parking lot opposite the Taj. After they had left Pandey parked the taxi, collected the slip from the parking lot attendant and waited patiently for their return. They returned after some time and he drove them back to Andheri where he was paid his balance. Then they said that they wanted to hire his taxi again for the next day. The pickup would be from the same spot around 10 in the morning. They had won his confidence and he was quite happy to oblige.

The next day only the couple and their two daughters boarded the taxi. They had a fairly big bag that would not fit in the dickey. Pandey offered to keep it on the overhead carrier, but the man insisted that it be locked in the dickey as it contained valuable articles. So to make room for the bag in the dickey, Pandey shifted the tools to the floor of the taxi. With the bag safely locked in the dickey, the man went away to make a call. On his return, they began their journey again to the Gateway of India. As they reached the Gateway, the man asked Pandey to park the taxi in the same Pay and Park. He was anxious and impatient when a friend hailed Pandey and got chatty with him. Before alighting, the man informed Pandey that they were leaving the bag in the dickey in his safe custody and repeatedly cautioned him not to leave the taxi.

Though he had promised not to leave the taxi, Pandey had to answer what we insist on calling in police parlance the 'nature's call'. So he paid the parking attendant ten rupees for keeping an eye on the taxi in his absence and rushed to the urinal which was a short distance away. Just as he was stepping out of the urinal, he heard the sound of the explosion. There was chaos all around and, for a while, he could hear nothing. Pandey had suffered a temporary hearing loss and tinnitus (ringing in the ears). After some time, he made his way through the smoke to the parking lot. Dead bodies were lying on the ground and the injured were writhing in pain, fighting for their lives. He looked for his taxi and could not believe what he saw. There was only a big crater where he had parked it! And what looked like his taxi was lying some thirty feet away, completely mangled! He was stunned and just did not know what to do.

The seriousness of what had happened to him began sinking in. *Could it be that I have had a miraculous escape? Could it be that the bag of valuables that I had locked in the dickey with my own hands was a bomb? Could it be that the man who kept asking me to remain in the cab wanted me to die in the cab?* The thoughts were horrid and terrifying.

Pandey slowly walked towards a pavement, sat down and tried to calm himself. His escape from the jaws of death was so overwhelming that it took him a long time to collect himself. The people around him were busy with the rescue operations. They had no clue what had happened to the man who sat bewildered on the pavement, not injured and yet holding his head, wondering what he was supposed to do next. After some time, he pulled himself together and walked up to the Colaba police station. The officers on duty were busy managing the crisis. He told them that it was his taxi that had left that big crater in the parking lot and landed thirty feet away.

He paused to control his anguish and I remembered Sant Kabir's famous *doha* that my mother often quoted:

Jako rakhe Saiyan, maar sakey na koy
Baal na banko kar sakey, jo jag bairi hoy

(He whom God protects, no one can kill. Even if the whole world turns into his enemy, not even a hair of his can they harm.)

As I probed further, I found that he could vividly remember the faces of the passengers. He had had ample opportunity to observe them at close quarters, on two successive days and that too for a good three to four hours each day! Here was a witness who had the ability to help us get their likenesses done and identify them! A god-sent! He was the salvager – the biggest aid in locating the family of four and their ringleader who wanted to park the bomb in the compound of the Taj. So I immediately instructed my Crime Branch officers to arrange for good sketch artists who could sit patiently with Pandey and draw the sketches. The officers and the artist did a splendid job and the sketches were meticulously prepared the same night.

Now we had to activate our informants from Azad Nagar and figure out who amongst our officers had a good khabri network in and around Azad Nagar? Inspector Vinayak Sawde had worked at D.N. Nagar and Juhu police stations. An experienced hand, Sawde had worked with me earlier. He knew the area like the back of his hand and had a good network of informants. So I immediately sent for him. I told him to leave everything else aside and immerse himself wholeheartedly in this investigation. 'Sir, if they indeed are from that area, rest assured, I will get them for you!' promised Sawde before taking my leave.

C.D. Barfiwala lane is the dividing line between Juhu and D.N.Nagar. There is a narrow connecting road between C.D.

Barfiwala lane and Azad Nagar, generally used by the nearby Junaid Nagar hutment dwellers. There is a tea stall at the mouth of the approach lane, a popular hangout for youngsters and local busybodies and an ideal spot for gossip and information. Sawde started mingling with the people there and discreetly shared the sketches with some of his informants in the area. Soon a man approached Sawde and hinted that he had some useful information. He, however, requested Sawde to meet him at another spot the next day. At the next day's meeting, Lady Luck smiled on us. A rarity indeed! The informant said that he had seen the persons in the sketches in the area, but was positive that they were not from the locality. Instead, they used to come there to meet one Ashrat Ansari.

Sawde excitedly rushed to me to report the breakthrough. The sceptic and doubting Thomas that I am prompted me to question Sawde if the informant was hundred per cent sure. Sawde said he was. Still, I did not want to take any chances. I asked Sawde to go back to him and reconfirm. Sawde said, 'Sir, why don't *you* meet him to judge if he is telling us the truth?' So it was decided that in order to protect the informant's identity, I should meet him discreetly at some nondescript location. Sawde brought the informant in a private car to the service road which runs parallel to the Kennedy Seaface (Marine Drive) where now stands the Police Memorial to the officers and men martyred in the 26/11 terrorist attacks. Both Sawde and the informant then got into my car. Sawde sat in the front seat, the informant in the back seat next to me and I began questioning him.

'Sawde *Saab* says you have recognised the persons in the sketches. How are you so sure that the sketches are of the same people?' I asked him.

'Sir, the older daughter is very attractive and smart,' he said, lowering his gaze a little. Perhaps he felt a little foolish and embarrassed at what he was saying. 'She was well-dressed and stood out. I was curious to know who the strangers kept visiting, along with such a pretty girl. So one day I followed them and found that they had come to see Ashrat Ansari. After a while, Ashrat and they left the house together.' A few more questions and he confessed that he felt a tinge of jealousy for Ashrat's good luck. I felt that he was telling us the truth. Still, to be doubly sure, I gave him an hour to think it through, after which I went back to talk to him and he stuck to the story. The next step was to nab Ashrat, without alerting his accomplices, in a neat and clean pickup.

Ashrat Ansari did not figure in our records. His father, a carpenter, hailed from Bans Bareily in UP and was settled in Mumbai since 1979. One of his brothers had stood for municipal elections. Another brother was a cable operator. Ashrat was in his late Twenties. He had studied till the ninth standard in the Marol Urdu School and begun working as a zari worker. In February 2002, he was working in a zari workshop in Surat when riots had erupted after the Sabarmati Express compartment carrying *kar sevaks* from Ayodhya was burnt down in Godhra.

A Crime Branch officer without khabris is like a car without petrol or a warrior without a sword. Good khabris are like gold dust, priceless but hard to collect. For they are slippery customers. First of all, how far can a khabri be trusted? Most often he is from the same background as the suspects and has an axe to grind with them. How does one secure the khabri so that he does not carry information to some other camp or to persons who can alert the culprits themselves? How does one ensure his safety, so that the culprits don't eliminate him? Then whenever a sensational crime takes place, there is tremendous competition among the investigative agencies to detect it. Sometimes the competition helps, but at times things get complicated, all in good faith. For instance, when the khabri provides information to multiple agencies. Who can incentivise him better? So you have instances of officers of one agency picking up the khabri and ending up guarding him against the other agencies. At such times, the informant becomes extremely important to the officer, more than even his wife! The officer has to secure and shepherd the informant, keep him safe and cocooned in hotels or secluded places with trusted men of the unit living with him to guard him. This happens in all the police forces all over the world and leads to situations bordering on the comic. Or rather tragi-comic, when the pressure on the investigators starts mounting as the press, politicians and public start baying for their blood. And then all becomes fair, as in love and war, and particularly if it is the war against terror, so paramount is the urgency to foil the nefarious designs of the terror modules and save innocent lives. Sometimes officers are tempted to take shortcuts which can either pay off or backfire. Policemen are only human after all. And to match the wily masterminds of terror, they need as much luck as investigative skills.

Now, in this case, it had come to light that the taxi used for the Gateway blast had been hired from Azad Nagar at the S.V. Road junction. With this input, not just the local police station, even the press began detecting the case. Then some officers of the local police station learned of Sawde's khabri – the local guy that he was – and couldn't resist picking him up. 'So! You are talking to the Crime Branch, huh? You could not come to us?' They felt offended that he had bypassed them. Some choicest vernacular abuses that come naturally to an angry policeman must definitely have been added to these questions. It made Sawde rush to me, harried and frustrated. *'Sir! Apna khabri uthaa liya!'* (Sir! Our informant has been picked up) he wailed.

This was dangerous and needed swift intervention. I immediately called up the local DCP and the Senior Inspector, requesting them to leave the man. We had reached a very crucial stage. Any action on their part, however well-meaning, could jeopardise the investigation and alert the module! Both appreciated the gravity and a relieved Sawde rushed out to take charge of his khabri.

Then the local police put their finger of suspicion on a housebreaker from their area and went to his house to enquire, only to learn that he had anticipated their arrival and left the area on a motorcycle, riding pillion with someone. So his relatives were summoned to the police station for further enquiry. As the family was being questioned, news came that the suspect had met with an accident in Ajmer and had died on the spot. The body was brought to Azad Nagar for the last rites. The local sentiment had turned anti-police, though the poor police had nothing to do with his death. Ashrat Ansari was one of the mourners in the funeral procession. We were closely monitoring the situation. 'Should we pick him up after the funeral?' My officers asked me. I said no. Let us wait, we need a clean pickup.

We had deputed two 'zero numbers' and two constables in the area for keeping tabs on Ashrat's movements. Zero numbers are a unique category of 'policemen'. I don't think we have this term in any other place than Mumbai. These are ordinary citizens who are sort of satellites to our officers and constables in some of the specialised units like the Crime Branch, Narcotics Cell, ATS or even Police Station detection squads. Often, they are people who just enjoy rubbing shoulders with cops and the importance they derive from their proximity to the police. They are prepared to run all kinds of errands or help out in surveillance and get a 'high' from their closeness with the police machinery. The police cannot be omnipresent, especially in huge cities like Mumbai, and need people's cooperation in keeping vigil. A policeman, try as he may, often finds it hard not to stand out. Thanks to his training and grooming in Service, peculiar mannerisms get ingrained in his persona and essential nature. Over a period of time, the air of authority seeps into his demeanour. Therefore, to carry out delicate watch and surveillance operations, it is the 'zero numbers' who come in handy. They can dexterously and expediently adapt to situations and locales. They easily merge with crowds, as vegetable vendors, sweepers, courier boys and waiters. It is like outsourcing police work to private citizens. With the help of zero numbers, Sawde and team had their eyes open and their ear to the ground in Azad Nagar.

In another significant development, the manager of the Minara Masjid in Memonwada came to the Pydhoni police station and reported that they had found a letter in the masjid from an organisation called Gujarat Muslim Revenge Force, begging forgiveness of the Mumbai Muslims injured or dead in the blasts. In addition to claiming responsibility of the Monday blasts, the letter gave a deadly assurance that henceforth they would be giving a thirty-minute notice of the blasts. So, more was yet to come. And, again a race against time to identify and nullify this module!

But we did not have to wait for long. On 31 August, with the alerts from the zero numbers and constables, Sawde succeeded in achieving a clean pickup of Ashrat, assisted by Police Sub Inspectors Suryakant Talekar, Vijay Kandalgaonkar, Jitendra Vankoti, Pramod Toradmal, Head Constable Narayan Subarao Patil and Police Naik Hindurao Dagadu Chincholkar and staff. We had reached Ashrat through secret information and I needed to satisfy myself as regards his role and complicity. Depending upon his interrogation, I had to coordinate further operations to get hold of the rest of the members of the module. The nearest quiet spot where I could join the team was the vicinity of the Aarey Milk Colony. That was the only available locale where Ashrat could be questioned away from prying and inquisitive eyes. I asked Sawde to park their vehicle in a *tabela* (cowshed) in Aarey so that I could join them before Ashrat was taken to a Crime Branch unit for the necessary formalities. I rushed to the tabela and despite the tension in the air, found the whole thing quite surreal and farcical.

Besides the Mumbai Crime Branch, the only other species present in that strange interrogation room were the buffaloes who serenely pretended to be expert interrogators. Of substantial stature, chewing the cud with complete nonchalance, as if this was not the first nor the deadliest terrorist they had met! They were only mildly interested in the proceedings and let out an occasional moo as if egging us on to be done with it and wind up fast; this case was solved and they had more complicated plots to unravel. For me and my colleagues, however, this was the first time that we were confronting a suspect surrounded by fodder, mud, dung cakes and the invigorating smell of bovine excreta. That too in the hot and humid Mumbai weather!

Ashrat was still making a valiant effort to confuse the officers and deny his involvement, but seeing me arrive on the scene, his expression changed. 'So! From all the criminals in the world, I find *you* responsible. You think I am firing in the air? You think I would waste my time with you if I did not have clinching evidence against you?' I asked him without even raising my voice. The tabela backdrop and my sudden entry were far from pre-planned, but were so dramatic that they could have appeared choreographed. They did not fail to make a seismic impact on Ashrat who did not take long to admit his guilt. In no time his bravado deflated and he began singing.

The bearded man and his family, who had tricked Shivnarayan Pandey into planting the car bomb at the Gateway, turned out to be Sayed Mohammad Hanif, an auto rickshaw driver, his wife Fehmida and their two daughters. They lived in Chimatpada at Marol Naka. The man who had taken the family to the Gateway on the first day was Nasir, the ringleader of the ground operations and also a prime conspirator. The module was responsible for planting four bombs: the unexploded bomb discovered on the BEST bus on 2 December 2002 at SEEPZ; the bomb that had exploded on the BEST bus on route number 340 at Ghatkopar on 28 September 2003; and both the bombs that had exploded on 25 August 2003 at Zaveri Bazar and at the Gateway of India.

When Ashrat disclosed Hanif and Fehmida's role, it needed to be checked if they were in their house. So I decided to send a team into the chawl posing as municipal health officers, carrying out a survey for which we needed a lady officer. Assistant Police Inspector Gopika Jahagirdar, working at Dindoshi police station resided nearby. She was summoned and with her, the 'survey team' comprising Sub-Inspector Sudhir Dalvi reached the chawl. They went door to door, with Ms Jahagirdar asking questions on the vaccination status of the children and the like. Fehmida did not let the team in and provided all the answers standing in the doorway, saying that her husband was not home. So we kept a team stationed discreetly outside the chawl to watch for Hanif's return. I was being regularly updated about their 'exploits'. The team even mistook another auto rickshaw driver for Hanif and fearing that he was trying to flee, gave him a long *Bollywood-ishtyle* chase, before discovering their mistake. After Hanif's return, the team with Ashrat reached the house and picked up Hanif, Fehmida and their daughter Shaheen (name changed to protect the minor's identity). The Prevention of Terrorism Act, 2002 or POTA was applicable to the conspiracy for the four blasts. With leads from the arrested accused, we recovered explosives, detonators and other incriminating material. Hanif, Fehmida and Ashrat were produced before the POTA Special Court. Shaheen was found to be a minor and was produced before the Juvenile Court in Dongri.

With the arrest of these accused, we could unravel the entire conspiracy which was hatched in Dubai by ISI agents and the banned Lashkar-e-Taiba (LeT) which is an active Islamic militant organisation operating from Pakistan. LeT was founded in 1987 in Afghanistan with funding from Osama bin Laden and has its headquarters in Muridke near Lahore. Its object is to introduce an Islamic State in South Asia and to 'liberate' Muslims in Kashmir.

They operate several training camps in Pakistan occupied Kashmir (PoK). Despite international disapproval, the ISI continues to give the LeT complete support and protection. The 2001 terror attack on the Indian Parliament was part of their systematic plan of attacking Indian civilian and military targets.

In Dubai, the LeT has its agents in and around the mosques and labour colonies where a large number of Indians reside. These agents actively scout and indoctrinate Indian Muslims and recruit them as terror operatives. After the Godhra riots, to incite hatred and spread anti-India sentiments amongst the Indian Muslims, the LeT and the ISI created cassettes, audiovisuals and pamphlets specially designed to paint a bleak picture of the plight of the Gujarati Muslims and used them to turn Indian Muslims against the Indian State. From such brainwashed Indians, they chose recruits for terror modules. The moment a recruit was indoctrinated enough, the ISI would send him back to India, promising a salary equivalent to the amount earned in Dubai. He was then asked to lie low till they signalled him to wage 'jihad'. Such operatives lying low and ready to launch terror attacks are known as sleeper cells.

Hanif was one such sleeper cell. He had worked in different jobs in India and the Middle East. Then in 2000, he had moved to Dubai and got drawn into the LeT dragnet. Atrocities committed on Muslims in Gujarat was a regular subject of speeches and discussions in the masjid he attended. The doctored CDs they showed him on the Godhra riots had the desired effect and he began thinking and plotting revenge.

Two other Indian Muslims were also part of this group – Zahid and Nasir. Nasir was in his early Thirties and had done his schooling in Mumbai. In 1996, he had gone for employment to Dubai, where he was scouted and indoctrinated. He was introduced to Hanif at the LeT office at Deira Dubai. Zahid was Zahid Yusuf Patni. He came from Naya Nagar in Mira Road near

Thane and was a schoolmate of Ashrat Ansari. After coming under the spell of the LeT, he had begun collecting money in Dubai to fund terrorist activities in India. After his return from Surat, post the Godhra riots, Ashrat Ansari had met Zahid in Mumbai and shared his desire to avenge the atrocities committed on Muslims in India. So Zahid got Ashrat Ansari on board.

Sometime in August 2002, the Pakistani motivators met the three indoctrinated Indians at Nasir's house in Dubai to convince them that they must avenge the Godhra riots by causing explosions in India and promised complete support. The trio agreed to do their bidding. With further intense indoctrination at the LeT office in Deira Dubai, Nasir emerged as the ringleader to act as the link between the ISI and LeT handlers in Dubai and Hanif and Ashrat in India. With the blessings of the handlers, the trio floated the 'Gujarat Muslim Revenge Force' and began selecting their targets. Besides targeting the mass transport system in Mumbai, they had ambitious plans of attacking the Mumbai Airport, the Crime Branch office, the Bhabha Atomic Research Centre (BARC), the refineries, the garba revellers at the Navaratri festival and a Jain temple in Chembur. They had even conducted reconnaissance of the water supply line to Mumbai near Bhiwandi and the power supply lines on the Gujarat and the Mumbai-Goa Highways.

Hanif returned to India in September 2002 and began plying an auto rickshaw. Nasir returned in October 2002 and began residing in Sarvodaya Nagar in Ghatkopar. In the last week of November 2002, Nasir, Hanif and Ashrat got together to plan the nitty-gritty of terror attacks. It was Nasir who decided on the targets, worked out the logistics, arranged the funds and procured the material for making bombs. As per his directions, Ashrat and Hanif planted the bomb that was discovered unexploded on the bus at SEEPZ Depot on 2 December. They had gone together to the bus stop, but only Ashrat had boarded the bus and left the bomb under the seat.

Not easily disheartened, they selected Ghatkopar for the next attack. It was Hanif's wife Fehmida, their committed supporter and accomplice, who now accompanied Ashrat to plant the bomb. In Hanif's loft, they prepared a bomb using forty-four gelatine sticks. Then Ashrat and Fehmida went to Andheri and boarded the ill-fated BEST Bus on route number 340. They occupied the back window seat and slid the bag with the bomb underneath. They had bought tickets for Asalfa, but alighted earlier and returned home to savour the success of their mission on television news. This time they were lucky.

Emboldened by the success, they planned to explode more powerful bombs to target Mumba Devi and the Gateway of India. Thereafter, it was brisk activity for the module. On 24 August, Nasir took Hanif, Fehmida and the girls in Pandey's taxi to the Gateway in the morning and selected the parking lot for planting the bomb. The same evening, he took Ashrat to Zaveri Bazar and designated a spot in the crowded area to park the other taxi bomb. The time for the explosions was fixed at 1:00 p.m. The success on the bus in Ghatkopar had taught them how to keep pace with the timer devices. They had now perfected and mastered the ghoulish art of timer devices. This time the charge was deadlier and all that they had to do was to make certain that there was not the slightest delay at any step.

The next day, the terror module put into effect their demonic plan. Two bags containing a bomb each left Andheri that morning: one for Zaveri Bazar and the other for Gateway of India, in two separate taxis. Their timers were ticking away to kill and maim innocent Mumbaikars who were heading to those spots that very minute from different parts of the city, never to return to their near and dear ones, oblivious that death was only a couple of hours away.

Ashrat could not find parking space at the spot determined by Nasir and settled for the nearby taxi stand. He then pretended that he was expecting a man to collect the bag kept in the dickey. After a while, he informed the ill-fated driver that since there was no sign of the man, they would have to return to Andheri; but before that Ashrat would quickly buy a few goods from the shops. So saying he left the hapless driver waiting in the taxi to guard the bag and began walking towards Charni Road. After he had walked some distance, he heard the sound of success that his ears were so eagerly yearning for.

Their task accomplished, the saboteurs phoned Nasir from PCOs and quietly went back to the safety of their homes to gloat over the news coverage of their accomplishment.

Now the immediate task of the Crime Branch was to get hold of Nasir. We launched a massive manhunt. Nasir's real name turned out to be Abdul Rehman Saiyyad Ali Aydeed. He had set up bases at Salala Barkus Maisram in Hyderabad and at Naya Nagar on Mira Road. Late in the evening of 12 September, information was received from a reliable source that Nasir was to come to the Ruby Mill Compound near Ruparel College. A trap was laid and instead of surrendering to the police, Nasir chose to defy them. The police retaliated and he was killed in the encounter. The Bomb Detection Dog Squad was called for the search of his car. A huge cache of arms, ammunition, explosives, detonators and other bomb-making material along with objectionable documents pertaining to the Gujarat Muslim Revenge Force were found in his vehicle and from his house in Naya Nagar. Senior Inspector Dilip Patil, Inspector Dinesh Ahir, Sub Inspectors Kedar Pawar, Sachin Kadam, Atul Sabnis, Nivritti Kolhatkar and Raju Utekar were the officers who took part in this operation.

Struck by remorse at his part in the heinous crime which had killed and maimed innocent people, accused Zahid Yusuf Patni surrendered to us on his return from Dubai. He gave us further valuable information on the conspiracy and turned approver in the trial which helped us nail the culprits.

A huge weight lifted off my shoulders, now that we had solved the mystery of the GMRF. This detection appeared to have dealt a severe blow to the 'jihadi' modules targeting Mumbai because for quite some time thereafter, the spectre of terrorism lifted its shadow from the city. Mumbai had a welcome respite from terror, at least till the 2006 serial train blasts.

The two daughters of Hanif and Fehmida had been brought up in a very conservative manner. We had to send them to the juvenile home and later the grandparents took charge of the children. The charge sheet was filed in February 2004 against the arrested accused. The trial court sentenced Hanif, Fehmida and Ashrat to death. The High Court confirmed the death sentence in 2009 and now their appeals are pending in the Supreme Court.

Clean pickups of terrorists are not possible unless you have in your team intelligent officers and constables ready to put their lives at risk. Their experience, finesse and professionalism in handling such operations make all the difference. It is easy to deride the police and dismiss them as a corrupt lot, good only at collecting *haftas*. Little do the critics and detractors know of the perilous and high-risk work that the crude and awkward looking constables undertake to nab dangerous criminals, especially terrorists and members of organised crime syndicates. It is the need of the hour to devise a system to take better care of these officers and men, and make our detection and specialised branches expertise-based rather than tenure-based as they are today. It is these officers and men who put their lives at risk while in the line of duty, that enrich and enhance the track record of the Mumbai police and its Crime Branch giving them the aura and legendary status that they have come to acquire.

I interrogated all the accused in this satanic conspiracy. Out of all the accused I quizzed in this case, I found Fehmida to be the most radicalised and the hardest nut to crack. She also had an eighteen-year-old son, but she had assiduously kept him out of this plot. I remember saying to her, 'Tell us the truth, for the sake of your daughters. You have been so unjust to them. You have involved them in this serious crime. Such young girls who are completely dependent on you. How could you do it? How could you be so stone-hearted as a mother? Do you realise what you have done? What if your house is sealed as terrorist property and your children are thrown on the streets?'

Only when the gravity of these lines sank in that she broke down and emerged out of some kind of a bubble that she seemed to be living in. Out of the trance, she begged us to save her young daughters, whom only months ago she had used without qualms, as cover for dangerous terror operations. She had made them travel with a deadly bomb primed to explode and perilously ticking away, barely at four feet distance, in the boot of the taxi. Had it gone off earlier, the minors would have been blown to smithereens for no fault of theirs. I had not come across a precedent of a woman terrorist exposing her own minor offspring to such a grave risk. The woman was inexorable and callous. That she should have used her daughters for such dangerous work and not her son, also illustrated a peculiar mindset. As if the daughters were perfectly expendable!

20

Banished to the Wilderness

Between the Ghatkopar bus number 340 blast and the Gateway of India and Zaveri Bazar blasts, we were trying hard to ascertain the origin of the prescient apocalyptic emails. The effort had hit a dead end because the agencies stated that under the strict US privacy laws, we were not allowed to probe beyond a certain limit. Their servers were abroad and it was not possible for us to get to the root of the matter.

One evening, when I was busy with the blasts investigation, Assistant Police Inspector Ramesh Mohite, head of the Crime Branch Cyber Cell, came to see me. He had arrested a young hacker for hacking into the networks of banks and withdrawing money. Mohite wanted me to interrogate the man. I told him I was busy with the blasts investigations which were urgent. He saluted me and left, but looked thoroughly dejected. He was a conscientious officer, doing his job well, and here I was, not giving any importance to his work! That's what the look on his face said and I realised that I had erred. So I immediately sent my orderly Shashi Naik after him and called him back.

I asked Mohite to bring the hacker before me. Soon the hacker, Amit Tiwari, was brought before me and I began interrogating him. His father was a Military Intelligence Officer. When he said this, I was disgusted and rebuked him, 'You are an Indian Army officer's son and doing this sort of work? Shame on you!'

'I will work for the country, sir. Just give me a chance,' he pleaded.

The moment he said that, my mind went to the emails received from the Gujarat Muslim Revenge Force (GMRF). 'Will you help me detect where these emails come from?' I showed him the emails and asked him. I was desperate to crack their origin and he was a bright chap. He agreed. He asked for a laptop with a fast internet connection. I immediately directed my men to hire a room. They soon arranged a room in a lodge near the Babulnath temple. I used my contacts and got a shopkeeper to open his shop that night at Lamington Road to procure a laptop. I got in touch with Hathway Cable network and asked them to provide a high-speed internet connection which they provided immediately. By 4 a.m., Tiwari was in business and set to roll. Unfortunately for us, despite a lot of effort, he did not succeed. He said that proxy servers had been used to send these emails and we got nowhere.

Later this young man came out on bail and would sometimes give us alerts which I would pass on to the Commissioner of Police R.S. Sharma in good faith for verification and was wholly unaware of the two powerful lobbies within the IPS at work. I was singled out for being close to R.S. Sharma who had superseded quite a few senior IPS officers to get the coveted Commissioner's post. Also, since I had succeeded in detecting and nabbing the module responsible for the series of blasts thereby earning plaudits from the state government, I had stepped on the toes of certain powerful seniors. They anticipated that since my promotion was due shortly, I could be posted to IGP/ Joint CP posts in the city.

So taking the emails issue and saying that they were false, I had a CBI (Central Bureau of Investigation) inquiry slammed on me. It was contended and suspected that I was deliberately trying to generate false alerts to enhance my own importance. This inquiry went on for two years and took a huge toll on my peace of mind. This is what we expose ourselves to while gathering Intelligence which is a thankless task often brushed aside as a ceaseless professional hazard. On the other hand, getting blamed for Intelligence failure is the perennial tragedy of our lives. Damned if you do, damned if you don't.

Fortunately for me, the cyber cell staff and other Crime Branch teams deposed in my favour and said that whatever had been done was done in good faith and in the larger interest of the nation. A certain group of senior officers was frightened that after the detection of the Gateway of India and Zaveri Bazar blasts, my importance had risen and I might displace some officers from their posts. So they conspired to start the inquiry against me. However, despite the CBI inquiry, my good record foiled their bids to stall my promotion as the Promotion Committee promoted me and I was made Special Inspector General, Protection of Civil Rights on 27 November 2003. After four to five months there, on 1 March 2004, I was taken to the Anti-Corruption Bureau (ACB) as Special Inspector General (Maharashtra State). The same group of officers then got alarmed that I might institute inquiries against them. They began making a grievance that I could not be posted in the ACB when there was a CBI inquiry going on against me. Back I went to the DG office and was posted as Special Inspector General (Training and Special Units) for Maharashtra State on 21 July 2004. My job was to look after all the recruitment and training of officers right from constables to Deputy Superintendents of Police in the state.

Now one of the charges against me in the CBI inquiry was bogus emails, or that I was generating these emails. In fact, the Cyber Cell was using the hacker and everything was done in their presence, even after his release on bail. The hacker was used purely to get the source of the emails sent to the TV channels. His 'expertise' was being used to prevent future strikes. The officers of Cyber Cell had monitored his activities and brought the information to me which I had promptly passed on to the CP, Mumbai. Beyond this, I had had no role to play.

Another charge against me was about the Zahoor Markhanda encounter by Mumbai police under Vijay Salaskar. Zahoor Markhanda was a Dawood gang operative and had a criminal record. The charge against me was that I had engineered the killing of Zahoor Markhanda at the behest of the rival gang. His encounter had happened when I was CP, Railways. I was nowhere connected with it.

Next it was alleged, that my wife had declared five crores in the Voluntary Deposit Scheme of the Income Tax (IT) department. I told the CBI investigators to write to the IT department and ascertain the facts. The IT department wrote back saying there was no such disclosure.

The next charge was that my father, being from the film industry, had been a friend of Sanjay Dutt's father and so I had helped Sanjay Dutt. In fact, it was my investigation that had led us to the role of Sanjay Dutt and it was I who had arrested him.

It was actually a preliminary inquiry which, as per the norms, should have been over in six months. It went on dragging for two years while I was in the DG office in charge of Training. The CBI kept summoning me and I was frustrated. Nobody would tell me anything about its outcome. D. K. Sankaran, an IAS officer of the Maharashtra cadre, was then Special Secretary (Home), in Delhi. One day, in absolute frustration, I just rang him up and spoke my mind. I told him how I was being made a victim of a conspiracy and departmental jealousies. After a few days, he phoned back and said that he had called for the file and found that there was absolutely no truth in the allegations and the same was mentioned on the file! I was surprised because nobody had told me this. All that was being said was that there was an inquiry pending against me. My reputation was being tarnished through whisper campaigns and word of mouth untruths. 'Chinese Whispers' is an effective and deadly tool employed to destroy careers in the police department and the unfortunate truth is that the IPS officers behind such smear campaigns are those who are regarded as 'honest' officers in the Maharashtra cadre. I refuse to bracket them in the category of the honest. Honesty does not mean only not accepting bribes, etc. Mental integrity also is a crucial component of character. Sadly, they were sorely lacking in that virtue!

I later learned that some of my senior officers and detractors had gone to the CBI office to check on the status of the inquiry and when they found that there was no substance in the charges, they asked the CBI officers to ensure that the inquiry was made to drag on so that my career progression was halted.

At such times, besides the feeling of victimisation, despite knowing that you have done nothing wrong, you feel dirty and filthy. Then comes the thought, why did I put in so much hard work? Then you tell yourself, I will not work hard henceforth. Still, your training and conscience tell you, no, you will do your duty!

After being side-lined to the post of IG Training, I would attend the annual crime meetings and the half-yearly crime conferences where I was deputed to take down the minutes! I could see some of my colleagues gloating over my plight. It used to be humiliating and unbearable. When you have not done anything wrong, it is so difficult to withstand such an ordeal. The punishment postings proclaim that your career is over. You hear snide remarks like 'hero to zero'. You learn how some of your detractors have announced that you will never ever climb the steps of the Crime Branch again. Newspaper articles about inquiries against you are skilfully planted. The whole world comes to know when an inquiry is launched. When you are exonerated, no one even gets a whiff of it, for the newspapers are conveniently silent!

For the family, it is really hard. They suffer the most. Right through these trying times, Preeti was my 'Rock of Gibraltar.' Steadfast and unflinching. She silently and stoically suffered my regular mood swings and anger outbursts. She was the ever-present punching bag at home, absorbing the 'short fuse' of a bitter and disillusioned husband whilst simultaneously handling the needs, demands and tantrums of two growing adolescent boys.

The other two props were my sister Poonam and of course, Mama. However, Mama was not keeping well. Ten years ago she had been diagnosed with breast cancer and had to undergo surgery and chemotherapy. Though all of us were trying to lend a helping hand, Mama's chief caregiver was Poonam who handled and managed the entire medical treatment and follow-ups with sincere devotion, letting the rest of the siblings and their spouses concentrate on running their own lives and managing their young families. Despite Mama's delicate state of health, she loved going on small journeys to the temples she wanted to visit. Mama expressed her desire to visit Dharamshala, her birthplace in Himachal Pradesh that she had not visited for decades. Though it was going to be a long and strenuous journey, so firm was Mama's resolve that it was decided to risk it. Despite the strain, Mama covered all the spots, including her old ancestral home. She met a few people in the neighbourhood who could remember her and her family, besides halting at the numerous small temples that dot the countryside. She was a Ram bhakt and wanted to visit a particular Ram temple. The only description she could give was of a tree nearby which was a favourite haunt of parrots! Ultimately, the driver of the hired car managed to find such a temple. Mama eagerly entered it but to her dismay, the idols of Ram, Sita and Lakshman did not match the images in her memory. Just then the priest closed the *garbhagriha* – the sanctum sanctorum of the temple – to change the deities' regalia. When the doors opened, Mama was overjoyed. The idols were just the way she remembered them! God had fulfilled her desire and gave her darshan in the finery that she wanted for Him. He knew it would be her last visit!

She returned from Himachal completely enthralled by her

adventure. And just when we were thinking that she was out of the danger of recurrence, the disease struck again. The year 2006 saw her frequently falling ill. Medical investigations began and we found her going unusually quiet, probably because she had sensed that she did not have much time. When she got no relief, we ultimately admitted her to the Holy Family Hospital where the final diagnosis was arrived at. I still remember how lost and helpless I'd felt when the doctor notified us that the disease had spread and there was nothing more they could do. The advice was to take her home and make her comfortable.

It was a shock. I remember getting agitated with the doctor and asking him how there was nothing he could do when it was his job to save lives! Quite foolish of me, as I see it now, but I was frustrated and incensed. The other family members were desperately trying to calm me. At last, I went into the washroom and sobbed uncontrollably. The day we'd lost Dad kept coming back to me. Within seconds of his death, Mama had disappeared inside the room and emerged without *sindoor,* the vermilion powder that married women wear in the parting of their hair in some communities. Then she had held her calm and not shed a tear until the body was lifted and carried outside for the final journey. Tears ran down her cheeks, she looked so vulnerable. I had hugged her and said, 'Mama, your children are here for you! We will look after you!' Then had followed our long struggle and she had led us through it, instead of us looking after her, with the sheer strength of her character and her prayers. I despaired if it was all over?

We took her home and tried our best to make her as comfortable as possible. Every evening at seven I would leave my office and go to Bandra, only to watch her deteriorate rapidly. Soon she was totally confined to bed. Palliative care was the only treatment. The house was now a small nursing home. Sitting by her bedside and holding her hand when she could hardly talk coherently, I would remember her sitting in the veranda and waving out to me as I passed by in my car from or to my office on Carter Road. I was then the Additional CP (West Region) and unable to stop by because there was always some important meeting or urgent task to attend to! Would I be forgiven for all the visits promised to her that I had to cancel the last minute! My sitting here now when she was so drowsy, drifting off to another world, and when she could hardly comprehend or speak – of what use was it!

After Diwali, her medical condition worsened and we never realised when she had slid into a coma. Just then, I was asked to visit Russia, for an important assignment, with another colleague. I was not keen to leave Mama in this state, but Preeti and Poonam insisted that I went. Mama would never have us skip our work for anything, they reminded me. The monsoon memories of Mama wading through the waterlogged St Paul's Road and dragging us to school had a deep meaning. Duty first. So I went to Russia and dreaded every moment there, expecting the call any minute to say that she was no more, but she held on.

The end came just before midnight on 31 December 2006. After spending the evening at her bedside, Preeti and I were on our way home. We turned back when we received the call from Poonam to tell us that she was no more. The streets of Bandra were lit with fairy lights and the world around us was ushering in the new year with fireworks and music. As if the exit of a good soul is a celebration in itself! It was only then that the true meaning of the word orphan began sinking in. The next day was the funeral. Mama had left with Poonam detailed instructions on the manner she wanted the last rites to be conducted. We followed them meticulously.

Mama's passing meant losing a great source of strength, not just for me, even for Preeti. My children were deeply attached to her and took a long time to reconcile to her absence. This was the first death they had seen in the immediate family.

Hiding my emotions from Mama had always been a futile

exercise. She would always make out if something was wrong with me. Probably all mothers are made that way. They can feel the pulse of their children better than their own! So whenever I was melancholic, and down and out, feeling let down and treated unfairly, she would know. She took pride in my achievements and followed my career without asking too many questions. When I was banished to the wilderness these last four years, she would occasionally bolster my spirits by saying, 'Only the fruit-bearing trees get stones hurled at them. Your fruit is your good work. So stones are bound to be thrown at you.' And she waited patiently for the tide to turn, with unwavering faith. She was right in her belief and conviction. Soon I would be conferred the President's Distinguished Service Medal, but my dear Mama would not be there to see me receive it. Nor would she be there to watch me strain every sinew and gird myself for the Herculean battles awaiting me in the proximate horizon.

21

For the Luck of the Pot

Matka King Dies in Road Accident!

Said *The Times of India* of 14 June 2008, and went on in detail:

> Worli based matka king Suresh Kalyanji Bhagat (52) was killed along with six others in a truck-jeep collision near Alibaug on Friday afternoon. Son of the matka (gambling) king of 1960s, Kalyanji Bhagat, Suresh was returning to Mumbai in a Scorpio jeep with six others after attending a hearing in the Alibaug court regarding a pending narcotics case. At 1:45 pm near Dharamtar bridge on the Alibaug-Pen road, their jeep had a head-on collision with a truck going to Alibaug. According to the police, it was the truck driver's fault. The driver is absconding. Talking to TOI, Raigad superintendent of police Pratap Dighavkar said, the seven victims were travelling in the Scorpio that belonged to Suresh Bhagat, who is said to be a matka king staying in the BDD Chawl area (Worli). According to the Poynad police, the mishap occurred around 16 km from Alibaug town. All the seven persons travelling towards Mumbai in the Scorpio were killed in the collision, said an official.
>
> The other six victims were identified as Dharmendra Kumar Singh (38), Ramesh Bhagwan Salunke (28), Tushar K. Shah (34), Valmiki Sitaram Pawar (35), Milind Kadam (47) and Kamlesh Ashok Kamble (24). Kamlesh succumbed to injuries after he was rushed to Sion hospital. Going by the damage done to both the

> vehicles, it was a high-impact collision. Bhagat used to operate the Kalyan matka, which was earlier managed by his father. He reportedly had several matka dens in Vashi as well. According to the Mumbai police, he had extended his branches to Gujarat and Rajasthan.
>
> Suresh had been arrested a few times since 1997 for possessing narcotic substances. In 2004, he was held along with 21 others in a police raid. Suresh was also arrested in August 2000 and released on a bail of Rs 25,000.

Unless he was a matka punter, to the reader browsing the morning papers with sips of his favourite brew, it was just one of those serious motor accidents, endemic on single lane highways. The TV reportage of the earlier evening too had dedicated prominent coverage to the fatal accident. In any case, he would have no inkling whatsoever of the flurry of activity it had triggered in the Mumbai Crime Branch where the news had reached within hours of the accident.

The Poynad police station, under whose jurisdiction the accident spot fell, had learned about it on the telephone. When they reached the spot, the truck driver was nowhere on the scene. The impact of the collision was so massive that though a sturdy vehicle, the Scorpio was completely mangled and swept off the road into the paddy fields. The dumper truck was on the road but had its front severely damaged. The police rushed the injured to the hospital and, on the basis of their own report, registered the crime under sections which covered death by rash and negligent driving, by rash or negligent act not amounting to culpable homicide and by lesser offences such as failure of the driver to do his duties in case he causes an accidental injury to anyone.

Was it too much of a coincidence that just a few days prior to this accident, the Crime Branch had received for an enquiry a complaint made by the same Suresh Bhagat to the Mumbai Police Commissioner stating that he apprehended a threat to his life? And that too from Jaya Chheda – his ex-wife, their son Hitesh Bhagat and two others, Suhas Roge and Kiran Pujari! He had said that these persons wanted to eliminate him to usurp his entire matka business.

What was it about the matka business, that to wrest its control, even patricide was a small price to pay in the 'First Family' of the matka world? In the family which had already amassed a huge fortune, which could last them for generations to come. Well, the stakes were such. Knowledgeable sources estimated that the daily take-home for the matka owners could touch even a neat one crore rupees!

Matka is nothing but a lottery, or gambling with numbers. Called *ankda jugar* (literally 'figure gambling'), it had been popular in the city even in the pre-Independence days when the lucky numbers were based on the figures of opening and closing rates of cotton sold on the New York Cotton Exchange. The figures were then transmitted to the Bombay Cotton Exchange in Sewri via teleprinters. With rapid industrialisation and the growth of textile mills, ankda jugar lured the industrial workers in Mumbai as a source or rather a hope of quick money. Much like liquor, it became the despair of many a working class family. Gambling or matka dens mushroomed in and around Girangaon which became a hub of the gambling business. All would have been well for the 'entrepreneurs' in the field, had the business been legitimate, which it was not.

The Indian approach to gambling is curiously ambivalent. Sociologists say that even the Vedas have references to 'games of chance'. Dice have been found during excavations at the Indus Valley civilisation sites. Our epics and mythology have interesting stories woven around gambling. Together they acknowledge that games of chance, wagering and the cheating that goes along, have been an integral part of our life and society since time immemorial.

The first ever game of dice is believed to have been played by none other than Shiva and Shakti – Lord Shiva and his consort Goddess Parvati. The famous caves at Ellora near Aurangabad has a sculpture depicting this divine game of dice. One version goes that Shiva loses everything to Parvati, leaves her and becomes a hermit. Then Lord Vishnu intervenes, reverses the trend and makes him win it all back. Parvati harbours a nagging suspicion that Shiva is cheating. It is then that Lord Vishnu puts to rest the doubt by explaining to her that Shiva is not cheating and that the dice moves as per Lord Vishnu's wish. There is, of course, a deeper philosophical meaning to the story: the detachment of Shiva from Shakti; the shaping of the universe through the game of chance; the overall divine control over destinies and the freedom of choice one has within the parameters of that control; the need to exercise self-restraint and so on. What is interesting though is that it is believed that the game was played on the day of Diwali and that Goddess Parvati was so pleased with it that she declared that whosoever plays dice or gambles on Diwali day will be blessed for the rest of the year by Lakshmi who is Lord Vishnu's consort and the Goddess of wealth and prosperity. So, in many parts of the country, there is a tradition, even among the conservative and the elite, of playing cards on Diwali, after the worship of Goddess Lakshmi, with at least nominal stakes.

The Gujarati community has a tradition of playing cards with stakes for almost a month, before and on the night of Janmashtami – the birth of Lord Krishna. On Janmashtami night, conservative Gujarati families including the womenfolk who observe a fast for the day, play cards as an auspicious token. Sociologists say that in ancient times, among the prosperous elite, opulent living, promiscuity, gambling and drinking were accepted forms of indulgences which later even the lower rungs of the social ladder began to imitate. The epics portray that in the reign of King Kansa, the ruler of Mathura, these vices reached Gomorrhean proportions prompting Lord Krishna to take birth to destroy the evils and restore order. In commemoration of this, for a month or so till His birth anniversary, society and religious sanction permit mortals to let their hair down and indulge in a few 'harmless' vices, after which one must get back to being good and pious again!

Lord Krishna, the most indulgent and tolerant of all the gods when it comes to human failings, is connected with another instance of the game of dice – *Dyuta* – in the great epic Mahabharata. In a game of Dyuta, King Yudhishthira gambles away his kingdom, his brothers and even his wife Draupadi. She has to invoke Lord Krishna who rushes to her help, to save her honour from humiliation. A chain of events follow, culminating in the two branches of the family fighting out the Great War of eighteen days to establish their claim over the throne. On the battlefield, Lord Krishna reveals the *Bhagavad Gita* to the wavering Arjuna to help him gather his nerves and fight. In the tenth chapter of the *Bhagavad Gita*, Lord Krishna describes his several manifestations and his opulence in all its glory. He is all-pervading, and he is the essence of all forms of good and all forms of evil. 'I am the gambling of the cheats!' He declares. So, of all the instincts and prowess of the cheats, it is the gambling instinct that is the supreme manifestation, equated with god.

For a culture that tended to look upon gambling so indulgently and sanctioned its use to mark religious-based festivities, treating it as an illegal activity seemed to have created a delicate problem, both for the police as well as for the moral guardians, who after all came from the same society and cultural background. Unlike other hardcore and traditional crimes, gambling was perhaps regarded as a lesser evil and treated lightly by society and its law enforcement agencies. When forced underground, it was to spread its tentacles insidiously and develop the capability of subverting the entire system. Bookies would thrive and the gambling den owners would rake in the moolah right up to the eighties. The money made out of it was cleverly laundered to start legitimate businesses and to create benami properties. A full-fledged underground industry developed around it, with many mouths feeding on its smooth running, and doing everything in their capacity to ensure its continuation.

Kalyanji Bhagat was one such bookie from the Kutchi community, a hardy people from the drought and famine-prone Kutch region of Gujarat, an erstwhile princely state. Forced to migrate in search of livelihood, they settled not only in Mumbai but in different parts of the globe, making fortunes with hard work, thrift, sharp business acumen and an inherent penchant for taking risks.

Kalyanji was from a farming family and came to Bombay in 1941. It is believed that 'Bhagat' which means 'devotee' was the title conferred on his family by the ruler of Kutch for their piety and religiosity. Living in a small tenement in the BDD chawls in Worli, Kalyanji did an array of odd jobs, including hawking spices door to door and managing a provision store. But the burning desire to make more money and in the shortest possible time gravitated him into the world of ankda jugar. Kalyanji began receiving and underwriting bets on the New York Cotton Exchange figures. Finally, the prayers and devotion of the 'Bhagats' was answered as Goddess Lakshmi opened the doors of prosperity to Kalyanji Bhagat.

Then came a turn of events that challenged Kalyanji's ingenuity. In the mid-fifties, the figures of the cotton rate became too predictable to wager bets on, and in 1961, even the New York Cotton Exchange stopped the practice. Kalyanji was looking for alternate strategies and options to keep the business going. Taking a cue from the American numbers' game and lotteries, he hit upon the idea of 'the luck of the pot' – the simple way of drawing lots from chits in a pot. The name he chose for it was matka which in colloquial usage means the regular earthenware pot. In 1962, he started the game matka from a notional pot. Initially, he used packs of picture cards to draw the winning figures. He must have been a master of human psychology and a marketing guru. Without any formal training in sales and marketing, he succeeded in building a brand out of the simple name he had given to his business. It became hugely popular with gamblers in the city. To win his customer's trust in the authenticity of the operation, he instituted a syndicate to oversee the process of picking cards. Also, even the poorest punter could wager a bet and genuinely felt that he stood a good chance to win, as bets would be taken even with a single rupee and on single digits.

Like all illegal activities, with bribery and corruption, Kalyanji's 'Worli Matka' or 'Kalyan Matka' began spreading its tentacles all over India. People from all walks of life, the wealthy including film personalities, got hooked and stories of fortunes made or lost in a matter of hours began circulating, adding to the charm and aura of matka. Soon it shifted from Worli to Zaveri Bazar and another sharp mind was drawn to it from a community close to Kalyanji's, in geographical proximity as well as in business acumen. This was Ratan Khatri, a Sindhi, who joined Kalyanji as a manager. The matka also acquired an international dimension as punters began betting from the Middle East and the USA. In 1964, Khatri broke away from Kalyanji and formed 'Ratan Matka'. Such breaking or branching away did not matter much from a financial perspective. The 'daily turnover' had already reached close to a whopping one crore, which meant that there was still enough to go round even if more players entered the business. It soon led to the creation of multiple matka kingdoms with names like Vasant Shah and Pappu Savla getting added as chieftains.

Kalyanji Bhagat died in 1993 and of his three sons, Suresh Bhagat took over the business. The going was good until the underworld dons, on the lookout for as many greener pastures and milch animals as possible, turned their attention to matka. Crime syndicates soon began extending 'protection' and 'security' to the matka kings for hefty fees and for a share in the booty. Violence therefore could not be far behind! In 1998, Vasant Shah was murdered, allegedly by the Arun Gawli gang, to protect the interest of the rival matka king Pappu Savla.

When it became increasingly apparent that the matka operators were getting linked with the underworld and pumping money into it, the law enforcement agencies soon focussed their attention and became harsher, forcing the matka business to shift out of Mumbai to states like Gujarat, Rajasthan and Madhya Pradesh. Moreover, with the advancement in technology, punters started turning to newer variations of gambling, like online gambling and betting on cricket matches. The old-timers began complaining of deterioration of 'standards' and 'values' in the matka operations. The old matka kings had an aura around their persona which thrived on the myths linked to them: they adhered to certain norms and ethics which they never compromised on; their lucky draws were genuine; the numbers were announced by following set rules; they did not mind suffering losses; they did not rig the draws; they were generous to a fault with their staff, managers and 'franchisees'; they were philanthropists.

The Gen-Next, however, had no such aura or qualms. On the contrary, it was perceived as lacking in commitment to the clients and patrons. With modern technology like computers, cheating became easier and it was suspected that to ensure maximum profits for the owners, draws were now regularly being rigged. Only those numbers were declared winners on which the least bets were received. Though it was difficult to estimate the exact figures, in 2008, the daily profit accruing of the entire business was rumoured to be around rupees one crore.

Despite the astronomical wealth, Suresh Bhagat's personal life was far from happy. In 1979, he had an arranged marriage with Jaya Chheda, daughter of a man who was much respected in the Kutchi community. The marriage was celebrated with much pomp and fanfare at the Brabourne Stadium. Those who knew him said that like his father, Suresh was kind-hearted and generous, with not a very lavish lifestyle. He was frugal and thrifty. He enjoyed simple pastimes like listening to Hindi film songs. However, he soon became addicted to drugs and, as a consequence thereof, began losing his grip over the network of bookies. Jaya Chheda had learnt the ropes from her husband and, as he lost control, she stepped in to fill the vacuum. Probably, the bookies had also started depending on her. Within the extended family, too, she was quite unpopular. She soon began getting more and more frustrated with Suresh's downward slide and was hell-bent in not allowing the business to fall into the hands of Suresh's brothers. She began seizing control and succeeded to a large extent, with the help of her own trusted relatives and cronies. Some estimated that she took over nearly eighty per cent of the matka empire worth hundreds of crores and her daily net earnings from matka were thought to be in the vicinity of twenty-five lakhs and above.

Suresh's drug addiction and his frugal lifestyle soon became a bone of contention between 'the first couple of matka'. The arguments and altercations became more frequent and bitter. The rift soon culminated in a divorce. Their only child Hitesh, though in his early Thirties, was a spoilt and pampered brat. He was the antithesis of his father. Flamboyant and a worshipper of the good things in life. A flashy playboy! The mother had gifted him a Lamborghini for one of his birthdays. During one of his speed rushes, he had crashed it on a lamp post causing extensive damage to the car. The mechanic and the spare parts had to be flown in from Italy.

After the divorce, Jaya began staying with her parents in Pantnagar in the eastern suburbs, but she continued to control the matka business. Hitesh continued to stay with the father but was on the side of his doting and pampering mother who was fiercely protective about him. What had complicated matters further between the couple was Jaya's friendship with a dubious and ambitious character, an Arun Gawli acolyte called Suhas Roge. He used to be Suresh Bhagat's bodyguard and also ran a non-descript newspaper called *Mumbai Crime*. The intuitive Suresh Bhagat had sacked him as Roge had his eye not only on Suresh Bhagat's wife but also his matka business. The relationship between Roge and Jaya soon developed into a torrid affair. It became their mission to gain full and complete control over Suresh Bhagat's matka business. This would not have been possible unless Suresh went out of it completely. They hit upon a devious strategy to get Suresh out of their way by getting him entrapped in a series of narcotics-related cases. They planted drugs in his car and tipped the police about it. Suresh kept finding himself frequently behind bars, but to the dismay and frustration of Jaya and Roge, like the legendary phoenix, Suresh would get released on bail and be back in charge. Suresh, too, did not want to let go of the goose that laid the golden egg and the power that accrued to the owner of the goose.

Then, one day, even Hitesh was arrested in a narcotics case along with his father, which clearly was not part of Jaya's design. This infuriated Jaya no end. Her anger knew no bounds and she decided that Suresh had to be eliminated at all costs. She planned to execute the murder with the help of Suhas Roge and his men. Tempting them with handsome rewards, she began hatching the conspiracy. Suresh somehow got the whiff of the plans and, in April 2008, he complained to the Commissioner of Police, Mumbai that he feared danger to his life from Jaya and her cohorts. When he felt that his pleas were not receiving the requisite attention and seriousness from the police, he even filed a writ petition in the Bombay High Court.

When such was the background, the news of the accident which reached the Crime Branch on the afternoon of 13 June was bound to raise our suspicion. Our hackles were further raised when an informant contacted me shortly thereafter to confirm that there was more to the accident than met the eye and that the conspirators were all geared up to ensure that the local police treated the case as a simple accident.

I immediately shared the information with Pratap Dighavkar, the Raigad Superintendent of Police, and he promised to take immediate steps to look into the matter. Since we were enquiring into the recent complaint of Suresh Bhagat, I dispatched Inspector Ramesh Mahale to Poynad to enquire further and assist the local police. In the meantime, Superintendent of Police, Raigad directed the local Crime Branch of the district to start a parallel investigation. From the mobile numbers written in the driver's cabin of the truck, they contacted the truck owners Anand Patil and Ajimuddin Maula Saheb Shaikh, who lived in Dahisar. The Raigad Crime Branch team immediately rushed to the house of Ajimuddin and after questioning him got the details of the absconding driver Pravin Shetty, an electrician, who was traced on 14 June itself.

Suresh Bhagat's siblings levelled serious allegations against Raigad police and cast aspersions on the integrity of their investigation. On the night of 13 June itself, R. R. Patil, the then Deputy Chief Minister and Home Minister, had enquired about the accident case and sought my opinion about its authenticity. I had informed him what my source had conveyed and expressed my strong suspicion that the accident could have been stage-managed. With this background, the government of Maharashtra transferred the investigation of this case to the Mumbai Crime Branch on 1 July. In the meanwhile, it had become more than clear that the offence came under the provisions of the Maharashtra Control of Organised Crime Act (MCOCA) which was applied to the case and the investigation was now under ACP Duraphe of the Crime Branch. Conspirators Jaya Chheda, Kiran Pujari, Harish Mandvikar, Suhas Roge, Hitesh Bhagat and Kiran Amle were evading arrests. Hitesh was arrested from Hotel Sun and Sand in Goa where he was ensconced with a starlet. Not surprisingly, this tip-off was received from a pimp who supplied high-end escorts! Jaya Chheda, Suhas Roge and Harish Mandvikar were arrested from Daman. Kiran Amle too was arrested.

The team led by ACP Duraphe and Inspector Mahale painstakingly conducted a thorough investigation tracing a shocking chain of circumstances that pointed to nothing but the absolute guilt of Jaya Chheda and her co-conspirators.

The boon to investigators in Kaliyug is mobile telephony which ensures that howsoever a criminal may try to cover his or her tracks, the truth will come out and Satyayug will shine bright even in Kaliyug. The Call Detail Records (CDRs) and Cell ID records of the cell phones of the conspirators, their drivers and friends left clear imprints of how they were all in touch with each other. Substantial cash paid by Jaya Chheda to Pujari, Mandvikar and associates was recovered and seized. It was confirmed that Jaya, Roge and Hitesh had engineered police raids on Suresh Bhagat to get him arrested for possession of narcotics through Kiran Pujari who was paid handsomely for his role. Kiran Pujari operated as an informer to various investigative agencies. He had also positioned himself as an influential social worker and hustler who 'got jobs done'. Things came to a boil when Suresh Bhagat filed the writ petition before the High Court against Jaya and her cohorts. The conspirators met at Jaya's place where Suhas Roge declared that he would 'ensure a permanent solution for Suresh Bhagat'. Jaya, the consummate manipulator, needled him that he merely talked and never acted. Piqued by this ridicule, Roge vowed that he would get Suresh Bhagat killed in a fake motor accident on his return to Mumbai from the Alibaug court, provided Hitesh Bhagat was not travelling with his father at that time. For the court hearings, Hitesh used to travel to Alibaug in the same car as his father. The 'Fixer' Kiran Pujari's help was needed to ensure that the police machinery treated this homicide as an accident. Kiran Pujari assured all help. Roge then contacted Harish Mandvikar, a 'bhai' from the slums of Borsapada in Kandivali, and gave him the *supari* or contract to eliminate Suresh Bhagat in a motor accident for seventy lakhs. Mandvikar was the archetypal local goonda-turned-social worker who had also formed a Dahi Handi mandal in Borsapada, of which his friends, electrician Pravin Shetty and cable operator Kiran Amle, were also members.

Dahi Handi is again a festival connected with Lord Krishna. It recreates the joy little Krishna spread with his innocent pranks in Gokul where he grew up among the community of cowherds. Dahi means yoghurt and handi means earthen pot, incidentally another name for matka. The festival has now reached many parts of the country, but it originated in Maharashtra and is observed with great fervour in Mumbai and Thane cities. It falls in the rainy season, the day after Janmashtami (Gokulashtami) which is the eighth day of the waning moon in the month of Shravan.

The main activity of the day is mimicking young Krishna and his friends who formed human pyramids to raid the earthenware pots of cream and yoghurt hung out of their reach by the harried housewives of Gokul. Forming human pyramids in the streets is not an easy job, especially when it rains or when spectators throw water on the participants to prevent them from breaking the handi. It needs practice and coordination, with sturdy team members manning the base and the lighter, nimble-footed ones making the higher tiers. The one who goes to the apex to break the handi is usually a child. The participants are called 'Govindas' and they start practising for the day well in advance. On the day of the festival, dahi handis are tied high up in the streets and cash prizes are declared for the group that manages to break them. To the tune of traditional songs and slogans, Govindas roam all day long, from locality to locality, and try their luck at breaking as many pots as possible and bag the prize money.

Originally the festival was a fun-filled day with just a little bit of cash incentive thrown in for the youth to show off their skills. Over the years, like everything else, it has got highly commercialised, criminalised and also politicised. The informal groups of Govindas are now Govinda *'pathaks'* (squads) who don specially made T-shirts and are carted from handi to handi in trucks, escorted by their 'generals' on motorcycles and in cars. They are backed by organisations called Govinda or Dahi Handi 'mandals' (circles or groups) that are sponsored by local bigwigs or dons or political parties. The prize money now runs into tens of lakhs of rupees and even film stars put in their appearances at the venues to affirm their solidarity with the sponsors.

The height at which the handis should be hung is a contentious issue, but Govindas vie to make pyramids as high as nine human tiers and keep sustaining grievous injuries in the process. Of late, girls have started breaching this male bastion. Even the Spaniards now make it to Mumbai to take a shot at the pots, giving this Indian festival an international flavour! Whether this simple annual street sport will eventually take a new avatar into a mega league sport is anyone's guess. For the police, however, the day is no fun and frolic. Keeping an eagle eye on the lumpen elements who take to the streets on that day, crowd and traffic management and not to mention preventing a communal flare-up, are issues uppermost whilst planning elaborate police arrangements for the celebrations.

The Dahi Handi mandals, thus, become a tool to exercise control over the community and draw young people to crime syndicates and political parties who use the festival to recruit, cultivate, organise and reward cadres. Harish Mandvikar ran one such mandal in Borsapada and, in furtherance of taking the supari, formed a pathak of his followers to eliminate Suresh Bhagat.

The conspirators had originally planned the 'accident' for 15 May 2008 which was the date for the hearing of the narcotics case in the court at Alibaug. Jaya had to devise some excuse to keep Hitesh away from the court on that day. She instructed Hitesh's Advocate, Somet Shirsat, to secure an exemption for Hitesh on health grounds, which the advocate promptly did. Thus, she ensured that Hitesh would not be in the car on 15 May.

Mandvikar had a friend called Ajimuddin Shaikh who owned a dumper truck which Mandvikar regularly hired for the Dahi Handi festival. Mandvikar approached Ajimuddin and said that he needed the truck for some work. Ajimuddin did not have a driver, but Mandvikar said that he would arrange for one. When asked about the nature of the work, Mandvikar said that he wanted to use it to break someone's limbs! Ajimuddin baulked at the answer and when Pravin Shetty came to pick up the truck, Ajimuddin asked him if they were really going to break someone's limbs. Pravin Shetty denied it and asked him to have faith in them before driving off with the truck. However, on that day, the truck reached the designated accident spot late and the plan was aborted. Pravin Shetty returned the truck to Ajimuddin in the evening. Suresh Bhagat had escaped death, but not for too long.

The next date of hearing was fixed for 13 June 2008. Suresh Bhagat's luck was fast running out and his days were numbered. On 12 June, Jaya asked advocate Shirsat to convey to the court that Hitesh was still bedridden. So the next day, Hitesh did not accompany his father to Alibaug to attend the trial. Mandvikar again arranged for Ajimuddin's truck to be picked up by Pravin Shetty who told Ajimuddin this time that they needed it to get some machinery on hire from Chiplun in Ratnagiri district.

Mandvikar and Kiran Amle were in Alibaug to keep close tabs on Suresh Bhagat's movements that day. Suresh Bhagat, his nephew Tushar Shah, his armed bodyguards Dharmendra Singh and Milind Namdeo Kadam, his advocate Kamlesh Bhagwan Salunkhe, servant Valmiki Sitaram Pawar and one Kamlesh Ashok Kamble went to Alibaug by the Scorpio to attend the court. After the hearing, they left the court around 1 p.m. in the Scorpio for the return journey to Mumbai. Harish Mandvikar began following the Scorpio in a Maruti Swift car driven by Kiran Amle.

This time Pravin Shetty was punctual and stationed with the truck near the Vadkhal village on the Alibaug-Panvel road. Mandvikar was in constant touch with him on Kiran Amle's cell phone. As per the plan, Pravin Shetty drove the truck up to the Dharamtar Bridge and parked it at the corner of the Alibaug-Panvel road near Shahbaj village, waiting for the signal from Mandvikar to advance. Mandvikar called Shetty and made sure that he advanced in time to spot the approaching Scorpio. Taking a cue from Mandvikar, at the opportune moment, Shetty revved up the truck and hurtled headlong into the speeding Scorpio as it neared Fauji Dhaba. He jumped off the truck in time to save himself, but still injured his nose and head. The ill-fated occupants of the Scorpio stood no chance whatsoever. Pravin Shetty then took to his heels through the paddy fields and, after a while, came to Sai Kutir, a restaurant at Vadkhal Naka, which had a public phone booth. On being questioned about his injuries, he gave the restaurant staff the cock-and-bull story that he had had a fight with the cleaner of the truck he was driving and the cleaner had hit him with an iron tommy. From the telephone booth, he established contact with Harish Mandvikar and Kiran Amle who instructed him to wait there. A short wait later, the former picked him up in the Swift to ferry him back to Kandivali.

Around 2 p.m., Mandvikar called Ajimuddin and informed him about the accident. When Ajimuddin learned that seven persons had been killed, he was shocked and annoyed. This was followed by the Poynad police also calling him and informing him about the accident. Mandvikar assured Ajimuddin that he would cover all his losses and more. However, it also dawned on him that Ajimuddin could spill the beans. So he sent two men to him with ten lakhs, but Ajimuddin did not accept any money on the bizarre ground that instead of just one, they had killed seven persons! Ajimuddin met driver Pravin Shetty and told him that he would have to accompany him the next day to Poynad police station. With the help of another friend, Ajimuddin took the injured Pravin Shetty to a private hospital for treatment. The attending doctor was informed that Shetty had accidentally got hurt by the shutter of his truck. The doctor advised hospital admission, but Shetty declined, giving a written excuse that he had some important work to attend to. He then went to Kiran Amle's house from where he was later picked up by the police.

At the time of the murder, Suhas Roge was in Mumbai. About two hours after the murder, he met and briefed 'social worker' Kiran Pujari about the day's happenings. Kiran Pujari assured all the help with the authorities to ensure that the murder would pass off as an accident and no further action would be initiated. He had the contacts and the financial clout to ensure the 'cover-up'.

Mandvikar had already received ten lakhs from Jaya Chheda for the job. After the accident, he reported his success to her and she sent him an additional thirty-five lakhs through Roge on the same day. She assured him that she would pay the remaining twenty-five lakhs as soon as the dust settled.

Hitesh Bhagat who was supposed to be ill and bedridden had flown to Bangkok with a friend, eleven hours before the murder, on tickets booked three days earlier. They returned on 14 June 2008 and checked into a hotel room booked in the name of the friend. Thereafter, until his arrest in Goa, Hitesh stayed in different hotels in Mumbai and Goa in rooms booked under the names of his friends.

Accused Kiran Pujari and Ajimuddin Shaikh turned approvers for the prosecution in the case.

In all, the accused made twenty attempts to secure bail from the High Court alone. Four of the accused even approached the Supreme Court for bail. But none of these attempts succeeded.

At the trial, Special Public Prosecutor Kalpana Chavan examined eighty witnesses for the prosecution. The accused tried every trick in the book to tempt some key witnesses to make them turn hostile. A few witnesses did fall prey to the allurements, but it failed to make any dent in the prosecution case. One attempt to make a key witness turn hostile backfired to such an extent that a trap was laid and the person offering the bribe was arrested. An offence was registered against him and the bribe amount of one crore was seized and deposited in the state coffers. A battery of renowned defence counsel appeared for the accused but in vain. On 31 July 2013, Judge S. G. Shete sentenced all the six accused to imprisonment for life.

25 August was the date on which Dahi Handi was celebrated in 2008. It must have been a sombre affair for the Borsapada Dahi Handi mandal that year, and every year thereafter, what with the cream of its leadership cooling their heels as state guests! Leaders who should have confined themselves to making human pyramids and snatching some pure joy out of the earthenware pots filled with curd and cash! Instead, they had opted for and lunged at the elusive matka, the attractive but hopelessly unsavoury notional pot that has rarely brought lasting pleasure to anyone. They had ventured into dangerous and unknown terrain at their own peril and played a losing gamble. Hopefully, their failure has served as an eye-opener and a salutary example for the other Govindas who might have seriously considered following in their footsteps.

22

Breaching the Citadel

It was a dull morning, like most Monday mornings in Mumbai, and a little grim, for it was nearing the end of Chaitra – the month that brings in the hot summer. It was particularly sombre for the Marathi heartlands of Mumbai. They had finished three festive weeks celebrating the fight of Good over Evil.

First, they had Gudi Padwa – the Marathi New Year day, reminding them, among other things, of the coronation of Lord Rama on his return to Ayodhya after the victory over Ravana. Then came Chaitra Navaratri – nine nights to worship nine forms of Shakti – the Goddess of strength who never failed the righteous. It culminated with Ram Navami – the birthday of Lord Rama. The following day, 14 April was the birth anniversary of a great icon of modern India – Dr Babasaheb Ambedkar. Another big day for the fight for justice. Just seven days from Lord Rama's birthday came the birthday of his loyal follower and general – Hanuman – celebrated with great fanfare on Sunday, 20 April. In between snuggled Mahavir Jayanti – the birth anniversary of the founder of peace-loving and non-violent Jainism whose affluent followers had done all the right things to mark the day.

And today it was 21 April 2008. Good food, blaring music, rituals, sermons and speeches were over and Mumbaikars were preparing to go back to the daily boredom of ordinary life. Their tired police force expected a little respite after the elaborate bandobasts deployed to ensure that no one gave cause to anyone to feel offended on behalf of their communities.

It was still the early hours of the morning. The sun had not yet unleashed its fury and people were busy getting their milk, bread, eggs and newspapers. In the heart of the city, a chawl – a large residential building divided into many small, one or two-room tenements offering basic accommodation to its inhabitants – had awakened to a daily routine. A *paperwallah,* with the usual bundle of newspapers under his arm, entered and hurried past the young boys at the big gate who were still stifling their yawns. Then entered the *doodhwala* – the milkman – carrying his packets, as usual. Residents who had to leave early were rushing out, clutching bags with lunchboxes, to catch buses and trains. A black and yellow taxi, piled with overhead luggage, entered the gates. Inside was a fatigued couple just off an overnight train, yearning for a good cup of tea and a hot bath.

The paperwallah soon finished dropping the newspapers and the doodhwallah his milk packets. Old friends that they were, and a little lighter in their load now, they stopped in the passage to greet each other for a brief banter before leaving the chawl. Just then the paperwallah remembered that he had to make an important call. The days when anyone and everyone could own mobile phones were already here. He dialled a number to deliver an important message. As he disconnected, the doodhwallah cracked a good joke. The paperwallah slapped his back in appreciation, bid him *au revoire* and made his way to the gate.

Just as he reached the gate, a car arrived. He helped the boy at the gate to open it for the car.

As for the doodhwallah, he appeared to be a little relaxed today. Instead of leaving the chawl in a rush, he stopped to keep the lift waiting for the visitors who got off the car. Four impressive gentlemen took the lift to the second floor. The man they wanted to meet was there, a lean, swarthy man, with a large moustache, engrossed in a conversation with two men in black coats – lawyers on way to courts who had made an early morning detour for an esteemed client. He looked up at the four men and gaped. Had he recognised them? Of course. He was Arun Gawli and these very men had arrested him fourteen years back for murder. The murder was of Ramesh More, the Shiv Sena legislator. And he knew why they were here today. For the same reason that they had arrested his brother Vijay a few weeks back.

Gawli knew his game was up. He got up and requested the officers to let him wear his trousers and use the toilet. He was permitted to do so, albeit with the toilet door ajar. He was taken by the lift to the ground floor. Just then a few ladies rushed to the ground floor and started shouting slogans, condemning the police action. They were in too much of a shock to do a good job of it. The Deputy Commissioner with more reinforcements had already entered Dagdi Chawl. Dagdi means 'made of stone'. Gawli's famed stone fortress had finally been breached.

The paperwallah was Constable Asam Farooqui. Constable Mahesh Bagwe was the doodhwallah. Constable Arun Adam accompanied by a lady constable were the 'outstation passengers' in the taxi. The four officers who took Gawli under arrest were Assistant Police Inspector Dinesh Kadam and his team comprising Crime Branch officers Dhananjay Daund, Shivaji Sawant and Constable Rajendra Ramade. They had been waiting at Jacob Circle, 150 metres from Dagdi chawl for Farooqui's call. *'Doosare maale pe baitha hai.... Do vakeel ke saath,'* (He is sitting on the second floor with two advocates) he said.

Gawli was bundled into the police vehicle and with sirens blaring was whisked away to the Crime Branch Unit III office at N.M. Joshi Marg. The entire operation took no more than fifteen minutes. These were probably the longest fifteen minutes of my life. I was the Joint Commissioner of Police (Crime) and responsible for this entire operation. Had it gone out of control, the buck would have stopped at me. Even a minor error or a few minutes' delay by the paperman, milkman or the passengers in the taxi could have jeopardised our entire plan. The pessimist that I am, I was not at all sure that it would go this smoothly. So when the team phoned me to report success, immediately after they left Dagdi Chawl with Gawli, I pinched myself to check if it was not a dream.

Gawli had floated a political party called the Akhil Bharatiya Sena and was elected to the Maharashtra Legislative Assembly. The proper procedure had to be followed to arrest a sitting MLA and we immediately informed the Hon'ble Speaker of his arrest.

So now Arun Gawli was under arrest for an offence registered on 25 March 2008 by Unit III of the Crime Branch. It was lodged by a builder called Nandkumar Naik who owned a firm called Chaitanya Developers which constructed buildings for the Slum Rehabilitation Authority (SRA). Sometime in 2005 his office received the first 'tele-summon' from Dagdi Chawl: *'Nandu naik la Dagdi Chalit bhetaila sang,'* said the messenger who called himself Raju. It meant: tell Nandu Naik to meet us at Dagdi Chawl. Calls from the Dagdi Chawl, or from Dubai or Malaysia are the most dreaded of calls for a Mumbai businessman. Their initial response is generally how Naik reacted. Out of fear, he avoided attending to the calls himself and neither did he have the courage to approach the police.

When three or four of his calls did not elicit the desired response, Raju scaled up the pressure. The next call said that since Naik had not turned up at Dagdi Chawl even after four calls, he will have to be eliminated. Naik and his partner checked the telephone number. It showed that the calls were from the Byculla Exchange, the exchange under which came Dagdi Chawl. Naik's office staff was terrified. So Naik had no choice but to answer the next call himself which came in November 2005. Raju greeted him with the choicest of abuses, directed him to be at

Dagdi Chawl at 6 the next evening and said, 'If you don't come to Dagdi Chawl tomorrow, we will send you up in the clouds.'

After a sleepless night, Nandkumar Naik stood on the pavement of Dagdi Chawl at 6 o'clock sharp the next evening. To his surprise, nobody contacted him and he returned home after a wait of one and a half hours. This was the gang's way of testing the victim's intentions. Had he come genuinely to bow before 'Daddy' or was he part of a trap?

After a couple of anxious days, Naik received a call from Raju in the morning, asking him to come sharp at noon to the Dagdi Chawl gate. Fear carried Naik to Dagdi Chawl and after a short wait, he was approached by a man who asked his name. When Naik gave his name, the man said that he was Sudhir Ghorpade and it was he who had made all the calls as Raju. Ghorpade led Naik inside Dagdi Chawl to a room which he called '*bhajanachi kholi*'. The black humour hidden in this nomenclature was enough to send shivers down Naik's already broken spine. It means 'room where prayers or hymns are sung'. After a short wait in the 'prayer room', a man in his early forties entered. 'I am Vijaybhau Ahir, Gawli's brother. Big builders in the Dadar area have given us fifty lakhs each. You must give us twenty-five lakhs,' he told Naik. Naik begged for Ahir's mercy and said that he was doing very small SRA work and could not pay twenty-five lakhs. Ahir then agreed to make a special case and settled for ten lakhs. Naik put up an Oscar-winning performance, crying about his family liabilities. He got the amount further scaled down to seven lakhs to be paid in instalments.

From December 2005 Ghorpade began visiting the office of Chaitanya Developers to collect the instalments, the last of which was made in May 2006. Naik hoped that his ordeal would now be over, but it was not so. During the Navaratri festival, Ghorpade again descended on Chaitanya Developers and extorted one lakh as donation. In June-July 2007, the extortion calls began again.

Naik chose to ignore them but then a ruffian calling himself Dinesh Narkar came to the office and delivered a fresh invitation to Dagdi Chawl. When Naik did not comply, Narkar again paid a visit to Naik's office. This time he placed a revolver on the table, yanked out the telephone wire and slapped the employee who told him that Naik was not in the office. He carried out a search of the office which did not yield Naik. He left, but not before delivering an ominous threat, 'Death would soon visit Nandkumar Naik if he does not come to Dagdi Chawl.' Then after five to six days, Narkar suddenly landed in Naik's office and made Naik speak on the phone with Vijay Ahir. Ahir abused him and asked him to come immediately to Dagdi Chawl. Naik begged for forgiveness and asked for some time.

On the evening of 24 March 2008, Naik's office received a call that the next day Vijay Ahir would be sending Dinesh Narkar for three lakhs. When Naik expressed his inability to pay, he was told that he would be eliminated if he did not pay up.

Now Nandkumar Naik and his partner were in a state of despair. They could bear the ordeal no more and decided to approach the police. So the next day, instead of waiting for Narkar, Nandkumar Naik ended up at the Crime Branch Unit III office in the compound of N.M. Joshi Marg police station and registered an offence under the provisions of the Arms' Act along with extortion and criminal intimidation. The investigations began. Soon Dinesh Narkar, Sudhir Ghorpade, Vijay Ahir, Pratap Godse and a few others were arrested. Pratap Godse was the President of Akhil Bharatiya Sena's Saki Naka unit and Sudhir Ghorpade was a Central Railway employee. Sustained interrogation revealed that Arun Gawli, the sitting MLA representing the Chinchpokli constituency, was himself actively involved in this extortion. So naturally, we had to arrest Gawli.

Not for nothing was Gawli called 'Daddy' by his gang. He had created a protective umbrella for his members. Like other gangs – of Dawood, Chhota Rajan and Amar Naik – Gawli's gang was run like a 'Company' with a 'human resource management' policy in place. Dagdi Chawl looked a chawl like any other, but it was a cleverly manned citadel housing the 'Corporate Office' of the gang. It was well-nigh impossible for the police to come anywhere near Dagdi Chawl.

The gang had a multilayer system of keeping a watch in and around Dagdi Chawl. The outer circle of 'watchers' sometimes had very young boys aged fourteen to sisteen years. They kept a watch for any police or rival gang activity in and around Byculla railway station, S. Bridge, Bakri Adda and Byculla Fire Brigade station. Then there was an inner circle on watch duties in and around the surrounding buildings on Dagdi Chawl's immediate periphery. Lastly was the innermost circle who performed 'close proximity' duties for Daddy and the other important gang leaders inside Dagdi Chawl. They carried weapons in case of an attack. In the 80s and through the 90s, the monthly salaries of watchers on these three circles were rupees 5,000, 10,000 and 15,000 respectively. These were princely sums then.

The gang also paid a one-time compensation to the family members of gangsters killed by the rival gangs or in police encounters. Members killed in police encounters were paid one lakh each while those killed by a rival gang were paid only 50,000 rupees each as their death was attributed to their own negligence! Even a pension scheme was started and its amount depended on the rank of the member in the hierarchy, based on his 'performance'. All these amounts were revised to be in sync with the rising inflation.

The gang also had a 'legal cell', responsible for engaging, liaising with and briefing the lawyers handling their court cases. Once the trial commenced, the legal cell had to win over or threaten the prosecution witnesses and induce them to turn hostile to ensure acquittals. All this was done very surreptitiously, most times without the investigating officer even getting a whiff of it. The gang also looked after members' welfare inside lock-ups and jails. Jails like the Arthur Road Jail, Mumbai, the Harsul Jail in Aurangabad and the Amravati Central Jail had a room or a house rented nearby where cooks were hired to dish out meals for the incarcerated gang members and *dabbas* (tiffin boxes) would be ferried to the jail in auto rickshaws and small cars throughout the day.

With such a security system in place, and manned by such loyal employees, policemen in uniform would be identified some distance away from Dagdi Chawl. Our previous experience revealed that the moment police presence was noticed, the women and children in Dagdi Chawl would form a human wall and prevent the police team from reaching the second or third floor where Gawli resided with his family. Gawli would disappear in the maze of rooms or hidden cavities inside the chawl and get ample opportunity to create a mini 'uprising' in the area.

So how do we breach the fortress? How could we ferret him out of Dagdi Chawl? To chalk out the plan, ACP Ashok Durafe, Assistant Police Inspectors Dinesh Kadam and Divakar Shelke assembled in my office along with the Deputy Commissioner of Police and other senior officers. Everybody was unanimous in their view that surprise and swiftness were the only way we could achieve it. The entire operation had to be planned to the minutest detail and executed with surgical precision and dexterity. After a lot of intense brainstorming, a detailed plan was drawn. A minute study was made of the regular visitors to the chawl and we picked good actors from among ourselves who could play a milkman, do newspaper delivery rounds and arrive in a taxi like outstation guests. Such jobs cannot be done by all and sundry. For instance, I am totally unfit for them. With my height and features, I am sure to stand out like an eyesore and no disguise would succeed in making me merge with any surrounding.

So while Mumbai observed with fanfare a symbolic fight for justice and victory of good over evil, my team and I thought and thought and worked out all the nitty-gritty to play out our roles in the actual fight for justice. Finally the day after the Hanuman Jayanti we took our positions in the field and struck. Fortunately, it was one of those rare days when everything worked our way.

I had submitted a proposal to the Commissioner of Police, Hasan Gafoor, requesting the Maharashtra Control of Organised Crime Act (MCOCA) to be applied to this case, which was duly granted.

As we were busy taking all the possible care to build a watertight case against Gawli, on 26 April 2008, the Central Intelligence Unit (CIU) of the Crime Branch received information that a group of accused were planning to enter and loot a jewellery shop in Kalbadevi. It was called Prakash Gold Palace. Inspector Shashank Sandbhor assisted by Assistant Police Inspector Ajay Joshi laid a trap and five men were arrested, just as they walked out of Hotel Govindram Lachiram which is adjacent to this jewellery shop. One of the accused, Vijay Kumar Giri was found in possession of a country-made handgun without a butt along with one live cartridge. As is the practice, the CIU registered an offence of preparation to commit dacoity at L.T. Marg police station and took over the investigation. The interrogation revealed that the accused were members of the Arun Gawli gang.

Since Unit III was investigating the activities of the Arun Gawli crime syndicate, the Senior Inspector of the Central Intelligence Unit requested Unit III to take custody of the five gangsters arrested for the Prakash Gold Palace case. Unit III took them into their custody and the interrogation began. It was a very capable constable called Chandrakant Raut who elicited extremely important information from the accused. The country-made handgun seized from the four gangsters at Kalbadevi had been used in a very serious murder case in March 2007 – the murder of Shiv Sena Corporator Kamlakar Jamsandekar which had taken place at Saki Naka when I was posted as Special Inspector General (Training) at the DG office.

In a toughly fought contest in the Mumbai Municipal Corporation elections, Shiv Sena's Jamsandekar had defeated his main opponent Ajit Rane, a candidate fielded by Arun Gawli's Akhil Bharatiya Sena to capture the Mohili Village (L Ward) seat. A month later, on 2 March 2007, around 16:45 hours, Jamsandekar was sitting in his house in the Rumani Manzil Chawl in Asalpha Village near the Mohili Pipe Line. He was reading the newspaper, with one eye on the news bulletin running on TV. His wife was out attending a function at a nearby school, his daughter Sayali was packing her school bag for the next day and his niece Manali was in the kitchen. Suddenly Manali heard a big sound like the bursting of a firecracker and rushed out to check. Two unknown persons were fleeing from the room. Her uncle was slouched on a chair with blood oozing from his head. She started screaming hysterically for help. The neighbours rushed in and contacted the police. The police arrived immediately and rushed Jamsandekar to the Rajawadi Hospital where he was declared dead before admission.

The Saki Naka police station registered an offence of murder and commenced the investigation. The only piece of evidence found from the scene of offence was the butt of the gun used by the assailant. It had detached itself after firing. The revolver itself was never found. The investigation indicated political rivalry in the Corporation elections to be the motive and led to the arrests of Ajit Rane, Pratap Godse and five others. Soon the investigation was completed, the charge sheet against the seven men was filed and the case was duly committed to the Court of Sessions.

The accused in the Prakash Gold Palace case had not only revealed that the butt recovered from the scene of the offence of the Jamsandekar murder was detached from their handgun seized at Kalbadevi, but it was also they who had committed the murder. A very excited Assistant Police Inspector Dinesh Kadam came into my chamber to break the news to me.

'But then what about the men arrested and charge sheeted by the Saki Naka police station?' I asked him.

'Sir, Gawli himself had taken the supari of thirty lakhs to kill Jamsandekar. He had assigned the task to two teams of hitmen. The hitmen arrested by the Saki Naka police station were dilly-dallying and not completing the task. So Gawli deputed the second team of Vijay Kumar Giri, Ashok Kumar Jaiswar, Narendra Giri and Anil Giri to accomplish "Jamsandekar's game". And they did it.'

I instructed Unit III to take over the investigation of the Kamlakar Jamsandekar murder case and probe the offence in its entirety. On 20 May 2008 I granted prior approval as per legal procedure, to add the provisions of MCOCA to the Jamsandekar murder case.

Our investigation revealed that Sahibrao Bintade, the political mentor of Kamlakar Jamsandekar, and his partner Balu Surve also dabbled in real estate. Over a period of time, disputes arose between Sahibrao Bintade and his protege Kamlakar Jamsandekar over politics as well as property. Matters got further compounded when the property belonging to Sahibrao Bintade and Balu Surve was demolished by the Municipal Corporation. They suspected it to be the handiwork of Jamsandekar and decided to get rid of him. Through contacts, they approached Gawli and gave him a supari for thirty lakhs. *'Jamsandekar yanche kaam hovun jaeel. Tumhi kalji karu naka,'* (Don't worry. The job of Kamlakar Jamsendekar shall be done) Gawli assured them as he took his thirty lakhs. As per the promise, Gawli accomplished the task through shooters Vijay Kumar Giri and Narendra Giri alias Kandi. Those arrested by the Saki Naka police station was the other team who were made to surrender as proxies to derail the investigation. This was a definite ploy, a conspiracy to enable a big fish like Gawli escape the clutches of law.

Gawli had never been convicted in his entire criminal career spanning nearly three decades. He had ample resources to hire top-notch lawyers to defend him. We were all convinced as regards his active role and complicity in the Jamsandekar murder and the Crime Branch arrested him for it. After a painstaking investigation, his role was very clearly brought out by my investigating team, but the evidence had to withstand judicial scrutiny. I, along with other senior officers in the Crime Branch went very minutely into the evidence. The evidence seized also showed that the money extorted from businessmen like builders, estate agents, cable operators and from bootlegging and gambling joints used to be deposited in the gang's 'treasury' which was called 'Mothi Bank' (the Big Bank). Records of transactions and amounts received by gang members were maintained in exhaustive registers which were regularly checked by Gawli himself.

The highlight of this investigation was that seven members of the Gawli syndicate gave their confessional statements in which they clearly described the role played by Arun Gawli in the conspiracy. The ballistic report too proved that the handgun seized from the accused at Kalbadevi was the same weapon which had fired the fatal shots at Jamsandekar.

The trial of this murder case commenced after I was promoted to the post of Additional Director General of Police of the Anti-Terrorism Squad (ATS) in March 2010. Despite the tremendous pressure of work in the ATS, I regularly kept myself abreast of the progress of the Jamsandekar murder trial. ACP Duraphe, Assistant Police Inspectors Diwakar Shelke and Dinesh Kadam and Sub Inspector Yogendra Chavan kept me updated.

We had our apprehensions that the Arun Gawli gang would use all the 'tactics' at their disposal to ensure the acquittal of their 'Daddy' and his co-accused. A very important witness in this case was Ramchandra Gurav alias Dhaktya. Gawli's 'legal cell' realised that this witness had to turn hostile if Gawli had to get his acquittal. A Gawli gang team reached Kankavali in district Sindhudurg where the witness resided. They gave him 25,000 rupees in cash, threatened him that if he did not retract his statement in court, he and his family would be wiped out.

I was sitting late in the night in the ATS office for some important work when Dinesh Kadam reported this disturbing development. I directed him to immediately dispatch a team to Kankavali to ensure that proper investigation was conducted to probe into this incident. I then spoke to the Superintendent of Police, Sindhudurg and explained to him how important the witness's testimony was to the outcome of the trial which was at a crucial stage. I informed him that the witness would be reaching the police station to lodge a complaint about the threat and produce the 25,000 rupees as inducement amount. I requested him to provide protection to the witness. We received complete cooperation from the Sindhudurg police.

We could bring to the notice of the MCOCA court how the gang was trying to tamper with witnesses. Very significantly, at this very time, Gawli got himself admitted at the Jaslok Hospital, primarily to create an alibi for himself. Another attempt the gang made to browbeat witnesses was reported in Saki Naka. Jamsandekar's widow, Komal was now the Shiv Sena corporator. Some of the banners featuring her picture were found defaced ominously – just the head was cut out from the banners and it created panic. Our team gave her confidence that she must lodge a complaint which she promptly did.

The trial proceeded under such trying circumstances and our hard work ultimately paid off. All crucial witnesses appeared before the court and supported the prosecution completely. On 31 August 2012, the MCOCA court sentenced Arun Gawli and his co-accused team members to rigorous imprisonment for life and also ordered them to pay a fine of seven lakhs each.

'The prosecution has succeeded in unearthing the perpetrators of crime as well as the role of the kingpin of the organized crime syndicate Arun Gawli,' observed the learned judge. Gawli prayed for leniency on the ground that he was sixty years old and his wife, children and aged mother were his dependents. He prayed that the period spent in jail as an under trial prisoner be offset against his sentence and he be released. The learned judge refused the relief and recorded, 'I haven't found any repentance on his face.'

Ganglords possess various 'attributes' or 'qualities' which make them 'the first among equals' in gangs and helps them survive gang intrigues. Some are known for their daredevilry or fearlessness. It is something out of the ordinary that sustains them and makes them stay afloat in the midst of cut-throat competition and rivalry, both from within the gang and outside. They need vital and real-time Intelligence to know what is happening within their gang as also among other gangs. The history of the underworld has instances galore where gang leaders have been killed by their own lieutenants or associates in the fight for intra-gang supremacy. Ambition can be a dangerous trait in the gang hierarchy. So the life span of a gangster and more specifically a gang leader can be ruthlessly short.

Arun Gawli like his two contemporaries, Dawood Ibrahim and Chhota Rajan, has survived the trials and tribulations of gang intrigues because he possesses all these essential attributes. Like Dawood and Rajan, his in-depth planning of gang killings, his ruthlessness in dealing with foes and his ability to survive for nearly three and a half decades are ample testimony to his cunningness and fox-like nature. Over a period of time, Gawli established a tremendous hold in and around the Byculla, Chinckpokli and Umarkhadi areas. His contacts amongst the lower echelons of the police department are also well known.

The Kamlakar Jamsandekar murder case is the one and only case in which Arun Gulab Gawli, the dreaded gangster of Mumbai and a legislator, has ever been sentenced. Until then, he had successfully managed to elude conviction, even though a multitude of cases were registered against him and investigated. If not for the hard work, diligence and commitment put in by the officers of the Crime Branch, Arun Gawli would have once again, like in the past, made a mockery of our justice system and continued to hold court in his citadel, pretending to be the messiah of the downtrodden, meting out death on behalf of the unscrupulous and collecting revenue for the services rendered.

And since that early morning breach of the Dagdi Chawl on a fateful day in April 2008, the ominous gates of the once impregnable citadel have never been shut!

23

The Mystery of the Mournful Walk

Constable Hriday Mishra had just finished his exercise. He resided at distant Kalyan, a good sixty kilometres away from Mumbai. He tried hard not to miss his daily regimen of walk and exercise, defying the erratic duty hours inevitable in his job with the Mumbai police. He had to report for duty at Unit II of the Crime Branch, located at Saat Rasta. A quick bath and then off to the railway station, but not without some breakfast. For you never knew when your next proper meal could be. Perquisites of working in the Mumbai police and its legendary Crime Branch! Just then his phone rang. It was an old friend who kept him 'well-informed'.

'Sir, aap kahan hain? Kalachowki main ek badaa kand hua hai!' (Sir, where are you? A serious crime has taken place in Kalachowki), said the man and straightaway began his story. His excitement made words sputter or tumble out in top speed. Mishra found it extremely difficult to follow the narration which sounded like an auction chant.

'Speak slowly! I can't follow what you are saying!' said Mishra and the man calmed down a little. He inhaled deeply, appearing to have steadied himself before he spoke into the phone once more, this time in a more composed tone. He began the narration all over again and conveyed that early that morning, around 5:30 a.m. on 27 October 2009, which was a Tuesday, two motorcycle-borne assailants had killed a woman and injured her husband while the couple was on their morning walk. This gruesome act had occurred on the lonely stretch of road near Wadia Baug in Lalbaug and the motive was robbery. The husband had resignedly given up his gold chain and cash, but the wife had refused to surrender her earrings. She had to pay for her foolhardiness with her life. A scuffle had ensued during which the robbers had slashed the woman's throat fatally, and injured the poor husband who had tried to intervene to come to his wife's assistance.

'Slashed the woman's throat? The chain-snatchers did this?' Mishra interrupted his friend in disbelief. Chain-snatchers seldom killed their targets!

'Yes, slashed her throat!' The man confirmed. A passing biker had spotted the victims and alerted the Police Control Room. The couple was rushed to the KEM Hospital where the woman was pronounced dead on arrival and the man was admitted to the Intensive Care Unit (ICU). Besides the chain and the cash, the robbers had also decamped with the man's cell phone.

Mishra's informant knew the injured man whose family owned Shah Vijpal Veerji & Co – a grocery store in the area. The couple were Kutchis and had a ten-year-old son who was not yet informed of his mother's gory death. Mishra's friend felt that the killers could be tracked if the stolen cell phone was monitored and requisitioned Mishra's help in ensuring this. 'Don't worry. I will speak to my seniors and see that it is done. I will!' Mishra promised. 'Just text me the man's name and his cell phone number.'

The caller hung up and in a few seconds Mishra's inbox had the number and the name which was Jitin Dedhia. Mishra forwarded the message to his senior-in-charge, Inspector Dinesh Ahir instantaneously. He then dialled Ahir's number and promptly elucidated the details to him, stressing on the imperative need for surveillance on the number to trace its last location. Dinesh

Ahir, an experienced crime-hand himself, appreciated the validity and urgency of the point and promised that he would ensure it.

As he rushed to the railway station to catch the 9:03 train to Mumbai, Mishra's mind kept going over the incident. The unfortunate victim would be filing her FIR at the Kalachowki police station now, only if she had without confrontation, taken off her earrings in time and handed them over to the crooks! Chain-snatchers killing their victims! What a terrible trend for the city.

Intrigued, Mishra couldn't help but dial his close associates and colleagues, Irfan Khan and Anwar Memon, even as he waited for his train on the crowded platform. Both Irfan and Anwar were constables from the Crime Branch. The three had joined the police force together and they enjoyed working together. As expected, even Irfan and Anwar were shocked when they heard Mishra recounting the facts. Murder at the hands of chain-snatchers was an absurdity! Mishra asked both to hurry up to work and be prepared for a busy day ahead. In all probability, there would be no returning home tonight, or even for days, as it often happened with Crime Branch detectives sent to hunt out dangerous criminals. Mishra boarded the crowded train like a seasoned athlete and stood in the compartment like the proverbial sardine. As the train chugged into Dombivali station, his phone rang. He saw the name 'Rakesh Maria' and answered the call immediately, 'Jai Hind, sir!'

'Jai Hind, Mishra. Kaise ho? Aur kahan ho? Aur yeh chain-snatching mein jo zakhmi hua hai Kalachowki mein, uska number tumko kahan se mila?' (How are you Mishra? Where are you? And where did you get this number from – of the man injured in the Kalachowki chain-snatching?) I asked Mishra.

And then I realised that I should have given him some time to answer the first two questions before adding the third. Poor Mishra, without breaking protocol, answered all my questions chronologically adding the mandatory 'sir' at the end of each sentence. Then I conveyed to him that it was indeed Jitin Dedhia's number and that not only had Inspector Ahir immediately shared his information with me, we had lost no time in putting the number on surveillance. From his tone, I could perceive that Mishra was happy that his seniors had accorded importance and priority to his input and taken his call seriously. 'Mishra, I want your team to solve this murder at any cost. Catch the culprits and get them before me within twenty-four hours. Get cracking,' I said to him.

'Yes, sir, definitely, sir!' Mishra promised with conviction in his voice. The crisp 'Jai Hind, sir' and 'Yes, sir' in the crowded Kalyan local must have attracted the attention of his fellow passengers. They must have gawked at him with wonder and curiosity as if he were from another planet altogether. Men posted in the Crime Branch do not wear uniform on duty and it is difficult to detect the cop in them unless they display such giveaway behaviour. During my interactions with the officers and constabulary, I encouraged them to grow beards, sport long hair and wear attire that would help them merge and mingle with the general public. This would go a long way in the collection and garnering of much-needed information and actionable Intelligence, I would tell them.

I was the Joint CP (Crime) then and when Dinesh Ahir told me about Mishra's call, I had a gut feeling that Mishra could be our 'point-person' to help the Crime Branch get vital clues to take the investigation forward. I knew Mishra from before. I had headed the Recruitment Panel that had selected Hriday Mishra, Anwar and Irfan when they were enlisted as police constables in the Mumbai police. All three were promising candidates, bubbling with sincerity and confidence and full of the alacrity that comes of being keen sportsmen. Mishra was the Maharashtra State School Champion for the javelin throw and I had recruited him as a constable in 1998. Irfan Khan and Anwar Memon were outstanding basketball players. They had represented Maharashtra at the national level. Both were from Nagpada. Ever since the recruitment of these three constables, I had regularly followed their progress and encouraged them to cultivate informants and evince keen interest in investigations. Finding them receptive to motivation and ever willing to take up challenges, I had brought them into the Crime Branch in 2008.

The local police had already registered the First Information Report on the basis of Jitin Dedhia's account. He had stated, from his hospital bed, that when he and his wife Beena came close to the deserted stretch near Wadia Baug, suddenly two men on a motorcycle had pulled up near them. The men had covered their faces. The pillion rider got off, approached the couple and menacingly ordered Beena to hand over her earrings. Jitin was urging her to give up her earrings, but she refused to do so. The killer then slashed her throat with a knife. Jitin tried to resist him, but he attacked Jitin too with the knife and slashed his forearm and finger. Jitin's gold chain and his wallet which contained some cash were also snatched. In the scuffle, Jitin also lost his cell phone. The robbers then made good their escape and vanished on their bike.

Given the early hour of the chilly October morning, there were very few passers-by and they did not intervene. However, a witness called Gaikwad saw the victims, informed the Police Control Room on his cell phone and left for the police station. A short while thereafter, a police wireless van had arrived on the scene and rushed the injured couple to hospital. Jitin also provided a general physical description of the two assailants.

By the time the Crime Branch team reached the scene of offence, an alert had been issued to all the police stations and Mobile units in the metropolis to maintain a lookout for the bike-borne assailants and the local police had commenced their investigation. Jitin's mobile was not found on the spot and in all probability, the assailants had taken it away. The good Samaritan who had contacted the Control Room and rushed to the police station had in fact gone to the neighbouring police station. He was re-directed and taken to the Kalachowki police station to record his statement. A reconstruction of the scene of crime reached the conclusion that the assailants had taken the G.D. Ambekar Road and disappeared in the direction of Parel Tank Road.

The news of the deadly attack on peaceful morning walkers was widely flashed on the breakfast news and spread shockwaves through the city. The next day's newspapers accorded front page publicity to the incident, discussing and lamenting the growing incidents of violent chain-snatchings and assaults. There was a wave of sympathy for the victims' family when it was reported that the couple was planning their son's birthday which was on Thursday that very week. The plight of the Dedhias was perceived as the utter failure and incompetence of the Mumbai police. The refrain was that the police were busy providing security to the VIPs and had no time for the ordinary citizen.

The next day, the Shiv Sena which had received a setback in the recent Assembly elections, decided to take it upon itself the task of protecting morning walkers in the city. Their Executive President directed the cadre to form a 'Bhagwa (saffron) Guard'. Under the leadership of the Shiv Sena Shakha Pramukhs (Branch or Unit heads), the Bhagwa Guard would patrol gardens, parks, sea-faces and grounds in the early morning hours.

The police effort towards nabbing the assailants continued unabated. Sketches of the culprits were drawn and circulated among all the police stations and special units of Mumbai police. The consequent result was that many suspicious characters were rounded up for further probe. Police stations were also directed to look out for motorcycles lying abandoned or unattended and to verify their ownership. The last location reported on the stolen mobile was Sewri and, it was quite possible, that the motorcycle was abandoned in Sewri and its surrounding areas.

The pressure was mounting steadily on the Mumbai police in general and the Crime Branch in particular, when Constable Irfan Khan got information that a chain-snatcher, reported to be closely resembling the circulated sketch, had acquired a new bike. He was a history-sheeter who had a number of chain snatchings to his discredit and lived near the J.J. Flyover Bridge. He was brought to Unit II and subjected to sustained questioning. He kept saying, 'Sir, for such a small job where is the need to commit a murder? Why would I use a chopper? Such small robberies I can easily do on railway stations. I don't need to hurt the target for it. Sir, you know that well.' The Unit thoroughly checked his movements on that fateful day and arrived at the conclusion that he, indeed, was not involved in the murder.

It was during this time that Fate appeared to tilt a tad bit in our favour. Two important witnesses had come forward to volunteer information. One was a local resident who confirmed that there were very few people on Ambekar Road when he had set off for his walk in the wee hours of the October morning. On the way back, opposite the Veterinary College, he had seen a speeding motorcycle dash against the iron sheet barricades erected around the monorail construction. Both the riders had fallen off the motorcycle, as it tilted on its left, with the impact. He had run forward to help, but they quickly picked themselves up and rode off towards Bhoiwada. He further noticed that the pillion rider was limping and also heard him abuse the driver in Hindi as he hopped back on to the bike.

The other witness, too, was a morning walker. He happened to be on a bridge some distance away but overlooking the murder spot. He had heard shouts from the direction of Wadia Baug and had looked down from the bridge. He saw the stabber standing near a man who was screaming and a woman lying on the road. He also noticed another man waiting for the assailant on a motorcycle nearby. Then both the suspected accused sped away towards Bhoiwada. This witness had to walk some distance to take the stairway to descend from the bridge and it took him some time to reach the spot. But, by then, the police wireless van had shifted the injured couple to the hospital.

All the police stations in the city started a concerted drive against chain-snatchers since it was presumed that the murder was a botched-up chain-snatching episode. The heightened police vigil and the questioning of history-sheeters were helping the city police to prevent and detect petty street crimes. Unfortunately, no clue was in sight to detect the murder of Beena Dedhia and bring the cold-blooded murderers to book! We once again found ourselves facing a dead end.

In the meanwhile, Constable Anwar Memon's persistent efforts led to what looked like a useful piece of information: a history-sheeter from Delhi used to fly down, at least once a month to Mumbai, snatch three to four chains and take the return flight that very evening. Without further ado, a Crime Branch team took off for Delhi to work on this lead, taking the informant along.

A trap was laid and they lay in wait at the gate of the suspect's housing colony. Taking a cue from the informant's signal, they stopped a man on a motorcycle as he arrived at the gate. On being questioned, he said that the suspect they were looking for was not him, but rather his older brother and took them to his house. The door opened and they were greeted by another brother. The latter, in turn, informed them that the brother they were looking for lived in a house a little distance away. The brothers then took the team to the other house, only to find that the bird had flown the coop, with wife and three children, and in his own Innova!

Obviously, the loving and close-knit family had played some role in his escape by deliberately delaying the police's arrival at the actual residence and facilitated the culprit to flee. The miffed Crime Branch team was not going to take it lightly. Their egos bruised, they compelled one of the brothers to join the chase that took them all the way to Jaipur. Every time they reached a location, the chain-snatcher was somehow always one step ahead. So they issued a 'loving invitation' to the 'cooperating' brother to be their guest at Mumbai which he accepted. As anticipated, this news had to route its way to the man on the run. He called the team on his brother's mobile phone and pleaded his innocence. He promised to be in the Unit II Crime Branch office at the earliest and on his own, but the once bitten, twice shy team was in no mood to take any chances. As soon as they flew back to Mumbai and reached the Unit II office with the guest, they received a call from the chain-snatcher who was waiting outside their office! The high-flying chain-snatcher produced his alibis along with his Delhi-Bombay-Delhi ticket which was prior to the murder in Kalachowki. He was closely questioned and after confirming that, indeed, he had had no role to play in the murder under investigation, he was allowed to go. We were back to square one!

As all this was happening, the activists, the police baiters and the press were getting restless. There was a women's morcha (march) on the Kalachowki police station and also a morcha on the Mantralaya to protest against the alleged police inaction, apathy and incompetence. The Bhagwa Guard had begun their promised patrolling, wearing saffron T-shirts and armed with sticks in their hands. Alert citizens helping the police keep vigil are always welcome, but not when it is done to create an impression that the police are inert when they are actually engaged in plenty of behind the scenes hard work that cannot be disclosed for obvious reasons!

We seemed to have reached a dead end in the Beena Dedhia murder case. I was goading the Crime Branch officers and men, constantly taking updates from them and exhorting them to think out of the box. As Joint CP (Crime), I had evolved the practice of holding weekly crime review meetings in my office and it was specifically designed to improve communication and make every officer and constable develop a stake in our work. My instructions were that not just officers, even constables had to attend these meetings, keeping only a skeletal staff at the unit offices. During the weekly crime review meeting, each officer and constable had to tell me what he or she had done in the past seven days and what was on the anvil for the next seven. Even constables were encouraged to discuss strategy, crime trends and information on the underworld and terror fronts. Their opinions were valued and they were motivated to go out in the field and work on Intelligence.

After the review meeting of Unit II that week, my PA, Sayed Waheeduddin informed me that Constables Mishra, Anwar and Irfan wanted to see me. I called them in as soon as I got the time.

'Sir, we want to discuss the Dedhia murder case with you,' Mishra began. I was only too happy to. Mishra had decided to re-visit the case, dissect the minutest fact from the very beginning instead of just going by the information they were receiving now. The three constables stood convinced that they ought to unravel the case and take a close look at it, thread by thread. Perhaps there was some tiny detail that had missed our eye. Could Jitin Dedhia throw light or give us some clue that he had inadvertently forgotten to mention? Something innocuous to a layperson, but a matter of deeper probe to a professional investigator! In any case, why not see what he was up to now, Mishra thought. Taking Irfan and Anwar with him, they went unannounced to Jitin Dedhia's house. To their utter surprise, Jitin met them with great reluctance and when he did, he appeared not like a morose bereaved husband, but quite hostile!

'Sir, we are here with a firm belief that only you could give us some detail which can lead us to the culprits – some clue that has escaped our notice so far,' Mishra explained to Jitin. To his surprise, Jitin's demeanour and bearing showed a complete lack of interest. His attitude towards his unexpected visitors was that of hostility and aversion. He rudely said to them, 'How many people do I have to repeat the same story to!'

The trio was taken aback at his tone and expression. They expressed regret and gently persisted with their questions: 'Sir, along with the cash, what else was there in your wallet? Credit, debit cards? PAN card?'

'All were taken away,' said Jitin.

'So then which were the banks? Could you tell us?'

'I have already replied to these questions,' came the answer.

'Sir, could you give us a little "demo" of how the incident had happened? How did they accost you and how did the struggle happen?'

'This has been asked to me so many times! I am exhausted,' Jitin answered with a mask of absolute disinterest. Just then some visitors came to meet Jitin and the Crime Branch trio decided that it was time to tactically withdraw and take their leave. They had mulled over the way the meeting had gone and felt that they must share it with me.

'Sir, something is not right. His expressions, the way he spoke, it was as if he did not want to talk to us,' said Mishra, shaking his head.

The certainty in Mishra's voice got me thinking. I thought hard. These three men were practical investigators. Their assessment of individuals and situations alike, as well as their instincts, were their guiding lights. Consequently, if they got this uneasy feeling, it could not be brushed aside. 'Tell me what exactly did you feel when he was talking to you,' I said.

'Sir, he is hiding something!' they said in unison. And they again described the lukewarm reception and hostile response of the supposedly distraught husband.

'Kuchh lafda hai kya? Aurat ka chakkar toh nahin?' (Is there some scandal? Not an affair with a woman?) I asked them.

'Find out more about this Jitin. Make enquiries. What type of a man is he? Keep him under observation. And study his CDRs thoroughly and keep me informed.' I said. (CDR stands for Call Details Record.) The three men saluted me and took their leave, their faces lit up because I, the Joint CP Crime had appreciated and valued their assessment. As for me, it was the first time I felt that we were finally really on to something in this case. After decades of experience in separating the grain from the chaff and the truth from the heap of lies, the investigator's gut and brain develop sensory appendages or antennae! I was now getting this premonition of a positive signal in the air!

After leaving my cabin, the trio arrived at a division of labour. Anwar and Irfan would concentrate on field work; Mishra would study the call records. He promptly requisitioned Jitin's CDRs for the past one year.

As I kept brooding over what more we could do to identify and net the killers, Mishra's painstaking research was throwing up some interesting findings. It was not as easy to study CDRs in those days as it is now. The Unit had only one computer which took care of all its work, so Mishra had to check the CDRs manually. He would check the closely printed CDRs whenever and wherever he got the opportunity, even in trains and buses and late in the night at home.

He found from the study of the CDRs that Jitin had been talking to a particular number for long durations perhaps suggesting a different kind of a relationship with the owner of the other number. So Mishra decided to check out this number and dialled it. It was answered by a lady. Mishra said to her, *'Hum yahan taxi leke khade hain. Aap haspatal kab chalengi?'* (I am waiting here with the taxi. When will you leave for the hospital?)

To Mishra's luck, the woman was neither waiting for any taxi nor was she planning to go to a hospital. Naturally, she said that he had dialled the wrong number. Mishra begged her pardon, disconnected the call and without dilly-dallying, called for the one year CDRs of this number. A perusal of this new CDRs showed that the long conversations with Jitin were mostly in the afternoons. However, from July, this number had switched to another number for similar long conversations. Correspondingly, Jitin's number had, for some inexplicable reason, stopped all contact with this number from July! Mishra then called for the six months CDRs of this new number. It was registered in the name of a person whose address was in Lalbaug which is in central Mumbai.

Mishra painstakingly went through the CDRs and made a startling discovery. On the day of the murder and around the time of the murder, there were two calls, lasting barely seconds, from the Lalbaug number to another number. One was at 5:10 a.m. and the other was at 5:25 a.m.!

Did this new number belong to the killer? Mishra urgently requisitioned the CDRs of this new number and got it the very next day. Not only did it reflect the two suspicious early morning calls, at the first call the location of the phone was in Sewri and at the next call the location was in Kalachowki, near the spot of the murder! It also showed that around 5:10 a.m., the recipient of the two short calls had, in turn, called another number! Logically, Mishra made an urgent requisition for the CDRs of the other new number. The CDRs revealed that this new number was at Antop Hill at 5:00 a.m. and at 5:30 a.m. it had also come to Kalachowki near the scene of the crime!

Had he stumbled upon the numbers of the killers? Were they dispatched or summoned by the Lalbaug number to the spot of the murder?

Who was this person from Lalbaug? Was he the murderer? Or was his SIM being used by the murderer to get in touch with the two other numbers who were at Kalachowki around the time of the murder?

With a head pounding with these questions, Mishra first shared this pivotal and mind-blowing discovery with Irfan and Anwar, and then with Inspector Dinesh Ahir who, along with Mishra, then rushed to me with the CDRs. When Mishra explained the entire business to me, I was speechless at his sheer industry. The two SIM cards that had rushed to Kalachowki, just before the murder, were crucial. On the Crime Branch hotline, I immediately directed the Additional CP (Crime) to commence the interception recording of the two numbers and directed Dinesh Ahir and Mishra to maintain strict confidentiality about this vital discovery.

Although a new and seemingly concrete line of the investigation appeared in sight, much remained to be done. The immediate task now was to track down the person who was using the Lalbaug number. Anwar and Irfan, who had taken it upon themselves to do the field work, soon found out that it was a man called Ganesh Samal. He sold *Chinese bhel* (a popular variation of the famous Mumbai street food bhel, arrived at by adding Chinese sauces) from a cart on the street at Lalbaug. So, Mishra, Anwar and Irfan traced the cart and managed to whisk away the man quietly to the Unit office. What Ganesh Samal told them was enough to confirm the trio's hunch that Jitin Dedhia had good reasons to avoid nosy Crime Branch constables like the plague!

Samal said that the SIM in question was one of the pair that he had obtained from MTNL. He had given it to his wife Gitanjali, who was employed in Shah Vijpal Veerji & Co, the grocery shop owned by the Dedhia family. The SIM was being used by Jitin when the murder happened. The needle of suspicion was moving closer to Jitin Dedhia, but a lot of ground had still to be covered before we could be absolutely certain that our presumption was incontrovertible. Fortunately, the Samals appreciated the gravity of the matter and cooperated with the Crime Branch, maintaining complete secrecy till the whole conspiracy was unravelled.

The job at hand now was to trace the two killers through the two SIM cards that were active in Kalachowki in the early hours of that morning. From the call intercepts, we began gleaning information, bit by bit, on the men on the Crime Branch radar. One of the suspects appeared to be a North Indian taxi driver. So Mishra, himself a North Indian, felt that if he spoke to 'Target-1' in his typical north Indian Hindi, it would work. So he gave it a go.

'Hello, bhai. Kya haal hain? Gaadi theek chal rahi hai?' Mishra asked in his typical Hindi. (Hello brother, how are you doing? Is the car running well?)

'Haan, bhai, sab theek hai, raat mein gaadi driver ko diya hai. Lekin bhai, pehchana nahin!' (Yes, brother, all ok. At night the car is with the driver. But I can't place you, brother!) Target-1 had begun his reply with equal warmth, but then realised that he did not recognise the querist! So he added a question which was safe enough to not offend the caller and yet help him pinpoint his identity: *'Kahanse bol rahe ho?'* (Where are you speaking from?)

'Saki Naka mein hoon,' Mishra answered using subterfuge to attain his goal. I am in Saki Naka. It meant neither here, nor there. There was a long pause as Target-1 assessed the import of this answer. He had to say that he could not recognise the long-lost friend. *'Yaar, pehchana nahin!'* (Buddy, I cannot place you!) He confessed.

'This is Shuklaji! We had met in Saki Naka, remember? I too drive a taxi!' Mishra went on glibly and the poor target had to lump it. A Mumbai cabbie meets so many of his tribe all day long. It is humanly not possible to remember each and every one of them. So the man accepted Shuklaji and after some more small talk, Mishra concluded the call.

The next day Mishra dialled Target-1 again and was relieved to be recognised, for before he could say anything, he was met with a 'Yes, Shuklaji! How are you!' So now the friendship could surge forward. Mishra shared with Target-1 a bit of great news that Shuklaji was intending to purchase a new taxi and the rest of the conversation was an earnest exchange of thoughts and suggestions possible only between two Mumbai cabbies. Little did Target-1 know that what Shuklaji was looking for was a clean pickup for his newfound friend, Target-1 who turned out to be the twenty-two-year old Nazim Kalam Khan.

With Target-1 ironed out, unwavering focus was directed towards tracing his co-assailant, Target-2, the other contract killer who was from Moradabad, in UP. He had a fresh fruit juice stall in Kalachowki. Mishra, Anwar and Irfan went to the juice shop and ordered juice. Even as the juice was being prepared, Anwar dialled a number and said to the man running the shop, *'Arre, bhai ka number kitna try kar raha hoon, magar lagta hee nahin,'* (I have been trying bhai's number but I can't get through). The man promptly said, *'Bhai gaon gaye hain,'* (Bhai has gone to his village). So was there any other number he could be contacted on? There was a shop to be rented and the rent had to be discussed with bhai. The man complied unsuspectingly and handed Anwar a number. The name of Target-2 was Hasaruddin Munnan Malik.

Once outside the shop, they dialled the number. *'Hasaruddin bhai, Salaam Aleikum! Kaise ho?* (Hasaruddin bhai, Salaam Aleikum! How are you?) said Anwar as soon as the call was answered.

'Waleikum Assalaam, bhai! Mein gaon mein hoon,' (I am in my village) came the answer.

'Raju bol raha hoon, Hasaruddin bhai,' said the caller and then immediately added, *'Arre sorry bhai! Traffic mein hoon, thodi der mein call karta hoon,'* (This is Raju. Oh, sorry bhai! Right now I am stuck in traffic, so I will call you after some time), he lied. 'Ok, bhai,' said Hasaruddin and the conversation ended.

The number was then used to narrow down Hasaruddin's current whereabouts. The details of Hasaruddin's number threw up his location which was traced to near Moradabad, in UP. A Unit II team left immediately for Delhi by flight. The team had asked an acquaintance to pick them up in his Innova and take them to Moradabad.

On reaching the local police station near Moradabad, the team informed them that they had come from Mumbai and needed help to track down an accused. To their utter surprise, the officer-in-charge looked at the address and said, 'Is it for the same offence? The one for which you had come last time?' 'Yes, it's the same offence,' said our officers, though they had no clue whatsoever about what the officer was talking about. Looked like the other members in Hasaruddin's family too had chequered careers! The officer then contacted someone in the village and informed the team that the accused was not in the village, but his older brother and father were. Would their statements do? Of course! The team reached the village and found, much to their joy and surprise, that the older brother was none other than Hasaruddin himself and he was ready to accompany them to the local police station to record his statement. The team immediately took Hasaruddin to the police station. It was only then that the team realised that Hasaruddin's younger brother had eloped with a minor girl from Mumbai and an offence of rape was registered against him. The brother was untraceable, prompting the Mumbai police to pay regular visits to the village to nab him. At the police station, they announced to Hasaruddin that he would have to accompany them back to Mumbai to record his statement as only he could convince the superiors that his brother was really untraceable. They said they were dead tired. The constant movement and activity had burnt the team out completely. So drained they were, that instead of saving money, they would prefer to fly down, him included, to Mumbai and their bosses would understand.

I had been keeping track of and monitoring the operation right through via mobile telephone. I was under a lot of stress. The level of difficulty and danger that accompanies the execution of such operations in unfamiliar territories is most often understated. The team risks their lives and every move is fraught with danger. Although they were my men who were out in the field, trying their best to close in on the co-assailant, the burden of pressure had cast its shadow over me as well. A slight slip and months of hard work could simply be washed down the drain. The creased lines of my forehead smoothened out momentarily and I could heave a sigh of relief and relax a little only when the team conveyed to me that they were on their way to Delhi with Target-2 to catch the first available flight to Mumbai.

The Innova driver they had hired accelerated his pace to transport them to Delhi Airport to catch the earliest flight to Mumbai. As they began settling his bill, he stood before them with folded hands and said, 'Sir, I am a small man. You are doing such great work for the country. Let this be my contribution. I don't want your money. I am lucky that I had this opportunity to do a good deed.' He was the same man – the suspected chain-snatcher they had chased with his brother from Delhi to Jaipur and to Mumbai and persuaded him to appear before them to clear his name. It seemed as if he had turned over a new leaf after his brush with Unit II.

Jitin Dedhia was kept under close scrutiny and his movements were being monitored. Target-1 Nazim Kalam Khan was also under surveillance. The police cannot be omnipresent, especially in mega cities like Mumbai where they are seriously understaffed. They perpetually need people's cooperation to undertake delicate operations by merging with the crowds and stepping in where the police cannot. Irfan and Anwar, whose job it was to do field work, had pressed into service their zero numbers, the unique category of private citizens who are prepared to run all kinds of errands for the police and help them in surveillance. The call intercepts assisted Unit II in getting leads to the spots Nazim was frequenting and the persons he was hobnobbing with, like garages and mechanics. Working in perfect coordination with the zero numbers, the team secured a clean pickup of Nazim Kalam Khan. This task was accomplished when Nazim came to a garage to fetch his taxi after repairs. Using zero numbers, motorcycles and friends driving taxis, the clean pickup was achieved with clockwork precision and professional finesse.

The suspects were kept in different rooms and interrogated separately. Within ten minutes, Nazim began weeping and confessed that he had committed a serious crime. In his wallet, he still carried a passport size photograph of Beena Dedhia that was provided to him by Jitin to help him identify her, with the name Beena Dedhia written on its back in Jitin's hand. Nazim said that he was finding it impossible to sleep from the day of the murder. The minute he shut his eyes, he would be haunted by the image of Beena just before she breathed her last on the pavement. Hasaruddin, too, confessed to his crime. They were introduced to Jitin by Hasaruddin's friend, Rajanikant Wagh aka Chhotu who worked at the newspaper stall adjoining Hasaruddin's juice centre. Together they had taken the supari (contract) of one lakh rupees from Jitin Dedhia to kill his wife, Beena.

Soon, Jitin Dedhia joined the wagon of visitors to the Unit II office. The tension was writ large on Jitin's face as he was ushered into the Unit II office that day. He noticed that unlike in the past, the atmosphere was quite cheerful and the officers and men actually seemed to be in a celebratory mood, not their usual grim selves. Something was amiss. As he sat down in a chair, he was asked, *'Jitin Dedhia sir, ab toh sach bataao ki kya baat hai?'* (Tell us, at least now, sir, what is the truth?)

This was followed by a deafening silence for almost two long minutes. No one spoke a word. The officers and men just waited. And then Jitin Dedhia broke down and wept bitterly. Nobody felt sorry for him and his fate. He confessed that his relationship with Beena had soured. She was rude and cantankerous. Matters were further compounded when he fell in love with Rupal Chheda, the wife of Beena's brother, who reciprocated his feelings. Beena was unwilling for a mutual separation and, hence, Jitin decided to get rid of her. He needed professional killers to achieve his goal and he found them in Nazim and Hasaruddin through Chhotu who was a friend of Hasaruddin. They hit upon the novel idea of making it look like a chain-snatching episode gone horribly wrong. Their earlier two attempts to murder Beena did not fructify. One was at a spot near an ice cream parlour near the Don Bosco School, Wadala and the other at Kapad Bazar near Chitra Cinema at Dadar. Jitin had taken Beena to both the spots on the pretext of a post-dinner motorcycle drive for ice cream, but the places were too crowded to pull off the murder. It would have been too risky to commit the murder there and they were forced to postpone their diabolical plan.

Their mission accomplished, Inspector Dinesh Ahir, Assistant Police Inspector Vijay Shinde, and Sub-Inspector Surendra Jadhav and Constables Hriday Mishra, Irfan Khan and Anwar Memon wasted no time to come and see me. The manner in which the three constables had taken the initiative and enabled Unit II to detect this sensational case proved that investigative talent did not depend on rank and it surfaced with delegation. As I got up from my seat to shake hands with each of them, I couldn't help but say aloud what I was feeling: 'Crime Branch is not dead. Crime Branch is very much alive!' The reason for this outburst lay in the severe criticism and ignominy the Crime Branch was facing – as if we were a dead arm of the Mumbai police. My words were but a sincere recognition of their hard work. I immediately called the Additional CP (Crime) and DCP Nisar Tamboli and announced that Unit II had solved the Dedhia murder case.

'Now I want you to get me the entire chain, with each and every link,' I said to the team as they took my leave. They promised they would do just that and left.

Accused Chhotu and Rupal Chheda, too, were arrested. As the investigation progressed, it revealed gruesome and shocking details of the murder. After slashing Beena's neck with the knife,

Nazim saw blood oozing out of the wound and had lost his nerve. He began running away. Seeing this, Jitin had shouted out to him that if he did not finish the job, all of them would get caught and then he, Jitin, would be compelled to tell the truth to the police. These words had the desired effect and pulled Nazim back to finish the gory task. He inflicted more lethal stab wounds on Beena to ensure that she did not survive. Jitin also prompted Nazim to slash his hands to make it look like he too was as much a victim as Beena, and that he had tried desperately to defend her.

The supari amount paid to the contract killers was just a paltry lakh of rupees to be shared among three of them. It was not a princely sum, but that did not shock or surprise me at all. I had seen murderers charge even less. A murder for just forty rupees!

It was one of the earliest cases I had handled when I was DCP (Detection) in the early '90s. The victim was a man working in the Mazgaon docks in one of the technical departments. He would often be on night shifts. He lived in Deonar in the Shivaji Nagar slums with his young wife. Their house was divided into two parts, one of which was rented out to a young tenant. The vast age gap between the husband and wife coupled with the irregular night shift working hours were bound to have disastrous consequences for the marriage. The wife and the young tenant soon began an affair. Such things seldom remain hidden and the husband began suspecting her fidelity. This led to verbal lashings and physical bashing of the wife. The latter could not take it any longer and so she and her paramour decided to get rid of the abusive husband. The paramour found a young rag-picker, barely eighteen or nineteen years of age, and entrusted him with the task of killing the husband. As per the plan, the woman added a sedative to the husband's dinner one night and he fell into a deep slumber soon after consuming it. The paramour and the contract killer then smothered him with a pillow. The body had to be disposed of. The contract killer chopped the body into pieces and carried the pieces in plastic bags to the nearby

Deonar dumping ground where he scattered them all over. The woman then pretended that her husband had abandoned her and disappeared. However, sometime later, the Crime Branch received a tip-off and the young contract killer was picked up. He duly confessed. But after the initial shock, my curiosity got the better of me when he stated that he had charged only forty rupees to carry out the killing and to also dispose the body! Why forty? Because the monsoons were fast approaching and he desperately needed to cover his shack with plastic sheets which cost him forty rupees! He lived in abject poverty in a structure that was just four bamboos covered with a sackcloth. It is not just greed, even a bare necessity – financial desperation – that motivates contract killers to accept jobs. And when need is the driving factor, one does not have to be a professional. How cheap is human life in this Mayanagari that is Mumbai, I learnt in this case, albeit with a heavy heart.

True to their words, Unit II investigated each and every link of the Dedhia murder conspiracy thoroughly and tried to build a watertight case. Hasaruddin's bike was used for the murder and the accused had changed the digits on its number plates to evade detection. The shop which customised the new number plates was traced. The bike bore the dents and scratches it had sustained when it had dashed into the monorail construction barricades while escaping. Scrapings of the paint from the iron barricade sheets and from the bike matched in the Kalina Forensic Science Laboratory. The lodge in Thane where Jitin used to take Rupal for their romantic trysts was also located. Jitin had made entries in the lodge register in his own hand. Nazim led the police to the murder weapon – a knife and his bloodstained clothes which he had hidden. The shop from where the knife was purchased was also traced. The two men on morning walks also identified the two killers in the Test Identification Parade. The Crime Branch had an absolutely watertight case.

Yet, the trial court discharged Jitin Dedhia and Rupal Chheda although they had not filed a discharge application. The Crime Branch went into appeal in the Mumbai High Court and succeeded in getting the discharge order set aside against Jitin, but not against Rupal Chheda. The trial concluded in 2012. Special Public Prosecutor Rohini Salian examined thirty-five prosecution witnesses. The accused were represented by an array of reputed lawyers. The court convicted the three prime accused – Jitin Dedhia, Nazim Kalam Khan and Hasaruddin Malik for the cold-blooded killing of Beena in the staged chain-snatching and sentenced them to life imprisonment.

This case was a classic whodunit where the unlikeliest person turns out to be the murderer. The prime witness in the gruesome murder was the husband of the victim and he was himself injured in the attack. Left to look after his ten-year-old son, whose birthday was just two days after the wife's murder, he was the object of profuse public and media sympathy. By all appearances and accounts, he had been brave and tried his utmost to defend and protect his 'foolhardy' wife who had clung needlessly to her gold earrings, when he was asking her not to.

In the circumstances, the villains who were gladly sentenced by all, even before the trial and without a trial, were the Mumbai police. And why were they guilty? Because they had not foreseen the murder. Because their patrolling van was not on that secluded stretch of road at the very moment the killers, engaged by the husband, had succeeded in eliminating the wife, and escaped. Because the first informant was the last person to give them any leads, having committed the crime himself. Because the contract killing was cleverly disguised as a botched-up chain-snatching episode, never to be detected.

Against these overwhelming odds, Constables Mishra, Anwar and Irfan, by the sheer dint of perseverance and hard work, and by using robust common sense, had cracked the seemingly hopeless case merely in one and a half months when I had placed a tall order on them to bring me the accused within twenty-four hours! A marvellous job any investigator would be envious of.

In the overburdened police force like ours, it is extremely difficult to motivate the constabulary and give them an opportunity to prove themselves. They are pressed into service to perform guard, picket and escort duties which are no doubt important, but have little to do with specialised tasks like detection and investigation. As a result, this valuable manpower, which forms nearly eighty per cent of the Force, and which can be converted into brainpower, is lost. With long duty hours and poor living conditions, constables suffer in health and are far from the level of fitness they must possess even if they are to do just bandobast duties. They sink into apathy and lethargy that comes with repetitive monotonous work and it is very difficult to pull them out of the rut.

The manner in which the mystery of the 'mournful morning walk' was solved by the Crime Branch proved that our constables have a lot of latent talent and can work wonders. They only need an opportunity to use it and hone their skills.

24

Neither Forgive, Nor Forget

'Sir, API Honrao is here. He wants to see you,' said my PA Sayed Waheeduddin on the intercom. It was a busy afternoon, sometime in early July of 2010, in the Anti-Terrorism Squad (ATS) office which was on the first floor of the old stone building opposite Hume High School in Nagpada, on the arterial Sir J.J. Road.

Assistant Police Inspector Anil Honrao, attached to my Thane unit, was a conscientious and hardworking officer. Not the type to just drop in to remind you that he existed. When he came calling, it meant something. So my immediate response was an eager, 'Send him in!'

I pushed aside the files I was going through as API Honrao walked in and gave me a smart salute.

'Yes, Honrao! Please take a seat,' I said. He quietly slid into a chair. What a perfect asset he was for the police department in surveillance and undercover operations! Didn't look a policeman at all. With a little bit of change here and there, in his clothes and accessories, he would easily pass off as anyone on the street, a bank clerk, a travel agent, a '*Xeroxwalla*' (photocopying man) near the railway station, an estate broker, anything. A chameleon who had infinite patience for long hauls and a good network of informants.

'Tell me! What brings you here?' I shot out my question without wasting time on pleasantries.

'Sir, aapne Mussadiq Wahiduddin Quadri ka naam suna hai kya?' (Sir, have you heard of the name Mussadiq Wahiduddin Quadri?) asked Honrao.

'Yes, Honrao! Jo Jalees Ansari blast case mein andar hai, woh?' (That man we had arrested in the Jalees Ansari blast case?) My antennae had immediately caught a signal.

'Ji, sir, bilkul theek, sir!' (Yes, sir, you are right) said Honrao, betraying just a flicker of a smile. I guessed that it was a tribute to my memory and he was patting my back, mentally.

'Sir, khabar hai ki Quadri zinda hai aur Golconda, Andhra mein rehta hai,' (Sir, we have information that Quadri is alive and living in Golconda in Andhra Pradesh).

'Kya bol rahe ho? Pucca?' (What are you saying? Are you sure?) I almost screamed. 'Was he not found murdered in his house in Mumbra? Dead body identified by his wife and brother?'

'Yes, sir, lekin woh sab naatak tha,' said Honrao, now clearly enjoying himself. I was speechless. This was incredible. Obviously, he meant that the murder was stage-managed.

'Sir, our Head Constable Raju Pathare received the tip-off. We made some enquiries and feel that there is some substance in the information,' said Honrao.

Forgetting all about the HUJI (Harkat-Ul-Jihad-Islami) and the JeM (Jaish-e-Mohammad) that I had been thinking about minutes ago, I immediately sat down for a refresher course on the 'Quadri Murder'. Who was Mussadiq Wahiduddin Quadri? How had he managed to die in our records?

The story went back to the late 80s and early 90s. Even before the Babri masjid demolition, major cities in India and especially Mumbai had been rocked by a series of bomb blasts. Mostly low-intensity blasts, they were designed to create panic among the general public and undermine the morale of the police and law enforcement agencies. IEDs (Incendiary Explosive Devices) were planted on trains, buses and also in places of religious worship like gurudwaras. One blast had occurred in the canteen in the compound of the Azad Maidan police station, near the Esplanade Court Complex, in August 1993. Prior to that, there was a blast at the Worli Police Headquarters in January 1990. In March 1990 there were blasts in the Mahim police station, at the SB-I (Special Branch) CID office and in a patrolling jeep at Bhoiwada police station. After the serial blasts of March 1993, similar devices were planted once again at police stations: at Gol Deol (Round Temple) Police Chowki at V.P. Road in April 1993; at Bhoiwada Police Chowki in August 1993; and in the Gamdevi police station in September 1993. An IED device planted at the Abid Road police station in Hyderabad city in Andhra Pradesh also had a striking similarity to this pattern.

The audacity of the attacks on the police force was disturbing. If we did not get to the root of the conspiracy, we would lose faith in our own abilities. All the investigating agencies were alert. The breakthrough was achieved when based on credible information received by the Central Bureau of Investigation (CBI) in the early hours of 13 January 1994, a joint team of the CBI and Bombay Police arrested the mastermind of these blasts. He was Dr Jalees Ansari, a practising MBBS doctor from Mominpura area of Bombay. As the recently appointed DCP (Detection), I was part of the team which carried out the operation. More than a dozen members of Dr Jalees Ansari's module were arrested and indicted.

Mussadiq Wahiduddin Quadri was arrested on 14 January 1994, as an important associate and co-accused of Dr Jalees Ansari. A man in his early Thirties, Quadri resided in Mumbra which is part of Thane, a district adjoining Bombay. His ostensible source of income was selling *ittar* (perfumes). However, he was acquitted in 1998 and changed his career path. Instead of selling ittar, he formed a gang of robbers and to his credit, till 2001, he had as many as five offences registered in his name. He was arrested again but managed to secure bail.

In August 2003, on Independence Day, the Mira Road police station in Thane district registered an offence of murder which was indeed peculiar. Residents of a block of apartments found smoke emanating from a neighbour's flat and called the police. Inside the flat was found a badly burnt corpse. Not only was it burnt, but the head was also missing! It was Mussadiq Wahiduddin Quadri's flat. The neighbours could not identify the body and the police tried to contact the family. Quadri lived there with his wife and brother. They turned up and identified the body as that of Mussadiq Wahiduddin Quadri.

Who could have murdered him? With his career in crime, he could have had many enemies, but the wife and the brother said that they suspected Chhota Rajan, the 'Hindu don' who had embarked upon killing all those suspected in the bomb blast cases.

I, too, had moved on and was now Additional Commissioner of Police (Crime) in the Mumbai Commissionerate. News of this important development reached the Crime Branch and we were alerted. However, the mystery remained unsolved. No one was arrested for Mussadiq Quadri's murder. No informant could give us any clue about the strange fact of his decapitated body. It remained a thorn festering under our skin and had now decided to come out, seven years later, when I was the Additional Director General of Police heading the Anti-Terrorism Squad, Maharashtra.

Quadri was now reported to be in Golconda in Andhra Pradesh (now Telangana). A famous fort city and a tourist attraction, Golconda is also known for its ancient diamond mines said to have produced several famous diamonds like the Koh-i-Noor and the Daria-i-Noor. Now it was for the Maharashtra police to mine a rare gem from Golconda, a criminal who had thrown dust in our eyes and put us off his scent for seven years.

After Honrao had jogged my memory sufficiently, I decided that he had to go to Golconda himself to confirm the veracity of the information and nab Quadri. After an in-depth discussion on the modalities of the surveillance, Honrao left to prepare his team. He was to be accompanied by Head Constable Ashok Kokate and Police Naiks Sudhir Mhatre and Rajesh Kshatreya.

Honrao and team began their surveillance under the garb of ordinary tourists, visiting the Fort and other spots. Quadri was earlier working in the ittar business and it was quite possible that he could be trading in it, as it is a thriving trade around Hyderabad which is just eight kilometres away. So the team began making enquiries with ittar merchants, tempting them with queries about procuring large quantities. One name that surfaced was 'Imran', who also appeared to have some links with Mumbai. With a very sketchy profile, the team had to now find his address which strangely the merchants could not give. All they could say was that he lived in the Arab Basti of Golconda.

Now Honrao and team had to scour the Arab Basti if they had to glean more information. Strangers frequenting a small town locality are bound to raise suspicion. Soon some locals began asking uncomfortable questions and it looked as if the team would have to give up the investigation track. Just then they caught a lucky break. They found out that Imran used to visit a particular masjid for namaaz. Mustering all their professional skills, Honrao and his team managed to ferret out more information from this tiny detail. At the end of a very painstaking operation, not only was it confirmed that Imran was Mussadiq Wahiduddin Quadri, but it also came to the team's knowledge that he was desirous of getting married and had given an advertisement in the matrimonial column of a local newspaper!

The copy of the matrimonial advertisement was now in our hands. It sought alliance for Imran Abu Mansur Hassani, the new avatar of Mussadiq Wahiduddin Quadri. Getting hold of it was the biggest achievement for Honrao and his team. It had a Post Box number and also a mobile number. Honrao passed it on to me and we commenced the telephonic interception of the number. We could now pinpoint Quadri's whereabouts and pass them on to the team. Very soon, Honrao actually saw Imran and confirmed that he was none other than Mussadiq Quadri. He informed me that it was a positive identification.

Not only was Quadri alive and kicking, but he was also chatting with potential brides who were totally oblivious to the real profile of the groom. We were also concerned about the plight of the brides, given that the groom was to be arrested by us soon. I told Honrao that we must arrest him before he gets married if we could, to save the innocent bride-to-be. However, apprehending Quadri in Golconda and getting him to Mumbai would have been a cumbersome project, given the communal situation prevalent there. Just then Lady Luck smiled on us. Or she was probably more concerned about the bride-to-be than us. We heard Quadri telling someone that he was planning to come to Mumbai. This was a heaven-sent opportunity. All that we had to do, the ATS and I, was to organise a 'reception committee' in Mumbai for the eager groom.

I instructed the team to follow Quadri till he boarded the bus scheduled to depart for Mumbai. They followed my instructions to a tee. On 5 October 2010, once we had confirmation of his boarding schedule, at the first stop of this bus in Mumbai which was at Maitri Park in Chembur, he was arrested. He carried a .32 pistol, and some live ammunition, but we gave him no chance to use it. He also carried an election card and a driving license issued on his Hyderabad address in his new name. The team that secured the arrest comprised, besides Anil Honrao, Rajan Ghule, Jitendra Agarkar, Prakash Patil, Shailesh Gaikwad and Anil Bhawari.

During his interrogation, Quadri said that he had deliberately befriended a man who resembled him in physique and brought him over to his flat for a drink. He then murdered the man in his flat, beheaded him and set the body on fire. He burnt the body so as to make it impossible for the police to get the victim's fingerprints. Had we got the fingerprints, we would have ascertained from our records that it was not Quadri. With the head and knife in a bag, he left for Bhayandar in a taxi. He threw the bag in the creek and left Mumbai for Nashik and then to Manmad. From Manmad he took a train for Hyderabad. He also revealed that to make his identification impossible, he had wanted to alter his face with plastic surgery. He had tried getting it done at Malegaon near Nashik, but due to some health issues, the surgery could not be performed. Further investigation also indicated his involvement in a case of theft and smuggling of valuable antiques.

So that ended the reincarnation 'Imran Abu Mansur Hassani of Golconda' and we got back our original Mussadiq Wahiduddin Quadri of Mumbra. Not just a robber any more, but a full-fledged murderer, who had a lot to tell us. Quadri stood trial which concluded in March 2019 and he was sentenced to life imprisonment by Additional Sessions Judge H.M. Patwardhan of the Thane sessions court.

It proved that neither did we ever forgive, nor did we ever forget. It also proved that we had officers and men who were capable of intense hard work and amazing feats. The way Honrao and his team handled the three months long tedious surveillance in Hyderabad was truly exemplary. It reminds me of a failed surveillance that had taught me a good lesson, that one needed to pick and choose the right officers for sensitive and important tasks. It is not everyone's cup of tea. Not everyone can be Honrao.

Sometime in mid-1994, we were chasing one Simon Thomas Neduncherry aka Sanu. He had formed a group of sharpshooters and was executing killings at the behest of Sharad Anna aka Sharad Shetty, a Dawood Ibrahim acolyte. After much legwork, information was received about a public telephone booth that Sanu frequented, to make calls to Sharad Anna who was in Dubai.

I immediately formed a team from the officers who were readily available in the concerned Crime Branch Unit and instructed them to keep a close watch on the booth. Sanu's photograph was also provided to them. This surveillance went on for a couple of months but did not yield any results. It appeared that Sanu had stopped using the booth and eventually I had to call off the surveillance.

On 16 June 1995, nearly a year later and after a hard chase, we managed to arrest Sanu and a couple of his associates, who were carrying sophisticated automatic pistols. More than rejoicing over the arrests, I was really eager to know how our surveillance of the phone booth had come a cropper.

I was aghast when Sanu very coolly told me that he had been tipped-off about the police surveillance by the booth attendant. I immediately sent a team to fetch the attendant for questioning.

'*Saab*, one of your policemen showed me Sanu's photograph. He said that they were sitting in the tea shop across the road. He told me that as soon as the suspect came to the booth, I should signal them,' said the booth attendant. My head went into a spin and I did not know whether I should laugh or cry.

Now the phone booth attendant was a good friend of Sanu. He wasted no opportunity to send an alert to Sanu that the cops were keeping a watch on the booth to arrest him. Further enquiries revealed that after nearly a fortnight of tedious and boring surveillance on the telephone booth, monotony had set in the minds of the Crime Branch team. They shifted to the tea shop opposite the telephone booth, entrusting the job of signalling Sanu's arrival to the telephone booth operator. That sounded the death knell of the Crime Branch surveillance on Simon Neduncherry aka Sanu and this despite correct and accurate information. All because I, as a leader, had entrusted it to a team that just could not handle the boredom and pressure of a long period of lying in wait.

I could do nothing about my anger. This was just human nature and, as leaders, we had to factor it into our operational plans. Failures taught you much more than successes. And therefore, when you had very sensitive operations with little time for planning, one tended to depend on men who had proven mettle and aptitude for such tasks.

25

Fixed and Stung!

With the spate of gangland killings soaking the streets of Mumbai in a bloodbath, the Crime Branch was desperately on the lookout for desperadoes who were ready, at the slightest bidding of their remorseless masters, to kill and get killed. Eliciting information on their movements and whereabouts was a constant process and for that purpose getting hold of associates who were even remotely connected with them was of utmost importance. Often these efforts turned out to be wild goose chases, but then there were instances when they yielded amazingly unexpected results, as it happened in this instance.

When we were in pursuit of Sunil Sawant aka Sautya and his henchmen, on 15 February 1995, late in the evening around 10 p.m., Dinesh Kadam came to my cabin and said that his team had picked up a close associate of Sautya and wanted me to question him. I asked them to bring the minion in. We were looking for acolytes who 'took supari' from Sautya to arrange the killings, handled his funds or organised resources to fund shooters who executed the killings. The man was brought in. He was in his early Thirties and a glance at his clothes and the gold rings on his fingers gave the impression of his financial well-being.

'Bahut paisa kamaya hai kya?' I asked him. *'Contract lete ho? Dete ho? Batao kaise paisa banate ho.'* I asked him. (Amassed a

lot of money, have you? You take contracts? Give contracts? Tell us how you make money).

'Nahi, saab, main gareeb aadmi hoon,' (No, sir, I am a poor man) he said with folded hands.

As soon as the sentence ended, he was grabbed by the scruff of his neck and given a tight slap by Constable Adam who was standing behind and could not bear the lie.

'Sir, saala khota bolto. Mercedes aahe haramichi,' (The bastard is lying. He owns a Mercedes) said Dinesh Kadam as the man winced.

'Owns a Mercedes? And says he is poor?' I said. 'That means you are hundred per cent involved in underworld "supari" activity. Tell us straightaway. Or you want us to find out? We will find out any way.'

'No, sir, I make money in match-fixing,' he said.

'What do you do? Come again?' I asked him. What was he talking about? What match? What does he fix? Is it a distortion of the word matchmaking? Was he into some high profile call girl racket? Flesh business?

'Sir, I have nothing to do with contract killing. I have never hurt a fly. I promise you I am not a murderer. I only do match-fixing. I fix cricket matches and horse racing for Sautya, Sharad Shetty and Anees Ibrahim,' he said.

I had neither any interest in nor knowledge of horse racing. But I was an avid cricket lover. I could not believe what he was saying. Then he explained how match-fixing worked and all of us gaped at him – aghast and in utter disbelief.

'I don't believe you,' I said as he ended his narration. All those boundaries and sixers that my heart jumped at, all those ducks and wides and no-balls that I cursed at, all those breathtaking last overs that I bit my nails for – was it all a hoax? Were my idols ordinary mortals? The men who wore my national colours were playing with my emotions?

'Sir, if you don't believe me, *savere India New Zealand ka match hai. Main aapko kal hee dikha sakta hoon kaise fixing hota hai.'* He was saying that the very next morning he could demonstrate to us how he fixed matches. The New Zealand Cricket Council was established in Christ Church on 27 December 1894. To celebrate its centenary, a quadrangular one-day cricket tournament was being held in New Zealand. The participating teams were South Africa, India, Australia and the hosts.

'Ok. You can use the phone here and we will observe,' I said.

'No, sir. There is a particular PCO ISD booth in the suburbs from where I make the calls. I have to keep calling continuously and receive calls in return. If I use another number, it will arouse suspicion; so I will have to use that very number. I cannot use your phones. I will speak to the players from the same booth. You can see and hear me speak.'

Having no other option, I asked Dinesh Kadam and his team to go with him to the booth and observe 'the fixing'.

The match was in Napier on 16 February 1995 early morning India time. My mind was in a state of shock, but my heart still had an ember of hope that what the 'fixer' had stated was untrue. Curiosity prompted me to camp in office that night. In the early hours of the morning, just before the start of the match, I got a call from Dinesh Kadam. 'Sir, they have decided that India is to lose the match,' he informed me in a voice tinged with sadness.

I turned on the television. India were the odds on favourites and expected to cruise through the match. However, against the odds, India was bundled out for 160 in 45.5 overs. New Zealand made 162 for 6 in 32.2 overs. It was a shocker, the proof of the pudding.

Later, Dinesh Kadam explained to me how the 'fixer' had established communication with the players. At the pre-fixed time, he started talking to a player who was speaking for himself and two other players from the Indian team. Not only were they getting money from the Dawood Ibrahim gang for fixing, but they were also laying bets with their own money to make more money. A senior member of the team support staff was deputed as the 'Bagman', the intermediary who acted as the delivery boy or running man to collect and distribute the cash and earn a share in the booty. Knowing the outcome of the match, the trio were assured of returns and, thus, made money both ways. We were informed that an estimated forty-three crores were raked in by the bookies that day. I was heartbroken. It put me off cricket forever.

Further enquiries revealed that 'Mr Fix-it' had really nothing to do with contract killings. As we often need to, for Intelligence gathering, a conscious decision was taken to cultivate him as an informant. He could not be exposed to the gang. He could not be thrown to the pack of wolves that were bound to eliminate him no sooner than they got the slightest whiff of his speaking to us. The strategy paid off and his cooperation proved invaluable in getting crucial actionable information on the underworld.

On 12 July 1996, after completing two years and seven months as DCP (Detection), I was transferred to the post of Assistant Inspector General of Police (Establishment) in the Director General of Police, Maharashtra office.

With the revelation about match-fixing, my interest in cricket had waned and was now barely limited to appreciating the finesse and style with which certain players played on the field. Not for the patriotic fervour, but for just the technique and artistry. Sadly, I had stopped pining for Indian wins. As a police officer, it was not difficult to get complimentary passes or pavilion tickets. But I no longer craved to watch matches live. So it made absolutely no difference to me that the final of the Titan Cup was to be held in Mumbai on 6 November 1996.

The Titan Cup was a triangular One Day International (ODI) cricket tournament to be held in India between 17 October and 6 November 1996. The participating teams were the national cricket teams of South Africa, Australia and India. South Africa's 1996-97 tour of India was to commence with the Titan Cup. They were the hot favourites as they had won the 1996 Pepsi Sharjah Cup and five out of their six matches in the 1996 Cricket World Cup. Australia were the runners-up in the 1996 World Cup. They were the second favourites. India had not won any ODI competitions in 1996. Things looked grim and dismal for India. The tournament began and as expected, the runaway favourites South Africa were winning all their round-robin matches with consummate ease.

Meherunnisa, the charming bar dancer who had given me information on Sunit Khatau's killers, was regularly in touch with me. Often, she would have no personal work but just wanted to express gratitude and would call me. For instance, whenever she heard any 'strange' piece of news which she felt I *ought* to know, she would call me and keep me informed. Some particular underworld character frequenting a particular joint; some dubious chap suddenly showering a lot of money in bars, which could mean that a not-so-above-the-board deal had gone through; some tidbits of information or gossip that could have a basis in reality and help us be vigilant. Meherunnisa used to be abreast of the crime beat stories. If she figured out that there was a serious detection or that some controversy was causing me anxiety, she would invariably call me and ask with concern, *'Sir, aapka photo akhbar mein dekha. Bahut tension mein lagte ho!'* (Sir, I saw your photograph in the newspaper. You seem to be under a lot of tension!)

I remember once she had called up when there was a major outcry about our work and she'd asked me with genuine concern, *'Sir, kitna kaam karte ho*! (Sir, you work so much!) The only way I can do anything for you to make you feel lighter is to entertain you. The session will really work wonders for you. Please tell me if I can do something.'

As embarrassed as I was amused by this concern, I hastily

assured her that I was fine and she need not worry. 'Just pray for me, Meherunnisa, and give me khabar if you really want to help me! That's what I need if I have to do any good work,' I told her. Preeti knew of Meherunnisa as she used to call up even on my residential landline sometimes. That evening when I reached home, I mischievously told Preeti about Meherunnisa's concern about my stress levels and the therapy she had offered to help out with.

'Looks like for the first time a police officer's wife will commit an encounter!' Pat came the reply and we both burst into laughter.

Now just before the Titan Cup finals, I got a call from Meherunnisa.

'Sir, it's time you make some money. Enough of just *gadha-majoori*! (*Gadha* meaning donkey and *majoori* meaning labour.) I can give you a tip!' she said.

'Yes, Meherunnisa, what are you up to these days?'

Meherunnisa was on top of the world. A very important South African cricketer had taken a fancy for her and she wanted me to benefit from the manna that was falling from the heavens.

'Sir, in this Titan Cup final, India is going to win. Please lay a bet on India,' she confided in me. I laughed, thanked her for her concern and the tip and she rung off.

During the period Amarjit Singh Samra was the DGP and he was going to the Wankhede Stadium to watch the day-night final match. He needed two extra tickets as he wanted to take some guests along. He asked me if I could manage two more tickets to oblige his guests. I told him that I was not going and he could have my two tickets.

'Don't you want to watch the match, Rakesh?' He asked me, surprised to find me totally disinterested because he knew I played cricket and how much I loved the game.

'No, sir. I know the outcome of the match. There is no need to go to the stadium.' I answered.

'What is the result of the game?' he asked.

'India, sir. You can bet on India,' I answered.

'You are a sceptic. Dealing with crime and criminals makes you only see the negative.'

'Sir, it's just a matter of time and you will know if I am right,' we both laughed and I left his chamber.

India made a measly 220 for 7 in 50 overs. During the break between the two innings, I received a message that I should speak to the DGP at the Police Control Room set up inside the Wankhede Stadium. Alarmed that there could be some emergency, I immediately followed the instructions. To my relief, there was no emergency. Samra was only very eager to prove my 'prophecy' wrong and said, 'So, Rakesh? You said India will win! Doesn't look like!'

I said, 'Sir, wait and watch. *Abhi toh match baaki hai. Aadha hi hua hai.*' (The match is still on, just half of it is over), I told him. And then South Africa capitulated for 185 in the 48th over!

This information that I had on betting really 'stung' me when I was the Commissioner of Police, Railways. Aniruddha Bahal, a journalist from the now-defunct *Tehelka* magazine wanted to interview me on betting and understand how the matches were fixed. He tried to seek my appointment through various common contacts, but I declined. He was very persistent and dogged in his pursuit. Then one day a very senior and respected Test player phoned me and convinced me that Aniruddha was a young and upcoming journalist, that he would talk to me strictly off the record and not mention my name. So I agreed to meet him and he came to my office at Byculla. There were three visitors' chairs in front of my table. He took the chair on the extreme right and kept a briefcase on the middle chair. This seemed odd and something out of the ordinary. People never place bags on tables or chairs especially when they visit senior officers. I felt a little uneasy, but since a senior cricketer had recommended him to me, I let it pass. I did not want to be rude and insult him by asking him to keep his bag outside. He asked me questions and I explained to him whatever I knew. After he left, I called the police orderly, Prabhakar Khetale, and asked him how he had allowed the visitor in with the bag. The orderly replied that Bahal had said that he had just arrived from outside Mumbai and assured him that he had only some clothes in the bag, and that he had offered to keep it out if I insisted.

Months later, one evening when I was in office, Preeti called me, 'Did you give an interview on TV on cricket?'

'What interview? Where?' I was racking my brains, trying to remember. Then I switched on the TV and saw my goose being cooked. I immediately telephoned Preeti and instructed her to pack our bags and go to Mama's house in Bandra. My fears were not unfounded. Our house in the Haji Ali Government Officers Flats was invaded by OB vans and the press. I felt utterly foolish and realised that I had not been professional. Perhaps, it was the first time ever that a police officer was the object of a sting operation. And it had to be me, the cop who was expected to sting criminals. I felt miserable and betrayed.

In 1997, the Chandrachud Committee was instituted to investigate into the match-fixing scandal that had not only rocked India, but the cricketing community as a whole. I was called before the Committee and had an informal discussion with the revered retired Justice Chandrachud who wanted to know why I had not booked the players and bookies. I explained how the focus of our investigation was on contract killings and how we were cultivating sources for getting valuable underworld information for that. Our primary objective at that juncture was against the underworld and terrorists and that saving human lives was a greater priority. And under what Act will one book these rogues? The Prevention of Gambling Act? And what is the punishment for gambling? There was no stringent legislation to make these acts culpable.

In 2013, when I was Additional Director General of the Anti-Terrorism Squad (ATS), Maharashtra, my brief was to prevent, detect and investigate activities related to terror, organised crime, counterfeit currency, illegal arms, ammunition and narcotics. In the first week of May 2013, a reliable source came to me with the information that a suspicious number was frequently speaking to Pakistan. I immediately formed a team comprising ACP (Technical) Pratik Deshpande, Police Inspector Rajesh Bagalkote, Assistant Police Inspector Yogesh Chavan, and staff to work on the information. We immediately obtained the mandatory permissions to monitor the suspect number. However, to our amazement, what we found had nothing to do with terror. Instead, it was 'spot-fixing'. The Indian Premier League (IPL) 2013 was on. It was Umpire Asad Rauf, a Pakistani, who was making regular calls to Pakistan. Though the calls were innocuous, it was his conversations with Vindu Dara Singh, son of Dara Singh – the veteran wrestler, actor, film producer and politician who was an idol for millions of Indians for his patriotism – that shocked the wits out of us. Vindu was talking to Rauf and getting information on various aspects pertaining to the matches. Moreover, Gurunath Meiyappan of the IPL team Chennai Super Kings was also part of the conversations and Vindu was in touch with him as well. Sanjay and Pawan Jaipur, the Chhabra brothers who are owners of 'Motisons' Jewellers in Jaipur, were part of this nefarious activity as well.

Now we of the Anti-Terrorism Squad, in any case, did not have the mandate to go after betting. My officers said, '*Saheb, apan he kase kay thambvoo shakato?*' (Sir, how can we put a stop to this?) We were maintaining a watch to see if there were any terror or narcotics links to the whole business when we could have stepped in and considered how to deal with it. Just then the Delhi police team came to Mumbai based on their own Intelligence and arrested S. Sreesanth of the Rajasthan Royals on 16 May for spot-fixing. Along with him, they also arrested two of his teammates,

Ankit Chavan and Ajit Chandila on charges of fraud, cheating and criminal conspiracy.

The next afternoon, I received a call from the office of the Home Minister R.R. Patil. The Home Minister had convened a meeting at the Sahyadri Guest House and wanted me to attend it. The subject matter of the meeting was not mentioned. All I was told was that the DGP Sanjeev Dayal and Joint CP (Crime) Himanshu Roy would be there. The meeting commenced and R.R. Patil was livid. How come the Delhi police came here and picked up the suspects and we did not have any Intelligence? He was questioning Himanshu Roy who was the head of Mumbai Crime Branch. Poor Himanshu Roy offered an explanation, the Crime Branch was working on certain concrete leads and activating sources, etc. Then R.R. Patil turned to me and asked if I had any information, *'Maria saheb, aplya kadey kahi mahiti aahe ka?'* He generally addressed senior officers as *saheb*.

The sting conducted on me when I was CP (Railways) was well known and R.R. Patil must have expected, or rather, hoped that I would have some information on the IPL spot-fixing. But even he could not have imagined in his wildest dreams what my ATS team had just stumbled upon. It was so fortuitous that I should have the information that he was looking for. I told him about our discovery.

'Can you give the tapes to Mr Roy?' he asked excitedly.

'Of course, sir, I would be only too happy to,' I answered.

He then told Himanshu Roy that he wanted the Crime Branch to carry out a thorough probe and book all those involved. The meeting ended on a positive note. The next day I sent Additional CP (ATS) Amitesh Kumar with our tapes to the Crime Branch and also sent an official letter to the Joint CP (Crime) Mumbai, asking to initiate the necessary legal action. Amitesh Kumar briefed the Additional CP of the Crime Branch. Subsequently, the Crime Branch arrested Vindu Dara Singh on 21 May. On 24

May, Gurunath Meiyappan was called and arrested. The Chhabra brothers, Sanjay and Pawan Jaipur had in the interim fled to Dubai. They were arrested later, after their return.

As a consequence of the actions taken by the Delhi and Mumbai police, the Mudgal Committee was appointed by the Supreme Court in October 2013 to probe into spot-fixing.

Based on its findings, Rajasthan Royals and Chennai Super Kings were debarred from the IPL. Umpire Asad Rauf fled to Pakistan as soon as he got a whiff of the Delhi police action and was taken off the elite panel of umpires. It also came to light that some Pakistani cricket players were in touch with Mazhar Majeed, a bookie from England, and they were rigging even international matches.

It is a Herculean task for ordinary citizens to pursue sports of any kind in Mumbai. Lack of facilities, resources and time are the perennial obstacles in the path. The only way most Mumbaikars can indulge in sports is through the vicarious pleasure derived from radio or television coverages which offer some diversion and respite from their day-to-day hardships and strife. Of all the sports, cricket enthrals them the most, since there is hardly a Mumbaikar who has not wielded a bat and turned a ball, be it in his alleyway or on a green patch. There is more than an iota of truth when it is said that cricket is a religion in India. A good performance by the Indian cricket team gives every Indian a feeling of wellbeing and unfettered joy that nothing else does. In his drab and dreary world, the success of a cricketer is perceived as if it were his own achievement.

The plight of a Mumbai cop is even worse. He has neither the time nor the energy left after the long and tedious hours of duty for the bare minimum exercise which is necessary to keep himself fit. So overburdened and stretched is he, that leave aside playing a sport for fun, following a sport on TV or radio is also a rarely fulfilled wish.

Even then, while working perpetually under intense pressure, the only way for one to maintain a close association with sports was through the radio and TV coverage. Cricket was always a source of pure unadulterated joy and watching even a replay of a good game of cricket was like a tonic, a stress buster. But alas, this was not to be. As a cop, you are accustomed or habituated to seeing the dark underbelly of the society all the time and in all its ugliness and gore. But even a cop deserves some unbroken dreams. It was, indeed, my misfortune that I had to witness the nadir of my favourite sport from such close quarters that I should turn totally indifferent to its results, never to trust any win or a loss in the game again.

26

Stop It If You Can!

> Here again, the INDIAN MUJAHIDEEN addresses the escaped multitude of faithless disbelievers, praising our Lord for humiliating you by our hands at Ahmedabad and Surat and calming our hearts by chastising your bodies with disgraceful punishment....

Thus began the terror email received by India TV on 23 August 2008 that had pulled us, the Crime Branch of the Mumbai police, straight into the nucleus of the Gujarat blasts. After the sinister beginning, it went on to forewarn about 'successive' and 'severely intensified attacks' and 'lethal strikes to shatter all the fabricated lies about busting the terror module behind the Ahmedabad blasts', calling the ATS Mumbai, ATS Gujarat, and the ACB and Gujarat police fools. It ridiculed the prestigious Intelligence Bureau (IB) by calling it the 'Ignorance Bureau' and promised to carry out the next attack right under their 'close vigil' and 'critical surveillance'.

The Ahmedabad blasts had occurred on 26 July and the next day in Surat, several unexploded bombs had been discovered. The mail glossed over the reason why the bombs planted in Surat had failed to detonate:

> You boast of defusing our thirty bombs planted at Surat which your foren'sicks' claim to have failed due to defective IC's. But

> we know better! You are nothing but victims of our terrorizing plan that turns you helpless when the Wrath of Allah descends on you. Just think O numbskulls! How many microchips can be faulty? One? Or two? Or all thirty at the same time? This is another threat to those filthy Hindus of Surat who have failed to take heed and a reminder to Narendra Modi that it is not over, by Allah in whose hands rest our lives! It is just the beginning.

It then proceeded to notify that the 'Indian Mujahideen' (IM) were now much more resolute and better organised and added:

> Our 'homegrown' unit is steadily multiplying, silencing all the noise you make about the eradication of the 'radical elements'.

Threatening 'deadliest' fidayeen attacks, and warning that all efforts to suppress jihad would go in vain, it boasted that not a single perpetrator with even the minutest role in the blasts had been arrested so far and the investigators who said they had arrested the masterminds had no clue whatsoever as to who it was. It said that the Indian Mujahideen was in no way associated with the Students' Islamic Movement of India (SIMI) but were,

> an absolutely self-reliant and self-sufficient group with each and every individual committed only to Islam and Jihad, with our fundamentals of intense hostility to Kufr (disbelief) and utmost affection for Muslims.

It warned that action against the SIMI would only further and smoothen their progress. It accused *The Times of India* of carrying out false and deceptive propaganda against the SIMI and unnecessary bragging about the ATS and cautioned that both these actions were going to lead to the bloodiest massacre ever witnessed in history. And it concluded with an ominous warning: 'Just hold on! The countdown of your devastation has begun.'

The email also contained photographs of cars captioned, 'Our Favourite Toys', 'The cars that devastated' and of IEDs (Incendiary Explosive Devices) captioned 'Weapons of Mass Destruction'. The sender had authored the email as 'AL-ARBI' and the email address was alarbi.alhindi@gmail.com.

The audacious mail was telling me what I already knew: that at any moment, innocent people could fall victims to fanatical terror strikes not only in my beloved city but anywhere in my country. That some fiends were planning those strikes every breathing moment of their lives. That, even as I was going through the email before me, some jihadi could be boarding a train with a pressure cooker packed with explosives and a timer ticking away mercilessly within. That some desperado could be parking a bicycle with a deadly tiffin box in a busy market that very minute. That some villain could be packing a car with explosives and some zealot could be holding indoctrination sessions converting normal human beings into killing machines in the name of god.

And I was right in the thick of things, in charge of the Crime Branch of Mumbai city for almost a year. To be precise, from 18 June 2007, quite unexpectedly.

The unexpected had happened around 4 p.m. on 17 June 2007. I was at my desk in the DGP office at Kala Ghoda as Special Inspector General of Police (Training and Special Units) Maharashtra State, when I had received a message from the DG Control Room that R.R. Patil, the Deputy Chief Minister and Home Minister, wanted to see me immediately in the Vidhan Bhavan (the State Assembly). The monsoon Session was on. What could be the matter? I was in charge of Training. I could think of no issue relating to my work that could have made it to the floor of the House. Worried, I had immediately rushed to the Vidhan Bhavan to find R.R. Patil waiting for me. Sensing my anxiety, he smiled and said, '*Maria Saheb, amhi appli Joint Commissioner (Crime) chya postingsathi order kaadhat aahot.*' (We are issuing orders for your posting as Joint Commissioner of Police {Crime}). That's what he was saying! I simply couldn't believe my ears. Before I could say anything, he added, 'We want you to revitalise the Crime Branch's working.' I tried to absorb the full import of the sudden change that was engulfing me. Over the next half an hour or so, he gave me a briefing on the government's concerns over the criticism it was facing for the perceived listlessness in the Crime Branch.

The first thing I did on emerging out of the meeting was to call Preeti to share the surprise. She was as nonplussed as me. Then I straightaway headed to the office of Dr P.S. Pasricha, the DGP. 'Yes, *puttar*, I knew it was in the offing!' Pasricha told me, using the Punjabi word for 'son' which he used when in one of his happy moods. Around 7 p.m., the press started calling and I learned that the orders for my transfer had been issued.

It was a *déjà vu* moment. This was the second time that a Deputy CM had called me personally to convey the decision of my transfer back to Mumbai police to get back their grip on controlling crime. The first time was in November 1998 when Gopinath Munde of the BJP had posted me as Additional Commissioner under Ronnie Mendonca. Manohar Joshi of the Shiv Sena was the Chief Minister then. Now the Congress and the NCP were in a coalition in Maharashtra. The Chief Minister was Vilasrao Deshmukh of the Congress and the Deputy CM and Home Minister was R.R. Patil of the NCP.

The next day I took charge and called on Commissioner of Police, D.N. Jadhav who received me very warmly. As I entered my new office as the Joint Commissioner, I could not help but remember what my detractors had prophesied when I was sentenced to obscurity in 2003 – that I would never ascend the steps of Crime Branch again. One of them had even ridiculed me in a meeting with his juniors, calling me 'hero to zero'. And here I was! Back! Back as the only officer to have made it to all the three important posts in Mumbai's legendary Crime Branch – the sensitive top posts of DCP (Detection), Additional CP (Crime) and Joint CP (Crime)! If this was not vindication, what else was it?

My plate was overflowing with tasks as if to compensate for the three and a half years in the DGP office when I was completely sequestered from detection and investigation. The underworld was rearing its ugly head again and in addition to tackling conventional crime, there were also the dark clouds of terrorism casting a pall of gloom all over the horizon. A spate of bomb blasts had been plaguing the country since 2005 – despite the intermittent arrests of perpetrators by various security agencies. With memory blurred by the passage of time and numbed by a decade of barbaric violence, it is bound to be difficult to recapture the impact of the terror the bombs had unleashed – even the unexploded ones – unless we jog our memory:

- At 4:00 p.m. on 23 February 2005, at the famous Dashashwamedh Ghat on the Ganga, an explosion killed seven persons and injured nine. The ghat located in the holy city of Varanasi is a sacred bathing place for Hindu pilgrims. Initially dismissed as an LPG cylinder exploding at a tea stall, subsequent developments were to unravel an altogether different and sinister story.
- On 28 July 2005 at 5:15 p.m., an explosion ripped through the unreserved compartment located a couple of bogeys behind the engine of the Delhi-bound Shramjeevi Express, soon after it had left Jaunpur station in Uttar Pradesh. Luckily the motorman had managed to halt the train and prevent derailment, but it could not save thirteen passengers and caused severe injuries to another fifty. Initially thought to be an illegally transported leaking gas cylinder, it turned out to be an IED with explosives and a timer device.
- 29 October 2005 was Dhanteras, the evening with which the Diwali festival commences and when the masses throng

the markets for picking up last minute gifts and other things considered auspicious for the occasion. Three deadly explosions targeted low-budget shoppers in Delhi that evening. The first bomb exploded at the Nehru Market in Paharganj which was packed with Diwali shoppers. Those nearest the bomb were blown to smithereens. Unable to bear the shock, a shopkeeper just across the blast site suffered a heart attack. Fourteen minutes later, the conductor of a DTC bus spotted a suspicious bag under a seat and alerted the driver. They made all the eighty passengers alight from the bus and drove it to a less crowded area. Kuldeep Singh, the driver, opened the bag and noticed some wires and a clock inside. The bomb exploded just as he was throwing it away. He regained consciousness in hospital only to find that he had lost his eyesight permanently. Four minutes later, the deadliest of the three bombs went off amidst shoppers thronging the popular Sarojini Nagar market. The final toll was sixty-seven killed and more than 200 injured.

- On 7 March 2006, a Tuesday, the holy city of Varanasi was hit again, this time with serial blasts. The first to go off was at 6:20 p.m. at an important temple – the Sankat Mochan Mandir – where long queues of devotees waited with offerings to catch a glimpse of the presiding deity, Lord Hanuman, for the auspicious Tuesday darshan and attend the evening arti. The bomb was hung on a peepul tree and it accounted for ten lives and injured more than forty. Within minutes, another bomb exploded in the waiting area at the Varanasi Cantonment Railway Station, claiming eleven lives and injuring close to fifty. A third bomb was found unexploded in Gowdhulia Market near the Dashashwamedh Ghat. If that was not enough, six bombs were reportedly defused from other areas in the city. Fortuitously, there was no communal backlash. The devotees behaved most responsibly and participated in the evening prayers with even more fervour and passion.
- On 7 July 2006, seven first-class compartments of local trains originating from Churchgate station in Mumbai were targeted

during the evening peak hours with powerful blasts. Stations affected were Mahim, Bandra, Khar Road, Jogeshwari, Borivali and Bhayandar. The targets appeared to be the city's upper-middle-class residents of the western suburbs, the relatively affluent and predominantly Gujarati businessmen and traders who preferred the speedy local trains to commute to the busy market areas. The death toll was 209, while 714 people were injured.

- On 8 September 2006 in Malegaon, three devices exploded, causing a stampede in the communally sensitive town in Maharashtra. It was 1:15 p.m. after the Friday prayers on the holy day of Shab-e-Baraat in a Muslim cemetery, adjacent to a mosque. As the devotees rushed out in panic, a stampede broke out, killing and injuring more innocents. The injured were rushed to local hospitals on every available mode of transport, including handcarts. The seriously wounded were rushed to Nashik, about 100 km from Malegaon. Curfew had to be imposed in the town and state paramilitary forces were deployed in sensitive areas to prevent riots. The death toll was thirty-eight, and 125 were injured.
- On 18 May 2007, the historic seventeenth century Mecca Masjid in Hyderabad's old city area, close to the Charminar, was targeted by an explosion around 1:15 p.m. near the wazukhana, killing eight people and injuring fifty-eight others. It triggered rioting by a Muslim mob and the police were compelled to open fire which killed five more people. (Hyderabad was the capital of the southern State of Andhra Pradesh, later divided into the states of Telangana and Andhra Pradesh.)
- On 22 May 2007, three explosions rocked the busy market area in Gorakhpur city in Uttar Pradesh. The blasts did not cause much damage, thanks to the faulty packaging of the bombs. There were no casualties, but six people suffered injuries. Gorakhpur is famous for the Gorakhnath temple which is a major pilgrimage site and the city also has a history of communal violence. However, no communal violence erupted.

The terrorists were determined to keep targeting our vibrant cities and sensitive locations that June when I took charge of my post as Joint CP (Crime), Mumbai. The local police and other specialised investigative agencies were under severe pressure to discern the right leads from the numerous conflicting signals they were receiving. Our own ATS, under the able stewardship of my colleague Hemant Karkare, was toiling hard on the job. The Crime Branch also had to be equally alert and active. Not only because Mumbai has always been a prime target, but because terror often takes help from ordinary crime. Prosperous commercial centres like Mumbai are hubs and nerve centres of various forms of crime. The Urbs Prima specialises in providing quick custom-made solutions to facilitate clandestine activities and shady deals. You never know when some tangible information in a conventional crime can land in your lap giving vital leads to a completely different genre of crime, maybe even terror. I was goading my Crime Branch officers and men to keep their ears to the ground when more explosions followed:

- On 25 August 2007, it was the turn of Hyderabad to get hit by serial blasts. Two bombs went off that evening: one at the Lumbini Park which has popular tourist attractions like boat rides and laser shows, and the other at the Gokul Chaat Bhandar which is a popular street food eatery. A third which had failed to detonate was discovered at Dilsukhnagar. The blasts took forty-three lives and injured close to sixty people.
- Next, on 11 October 2007, at 6:12 p.m., a bomb exploded in a courtyard of the Dargah of Khwaja Moinuddin Chishti in Ajmer, a shrine revered by both Hindus and Muslims alike. It was the holy month of Ramzan and the evening prayers had just concluded. Devotees had gathered in the courtyard to end their fast. The bomb had been concealed in a tiffin box. It killed nineteen people and injured seventeen. The police reported that a mobile phone appeared to have been used in the explosion.

- Then on 23 November 2007, in the afternoon, the courts and lawyers in three towns of Uttar Pradesh were targeted by terrorists: three explosions went off in Varanasi Civil Court, two in Faizabad District Court and one in Lucknow Court where another bomb was discovered unexploded. Eighteen lives were lost and eighty-one were injured. For the first time, an email had been sent to TV news channels from a New Delhi cybercafé a few minutes before the blasts. And for the first time, someone calling themselves Al-Hind Mujahideen claimed responsibility. The mail was sent from the email id: guru_alhindi @yahoo.fr. The reason for targeting the courts and the lawyers was owing to the grouse that the UP police had framed innocent men under false charges and the lawyers had beaten the accused. They were referring to the arrests of three Pakistani Jaish–e–Mohammed (JeM) operatives who had been assaulted by the lawyers when they were produced before the Lucknow Court. Moreover, the UP Bar Association lawyers had refused to defend a Varanasi serial blast accused. Hence, the wrath on the courts and the lawyers.
- On the evening of 13 May 2008, seven locations in the 'Pink City' Jaipur, the peaceful capital of Rajasthan, were hit by nine explosions. It was a Tuesday and again a Hanuman temple was among the targets. A tenth bomb was later found and defused. The blasts that took place within fifteen minutes in a two km radius killed sixty-three persons and injured 216. People escaped from one blast only to be faced by another. The next day, on 14 May, two TV news channels received an email claiming responsibility for the blasts from someone calling themselves 'Indian Mujahideen'. The email id was: guru_alhindi_jaipur@yahoo.co.uk. The mail was also accompanied by a video which showed a bicycle with a bag on its carrier and with its frame number clearly visible. The number was that of one of the bicycles used in the blasts.
- The email id had been created moments before the despatch of the email and was traced to a cybercafé in Ghaziabad. Relying on the Holy Quran, it threatened to demolish 'the

faith of the infidels of India' and claimed responsibility for all the blasts since the Dashashwamedh Ghat explosion. It demanded that India stop supporting the US, expressed anger about the Babri demolition and the Gujarat riots, and spewed venom against BJP leaders Narendra Modi, L.K. Advani and Atal Bihari Vajpayee. Akin to some of the earlier blasts in UP, the bombs in Jaipur too were placed on bicycles.

- On 25 July 2008, Bengaluru, the capital of the southern state of Karnataka and the Information Technology (IT) capital of India, was shaken out of its comfort zone when nine low-intensity bombs exploded during lunch hour in its busy areas, leaving one person dead and twenty injured. The next day, an unexploded bomb was found in a mall and defused. The explosive used was ammonium nitrate and urea but, for the first time, sophisticated microchips were found to have been used to set the date and time of explosions.
- On Saturday, 26 July 2008, Ahmedabad, the largest city of Gujarat and an important commercial centre was devastated by twenty serial blasts going off within an hour at thirteen locations in crowded areas. They killed fifty-six and injured over 200 people. After about half an hour or so, just as the worst seemed to be over, two more bombs went off, one at the Civil Hospital and the other at the L.G. Hospital where the victims of the earlier blasts were being rushed. Five minutes prior to the blasts, a fourteen-page email titled 'The Rise of Jihad' was received by some TV news channels and news agencies with the subject line: 'Await 5 Minutes for the Revenge of Gujarat'. Sent by the 'Indian Mujahideen', it enumerated perceived atrocities against Muslims in India and issued a warning: 'Ahmedabad will see death five minutes from now. Stop it if you can!' It was signed as Guru-Al-Hindi Al-Arbi and was sent through an e-mail id alarbi_gujarat@yahoo.com.
- The next day, 27 July 2008, was far from the usual relaxed Sunday for the prosperous diamond city, Surat, another vibrant commercial centre in Gujarat with an annual turnover of thousands of crores from the diamond and textile industry.

Surat had literally been sitting on more than twenty bombs which providentially had failed to explode! The previous day when Ahmedabad was reeling under terror, a municipal cleaner in Surat had found a packet on a road near a hospital and taken it home, thinking it to be some electronic gadget. He had forgotten all about it until the next morning when he learned about the Ahmedabad blasts and promptly informed the police. They swung into action to look for suspicious objects and found a Wagon R loaded with explosives. The police immediately convened a press conference and alerted the public, urging them to stay indoors and not crowd public places. People adhered to the instructions and soon report after report of bombs being discovered and defused in different parts of the city began making it to newsrooms. One more car carrying live bombs and explosives was discovered. The bombs had timer devices with faulty microchips. The police also found knives, packets of nuts and bolts, petrol, chemicals, detonators, timer devices and gelatine sticks. Citizens watched television news in horror, struck by the destruction and the mayhem the terrorists would have caused, had events panned out as per their diabolical designs that Saturday.

- The Ahmedabad blasts had a peculiar feature: their primary targets were multiple iconic locations in the city. At locations within a radius of around five kilometres, more IEDs were planted, primed to go off a short while after the blasts at the primary targets. This was done with the express intention of hitting at the emergency and administrative services rushing in to give care to the injured and also at the security forces cordoning off the blasts and other strategic sites. The heartless terrorists had identified the nearest hospitals to plant more bombs which were designed to explode precisely in time to strike at the people rushing there: the civic and police officials, political leaders and even the good Samaritans streaming in to donate blood. The idea was to cause fear and panic to demoralise the public and the administration, and thereby undermine the authority of the State. But, what was significant for Maharashtra and Mumbai, were two important facts.

- Firstly, the warning email had been sent from an IP address of an internet connection located in Navi Mumbai. It turned out to be a plush fifteenth floor Navi Mumbai apartment that housed an American expatriate named Kenneth Haywood. He was totally bewildered when the police reached him to verify the facts. It turned out that the terrorists had hijacked his unsecured Wi-Fi network to send the deadly mail!
- Secondly, all the four cars in which bombs were planted in Ahmedabad and Surat – two in each city – had been stolen from Navi Mumbai. The two used in Surat were stolen from Vashi and Panvel on the night between 7-8 July 2008. The other two that exploded in Ahmedabad – a Wagon R and a Maruti 800, were stolen on the night between 14-15 July 2008.

The forest fire in distant lands was now coming closer to our part of the woods. It spelt death and destruction, but also provided the Mumbai Crime Branch with some definite direction and clues to work on, instead of groping for needles in haystacks. Who were these perpetrators who had stolen those cars from our backyard? Who had sent that terror email from the house next door? Navi Mumbai and Thane may be different cities for administrative convenience, but for criminals, they are almost a single unit, closely linked for all practical purposes, like a single human body is for an insidious virus, bacterium or an allergen.

We sank our teeth into the vital inputs provided by the email and the four stolen cars to look for definitive leads, but before a month could elapse, the terrorists had despatched the email to India TV dated 23 August by stepping right into our own territory. They were cocking a snook at us and we could not let the affront go unheeded. They had hacked into an unsecured Wi-Fi connection of Khalsa College located within the jurisdiction of our Matunga police station. An FIR was immediately registered at the Matunga police station and the Crime Branch was galvanised into action. They were asking for a retort and the Crime Branch did not want to disappoint them!

Crime, like bespoke tailoring, has its specialisations. You have master cutters who will do only men's suits and dressmakers who are 'specialists in ladies' salwar-kameez'. And just as a *sherwani* maker will not make a *lehenga*, a pickpocket will not indulge in housebreaking and a car thief will not waste his time on a bank fraud. Motor vehicle theft is a very niche crime, not every criminal's cup of tea. Within the niche, there are further super-specialities: four-wheeler theft, two-wheeler theft, theft of trucks, dumpers, tempos and so on.

Car thefts don't happen randomly. They are carried out to fulfil specific orders, placed for different makes of cars. For the car thieves, the makes have code words, mostly borrowed from the kingdom of animals, birds, fruits and vegetables. A stolen Scorpio becomes a Cheetah and, in 2008, a Cheetah in the grey market cost 3.25 lakhs; a Qualis cost a little above three lakhs and was called Koyal or Coolie; a Tavera, called Tamatar (tomato) cost 3.5 lakhs. In the 2.25 lakh bracket fell the smaller makes: Santro called Santra (orange), Alto called Aloo (potato), Zen called Jamun (syzygium jambolanum), Baleno called Pyaaz (onion) and Swift called Mendak (frog). Wagon R called Baingan (brinjal), Bolero called Babloo, and Innova called Eno cost around three lakhs.

Like the fruit and vegetable market, the market for stolen vehicles is a seasonal one. For example, on the eve of elections in Uttar Pradesh and Bihar, there is a sudden demand for Scorpios, Taveras and Innovas – vehicles that are most convenient and hardy for campaigning. Demand also varies by region: Innovas, Scorpios and Taveras are more in demand in states which have a very demanding terrain, like the Northeast. Then there is a niche market for stolen Pajeros, in places such as Delhi, Haryana and the surrounding areas where it is a symbol of status and power.

After a party in need of a stolen car places an order with a gang for a particular make of a car, a countrywide search commences for the car documents of that make, genuinely written off in a road accident. Once located, the papers of that vehicle are 'bought' by bribing the staff of the concerned RTO. Simultaneously, from the 'database' of car thieves, a headhunt commences for a suitable operative who is proficient at stealing the vehicle. He is called a 'Machine'. The Machine does thorough research to understand the routine of the owner and the topography of the locale where he parks the vehicle etc. Once he has mastered all the parameters, the Machine decides the right time and place for the theft. The vehicle is then neatly swiped and takes the identity of the vehicle destroyed in the accident.

Before a stolen vehicle reaches its final destination, more often than not, it gets a makeover, in addition to a fake or forged number plate and papers. There are specialists and exclusive garages and mechanics who do these jobs as not everyone has the wherewithal to get into such a business. Then very often, the stolen vehicle is driven from one state to another in stages, by different drivers, like a relay race. The relay drivers are kept in the dark about each other's identity. This is done because in the eventuality of a driver falling into the police dragnet, he is at a loss to give the police any clues about the thief or the final delivery point. There are cut-offs in the entire crime chain. Then there are territorial norms. Certain gangs operate only in certain areas. They will not trespass into others' areas. From Mumbai alone, an average of a whopping 3,500 vehicles are stolen every year!

Vehicle theft is, therefore, one of the most organised of crimes and since the terrorists had chosen to rely on the stolen car market to pack the explosives, we had a good chance of car thieves leading us to them. And in any case, I needed officers steeped in the knowledge of methods of the game, officers with expertise in dealing with motor vehicle-related crimes in Mumbai and surrounding areas, with a network of reliable informants in the field. I found such an officer in Senior Police Inspector Arun Chavan who had extensive experience in cases of motor vehicle thefts and jewellery heists. I immediately summoned him.

'*Arun, humko jaldise jaldi pataa lagana hai ki kisne aur kaise chaar gaadi Navi Mumbai se chori karke Gujarat bheji hain. Baaki sub kaam bajoome rakhke tumko iske pichhe padnaa hai,*' I said to him in our Bambaiya Hindi – perhaps the briskest communication aid in the world. (We must immediately trace out who stole the four cars from Navi Mumbai and how they were delivered to Gujarat. You need to put all other work on hold and just get after this task.)

Then I explained to him what I was after and all the facts that had come to light so far. He heard me out and enlightened me on certain intricacies of such thefts to update my knowledge. '*Sir, aap chinta mat karo. Yeh kaam aap mujhpe chhod do,*' (Don't worry, sir. Just leave the job to me) he assured me as he got up to leave. The interaction made me feel confident that I had found the right officer to lead the team.

As promised, Arun Chavan and his squad comprising Assistant Police Inspectors Nandkumar Gopale, Shripad Kale and Ajay Sawant, Head Constables Prahlad Madane, Viresh Sawant and Subhash Ghosalkar immersed themselves totally in the task. I waited nervously for their efforts to fructify and followed up continuously. Ultimately it was Head Constable Prahlad Madane who got us the crucial information. A group of car thieves regularly came from Indore to steal vehicles from Mumbai, Navi Mumbai and Thane and they were the ones who held the key to this puzzle. Armed with this information, the team now began to work day and night to trace the path traversed by the four stolen vehicles to reach Surat and Ahmedabad. They meticulously went from spot to spot, making enquiries with the lodges and dhabas where motorists halt for rest, chatted with the employees in garages, mechanics and toll booths, checked the CCTV footage wherever available. The hard work paid off and they finally tracked the route taken. It was Panvel – Vashi – Thane – Ghodbandar Road – Virar – Charoti Naaka – Valsad and then to Surat and Ahmedabad.

Armed with this information, the next crucial step was to get the 'Machines' who had stolen the cars. It was again Head Constable Prahlad Madane who got us further information on the Indore gang. With fresh inputs, the team succeeded in luring two suspects to Mumbai, sometime in the third week of August. Both hailed from the Khazrana area in Indore. One was Mohammad Mubin Abdul Shakoor Khan alias Irfan, a history-sheeter in car thefts with offences committed in areas like Andheri, Juhu, Saki Naka, Nala Sopara and Dharavi. He had nearly twenty-five registered cases of car thefts to his discredit. His career in crime had begun as a bag-snatcher in trains and he had graduated to car thefts in 2001. I wondered if my posting as Commissioner of Police (Railways), when we had tightened the screws on thieves and robbers on the railway network, had been instrumental in his change of field and specialisation! The second thief was Amin alias Raja Ayub Shaikh, a youth who had studied up to class VIII and in whose account there were car thefts and even other thefts recorded at Juhu and the Mumbai Crime Branch.

The suspects were brought for questioning one night around 10:30 to a Crime Branch safe house as we had to maintain utmost secrecy about the leads. I was at a friend's residence for a long-pending dinner fixed with great difficulty, thanks to my erratic schedule. My host was thoroughly disappointed when I announced that I had to leave early for a pressing call of duty. I sent Preeti home in our car and rushed to the safe house in an unmarked vehicle. The DCP and ACP Ashok Duraphe were both present and the air was charged with tension. As expected, the suspects were in no mood to give anything away. It was only around 3 a.m., with patient and skilful interrogation, that they confessed that they had indeed stolen the four vehicles from Navi Mumbai. But at whose behest?

'Sir, ek Afzal Mutalib Usmani namka banda hai. Usne humko order diya tha gaadi ke liye,' (There is a chap called Afzal Mutalib Usmani. He had placed the order for the cars) they said.

'Tumko hee order diya? Doosra koi nahin socha usne? Yani achhi jaan pehchan wala admi lagta hain tumhara!' (He only found you to place his order? He did not think of anyone else? That means he is very well known to you!) How did Usmani think of them? Why did he not contact some other car thieves? 'Where and when did you meet him first? You think we don't know? Why are you avoiding eye contact?' I asked them sternly.

Again the patient game of chess resumed and out came the important revelations that we were so anxiously waiting for. In 2006, Mubin was arrested in a car theft and had to spend eighteen long months in jail where he made friends with another inmate called Usmani alias Afsar Afzal Khan alias Raju. After his release sometime around April-May 2008, Afzal Usmani called Mubin to Mumbai for 'business'. They met outside the Vashi railway station and Usmani asked him to arrange for four stolen Scorpios. Stealing so many Scorpios was not an easy task. It could not be done in a jiffy. It was time-consuming. Mubin explained all this to Usmani who settled for Wagon Rs and Maruti cars with LPG cylinders which perfectly fitted the bill.

Usmani's interest in this theft ran so deep that he accompanied them while stealing the vehicles and also to Surat and Ahmedabad for delivery. The trio first parked the stolen cars in a car parking lot. A smart move, as the police rarely look for stolen vehicles in car parks.

Now it was imperative that we got hold of Afzal Usmani. More searching questions revealed that Afzal Usmani's association with them was deeper than just the four vehicles supplied for the Gujarat serial blasts. He had, earlier too, bought stolen vehicles from them for use in his tourist taxi business! Which meant that they should be able to lead us to Usmani! 'There is a stolen Maruti Zen that we had sold him,' tumbled out the details. 'It is kept in a safe place and we too use it when we are in Mumbai for our business,' they disclosed to me.

That was it then! Excited that we were at last on the right track, I enjoined the team that now with the help of the Maruti Zen they had to get me Afzal Usmani. Arun Chavan was confident that it would be a matter of a few hours. And I too was confident, for they had done such good work so far! So I left for home at about 7:30 in the morning, whistling under my breath and in a happy mood, as if I had just won the national lottery. I imagined that Arun Chavan would call me any moment to say, *'Sir, Usmani milala*!' (Sir, Usmani has been found!)

So imagine my happiness when Arun Chavan gave me a call late in the afternoon. Seeing his number on my mobile, my heart leapt with joy. Words of choicest praise were poised on the tip of my tongue to gush out for him and his team. What I heard instead was a small and forlorn voice, 'Bad luck, sir! *Tey doghe palaale, sir!'* (Both of them have run away, sir!)

The words 'bad luck, sir' always gave me the jitters. It used to be the favourite phrase adopted by officers reporting fiascos. Instead of saying 'our mistake, sir' they would put the blame on fate. Thankfully, they did not stretch it to karma! The words exploded in my ears like hand grenades hurled through the phone. And how did we manage to snatch this defeat from the jaws of victory?

The answer was straight out of a Charlie Chaplin slapstick comedy, funny in a bleak, black-and-white way. Three of our chaps, including our star Prahlad Madane, were taking the duo in a private vehicle to track the Maruti Zen. On the way, at a tricky spot somewhere near Chunabhatti, the vehicle broke down and our chaps could not get it going. Being experts at getting stubborn vehicles to sputter back to life, the thieves offered to take the wheel and the offer was blithefully accepted. The duo got busy and as the next step, the cops had to get down and give a push to the stuttering car. It started, and not to waste the golden opportunity that fate had made their tormenters offer them on a platter, the thieves revved the vehicle and made good their escape from what promised to be a long stay behind bars.

Arun Chavan must have been thankful for modern technology that he did not have to face me in person to break the calamitous news. Naturally, I spared no words to blast him through the phone. The most decent rant came towards the end of my long tirade: *'Tum log ghar banaate bhi ho aur khud hee usko aag lagaake vaat lagaatey ho! Full satyanash!'* (You build the house and then set it on fire yourself and mess things up! Complete disaster!) That's exactly what they had done. Seasoned officers and men had wasted their own good work – their finest detection. I could do absolutely nothing but rue the naivety and credulity of my team!

'Give me a few more days, sir. Please give us a few more days. We will surely get them,' Arun Chavan kept pleading. Ultimately I ended my bit in an equally dejected tone, 'Chavan, will you be able to do it in this lifetime of mine?' So distraught was I!

With Usmani's name and role disclosed, we began studying his crime record and antecedents. Afzal Usmani was a henchman of Fazl-ur-Rehman, an extortionist who operated from the Gulf. Usmani was a wily desperado, known for opening fire unhesitatingly to make victims cough up money. In one case he had opened fire at a shop selling firecrackers! In another, he had indiscriminately fired in Hotel Sea Princess at Juhu. He had also been arrested for the murder of the owner of a shop selling granite and marble. The hapless man was an unintended victim. Usmani had fired randomly to terrorise another businessman and the marble trader had received the fatal bullet. The officer who had arrested him for this offence was none other than Vinayak Sawde of Unit 8 of the Crime Branch, the same officer who had helped me crack the Gateway and Zaveri Bazar blasts.

As we continued to work zealously on these leads, on 13 September 2008, New Delhi was shaken up by explosions in a crowded shopping area, killing eighteen and injuring close to a hundred people. Around 6 p.m. in the evening, the first blast took place at the busy Ghaffar Khan Market in Karol Bagh. Then within a span of half an hour, four more blasts followed – two in the popular shopping area of Connaught Place, and two in a market at Greater Kailash. Four bombs were defused, one at India Gate, two in Connaught Place and one on Parliament Street. Several shops were damaged and markets downed shutters. Security was tightened across the capital, at stations and hospitals, airports, cinema halls, malls and religious places.

It was yet again preceded by an 'advance intimation' sent to TV channels and the print media from an IP address in Mumbai, registered in the name of M/s Kamran Power Control Pvt Ltd located in Chembur, a suburb in eastern Mumbai. The email declared:

> We once again declare that our intense, accurate and successive attacks like the one you will see exactly 5 minutes from now, Inshallah, will continue to punish you even before your earlier wounds have healed. To dreadfully terrorize you this time, by the Will and Help of Almighty Allah, we are about to devastate your very first metropolitan centre, your 'most strategic Hindutva hub', your 'green zone' – yes! It's your own capital – New Delhi – with NINE MOST POWERFUL SERIAL BLASTS, Inshallah, that are going to stop the 'heart' of India from beating.

It went on to deride the Congress government at the Centre and the state governments of Gujarat, Maharashtra, Madhya Pradesh, Uttar Pradesh, Andhra Pradesh and Karnataka, accusing them of victimising Muslims in the blast investigations. They questioned the authorities about their claim to have arrested the masterminds of the blasts, '...then which "mastermind" executed today's attack? Which "terror Module" slapped your ugly face today?' It also boasted that all the operatives responsible for the Jaipur blasts were safe and preparing for further strikes, and derided the judiciary of Rajasthan.

They then mocked the Gujarat police that far from solving the Ahmedabad blasts case, they had not even been able to solve the mystery of a simple mail from the Indian Mujahideen, proving their lack of ability: 'It is very sad to see the bad condition of your cyber forensics who have still failed to find out our technique of sending the "Message of Death".'

It accused the Indian media of double standards when dealing with terror. According to them, the media harboured a bias against Muslims and favoured Hindu organisations. It listed instances of inadequate coverage to the blasts allegedly carried out by Hindutva organisations linked to the Rashtriya Swayamsevak Sangh or RSS.

The email gleefully pointed out that the Indian Mujahideen had initiated ways of making the Vishwa Hindu Parishad (VHP) and the RSS 'cry for their' sins and one such way was already demonstrated in the parking lots of the L.G. and Civil Hospitals in Ahmedabad. 'So next time whenever you are there in the hospital premises for the "blood donation" programme it is our assurance to you that we will be there too for our "blood reception" programme,' gloated the email over the carnage in the hospitals where the victims of the Ahmedabad blasts had been rushed.

The email also threatened the Mumbai ATS and the Chief Minister and Home Minister of Maharashtra. It lambasted the Congress for vote bank politics and for allowing the demolition of the Babri mosque, and for the Amarnath crisis. It said that the nine Delhi blasts had been planned for Ramzan in memory of the two 'martyrs' of jihad in Delhi and exhorted the Muslims of Delhi to reflect upon the glorious history of their ancestors and revive their forgotten obligation of jihad.

In short, the email attempted to portray the heinous acts of terror as a retaliatory measure from a home-grown terror outfit, rather than the desired outcome of the designs and machinations of an enemy power. However, the master whose voice it was, the trainer who had trained and prompted the voice, could not be camouflaged. He showed through phrases like '*your* very first metropolitan centre', '*your own* capital', 'blasts that are almost going to stop *the heart of India* from beating'. It was as if some inimical foreigners and their slave puppets were addressing Indians, not Indians addressing fellow countrymen that the authors claimed themselves to be. Intelligence reports indicated that with the Delhi blasts, 'Operation BAD' which stood for Operation Bangalore – Ahmedabad – Delhi, had been completed as per the directions of the Pakistan-based terror high command.

In the meanwhile, to atone for the disappearance of the two car thieves, Arun Chavan's team had put their noses to the grindstone. I could sense that they were avoiding meeting me in person but, being mulish, I pursued them doggedly, until one day luck finally swung back our way. It was Head Constable Prahlad Madane again who got us the lead. Usmani was at a place called Paschim Mohalla in Dhilai Ferozepur, which is in the Mau district of UP. He was reported to be coming to Mumbai by train to attend a court case.

Under Arun Chavan's command, I immediately dispatched Assistant Police Inspector Ajay Sawant and Head Constables Prahlad Madane, Subhash Ghosalkar and Viresh Sawant to UP for a search. They first reached Varanasi and then Paschim Mohalla late in the night. The next morning, when the team was about to start their search, to their horror and dismay they found the local vernacular papers screaming the news of their arrival: '*Ahmedabad bomb blast ki tehkeekat ke liye Bambai police Dhilai Ferozepur mein dakhil!'* Despite all their efforts to keep their identities masked, the papers were proclaiming that Mumbai police were in Dhilai Ferozepur to investigate the Ahmedabad blasts! The team quickly exited the village and headed for Varanasi, more determined as ever not to return without Usmani. Then they gleaned information that Usmani had rescheduled his train booking to Mumbai. He was to now board the train from the Belthara Road railway station.

The team immediately left Varanasi to reach Belthara in time to receive Usmani. Head Constable Viresh Sawant had worked in Unit 8 earlier and was part of Vinayak Sawde's team that had arrested Usmani. He was in a disguise so that Usmani did not recognise him. It was his job to identify Usmani and signal the others lying in wait at strategic positions on the platform. As expected, the team saw Viresh Sawant make the pre-decided sign to confirm that their target had appeared on the scene. Then the train arrived and Usmani boarded the compartment near the engine. Our chaps entered the compartment discreetly, one by one, prepared to keep a watch on Usmani throughout the journey. But before the train could start, Usmani, the shrewd and cagey customer that he was, sensed something amiss. He hurriedly got off the train and our chaps also followed suit. Usmani realised that he was not alone and broke into a desperate run. A long chase ensued along the tracks. It ended in Inspector Arun Chavan hugging Usmani tight like a long-lost friend. Usmani tried various stunts to get himself out of their clutches. At the Varanasi airport, on the return journey to Mumbai, he even pretended to get severe chest pain and was checked by a doctor. But the once bitten, twice shy Arun Chavan's team were taking no chances this time. They stuck to him like glue! Ultimately, he was arrested, produced before the court and remanded to fourteen days' police custody.

Now began the race against time to unmask the hidden hand behind the conspiracy! Easier said than done, given Usmani's track record as a hardcore criminal and now even more seasoned due to his jihadi links. Arun Chavan and his team began the Herculean task of interrogating him. The common perception is that it is very easy for the police to get the truth out of criminals when they are in custody because it invariably employs third-degree methods. It simply does not work that way. A vigilant judiciary and equally alert champions of individual liberty have ensured the promulgation of stringent guidelines and rules, making it well-nigh impossible for investigators to expedite and extract confessions by using third-degree. The accused have to be produced for a medical examination mandatorily every forty-eight hours. The examining doctors have to ascertain from them if they have been subjected to torture at the hands of the police. The doctors are legally bound to note their observations and make reports so that the courts get a correct and unbiased picture from independent medical professionals.

In offences of conspiracies motivated by ideological and religious fanaticism, the accused are more often than not thoroughly indoctrinated and live in a make-believe world which they find hard to shake off. Therefore, unlike underworld minions, they are tough nuts to crack. Moreover, they are also backed by activists, frontal organisations and lobbies which provide lawyers and ensure media support. In the case of jihadi terrorists, a majority of them are trained to create smokescreens, withstand sustained interrogation and anticipate questions two steps ahead. The educated and qualified among them are the most dangerous and difficult, for not only do they perfect the technique of chicanery in a disciplined and pledged manner, but they also harbour ideas of self-importance, as if their role is to lead the flock by example. Leading the interrogators up the garden path, making them commit errors to go after the wrong persons, and then crying themselves hoarse against the police for victimising the innocent, all these are tactics deliberately pursued and are all win-win situations for the jihadis.

Interrogation is an art and a game of patience and skill. Consistency, perseverance and thorough homework are the hallmarks of a good interrogation. As the Chief of the Crime Branch, it is paramount to understand and identify the strengths and weaknesses of one's officers and men. Who is good at cultivating informants? At interrogation? At paperwork? At field work? At public relations? Your success and that of the Crime Branch depends on your ability to pinpoint these qualities and utilise or avail them at the appropriate time. Arun Chavan and his team, with their excellent informant network on property and motor vehicle thefts, coupled with their meticulous legwork, had laid the foundation of this investigation. But now they had reached a *cul-de-sac*. Afzal Usmani and Arun Chavan's team had now reached a stalemate. We needed a fresh approach and a different strategy to unsettle Usmani. So I decided that Dinesh Kadam and team, whose track record of interrogation was quite impressive, be pressed into service.

Often, such a decision is mistaken by the previous interrogation team as an adverse inference against their professional competence and creates bitterness. As a leader, you have no choice but to resort to it and at the same time, do your best to clear the air and restore the confidence of the disheartened team. Time is of the essence, as you have just fourteen days of police remand. The more the interrogation drags on, the more the danger that the others associated with the crime will get time to cover their tracks and vanish, and more the time the accused gets to prepare his or her defence. You must do everything possible and permissible to bring the criminal out of his comfort zone and simultaneously keep all your officers and men assured that even the minutest of their contributions are genuinely acknowledged and appreciated.

Inspector Dinesh Kadam was in DCB CID (Detection Crime Branch, Criminal Investigation Department) Unit 3. The team that took over Usmani's interrogation along with him comprised

Sub Inspector Sambhaji Dhamankar, Head Constable Arun Adam, Police Naiks Shivaji Sawant, Shyam Sundar Patkar and Rajendra Ramade, and Police Constables Asam Farooqui, Chandrakant Raut and Mahesh Bagwe. Usmani must have indubitably been psyched and rattled by the sudden change in the team confronting him, in place of the earlier familiar faces. In the wee hours of the morning, I received the call I was eagerly praying for.

'Sir, he has admitted that he is working for the Indian Mujahideen. He stole the four cars at their instance, sir. *Sir, ab woh popat ki tarah bol raha hai!*' It was a euphoric Dinesh Kadam informing me that Usmani was now talking like a parrot. 'Sir, some of their men are living in Kondhwa in Pune. He has given us two names. Sir, one is Riyaz Bhatkal and the other is Sadiq Israr Sheikh from Cheetah Camp....'

The moment he said 'Riyaz Bhatkal', my memory disc swirled! This name had crossed my path when I was investigating the Zaveri Bazar and the Taj Mahal Hotel blasts in 2003. This was the same SIMI activist and chief indoctrinator who had disappeared the minute we had learned of his activities. He also had a brother working with him, who was equally adept at indoctrination!

Thus, the interrogation team succeeded in getting confirmation from Usmani that at the behest of Riyaz Bhatkal and along with the car thieves, Irfan and Amin he had stolen the four vehicles which were used as bombs in the Gujarat blasts. He further identified the vehicles in the photographs in the terror email of 23 August as the two he had driven with Irfan and Amin to Surat. His details of the route and the halts, and places where the number plates were changed, matched with the information collated by Arun Chavan's team and the information divulged by the car thieves, Irfan and Amin.

We also learned that the initial modus operandi of the module was to pack explosives in tiffin boxes or pressure cookers and load them on to bicycles which would be parked in crowded areas. However, such bombs inflicted only minor damage and the module was itching for a quantum jump in destruction. So they decided to use cars which could be packed with huge quantities of explosives and driven to the targets, just the way the 1993 blast accused had so devastatingly used the Commander Jeep for the Worli Century Bazar blast which had caused an entire BEST bus full of commuters to vanish!

Now we had to find Riyaz Bhatkal and Sadiq Israr Sheikh. It was yet again my ace team led by Arun Chavan which succeeded in arresting Sadiq. The accused trained by terror outfits are adept at dodging interrogators. The higher the rank in the module hierarchy, the more their knowledge of the crime. They are constantly assessing you, your expressions and body language, to gauge the depth of your information. It is very difficult for you as an interrogator to pretend to know what you do not. Your expertise as an interrogator depends as much on your ability to camouflage your lack of knowledge as on your knowledge about the whole conspiracy. The acting prowess and the attitude of 'I-know-everything-about-you-and-your-people' are what separates an outstanding interrogator from the run-of-the-mill investigating officer.

I again decided to use Dinesh Kadam and his team to discomfit and fluster Sadiq and make him talk, for we could not waste time. Luckily, the strategy worked and we began getting more details of the module that called themselves the Indian Mujahideen. Skilful interrogation led to a spate of arrests of Sadiq's recruits and associates like Mohammad Arif Badruddin Sheikh alias Arif Badar alias Laddan, Mohammad Zakir Abdul Haq Sheikh and Ansar Ahmed Badshah Sheikh whose training Sadiq had facilitated in Pakistan. At Sadiq's instance, some arms and ammunition were recovered from a garment factory in Sewri.

Sadiq owned up responsibility for the Dashashwamedh Ghat blasts, the Shramjeevi Express blasts, the Diwali-eve Delhi blasts, the Sankat Mochan Temple blasts, the Gorakhpur Market blasts, the Lumbini Park and Gokul Chaat Bhandar blasts in Hyderabad, the UP Courts' blasts, the Jaipur serial blasts, the unexploded bombs found in Bangalore, the Ahmedabad serial blasts and the unexploded bombs found in Surat.

Sadiq was working in CMS Computers Ltd in Mumbai, was married and was a father of twins. He had completed an Industrial Training Institute (ITI) course. In 1992, when the Babri mosque was demolished, he was in his early Twenties and was drawn to SIMI and Riyaz Bhatkal. One Salim 'Mujahid', brother of Sadiq's sister-in-law, brainwashed Sadiq further and put him in touch with Asif Raza in Kolkata. Asif Raza visited Cheetah Camp in Mumbai and Sajid also visited Kolkata to meet him at the Tipu Sultan Masjid. After staying with one Aftab Ansari for a few days, he was taken to Bangladesh and then sent to Pakistan on a fake Pakistani passport. He met Azam Cheema at the Lashkar-e-Taiba's (LeT's) Bahawalpur training centre and received arms training at Muzaffarabad. He was sent back to India via Nepal where the ISI agents took back his Pakistani passport. Twice subsequently he undertook terror training in Pakistan and also visited Dubai once.

From Sadiq, we learned that the Indian Mujahideen comprised around forty to fifty members who were divided into three groups: one based in Kondhwa in Pune, the second in Mangalore and the third was operating from a flat in Batla House in Jamia Nagar in Delhi. The Kondhwa and Mangalore subgroups were under the overall command of Riyaz Bhatkal and he had trained them mostly in Bhatkal. The Batla House subgroup was headed by Sadiq himself and a majority of its members were, like Sadiq, from Azamgarh in Uttar Pradesh and trained in Pakistan.

Both Riyaz and Sadiq were working under Amir Raza alias Rizwan. Who was this Amir Raza? To find the answer, we would have to go back to 2001.

In July 2001, Parthapratim Roy Burman, the thirty-five-year-old scion of Kolkata's Khadim Shoes was abducted and released after a ransom of four crores was paid by his family. Investigation of this crime exposed the links between jihadis and the Indian and the Middle Eastern underworlds. Aftab Ansari from Lalapur in Varanasi held degrees in journalism and law. He had directed Roy Burman's abduction from Dubai. Ahmed Omar Saeed Sheikh, a Briton of Pakistani origin and a graduate of the prestigious London School of Economics (LSE), was an Al-Qaeda operative. One of the three terrorists, including Azhar Masood, released by India in exchange for the hostages of the hijacked Indian Airlines Flight IC 814 in 1999, it was he who had provided the arms and collected the ransom money in Dubai. And the kidnappers in India were led by SIMI activist Asif Raza Khan, from Kolkata.

Asif Raza Khan, Aftab Ansari, and Ahmed Omar Saeed Sheikh had been inmates in Delhi's Tihar Jail in the mid-1990s. Asif Raza Khan, a SIMI and a Hizb-ul-Mujahideen man, was an accused in a TADA case; Ahmed Omar Saeed Sheikh, a British jihadi was accused in a TADA and Foreigners' Act case for kidnapping British tourists from New Delhi's Connaught Place; Aftab Ansari, an underworld operator, was an accused in a murder case. They had found common ground in jihad. After their release, Aftab Ansari jumped bail and escaped to Dubai, while Asif Raza Khan remained in India and conscripted recruits for jihad. Ahmed Omar Saeed Sheikh reached Kandahar in exchange for the Indian Airlines hostages and got close to Mullah Omar and the Taliban and also the Jaish-e-Mohammad (JeM) to become a trusted aide of Azhar Masood.

Then the trio hatched the plan to kidnap wealthy persons in India and use the ransom to finance terror. Asif Raza Khan was arrested in connection with one such offence in Gujarat and was killed on 7 December 2001 at Rajkot by the police when he had attempted to escape. However, he had already divulged the details of his links with the Al-Qaeda and the Jaish-e-Mohammed and the shocking fact that a part of the Roy Burman ransom money was diverted through hawala to finance the 9 September attacks in the US in 2001 and possibly, the attack on the Indian Parliament in December 2001. On 12 February 2002, Omar Saeed was arrested in Pakistan in connection with the kidnapping and beheading of journalist Daniel Pearl, the South Asia Bureau Chief of *The Wall Street Journal* who was based in Mumbai. He was in Pakistan to investigate the activities of the Al-Qaeda. Omar Saeed was sentenced to death and is presently on death row in Pakistan.

Riyaz 'Bhatkal' was Mohammad Ismail Riyaz Shahbandari. He came from the affluent Navayath community which has its roots in the Arabs who traded with and settled in the coastal regions near Bhatkal in Karnataka. In the late 80s these regions, like many others in the country, witnessed consolidation of Hindu organisations. Post the Babri masjid demolition, with rapid polarisation on religious lines, Bhatkal witnessed prolonged communal unrest. Riyaz Shahbandari was a young impressionable man then. His father owned a leather tannery in Kurla in Mumbai where Riyaz had received schooling in English as the medium of instruction to become a Civil engineer. His brother Iqbal became a Unani doctor and got drawn to the Tablighi Jamaat, a neo-fundamentalist organisation.

Riyaz got married to the daughter of an affluent shopkeeper in Bhatkal. His brother-in-law, Shafiq Ahmed, stayed in Kurla and became a leader of the SIMI. Riyaz also got drawn to the SIMI and came under the influence of its leaders like Abdul Subhan Qureshi, influenced by trans-border jihadi terrorism. He also got close to Asif Raza Khan of Kolkata and resorted to crime for funding indoctrination and terror. So the Riyaz 'Nevayathi' gang began operating in Kurla and the eastern suburbs, hounding soft targets like traders and businessmen for extortion. Youth from well-to-do families in and around Bhatkal and young professionals who were not traditional criminals were indoctrinated and convinced by the concept of 'Mal-e Ghanimat' – the fundamentalist interpretation of Islam which allowed and lauded the use of crime proceeds to further jihad. Riyaz Bhatkal's links with such crimes first surfaced around 2002 when he made an attempt on the life of a Kurla-based businessman called Deepak Pharsanwala. The huge wealth of the Indian business community could not only be used to fund terror in India, it could be sent through hawala to any part of the world to fund jihad across the globe. Teaming up with Asif Raza and using the funds generated by extortions and kidnapping, Riyaz Bhatkal and his brother Iqbal, indoctrinated and enlisted many recruits in India and Pakistan for terror operations. All manner of crime could now be committed without qualms, by involving committed greenhorns and also by indoctrinating seasoned criminals like Afzal Usmani and his associates like the vehicle thieves.

After the Indian government banned the SIMI shortly after the 9/11 attacks, it began morphing into alternate associations to carry out its agenda. For instance, Amir Raza, Asif Raza's brother, capitalised on Asif's death, painting it as police atrocity. Teaming up with Aftab Ansari and others, he formed the 'Asif Raza Commando Force' (ARFC) which carried out the American Cultural Centre attack in Kolkata in January 2002. Two motorcycle-borne attackers rode up in the early winter morning to the American Centre building. The checkpoints failed to deter the assailants who opened fire from an AK-47 assault rifle. Four constables and one security guard lost their lives and twenty people were injured. However, the ARFC could not withstand the heavy police crackdown that followed. Amir Raza had to flee to Dubai to join Aftab Ansari.

By then, their association with the Bhatkal brothers and Mohammed Sadiq Israr Sheikh had considerably cemented and consolidated. Sadiq, with his terror training completed in Pakistan, got back to India and with his friend Arif Badar, began a recruitment drive. He sent several youths to Pakistan in batches. The Bhatkal brothers, on their part, began recruitment and training in the southern states. Then at the earliest opportunity, goaded by the ISI, they began the terror strikes, selecting their targets punctiliously to terrorise and kill innocent Indians. Amir Raza and Aftab Ansari, directed and financed by the ISI, began arranging and coordinating resources for the three subgroups who were eventually to call themselves the 'Indian Mujahideen'.

The profiles of the terror operatives drafted by Sadiq and Riyaz Bhatkal showed that many of them were better educated than the recruits in the past and did not have a criminal record. Ten out of the twenty-one arrested were software engineers whilst additionally, one was a Mechanical engineer and one was an MBBS doctor.

The module needed a base in Mumbai and Maharashtra. They hired space at the Sewri Cross Lane in Mumbai and two flats in Kondhwa, Pune – one in Ashoka Mews and the other in Kamaldeep Apartments which the Bhatkal brothers used for regular meetings and for terror operations. We raided the rented premises used by the module and seized jihadi training material like CDs, DVDs, books, pistols, cartridges, sedative drugs, tents, hand gloves, balaclavas, airguns, knives, commando jackets, vacuum suction for climbing walls, and other such materials including anaesthetic drugs which were used in abductions. We also seized laptops, routers, hard discs, pen drives, a Wi-Fi spot finder, signal detector and other such incriminating materials used in the terror conspiracy.

Anwar Abdulgani Bagwan, a doctor and graduate of the reputed B.J. Medical College of Pune, was an active member of the module. He had received jihadi training in Bhatkal. He was in charge of a Primary Health Centre (PHC) in Jogwadi in Pune. It was he who had entered into the leave and license agreements for the Kamaldeep and the Ashoka Mews flats in Kondhwa, Pune.

Interrogation disclosed that the module was actively planning several abductions to finance their terror activities. Bagwan had procured in his own name sedatives and anaesthetic drugs from the pharmacy of KEM Hospital and also from the PHC of which he was in charge. They were meant for use in training terror operatives in the 'art' of kidnapping. Bagwan had trained Anik Shafiq Sayed aka Khalid in administering sedatives and anaesthetic drugs to abduct victims. The module had been planning to abduct builders and jewellers in Pune. A list had been drawn up and initial reconnaissance of the targeted victims was also conducted. However, the arrests neutralised the module's nefarious designs in the bud.

Interrogation unveiled the 'media cell' of the module which had perfected the technique of sending the deadly emails that they boasted of with great pride, the most crucial part of the psychological warfare unleashed to spread terror. Prior to the Ahmedabad blasts, they had used cyber-cafes to send terror emails and also to check their intragroup communications, until two of such emails were traced back. The police then began maintaining a vigil on cyber-cafes and the module was constrained to avoid them. This necessitated the need for special techniques to send and receive emails without detection. A qualified and committed cadre to render such a service was the only solution and, thus, began the search for such a specialised job. Arrested accused Mansoor Peerbhoy filled the role to perfection and was a key find. He was helped in this task by Mubin alias Salman Kadar Sheikh and Asif Bashir Sheikh. Asif was a Mechanical engineer, terror-trained at Bhatkal. Salman had only passed class XII, but was skilled in computers and groomed by Mansoor Peerbhoy.

Mansoor Peerbhoy came from a respectable and well-to-do family in Pune. His father was a retired onion and potatoes wholesaler, his brother was a doctor who was settled in London and his sister was a language and diction teacher. After securing ninety-three per cent marks in his class XII Board Exam, Mansoor had found admission to BE (Computer Engineering) in the Vishwakarma Institute of Technology in Pune and stood third in Pune University in the final engineering exam. His wife was a doctor and they had a two-year-old daughter.

In 2004, Mansoor was drawn deeper into religion. He would practise I'tikaf meditation during Ramzan and began frequenting an organisation called Quran Foundation to learn Arabic. It was here that he was spotted by Asif Sheikh and Aniq Sayed as ideal recruit material for jihad. The 'atrocities' against Muslims and the lack of leadership in the Muslim community were the points of discussion and soon sowed the seeds of jihad in Mansoor's fertile mind. Slowly, but surely, he was led on the path of radicalisation to believe that it was his bounden holy duty to wage jihad.

Systematically trapped by jihadi scouts on the lookout for recruits with a good knowledge of computers and internet communication technology, in January 2007, Mansoor was found ripe and ready to be taken to the flat in Ashoka Mews in Pune. There, Asif introduced him to a pair called Ahmedbhai and Mohammadbhai – as a storehouse of 'knowledge' on Islam. They were none other than Riyaz and Iqbal Bhatkal. The masterminds now took charge of the new prey and steered him deftly towards their goal: using his knowledge and expertise to learn how the members could communicate safely and securely with each other and the outside world without getting caught by the prying eyes of the Intelligence agencies.

In August 2007, Principal Engineer Mansoor was sent to the US by his company Yahoo Web Services, for some work. He utilised the visit to buy equipment like a spy camera and a radio frequency signal detector for terror work. While there, he had managed to hack into the VHP's website.

In the first week of May 2007, Iqbal Bhatkal asked Mansoor to register for a workshop on ethical hacking of websites and wireless, scheduled in Hyderabad. The fee was hefty – nearly 60,000 rupees. The diehard jihadi that he was now, Mansoor even paid for the course out of his own pocket. The course was in the third week of May and Salman had joined him for the stay in Hyderabad as his understudy. On 18 May, Mansoor learned of the blast at the Mecca Masjid when he was praying in a mosque. He rushed to the hospital with Salman to donate blood. The Mecca Masjid blast strengthened his resolve to wage jihad, to the delight of Ahmedbhai and Mohammadbhai who took every care to press the Quran and the Hadith into service to motivate the media cell to seek revenge. Subsequently, one Saturday morning they were taken to Sinhagadh near Pune to witness what looked like a Hindutva activity where young Hindu boys and girls were being taught to wield lathis and also the nuances of other martial exercises.

The task entrusted to Mansoor was to find unsecured Wi-Fi connections whenever he was on the move, in Pune as well as outside. He found several in Pune which the Bhatkals decided not to use as they did not want the police to get any inkling of the module's base or existence there. Riyaz Bhatkal instead directed Mansoor to go to Mumbai and look for unsecured Wi-FI connections. Mansoor, accompanied by Salman, Asif and Akbar Chaudhary, visited Mumbai and Navi Mumbai every Saturday in June 2008, in Akbar Chaudhary's car. While seeking assured internet connectivity for the despatch of their messages predicting doom, they scoured Colaba, CST, Sanpada, Sion and Chembur and identified unsecured Wi-Fi connections. From Lamington Road in Mumbai, Mansoor also bought two laptops for his terror work on two different dates, paying a good part of the price from his own earnings.

On Riyaz Bhatkal's directions, on the morning of 26 July, Mansoor, Mohsin and Salman drove down to Mumbai. The time for the 'Stop it if you can!' dispatch was 6:45 p.m. Taking care to reach the vicinity of Kenneth Haywood's apartment block well in time, they posted the mail by hacking into his unsecured Wi-Fi that they had already identified. With the job done, Mohsin took the car back to Pune. Salman and Mansoor returned separately by road. They did not want to be caught in the police nakabandis (checkposts) they expected to be put up on the roads after the blasts.

On the evening of the Ahmedabad blasts, Iqbal Bhatkal had arranged a celebratory dinner for the module at Kamaldeep Apartments. All the operatives attended the party and patted their own backs for the successful execution of the carnage in Ahmedabad. The callous men gloated over visuals of their fellow citizens who were killed and maimed under the garb of jihad.

When Gujarat police effected some arrests in connection with the blasts, Iqbal Bhatkal decided to shoot another email to the media. Mansoor finalised it and was ordered to send it from Mumbai. On 23 August 2008, with Asif, Salman and Akbar he came to Mumbai. This time he used the unsecured Wi-Fi connection of Khalsa College. Similarly, on 13 September 2008, they hacked the unsecured network of Kamran Power Control in Chembur to send the warning email for the Delhi blasts.

Since Sadiq Israr Sheikh had spilt the beans about the terrorists holed up in Batla House in Delhi, I formed a team under Inspector Shashank Sandbhor and sent it to check the area surrounding it which is in Jamia Nagar, a predominantly Muslim neighbourhood. The team included officers like Assistant Police Inspector Ajay Sawant and Head Constable Prashant Madane drawn from Arun Chavan's squad and some from Dinesh Kadam's unit. I had the team flown by a late night flight to Delhi. The team reached Jamia Nagar in the wee hours of the morning. Sadiq had provided us with Atif Amin Shaikh's phone number and we had obtained the requisite go-ahead to track and monitor the conversations. It was Ramzan and the area was bustling with activity. Sandbhor was in constant contact with me. As per his assessment, it was quite impossible to carry out a successful smoking-out operation in Batla House, so crowded was the place, with narrow lanes and by-lanes. The best and only option was to do clean pickups of the jihadis whenever they ventured out far away from their holes or burrows, so as not to alert their associates.

On 18 September, we learned from his conversations on the phone that Atif Amin Shaikh was to meet a girl at the Delhi Interstate Bus Terminal around 4 p.m. the next day. We decided that it would be an ideal location to pick him up. He would be on a motorcycle with a friend. Sandbhor and team got down to planning the nitty-gritty of how to accost him.

However, on 19 morning, all of a sudden, there was news on TV about an on-going encounter in Batla House! My heart skipped a beat as I thought of my boys fighting for their lives in the Batla House flat. The terrorists were expected to be armed to their teeth. What could have prompted Sandbhor to raid Batla House without informing me and abandoning the bus terminal plan? I immediately dialled Sandbhor. To my absolute relief, he answered the call. It was not the Mumbai Crime Branch team who had engaged with the terrorists. A Delhi police team, who had also been pursuing the information about terrorists being holed up in the house, had entered it. An exchange of fire had ensued in which a decorated officer of the Delhi police, Mohan Chand Sharma, Inspector of the Special Cell, lost his life. He had won seven gallantry medals including the President of India's Medal in 2009. He was posthumously awarded India's highest peacetime military decoration, the Ashoka Chakra, on 26 January 2009. Two terrorists were arrested and two were killed, including Atif Amin Shaikh. I immediately ordered my team to pull out and return to Mumbai.

Shortly thereafter, D.P. Sinha, Joint Director of the Intelligence Bureau came to Mumbai and a meeting was scheduled one late afternoon where he was to brief senior Maharashtra police officers. Hasan Gafoor was the Commissioner of Police, Mumbai. I was busy in the morning in my office, preparing for the meeting, when I got a call from Arup Patnaik who was the Additional DG in charge of Highway Safety Patrol, Maharashtra.

'Drop in at my office, Rakesh! I have some important information for you which will prove useful,' he said. All information was welcome and I rushed to his office which was located at the Old Customs House. When I entered, I was surprised to see that Patnaik was not alone. 'Meet D.P. Sinha, Joint Director of the IB,' Patnaik introduced me. The man who was to meet me in the afternoon was right before me. What I learnt thereafter was even more surprising and disquieting. D.P. Sinha carried some grave misconceptions about me and was curious to find out more. He had dropped in at his batchmate Arup Patnaik's office and my topic had come up for discussion. Patnaik was stunned to hear the extent of the misinformation and realised that the groupism prevalent in the Maharashtra senior police ranks was at its root. Fortunately for me, Patnaik had observed my work from close quarters and was in a position to vouch for my good work. He told D.P. Sinha that either it was plain mischief to tarnish my reputation or a case of Chinese whispers. In any case, in all fairness, Patnaik felt that Sinha should meet me personally and judge for himself. Sinha had agreed and that is how I was in Patnaik's office that morning.

We had a protracted discussion thereafter and Sinha asked me several questions. I explained to him how I had tried to concentrate solely on my job, refrained from taking sides and in return how I had been hounded with so many inquiries and disinformation, continuously picked up for special vilification and driven to despair. As I left, I felt a little lighter that at last, I had been able to unburden myself to a sufficiently senior officer in the Union government. For this, I was totally indebted to

Arup Patnaik who had stepped in like a guardian angel at a crucial juncture.

Later that afternoon, I reported for the 3:30 meeting of senior officers. D.P. Sinha began his address by saying that the Intelligence Bureau had information about a terror module in Maharashtra and Mumbai. As he progressed with the details, it was clear that he was referring to the Indian Mujahideen. I felt it was time I told them that we had them in our bag.

'You are absolutely right, sir,' I said. 'I have arrested twenty-one of them.' There was a pin-drop silence in the room. All were startled except the CP, Hasan Gafoor. I saw a smile light up his face, perhaps his brightest, for he was not a man given to public display of emotions. I had kept him in the loop. He knew that I had reached a breakthrough and we were to go public any minute with our findings.

Then I addressed the meeting and explained in detail what we had unravelled about the module's involvement. The DG congratulated the CP and me and I said that more than me, the credit went to my officers and men who had toiled hard on the case and maintained utmost secrecy.

Then D.P. Sinha and Datta Padsalgikar, who was the Joint Director IB, West Zone, sat in my car and we came to the Crime Branch's N. M. Joshi Marg unit where all the arrested accused were housed. For the next couple of hours, D.P. Sinha interrogated them and was satisfied that we had apprehended the right bigots. He assured us all help and left for Delhi the next morning.

The interrogation had also thrown up information that Riyaz Bhatkal was in Ullal, in Karnataka. Our team led by Arun Chavan flew to Mangalore on 29 September. They traced Bhatkal's movements in Ullal and pinpointed the house he was staying in, with his wife and child. Not knowing the local language proved to be a major handicap for our team, as they clearly looked out of place in the rural South Indian surroundings. Through the IB, I contacted the Range IG and got the local police on board. I also sent the DCP and Inspector Dinesh Kadam to join the team as additional help. The local police advised us that the operation be carried out in the early hours of the next day. Accordingly, all plans were made and the raiding party reached the house the next morning. However, to their utter shock, they found the press already there! To add insult to injury, the birds had flown the coop, leaving behind some hand grenades, cash worth eleven and a half lakhs and a pot of warm tea on the gas stove! Despite all our efforts, including following up his leads to the Indo-Bangladesh border, we could not lay our hands on Riyaz Bhatkal thereafter. Soon he managed to cross the border to seek shelter under the wings of his Pakistani masters.

After the arrest of Sadiq Israr Sheikh, my teams toiled relentlessly and managed to arrest a number of IM operatives swiftly. I realised that one of the ways the radicals and activists created confusion in the minds of the general public was by discrediting the police through false and malicious propaganda by alleging atrocities, high-handedness and unfairness. In this game, the police machinery, despite its good work, almost always does badly, for we have neither the time nor the inclination to manipulate the system. Looking at the track record of terror modules, it was only a matter of time before we would be at the receiving end to face such false allegations which were designed to divert our attention from detection work. To inspire confidence in the citizens that we had indeed busted a dangerous terror module, I thought that I must call some respected and reputed members of the society or 'influencers', who will judge the worth of our claims independently and negate the negative publicity that would soon be unleashed to hound us. My officers were apprehensive when I expressed this view, but I said that our conscience is clear and hands are clean. We need not worry on any count.

So, in a very unusual move, I called a few eminent persons to the lock-up at Jacob Circle. They included senior journalist Kumar Ketkar, film director Mahesh Bhatt, litterateur Javed Akhtar, social activist Teesta Setalvad and some senior maulanas to meet the arrested accused. They met and interacted with each accused without the police being present in the room and came out visibly shocked and astounded at the level to which the youth were indoctrinated. They were also pained at the resultant hardening of the souls of those young zealots and the cruelty they were capable of unleashing. And most of all they were flabbergasted that such highly qualified young men could be so regressive. Not one of these esteemed personalities expressed any doubt that we had not caught the right perpetrators of crime. The accused also told them the whole truth and did not level any allegations whatsoever against us.

A couple of days later, senior advocate Majeed Memon who was engaged by the Peerbhoy family came to meet Mansoor Peerbhoy with his parents. The parents, good souls that they were, were totally heartbroken to learn that the apple of their eye had committed such heinous crimes. They were in a state of shock and despair.

'Tu toh hamare budhape ka sahara hai! Yeh kaise kiya tuney?' The poor mother asked Mansoor. (You are our support in our old age. How could you do this?) But Mansoor showed no feelings, let alone remorse. He calmly and without any emotion told his mother that his first duty was towards Islam and the parents came only second! They were then allowed to talk to him within our sight, but out of hearing. Towards the end of the interview, Majeed Memon and the Peerbhoy couple informed me that Mansoor was willing to confess and turn an approver. I said we would definitely consider the request and he should make a proper representation and take it up before the court. But then to their dismay, Mansoor refused point blank and said, 'How can I betray my fellow jihadis?'

Our investigating officers meticulously started collecting all the possible evidence to connect the events in the conspiracy and did a remarkable job, amidst all the other duties they had to carry out in the aftermath of the 26/11 strike. As expected, teams of investigators from other states began descending upon Mumbai to take charge of the accused that we had arrested to detect the blasts they had carried out in those particular states. Our breakthrough thus created a ripple effect and gave impetus to a nationwide effort of digging out the roots of this conspiracy.

What do we make of the Indian Mujahideen? Was it really 'home-grown terror' as they would like us to have believe? The answer to this lies more outside India than within. The rise of the Indian Mujahideen coincided with the rising embarrassment of Pakistan as the land of terror – sponsoring and nurturing organisations like the LeT, JeM and the HUJI. The world had no choice but to accept what India had been crying hoarse about all these years. To counter the now irrefutable criticism, Pakistan was desperate to show that their one-point programme – the Balkanisation of India – was the wish of disgruntled elements within India itself. They were at pains to show the world that India was producing its own home-grown jihadi terrorists who wanted to destroy Indian democracy and the Indian State and that there was no need for Pakistan to sponsor terror to destabilise India. The 'Indian Mujahideen' was nothing but an outcome of that strategy.

An interesting bit of fact assumes some significance in this context. Shortly before the Jaipur blasts, there was a meeting at the McDonald's restaurant just outside Andheri (West) railway station. It was attended by Riyaz Bhatkal, Sadiq Israr Sheikh and Atif Amin Shaikh alias Bashir. The discussion was regarding a grievance they harboured. They felt that despite all the 'great work' that this terror group was doing, they were neither getting enough credit nor recognition, in a consolidated fashion! For instance, their last two terror emails had gone from two different identities. Now they needed to show that it was the handiwork of the same group. Their strikes were looking like gigs put up by small-time actors. Not the blockbusters that the bosses in Pakistan wanted to project. So no one was taking them seriously! The Pakistani masters were getting uncomfortable and desperate. After all, they were frantically trying to create an impression that there was a massive home-grown Indian jihadi movement, which was hell-bent in defeating the Indian State. All they got after every blast was just some speculation all around and the responsibility claims made no impact whatsoever on the great Indian Juggernaut. So it all looked very ad-hoc! Not a grand indigenous plan that they wanted to make it look like. The Pakistani handlers asked their minions to get their act together. So now they needed to show that all the terror strikes were the handiwork of the same group and the group was self-sufficient, freshly radicalised home-grown jihadi terrorists who had nothing to do with any external power or terror outfits, nor with the erstwhile avatars like the SIMI. The meeting in McDonald's, ironically an Uncle Sam establishment, and a perennial target of jihadi terror in Mumbai, was called at the behest of Pakistan, only to discuss and decide what they must call themselves if they had to deliver the desired outcome to Pakistan.

They juggled with several sobriquets and monikers. The first name they toyed with was *isaba* – an Arabic word for a battalion or a militia or a gang. Next, they thought of *furqan* which means one who knows the difference between *haq* and *batil* – right and wrong. After considering all these titles, it occurred to the participating jihadis that there was nothing Indian about those names! It then dawned on them that the word 'Indian' has to figure in whatever name they chose. So they abandoned all the earlier options that seemed so contrived and alien and decided to call it 'Indian Mujahideen' – a no-brainer really! And that was all that was Indian about it. An outfit to destroy India, and still calling itself Indian!

How 'Indian' could they be then, was anyone's guess, but stopping them if we could, was entirely our job. No guesses there. No two opinions. And we were determined to do it.

Stop it if you can! That was the challenge they had thrown at us. And stop them we did. The profound relief that we educed was almost like stopping a demon in his tracks – a demon who had tasted blood and begun relishing it. A demon addicted to terrorising hapless innocents and getting a high out of it. A demon like the ones straight out of our mythology whose arrogance would surely be its undoing.

27

Thou Shalt Not Escape!

'*Sir, suna kya? Usmani bhaag gayaa!*' (Sir, have you heard? Usmani has run away!). It was a khabri.

'*Kya? Kaun bhaag gayaa?*' (What? Who has run away?) I asked.

But even as I was saying this, the name 'Usmani' clicked; the cursor dived and tapped on the right-side window in the deep recesses of my mind. It is not as common a name as Mohammed or Ahmed. The portly image of Afzal Usmani settled before my eyes.

'*Indian Mujahideenwala Usmani?*' (The one from the Indian Mujahideen?)

My question had coincided with the khabri's answer which was identical, save for the tone: '*Indian Mujahideenwala Usmani, sir.*'

Oh no! I literally groaned. The ordeal that my Crime Branch team had gone through to lay their hands on Afzal Usmani, began unwinding itself like a reel out of a spy thriller as I asked my next question, '*Lekin woh toh apne custody mein thaa na? Bhaag kaise gaya?* (But he was in our custody, right? How did he manage to run away?)

'*Sir, court mein laya tha, vahaan se bhaag gaya,*' (He had been brought to the court. He has run away from there).

It was late in the afternoon on 20 September 2013, and I was sitting in my office – as the Additional Director General, Anti-Terrorism Squad, Maharashtra. I immediately began gathering more details on the escape from official sources. A team of Navi Mumbai police had brought Afzal Usmani to the Mumbai Sessions Court near Kala Ghoda that day, from the Taloja jail where he was lodged. The escort party was led by Assistant Police Inspector Ramchandra Chopde of the Nerul police station, and Assistant Sub Inspector Deshmukh was in charge of Usmani. The Supreme Court has laid down that handcuffs or other fetters shall not be forced on prisoners – convicted or under trial – while lodged in a jail anywhere in the country or while in transit from one jail to another or from jail to court and back. So the next best thing for officers escorting such prisoners is to hold their hands like ardent lovers and stand. Sometimes it gets monotonous, humdrum and tedious. Attention wavers and drifts, especially in the hot and humid weather of Mumbai and in congested places like crowded court corridors.

The escort party was waiting with the prisoners in the open verandah outside the courtroom. One person was found missing in the headcount. That head was Afzal Usmani's. He had taken advantage of the chaos and flown the coop. The place was bustling with activity and a man could easily merge with crowds of litigants, lawyers and staff rushing around. The area also has excellent public transport connectivity and a person can be miles away in no time to conceal himself in the thickly-populated areas on the periphery. Naturally, the hunt for Usmani proved futile and led us nowhere. The slippery customer that he was, he had made himself scarce in no time. Consequently, an offence of escape from custody was registered in the local Colaba police station around 4:30 p.m.

Considerable hard work coupled with extreme stress levels had gone into busting the Indian Mujahideen module and in quickly arresting a large number of conspirators and operatives. It had brought great relief and respite to the metropolis and its overburdened police force. Despite the 26/11 attacks that followed soon thereafter to create a siege-like situation in the city, the

Mumbai Crime Branch had managed to file the first charge sheet in the Indian Mujahideen case in early 2009. The task to look out for the absconding accused was still on. We were in 2013 now, and the terrorists, fuelled and goaded by their masters across the border, were itching to get back at us, as was evident from the German Bakery attack in Pune in 2010 and the July 2011 serial blasts at Zaveri Bazar, Opera House and outside Dadar railway station.

How this radicalised hardcore criminal had helped the Indian Mujahideen graduate from tiffin box bombers to car bombers, the 'value addition' he had made to their terror operations, had to be revisited and explained to the subordinate officers and men of the ATS. I immediately convened a meeting of the heads of all ATS units of Mumbai and Thane. In addition, the meeting was also attended by DCP (ATS) Pradeep Sawant and the Additional Commissioner, Amitesh Kumar – both dynamic young officers and assets to the ATS.

I impressed upon them how dangerous Afzal Usmani was. His being on the loose could increase the potency of the Pakistan-fed jihadi modules manifold who were constantly trying to regroup and launch attacks. Usmani, with his contacts in the underworld and propensity to undertake desperate missions, was of immense value to them, and more so because he was thoroughly indoctrinated and a committed jihadist. These instructions were also reiterated telephonically by me to all the ATS unit heads in Aurangabad, Nagpur, Pune, Akola, Nanded and Nashik which are headed by Senior Inspectors. Aurangabad also has a DCP (ATS) at its head, while Nagpur and Pune had ACPs. Naveen Reddy was the Aurangabad DCP (ATS), and the DIG (ATS) for the rest of Maharashtra was Sanjay Latkar, who was based out of Pune. Both were very competent and conscientious officers. So I asked all these officers to immediately spread out into the field, activate their sources and leave no stone unturned to ferret Usmani out.

Obviously, Usmani's relatives, friends and associates were now on our radar. I directed the Mumbai units to ascertain the list of visitors who had met Usmani in jail. Who used to meet him in the sessions court when he was brought for his court appearances? With whom could he seek refuge? Who would help him escape? Who would harbour him? These were the questions we needed answers for. And quickly!

The Kalachowki unit of the ATS was headed by my old and experienced hand, Dinesh Kadam. The unit got a whiff that immediately after his escape, within about forty minutes, Usmani had visited his cousin, Akmal Dawood Usmani who lived in Sewri, borrowed some money from him and left immediately. Then the unit also got wind that 'coincidentally', from the date of Afzal Usmani's escape, his sister's nineteen-year-old son, Javed Nurul Hasan Khan was also not to be seen around his home in Dharavi where he used to normally hang out. What was more significant was that this Javed would frequently visit Usmani in jail and also when he was brought to court. And now he was nowhere to be seen! The unit now began working on finding out more about Javed's friends and his hideouts. They were searching high and low, but there was no sign of both. It was as if both had vanished into thin air!

A month went by, and a very stressful month at that, haunted by the dreadful anticipation of renewed terror strikes. It was then that out of the blue a 'zero number' conveyed to the Kalachowki unit the glad tidings that the prodigal nephew was back in good old Mumbai and was reportedly moving around in Govandi, Kurla, Sion and Mahim – areas which are close to Dharavi. Our vigil intensified and on 25 October, the informant confirmed that Javed would be coming around 9 p.m. to Hotel Delux on L.B.S. Marg in Kurla.

'Sir, woh Javed Mumbai wapas aa gaya hai!' (Sir, that Javed is back in Mumbai) announced Dinesh Kadam.

'Apneko abhi ek yehee mauka hai, Dinesh! Perfect plan karo aur pakad lo usko! Saala haath se nikalna nahin chahiye!' I could feel my pulse race as I said this. (We have only one chance, Dinesh. Make a perfect plan and arrest him! The scoundrel must not get out of your hands!)

We had a detailed discussion and Dinesh Kadam formed a team to lay in wait for our target, comprising Assistant Police Inspector Susheel Kumar Shinde, lady Police Sub Inspector Sahara Shaikh, Assistant Sub Inspector Sanjay Chavan, Head Constable Srikant Shelar, Police Naik Mahesh Bagwe, Police Constables Asam Farooqui, Manohar Shinde, Mahesh Mule and Amit Mhangade.

So, around 8:30 p.m., a car suddenly broke down just outside Hotel Delux on the busy L.B.S. Marg. The driver and his mate had to call a mechanic. Fortunately, he came immediately and got busy rectifying the mechanical defect.

A man on the pavement near a paan stall was waiting anxiously for a friend. He kept calling his friend to ask where he had reached. *Kidhar pahuncha, bhai! Aur aadha ghantaa lagegaa?* (Where have you reached, brother? Will it take you half an hour more?)

A Muslim lady in burqa stood talking to a man in a Pathani suit who was wearing a skull cap and sitting on a bike parked near the pavement.

A table in the restaurant was taken by a group of three who began discussing some serious matter, going through a sheaf of legal papers and documents, which looked like a court case. They placed their order and said that they were expecting two more persons to join them.

Around 9:30 p.m., the man waiting at the paan stall finally looked relieved that his friend was approaching. He threw his half-smoked cigarette on the pavement, stubbed it out with his shoe and began walking to receive his friend.

The mechanic shut the bonnet and wiped his hands with the

dirty rag in his pocket, with a disgusted look on his face, as if preparing to box a few ears if he could.

A young man was climbing the steps of the restaurant. The men with the legal papers were winding up their meeting as they had received a call that their lawyer would not be able to meet them that day. They were settling the bill.

If the young man was hoping to meet some friend in the restaurant, he would have to wait. For he could not spot the face amongst the guests and then froze for a second. Something was not right. God gifts criminals with a sixth sense, especially those who are on the run. Their alert mechanism is alive in full zing with antennae out to catch signals to sense when there is a cop on the lookout around. They get vibrations – *Khatraa hai!* (Danger around!) The young man now looked scared and turned. He rushed towards the door and when he heard the men with the legal papers push their chairs back and stand up, he sprinted out with the three men in hot pursuit. Out on the road, the car owner, his friend and the mechanic too joined the chase. The man waiting for his friend at the paan shop and the amorous couple were not far behind. They were now on a bike! Luckily the chase ended in a short while to enable an ecstatic Dinesh Kadam to dial a number. I pounced on my phone as soon as it rang. *'Sir, mil gayaa!'* (Got him). Just two happy words.

It did not take us long to get the entire account of the *mamu's* (maternal uncle) escape from his devoted *bhanja* (nephew). For quite some time, Afzal Usmani had been observing the routines, duty patterns and habits of the policemen in the escort party and biding his time for the opportune moment to slip off. His research sufficiently completed, on the day of the hearing – 20 September – Javed chose to stay home instead of going to the Sessions Court to meet his mamu. He had helped himself to 5,000 rupees from his mother's savings which she used to keep for a rainy day. He had also packed a small bag for the overnight stay for two men.

He finished his lunch, kept the door ajar and sat fiddling with his cell phone. It was near teatime that the door opened and Usmani entered the house, wearing chocolate-coloured trousers and a white kurta.

'Come, let's go!' Usmani urged Javed. 'Have you kept the money ready? Let's get out of here!'

It was not for nothing that Javed was a frequent visitor to meet the incarcerated Afzal mamu. Javed was totally in awe of his uncle to the point of veneration. For him, Afzal mamu was everything, with his great trigger-happy reputation in the underworld and his subsequent 'reformation' in the cause of Islam. Usmani had been indoctrinating Javed and grooming him to be a terror recruit with such fervour that Javed was completely under his spell.

So the dutiful disciple picked up his bag and they left the house, walking down 60 Feet Road. Usmani took off his white kurta and threw it in a gutter. He was already wearing a blue T-shirt under it. Then he walked nonchalantly to Mukund Nagar with Javed in tow, all calm and composed. Next, Usmani entered a barber shop called Vinayak Hair Cutting Saloon and relieved himself of his moustache and beard. He also pampered himself and Javed with a good head and facial massage. The makeover was now complete. He was ready to face the world in a new avatar. But not without caution. No undue risks. So the mamu-bhanja duo bided their time till dusk fell over the city and only thereafter did they board a BEST bus to Khar. Then an auto rickshaw ferried them to Borivali where they boarded a private bus to Gujarat from the stop outside the Borivali National Park. Reaching the Vapi railway station around midnight, they boarded the Gorakhpur-Awadh Express around 1:30 a.m., reaching Lucknow at 7 the following morning. From Lucknow, they took a bus to Fakharpur in district Bahraich. A *ghoda gadi* (horse cart) took them to village Tatehara in Lalpur to the house of Salma Khatoon Fakhruddin Khan, Javed's older sister.

From Tatehara, Usmani crossed over to Nepal, but not before convincing Javed that he should stay put in Tatehara and continue with his education in Bahraich. He did not want Javed to go back to Mumbai at any cost. The obeisant nephew began looking for admission to a suitable college. However, he needed his educational certificates. So he had no alternative but to go back to Mumbai to collect them, or so he said. Rather, he must have felt like a fish out of water, in a remote corner of the country that his uncle had left him to dry out. He was perhaps pining for the exciting life in Mumbai that a nineteen-year-old finds so alluring, especially when he is mixed up in the wrong crowd. So, much against his uncle's advice, Javed had come to Mumbai. Knowing full well that the police would be on the lookout for him, he exercised utmost caution not to come anywhere near his own house. He had also avoided staying with friends or relatives. He knew that they would definitely be on the police's radar. Instead, he stayed with some friends of his friends who lived in Govandi and this had made our task of ferreting him out more arduous.

From Javed's disclosures during the interrogation and also from reliable information received from our own sources, it appeared that Usmani was nursing some big career plans for himself. With all the top leadership of the Indian Mujahideen behind bars, he was seriously dreaming of slipping into their shoes. We had to nip his monstrous ambitions in the bud. We had to get this dangerous fugitive back to where he rightfully belonged – behind bars.

'So, now where is your Afzal mamu?' Javed was asked.

'He keeps shuttling between Nepal and Tatehara, sir. If you go to Tatehara, you will be able to get him for sure,' said Javed.

On 25 October 2013, Dinesh Kadam promptly relayed this vital information to me over the telephone. Despite the late hour, it was imperative to form a team and dispatch them on the mission without losing any time.

I had to handpick officers from the Anti-Terrorism Squad (ATS) and men of proven skills for the team, who were not only astute with a presence of mind and quick thinking, but also possessed the derring-do which was needed for a chase in a totally unknown and hostile terrain, which was close to the notorious Indo-Nepal border. Dinesh Kadam could not be spared. He had to remain in Mumbai to continue Javed's questioning and to act as a link between Javed and the events that would unfold in Tatehara during the chase. ACP Mangesh Pote, who had worked with me in the Crime Branch, was not only an experienced officer, but was also cool and composed. Under him, I selected a team comprising Police Inspector Shital Raut, Assistant Police Inspector Anil Honrao, Police Naiks Namdev Kale and Mahesh Bagwe, and Police Constables Asam Farooqui and Anwar Memon. Shital Raut of the Vikhroli unit was a dashing young officer. A basketball player, he had represented Maharashtra at the national level and I had watched him closely both on the sports field as well as in police work; Anil Honrao was the proverbial chameleon, an asset for covert operations; the Constables and Naiks too were veterans who had helped me in several operations.

The team could not get so many seats on the same flight to Lucknow. So they were split into two groups, one headed by Pote and the other by Shital Raut. The indefatigable and enthusiastic Amitesh Kumar and Pradeep Sawant ensured that the teams flew out that very night so as to reach Lucknow early next morning. The first to reach Lucknow was Shital Raut's team. Information about Javed's arrest was bound to reach the terrorists soon and we simply could not afford to waste any time. Therefore, without waiting for the other team to land, they hired a Tavera and reached Fakharpur. Discreet enquiries with the local populace confirmed that some 'new person' had come to stay in Usmani's niece's house. Who was this person? And how does the team get to check the house for the presence of the 'new man'?

Quite simple. In the afternoon, the house was visited by some policemen in plain clothes who said that they had information that *patta jugar* (gambling with cards) was being played in the house and that they wanted to carry out a search. They were permitted to do so, but they were unable to locate 'the new man' inside. When informed about this, I was aghast at the SNAFU (Situation Normal All Fucked Up)! I could not demoralise the team. But I could not resist cursing under my breath in as mild a voice as possible.

'Why did you not make sure before entering the house that he was inside?' This was one of my standing instructions to the teams even in the past for such operations! They had no answer. They were so keen to not waste time that they had risked a dangerous wager. Luckily no one in the house suspected anything. On the contrary, they gave our team information about the houses that actually ran gambling dens inside!

If not in that house, where was Usmani? I conveyed the information to Dinesh Kadam. *'Tumhara banda bol raha hai ki woh Tatehara mein hai.* But he is not. *Jhoot toh nahin bol raha hai na?'* (Your Charlie says that Usmani is in Tatehara, but he is not. I hope he is not lying by any chance?)

Dinesh confronted Javed who said that the only way to get Usmani's precise whereabouts was to get hold of a man called Fakhruddin, a resident of Tatehara. I told Shital Raut that the team must now aim for a 'clean pickup' of Fakhruddin. They skilfully managed to get hold of a local villager who could identify Fakhruddin. I began discussing with Shital Raut to understand how he could achieve a clean pickup. Soon a plan was chalked out. As per the plan, the team lay in wait for Fakhruddin around a paan shop he frequented. The team picked him up as he was walking away from the shop and brought him to a waiting Tavera. He was quite rattled, but when questioned, he feigned total ignorance, 'Sir, I have no idea what you are talking about! I don't know where Afzal Usmani is.'

Shital Raut immediately conveyed the development to me and I contacted Dinesh Kadam.

'Sir, woh Fakhruddin jhooth bol rahaa hai. Usko sau takka pataa hoga maama kahan hain. Badi dosti hain maama se uski,' (Sir, that Fakhruddin is lying. He will hundred per cent know where maama is. He and maama are great friends) said Javed when Dinesh Kadam told him about Fakhruddin's response.

'Toh abhi bol, tere Fakhruddin se sach kaise bulwaneka?' (Then tell us now, how do we make your Fakhruddin tell us the truth?) Dinesh Kadam asked Javed, *'Kya karta hai yeh Fakhruddin? Kya kaam dhanda karta hai?'* (What does this Fakhruddin do? What work does he do?)

Javed said that Fakhruddin was a hawker in Mumbai. He sold roasted *moongfali* (peanuts) and fruits from rented handcarts. By now, Pote's team had also reached Tatehara. This information was passed on to Pote and Raut who were now seated in the Tavera with their dear babe in the woods – Fakhruddin.

'So! You are a hawker! You rent handcarts in Mumbai? What do you sell? Moongfali? We know everything about you. Do you want to continue selling moongfali? Or you want to break stones in jail? Decide fast. We don't have all the time in the world. Tell us. Looks like you want to stop work!' Fakhruddin was now facing a barrage of browbeating propositions about his future business scenario, *'Mumbai mein entry band kar dega. Sab cheez jabt karenge.'* (You will not be able to enter Mumbai. All your assets will be confiscated). Fakhruddin's face slowly changed colour. And then came the trump card. 'Now we want you to speak to someone you know!' A cell phone was put on the speaker mode and Fakhruddin was startled to hear the voice, *'Assalam Aleikum, Fakhru bhai. Javed bol raha hoon ji!'* (Greetings, brother Fakhru! This is Javed). Fakhruddin's face now turned totally pale as Javed informed him that he had told the Mumbai police everything. It was then that Fakhruddin came around and accepted the facts that he had been denying all this while: yes, Usmani was a good friend. Yes, he had come to Tatehara and had crossed over to Nepal. Yes, he kept visiting Salma's house from Nepal. Yes, he was here a few days ago. But....! But, Usmani had left for Nepal only the day before.

The team was utterly dejected to hear this. It meant that the search for Usmani in the biting October cold, so difficult to handle for those living in the south of the Vindhyas, was not over yet. Again Fakhruddin was cautioned that he had aided and abetted the escape and he could be made an accused in a criminal case. His entire business in Mumbai would come to an end, he would be declared 'persona non grata', unless he cooperated with us and got Usmani back to India.

Cornered, Fakhruddin acquiesced to squeal on his friend. He divulged that there was another individual by the name of Aslam, a man in his mid-Twenties, who held the key to Usmani's whereabouts in Nepal. Aslam would be able to take us to the village. These words lifted the team's plummeting spirits. At last, there was a ray of hope. Aslam was in Nepal. Fakhruddin rang him up and called him over for an important meeting, without disclosing any details. He arrived for the meeting only to be introduced to Fakhruddin's esteemed guests from Mumbai who made it amply clear how determined they were not to go back to Mumbai without their mutual friend, Afzal Usmani. Maintaining complete secrecy and unmitigated cooperation were a must. If not, the search across the border was bound to be stymied.

With such preparation, a determined team, comprising Shital Raut, Asam Farooqui and Namdev Kale saw Aslam off at the border checkpost and began their long, agonising and tortuous wait. Aslam turned out to be a true friend of Fakhruddin's. He took utmost care to ensure that his new friends remained in the shadow, while he managed to get Afzal Usmani to a local bar. It was a sozzled Afzal Usmani, now called Irfan Qureishi, who sat slumped in a vehicle that halted at the border checkpost to enter India that night. Provided, if all went well.

But it did not. I was at the house of my friend Vidhu Vinod Chopra – the well-known film producer and director – for dinner that night. Right through the evening, I kept excusing myself to find corners where I could speak to Pote, Raut and Dinesh Kadam without being overheard. Suddenly I received a call from Raut, saying that they needed one lakh fifty thousand rupees in cash at the border checkpost. What for? The Nepali border guards had found 'Irfan Qureishi' reeking of alcohol. They were informed that he had just attended a *daawat* (feast) and indulged himself a little too much. But the knavish border guards categorically told Aslam that the price to let the drunk friend to cross the border without a medical test was 1,50,000 Indian rupees. Now how was I to manage this devil of a job, sitting here in Mumbai?

Vidhu sensed that I was in some deep thought and trouble.

'What's the matter, Rakesh?' He asked me.

'I need one lakh fifty thousand rupees to be delivered in Nepal to my team this very moment, for a work of great national importance! And I cannot share any more details with you.' I answered.

'Ok,' said Vidhu, sensing my anxiety as if he were part of the ATS. 'I have a friend who is from Nepal. Director of Photography Binod Pradhan. I will speak to him and see if he can help us.' He immediately dialled Binod Pradhan's number and told him that he needed a lakh and fifty thousand to be delivered to the border checkpost for a very important work of the police department. He however added that he wouldn't be able to furnish any more details. Pradhan said that he could arrange it, but it would take time. He would have to send the money by car from Kathmandu and the journey would take eight hours.

'Rakesh, he says he can certainly do it but the money will take eight hours to reach. Will do? Shall I say yes?' Vidhu asked me.

It was simply out of the question. We could not afford an alert Afzal Usmani declaring to the Nepali border guards that he was not Irfan Qureshi. So I thanked Vidhu and said we could not wait that long. Then with a heavy heart, I called up the team and told them that that they would have to manage the situation on their own. There was no way I could arrange any money to be delivered to them at that hour and at that location within the stipulated time. Needless to say, they managed. After some good bargaining with the guards, some gold rings came off their fingers, some gold chains were added to the kitty and the vehicle was allowed to cross the border and enter India.

Thus on 27 October 2013 at 3:30 in the morning, Aslam and Fakhruddin left a bewildered Afzal Usmani at Rupaidiha railway station from where ACP Pote and the team picked him up and drove him straight to Lucknow. Afzal Usmani was dishevelled and he was smelling like the putrid remains of a dead rodent. Therefore, he was given a good haircut, shave, bath and some new clothes. Then he was photographed and the picture was sent to Pradeep Sawant and Amitesh Kumar in Mumbai for obtaining permission from the Director General Civil Aviation (DGCA) to permit him to fly on a commercial flight. Looking at his past record, he was capable of creating a ruckus at the airport. At the time of his last arrest in 2008, he had feigned chest pain at the security check at Varanasi airport and we had to get him examined by a doctor to prove that there was nothing the matter with him. So we had to be extremely cautious with him, leaving nothing to chance.

The Colaba police station case was transferred to the ATS and Police Inspector Bajrang Parab, yet another meticulous and hard working officer took up the investigation. Afzal Usmani was found carrying a driving license under a false name of Waseem Sattar Khan which he had obtained from the RTO office of Bahraich district. The investigating officer dug out all the papers pertaining to the license from the RTO which proved the offence of falsification of documents. In his defence, Usmani had taken an audaciously incredible stand that he had not escaped from lawful custody, but was abducted by the police and kept in an unknown place to compel him to turn an approver in the case. It was the application for the driving license which was submitted at the Bahraich RTO that had helped the prosecution punch holes in this defence. The application, which needs biometric verification now, was made during the same time when Usmani was supposed to have been abducted by the police!

On 20 January 2016, for falsification of records and documents, Usmani was awarded five years rigorous imprisonment and a fine of 10,000 rupees along with two years of rigorous imprisonment for escaping from custody. The entire escort team from Navi Mumbai was suspended for their negligence.

Getting a dangerous fugitive from across the border, and that too from a village where communities are close-knit is extremely difficult. The resourcefulness and never say die spirit of ACP Mangesh Pote, Inspector Shital Raut and their team alone made it possible for me to beat a treacherous and crafty criminal at his own game, and that too with the help of his own associates. The role and professionalism of Dinesh Kadam and his team, also deserves special mention. It was they who got the vital initial breakthrough that led us to the Afzal Usmani trail. Afzal Usmani had to grudgingly accept that he was completely outwitted by the ATS teams. He could not conceal his admiration for them and confessed to Pote and Raut on the way from Rupaidiha to Lucknow, *'Saab, apne baraabar waqt par mereko utha liya.Warna main Pakistan jaane wala thaa!'* (Sir, you picked me up at the right time. Or else I would have gone to Pakistan!)

28

Gathering the Ashes

Shehar sunsaan hain, kidhar jaayen
Khaak bannkar kahin bikhar jaayen

(The city is ghostly silent, where should one go?
Turn into ash and get scattered anywhere)

Nasir Kazmi's lines came to my mind as I braced myself to walk up to the Commissioner of Police that day and unburden my soul.

'Sir, aapko pataa nahi aapne muhjko kaise fasaa diya hai!' I said to him. (Sir, you don't know what a fix you have put me in!)

'Why? What happened?' Hasan Gafoor asked me in surprise.

'Sir, I was rushing to Colaba that night, but you put me in the Control Room! And now I get vibes from some quarters as if I was ensconced in the Control Room and was sending others to their death. Sir, I wish I had died in one of those battles rather than survived to see this day! My only crime is that I am alive!'

The criterion for having performed duty during 26/11 was either being dead or being injured. Anybody, who had not done either was not deemed to have done much. The atmosphere around us was very sad and depressing. The city was once again limping back to normalcy and its police force was combatting the demon of demoralisation with determination. The blame game was gathering speed.

On the political front, Chief Minister Vilasrao Deshmukh (of the Congress) had tendered his resignation on 3 December 2008. Faced with allegations of inept handling of the attacks and insensitivity, he had accepted moral responsibility and stepped down. His Deputy and Home Minister, R.R. Patil (of the NCP), had already resigned on 1 December 2008. A month later, on 30 December 2008, the government appointed the 'High-Level Enquiry Committee (HLEC) on 26/11' to probe into the police and the administration's response to the attacks. It was a two-member committee comprising former Home Secretary Ram Pradhan and former IPS officer Vappala Balachandran. Ram Pradhan, a retired Indian Administrative Service officer, had served as Union Home Secretary and Governor of Arunachal Pradesh. He had held Secretary-level positions at the national and international levels in the areas of Defence and Home. He had played a major role in the Assam and Mizo Accords. Vappala Balachandran, a national security Intelligence specialist, had served seventeen years in Maharashtra and nineteen years in foreign Intelligence service. He had retired as Special Secretary, Cabinet Secretariat, Government of India. He was also a highly respected columnist and author. The Committee came to be known as the Pradhan Committee.

The CP was being accused of incompetence and passivity. It was the classic case of a dilemma that kings and generals face. Should they be leading from the front or should discretion be the better part of valour? Should their judgement and action be ruled by sensible caution or by heroics to fetch them applause from the gallery? Why had he stationed himself near the Oberoi? Why did he not sit in the Headquarters in his own office or in the Control Room? Why did he not visit all the spots instead of being stationed at just one?

Even in the days of modern communication, where you are 'connected' all the time, is a general supposed to be on his seat in his cabin all the time, or visit all the fronts just to prove that he is there? And if he does stick to his cabin, it would be cited as a lack of leadership qualities and the inability to show solidarity. If he visited all the active spots, with his convoy and the media in tow, he would be accused of diverting his deputies' attention and focus. If he is the quiet and unassuming type, not vocal and given to easy camaraderie with the media, he digs his own grave. If he is the opposite, he is called the publicity-hungry reckless cop in love with himself!

All this had a striking similarity with the aftermath of the 1992-1993 riots. The only difference was the identity of the King – the wireless call sign for the Mumbai CP – that has survived all other changes. Then, the King was a Shrikant Bapat, a Hindu. Now it was a Hasan Gafoor, a Muslim. Then, the King was shunted out and made to face a Commission of Inquiry. Now, he was still around, counting his days and facing a high-level inquiry. A much lesser ordeal, but enough for a fatal setback and a slow death to a sensitive man and a good officer. As expected, he was shunted out six and a half months after the attack and made Director General, Police Housing Corporation.

Along with the work of detection and investigation of the attacks, all of us were now presenting facts before the Pradhan Committee so that they could assess how we, as a Force, had dealt with the challenge, and what had gone wrong. They began visiting the places connected with the attacks and interviewed officials. The mind was crowded with various questions, making sense of the inputs and trying to understand the flow of events, when I received a shock which I least expected.

I was genuinely fond of Ashok Kamte and wished him nothing but the best. I shared his love for sports and admired his passion for fitness, his energy and his commitment to work. I had requested the CP that he be placed with me in the Crime Branch, but my request had been turned down and he was posted to the East Region as Additional Commissioner. This may sound trite but his death had come to me as a personal loss and Preeti had immediately rushed to Pune to meet his wife, Vinita Kamte, after Ashok's funeral. It had never occurred to me that I could be held even remotely responsible for the deaths of Ashok Kamte, Hemant Karkare and Vijay Salaskar. One evening, Vinita Kamte called Preeti and sought a meeting with me. I was neck-deep in work and said that I could only see her late in the evening. She agreed and came to my house at 10:30 p.m. as decided. I returned home earlier than usual to receive her. She was accompanied by her sister, Revati Dere Mohite, then an advocate practising in the Mumbai High Court and later elevated to the High Court Bench.

The conversation began. The first topic that she broached was the unfair treatment meted out to Ashok Kamte in matters of postings. Why was he posted to the East Region when he deserved to be posted to the West Region, she asked me. I said that I had no idea about it, but I had wanted him to be in the Crime Branch with me. I told her that I had requested the CP, but my request had not been acceded to.

She kept asking for minute details of the incident at Cama Hospital and Rang Bhavan lane where Karkare, Kamte and Salaskar had fallen to the terrorists' bullets. I wasn't myself sure of how exactly things had panned out. The investigation was at an infancy stage and she expected me to have all the facts and time of the incidents at my fingertips. From the way she was putting the questions to me, I felt as if I was facing an inquisition. I sensed that she had come with some preconceived notions and had an animus towards me.

My doubts were confirmed in a short while and I could not believe my ears. She was of the view that the Control Room had not sent adequate and timely manpower and help to Cama Hospital which had resulted in Ashok's death! I explained to her the challenges we had faced and how we had tried rushing all possible help to Cama, but she appeared to be in no mood to appreciate. I could understand her grief and sentiments and was most patient with her.

She asked me how Ashok had gone to Cama Hospital when he was asked to go to Hotel Trident. I was confused and totally surprised and said I didn't know. Trident? I began thinking. She said that the CP had ordered him to go to Trident. This was a complete surprise to me. I began wondering. If the CP had asked him to go to Trident, why had he been asking for orders? I remembered the operators telling me that he was asking for orders, that he was nearing the Taj and was finally near Zone-I office when I had directed him to go to Cama! I was clueless.

Where were the other South Region officers? What were they doing? Shying away from the action? She asked. She derided my colleague Deven Bharti, Additional CP Crime Branch, for the action he had taken at Cama Hospital where I had directed him. 'Does he think he is Hanuman that he could have jumped from that tall building next to Cama Hospital and killed the terrorists!' She remarked, referring to the monkey-God from the Ramayana, Lord Rama's General and emissary. I heard her, aghast. That night, taking positions in nearby buildings to contain terrorists was a tactic tried out even at the Oberoi. It may seem ridiculous, but the DGP himself had dispatched our officers – Additional CP (ATS) Parambir Singh and team – to the NCPA buildings opposite the Oberoi to take aim at the terrorists in the hotel. Later even the National Security Guards (NSG) had joined them there. Even at the Chabad House, the same tactic had been adopted by ACP Isaque Ibrahim Bagwan. I was trying to explain how everyone had tried their best, but she was in no mood to listen.

Another fact that she wanted to know about was the identity of the officer whose bullet had injured Ajmal Kasab. Who had opened fire and who had injured Kasab in the Rang Bhavan lane? I was on my guard now. It would all depend on the forensic evidence about the bullets which were found and matched with the weapons and injuries. The courts would decide the matter and not I, I said to her. I did not want to commit to anything unless I was sure.

Ashok had opened fire and he had injured Kasab, she said. But then she also said something that was too harsh. She said that I would only give credit to my Crime Branch officers for this feat and not to Kamte. I could not bear this charge. The suggestion that I would rob any policeman of credit for his bravery and skills, and that too a sterling officer like Ashok Kamte, was just not acceptable. And after this charge I did raise my voice a little. 'Don't paint me with the same brush as you would paint others,' I said sharply. 'My Crime Branch officers' meant Salaskar who had laid down his life and Arun Jadhav who had miraculously survived to tell us the story. I was being accused of trying to get them credit for the injuries suffered by Kasab! Seeing how it had disturbed me, Revati Dere Mohite controlled Vinita Kamte. Shortly thereafter the ladies left my house, leaving Preeti very upset and me sitting dumbfounded in my chair. I could not remember any instructions being issued to Kamte to go to Trident. The Control Room staff had not informed me about any such input. I was sure of it. And now his wife had just accused me of diverting him from the Trident to Cama and not sending enough reinforcements to him. In short, I was responsible for Ashok Kamte's death! As if that morning I had got up and said to myself, today I will kill three officers of Mumbai police and worked towards it and achieved it by taking charge of the Control Room in the night!

As the full import of what she had said began sinking in, I was heartbroken. Was she seriously convinced that there was negligence in rushing help to Cama and I was responsible for it! Is this what people called 'stars'! Was it just a simple misunderstanding? Or could some of my dear 'friends' be deliberately spreading this venom and misleading people to believe the falsehood? Slowly I realised that a whisper campaign was afoot against me yet again. The media picked up the story. Some sections of the press and some activists began spreading theories that the three officers had been deliberately killed and that a conspiracy to kill Hemant Karkare was the root cause of the entire incident!

When I had shared my plight with Gafoor that day, he had smiled and said, 'It was entirely my decision, and I had the right to take it, as the head of the Force. Assigning jobs to my officers is entirely my prerogative and I stand by it. It was a good decision. You did a splendid job,' he said. As it did not lessen my anguish, he added, 'Stop worrying yourself over it and don't pay attention to your detractors. This Force is plagued by a lot of dissatisfied and jealous souls. I need you alive and working on the job ahead. That is more important.'

Soon I received a request from Vinita Kamte that Ashok's father, the retired Lieutenant Colonel Kamte would like to meet me at his residence. I said I would be most happy to, and went to his house at Napean Sea Road one morning with Preeti. Vinita Kamte was also present and Ashok's father received us with great warmth. The long tradition of uniformed service in the family manifested through his every gesture and expression. The painful incident at Cama was the topic of our discussion and I sincerely explained to him whatever I knew. I had nothing to hide or be ashamed of. I had done my best. The true-blue Indian Army soldier listened to each and every fact with complete attention and asked me very pertinent and significant questions with great composure. In the end, he said, 'I think they ought not to have gone in the same vehicle!' This sentence was not to the liking of Vinita Kamte and she gave vent to her anger in no uncertain terms. We just listened to her patiently and left the house after a short while. How I wish I had met the gentleman to discuss some happy tidings, in the company of his son, and not to dissect the circumstances of his son's death!

Days went by and even that uniquely gruesome night between 26-27 November 2008 in Mumbai became just a number, like 9/11. The former was in November and the latter was in September, but that did not matter for people who love coining catchy, convenient and clever terms. The 2008 Mumbai attacks, or better and shorter still, just 26/11! People became figures and statistics:

Lives lost 166.

Break up: 122 civilians, 26 foreigners, 18 security personnel.

Injured 304.

Break up: 241 civilians, 26 foreigners, 37 security personnel.

Nine terrorists killed. One captured alive.

Loss and damage to property: Rupees 155,73,12,971.00.

Whether 26/11 was or was not 'India's 9/11' also became a contentious issue with some who had the time and appetite for such discussions. Comparisons are not always odious. Sometimes they are welcome, especially when they help you aim at improvement. It's just that whilst at it, people lose sight of the fact that they are comparing unequal entities. The word 'unprecedented' can look like an excuse to an increasingly sceptical world – a world that expects 'professionalism' and 'ever-preparedness' from our security agencies who are always being compared with their Western counterparts. Even then, one has to admit that 26/11 *was* unprecedented, in some respects just for Mumbai and its police force, and in some respects for the entire world. And once again, like the 1993 serial blasts, others learned at Mumbai's cost.

Terrorism is a hydra-headed monstrous phenomenon and it has raised its ugly head in all the nooks and corners of the world. Events of the past few decades have conclusively proved that no country, state or nation is immune to the threat of terrorist attacks, even those which support and harbour terrorists. Terrorists, both home-grown and foreign, have exhibited their capability and ability to strike almost at will, using the time, place and method of their choice.

Then what was so unique and unprecedented about 26/11? The magnitude as well as the sheer ingenuity of its conception. The conspiracy was hatched, and the terrorists were trained, equipped and launched from foreign soil. The ingress was through the sea route, a route hitherto unchartered and unimaginable and absolutely audacious in its planning. The terrorists were equipped with automatic weapons, hand grenades, RDX explosives and sophisticated pistols. They had the latest scientific technology of Global Positioning System (GPS), satellite phones, and Voice Over Internet Protocol (VOIP) Services, to communicate during the entire operation.

Previous terrorist attacks in Mumbai had turned into a stereotype. The terrorists would plant the Improvised Explosive Devices (IEDs) at public places like venues of religious, political and cultural importance, tourist spots, vital installations, offices of security agencies, areas of critical infrastructure and public transportation systems. This is how attacks were launched at the Parliament House in New Delhi on 13 December 2001; in Akshardham in Gujarat on 24 September 2002; at the Indian Institute of Science in Bengaluru on 28 December 2005; and the Central Reserve Police Force (CRPF) camp in Rampur in UP on 1 January 2008, to name just a few. However, these were one-off attacks, concentrating on singular locations. The security agencies were left with the task of cordoning off the affected locations, sifting or collecting evidence, unearthing the conspiracy behind the attack and arresting the accused involved. Of course, in addition to this, the immediate task of the security forces as the 'first responders' was the transportation of the injured to nearby hospitals and also the removal of the dead bodies from the scenes of attacks.

This time, however, it was an unprecedentedly unique and chilling experience for the security agencies. Now they had to counter a series of attacks that employed combined tactics: simultaneous bomb blasts, grenade attacks, random and indiscriminate firing at crowded locations, hostage taking and prolonged sieges to attract eyeballs. Terrorism is theatre and that too, for large international audiences.

There is absolutely no denying the fact that a terrorist attack was indeed anticipated in the city, but not in this audacious manner. These terrorists were trained commandos, equipped with the latest weaponry and sophisticated gadgets, whereas we – the local police – were the first responders armed with our usual standard weaponry, though not lacking in any manner in courage and valour. This was an open act of war. The perpetrators were all out in the open and they had come prepared to die. For the first time, security agencies in Mumbai worked from a position of strategic disadvantage, whereas the perpetrators were dealing from a position of strength. We did not have the domination or the authoritative advantage that we were so used to while dealing with internal security matters. Sirens heard, and people would start running! No! Today, we had face to face confrontation with adversaries who were not ready to withdraw. The confrontation was with AKs and hand grenades. It was not a level playing field! And the difficulties were further compounded by the loss of senior officers – the commanders – so early on in the fight that it had quickly spiralled and spilt over to the streets, with the potential of leading to an immense loss of morale.

It brought home to us the lesson that what we need is an ability to foresee all possible types of scenarios, even at the cost of being accused of unwarranted paranoia and fear psychosis. Prepare to counter the enemy like an army and rehearse the preparations, all the time. Appreciate the potential and vulnerability of all possible targets. Prioritise them and conduct regular security audits. Prepare for the worst. Who knows, the next attack could be biological, chemical, radioactive, or even nuclear! Become foretellers of Doom!

After the 9/11 attack, the Americans had set up the 'National Commission on Terrorist Attacks Upon the United States' to prepare a complete account of the surrounding circumstances. It studied their preparedness and immediate response, and was popularly called 'The 9/11 Commission'. An important witness examined was George Tenet, Director CIA. The Commission confronted him with the obvious charge that it was a colossal failure of Intelligence. He had replied, with all the humility at his command, that it was not. Rather, it was a failure of imagination, he had said. Something similar had to be said here, and its fallout had to be accepted and worked upon.

Naturally, police forces from across the world came to us to understand what we had encountered. That in itself was unprecedented. I don't remember spending so much time on this aspect when we'd handled the serial blasts of 1993 which were also the first of its kind. This time, however, the international community was not indifferent to Mumbai's plight because they could not afford to be. They were no longer insulated from it. This time their own citizens had been targeted, unlike in the earlier blasts in local trains, buses, markets and temples. So this time around, I had to meet senior Intelligence teams from different countries, brief them in detail and learn from them.

As a security professional, I had a lot to learn from this terrible disaster. I had always been a field and investigations man, but again the Hidden Hand, Destiny or God, whichever one may choose to believe in, through the wisdom of my boss, had placed me in the Control Room! Each one placed in such situations has his own peculiar predicament. When you have a choice, you weigh the pros and cons – should I be doing this or the other? And when you don't have a choice and you have to do what is placed before you, as it often happens in uniformed service, a niggling doubt arises – what am I good at? And should I be somewhere else and doing something else? It would be dishonest to pretend that such thoughts do not enter one's mind, though it is equally true that once you take up the task, the Service trains you to give your best and your hundred per cent to see it through. The generalist in you takes over and draws out all your rich and varied experience to arrive at the best possible decisions in the given circumstances.

When the reports of casualties were coming in, and when my colleagues were sharing their scenarios and explaining their difficulties to me, initially I did feel a little uncomfortable. Here I am, confined within these four walls, instead of joining them in the field to strategise and to face the bullets and bombs. They are dying and I am just speaking into these phones, issuing advisories! But then that in itself is a test and part of training – controlling the bravado and the itch to go out in the field! To admit that when faced with warlike operations of this nature, it is so important for officers in higher commands to live, survive and lead, rather than offer themselves on a platter to the enemy who would love to see your force rendered rudderless! It doesn't always work to do the cowboy stuff, like the Marshall of Lawless – my teenage hero!

Monitoring a sudden operation from a distance of this mammoth and complicated a nature, was an eye-opener. I may be wrong, but I do not think any other senior IPS officer, at least in the Maharashtra cadre, has had this exposure which gave me so much practical insight into the city's disaster management, from a policing perspective. It also made me realise the importance of Control Room operators, always the unsung heroes in all our operations. We know the theoretical aspect of its operations and there are occasions when you pay a fleeting visit to a Control Room, say for instance when you are deputed on night rounds. But that does not give you much understanding of its practical difficulties. It was the first time that I had spent so much time in the Control Room.

I realised that my own experience in the detection and investigation of serious crimes also helped a great deal in shaping our response to the detection and investigation that we had to launch almost immediately after the attacks began. This again was a unique feature of this operation. Detection and investigations began in right earnest starting from the false alarm about the suspected shooter at the Leopold Café and the raid on the hotels around the Taj to look for the handlers. It was quickly followed by Kasab's arrest, the steps to secure the hard evidence on the chaotic streets, Kasab's interrogation, the seizure of the dinghy and the search for Kuber – the fishing boat that the terrorists had hijacked to penetrate Indian waters. My placement in the Control Room was, in a way, a boon for ensuring that all these operations went on smoothly and with the due care they warranted, simultaneously with the action unfolding on the field. Nobody is indispensable and the world can go on without Rakesh Maria. But at that critical juncture, if I too had been grappling with the terrorists inside say the Taj or the Oberoi, where I was sure to rush had the CP not drafted me to the Control Room, I wonder how we would have steered the detection and investigative part amidst the mayhem.

Fifty-five hours! Why did it take us that long? Well, there were hundreds of patrons in the two hotels. We had to do our best to rescue as many as possible. The entire operation was conducted with the objective of saving lives and minimising collateral damage, rather than merely nabbing the terrorists. The Mumbai approach was intrinsically very different from say, that of Lahore, as was evident in the attack on the Manawan Police Academy on 30 March 2009, or of the Russian authorities as was evident in the Beslan School Attack on 1 September 2004, when the security agencies gunned down the terrorists with scant regard for hostages' lives or collateral damage.

Why is our Mumbai such an attractive target? Obviously, because a successful attack on Mumbai means a decisive blow to the economy and reputation of India. Mumbai makes for a strategic target as it gets a lot of international attention. The city has high internal mobility and a large floating population. The fast-paced life ensures that often neighbours do not know each other. So it gives complete anonymity to its residents. India's borders are so porous and Mumbai has such ethnic and language similarities with our inimical neighbour, that infiltration into the city and camouflage is fairly easy. Therefore, Mumbai is relatively an easy target, when compared to other Indian cities.

Why is it that we are never well equipped? Every year proposals and requisitions are sent for better and enhanced equipment and infrastructure, but what gets sanctioned is hardly commensurate with the need. Our reform and modernisation, in equipment and training, unfortunately gets attention only after a serious incident when the political masters get jolted out of their other preoccupations and commitments. It is only then that the red tape loses its grip.

Armed with such thoughts and musings, and handling a multitude of other equally pressing matters, I appeared before the Pradhan Committee thrice. In the meanwhile, in March 2009, Vinita Kamte applied to the Information Officer in the CP's office under the Right to Information (RTI) Act, asking for the written transcripts and audio tapes of the Control Room conversations. The Information Officer reports to the DCP (Operations) who in turn reported to K.L. Prasad, Joint CP (Law and Order or L&O). The DCP (Operations) opined on the file that since the Crime Branch was investigating the matter, and considering the sensitivity of the matter, the opinion of the Joint CP (Crime), i.e., my opinion may be sought. The Joint CP (L&O) concurred with it and asked for my say in the matter. Since the case was sub judice, I immediately asked for the report and remarks of the Investigating Officer (IO) of the 26/11 investigation. IO Ramesh Mahale, after consulting Public Prosecutor Ujjwal Nikam, was of the opinion that parting with the information at that stage may impede the investigations. He also mentioned that the trial court had forbidden transmission of audio and video recordings by an order dated 23 March 2009 passed in connection with another request. This was conveyed by me to the Joint CP (L&O). The Information Officer rejected the application under the relevant provisions of the RTI Act which lay down that there was no obligation to provide information to a citizen if parting with it would impede the process of investigation or prosecution of an offence.

The trial commenced on 16 April 2009 at the Arthur Road Jail and the Crime Branch officers got busy with the task of ensuring the presence of witnesses before the court and briefing the prosecutor on a daily basis. In the same month, Vinita Kamte filed the First Appeal against the Information Officer's order before the DCP (Operations). Though I was not the Information Officer and nobody to approve or disapprove the supply of information, she solely blamed me for the rejection, accusing me of harbouring mala fide intentions and covering up my alleged acts of omission by taking shelter under the exception provided by the RTI Act! In fact, my role had been that of a conduit, to just convey the opinion of the Public Prosecutor and the IO to the Joint CP (L&O) so that he could communicate it to the Information Officer. Even though the Information Officer is subordinate to the Joint CP in police hierarchy, under the RTI Act, he functions independently and his superior has no role to play in the discharge of his statutory functions as the Information Officer.

I felt that the application was singling me out. On that fateful night, and when the unfortunate incidents at Cama were unfolding, I was not the only senior officer present in the Control Room. K.L. Prasad was also there till he was directed by the DGP to proceed to the Taj where he had reached much after the siege at Cama and the Chhatrapati Shivaji Terminus (CST) had ended, and much after the encounter at Girgaum Chowpatty. The DGP had ordered him to rush to the Taj as he had felt that two senior officers need not be in the Control Room and DCP Vishwas Nangre Patil needed help. Even in giving Vinita Kamte the information she had asked for, mine was not the only desk that her application had touched as it had travelled its course before being decided. The decision was based on the opinions of the Public Prosecutor and the Investigating Officer. Therefore, I began getting a feeling that the application was made with a predesigned intent of targeting me.

In May 2009, the DCP (Operations) allowed the First Appeal partly, on the ground that the charge sheet was filed in the case and, therefore, giving her information may not impede the investigation. So he gave her permission to take inspection of the documents and listen in to the recorded conversations, directing the concerned officials to coordinate with her. I was extremely busy with my own work in the Crime Branch and had nothing to do with the Control Room and the work of the Information Officer. I was not involved in collating or handing over the information to Vinita Kamte or communicating with her. It was all being handled by the concerned officials under the Joint CP (L&O). Sometime later I learned that she was given the date and time for inspection of records and she had availed of it with the assistance of two lawyers. I was told that she was provided with the Control Room's wireless logs that she had asked for, both, the Ericson channel which is for communication between all police station mobiles, walkie-talkies and the Control Room, and of the Motorola channel which is for communication between senior officers.

All the records that were handed over to Vinita Kamte from time to time were being handled by different officers and different branches who were ready to explain their method of recording and preparing them, or copying them, and all the technical details that went into the process. I was not the only man in the Control

Room that night and nor was I the single repository of all the calls of all the channels and lines, or the only man taking down details from callers and giving all the instructions. I was neither with all those officers and wireless operators who were out on the field shadowing their respective bosses to convey correctly and promptly the vital details of the actions from the ground. But if negligence had to be attributed, and responsibility had to be fixed for all of it on one person, well, I was the man to bear the cross! For, I was the man placed in charge of the Control Room that night!

The Pradhan Committee submitted its report dated 18 April 2009 to the Chief Minister. They had examined fifty serving or retired officials, some more than once. There was an uproar when the government refused to table the Report in the House and tabled only an Action Taken Report.

On 25 November 2009, there appeared a report in *The Times of India* under the heading '26/11 a Year Later, ACP Kamte's Wife Alleges Cover-up'. It was a reportage of the function which was organised for the release of the book titled *To The Last Bullet –The Inspiring Story of a Braveheart*. From the report, it was clear that in the book, Vinita Kamte had directly accused me of inept handling of the Control Room, and callousness towards my colleagues in the field that night.

I was deeply anguished and upset by the allegations in the news report. While I felt that there was an urgent need to refute them in public, I would never do so myself, as I was aware of my responsibilities as a police officer and would never dream of jeopardising the ongoing trial which was crucial to India's war against terrorism. My entire career and reputation, and the name and prestige of the Mumbai police was at stake. The three slain officers were my dear colleagues and esteemed members of the Force. I did understand the trauma suffered by Vinita Kamte. To be accused of harming the three men facing a terrorist attack that we were all fighting together irrespective of rank and designation, was unbearable. The suggestion that I had behaved callously and irresponsibly towards them was preposterous. I wrote a letter to the Additional Chief Secretary (Home) requesting appropriate steps to set the record right so that the people get the true picture and not lose faith in me and my colleagues who had manned the Control Room that night.

Vinita Kamte's book continued to draw plenty of media attention and my alleged inept handling, callousness and cover-up got a good deal of publicity which I suffered silently. She continued to agitate over issues in different forums and the burden of the accusations continued to weigh me down, raising its ugly head every now and then. I began getting calls from friends, acquaintances and even respected political leaders cutting across party lines.

I was called by Home Minister R.R. Patil for a meeting. I told him that I was prepared to resign if the government did not refute the allegations by making public the true facts on record. He tried to soothe my anguish and assured me that the government would set the record right at the appropriate time.

Then the Pradhan Committee Report found its way to the media and it led to a further uproar. Ultimately, the Report was tabled before the House on 21 December 2009. Questions were raised in the Assembly over the incident in which Hemant Karkare, Ashok Kamte and Vijay Salaskar had lost their lives. They were based on the allegations levelled against me in Vinita Kamte's book. The IO briefed the Home Minister thoroughly who defended our actions on the Floor of the House and appreciated the work of the Control Room.

The Report was received with mixed reactions, as is expected when any such reports are tabled. Some found fault with the reasoning that had praised the police but hanged their leader, the CP. Many thought that the Report was biased against Gafoor and was pro-DGP. However, the Report created a template for a future police structure to avert, handle and tackle terror attacks in the Urbs prima. An important study coming from two professionals who had a deep understanding of police working, the Report is an important document.

The Committee had attempted, in its own words, to analyse how far the existing procedures, instruments and administrative culture were to be blamed for the perceived lapses. Their stress was on identifying systemic failures. It was heartening to read that they had not found any serious lapses in the conduct of any individual officer. The Committee said:

> ...the general police response to the terrorist incidents at five places was swift and according to the standard law and order response to such incidents. However, a perusal of the control room log would indicate that they were handicapped by the initial lack of full information. The simultaneous attack at five different places, with a constant stream of calls coming in, had obviously overloaded the communication system.

As regards the Control Room, they had some good words to say:

> ...the Committee has noted with appreciation the role played by Shri Rakesh Maria, Jt CP(Crime) in the C/R in handling a very serious crisis situation extending over three days. The Committee is also appreciative of the dedicated work performed by Control Room staff including officers, Wireless operators and men in maintaining records.

However, the Committee also said that they had found instances of lack of intelligent appreciation of threats, handling of Intelligence, maintaining a high degree of efficiency in instruments specifically set up to deal with terrorist attacks and lack of overt and visible leadership in carrying out operations to face multi-targeted attacks.

On the factual front, one observation of the Committee was that it was perhaps not necessary for Hemant Karkare and others to have travelled along the Badruddin Tayyabji Lane (Rang Bhavan lane) to rescue Sadanand Date as the rear gate of Cama was broken open to allow Date's wireless operator Sachin Tilekar to exit. They had interviewed both Tilekar and Arun Jadhav who also said that Salaskar had taken Tilekar out through this gate and sent him to the hospital in a Crime Branch vehicle.

The decision of the three senior officers to go by the Rang Bhavan lane in one vehicle to confront the terrorists from the front gate was indeed an unfortunate one. But as is the axiom, the man on the spot is the best judge, and three experienced officers, and one of them the head of the ATS could not have acted without reason.

The eyewitness accounts for the battle near Cama were quite cogent. Of them, Arun Jadhav had deposed in the trial court in July 2009 that one policeman had come out of the rear gate of Cama in an injured condition. As he was approaching them, there was firing from the direction of the hospital and Kamte had retaliated from his AK-47. They took the constable out and he informed them about the officers injured inside the hospital. Then there was a discussion amongst Karkare, Kamte and Salaskar. Karkare had said that they should all go to the front gate of the hospital as there was a likelihood of the terrorists exiting from there. They took ACP Bhambre's Qualis and began moving in that direction. As they proceeded towards the Special Branch-I office, they received a wireless message that two terrorists were hiding near a red car in the Rang Bhavan lane and, therefore, Kamte directed Salaskar who was at the wheel, to slow down the vehicle and proceed further cautiously. Jadhav then described how the terrorists had sprayed them with bullets, how he, Karkare, Kamte and Salaskar had retaliated, and how they had all sustained serious injuries that had incapacitated them.

I found of great significance two exchanges of messages with Karkare which were on the Ericson channel, used by senior officers.

The first was his exchange with the Control Room from 23:24 to 23:30 and began with Karkare conveying that they were at Cama Hospital, after which he proceeded to describe the situation: there was firing and blasts. Three-four, probably grenade blasts, had occurred in five minutes in their presence. Therefore it was necessary for them to 'encircle' and they were near the SB-II office. He asked for a team to be sent from the front side of Cama Hospital and informed that it needed to be coordinated to avoid cross-firing. He had said that Joint CP (L&O) K.L. Prasad would be present in the Control Room and should be asked to request the Army for commandos. In three minutes, the Control Room asked him for a confirmation if he needed help from the front side of Cama Hospital. At that time he had replied that ATS's Quick Response Team (QRT) was there and just then a team of the Crime Branch had also come to the Special Branch-II side. He needed help from the other side as they would have to encircle and lay a cordon. He repeated that through Prasad a request be made to the Army authorities. The Control Room had replied that they had noted his message.

Then about half an hour later was the second exchange of messages. It was between the Control Room, Karkare and Joint CP (Traffic) Sanjay Barve. The latter was asking the Control Room to give a call to Karkare's walkie-talkie. The Control Room had tried Karkare's walkie-talkie and also the wireless set on his vehicle, but there was no reply. Barve's speech kept getting cut, but finally, he managed to give a message at 23:57 to the Control Room for Karkare, asking him to send two armed Assault Teams to the Oberoi, from the ATS teams or from the teams available with Karkare, which he could arrange. Before the Control Room could pass on the message, Karkare himself came on the walkie-talkie. After learning that Barve was trying to contact him, he called Barve. The conversation was as follows:

> 23:58 – Barve to Karkare: We need two Assault Teams to cover Trident Hotel on the southern side. Can we get them for Assault Team five each. Over.
>
> 23:58 – Karkare to Barve: I am at Cama Hospital. Four-five people seemed to be holed up here. Many grenade blasts, lot of fire. The teams are here, but I don't think we can get Assault Team. I will check if there are two QRT teams here. One Crime Branch team is also here. Four-five people are in the building. Patients are outside we are cordoning it up and then apparently one team inside. Over.
>
> 23:58 – Barve to Karkare: Received correctly, sir. If a spare team from other part of the city. From southern side we need to cover them for total cordoning off this side also. Over.

The next minute, Karkare ascertained from Barve his exact location near the Trident and advised Barve to block the traffic entirely to prevent the terrorists from escaping. Barve said that he had already done so. This was the last time that Karkare had spoken on the wireless.

These conversations clearly showed that Karkare was completely aware of the shortage of trained manpower which was required for the operations and was requesting that Army commandos be requisitioned. (He wasn't aware that Prasad and I had already initiated requisitioning force from the Army and the Navy and at that very moment, I was in touch with the concerned authorities.) The conversations make evident that at 23:58, without waiting for the arrival of Army commandos, Karkare was planning to throw a cordon with the available force at his disposal, despatched by the Control Room or teams that had joined him on their own. The conversations establish the fact that simultaneously, as the head of the ATS, Karkare was also trying his best to allocate manpower under his command to the other active spots.

If these messages were carefully read in conjunction with several messages on the Ericson channel, which is for communication between the Control Room and all wireless mobiles, it was obvious that during this time, the Control Room was busy and committed towards arranging for and diverting Striking, Assault Mobiles and other manpower for Cama from the scarce resources available. It is equally clear that Karkare was not alone in this predicament. The officers in charge of the Taj, Nariman House and the Oberoi were also facing similar situations and making substantial attempts to lay cordons and send in teams, all from the available manpower. It is a matter of pride for the Mumbai police that none of these brave officers exhibited any remonstrance or showed any frustration. All of them tried to accommodate each other like a family and did their best to share resources and meet the challenge. If read in the proper context, the wireless messages put to rest all doubts and misgivings about the Control Room's response to Karkare's calls for reinforcements for Cama.

It was clear that the incident at 'Cama Out', as it came to be called in the trial, was just one of the unfortunate incidents that night. What the Mumbai police and its Control Room had handled that night was many times more, in terms of horror, gravity and sorrow. It was pure distilled terror. When we were immersed in it, we knew it was huge. But how huge, that could be only gauged after going through the voluminous record and evidence that was gathered.

29

It Was War

How did it happen? How?

As I piece it all together, I cannot but be struck by awe. Awe at the ordeal that all the victims had faced that night; awe at the enormity of the challenge that the entire police force had faced that night; awe at what all of us had faced in the Control Room that night; awe at what the auxiliary services had faced that night.

Of course, we knew how tough it was even while handling it, but it was only much, much later, as the investigation progressed and we began presenting facts to the Pradhan Committee, when fingers were being pointed at us and we began providing answers, and when the trial progressed, that we really began to understand how the multi-targeted attacks had begun, how the crisis had developed, and how it had been handled by different people. Now, with the benefit of hindsight, the enormity of it all hits you even harder.

How had it started for me? The first thing that I vividly remember is the charged atmosphere in the Control Room, and my wireless operator anxiously slipping a question through the scores of queries that were waiting for my answers. He asked it in a manner as if he knew that I would explode at his foolishness to have put the question in the first place.

'Sir, madam vichartaat ki Kunal la bus stop varun parat bolvayche,

ki jau dyayche camp la?' (Sir, madam wants to know if Kunal should be called back from the bus stop or should she let him proceed for the camp?)

'Kunal.... Camp....?' I stared at him blankly. I had forgotten that I had a family and my eldest son was about to board a bus to Pravara Nagar with his team to play a tournament. That just over an hour back I had given him a pep talk to go give his best and make his team reach the top. 'Let him go!' I snapped at the operator. And as I did, a strange thought flashed through my mind – let him go, so that at least one in the family survives! It may seem silly now, but honestly, that is what had crossed my mind then, and I had not even a moment more to waste on the thought.

'Could you come home early today? He is a little nervous. Some time with you will work wonders,' Preeti had pleaded in the morning. Kunal was to play in the Maharashtra State Inter-District Basket Ball Championships. Based on the performance, he would be selected for the state team to participate in the nationals. It meant the world for him.

The past few months had been very difficult. Almost every day I would return home well past midnight and some nights, not at all. We had busted the Indian Mujahideen (IM) module, but there was no respite. The atmosphere was tense, with alerts indicating that Islamist terrorists were planning more strikes in Mumbai. For instance, in June, we had an alert that sites in south Mumbai like the High Court, the DGP Office, the Department of Atomic Energy and Leopold Café were on the list of targets. They fell in Zone-I where the DCP was Vishwas Nangre Patil. He had immediately alerted the Senior Police inspectors under him, visited the areas several times, alerted the respective managements, including the owner of Leopold, and even removed the hawkers with the help of Municipal authorities.

Another major alert had been issued on 9 August 2008 by

K.L. Prasad, Joint CP (L&O). It indicated 11 August as the date the terrorists had set for bomb blasts in Mumbai. Amongst the targets were some prestigious and iconic establishments in the South Region of the Commissionerate: Hotels Taj Mahal, the Oberoi and President; railway stations Chhatrapati Shivaji Terminus (CST), Churchgate and Marine Lines; the prominent bus stops at Nariman Point and Backbay; the Colaba Market and the Sassoon Dock; the World Trade Centre and the Bombay Stock Exchange.

The Stock Exchange had been a target before, in the 1993 serial blasts. Destroying the Taj had been on the terror agenda for long, as evinced by the 2003 'Gujarat Muslim Revenge Force' (GMRF) blasts at the Gateway and Zaveri Bazar. Now the Oberoi had made it to the list. It is the old name by which Hotel Trident is still known. Since the 70s, 'Taj and Oberoi' is a phrase used by Bombayites to describe the height of five-star luxury and it has survived the renaming of the latter. CST is the new name for old VT – the Victoria Terminus which is an iconic UNESCO heritage structure.

All those responsible for the security of these establishments were informed about the alerts. The DCP visited the areas again and gave specific instructions to his subordinates. Sanjay Amrute, the Senior Police Inspector of the Marine Drive police station, wrote a letter to the Security Manager of the Trident, listing the steps needed to augment their security, such as X-ray check of guest baggage and deployment of armed security guards by obtaining gun licences from the police. He also held a meeting of representatives of prominent establishments in his jurisdiction like corporate offices, hotels, malls and multiplexes, and briefed them on the threat perception and the action warranted.

Mercifully, 11 August had passed without any such incident. However, another alert came in the last week of September, warning of an impending Lashkar-e-Taiba (LeT) attack on

Hotel Taj Mahal Palace. The alert also included Taj Land's End in Bandra, the J.W. Marriot in Juhu, Sardar Vallabhbhai Patel Stadium in Worli and the Juhu Air Field.

Almost as a forewarning, on 20 September 2008, an explosives-laden truck had exploded in front of Hotel Marriot in Islamabad, leaving more than fifty dead and 250 injured. The DCP, accompanied by Deepak Vishwasrao, Senior Police Inspector Colaba, had visited the Taj and briefed their senior management and the security team. They had discussed several possibilities like terrorists planting explosives and suicide squads storming into the building, resorting to indiscriminate firing and ramming explosives-laden vehicles into the building. The Taj team was guided on various measures like CCTV camera positions, contingency arrangements, parking restrictions and prevention against aerial attacks. In another visit, the management was acquainted with the model security instructions which were issued for the Bombay Stock Exchange. They were advised to keep only the main entrance gate open, equip it with metal detectors, and to not allow any entry without frisking and checking. Strong double barricading on the entrance, with sandbags fortifications, was recommended, as also deployment of armed guards. The DCP had specifically alerted the management about the vulnerability of the Northcote gate. He had advised that it should be closed permanently and a strong iron grill should be installed. What is more, for a few days, two snipers had been deployed atop the Taj and also an armed guard at the main entrance. The DCP had also sent a letter listing the twenty odd steps to the Senior Police Inspector who in turn briefed the Taj management again to bring home the gravity of the alert. The owner of Leopold Café, Dinyar Jehani, was called and told clearly that he had to be extremely careful and deploy CCTV cameras and adequate security of his own.

The Crime Branch too was in a state of alert. We were working at breakneck speed to complete the investigations into the Indian Mujahideen case. Filing the charge sheet against the arrested accused, within the deadline, was top priority. Amidst all the pressure, for the first time in so many days, I had managed to come home around 8 p.m., and spent some pleasant time with Kunal and Krish and tried to infuse the atmosphere with positivity to make my kids feel that their father – despite his absentee status – was there for them and on top of things. All was well when Kunal left to catch his late night bus and I stepped into the shower, with a plan to enjoy an early dinner, a little bit of sports surfing on the channels and the much needed good night's sleep. However, when I stepped out, I found an anxious Preeti waiting with a frown on her face.

'There was a call on the hotline,' she said. 'Very abrupt. You had better call them immediately and find out.'

'Abrupt! What do you mean by abrupt?' I asked her.

'Well! He asked *"Saheb kuthe aahet?"* (Where is Saheb?) And when I said you were in the bath, he just cut the line. They are always polite. But today the tone was very curt. Weird!' she said, with a woman's intuition which is normally very good at foreboding trouble. I immediately picked up the hotline and learnt that firing had been reported in Colaba, at the Leopold Café, and some foreigners had been injured.

Leopold Café is a popular eatery in south Mumbai. It is on the busy Shaheed Bhagat Singh Marg in touristy Colaba which is notorious for drug peddlers. A must-do joint for foreigners, especially backpackers and the young lot keen to taste the city's nightlife, Leopold finds a special mention on travel sites and travel guides. A shoot-out around this time of the night in a Colaba restaurant smacked of a drug cartel at work. I must rush there, and immediately.

Instinctively, I grabbed the clothes I had discarded minutes earlier – a strict no-no otherwise – and simultaneously dialled Vijay

Salaskar, one of my bravest and most dependable of officers. He headed the Anti Extortion Cell of the Crime Branch. Salaskar said he would also rush to Leopold immediately. I also spoke to my Additional Commissioner, Deven Bharti who was in the western suburbs for some personal work. He said he would immediately rush back. Just then my cell phone rang. It was K.L. Prasad who too had received the information. I said I was rushing to Leopold Café and at the same time expressed a suspicion that was niggling me: 'Could it be a terror attack?'

'I'll come with you,' Prasad said and I replied, 'Yes, of course!'

I lived in Ambar Apartments, the official government quarters on Malabar Hill and Prasad lived in Avanti, the next building in the same complex. Within minutes, both of us were hurtling down the hill in my car, but not before receiving more disturbing news that firing was now reported near the Taj. Someone had opened fire on a police wireless van called 'Tourist Mobile' whose job it was to patrol the area around the tourist spot of Gateway of India, with a few constables armed just with lathis. The driver of the van was injured in the firing. Later we were to learn that the mobile van which was called Tourist-1 was shot at near the Leopold Café where she had rushed.

This was definitely much more serious than a drug cartel shoot-out! And we were carrying only our pistols. I immediately felt that my officers and I needed to collect more weapons from the Crime Branch Armoury and only thereafter rush to the Taj. I immediately began calling them to convey the change in plan and like me, Prasad too began instructing his juniors.

Salaskar had already reached Colaba. Both the Taj and Leopold are located in Colaba. I told him that things seemed much more serious and he should report to the Crime Branch office to pick up weapons and ammunition. As I finished, my phone rang and it was the CP, Hasan Gafoor. He wanted to know where I was. I said I was passing Islam Gymkhana and that Prasad was with me. I told him that my team and I were going to pick up our weapons from the Armoury and proceed to Colaba. But he had other plans for me. 'No, Rakesh. I want you to go straight to the Control Room and take charge. I want you to monitor the situation from the Control Room.' His directions were clear.

The Leopold Café firing was the first terror attack of the night and it was reported at 21:48. Just two minutes thereafter was reported the firing on Tourist-1 and the driver having been injured. Four minutes later came reports of five to six persons being injured at Leopold and of firing near the Taj. It was followed in two minutes by a call that 'sten-men' had entered a hotel and also the report of gunmen entering the Oberoi, firing with their weapons. This was quickly followed by the report of a taxi being blown up at Wadi Bunder in central Mumbai, four-five km away from the CST. Five minutes later, came the report that some trouble could be heard at the CST, confirmed immediately as firing at the railway station. In two minutes came the report of something untoward happening at Colaba Market, later to turn out as the attack on a Jewish establishment (Chabad House) in a building called Nariman House. In the next three minutes, at 22:06 a suspicious bag was reported lying near the gate of the Oberoi.

In just about fifteen-twenty minutes, the terrorists had struck at six locations in south and central Mumbai. All these calls were processed swiftly by the Control Room and the operational heads, as per the standard procedures, to spark off several chains of communications and corresponding movements of available manpower to the troubled locations.

Every police station had 'Beat Marshals', the motorcycle-borne policemen who patrolled fixed areas. They also had vans called 'Police Station Mobiles' with names like Colaba-1 or Colaba-2 (Colaba being the name of the police station). There were bigger vehicles called 'Striking Mobiles' under the control of the Additional Commissioners of Police of each of the five regions and also some under the Control Room. Then there were seven 'Assault Mobiles' under the City Anti-Terrorism Squad (ATS). Each had one Sub Inspector and five men armed with one 9mm pistol, one AK-47, one SLR (Self Loading Rifle), one Carbine and six bulletproof jackets. They were located at strategic points for tackling grave emergencies. There also were eight Quick Response Teams (QRTs) under the City ATS. They were a force of eight officers and forty-eight men below the age of thirty-five, ready to move at short notices in a team of one officer-twelve men. Under the Crime Branch came the Special Operations Squad (SOS), which was used for protecting the investigating or raiding teams. It had fifteen officers, twenty-two men and four drivers. Each officer/man carried either an AK-47 or an SLR or a pistol each. There were also the Riot Control Police (RCP) teams, each comprising eighteen men.

The Control Room had immediately alerted the respective jurisdictional officers and ordered nakabandi (roadblocks manned by pickets to check suspicious movements). The Beat Marshals had reached the spots and the Senior Police Inspectors and Assistant Commissioners of the concerned police stations were on their way. Not just the Police Mobiles of the three affected police stations (Colaba, Marine Drive and Azad Maidan), those of adjoining Cuffe Parade, M.R.A. Marg, J.J. Marg and L.T. Marg police stations were also directed to the spots. What is more, Mobiles of police stations a good distance away, like V.P. Road, D.B. Marg, Wadala and Sewri too were rushed, as were the Striking Vans of South Region, Zone-II, V.P. Road and J.J. Marg. The Bomb Detection and Disposal Squad (BDDS) was put on the job to deal with the suspicious object found near the Trident. While some officers and men were directed to the spots by their superiors, others had joined the operations on their own. The seniors rose to the challenge by leading the men from the front.

Deepak Vishwasrao, Senior Police Inspector, Colaba, under

whose jurisdiction fell Leopold Cafe, Colaba Market and the Taj, was on his way home but turned back immediately. Barely had he reached the police station when the trouble shifted to the Taj and he rushed thither. Coincidentally, DCP Zone-I Vishwas Nangre Patil was the DCP deputed on the routine night round. He reached the Taj at 21:55 where he was to remain throughout, as the CP himself had directed him to take charge of the situation. Within a short time, he entered the battlefield along with a few men. Rajvardhan, Deputy Commissioner (SB-II), learnt about the Leopold firing as soon as it happened. He was at his residence and rushed to the Colaba police station where he learnt about the firing at the Taj. He went to the Taj and joined Nangre Patil in the operation.

Police Inspector Bhagwat Bansode of Marine Drive police station (adjoining Colaba) was on night duty patrol. He reached the Oberoi in three to four minutes. Senior Police Inspector of Marine Drive police station, Sanjay Amrute had reached home after attending a meeting at the Trident. It was with the Special Protection Group (SPG) for Advanced Security Liaison for the Prime Minister's visit scheduled three days later. The Oberoi Security Officer informed him about the firing and he immediately left home for Marine Drive. The Additional CP (South Region) Dr Venkatesham, under whose jurisdiction all these locations fell, was monitoring the situation closely and was on his way to Colaba when he learnt about the firing at the Trident. As Nangre Patil was handling Colaba, he went to the Oberoi at 22:05. Around the same time, Senior Police Inspector Amrute joined him as did Vinay Kargaonkar, Additional CP (Protection & Security) on his own. Kargaonkar had heard the loud explosions from his house close by.

The CP received information about the firing at the Leopold Café and the Taj from the Control Room soon after the incident and immediately began monitoring the situation. He directed senior officers to attend to the Taj and Leopold and was proceeding towards those spots when came the report of firing at the Oberoi. He decided to go there. He reached the Oberoi, set up his Command Centre nearby and began issuing operational instructions, deputing senior officers to carry out specific tasks.

Isaque Ibrahim Bagwan, ACP, Azad Maidan Division, resided in Colaba. He was directed by the CP to rush to the Leopold Café. By the time he reached, the terrorists had already entered the Taj. Just then a big explosion was heard from the direction of the Colaba Market and he rushed to the location. It was called Panch Pairi, meaning 'Five Steps' – a name coined by the fishermen for the steps leading up to the narrow passage to Nariman House. He found that the terrorists were lobbing hand grenades and one casualty was reported. With just one wireless operator and with the help of the people who had gathered, he managed to throw a cordon to restrict the traffic in the area. IPS officer Hemant Nagrale, on deputation to the State Electricity Distribution Corporation, was at his residence in Colaba. He rushed to the Leopold Café on his own and helped remove the injured to hospital. From there he joined the operations at the Taj and began evacuating the injured.

Sadanand Date, Additional Commissioner of Central Region, had reached his residence on Malabar Hill when he learnt of the attack. He called Venkatesham to ask how he could help. Venkatesham requested him to go to the CST and Date immediately proceeded towards the railway station.

Within twenty minutes to half an hour of the attacks, senior officers had reached each of the active spots to take charge and even the State Reserve Police Force (SRPF) – the armed police battalions located in different places to assist civil police – had been summoned. As the police began grappling with events which were unfolding rapidly, messages from men and officers in combat began coming in. Within no time, reports of casualties started trickling in, with demands for ambulances, stretchers and staff to escort the injured to hospitals. Eyewitnesses at Leopold had described two gunmen opening fire. Officers at the Trident reported that there were two gunmen on a rampage with plenty of arms and ammunition. Faced with automatic fire and hand grenades, it did not take long for the men on the spot to realise that expert and specialised help – skilled and trained in handling terrorist attacks – was needed. Thus, demands not just for the SRPF – but also for the Striking, Assault and QR Teams began coming in. The Control Room began directing these teams to the spots, under the watchful eye of senior officers who were all listening in and issuing directions.

Several wireless networks called 'channels' are monitored from the Control Room. The five regions – South, Central, East, West, North – have their own dedicated channels and control rooms in their own jurisdictions. The Traffic Division has its dedicated channel and there is also a VVIP channel and a separate Motorola channel for communication among senior officers. Each of these dedicated channels function under the overall command of the main Control Room from where they are monitored round-the-clock by teams of operators working in shifts.

For the Police Control Room of Mumbai – the huge, densely populated and cosmopolitan metropolis – dealing with emergencies and panic-stricken callers speaking in a myriad languages and accents, is not uncommon. They are used to handling huge rallies and demonstrations, milling crowds and gargantuan festival processions, communal flare-ups and riotous situations, manmade and natural disasters like fires, building crashes, gas-leaks and flooding, and even hide-hit-hide terrorist attacks like serial explosions. Today, however, something way beyond their usual cup of 'cutting chai' had landed on their desks. They were receiving, on an average, five terror-related calls per minute. From 21:40 hours on 26/11 till 02:00 on 27/11, they had received 1,365 calls! And the callers today were braving hand grenades and indiscriminate firing from automatic weapons. The calls were more frantic; the struggle to find the right words was harder. Consequently, the task of comprehending it all and responding to all of it was all the more challenging. The fear of the Unknown was in the air.

I reached the CP's office at 22:27, along with K.L. Prasad, to take charge of what was virtually to be the War Room for the next three days. By then, the Control Room, led by ACP R. C. Tayade and Senior Police Inspector Sunil Tondwalkar, was already on the job with full concentration, doing everything possible as per the established practice and protocol. As a result, simultaneous action had begun at the Taj, Colaba Market, the Oberoi and the CST. The situation was rapidly worsening at all the four locations. A suspicious bag each was spotted at the Trident and also near the Taj taxi stand. Report after report of firing, blasts, hand grenade explosions, suspicious objects and activities were streaming in and call after call from anxious citizens asking to verify the news, seeking clarity and requesting for help. To counter the clogged lines and cut delays, all of us were using our cell phones which were a blessing.

From the minute I stepped into the Control Room, the officers began providing me with important inputs on the on-going operations and also sought my guidance wherever they felt the need. I had to speak to and provide verbal reports to top officials like the CP, the DGP, the Chief Secretary of Maharashtra and to the Ministry of Home Affairs (MHA) in New Delhi. I had to also liaise with the other security agencies such as the Central Reserve Police Force (CRPF), the National Security Guards (NSG), the Army and the Navy. Till the arrival of the NSG in the early hours of 27 November, I was literally on my feet without a morsel of food and with just a few sips of water to help me keep talking. The same was true for all the others around me, though they could do with a few sips of tea which is not my cup of tea, as I am literally a 'teetotaller'.

Almost immediately after our arrival in the Control Room, amidst reports of firing and grenade attacks, we began receiving reports that terrorists were walking the streets near the CST. The locations were near the Azad Maidan, near the Municipal Corporation building and near the offices of the Special Branches 1 and 2 which are in close proximity to the CP's office – the nerve centre of the city's security where the Control Room is located. The prospect of terrorists blasting their way into the CP's office was no longer a far-fetched scenario. There was palpable anxiety in the Control Room because the operators knew exactly where we stood. We had to make do with the skeletal manpower we had at our disposal. This was quite a crisis. To protect the CP's office, armed and well-equipped teams are deployed in what is called HO Striking Mobiles. At that given moment, however, these striking vans had been dispatched to the active spots.

Surrounding me to meet this challenge were forty to fifty men and women, on their desks, intently scanning their computer screens. Their faces were grim, necks craned and shoulders taut. Concentrating on each syllable and word, straining all their faculties to catch, grasp and decipher the terrible reports that were pouring into their ears through their headphones. Quickly jotting down the material details. Asking the callers to repeat themselves, seeking clarifications. Collating and connecting the messages. Making sense of the rapid flow of events. Understanding and imagining how things were panning out in topographies miles away; bridging the gap between the personnel in different locations; rushing precious manpower and resources in the most efficient manner possible; drawing their superiors' attention and seeking directions when required; running from desk to desk and to the desks of the ACP and the Senior Police Inspector on the elevated platform at the centre. In all, making all the possible efforts to counter the clogged lines to expedite action.

I was constantly talking on different cell phones which were being thrust at me by someone or the other – the Control Room staff, my own operator, the ACP, the Senior Police Inspector– or talking on fixed lines or the wireless sets of different channels whenever anyone contacted me there. Prasad too was issuing instructions to his juniors, taking calls, coordinating with the MHA and making important calls for requisitioning the Army. Not one of us had the time to take even a moment's pause. I was speaking to the Local Arms (LA) Division to get the material and manpower delivered, and to the head of the CRPF and to the SRPF. I was speaking to the CP, the DGP and the Chief Secretary to inform them of the steps being taken and requesting for their intervention where necessary. I was talking to the Traffic Division to facilitate the transport of additional manpower, and requisitioning buses. I was trying to contact the Army Chief at his residence in Delhi.

It is not possible for anyone to hear each and every conversation on the channels, and obviously, the operators could not and did not share with me each and every call and response. They tried their best to inform me about the major events and alerts and asked for my guidance whenever in doubt. Which meant that I was continuously engaged in and involved with some issue or the other and asking for verification of information, if necessary, before giving directions. It seemed like the longest night of our lives, full of crisis management every second. Every moment was packed with a multitude of activities to be internalised and responded to. Every message was important, each messenger seemed to be in a crisis and with so many 'I have to's' hovering over us.

The news of the attack had spread like wildfire. Anxious friends and families were tracing the whereabouts of their near and dear ones. Rumours had already started circulating. Some said that sixty terrorists had infiltrated the city. We were also receiving a number of panic calls. Nothing could be taken lightly, nothing could be discounted. We had to rush manpower to verify the information and act if necessary. And then I was informed that the crowd gathered at Leopold had found a suspect carrying a revolver! Though he was pleading innocence, they had roughed him up well and handed him over to the Colaba police. A quick breakthrough? Possible! I immediately directed my Crime Branch officers, who were already on their way to Colaba, to interrogate the man. Luckily for him, it was our seasoned officers who had reached the spot – Senior Police Inspectors Salaskar and Ramesh Mahale. The man turned out to be an armed guard of a guest dining at the Leopold. Caught unawares by the indiscriminate AK-47 firing, he had taken cover and escaped unhurt. He was indeed innocent and we let him go.

Amidst all those trying to get through to me, even my wife had somehow managed to contact me, 'irritatingly' anxious like any other mother. Was it safe for our son to board a bus that was to take him away from the city? Or should he be called back to the safe confines of our home?

From the War Room, anywhere seemed far safer that night than Mumbai, our beloved city that our enemies loved to hurt and harm repeatedly, and with more and more venom. We had no clue what we were up against. How many infiltrators? How far had they spread? What were their targets? The Indian Mujahideen had revealed a new trend in enemy tactics: engage the security forces at one spot and then add attacks at short intervals at secondary sites – on the periphery. They took pleasure in killing and maiming anxious friends, relatives, social workers, security forces and emergency service providers rushing to rescue the victims at primary targets.

Also, this was a new type of urban warfare which had not been experienced by Mumbai so far. An operation by *fidayeens* looking forward to getting martyred to secure their assured place in heaven, after causing maximum damage to the nonbelievers on earth. Where else were they headed? To the Bhabha Atomic Research

Centre (BARC)? To Tarapur? Our refineries? Our ports? Airports? Army and Navy establishments? These men on the rampage must be outsiders? And if so, was someone supporting them from this soil? Where were their hideouts? What next to come screaming through the wireless sets? Shouldn't my investigating teams be looking into something immediately, to get a hang of the plot? What should they be pursuing?

Despite the anxiety, every operator around me was fully engaged, giving their hundred per cent, responding to each call with exemplary equanimity and trying their utmost to rein in the hell breaking loose outside. And all this, while keeping their eyes peeled for the smallest bit of information – a watchful eye also on the TV monitors reeling off hysterical reporters covering the theatres of war. What could be the feelings of the men and women donning those noisy headphones as they watched some of their colleagues preparing to enter the battles, even as several others shared their plight and asked for help: hand grenades hurled at us! Send us automatic weapons! Send us bulletproof jackets! We need commandos! The repeated replay of an injured policeman being shifted on a motorcycle was tugging at my heart. Then what must be the feelings of the operators as they saw it? Hearts sinking with alerts of terrorists roaming the streets around our building? With the thoughts of some friends and family in and around the troubled spots? What do I do to keep their morale up?

Not that we had any time for inspirational speeches and huddles. To inspire and get inspired, we only had to do our job relentlessly. With the resolute scowls that it brought on, with an occasional grip on the shoulder or a small pat on the back, and grim smiles to convey and reassure that we were all one, under the varied epaulettes on our uniforms, and that each one of us was as important to the nation as the officer and constable out in the field, destined to face the enemy's bullets and bombs that night. We had to ensure that we functioned nonstop!

So in the midst of attending to queries of the Control Room staff and calls from different officers and Crime branch teams, I took a quick review of the security arrangements of the CP office's compound. I immediately directed ACP Tayade to take a round of the compound to alert and brief the guards. Just then, someone thought it necessary to express what all of us were thinking anyway: *'Sir, saare HO striking doosri jagah hain toh yahan kaise manage karenge?'* (Sir, how will we manage here now that all the HO Striking vans have been sent to other locations?)

'Dekho, iss compound ka kona-kona hum jaantey hain. Aur idhar hamaare paas hathiyaar bhi hain. Ek toh yahan hum unhe ghusne nahin denge! Aur woh yahan pahoonche bhi, toh unko khatam kar denge! Ismein mujhe koi shak nahin!' (Look, we know each nook and every cranny of this compound. And we also have weapons here. First of all, we will not let them enter. And even if they reach here, we will finish them. I have absolutely no doubt in my mind) I said. My words had the desired effect. Brows cleared as they saw my point. Then I also took some very basic and simple steps. I got the guards to stack movable furniture like steel cupboards, wooden tables and chairs near all the staircases and entrances to block easy access and to help us take cover in case of an attack.

The terrorists were first spotted on the staircase outside the CST and ten minutes later Azad Maidan-2 reported that two persons were walking along the lane of the Municipal Corporation building towards Metro Cinema. Immediately in the next minute, a Beat Marshal warned the Control Room that some boys with bags on their backs were walking in the lane near the Special Branch-I (SB-I) office behind the CP office's compound. The Control Room directed Zone-II Striking van to advance, but she was near the Corporation Building and reported firing. In the next few minutes, the Control Room continued to scout for more help for the SB-I office lane and asked Zone-II Striking, Malabar Hill-1, D.B. Marg-1 and also L.T. Marg-1 to rush there. The

Control Room also received reports that the suspicious bags near the Trident had exploded and a suspicious dinghy was found at Badhwar Park in Cuffe Parade! People had seen eight to nine men getting off the dinghy some time back, carrying bags.

At 22:50, Azad Maidan-2 reported firing near the Times of India (TOI) building which is opposite the CST, and near the SB-I office. The Control Room asked them to take the help of Zone-II Striking and HO Striking that were nearby and continued to look for other vans that could be rushed to the spot. Senior Police Inspector Azad Maidan was in the vicinity of Metro Cinema junction. Zone-II Striking was at the Municipal Corporation building – a short distance from the spot and reporting that firing was still on there.

Reports of trouble at the Taj and Oberoi continued streaming in when at 22:54, Senior Police Inspector M.R.A. Marg reported that two persons were firing in the TOI lane and his staff had retaliated. He said that taking advantage of the darkness, the men had run away in the direction of SB-I, towards the CP's office. Blasts continued to be reported simultaneously on the road in Colaba Market and near the Municipal Corporation building near the CST. If these were not enough, there had also come a report of a taxi being blown up at 22:53 at Vile Parle, a suburb close to the airport on the Western Express Highway!

So now we had two five star hotels, one train terminus and one residential building under siege in south Mumbai; terrorists prowling in the lanes around the CP's office, TOI building and Corporation building; one taxi blast in central Mumbai and one taxi blast in northern Mumbai. All in a span of just about an hour.

And suddenly, in four to five minutes – around 11 p.m. – a new active point emerged – the terrorists were now near the Cama and Albless Hospital, a hospital for women and children with around 370 beds, which was built in the 1880s with a donation from the philanthropist Pestonjee Hormusjee Cama. No one, even in their wildest imagination, could have ever thought that a hospital which selflessly attended to sick women and children from the poorer sections of society would ever see a brutal terror attack one day, with bullets and grenades.

The Control Room immediately began diverting manpower to Cama Hospital, beginning with two wireless vans of the L.T. Marg police station – L.T. Marg-1 and 2. L.T. Marg-2 was anyway at the Mahanagarpalika gate close by and reached Cama at 23:05.

By then, Deven Bharti, Additional CP (Crime), had returned to the CP's office. Meanwhile, the Crime Branch and the ATS were frantically on the lookout for terror-linked telecons. When trouble was reported from Cama Hospital, I directed Bharti to rush there with a team.

By then, Sadanand Date had also reached the Metro Cinema junction near Cama and learnt that the terrorists had entered the hospital. He immediately collected some officers and men from the junction. At 23:05, Senior Police Inspector Azad Maidan reported to the Control Room that he was going to Cama with Date and the Control Room in turn asked L.T. Marg-1 and 2 to report to Date at Cama. Next, L.T. Marg-2 was asked to check the servants' quarters since some injured were reported to be there, and L.T. Marg-1 was asked to go near the SB-I office. Meanwhile, Senior Police Inspector L.T. Marg was asked to join Senior Police Inspector Azad Maidan near the Corporation Bank. Two more Mobiles were directed to the area: Pydhonie-3 and V.P. Road-2 who were asked to come to the rear of the G.T. Hospital which is also in the vicinity.

At 23:08, the Control Room received Sadanand Date's location on the Motorola channel that he had reached Cama Hospital. Again in the next two minutes, the servants' quarters was a cause of concern as two injured persons were reported to have entered there and Senior Police Inspector L.T. Marg was specifically asked to rush there. Next, Beat Marshal-2 suggested that a van be sent to the lane along TOI from the CST to Cama. He was asked to take the help of M.R.A. Marg. Then at 23:13 Malabar Hill-1 reported that two men were firing inside the Cama Hospital and the next minute, Senior Police Inspector Azad Maidan reported to the Control Room that he and Date had reached the terrace of the hospital. Even as this was unfolding, DCP Zone-II asked for bulletproof jackets for the TOI lane and rushed an officer to fetch them from the Azad Maidan police station.

As Date, Senior Police Inspector Azad Maidan and the team reached the terrace of the Cama Hospital at 23:13, Additional Commissioner of East Region, Ashok Kamte asked the Control Room: *'Mananiya King Saranna vicharun ghya mala kontya spotla report karaycha aahe,'* (Ask the CP and let me know which spot I am to report to).

'Samajle, sir. Me call deoon vicharto,' (Understood, sir. I will call and ask) the operator replied and tried calling the CP, but could not get through. He came to me and asked me what he should do. *'Kamte sahebanna tyanche location vichara,'* I told him. (Ask Kamte saheb for his location).

So at 23:16, the Control Room asked Kamte his location and he replied: *'Ajoon pohochayla 10 minute. Tajmahal hotel la pohochayla 10 minitey,'* (Still, ten minutes to reach, ten minutes to reach Hotel Taj Mahal).

When the operator told me this, I directed him to ascertain Kamte's exact location which he did a minute later at 23:17. Ashok Kamte immediately answered, *'Wadala passing, Wadala passing.'* The Control Room replied that they had noted it and gave me the information.

It was very reassuring to know that a dynamic officer like Ashok Kamte was about to join the battle at the Taj. The situation needed all hands on deck. At the Oberoi, they were trying to extinguish the fire but with the gunmen on the rampage, the fire brigade was finding it difficult to enter. Senior Police Inspector Marine

Drive was asking for staff with automatic weapons, like the QRT. Some rescued guests had informed the police about many others trapped inside. A call was also received from ACP Azad Maidan that two men had entered DCP Brijesh Singh's residence which was in the compound of Azad Maidan police station which was very close to Cama! Deven Bharti was leaving the CP office's compound for Cama when he'd received this bit of information from the staff. He proceeded to the spot with his Crime Branch team, only to learn that terrorists had entered Cama Hospital. He immediately rushed to the rear gate of the hospital and in order to initiate effective action, he decided to go to a nearby tall building from where he could take a vantage position to aim at the terrorists. Immediately thereafter, he went to the terrace of the seven-storeyed Anjuman Islam Boys' Hostel which is next to Cama Hospital. Just then, Assistant Police Inspector Parab of the Crime Branch's Anti-Extortion Cell joined Bharti and informed him that Vijay Salaskar and his team had also reached the hospital's rear gate. Bharti immediately called up Salaskar who informed him that Karkare and Kamte were also with him at the rear gate. They had discussed the situation, Salaskar told him, and that they were planning to now lay a cordon around the hospital.

While on the terrace of the Boys' Hostel, Bharti received important information from an Intelligence officer: one person was in constant touch with the terrorists from a cell number, and was giving details of the police movements around the Taj! Bharti immediately informed me about this development and I ordered him to rush to the indicated spots around the Taj where the handlers seemed to be located. Bharti rushed with his team and began combing hotels Gulf, Godwin and Garden near the Taj. After much later they reported to me that only the cellular tower atop Hotel Godwin was being used to receive and transmit calls. The phone was being used by the terrorists inside the Taj. Obviously, there were no suspects to be picked up from Hotel Godwin. Thereafter, Bharti and team joined the officers and men outside the Taj and helped in the cordoning and rescue operations there.

Around the time that Kamte was reporting that he was passing Wadala, the Control Room had begun receiving frantic messages about the situation inside Cama. While L.T. Marg-2 said that firing had resumed at Cama, Senior Police Inspector Azad Maidan reported that it had again erupted on the terrace. At 23:19 a message was received from Date's wireless that he was on the terrace and asked for commandos to be sent there. The Control Room, in turn, asked Zone-II Mobile to send commandos to the terrace. At the same time, demands for bulletproof vests were received from other locations and Venkatesham was issuing directions to meet the demands. Just then, DCP Zone-II informed the Control Room that there were blasts and firing heard from Cama Hospital.

As Date and team were tackling the terrorists inside Cama, at 23:22 Kamte reported that he was approaching Zone-I Office: 'Approaching, approaching, Zone-I office.'

'Understood, sir,' replied the Control Room.

'Aadesh, Aadesh. Majhyasathi aadesh kay aahe?' (Orders, orders. What are the orders for me?) asked Kamte immediately.

The operator replied that he would ask me and let Kamte know. As he was consulting me, the Control Room again got a call from Date's team that two-three blasts had occurred and they desperately needed help on the sixth floor of the hospital. As the Zone-I office is situated very close to Cama, I felt that Kamte could reach Cama in no time. I was confident that he would be of great help in the operation. So I asked the operators to direct him there, which they did.

The situation at Cama Hospital was now in the hands of three senior officers, all of whom were equally capable. The senior-most was Hemant Karkare, Joint CP (ATS), who had been closely monitoring the situation right from the beginning and was in constant touch with the CP. He had reached his residence in Dadar in central Mumbai when he had received reports of the attack. He had immediately left home with the Z Category Protection provided to him by the Special Protection Unit (SPU) which included two Personal Security Officers and four bodyguards. Each was armed with a 9mm pistol and also had among them one MP5 automatic weapon and one Sten gun. He was also given a bulletproof vehicle and had, in addition, two QRT personnel with weapons. Karkare's vehicle had reached the Haj House on D.N. Road but could not proceed further due to the blockade and barricades set up by the police. Not one to waste any time, he had got down from his vehicle and met DCP Sanjay Mohite, Additional DG (Railways) K.P. Raghuwanshi and DCP Koregaonkar who were present there. He learned that after the firing at the CST, the terrorists had gone in the direction of SB-I office. Karkare put on a bulletproof jacket and a helmet. He took his pistol from his vehicle and proceeded on foot towards Cama, accompanied by his security guards – officers of the SPU, the constables, and the two QRT men. They reached the rear gate of Cama at 23:24.

The second officer was Crime Branch's Vijay Salaskar, a daredevil skilled in the use of weapons. He had two vehicles with him and men from the Anti-Extortion Cell. They were returning from Leopold to the CP's office to pick up weapons when they had heard of the skirmish at Cama. Grasping the seriousness of the situation they had straightaway rushed to the spot to assist Date and Karkare. The third was Ashok Kamte, a brave and outstanding young IPS officer and a sportsman, fit and agile, who had been asked to rush to the spot by me. He had reached Cama Hospital around 23:28.

By then, rumours and panic calls had begun putting a severe strain on our scarce manpower and resources. There was a report of some commotion around Mantralaya near the residence of a minister. A suspicious car was seen speeding near the Siddhi Vinayak Temple which has long been a terror target. There were scares of attacks on Hotel Four Seasons at Worli and the J.W. Marriott at Juhu which could not be taken lightly, as also several reports of abandoned or suspicious cars. Each report had to be attended to and followed up meticulously. People were trapped inside Nariman House, guests and staff at the Taj and the Oberoi, and patients and medical staff in Cama. Close combat was on everywhere and our officers and men were asking for bulletproof jackets and automatic weapons. The operational heads were initiating arrangements to make protective gear and arms and ammunition available at all the locations, but it was clear that we were not equipped to deal with the situation on our own, materially as well as in terms of training. Therefore at each spot, the senior-most officer was responsible for marshalling the resources, and for strategising and organising the response. The Control Room not only depended on him, but the officers and men assisting him at the spot as also their wireless operators for correctly reporting back the developments. These officers and their wireless operators became the eyes and ears of the Control Room that horrific night.

I immediately thought of soliciting help from the Navy. Mumbai is after all the headquarters of the Western Naval Command which has a formidable combination of well-equipped Naval bases and commandos at their disposal. We would have to obviously follow formal procedure for requisitioning their help. It therefore made sense to first brief the officers in-charge so that they were ready to take off by the time we got the approvals and the final orders. This would save vital time as every minute mattered. I had already begun working in that direction.

As mentioned earlier, Hemant Karkare was the most experienced officer at Cama and therefore his assessment was undoubtedly of great significance. He had informed the Control Room at 23:24 that he was at Cama Hospital where firing was on and some four to five blasts had occurred in his presence within a span of five minutes. Karkare wanted to encircle the place. He was near the SB-II office's side and asked the Control Room to send a team to the front of the hospital. He said it needed to be coordinated to avoid cross-fire and also requested that Prasad be asked to requisition commandos from the Army. He again repeated that they were near SB-II office, and that there was firing on the fifth and sixth floors and three-four grenade blasts had also been heard.

At that very moment, I was briefing Commander Bhutani of the Navy on the crisis we were facing and the desperate need to have their commandos to help us. Commander Bhutani assured me that he would send us the MARCOS (Marine Commandos) but needed permission from the Central High Command. I immediately began working on getting the permissions and also got in touch with the DGP to get the Central Reserve Police Force (CRPF) deployed for action at all the affected locations. Thereafter I spoke to the Commandant of the CRPF. The CRPF contingent left their barracks for the trouble spots around 23:40 even as I was speaking to the Chief Secretary to obtain orders for the Western Naval Command to send us the MARCOS and also for the Army to send us commandos for all the four locations. K.L. Prasad was also in touch with the Army and was coordinating to get a more trained force.

While I was liaising with various officials and agencies to requisition commandos and additional trained and well-equipped force, the Control Room was looking for more reinforcements for Cama Hospital and was calling the Striking Vans.

At 23:27, the Control Room confirmed with Karkare: 'Sir, you need help from the front side of Cama Hospital, right?' To which Karkare answered at 23:28 as follows:

> The QRT team of ATS is here. Just now a Crime Branch Team has come from SB-II side. So we need from the other side. We

need to encircle it and cordon. See if a request can be made to the Army through Prasad, Jt CP (Law and Order).

The Control Room assured him that they had noted his instructions. Around the same time, the Control Room heard from Date's walkie-talkie that all members of the police party were injured in the heavy firing on the fifth floor.

Thus, at the rear gate of Cama Hospital in Anjuman-E-Islam Lane, a large number of policemen had gathered. Led by Karkare, Salaskar and Kamte, they were now strategising on how to surround the hospital. They were also aware that trained commandos would have to be requisitioned from the Armed Forces for this kind of an operation. South Control and the Control Room were trying their best to look for more Striking Mobiles that could be diverted to Cama and other active spots where the situation was equally bad and the battles were intensifying. And Prasad and I were trying our best to requisition help from the Army and the Navy to get commandos and additional force.

At 23:30, Senior Police Inspector Colaba issued a warning from near the Taj, *'Amchya angaavar hand grenade taklet. Amhi just vachlo. Jar koni reinforcement asel tyanna precaution ghyayla sanga.'* He said that he had just escaped a grenade which was thrown at them and wanted to warn other forces if they ventured there. DCP Zone-II's walkie-talkie also reported a hand grenade explosion at Cama. The Control Room immediately warned CCR Striking-2, that was dispatched to Cama, about the grenade threat. A general warning was also issued to all about possible hand grenade attacks. At 23:36, ACP Bagwan told the Control Room: *'Me Colabyat payi-payi yet aahe. Majhyabarobar SRPF aahe, Ithehi firing chalu aahe. Pahila tyanni haat bomb khali takla aahe ...Amhala searchlight ani mothe weapon wale milale tar tyanna amhi barobar karu.'* (He was on foot, accompanied by the SRPF. There was firing going on. First, the terrorists had hurled a hand grenade.

He was asking for searchlights and saying that if he could also get men with 'big' {automatic} weapons, he would then be able to give a befitting reply.) The Control Room immediately began checking for the availability of force for Bagwan's aid and directed the nearby vans to reach the spot. Within a short time after the attack, Bagwan had called me to explain the situation. We were arranging SRPF for his help but before that, M.R.A.-1 had reached the spot. Bagwan deployed the three men with SLRs in the nearby buildings and thereafter an SRPF team reached him.

They had .303s and teargas shells. I later learnt that Bagwan had motivated the men by reminding them of Chhatrapati Shivaji Maharaj (the legendary Maratha warrior King): 'Terrorists have attacked us. You are brave, but don't let your morale go down. We are born policemen. We will defend this pass like the *mavlas* (the devoted peasants-turned-soldiers) of Shivaji Maharaj.' Bagwan had positioned the men in the windows and terraces of the surrounding buildings and succeeded in pinning the terrorists down by confining them to the building.

By then, the terrorists holed up in the Taj were hurling grenades from the windows on the police cordon. At 23:45, Senior Police Inspector Colaba requested the Control Room: *'Taj chya pudhchya bajula teen launches arms sahit pathvlya tar bare hoil.'* (It would be better if you could send three launches with arms to the front side of the Taj). He wanted to shoot down the terrorists who were lobbing grenades from there. The Control Room instantly called Mumbai police's launches, Sharvari, Aboli and Priyanka. Aboli replied that she was patrolling the sea near the Gateway. The Control Room conveyed this to Senior Police Inspector Colaba and he in turn asked them to deploy the Aboli in readiness in order to shoot terrorists who were taking positions in the windows of the third to fifth floors.

The Control Room was therefore trying its best to respond to all the calls by allocating manpower to different locations: the Assault

Mobile located at Washington House to the Oberoi; Assault Mobile at the Mantralaya to Cama Hospital; Assault Mobile from the American Centre to the Taj; Senior Police Inspector V.P. Road to the G.T. Hospital gate; L.T. Marg-2 to the main gate of Cama; Central Control Room Striking-II to Cama; and the QRT to Cama. The Superintendent of St. George Hospital had also requested for more force as the number of injured being brought in was increasing and they were apprehending danger.

At 23:48, Senior Police Inspector Azad Maidan Mobile reported, *'St. Xavier galli madhye firing chalu aahe. Madat pahije.'* (There is firing on in St. Xavier's College lane and help was needed.) Meanwhile J.J.-1 reported that she was taking Assistant Police Inspector Pawar to Bombay Hospital as he had been injured. Within two minutes, Pydhonie-3 said, *'G.T. Hospital la madatichi avashyakata aahe.'* (Help needed at G.T. Hospital.) The Control Room asked him: what kind of help? *'Gadbad waatatey. Samorun konitari manoos yet aahe asey lok sangtat.'* (Seems like some trouble. People say that someone is advancing from the front side.)

The South Control Room asked Senior Police Inspector L.T. Marg to come to G.T. Hospital and asked L.T. Marg-2 to go to Cama's main gate. The Control Room reconfirmed from the South Control Room – besides CCR Striking, which other Striking was at Cama? The South Control Room replied that Pydhonie-3 was at G.T. Hospital, and L.T. Marg-2 and Senior Police Inspector V.P. Road had also been dispatched. The Control Room then asked L.T. Marg-2 to go to GT Casualty with weapons as requested by Pydhonie-3. At 23:51, Senior Police Inspector L.T. Marg confirmed that he was at Cama Hospital.

While danger seemed to be lurking in the streets around St. Xavier's, G.T. Hospital, and St. George Hospital, frantic calls were also coming in from Vishwas Nangre Patil from the Taj asking for armed men in bulletproof vests as they were being attacked with hand grenades. Similarly, at the Oberoi too, they needed more armed men.

As the action was being planned by the three seniors led by Hemant Karkare at the rear gate of Cama Hospital, the Control Room continued to guide manpower to reach the spots where trouble had erupted. The terrorists who were spotted in a red car were now in focus as the clock struck twelve. The Control Room alerted Senior Police Inspector D.B. Marg, who was at Vinowli Girgaum Chowpatty, and HO Striking-2 that was near Cama, to come opposite St. Xavier's College near Metro since some terrorists had been spotted in a red car. At 00:03, HO Striking-2 asked for further description of the car and was asked to get it from Nagpada-1 who was already at the spot.

Firing was on in the vicinity of SB-I near Gate number 6, said Bravo-6 and the Control Room informed them that L.T. Marg -2 was already present there. Senior Police Inspector D.B. Marg reached Metro junction at 00:03 and the Control Room asked him to come to G.T. Hospital where Pydhonie-3 was positioned. L.T.-Marg 2 upon enquiry gave her location at the G.T. Hospital's main gate. Senior Police Inspector D.B. Marg asked the Control Room the exact spot that he should come to and he was told that trouble was brewing at G.T. Hospital. Senior Police Inspector V.P. Road countered this by saying that he had already reached the Casualty gate at G.T. Hospital, but that there was no trouble there. At 00:09, the Control Room told Senior Police Inspector D.B. Marg that firing could be heard at SB-I Gate number 6, and he replied that he had indeed come to G.T. but was taking a U-turn and was going back. The Control Room directed him to take the middle lane to Cama Hospital. At 00:11, the Control Room asked Senior Police Inspector L.T. Marg his location and he replied that he was at Cama Hospital. Meanwhile, the Control Room discovered that Azad Maidan-3 was at Mahapalika Marg and called her to Gate number 6.

At 00:11, the CP asked the Control Room to put him through to Hemant Karkare. The Control Room tried, but to no avail. After two minutes, at 00:13, Karkare's wireless operator informed the Control Room that Karkare had gone inside. At the same time, the Control Room asked Senior Police Inspector D.B. Marg whether he had reached St. Xavier's. He responded that he was waiting at the Metro junction and was not allowed to proceed further by the DCP who was himself present there.

In a span of about forty-two minutes (from 22:29 to 00:11), the Control Room had managed to direct to Cama Hospital as many as eleven Police Station Mobile Vans, three Striking Mobiles, one Assault Team, one SOS, one QRT, one ACP, four Senior Police Inspectors, one Riot Control Police Team from Naigaum which has eighteen men, and two Beat Marshals after receiving Karkare's call at 23:24. I later learnt that Senior Police Inspector Azad Maidan was on leave and his vehicle was being used by Assistant Police Inspector Vijay Shinde who had accompanied Sadanand Date to Cama Hospital. Thus, in all a minimum of a hundred police personnel had reached the area around Cama to help flush out the terrorists and rescue victims. They included four additional CPs (Date, Parambir Singh, Kamte and Deven Bharti) and three DCPs (Zone-II, Zone-V and HQ-1).

Even then, something unbelievable and unfortunate was to happen there that day. Rather, it was happening that given moment, even as the Control Room was labouring under the impression that an operation was still on in Cama. What no one could inform the Control Room in clear terms, probably because they themselves were not clear about the happenings, was the development that the very two terrorists, who were a little while ago engaged in a battle in Cama Hospital, had somehow managed to come out and were now walking on the streets. And Karkare, Kamte and Salaskar had left the rear gate of Cama, and they had got into ACP Pydhonie's Qualis and taken the Rang Bhavan lane towards Mahanagarpalika Marg, with driver Assistant Sub Inspector Bhosale, Salaskar's teammate, Arun Jadhav and two wireless operators.

The first time that the Control Room had heard of the ill-fated Qualis which was to play a major role in the unfortunate chain of events was at 00:14. Thereafter, the Control Room instructed Senior Police Inspector D.B. Marg to rush to the help of Nagpada-1 that had been fired upon. He responded that he was following a police Qualis van which had passed by the Metro junction and that there was firing from the vehicle! The next minute, DCP HQ-1 informed the Control Room that the van had gone along the road near Saifee Hospital – that they had started firing from Cama Hospital – and that it had then passed by the Metro Talkies along Charni Road. The Control Room immediately alerted everyone to watch out for the van and issued warnings to not go near it. (Anyone could approach it since it was a police vehicle.) The Qualis had taken the Maharshi Karve Road. In four minutes, Senior Police Inspector D.B. Marg reported that the vehicle was near *Free Press Journal's* office at Nariman Point and that hand grenades were being lobbed from it. The Control Room immediately directed Cuffe Parade-2 to the spot. The next minute, one Police Sub Inspector Wadekar reported from the Metro junction that the crowds gathered there had told him about a police car which had been hijacked! This was at 00:19.

Just then, the Dog Squad Mobile began asking for help:*'East Region saraanchya gadiwar firing chalu aahe. Jakhmi koni nahi. Tya thikani SB che office aahe. Tethe donh saunshayit laplay aahet tyani samorasamor firing keli aahe.'* It meant that Kamte's vehicle was being fired upon, that no one was injured, but two suspects were hiding near the SB office and had opened fire from the front. The Control Room immediately called M.R.A.-1, but there was no response. The very next minute, Cuffe Parade-2 asked for help at Nariman Point and Azad Maidan-2 reported that the Qualis had had a flat tyre.

While the Qualis was at the centre of attention, the focus of the battle at the Taj was now on the sixth floor where Nangre Patil was desperately seeking help to cover the floor. He had conveyed that there were five terrorists, three in a room and two in the lobby. He also added that he could see them on CCTV cameras and needed to cover the elevators and control the staircase. The Control Room assured him that Assault 3 and 6 were being sent to his aid with bulletproof jackets and weapons. Amidst calls that the terrorists in the Taj were destroying the cameras and there were suspicious activities in the NCPA opposite the Oberoi, came a report that the Qualis was now on its way to the Oberoi at 00:22. The Control Room immediately alerted the Senior Police Inspector of Marine Drive. Just then came a message that a police constable was found lying injured near the Metro junction.

And then flashed a very garbled message from an ACP Mobile, which was to be the game changer. The caller was speaking in Marathi and was obviously in deep distress, as he was unable to construct a single sentence. *'Qualis gadi Rang Bhavan yethun kidnap karun PI Salaskar, ATS Sir ani South Region Sir gadimadhye firing karun ti Qualis fire karate, State Bank of Mysore mantralayachya bajula gadi sodun paloon geli.'* (The Qualis car from Rang Bhavan kidnapped PI Salaskar, ATS Sir, South Region, Sir fired in the car, that Qualis is firing, State Bank Of Mysore near Mantralaya car left and ran away.)

'Who is speaking?' the Control Room asked him.

'Constable Jadhav,' came the reply.

'In which direction have they gone?'

'The terrorists have left this car and run away in a Honda City. Cannot say which direction.'

'Where are you? Are you injured? Who is kidnapped?'

'The terrorists have gone in the direction of the Mantralaya (State Secretariat).'

'Where are you? Who is in the car? Will send you help!' said the Control Room and also alerted Senior Police Inspector Marine Drive to look into the development and be alert for the absconding van. Jadhav then added that all the people in the van had been injured and the terrorists were moving in the direction of the Oberoi. The Control Room then spoke to Marine Drive-1 and Senior Police Inspector Marine Drive who directed Marine Drive-1 to proceed to Mantralaya to attend to Jadhav. The Control Room also alerted everyone that the terrorists had got off the Qualis, and had hijacked a Honda City. Jadhav then proceeded to give his exact location as Vidhan Bhavan – the State Assembly.

As the Control Room began making arrangements to attend to the injured in the Qualis, at 00:31, Ashok Kamte's wireless operator contacted the Control Room again, now from a DCP Mobile and said that they had been fired upon and had abandoned their car near the SB-I office. He said that the suspects were ahead and asked that a Mobile van be sent to him as he wanted to take charge of the car and suspected that the terrorists were hiding at a distance.

At 00:32, the Control Room instructed everyone to be on the lookout for a Honda City in which the police officers had been kidnapped. Cuffe Parade-2 immediately reported that the car was heading towards Mantralaya and was standing at a signal near them in the Marine Drive Jurisdiction. It was seen to be taking a left turn. The Control Room asked Cuffe Parade-2 to follow the Honda City.

At 00:33, came a report from Azad Maidan-3 that three men were lying in the St. Xavier's College Lane and that stretchers were needed to shift them. At this very moment, the Control Room was also guiding nearby vehicles to help the injured officers in the Qualis.

It was at 00:34 when Cuffe Parade-2 gave the correct description and number of the car that the terrorists had hijacked after abandoning the Qualis. It was not a Honda City, but a Skoda which had gone in the direction of Mantralaya after opening fire near the Assembly Hall. The next minute Marine Drive Beat Marshal also reported the correct number of the hijacked Qualis. Meanwhile, the Marine Drive Senior Police Inspector informed the Control Room that the three kidnapped constables had been traced, and that they were seriously injured and needed help.

At 00:35, the Control Room called Kamte's walkie-talkie and his wireless in the vehicle, but there was no response. But two minutes later, his operator called the Control Room from the East Region vehicle. 'There has been firing on our vehicle as well as on us. We were suspicious and therefore did not proceed further,' he said. He requested for a Mobile van to be sent near the SB-I office or the Crime Branch lock-up so that he could establish contact. The Control Room said that they had understood and asked him for his location and also directed Senior Police Inspector L.T. Marg to come to the SB-I office gate.

Then amidst calls for shifting the injured from the Qualis to the hospital, of the BDDS' operation which was underway at the Gateway, and reports of Zone-I and team taking positions to tackle the terrorists at the Taj, came a very cryptic message at 00:39. It was from Senior Police Inspector D.B. Marg. He announced: firing at Vinowli Chowpatty. In the car. We have covered.

The Control Room had immediately alerted four Police Mobiles, and the next minute came a very disturbing message at 00:40. It was Sarmukadam, Senior Police Inspector of L.T. Marg, who said, *'SB-I chya galli madhye madat paathvaa. Tithe 2,3 jakhmi aahet. Mala waatatey Kamte Saheb aahet. Tabadtob paathvaa.'* (Send help to the SB-I lane. There are 2-3 injured there. I think Kamte Saheb is one. Send immediately.) This was at 00.40.

At that very moment, Senior Police Inspector D.B. Marg was

seeking immediate help at Girgaum Chowpatty. The Control Room began directing nearby vans to the SB-I office lane to help Senior Police Inspector L.T. Marg. It asked Dongri-1 to come to SB-I office lane with weapons to assist Senior Police Inspector L.T. Marg who had reported about Kamte and the other two injured persons. This was at 00:41.

Just then, Senior Police Inspector D.B. Marg sent a clearer message from Vinowli: two terrorists captured. One fired upon. Our ASI injured. Send help immediately.

With the nearest available help having been diverted to reach the two spots, the operators rushed to me to report about these two developments: deep anguish at the news of the wounded colleagues and yet triumphant that at least two of the terrorists had been captured by our men.

Senior Police Inspector D.B. Marg gave further details of their feat: two terrorists have been hurt at Vinowli Chowpatty. They had come in the Skoda car. Send help to Vinowli Chowpatty. Send also the BDDS Mobile. We have captured the two terrorists.

Captured? Killed? Injured? It wasn't clear and we were very anxious. We needed the terrorists alive, needed all the information from them to save our city. If they were dying, we needed to keep them live. It is well known that a fidayeen is trained to commit suicide when caught. What if they swallowed some substance? I must have them handcuffed! With their hands tied behind, I thought to myself.

I immediately rushed to the channel to speak to Senior Police Inspector D.B. Marg. I said to him, *'Shabbas! Apan phar changli kamgiri keleli aahe. Ata ek kaam karaa, tyanche haat maage bandhoon tyaana police thaanes gheoon ya. Police thanet aalyaavar mala phone karaa.'* (Congratulations! You have done a very good job. Now do one thing, tie their hands behind their backs and bring them to the police station. Give me a call once they are at the police station.)

The Senior Police Inspector confirmed that he had the two terrorists and the Skoda car in his custody. I asked him to keep a Mobile van to guard the car and the spot. Without any further delay, I dispatched my Crime Branch investigating team to the spot to secure the site, collect evidence and carry out the investigation formalities. The Senior Police Inspector then said that both the terrorists had been injured and that they were shifting them to hospital. I enquired about the nature of their injuries and simultaneously directed my Crime Branch officers to take further steps for ensuring their safety. The angry policemen may find it hard to resist attacking the nabbed terrorist, you see!

Just then, at 00:47, Vishwas Nangre Patil got through to me and said that he was on the third floor of the Taj near the CCTV room and could see the movement of the terrorists. There were three in room number 671. He asked me to guide the Assault mobile accordingly and said that apart from Rajvardhan, he had three other associates with him. Praise and motivation, in minimum words, was due. 'Very good, Vishwas! I have directed the Assault Mobile to you. Well done,' I said. By then I had also succeeded in getting assistance from the Army and I could safely assure him, 'The Army columns are coming right now. Army columns surrounding the hotel.' We then discussed the positions they had taken, the movement of the terrorists and the use of the Assault and QR Teams.

With the capture of the two terrorists, and the Army and Navy on their way, I was beginning to feel a little hopeful that we would soon get a grip on the situation. But unfortunately, it was drowned in a pall of gloom a short while later. As I was speaking to Vishwas, at precisely 00:47, Karkare's wireless operator informed the Control Room that not just Kamte, even Karkare and Salaskar were injured and all were being rushed to hospitals. Two policemen who were found injured at Metro junction were also being rushed to the hospital. A driver of a government vehicle found in Rang Bhavan lane had also been injured, and even he was being shifted for medical aid. At 00:49, Senior Police Inspector L.T. Marg reported that Salaskar and Kamte had been fired upon. ACP Pydhonie had also rushed to the spot and was helping in shifting the officers.

Pushing aside all the negative thoughts about the injured officers from my mind, I immediately began issuing instructions to my Crime Branch teams to start questioning the arrested terrorists who were rushed to the B.Y.L. Nair Charitable Hospital. One of them was declared dead on arrival, but the other was alive. On my instructions, ACP Tanaji Ghadge and Inspectors Prashant Marde and Dinesh Kadam reached the hospital and began interrogating the captured terrorist. I was itching to go to the hospital to interrogate the villain. After all, only when you know the disease, can you find the medicine! Although I could not leave the Control Room just then, I was dying to know what the adversary had to say. I gave the officers strict instructions to keep me informed of every vital bit of information. They promised, and after a while, began calling me every few minutes to share important details of the questioning.

Just then, the phone rang and it was Inspector Nitin Alaknure from the hospital. He was sobbing uncontrollably. '*Sir, Salaskar gele!*' (Sir, Salaskar has left us!) I could not believe my ears. 'What?' That's all I could manage to say. The footage of Hemant Karkare getting into his bulletproof jacket to enter the battlefield kept being re-played on TV screens. It was as if the operation was still on and he was in charge and still in command. A little while later, the officers in hospitals rang me on my cell phone to say that even Ashok Kamte and Hemant Karkare were dead.

At 00:56, the CP called on the Ericson channel which is for communication between all wireless mobiles and walkie-talkie sets and can be heard by everyone in the field. He enquired about Karkare and Kamte's location and also wanted to know about Sadanand Date.

I wished the CP had not asked me for this information on the general channel. We had to avoid discussing it on the wireless! That was my first concern as the CP spoke to me. The news could have seriously demoralised the force! Speaking about officers' deaths and men amidst a war of this kind was a sure-shot recipe for pulling down the force's morale and even perhaps a consequent defeat. The entire force was listening in to our conversation on Ericson and I had to take care. I had received information that Salaskar was no more, but the CP had not asked me about him. So I kept quiet about the matter. I quickly decided that I must say something very guarded. So I told him that Date was in Cama Hospital and Kamte was near the SB office. What about Karkare, he asked. I said that he was at the CST, but that I would find out about his exact location and get in touch with him right away. The CP said that he only wanted to know if Karkare and Kamte were injured or were they safe? And also if Date had received any medical aid and if all other injured were being provided treatment. I said that I would find out. I told him that as for the report that there was firing on Kamte's vehicle, nobody was injured, but that I was not able to get through to Date and added that as soon as I had information, I would let him know. Gafoor then asked if I would be sending a party to rescue Sadanand? I told him that I had already done so and the Additional CP (Crime) and three units of the Crime Branch were already on the job.

After the conversation on the wireless ended, I immediately called the CP on his cell phone and told him whatever I knew. I told him that not just Kamte and Karkare, Salaskar and one Assistant Senior Inspector Tukaram Ombale had also died in the attack – one more gem, so far hidden, had succumbed to the bullets of the terrorist he had laid his life to capture alive.

Much as I would have liked to keep the deaths of the three senior officers under wraps for some more time, it was not possible, as the media got to know of it. As the news of the deaths spread, the atmosphere in the Control Room became heavy with sorrow. I believe that there is a very thin line between demoralisation and despondency. As a leader, one could feel the despondency in the air. If one happened to show even the slightest sign of helplessness, it could have dangerously percolated all the way down and spread out to the men and officers who were engaged in a terrible combat. If the Control Room felt bereft of solutions and ideas, it was bound to impact the operations in the field. So I had to pretend to be completely unshaken. I had to give them the confidence that all was not lost – we have arrested some terrorists; we have also inflicted damage on them! The Army and Navy were rushing with help. And we had lots to do.

Meanwhile, the bodies of innocent victims were lined up for medico-legal formalities. There were calls for more help at the hospitals where doctors were toiling hard to save the critically injured. People were still trapped in the Taj, Oberoi and Nariman House. We were still waiting for the Navy and Army commandos to join our teams.

'J.J. Hospital Casualty yethe ekoon 11 jakhmi aaley aahet. Daakhal zaley aahet. Donh mayat aahet. Plus donh bodyche paay aale aahet. Evdheech mahiti miltay. Savistar mahiti nantar kalavito.' (In all eleven injured persons have been brought to J.J. Hospital Casualty. Two dead have also been brought, along with just the legs of other two bodies. That is all the information received. Will give detailed information later.) This horrific message was relayed by J.J.-2 Mobile to the Control Room at 00:15. Such chilling announcements were not only made but also noted down by wireless operators.

The dance of death was still on, and the dawn which was about to break was not going to make much of a difference to the dark shadows leaping in our hearts. The ordeal was far from over and we had no time to grieve.

30

Straight From the Terror's Mouth!

'Sir, *aisa lagta hai ki issko maar dena chahiye!*' (Sir, feel like killing this man!) Muttered one of the most level-headed of my officers as they led me to a room.

Such was the pent-up anger; and he was echoing my own thoughts! I looked at all the grim faces around me. They had worked shoulder to shoulder with Vijay Salaskar. Some had worked under Hemant Karkare. All of them admired Ashok Kamte. And they were fiercely proud of the supreme sacrifice made by Tukaram Ombale. What if they lost their cool at their charge, at his warped mind! He and his co-conspirator, who lay in a morgue, were responsible for the maximum police casualties. How do I protect him from us? The guards had to be chosen with great care! I made a mental note of it, as I set my eyes for the first time on this ogre that they had brought from the B.Y.L Nair Charitable Hospital.

He was short and puny. And he had caused so much damage! I remembered reading somewhere a sentence attributed to Ian Fleming: 'Short men caused all the trouble in the world!' Could it be true? Such violent assault with weapons, was it some kind of compensatory aggression? The need to make it big?

He looked into my eye. Death held no fear for this zealot because he was made to believe that this kind of death was good for him. How do you interrogate such a fiend who does not fear death, who takes pride in the crime he has committed? He was not all that simple, his poverty, his earthy peasant background notwithstanding. Quite sly and wily, if my officers were to be believed. Once the initial shock of being caught alive had subsided, his audacity and care-a-damn approach were staging a comeback.

'Kithon da munda hain tu?' I asked and watched his reaction. There was a flash of recognition in his eyes. A familiar chord had been struck, in this strange distant land. From where are you, boy? I had asked him in Punjabi, the mother tongue I shared with this enemy of my motherland.

'Okara,' he replied.

That sounded familiar. Where had I heard of Okara? Yes, Preeti's father used to speak of it. I came out and dialled my father-in-law to get some basics about the place. Armed with it, I re-entered the room and began asking him questions about his village and surroundings. As I came to his family, I could feel an acute sense of anxiety descend into his tone and demeanour. *'Ma de naal gal karega?'* (Want to speak to your mother?) I asked him. He shook his head despondently. After I prodded him further, he conceded that he feared that America and India would bomb his village, now that his identity was revealed. He was Ajmal Amir Kasab of Faridkot in Pakistan. A boy who was very fond of his two younger siblings, a brother and a sister.

I had broken the initial barrier and I had found a chink in his armour. If all had gone well, he would have been dead with a red string tied around his wrist like a Hindu. We would have found an identity card on his person with a fictitious name: Samir Dinesh Chaudhari, student of Arunodaya Degree and P.G. College, Vedre Complex, Dilkhushnagar, Hyderabad, 500060, resident of 254, Teachers Colony, Nagarabhavi, Bengaluru. Ramesh Mahale, Prashant Marde and Dinesh Kadam would have been on their way to Hyderabad to find more about him. There would have been screaming headlines in newspapers claiming how Hindu terrorists had attacked Mumbai. Over-the-top TV journalists would have made a beeline for Bengaluru to interview his family and neighbours. But alas, it had not worked that way and here he was, Ajmal Amir Kasab of Faridkot in Pakistan, and I was asking him, *'Ki karan aya hai?'* (What are you here for?)

It was late on the night of 27 November and although more than twenty-four hours had passed, the havoc Kasab and his associates had wreaked on my city, all in the name of 'their' god, was still raging on at the Taj, the Oberoi and Nariman House, where now the National Security Guards (NSG) commandos had joined our men.

Grit, courage, bravery we had aplenty, but it was not enough to overcome these trained killing-machines who were programmed to hate India. The cowardly programmers were sitting thousands of miles away, ensconced in the cushy comfort provided by another country. Like skilled puppeteers, they were pulling the strings through satellite and cellular networks, watching their show live on television, assessing the impact and improvising as the act progressed, to elicit more and more gasps of horror and pain, and enjoy the blood they were drawing, like the mythical vampire. They wanted the strings completely hidden from the world, but they had reckoned without Allah. The strings were invisible, but they were not 'inaudible'.

To communicate with their handlers in Pakistan, the terrorists had used their own cell phones and also those of the hostages. The same was true of SIM cards; the calls were put through Voice Over Internet Protocol (VOIP) technology. The Anti-Terrorism Squad (ATS) had started intercepting and recording the conversations sometime after the attacks had begun, and shared important details with senior officers in the field on a need-to-know-basis. How meticulously the handlers were controlling the operation was apparent from the recordings of conversations between the handlers and terrorists.

In the Taj, about three and a half hours after the attack had begun, it went like this*:

> Handler (H): Media is showing that a big operation is on at the Taj. One of you keep an eye on the staircase. Wherever there is entry take a position, take position crouching and hiding, to stop them. Remove the mattresses in the rooms, gather the curtains, use alcoholic drinks, and set them on fire. Set two-three floors ablaze and then come down and sit.
>
> Terrorist (T): OK.
>
> H: Answering phones is a must, OK?
>
> T: OK.
>
> H: Whatever the media airs, we will keep informing you. That way you can adapt your methods. Don't delay setting the fires!

The enemy had managed to catch us unawares, penetrated deep into soft targets and was holding innocent people hostage. They were sworn to destroy and could do anything and everything, provided it maimed, killed and caused extensive damage and horrific destruction. On the other hand, our forces were committed to protect and save innocent lives because minimum collateral damage was the rule to be strictly followed. We neither had the equipment nor the training to achieve this by ourselves, while the terrorists were armed to their teeth with AKs and hand grenades. Operating within such constraints, our men desperately needed support from commandos who were trained to penetrate such sieges and rescue hostages. Therefore, despite our amazing feat at Girgaum Vinowli Chowpatty, a long haul was inevitable.

Shortly after midnight, I received confirmation that 200 National Security Guards from Delhi would reach us by 02:30.

---

* This is a literal translation of the conversation between the handlers and attackers.

I had immediately contacted DCP Zone-VIII Nisar Tamboli and DCP (Traffic) Nandkumar Chowgule to make arrangements to receive and transport them from the airport to south Mumbai without any delay. By 02:00, two teams of MARCOS, seven commandos each, were expected to join our men, one at the Taj and the other at the Oberoi. Until then, senior officers present at each location were utilising the available manpower. As leaders on the spot, they were the best judges of the situation and were cognisant of the steps that were needed to handle it. Besides speaking to our own Local Arms (LA) Division from time to time for reinforcements, I was doing everything possible to ensure that the Naval Commandos and the Army columns reached the locations speedily. However, this help was to take much longer to reach, than expected.

At 01:33, Colonel Sanjay had assured me that the Army columns had left Kalina. Senior Police Inspector Colaba confirmed that he had three of our Assualt Vans at the Taj, but they needed more help. Vishwas Nangre Patil was desperately demanding to know the expected time of arrival of the MARCOS. 'People are losing their lives. Looks like on the sixth floor they have killed two people. How long? How much time more? So that we can plan. Ask the seniors.'

'I am told that the commandos and the columns have already left for the locations. They will reach you shortly! I will talk to them and get back,' I told him. It was so frustrating and difficult to just keep on explaining the delay which was beyond my control. And then to motivate and reassure them, add sentences like 'you are doing a great job'! One meant it in right earnest, but felt so miserable, standing in the Control Room when your colleagues were in the thick of battle. Could I be of better help to them out there? Or should I be with the interrogating team? Would that make a difference? Or should I be listening in to the telephone intercepts? Brushing aside all such misgivings I continued at my own post doggedly, doing my best to carry out the multiple tasks that the CP in his wisdom had thought me fit for.

Just as we felt that we had neutralised at least two terrorists in the Skoda, Dr Venkatesham alerted me around 02:00 a.m. that the car had four terrorists, of which only two had been captured and the other two had escaped! This was baffling, but could not be dismissed. One never knew! Immediately a message was flashed to all the Mobiles to be on the lookout for two heavily-armed terrorists roaming or hiding somewhere in the vicinity. Along with this, there were several calls to check suspicious cars, taxis and objects, and the Bomb Detection and Disposal Squad (BDDS) vans were asking the Control Room which calls they should first attend to.

Around 02:00 a.m., the Quick Response Team or QRT reached the Taj, followed immediately by an Army column. The terrorists were in the midst of tearing bedsheets and tying up hostages, while Vishwas Nangre Patil wanted the Army to go to the sixth floor and start an assault operation. However, to our dismay, Captain Chehel, the Commanding Officer in-charge, refused to enter the hotel on the grounds that as per their orders they were to only perform cordoning operations. The MARCOS were now our only hope. Luckily, within four to five minutes they too reached the Taj. The senior officers began considering how our men could team up with the MARCOS when the CP sounded an important warning: not to mix our men with the MARCOS as the training differed completely. There was every danger that our men could become a hindrance rather than help, he had felt. Then there was yet another glitch that we faced with the Army. Senior Police Inspector Colaba reported that the Army column was declining to help them cordon off the area around the Taj. They had orders to only patrol around the Leopold Café! I had long conversations with the Commanding Officers yet again to sort out the issue. Despite our best efforts, we had received only two teams of MARCOS. For Nariman House, Isaque Ibrahim Bagwan, Assistant Commissioner of Police Azad Maidan Division, had to entirely depend on the State Reserve Police Force (SRPF).

The commando operations began, but the live TV coverage was making the task of the handlers in Pakistan easy. They began instructing the terrorists on how to counter our moves and inflict more damage. The terrorists had begun lighting fires. Around 03:30, the blaze in the Taj flared up and began spreading. Some of the trapped guests began sliding down the ropes made out of bed linen. The Control Room sent ten Fire Brigade engines to the Taj and arranged police escorts for taking their tankers to the nearby wells for refills. Then as luck would have it, the Snorkel lift which could reach the fifth and the sixth floors got jammed.

At 03:37, the the CRPF's Rapid Action Force (RAF) reported for joining the ongoing operations, but the NSG commandos who were expected to reach by 03:40 were still awaited. They were to be flown in from Manesar in Haryana, but the transport aircraft which could fly the entire team at one go was stationed in Chandigarh. Finally, a smaller aircraft from Delhi was made available. Transporting the full contingent now required multiple trips, and refuelling the aircraft and finding fresh crew for each trip took time.

The Control Room directed photographers to hospitals to take pictures of the dead bodies before they were shifted to morgues. Many were unidentifiable. The guests rescued from the Taj and the Oberoi had to be taken to safe destinations. They had to be handled sensitively and also to check if they had relatives or friends who were dead, injured, missing or trapped in the operations. Many of the hotel guests were foreigners. A majority of them had no friends or family in Mumbai. Anxious consular staff were trying to ascertain details of their own citizens among the rescued and waiting to take charge of them.

I decided to take all of them first to the Police Club near Azad Maidan, reassure and stabilise them, verify their identities and the details of the persons with whom they would be leaving, as we would need to keep further contact. I formed a special team to handle this delicate task and instructed the officers to deal with the traumatised guests with utmost courtesy. Moreover, there was every possibility that some terrorists or their local associates, if any, could mingle with the rescued guests and escape. To ensure that this did not happen, I needed a meticulous and experienced officer to supervise this very important work. I took Mahale off Kasab's interrogation for some time and put him in charge of the team.

By 05:00 hours, Bagwan reported that five to seven people were now seen on the terrace of Nariman House and there could be more inside. They had thrown hand grenades and opened random fire from the terrace. Ultimately, the NSG landed at the airport at 05:28 when the MARCOS at the Taj were re-assessing the situation for further action, while the terrorists at the Oberoi had opened fire on the nineteenth floor and were lobbing hand grenades.

DCP Zone-VIII, Nisar Tamboli and DCP (Traffic) Nandkumar Chowghule informed me that as per the NSG's standard procedure, their senior officers, led by Brigadier Sisodia, wanted to meet me first for a briefing. I immediately spoke to the Brigadier and explained to him that they would waste precious time if they came to south Mumbai to meet me, went back to the airport to brief their men and then returned with the contingent to the active locations. They accepted my suggestion that they should all start for south Mumbai immediately. The senior officers could meet me at the Control Room for the briefing while the contingent waited near Mantralaya which is at an easy distance from all the active locations. I also instructed Dr Venkatesham to keep our officers ready to brief them at each location.

Thus, the NSG was immediately transported in BEST buses to

the Mantralaya and their senior officers came to the Control Room. I explained to them the gist of Kasab's interrogation till then which meant that there were in all ten terrorists, out of which four were in the Taj, two in the Oberoi and two in Nariman House – the three active sites now. We discussed the basic details about weaponry and locations. They said that at the moment they had staff enough only for two locations and would first tackle the two hotels. After this quick briefing and exchange of information, they went to Mantralaya to brief their own teams. Immediately thereafter, the NSG reported at the two spots. Seeing the media assembled there, they made it clear to our officers at about 07:15 that they could not commence the operation if the media were not removed from the spots. Our officers immediately began persuading the media to leave but had a tough time achieving it.

Amidst all this, we were also receiving demands for more manpower to complete the formalities and paperwork at the hospitals, at the Coroner's Court and at the morgues. Also, important evidence had to be collected from various sites and it could neither wait nor be neglected. Statements of the injured had to be recorded. Some of them were extremely important eyewitnesses. The situation at the scenes of crimes had to be recorded. Each of these had to be done in the presence of independent witnesses called panchas who record the procedure followed and the articles found and collected. The recording documents are called panchanamas and they are extremely important at the stage of the trial of the offences. In addition to the work of supervising the Control Room, I formed eight teams of Crime Branch officers to work jointly with the local police station officers for all this work. To keep the lines free for the ongoing operations, we had to extensively use our cell phones and landlines as much as possible. I had also received orders from the CP to make an urgent report for the Ministry of Home Affairs (New Delhi) and was working on it simultaneously with the help of Control Room officers while doing my best to keep a track of all the other tasks.

There were several operational glitches that the Control Room was helping to solve such as a BDDS' light van which had got stuck in sand at Vinowli Chowpatty just when a suspicious bag was found on Tullock Road near the Taj which desperately needed to be looked into. Or, suddenly there was a frantic search for the walkie-talkie which was in the ill-fated Qualis and the scare that it could have been taken away by the fleeing terrorists. (It was luckily found in the safe custody of Senior Police Inspector Marine Drive.) There were several calls for the replacement of discharged wireless batteries and other technical help to keep the communication lines alive.

Equally if not more important, was the task to trace a boat floating on the Arabian Sea, manned just by the body of the Tandel (Captain) lying in its engine room, his throat slit like a sacrificial goat by expert hands of a *kasab* – a butcher. 'Ten of us came by a boat. We used an Indian fishing boat which we abandoned on the sea four miles from Mumbai. Then we sailed in a rubber boat to reach the shore,' Kasab had told the interrogating team. It was a boat that the fidayeens had hijacked on the high seas. They had killed the Tandel before leaving the boat to get into a dinghy. Additional CP Jagannathan whom the CP had sent to assist me in the Control Room had joined me by then. He and I contacted Commandant Bakshi of the Coast Guard. We shared the information with him and the need to locate the boat expeditiously. Thus, on another track, began the search for the boat and the important evidence it carried.

Later I learned that the conversation between the terrorists in the Taj and the handlers in Pakistan recorded on 27 November from 01:15 onwards also matched this account:

Terrorist (T): Salaam Aleikum!

Handler (H): Waleikum Assalaam! Are you not setting the fires? Have you not started a fire anywhere?

T: We are making preparations to start the fires. Not started yet. Gathering cloth.

H: My friend, do it fast! Want to ask you one thing, what did you do with the launch?

T: We left it!

H: Yes?

T: We left it just as it was.

H: The locks underneath were not opened for water?

T: No, in haste they didn't open and this work got spoilt. Left it and scooted.

H: Which work got spoilt?

T: There when we had to get down, when we had to sit in the boat?

H: Yes?

T: There were a lot of waves at the time and a boat approached us and everybody started shouting, 'Navy! Navy!' We then hastily jumped inside and bolted. Brother Ismail's satellite was left behind....

Then again the handlers checked about the Tandel:

T: I can see two big bus-like vehicles on the street outside. They have ladders on top. Both have come below the Taj.

H: My friend, do this, throw grenades. Quickly set the fires.

T: We are waiting for the other two (terrorists).

H: Ok, the chap who was with you in the boat, you killed him?

T: Yes, sir. Yes, yes, sir.

H: The chap who was with you in the launch, was he killed?

T: Yes, sir. He was finished.

H: How was he killed?

T: *Usey ribba kar diya* (unclear audio).

H: Is he in the boat or was he thrown into the sea?

T: No, he is lying inside.

H: Ok.

So we had a dead body and a GPS, drifting on the high sea in a boat. It could be lost forever if we did not hurry. We must get hold of it somehow. The handlers were also attempting to invigorate the terrorists by giving them feedback on the 'success' they had achieved so far:

H: How many hostages do you have?

T: As of now we are sitting with only one.

H: No issue, my friend, don't get vexed, my friend. You do your work, by Allah's grace devastation is rife in the entire Mumbai city. 260 are injured and some officers have been killed. Fifty fidayeens have entered and are firing at thirteen to fourteen places! By Allah's grace, the right kind of atmosphere is being created. There is absolutely no cause to be worried.

They wanted to hold distinguished persons like ministers, state officials and business heads, hostage:

H: In all probability, a helicopter may arrive because some ministers are trapped in your hotel. The media is also saying that some ministers are trapped in the hotel.

T: Really?

H: Now they are saying that the Prime Minister has asked for a helicopter to be sent to rescue the ministers. Then you start the fires. They are not opening the doors. So remove the curtains and burn them. If the rooms are set on fire, the ministers will burn and die.

T: Come, let's try....

While the Coast Guard was looking for the drifting fishing boat, the entire police force of the city was now looking for terrorists on the run, especially men with haversacks. Nakabandis were on at all the exit and entry points and junctions. All leaves were cancelled until further notice and all the men and officers on leave had to report on duty forthwith.

By 08:00 in the morning, the dead bodies of our martyred officers and men started reaching J.J. Hospital for the post-mortem. We needed to make adequate arrangements for their escorts and chalk out bandobasts for the funerals which were bound to attract huge crowds.

Meanwhile, Nariman House was now surrounded by our Force and firing had started there again. By 08:47, Bagwan reported that they had given a befitting reply to the terrorists' fire and felt that they had succeeded in killing one. Around 09:30, yet another bag was found in the Taj's main lobby containing seven magazines, five hand grenades, and cash and credit cards. It was only past noon when the NSG could systematically take charge of the Taj, floor by floor, checking for terrorists and rescuing the trapped patrons. The injured were being rushed to hospitals. The Control Room was keeping account of the dead and the injured from hospitals and police stations. The number of dead bodies at J.J. Hospital had increased manifold.

The handlers had received the extensive media coverage of Hemant Karkare's death with glee. They were using it as a prized trophy to boost the terrorists' spirits which were obviously sagging now that our Force had teamed up with the MARCOS. So this is how they went about it, with the terrorists in the Taj:

H: The media is saying that a Commissioner got killed some time back?

T: Good.

H: Alhamdulillah (Praise be to Allah). There has been a lot of damage. The media is saying that a Commissioner has been killed?

The conversations were interspersed with motivational speeches to ensure that the morale of the terrorists did not slump. An example of this was an exchange on jihad and martyrdom between the handlers and the terrorists at the Oberoi on 27 November around 13:13, as follows:

> H: God willing, it means that this time the issue is between *kufr* (infidelity) and Islam. We are followers who have been sent by Allah for His religion. I mean a martyr's death is big. But martyrdom should be such that it creates terror in the hearts of enemies. And the correct way is not to be afraid of martyrdom! A martyr's message has to be kept in the forefront.
>
> T: God willing!
>
> H: You have to fight in a way that they feel like Allah's tiger is chasing after them.
>
> T: God willing.
>
> H: God willing. Meaning the enemy should know that you are God's follower. The enemy is only terrorised by this.
>
> T: Yes.
>
> H: That you love death more than life!
>
> T: Yes.
>
> H: God willing, meaning martyr!
>
> T: God willing, pray!
>
> H: May Allah give you health, grant you success. Now the time has come to fight relentlessly, right?
>
> T: Right.
>
> H: They have a huge pride – isn't it – the Hindu brothers? Reduce their pride to ashes.
>
> T: God willing....
>
> H: Yes, you have to throw a grenade. Then you have to fire. Take a position and then come out. Don't just stand there. God bless

> you! We see that they are facing a lot of difficulties. The legs of their commandos are shaking and they are speechless. Your terror has penetrated deep inside, by the grace of God, really!
>
> T: God willing!
>
> H: God willing. We are watching on TV how their big leaders are not in a position to speak. The work that you have done, it has finished the jobs of top-class people....

Around 16:40, the Coast Guard helicopters located a fishing boat floating six nautical miles off the Mumbai shore. They lowered a jawan on its deck and reported that the boat was called 'Kuber' and that it was registered in Porbandar. Hovering over Kuber, they called Sankalp 46, the Coast Guard boat, to tow Kuber to the coast. Sankalp 46 handed Kuber over to Mumbai police's Patrol Boat 'Aboli' as they entered Mumbai police's nautical jurisdiction. There were several issues regarding naval and police jurisdictions and our investigating team had to carry out the formalities with great care. Many important articles were found in Kuber, including the pre-programmed GPS to facilitate the hassle-free voyage of the terrorists directly from Karachi to the desired shore in Mumbai.

In the meanwhile, the handlers and the gunmen started working on using some of the hostages to make demands on the Government of India as was planned, through live television interviews. The intercepts of telecons between the terrorists in Chabad House and the Pakistani handlers recorded from 14:35 p.m. onwards on 27 November bore testimony to this fact. Initially, the handlers did a detailed revision of the live interview with the TV channels that Babar Imran aka Abu Akasha would have to do. They were confident of Akasha's ability, compared to that of Umar, who was keen to talk to the media, but who they felt was comparatively *kachha* (immature). The 'revision' conducted by the Ustads (Mentors) was an eye-opener on how the press was manipulated by terror outfits:

T: How many people have been killed – as per the media?

H: The count runs into hundreds.

T: All right. God willing, God willing, God willing!

H: You have to protect yourself. The moment you see someone walking, doing something outside, on the rooftop, open fire. You don't know what is happening here.

T: God willing.

H: Ok, if I tell you that that Mexican woman there… if we get her to talk to the media, and she herself tells the media that this is what has happened with me, and I want to be saved. Then?

T: They will take immediate action.

H: But beware of one thing, she must not say how many of you are there or the number of hostages. It will benefit them greatly. It will bring a lot of pressure….

H: OK, hold on for a minute, lower the volume. The statement Jundalbhai had dictated – is that with you?

T: No, I burnt it last night. But I remember it. But it is not based on those examples.

H: Jundalbhai will dictate the statement to you.

Then another handler came on the line and dictated an Urdu couplet to Akasha that he could quote in the interview. Akasha gratefully wrote it down. He would be pretending to be a disenchanted Indian Muslim youth. The couplet was to make a very emotional appeal to his kinsmen to sacrifice their youth in the cause of Islam. After the couplet, Akasha was given several tips on strategy:

> Deliver your message, for it's very important. First, use a lot of Hindi, then switch to English. You needn't answer their questions, you persist with what you have to say; your own agenda. Remember, your message is going to be replayed by TV channels for hours.

Thereafter, Jundal came on the line and gave special directions on strategy and content to Akasha:

H: I had dictated those *jumlas* (punchlines or impactful rhetorical statements skilfully used by speakers to evoke instant applause) to you, hadn't I?

T: Yes, sir.

H: Do you remember at least a few of them?

T: I remember quite a few. But Vasibhai says that these are Star Media people. So don't speak about issues from 'there', but speak about Israel. About the alliance with Israel, the visits, the restrictions on Muslims, appointing Army Chiefs, not allowing rations to reach etc., all this should be included.

H: Yes, of course, all that should be included. The second thing. They will ask you where you are from, right?

T: Yes.

H: They will ask where are you from? Say: I am from Hyderabad in the Deccan; from the city. Ok?

T: Hyderabad. Deccan.

H: From the city, ok? And my area is Chowki.

T: Chowki.

H: Toli Chowki. Toli Chowki.

T: Toli Chowki, yes.

H: If you are asked about your organisation, say I am associated with Mujahideen, Hyderabad Deccan.

T: All right.

H: That's the organisation I am associated with. And if they ask you why you did what you did, then say it is because of the duplicitous policy of the government. You are writing it all down, aren't you?

T: Yes, sir. Yes, sir....

H: Duplicitous policy of the government. On the one hand, the government pats our backs, but on the other, the administration hammers our heads. The latest example of this is the Sachar Committee recommendations....The way the government declares concessions, but on the contrary, the administration keeps arresting Muslim youth.

Akasha finds the Hindi word *yuvak* (young men) dictated by Jundal difficult. It is derived from Sanskrit. So Jundal replaces it with the Urdu synonym *naujawan*, which he could handle and is popular in Hindi as well.

H: The future of the Muslim youth is ruined.

T: All right.

H: And give them the ultimatum that this is only a trailer of the movie, the real film is yet to be shown. Let the government know.

After drilling the *jumla* of the 'trailer and the film', Jundal told him to talk confidently, without hesitation. 'Keep giving your own standpoints and do not let the anchors ask too many questions!' Then they came to their demands:

H: All right? And one minute... they will ask you what your demand is?

T: Yes.

H: You first say, release all the Muslims in jails.

Jundal then listed all the other demands which Akasha jotted down diligently: hand over the Muslim states to Muslims; recall the Army from Kashmir and give Kashmiris their rights; begin the construction of Babri masjid immediately; hand over the land of the masjid to Muslims; sever all ties with Israel, which should stop atrocities on Palestine; on the Muslims. And Israel should not interfere in the affairs of Indian Muslims.

Later in the evening, Babar Imran aka Abu Akasha got through to the news channel, India TV and spoke to the receptionist who transferred the call to the newsroom. Akasha rattled off all the demands to a news producer mistakenly believing that he was live on air. Then the producer put him through to a female anchor. She let him announce his demands on a live telecast. Akasha came into his own, got into the groove and delivered his piece, clearly enjoying himself. Throughout the conversation, he used words and style that south Indians use while speaking Hindi, the way Jundal had trained him. Afterwards, the handlers congratulated him for his performance:

T: How did you like the interview?

H: Very, very nice. Mashallah from seniors, congratulations! Very happy, Mashallah! Marvellously presented.

T: He was trying to be very smart (referring to the news producer).

H: He was very crooked. Mashallah, you did well.

T: I insulted him in private.

H: Yes.

T: While he was trying to put the call through to a live broadcast, he told me that he was also a Muslim; Islam says this, says that.... I told him, you are a Muslim? Beware! He found it difficult answering me.

H: What are you saying!

T: He told me that two of our brothers had surrendered?

H: No! They are talking nonsense.

T: Yes!

H: Surrendered! That is nonsense. Since yesterday until now, they haven't been able to clear any location.

T: And what is his name? Where have the other brothers reached?

H: They all have reached their destinations.

T: Yes.

H: That's where they are. Alhamdullilah. They are fighting in the best way possible. The work is on. They have not been able to clear any place....

T: Good, good! Pray! Pray for grant of a martyr's death!

I could not spend much time on Kasab that night when I saw him first, but whatever little time I had, it had to make a lasting impact, and I think it did. He had not divulged the name of the boat to the team. With me, he began to call it 'Kuber Boat'. He no longer blamed his father for his entry into the Lashkar-e-Taiba or LeT. Now he said that he joined it on his own and enjoyed the prestige and respect it gave him in his village. The villagers who never took him seriously were now overawed by his jihadi status. He had so much to tell me. I looked at him wistfully as they hustled him out of the room and returned to my other tasks.

Arrangements were underway for the Prime Ministerial visit to the various hospitals. Each of the locations had to be carefully pre-checked as per standard operating procedures for likely terror attacks. The local police were under severe pressure and had to be supported by providing additional force to man not just the routes, but also the locations of the VVIP visits.

The NSG could reach Nariman House only around four in the evening of 27 November and by 06:30 in the evening, with winter dusk already enveloping the city, the Control Room was again arranging searchlights for the operation. The operations at the Oberoi and the Taj too were not showing any signs of nearing conclusion. The NSG commandos were entering each floor, checking the rooms and rescuing the guests trapped or hiding inside who had no clue if the persons trying to open their door were terrorists or security forces. The Control Room was receiving calls on behalf of trapped guests who had managed to pass on the details of their rooms to friends or relatives who in turn were relaying the information to the police officers in charge. Around seven in the evening, the commandos had managed to clear several floors of both the hotels. The NSG could not be deployed to guard the sanitised portions. For that, armed men wearing bulletproof jackets and helmets were needed at both the hotels. The CRPF's Rapid Action Force believed that it was not their job to man the cleared areas, and thus, reinforcements were needed from the local police and SRPF.

Around 19:00 hours it was reported to the Control Room that three terrorists had been killed on the first floor of the Taj, but one although injured, was still hiding in a portion of the same floor. Also, the work of opening the locked rooms with master keys was still underway. Even at the Oberoi, a similar situation was being faced. Although extra NSG platoons had now reached all the locations, the problem of guarding the sanitised areas and ensuring that terrorists did not enter them again remained. The Control Room operators conveyed the problem to me. I spoke to Prasad, Nangre Patil and Venkatesham and made arrangements to send additional manpower to both the hotels to guard the cleared areas.

Around 7:30 in the evening, as the NSG's operations intensified, major fires were reported from both the hotels, at the Taj under the dome, and in the new building of the Oberoi on the fourth floor. It was now obvious that the terrorists were adopting desperate measures.

The conversation taped by the ATS from 20:24 went like this:

T: Salaam Aleikum.

H: Waleikum Assalaam. How are you Fahadullah, my friend?

T: Abdul Rehman Bhaiyya has gone to Allah.

H: Well, is he near you?

T: Yes, sir. He is here.

H: May Allah accept him! My braveheart, persevere you must, you must be courageous and fight unrelentingly.

T: God willing.

H: Yes. Allah will help you. Where is the enemy?

T: The room is on fire. They are showing it on TV. I'm sitting in the bathroom.

H: Ok, ok. The media is showing that there's been a fire. Was it a rocket?

T: Rockets were thrown. Around eight-ten grenades were also thrown.

H: Where are you?

T: I am in the bathroom of a storeroom.

H: The fire won't reach there, isn't it?

T: No. There is water. Water.

H: Can you leave the room and go to another?

T: No, they have fixed guns at different points. That is what we were trying to do when Brother Rehman was martyred.

H: Oh.

T: The three galleries on the top floor are in one straight line. God willing, I expect them to come in.

H: Are Abdul Rehman's bag and things lying near you?

T: Yes, I have them.

H: All right, my friend. Be brave. Fight, fight with passion. All right! Pray! Pray now. Prayer at this time is highly granted.

T: Yes. What else, brother?

H: You keep fighting. Salaam Aleikum. Khuda Hafiz.

T: Where are the other brothers?

H: They are at it. They are fighting. The men in the Taj. The work is going on. Salaam Aleikum.

Despite all the bravado and the inspirational spiel from the handlers, it was quite clear that the surviving killing-machine in the Oberoi was finally exhausted and his morale was at its lowest ebb. The handlers seemed to be feeling some trepidation that he might be apprehended alive! Again in eight minutes or so they went:

H: Salaam Aleikum, Fahadullah, my braveheart, the war cannot be lost. You should come out and fight. Lob a grenade and try to come out of there. You can go to some other place.

T: I have thrown both the grenades.

H: Thrown the grenades?

T: Yes, sir.

H: How many Klashan (meaning, Kalashnikovs) magazines do you have?

T: I have only two.

H: How about the second one? How many does he have?

T: After he finishes with them, that's it!

H: Ok, with the three!

T: I said, let them come in, at least one will go.

H: There should be no situation of arrest. You must remember that.

T: No. God willing, god willing.

H: And only by fighting it out will this issue move in the right direction. It should not come to a situation that they throw a smoke bomb at you to make you unconscious and pick you up (alive).

T: No.

H: That will be a great loss. Fight by stepping forward, from wherever you can see. You cannot see anything from the window. Fire as soon as you see. Fire. Shoot a burst. That would cause a commotion and then you can try to get out.

T: Ok, I shall try, god willing.

H: Yes, my brother, put the barrel of the gun outside and fire a burst and with the firing of the burst, come out and fire on both sides and try to change your position.

T: All right, sir.

H: From where you are, you know that gunshots are flying from both the sides, and at least fifteen-twenty bullets can pass. Empty out an entire magazine and you can load the other magazine that is in your hand, and get away from there.

T: Ok, god willing!

H: You have to be courageous, my braveheart, do not be afraid. God willing if you are shot, it's success. God is waiting.

T: Yes, sir, god willing!

H: You have to pray.

T: God willing.

H: This is the time to pray, as prayer works! Man is firing and God is answering his prayers for his brothers, elders, ourselves.... make all the promises, pray.

T: All right, Inshallah.

H: All right. May God protect you. Be brave. Keep your phone in your pocket. Don't switch it off even for a minute for that's how we can keep in touch with you. Put it in the front pocket. Do not remove hereafter.

Fahadullah's mentors knew that he was feeling low and was exhausted. He had lost his buddy, had little ammunition and no provisions, and was just a whisker away from death's door. Alone, he was despondent and wondering what he should do next.

As for the handlers, what Fahadullah had done so far was quite enough. He was now completely expendable and had outlived his utility. The only worry and dread was that he may chicken out and surrender. Become an embarrassment and break the myth of fearless martyrdom for the cause of terror! If left to himself, un-goaded, he could just throw in the towel. So the coaches had to be there, to make certain that he fought. Now, these handlers only had a one-point programme – to ensure Fahadullah's quick death! They were trying their best to keep his morale up to get killed and kill as many as possible in the process.

Then a patient wait ensued. Ultimately, Fahadullah emerged out of the room and was gunned down, much to the relief of his puppeteers. Twenty-two hours after he had entered the Oberoi at their bidding, spewing fire and taking innocent lives. The operation could not be declared over until the entire hotel was scoured and checked for more gunmen and hidden explosives. This was going to take the whole of the night. Thus, the operation at the Oberoi got over only on the morning of 28 November.

At the Taj, the battle lasted even longer and ended on 28 November night.

At the Nariman House, as the standoff advanced and the security forces strengthened their positions, it was clear that the hostages had to be killed. The handlers discussed their utility with Akasha: 'As long as the hostages are alive, you will be spared; they are useful only till they are able to ward off the firing; when you feel that you are being cornered, first finish the hostages; there is no point leaving them alive; the Indian Army claims that they do their work without endangering the hostages; now efforts are on to save their lives; if they die, the relations with their countries will get spoilt and there will be an uproar.' Several such aspects were discussed.

However, there was a serious problem on hand: Akasha's buddy Umar was showing tell-tale signs of losing his nerve and Akasha was clearly worried. Hectic confabulations led to the decision that Umar had to rest and 'relax'. So the handlers told Akasha, 'Now if any of you is tired, like Umar is, take rest for an hour and a half. Let Umar sleep.' The handlers were preparing the fidayeens to get primed for the final battle. The message was clear: your end is near. Kill the remaining hostages and then get killed. Like the diabolical computer game, Blue Whale in which the administrators, thousands of miles away, seize control of gullible youth and prod them to commit suicide!

After Umar had 'rested', the actual preparations for killing the hostages began. The handlers were trying to understand the layout of the rooms and the place where the hostages should be made to stand or be kept so that the bullets fired at them should pass out through the windows and not ricochet to kill the killers themselves. After all, the puppeteers needed them alive for some more time:

> H: All right. Make them stand. Keep them tied if they are already tied up. Untie them if they are that way. (There was whispering in the background from the handlers' side: between the rooms. The room is small. It is a Kalashnikov bullet....There is a system, system. Do not fire within the room. The bullet will emerge from behind and hit. Ali got hit like this. Shoaib got hit like this. Umar got hit like this. Not the right thing! Make them stand in front of the door and then fire...)

More deliberations followed. Then Akasha and Umar positioned the hostages as per the directions of the bestial handlers who wanted to hear the fatal shots. So the call was put through. Typically and ironically, each of these murderous calls began with wishing each other peace!

> T: Salaam Aleikum.
>
> H: Waleikum Assalaam.
>
> H: Will the work be done now or not? (Killing of hostages).
>
> T: Now. In front of you. Was waiting for your call. In front of you.
>
> H: Say Bismillah! (Bismillah means 'Bismillah ir-Rahman ir-Rahim' – In the name of God, most Gracious, most Compassionate –

the Quranic phrase for good beginnings, the words with which Muslims begin any significant endeavour.)

T: Yes, sir.

H: Say Bismillah. (Sound of firing is heard in the background.)

T: Hello, hello!

H: Hello, Hello. Yes, sir.

T: Ok.

H: Yes, sir, yes, sir, now is one done?

T: Both done.

H: Both done?

T: Yes, sir.

H: Confirmed that both are done?

T: I did one, Umar did the other. Both. Alhamdullilah. With the same Klashan.

H: Speak a little louder.

(So Akasha repeats the news that his bosses were so eagerly waiting to hear. And they sounded relieved.)

H: Congratulations. May Allah accept!

Now with the hostages out of the way, preparations began to get the killers of the hostages themselves killed! And the tips began coming through the mobile phone: how to avoid crossfire. 'One buddy should sit in one corner and the other in another. Then you can open fire on the ascending commandos. Use all the ammunition remaining with you. How many grenades do you have...?'

As the handlers began discussing this, Umar felt uneasy and Akasha spoke up:

T: *The major problem of that my colleague normal courage is brought up that is why I closed him.* (Akasha was speaking in unintelligible

English so that Umar does not understand what he was saying to the handlers.)

H: Cannot make out what you said. Repeat.

T: *My colleague, my friend is normal courage. I want that his courage is brought up, his moral get up I closed him, that is why I closed him, otherwise he....*(in unintelligible English).

H: Yes, make him speak to me.

T: *He is some anxiety* (in unintelligible English).

H: No issue, God willing! God willing, he will stand up.

T: *He is feeling fatigue* (in unintelligible English). What do you feel?

H: You don't get anxious! We will explain it to him. God willing. Let me talk to Umar. God willing, he will accompany you. You don't worry. Now when martyrdom is to be achieved, it must be done with the head held high. God willing! I will convince him. How many grenades do both of you have?

T: Eight to nine.

H: Whatever you have, divide them equally. Also the magazines; fill the stray bullets in magazines. Load the guns with magazines and put on burst. And both of you fire wherever you see movement. And don't sit quiet, ok?

They then made Umar talk to the handlers:

H: Umar, how are you?

T: Alhamdullilah.

H: Yes, brother, what is the scene like?

T: The scene is ok.

H: Did both of you read the namaaz?

T: Yes.

H: Not fired yet, right?

T: No, not fired.

H: Now you have to roar like a tiger. God willing!

T: Now I will ask for a blessing.

H: Right, ask powerfully! The task is to give support to your mate. Regain your morale and stay together. After the namaaz, I will call you again. If you get separated, I will not be able to talk. So split only after I have called you again.

T: Yes. So, I shouldn't fire now?

H: Yes.

T: Not fire now?

H: If you see movement, fire.

T: All right.

H: The army is taking position. But don't you worry. I will call you back in ten minutes.

Umar was precariously close to a breakdown and they had to keep working on him to keep his morale up. On 28 November at around seven in the morning, the two men in Nariman House were told by the handlers that the security forces were preparing for the final assault. The media had been asked to move out. The handlers asked the terrorists to wash their faces, but they reported that there was no water as the electricity had been cut off. The handlers had not reckoned with this. So they told Akasha that it meant that their arrest was imminent. 'They want you to become desperate with hunger and thirst, so that they can arrest you. Some teams are on their way.'

The handlers began impressing upon the two fidayeens that there was now no point getting caught and they must go out and fight. Akasha had also reached the same conclusion by then, 'God willing, I am also thinking of the same. As it is, today is Jumma (Friday, the holy day for Islam). So we must attack them.'

Now the preparations began for the last stand and the fervour in the instructions increased. The fidayeens were being tempted to set goals quite unattainable as matters stood. Escape to the street and get away in a car to find a place with some food and water! Akasha said that he did not know driving. So the option of a motorcycle was also considered! Then a confused Akasha began to consider finding another room with a washroom. Water! Which meant he was not prepared to die as yet! The handler panicked. He began drilling into them that they had done such magnificent work that the Army was willing to lose ten-twelve commandos just to catch them alive. That eventuality had to be avoided at any cost. Akasha was horrified at the thought, for he said, 'God willing. Please pray! Even our corpses should not be touched by the Kufr! Please ask for this blessing. We are praying that we should not fall into their hands!'

The handlers advised them to pray: 'You pray: Allah! We are your followers. Fulfil our demands. Let their bullets make sieves out of our chests, but they should not be able to arrest us. My Allah! The potion we have come to drink, let us drink. Forgive us. Accept us!' The handlers were furtively reinforcing the fidayeen's desire to die. Then suddenly there was a commotion and the two terrorists announced that a helicopter had arrived, 'Hit! Fire! Heli, heli! A heli has come over us...! Firing has started!' They were being fired upon from inside the room and could be now heard taking cover and trying to leave the room. Even as this was on, the handler reminded them to keep the mobile phone in the pocket and use their bullets economically. It seemed as if they had succeeded in getting out of the room, but a little later the commandos had managed to get closer:

H: What's the scene like, Akasha?

T: I think a team has landed on the roof.

H: Fifteen men have climbed down on your rooftop right now.

T: Good, then should we stand in front of the windows and fight?

H: Can you see anything?

T: They are firing at the front room.

H: They have to climb down to reach you. They are clearing the upper floor. You take positions on the staircase. As soon as they come, start firing. They will have to get down from the stairs.

T: We are standing below.

H: It is quite likely that they first throw grenades.

T: Possible.

H: You take a position so that you stay in the room, but the stairs are within your range.

Now there was tremendous panic. The terrorists were befuddled. How should they position themselves? The handlers kept suggesting options. As regards ammunition, Akasha said they had only four grenades left. And then in a few minutes, he said that they had none. Four turning into zero in a few minutes indicated that Brother Akasha no longer was the eager jihadi, the man who a few hours ago had delivered an oracular message to young Indian Muslims. Alarm bells! The handlers immediately reminded him that he had four, and they were more than enough. Then they began giving options for the optimum use of the precious four grenades, 'Can you hide separately? That way you can cause maximum damage?' Not possible, said Akasha. The handler kept egging him on: 'These are the last moments. These you have to spend fighting with extreme determination!' he told Akasha. 'Yes. Because amidst this it has to end! Just as they begin. By waiting for another hour to two, you should not weaken. Fight bravely. God willing, your terror will spread. You will be remembered for life!'

Ultimately, one handler took matters firmly into his own hands. Without mincing words, he made it clear to Akasha that his time was up and there was no point in stretching his last stint:

H: My friend, don't wait for them to come and then to commence the attack. You start now. Throw a grenade at them and fire! It is the same thing. You fight for *dafaa* (time) or you fight in *gairiyat* (in detachment). For dafaa, you don't have enough weapons and the possibility of damage is more. Why not go in gairiyat?

The handler then convinces them that they should themselves launch an attack and surprise the commandos:

H: This is the last attack. Why not hold your heads high and fight! It will be a surprise for them! Bismillah! Open fire!'

The terrorists were goaded to come to heel and they tried to draw courage through the phone. Obviously, Umar needed more support:

T: Pray!

H: God willing, Allah tala, climb and start firing!

T: Pray that Allah saves us from the enemy, saves us from arrest.

H: Allah Ameen.

T: Tell the bosses, do pray.

H: God willing, we are praying.

T: Allah we should not be scared of death!

H: Allah, Allah Ameen!

T: All right, we are going up.

H: Bismillah, Bismillah! You are in Allah's hands!

T: Talk to Umar bhai. I think they are coming down.

H: You climb towards them!

T: All right, talk to Umar.

H: All right, don't talk. Go up! Shabash!

And then came the end.

T: Salaam Aleikum. Salaam Aleikum.

H: Waleikum Assalaam. Yes, sir!

T: I have been fired at. Last salute!

H: Which part are you hit on?

T: On the arms and on the legs.

H: May Allah protect you. Their people are getting injured too. (Sound of firing) They are going to hospitals.

T: In the first entry, we killed a commando! Bid final salute and pray.

H: We are praying.

T: Pray!

H: Listen!

But there was no one to listen to him at the other end. Finally, ACP Isaque Ibrahim Bagwan and team, and the NSG Commandos had got the better of Akasha and Umar. The hands of the kufr were stretching towards them and Allah was clearly in no mood to grant them their final prayers. God is one, His ways are strange, and His accounting method is perhaps best explained by the 'theory of Karma'. In any case, all this is too deep for the simple men in khakhi to understand. The only religion for them is their duty and they knew that they were fulfilling it faithfully.

The first time that I stepped out of the Control Room was on the morning of 29 November to attend the funeral of Hemant Karkare. His body was taken in a flower-bedecked open truck from his home in Hindu Colony in Dadar (East) to the Shivaji Park crematorium. People had lined up the long stretch to pay their homage to their beloved officer, raising cries of '*Hemant Karkare amar rahe*' (Long live Hemant Karkare) and '*Bharat Mata ki jai*,' (Victory to Mother India).

I lent a shoulder to his *arthi* (bier) and fought the tears welling up in my eyes as the thoughts of all the martyrs, my colleagues, crowded my mind. I was out of the Control Room after almost three days and into a world which looked quite strange. Bereft, all of a sudden, of so many of our finest men. It was bewildering and so hard to accept!

The media was jostling for sound bites, but I couldn't say anything to them. With a heavy heart, I headed home just for a bath one needed to have after a funeral and immediately rushed back to my job. There was so much, not just to be found out but to be proved.

Kasab had said that they were ten in all. But we could not take his word for final. What if by keeping these ten men in the dark, some other modules were also at work? Kasab was taken to the Sassoon Dock to identify Kuber and the articles lying within it. '*Ki karan aya hai?*' I had asked him that before. The answer to the next question was crucial for booking the guilty. '*Tennu kinne phejya aithey?*' (Who sent you here?) We had a fair idea of who it was, but that was not enough. The conspiracy against India had to be unravelled completely, and evidence gathered meticulously. The world would have to at last accept what it had been trying to push under the carpet all these years. The onus was yet again on the Mumbai police to bear the brunt and ensure that the proof of the conspiracy was presented meticulously and justice secured for India.

This is just the trailer, the film is yet to start. That was the 'jumla' the puppeteers had taught the puppets to parrot. Now it was our turn to say it to them, not for dramatic effect but in all seriousness, in all solemnity.

For most, the action had ended. For me, not yet.

31

The Trail of Terror

The city of Porbandar in Gujarat has a few things to be proud of. There is the Porbandar Stone, a yellowish-white limestone known in Gujarati as *makhanio patthar* (butter-stone) from which many a beautiful buildings in Mumbai are crafted. The Cama Hospital, designed in Medieval Gothic style by Khan Bahadoor Muncherjee Cowasjee Murzban, is one.

In its fabled mythical past, Porbandar is Sudamapuri – the city of Lord Krishna's impecunious childhood friend Sudama – his mate from Guru Sandipani's ashram. He could manage just a handful of beaten rice to carry for Krishna when he went to see him in Dwarka – Krishna's City of Gold, one of the seven sacred cities and another port on the long Gujarat coastline. How Krishna relishes the humble dish, how the joy makes Sudama forget seeking help to overcome his poverty, the way he returns empty-handed and the sweet surprise that awaits him there, is the story that Indian saints have been deciphering for ages. The simple inhabitants of Porbandar celebrate the divine friendship with a temple dedicated to Sudama, only second of its kind. The other is in Ujjain in Madhya Pradesh, where the Sandipani ashram is said to have been located.

In recent history, Porbandar is the birthplace of the Mahatma, the icon of peace, harmony, nonviolence and secularism, who, when in doubt and sorrow, turned to Krishna's celestial song, the *Bhagavad Gita*.

But, perhaps the least known feature of the all-weather port city is its maritime heritage, vouched for by the surrounding archaeological excavations dating back to the Indus-Saraswati civilisation. The navigational skills of Gujarati seafarers rarely gets due recognition, but live on in the intrepid spirit of its fishermen. Manmade boundaries mean nothing to this hardy folk, forced by the rising marine pollution to venture deeper into the high seas. Every year, several cases of 'India-Pakistan Maritime Trespassing' are reported. The violators are fishermen from both the countries, mostly operating along Gujarat and the neighbouring province of Sindh in Pakistan.

Hundreds of fishing boats are registered by their owners in Porbandar. The men operating them are aware of the ever-present danger of arrests and the distinct possibility of languishing in Pakistani jails. The boat-owners initiate negotiations for their return which may take years to fructify. Till then, the wives toil hard to make ends meet, supported only by a small daily compensation from the State. It is amazing how, despite this threat, these seamen continue to brave the turbulent waters to eke out a living with prayers on their lips and the Tricolour hoisted high on the masts.

On 25 November 2008, boat-owner Vinod Masani had cause to worry. His mechanised fishing boat M.V. Maa had returned to the Porbandar Jetty, but there was no sign of the other boat, M.V. Kuber. Both had sailed out together on 14 November. Tandel (Captain) Amarchand Solanki was leading Kuber's crew of four other *khalasis*: Ramesh Nagji Solanki, Natthu Nanu Harpati, Balwant Prabhu Harpati and Mukesh Ambu Harpati. Mukesh was a last-minute replacement of a regular crew member whose son had suddenly taken ill. Kuber and Maa had been together for a week before getting separated by a storm on the high seas. The last time the two Tandels had spoken to each other was on their walkie-talkies on 20 November at 10:30 in the night. Manish

Lodhari, the secretary of the National Fishworkers' Forum made enquiries with the Pakistani authorities in Karachi who said that they had not captured any Indian boat during the relevant period. Little did Lodhari and Masani know that Kuber was heading towards Mumbai, with Tandel Solanki at its helm, but with his crew replaced by ten merciless fidayeens carrying lethal weapons to attack Mumbai. To teach India, Israel and the West a lesson for their alleged atrocities on Muslims. Little did they know that the crude wooden trawler and its poor unsuspecting crew had been struck by a terrible manmade calamity on 23 November around noon.

> Our boat, the Al-Husseini reached the border between India and Pakistan near Jakhau around 12 noon. We spotted an Indian fishing boat in the waters and decided to seize it. Usman asked us to enter the engine room and told us that the minute our boat received a jolt, we should rush out of the engine room and jump into the Indian boat. We entered the engine room and Usman stood on the deck. He picked up a broken engine strap and began waving it. The captain of the Indian fishing boat thought that we were in trouble and needed help. He steered his boat towards us to touch the Al-Husseini. As soon as we received the jolt, all of us rushed out and jumped into the Indian boat. The five crew members were terrified. We immediately tied their hands and feet. 'Who is the Tandel?' we asked. The Tandel came forward. He said his name was Amarchand Solanki. We taped the mouths of the rest with sticking plaster and forcibly pushed them onto the Al-Husseini.
>
> 'Do you have enough diesel to last till Mumbai?' Abu Ismail asked Amarchand. He said that he had 700 litres in the tank and some more in barrels and added that although he did not know the way to Mumbai, the diesel would not suffice till there.
>
> Some diesel barrels and oil cans were immediately transferred from the Al-Husseini to Kuber. We also loaded some other stuff that we needed for the attack – haversacks, the rubber dinghy, her engine, and some provisions. We also shifted some excess

stuff from the Kuber to Al-Husseini. Then the Al-Husseini turned back to Karachi with the four captured Indians and we proceeded towards Mumbai.

Ismail started the satellite phone and began conveying our progress to our Lashkar-e-Taiba trainers in Karachi. With the help of the Tandel, we began our journey to Mumbai and kept checking the track with the help of the GPS.

Then Abu Ismail created three groups. The first had Abu Ismail himself, Nasir and I. The second had Javed, Hafiz Arshad, and Nazir Ahmed. And the third, Fahadullah, Abdul Rehman and Abu Soheb. Each group was supposed to take turns and keep a two-hour vigil. In the interim, Imran Babar cooked with the help of the Tandel.

Abu Ismail and Javed would be at the helm intermittently. Travelling thus, the Kuber came to a distance of five nautical miles off the Mumbai coast. We could see the hazy outlines of Mumbai's skyscrapers.

We had come close to Mumbai without any obstacle and now we had to just enter the city. We were thrilled at the very thought of entering Mumbai to kill people and teach India a lesson; also to America and Israel for harassing Muslims. I contacted Abu Hamza in Karachi and informed him that we were nearing Mumbai. He was very happy. 'Allah will help you in your task,' he said. 'What should we do with the Tandel?' I asked Hamza.

'We have eaten the four goats. Now you decide what you want to do with the goat in your possession,' he said. So I understood that the four captives who had been transferred to the Al-Husseini had been slaughtered. I discussed the matter with Abu Ismail.

I told him that killing the Tandel would be the best option and he agreed immediately. Then with the help of Abu Soheb and Nasir, I took Solanki to the engine room. Soheb and Nasir held his hands and legs. I held his hair, jerked his face up and slit his throat with a knife.

We left the dead body in the engine room and I changed my clothes. All of us came back to the deck. During the long journey, we had already discussed the tasks set out for each pair once we landed. Ismail now did the final revision.

He and I were to get off first and take a taxi to the CST. On the way, I was to plant a bomb under the driver's seat as I was taught during my training.

Soheb and Nazir Ahmed were to take a taxi to Leopold Café, open fire, throw grenades, and then as per the GPS and the videos of locations shown during the training, proceed to the Taj. On the way, Soheb was to plant a bomb in the taxi and Nazir was to plant RDX at a spot between Leopold and the Taj.

Javed and Arshad were to take a taxi straight to the Taj, open fire and throw grenades. On the way, Javed was to plant a bomb in the taxi.

Imran Babar and Nasir were to go to Nariman House with the help of the GPS. On the way, Imran Babar was to plant an RDX bomb.

After the eight of us got off, Abdul Rehman (Chhota) and Fahadullah were to take the dinghy to Hotel Oberoi, enter, and open fire and throw grenades.

Then Abu Ismail made us set our watches and said that he would give us the exact time of attack after landing. With a foot pump, we first inflated the dinghy, then took a bath and offered namaaz. In the morning, we were also given red threads to tie around our wrists. We also wore new clothes which were given to us by our LeT trainers with life jackets and waterproof pants to be worn over them. The Yamaha outboard engine was connected to the dinghy and it was then lowered into the sea. After the two of us had got into the dinghy, we first began lowering the equipment for the attack. Just then some of us felt that a ship was heading our way. There was a scare and someone shouted: 'Navy Boat! Navy Boat!' Taking it to be a naval boat, we jumped into the dinghy one after the other and took off towards Mumbai.

Abu Ismail was steering the dinghy and Nazir Ahmed was guiding him to Bhai Bhandarkar Machchimar Colony with the help of the GPS. Around 9 p.m., the speed boat reached the shore near Badhwar Park. Abu Ismail looked at his watch and told us that we must start the attacks by 9:45-9:50.

As decided, Abu Ismail and I were the first to get off the dinghy. We immediately discarded our life jackets and waterproof pants. The other three pair of men also got off at short distances and began walking towards the road....

Kasab was now with the Crime Branch giving a detailed account of how they had tricked the friendly khalasis from Porbandar into believing that the Al-Husseini was in distress, prompting them to extend a hand of friendship. As he was describing how they had killed the generous and munificent seamen in cold blood, calling them goats, I could see the fists of my colleagues clench and their eyes flash with fury. I could feel my own pulse racing. It did take an effort to rein in my anger.

Al-Husseini! Coincidence indeed. Yet another Al Husseini had played a major role in another unprecedented attack on Mumbai – the ISI sponsored 1993 serial blasts. That Al Husseini was not a ship, though. It was an apartment block in Mahim – key conspirator Tiger Memon's residential building used for the conspiracy, to make and store the car bombs and to give finishing touches to the conspiracy.

The offences for the attacks were registered at the respective local police stations. However, on 30 November, the government issued orders that the Mumbai Crime Branch would investigate the case. I appointed Ramesh Mahale as the Chief Investigating Officer (CIO) and under him, a team of ninety-eight handpicked men and women to painstakingly put together all the evidence – a mammoth task indeed. They worked arduously, day and night as if on war duty.

As the Joint CP in charge of the Crime Branch, Kasab was now my most 'esteemed guest'. Keeping this enemy alive was my number one priority. Anger and hostility towards Kasab were perceptible. The way the men and officers were reacting to him, I had to personally choose his guards for the entire period he would be with us. The ISI and the Lashkar were bent upon eliminating him by hook or by crook to obliterate the only living evidence of their heinous deed. We had received a letter from the Government of India that Kasab's security was entirely the responsibility of the Mumbai police and within it, of the Crime Branch. Specific Intelligence inputs had been received from Central Intelligence agencies that Pakistan was intent on killing Kasab and the Dawood Ibrahim gang had been entrusted with the task. The reputation of the Mumbai police, not just my job, was at stake if anything were to happen to him.

Initially, we would take him to the Detection Room for interrogation. All his medical check-ups were also conducted in the Crime Branch lock-up. We took strict precautions to ensure that he was not photographed and no photographs were given to the press. Therefore, it came as a rude shock when a picture of him sitting in a chair began floating in the media. I was livid. I cornered the officers concerned and asked, *'Gaddaar kaun hai?'* (Who is the traitor?)

All of them pleaded innocence. Their faces showed that they were not lying. Then they brought it to my notice that it was in all probability the handiwork of our own Central Intelligence agencies who had immediately dispatched their own officers to Mumbai to question Kasab. A message had to be delivered across the border that the most prime witness – and an accused – was in our hands, telling us all about their complicity and the conspiracy. This was particularly important because Pakistan was refusing to own up responsibility for the attack. They had completely disowned Kasab.

However, the photograph put us on a greater alert and we began interrogating Kasab in the very room where he was locked up. Two armed State Reserve Police Force (SRPF) platoons were deployed to surround and guard the premises. The innermost ring comprised unarmed police officers. The next ring was of armed police officers and constables. CCTV cameras were fitted at vantage points and monitored round-the-clock from a separate control room. Kasab's medicines for his injuries were kept under our lock and key. The water and food provided to him came from our own lunchboxes, picked randomly, but was tasted before being served to him.

I issued an order whereby only a select few were allowed to interrogate Kasab and under no circumstances, nobody, not even I, was allowed to enter the room without depositing the cell phones and other electronic gadgets outside the room. There were to be no exceptions whatsoever and a copy of the order was pasted at a prominent place. Some senior officers felt chagrined when asked to deposit their cell phones in the tray which was kept outside, but the duty officers did not budge, pointing politely to the order.

Kasab's police custody had to be extended a number of times with the permission of the court. In all, he spent eighty-one days in our custody – from 27 November 2008 to 19 February 2009. In order to steer the investigation, I personally interrogated him almost every day. It gave me a deep insight into the psyche of how terrorist outfits operated. Our daily interactions forged some sort of a bond between Kasab and me, and soon Kasab began addressing me respectfully as 'Janab' (Sir). In his confined world, I was now the supreme figure of authority, the highest that all the other men who controlled him looked up to. He was trained to follow a commander. I fitted the bill.

I soon realised that right from his childhood Kasab had been brought up to believe that India was Pakistan's numero uno enemy. He had no real knowledge or understanding of India or the world at large, except for a firm conviction that India, America and Israel were the greatest enemies of Pakistan and Islam. Naturally, because although he was twenty-one years old, he had studied only up to class IV in an Urdu-medium state school. He seriously believed that Muslims were not allowed to offer namaaz in India and mosques were locked up by the authorities. He felt that the azaan he heard five times a day in the Crime Branch lock-up was just a figment of his imagination. When we came to know of this, I instructed Mahale to take him to the mosque near the Metro Cinema in a vehicle. When he saw the namaaz in progress with his own eyes, he was bewildered. This was not how it was supposed to be!

What sort of training was this that turned humans into obedient fiends? Kasab's family of seven – parents, three sons and two daughters – was extremely poor. The father sold *dahi bhalla* (a popular snack) from a hand cart in Lahore where Kasab had joined him after leaving school. Kasab did odd jobs, drawing just 700 rupees a month. The financial strife led to frequent fights between father and son. One day, the father returned to his village and soon Kasab left home in a huff. He and his friend Muzaffar Lal Khan came to Rawalpindi in late 2007 in search of a better job and came in contact with LeT operatives who were functioning under the banner, 'Jamat-Ud-Dawa' after being banned in 2002. The boys decided to join the LeT for a simple reason that had nothing to do with jihad. They wanted to commit robberies to improve their financial status and wanted to get hold of some weapons and training to achieve their nefarious objective.

So in December 2007, the two boys went to the LeT office and enlisted for *Daura-e-Sufa* – the first lap of training at Muridke which was for twenty-one days. They were first converted to the Ahle-Hadis sect, given physical training and discourses on jihad. They were brainwashed to join the long war to liberate Kashmir and made to believe that martyrdom in war led to an assured berth in heaven, the greatest reward for a Muslim. They were also introduced to LeT founder Hafiz Muhammad Saeed aka Hafiz aka Hafiz Saab and his deputy in charge of Kashmir operations – Zaki-ur-Rehman Lakhvi. While Abu Fahadullah and Mufti Saeed were their trainers, Abu Hamza, Abu Al Qama aka Amjid, Muzammil aka Yusuf and Abu Umar Saeed also monitored the training.

Abu Hamza, a Pakistani, had carried out the December 2005 terror attack on the Indian Institute of Science in Bengaluru that had killed the renowned scientist, Professor Munish Chandra Puri and injured four others. Kasab told me that Abu Al Qama had made three reconnaissance trips to India by the sea in September, October and November 2008, but we were unable to confirm whether he had managed to enter Mumbai or not.

The next lap of training was called *Daura-e-Aam*, which was conducted in the hills for twenty-one days. They were trained in mountaineering, and also taught how to use, dismantle and reassemble sophisticated firearms like AK-47 which they called 'Klashan'. At this stage, Muzaffar Lal Khan chickened out and left Kasab to seek solace in the mentors. With them, he had found his metier. Instead of availing the three-month break that he got after this lap, Kasab remained at the camp, applying himself zealously to their *khidmat* (service). They included him in the next two-and-a-half months of advanced training called *Daura-e-Khas* near Muzaffarabad in Pakistan occupied Kashmir (PoK). It included the use of rocket launchers, hand grenades, satellite phones, GPS and map reading. Most importantly, the trainees were inured to endure hunger for sixty continuous hours while climbing mountains with heavy back-loads.

One day an unknown VIP visited the *Daura-e-Khas* training camp. He was introduced as 'Major General Sahab'. Obviously, with an Army background, he was a key figure and impressed the trainees a great deal. He interacted with them and carefully sought their feedback.

After *Daura-e-Khas*, Kasab was allowed a week-long family visit and also given some money. He also confided in me that he had received 1,25,000 rupees which he gave to his family for his sister's marriage. On his return, there followed a further training-cum-selection process. The twenty trainees were shown a CD which demonstrated in detail a fidayeen attack in Kashmir. Then Hafiz Saeed gave different names to all the candidates. Kasab was now called Abu Mujahid. Six of his would-be mates in the

Mumbai attacks, Imran Babar, Nasir, Nazir Ahmed, Hafiz Arshad, and Saquib became Abu Akasha, Abu Umar, Abu Umer, Abdul Rehman Bada (Hayaji) and Abdul Rehman Chhota respectively. There was one more trainee from Narowala in Shakargarh. He was named Abu Soheb.

Then followed an advanced training called the *Daura-e-Ribat* in which they were given an insight into the working of Intelligence agencies and the techniques of Intelligence gathering – how to detect if you are being tracked by sleuths? How to dodge them, throw them off your scent? How to keep a watch on or chase a target? How to anticipate the line of questioning and be two steps ahead in interrogations? These and other such tactics, including hostage-taking, were taught to the recruits. Major General Sahab visited this camp a few times to assess them. Towards the end of the training, he directed Abu Al Kaahfa to send them for acclimatisation training on the sea.

In 2008, Ramzan fell between 1 September to 30 September. The trainees were taken to the Karachi creek to a big vessel and taught to read maps, judge the depth of the sea, find directions with the help of stars and constellations, and use the GPS for sea travel. They were also trained to cast fishing nets to pass themselves off as fishermen. Thereafter, Hafiz Saeed and Zaki-ur-Rehman Lakhvi gave them motivational speeches for three days and six of the men were packed off to Kashmir for a fidayeen attack. Soon, some more trained fidayeens joined them. They were Ismail Khan, Fahadullah and Javed, known as Abu Ismail, Abu Fahadullah and Abu Ali, respectively.

How exactly were you given the task to attack Mumbai? Kasab was asked. On the thirteenth day of roza, they had attended a meeting addressed by Hafiz Saeed, Zaki-ur-Rehman Lakhvi, Muzammil, Abu Al Kaahfa, Abu Hamza and other leaders. The crux of the discussion was that the time was now ripe for jihad and India should be attacked. They wanted to attack India's financial strength – venues of public importance and places which were frequented by foreign tourists. Then Zaki-ur-Rehman Lakhvi announced Mumbai as the target and said that they would have to take the sea route.

'We were thrilled when we learnt that it would be Mumbai!' Kasab told us brazenly. He also boasted about how he was rated the best shooter in his group: 'One day when the meeting was on, Major General Sahab came in. He wanted to test our shooting skills. We were all taken outside the building and each of us was given an AK-47 and magazines. Ten targets were kept at a distance and we were asked to fire a single shot at his command. Then we were tested for rapid fire. My target had received the maximum number of bullets. So Major General Sahab congratulated me. He said to the others, "Firing should be like this young man's firing!"' Kasab glowed with pride as he recounted this.

Thereafter, Abu Kaahfa introduced them to one Zarar Shah, head of the media wing, who divided them into five pairs: Ajmal Kasab and Abu Ismail; Imran Babar and Nasir; Nazir Ahmad and Soheb; Hafiz Arshad aka Hayaji and Javed; and Abdul Rehman Chhota and Fahadullah. In the next four days they were shown India-centric indoctrination films in a special hall. The films were designed to convince them that in India, Muslims were perennially at the receiving end and were targeted systematically. They were made to believe that in India, Muslim women were subjected to atrocities, mosques were shut down and Muslims were not allowed to offer namaaz in mosques. Yet another film that they were shown was about the LeT attack on the Indian Parliament and which took pains to explain how the LeT had taken complete care of the fidayeen's families. The budding jihadis found it very reassuring. The films had the desired effect. Their passions aroused, the five pairs were now champing at the prospect of wreaking revenge on India.

I was amazed when Kasab added, 'Janab, they told us that Afzal Guru was involved in the Parliament attack and he was sentenced to death, but even then the Indian government was unable to hang him. Why? Because in your country executing the death sentence is very difficult. It takes ages!' Kasab sincerely believed, that just like Afzal Guru, he too would not be hanged any soon. He would frequently repeat this even to my colleagues.

The ten men spoke only a mixture of Punjabi and Urdu which was nowhere close to Hindi. It was therefore important that they learnt how to speak colloquial Hindi. The task was entrusted to Zabiuddin Ansari alias Abu Jundal, an Indian LeT operative. On 8 May 2006, the Maharashtra Anti-Terrorism Squad (ATS) had chased a Tata Sumo and a Tata Indica car on the Chandwad-Manmad highway near Aurangabad. Three terror suspects were nabbed in the Tata Sumo whilst the Tata Indica car had managed to escape in the direction of Malegaon. It was subsequently traced with forty-three kg of RDX, ten AK-47 assault rifles and 3,200 cartridges. The motive was to target political leaders who were accused in the 2002 Gujarat riots. Twenty-two accused were charge sheeted and Zabiuddin Ansari aka Abu Jundal was named as the main conspirator along with the absconding accused Fayyaz Kagzi. In May 2006, Abu Jundal had escaped to Bangladesh from where he fled to Pakistan on a fake passport obtained with the help of the ISI and LeT operatives. It was this very Abu Jundal who gave Kasab and his cohorts a fifteen-day training course in spoken Hindi and a whole lot of information on Mumbai. Kasab was in awe of Jundal for having recruited many Indian Muslims for terror and causing bomb blasts in India. He was told that for their loyalty, Jundal, his men and their families were well looked after by the LeT, what Kasab and his mates were also promised.

How did you plan the nitty-gritties of the attack? He was asked. Kasab told us that the original plan was to attack Mumbai on 27 September 2008, the day of the twenty-seventh roza. It was on the night of the twenty-seventh roza when the revelation of the Holy Quran is supposed to have begun and when Prophet

Muhammad was designated as the last prophet. Worship on this night is held equal in reward to worship of one thousand months and called Laylat al-Qadr, the Night of Power or the Night of Destiny. By killing the innocents in Mumbai on this holy day, the fidayeens and their bosses were hoping to please their god and get rewarded.

They had to penetrate the Indian waters undetected and reach Mumbai in time for launching the attack by hijacking an Indian boat. The targets chosen for a peak hour attack to ensure the maximum number of casualties included the Chhatrapati Shivaji Terminus or CST, the Taj Mahal Palace hotel, the Oberoi, Café Leopold and Nariman House. However, it was understood that several unknown factors in sea travel could cause delays. At places like Leopold, they were supposed to open fire indiscriminately. In the hotels, however, they had to take care that no Muslim was killed, and only focus on killing Indian, American, British and Israeli citizens. They had explicit directions to cause large-scale damage. 'You may be just ten in number, but the Indians should feel that fifty to sixty terrorists are at work. Our planning is geared for this effect. You have to do everything to make this impression last.' Each pair was allotted specific targets and explained the details of each attack. They were repeatedly shown video clips of the targets which were especially shot to show approach roads and layouts. They were also told the names of the various locations en route. The pairs were strictly told not to divulge the plans to each other, but during the long boat journey to Mumbai, they had discussed the plans amongst themselves. That is how Kasab had learned that Hafiz Arshad aka Abdul Rehman Bada aka Hayaji and Javed (Abu Ali) were to go to the Taj; Abdul Rehman Chhota aka Saquib and Fahadullah to the Oberoi; Imran Babar (Abu Akasha) and Nasir (Abu Umar) to Nariman House; and Nazir (Abu Umer) and Soheb (Abu Soheb) to attack Leopold first and then join the other pair at the Taj.

Kasab, Nazir (Abu Umer) and Javed (Abu Ali) were to plant a bomb each below the drivers' seats while proceeding to the CST, Leopold and the Taj respectively. RDX bombs were also to be planted in peripheral areas near the primary targets. The pairs attacking Nariman House, the Oberoi and the Taj were to establish contact with the media, declare that they had taken hostages, and pressurise the Government of India to liberate Kashmir. They were to misguide the media that they were disaffected Indian Muslims and pretend that they were many more in number than just ten.

How exactly did they embark upon the sea journey? Kasab was asked. On the fifteenth day of Ramzan, they were taken to a hilly area, where in addition to the firing practice, they were trained to assemble bombs with timers. They were also schooled to dismantle and assemble an inflatable dinghy and taught to remove its sea valve. They were trained to surreptitiously plant bombs below the driver's seat in running taxis. Soon their hair was cut and the beards shaved off. New clothes and shoes were purchased for them and they were also given watches set to Indian time. The labels on their clothes were removed to prevent identification. Their photographs were clicked to make fake identity cards to pass them off as Indian Hindus. To complete the Hindu impersonation, they were instructed not to forget tying the red sacred threads around their wrists before landing. They were then taken by a train to a LeT safe house in Azizabad in Karachi.

Just as they were gearing up for the attack scheduled for the twenty-seventh day of roza, Zaki-ur-Rehman Lakhvi came with the news that they would have to wait for a month-and-a-half! The boys were disappointed. 'We are completely primed and ready. No need to delay the attack!' They pleaded. Lakhvi assured them that the delay was not on their account.

Maybe the kind bosses wanted the boys to celebrate their last Eid on earth! Or maybe they were looking for a more opportune time to attack Mumbai? Like an evening coinciding with a one-day international cricket match when the city relaxes and least expects a disaster, except a disastrous cricketing defeat! Or they found the Mumbai police extremely alert, issuing as we had, advisories to various establishments? Or perhaps they wanted it to coincide with a day when a number of European Parliament Committee delegates on International Trade would be staying at the Taj ? As a matter of fact, a number of MPs were reported to have fortuitously left the hotel for a nearby restaurant shortly before the attack. The postponement is a mystery which we still have no answers to. So, while waiting patiently to hear from their masters, the terrible ten celebrated Eid cooped up with Kaahfa, their minder. The additional time was well spent. They were made to sharpen their skills, spend some more days on a ship anchored off the Karachi shore to ensure that they made no mistakes in reaching Mumbai with their deadly cargo.

In mid-November 2008, the revision began in right earnest with the help of maps and CDs. They also assembled ten RDX bombs, each weighing seven to eight kg. On 21 November 2008, the fidayeens were taken to another house in Karachi, situated near the creek. They met Zaki-ur-Rehman Lakhvi, Zarar Shah, Abu Hamza and Abu Kaahfa there. Abu Ismail was now designated the Emir (Chief) of the mission, entrusted with arms and ammunition, and explained how they were to be distributed amongst his men. Each pair was given 10,800 rupees which they shared equally. Zarar Shah gave each a mobile phone with Indian SIM cards which were to start functioning as soon as they entered Mumbai waters. However, they were strictly instructed to switch on the phones only after reaching Mumbai. Each mobile phone had only one number fed into it and they could contact their handlers just by pressing a button.

Lakhvi gave Abu Ismail certain phone numbers and one satellite phone. He wrote down in a diary the details of latitude and longitude. Abu Ismail gave each one of them an AK-47 with eight magazines, 240 rounds, eight hand grenades, a dagger, a pistol with three pistol magazines, twenty-one pistol rounds, a haversack, a water bottle, one kilogram of raisins, one headphone, three 9 volt batteries and a charger. They also received a separate sack each containing an eight kg RDX bomb as also a GPS. They filled the arms and ammunition in the haversacks which were then loaded on to a vehicle along with the sacks containing the bombs.

The day of their departure finally arrived. Early in the morning of 22 November 2008, the ten men got ready and offered namaaz. Around 6 a.m. they left for the creek on foot and reached the shore. Lakhvi was present there and gave a speech on how Hafiz Saeed was staking his reputation for the mission. 'Now it is your responsibility to make it a grand success. There should not be any lapse on your part to lower his prestige!' Lakhvi exhorted them. 'If you are caught alive....!' He didn't use any words to complete the sentence, he just picked up a fistful of sand and released it back on earth. The gesture made it clear that the mission had to end in their death or else Hafiz Saeed's reputation would bite the dust or come to nought!

Around 7 a.m. they left the Karachi creek in a wooden boat and after a couple of hours boarded the Al-Husseini. Their haversacks and bombs had already reached the ship, as had an inflatable dinghy, lifesaving jackets, rations like rice, flour, oil, pickles, cold drinks and milk powder and other necessities like match boxes, detergent powder, tissue papers, dental cream, towels, shaving and dental kits. That night they spent on the Al-Husseini. On 23 November, at about noon, they reached the Indo-Pak maritime border near Jakhau. They were like hungry birds of prey who were looking for an Indian fishing boat, and located the unsuspecting Kuber.

This is how, from 2007, with nearly a year of intense commando training and indoctrination, the LeT had prepared human killing-machines out of simple uneducated village boys and unleashed them on Mumbai. Mumbai, the microcosm of India. The symbol of India's resilience and good cheer that defies all its shortcomings. Our enemy wanted to break the Indian spirit yet again, by using just ten men who had been hoodwinked into it by brainwashing and promises of rewards in the afterlife for sadistic wanton killings in this lifetime.

What is jihad? What do you get when you do this? Kasab was repeatedly asked. He said consistently that martyrdom in jihad would take them to Paradise. 'Before embarking on the fidayeen mission, we have to shave and bathe! Savour delicacies! Offer prayers. That is what we did before leaving Kuber!' he said. They had relished kheer – a sweetened milk and rice preparation. Finally, they had embraced each other and bid goodbye. Kasab would be perplexed that the story consistently failed to impress us, despite the earnest enthusiasm and unflinching faith that he tried to infuse it with.

Within two weeks of the attack, the US FBI team arrived at the Crime Branch to gather inputs on the investigation and to question Kasab. Two of their officers were given access to interview him. Frustrated, they came to my office after an hour and reported that Kasab had only been railing against America, parroting all that he had learned at the feet of his trainers. You created poverty! You attacked Afghanistan! Bombarded by all his *gyan* (knowledge) and insolence, they were exasperated. So I took them back to Kasab's lock-up. Kasab immediately stood up respectfully when he saw me.

'Kistran gal karda pya? Siddhe siddhe jawab kyun nahi denda?' (What is this way of talking? Why are you not giving them straight answers?) I asked him in a firm voice.

He was taken aback. He said, 'But Janab, you never told me to tell them anything! How was I to know that I had to tell them everything?' I stared at him for a while and realised that he'd really meant it.

'Ok. *Now* I am telling you: answer all their questions and don't lie.' I said. He followed my instructions and answered all their questions without demur.

Late one night he was giving me some details. The conviction with which he spoke, prompted me to ask him again: 'What do you get when you do all this? How could you do it? Why did you do it?'

And he began earnestly, 'Janab, you don't understand. Our ustads have told us that when you die in jihad, your bodies glow. They start exuding a fragrance. Allah then receives you in heaven. Beautiful houries, fair maidens with limpid black eyes wait to serve you and they look after you. You get every possible luxury. Good life is there, not here on this earth.'

'Don't you feel any remorse at killing innocent people? Killing and orphaning children? People who had done nothing wrong? Nothing to you?'

'No, Janab,' he said, shaking his head. 'On the contrary, I am sad that *I* did not die. I should have died in jihad. It is the greatest misfortune of my life that I was not martyred.'

This was approximately three weeks after the attacks. Dinesh Kadam and I were interrogating him. We had not yet told him that all the other fidayeens had been killed in the attacks. He knew that his buddy Ismail had been badly injured, but not that he had died. I looked at him and could bear his insolence no more.

'Come with me. Get up,' I said and stood up. The others were taken aback.

'Where?' Their faces quizzed me. It was about 3.30 in the morning. I took Dinesh Kadam aside and told him what I wanted to do. He arranged for the vehicles. In a few minutes, the convoy was heading towards the J.J. Hospital morgue, with Kasab secured in one of the vehicles. The 'Jannat' (Paradise) where his nine mates lay in the freezer.

'Ye dekh! Yeh hain tere jihadi dost jo Jannat mein hain.' (Look at

them. These are your jihadi friends who are now in Paradise) I said, as he stared open-mouthed.

The stench was unbearable and was churning our insides. The faces were ghastly. A bullet had pierced a terrorist's eye. Some were very badly burnt, and the acrid smell of charred putrefying flesh pervaded the air.

'What do your ustads say? Fragrance, huh? Glow? Where is the fragrance? Where is the glow? Is this the fragrance? Is this the glow?' I kept asking him. He had no answer.

'If your ustads say that death in jihad gives you Jannat and your bodies glow and spread fragrance, and you get houries to serve you, why can't they go die in jihad themselves? Why do they send you? Because they want to enjoy the hell here? Are they not interested in dying in jihad and going to Jannat?' I asked him and his face contorted, as if all the blood had drained out of it. He sat down on the floor, holding his sides as if he wanted to vomit.

As we emerged from the morgue, I could see that he was totally dazed and shocked. A man cheated. Disillusioned. Taken for a rollicking ride. Even then, not once did he say, then or ever, that he was repentant. Not once did he say, *'Mujhse galati ho gayi'* – I have made a mistake. Not once did he say, *'Mujhe maaf kar do'* – pardon me. He knew that what he had done was unpardonable, whatever its justification.

Now I felt a little light. *Meri bhadaas baahar nikal chuki thee*, as we would say in Hindi. My suppressed anger was released.

The convoy came to the Metro junction, the stretch around which this monster had unleashed Death just a few days ago, killing my dear colleagues and innocent fellow citizens. I don't know what came over me again. I stopped the convoy and got out of my car. I made them take Kasab out. It must have been around 04.30 in the morning. The winter night was chilly and the temples and mosques had still not woken up the gods.

'Bend down and touch the ground with your forehead,' I ordered Kasab. Spooked, he meekly followed my instructions.

'Now say, "Bharat Mata ki jai",' (Victory to Mother India) I commanded.

'Bharat Mata ki jai!' said Kasab. Not satisfied with just once, I made him repeat it twice.

The schoolboy in me was standing in St Andrew's School before Father Rufus Pereira who expected his Head Boy to do things perfectly, however archaic and silly they may seem to some.

Immediately after the attacks, when the Indian media reported that the lone terrorist who was arrested alive hailed from a Pakistani village called Faridkot, their Pakistani counterparts were also obliged to launch a search. India demanded action against the Pakistan-based handlers and LeT bosses. A *Dawn* reporter confirmed the existence of an Amir Kasab in Faridkot in Okara near Dipalpur. His son had left home some time ago. A few journalists from *Dawn* visited Faridkot in the first week of December 2008 and located Amir Kasab, his wife and three children. They saw his handcart from which he sold dahi bhallas. He had initially refused to accept that the boy in our custody was his son. He denied that he had sold his son to the LeT. He said that his son had left home in anger for being refused new clothes for Eid. Thereafter, the village was besieged by journalists. The administration swung into action. The journalists were barred from probing any further. In a trice, the family disappeared mysteriously from the village. The first reaction of the Pakistani government was to consummately disown Ajmal Amir Kasab and the other attackers.

When we told Kasab that his government was not accepting him as their citizen, he felt sad and let down. Would you like to write a letter to your mother? To your ustads who are now disowning you? You can even write to your government. Ask for legal help. We will forward the letter through the Consulate, I suggested to him. He had refused to do any of this. However, after a couple of days, he expressed a desire, on his own, to write to his government. He was immediately provided with a pen and paper. He wrote the letter in Urdu, stating that he was a Pakistani national who had been arrested in India and requested that he be extended legal help. We forwarded the letter through proper channels, but the Pakistan government predictably did not respond. When the court offered to appoint an advocate for his defence, Kasab said that he wanted his government to provide him with legal aid. The learned judge made him write another application to his government and sent it to the Pakistan Consulate. There was no reply. Ultimately, Kasab had to settle for a court-appointed advocate.

While in our custody, one night I received a call that Kasab was unwell. My heart sank. Pictures of a dead Kasab, lying in the lock-up flashed before my eyes. He was my responsibility and if anything went amiss, we would be accused of torturing him to extract a confession. A doctor from the nearby government hospital was immediately summoned to visit and examine him. I rushed to the lock-up and discussed the diagnosis and prognosis with the doctor, something which I had never done due to work-related pressures, even for my own family. Kasab was pale and in a lot of pain. The doctor gave him some medicines and said he would observe him for a couple of days. We were all hoping that Kasab would recover through oral medication and not need hospitalisation. Every day the doctor would be brought to the Crime Branch to examine Kasab, taking care to ensure that the media did not learn of it. His condition however did not improve and the doctor advised him hospitalisation.

With no other option in sight, we were compelled to plan this new operation. Ashok Duraphe, Ramesh Mahale and Dinesh Kadam were my seasoned campaigners – dependable, cool, calm and composed. We sat down and decided that in order to keep him safe it would be best to admit Kasab to St. George Hospital. We placed a dummy in his place and quietly shifted Kasab to hospital. Led by Head Constable Mahesh Bagwe of Dinesh Kadam's unit, armed constables in plain clothes were on round-the-clock guard duty around him. Bagwe pretended to be Kasab's closest relative and stuck to him like a leech, and sat continuously by his bedside. Kasab was not even allowed to go to the toilet alone. He received three days of good medical care. He was kept in a General Ward with twenty-five to thirty other patients which made the task of the guards extremely difficult. Dawood Ibrahim had taken a 'supari' in his name from the LeT and ISI. The people of Mumbai were dead against him – he was undoubtedly Enemy Number One! Most resented what they felt was a fuss around him and openly said that he deserved to be hanged without a trial. Therefore, anyone could have attempted an attack on Kasab, taking advantage of his hospitalisation. History is replete with instances of the underworld attacking patients in hospitals. So we had to be very cautious and constantly be on our toes. Only one ward boy had suspected that the patient was Kasab and when my team realised this, the ward boy was 'persuaded' to stay with the patient for the entire duration to avert any leakage of information and media frenzy.

The Home Minister R.R. Patil came under severe criticism for a quip that he had made at a press conference which was misinterpreted as an attempt to downplay the gravity of 26/11. He probably did not realise that it would draw so much flak since he was not proficient in Hindi. He stepped down just five days after the attacks. Jayant Patil, an extremely articulate, soft-spoken and considerate man was given the Home portfolio. Always open to suggestions, Patil was a quick decision-maker. One evening I received a call from him. 'Where are you?' He asked. 'In the office, sir,' I said. 'Can you meet me outside Babulnath temple at eight in the evening? In plain clothes?' He asked me. 'Of course, sir,' I replied. He did not divulge anything further, so I felt it prudent not to ask for any details.

I reached Babulnath in an unmarked vehicle just a little before eight. As I was waiting for the minister's convoy, I was surprised to see a private car slowing down near me. Jayant Patil was at the wheel! Like ordinary citizens, with just the two of us in the car, we drove to the Arthur Road Jail. The topic of discussion was Kasab's security and the 'supari' given to Dawood to kill him. The trial would commence soon and Kasab would be transferred to judicial custody to the Arthur Road Jail, the popular name for Mumbai Central Jail, the oldest prison in the city.

If prisoners from two major gangs are kept in the same jail, there is every likelihood of violent skirmishes. So prisons in Maharashtra are unofficially 'allotted' to different gangs, out of practical exigency, and birds of a feather are made to flock together. The Arthur Road Jail, where Kasab would be kept in judicial custody is regarded as a Dawood Ibrahim gang prison where it would not be difficult for the Dawood gang to engineer Kasab's murder through some convicts or under trials! So what arrangements should we make to ensure that the Dawood gang did not succeed? Kasab had to be totally insulated from the other inmates. Further, Kasab would have to be taken to the trial court in Kala Ghoda every day. A major security hazard – a nightmare. So just as in the 1993 serial blasts case, the trial could be conducted in the Arthur Road Jail itself.

Jayant Patil and I introduced ourselves to the jail guards. They were surprised to learn of our identities and we were let inside after a flurry of activity. We had a long discussion with the prison officials and it was decided that Kasab's trial would be conducted in this very jail. For housing Kasab, a special cell in the prison was to be constructed which could withstand even a rocket attack!

The Government of India deputed a CRPF contingent for the peripheral security of the Arthur Road Jail. The Crime Branch was responsible for identifying the policemen to be deputed on Kasab's guard duty within the prison. We had to get their backgrounds carefully verified. They would work in shifts but would have to remain inside the prison for fifteen days at a stretch. To prepare food for Kasab and his guards, we identified cooks from different Police Training Schools and SRPF units. Their antecedents too were checked carefully and considerable planning went into shuffling their duties.

Then there was the problem of the nine dead bodies of Kasab's associates lying in the morgue where they were kept under heavy guard, with a red light glowing on the door. Pakistan was not ready to accept them. The Muslim burial grounds also refused, reasoning that the terrorists were not Muslims as their deeds were totally un-Islamic. Among the anti-India Islamic terrorist networks, there were efforts afoot to agitate for their burial and create shrines for the murderers. The government was at its wit's end to solve this vexatious issue. Home Secretary Chandra Iyengar, a hardworking and experienced civil servant known for her out-of-the-box thinking and I held a couple of meetings. The Navy was requested to give the bodies a burial on the high seas, but they expressed regret. The medical schools had no use for the bodies as they were highly decomposed and disintegrating. Time went by and a year later R.R. Patil was back in the saddle as Home Minister. The sensitive question of the dead bodies cropped up again. Ultimately, I chalked an operation with the help of the Additional CP and a team of officers and men which included Duraphe, Dinesh Kadam, Mahale, Police Naiks Patkar, Shivkar and Ramade, and Police Constable Farooqui. We kept both R.R. Patil and Chandra Iyengar informed about the goings-on.

A maulvi from a masjid was contacted at the eleventh hour and he agreed to perform the last rites of the killers. Keeping the morgue guards completely in the dark, Patkar, Shivkar and Ramade took charge of the bodies one by one, by following all the formalities. In caskets ordered from different dealers, the bodies were shifted to a waiting private ambulance. It was around midnight when the maulvi was blindfolded, put in a private vehicle and taken for a long drive outside Mumbai to a location I had identified and visited well in advance. Since the morning, the Crime Branch unit had been busy digging nine deep pits there. I had visited the site to ensure that the graves were deep enough. The vehicles driven by the policemen reached the chosen site. The maulvi was relieved of his blindfold. He solemnly performed the last rites, and read the janaza prayers.

At last, the nine enemies of India were interred, and were lent a shoulder by members of the Mumbai police, their sworn enemies. Wanted by nobody now except some mischievous activists for their own nefarious fissiparous ends. The maulvi was blindfolded again and left the site in the car that had brought him. The red light continued to glow on the morgue door. The guards outside kept guarding that door which no longer secured anything of serious consequence. The 'vigilant' journalists kept visiting the morgue to make sure that the bodies were still inside, waiting for the door to finally open for the breaking news pictures. Then one day, months later, the State Assembly began discussing the issue. The police officers sitting in the gallery held their breath as the Home Minister broke it to the House. The nine bodies had been given a proper religious burial at a destination that could not be disclosed for security reasons, he had said. The tight-lipped secrecy maintained by all my officers and men for this entire operation was a matter of pride for the Mumbai police. As their senior, I received appreciation on their behalf, from all the higher officials in the police as well as the state hierarchy, although no rewards could be declared for such work, however sensitive it may have been.

As the work of gathering evidence picked up pace, the missing pieces of the three-dimensional jigsaw began to fall into place.

There were many facets that could not reach the Control Room that night because the officers and men engaged in action were unable to convey them at the time. Many witnesses perished, many were critically injured and some did not understand the need to convey what they had witnessed.

When the ten terrorists had landed at Badhwar Park, there were hardly any local Kolis (fishermen) present there to accost them, thanks to the live telecast of the One Day International Cricket match in progress. Yet one Koli who happened to be there did question them. Bharat Tamore asked them who they were. 'We are students!' They had answered gruffly. He asked what work did they have here as students? 'How are you concerned?' They had retorted. Had there been more fishermen present there – generally a hot-headed lot who do not readily swallow insolence from anyone – the answer may not have gone unchallenged. The attack could have started at Badhwar Park itself. The instructions to the fidayeens were succinct: if confronted, open indiscriminate fire! Cause maximum damage!

Then there were the two taxi blasts. Kasab and Abu Ismail had hailed a taxi for the CST. Ismail sat next to the driver and Kasab sat behind. Kasab stealthily assembled the bomb and planted it under the driver's seat. After reaching the station, they first entered the washroom near Platform 13 and tried calling the handlers in Karachi, but the calls did not materialise. Then Abu Ismail assembled his RDX bomb and the duo took out their AK-47s and loaded them. Ready for action, they emerged from the washrooms. Abu Ismail placed his bomb at a nearby spot. Then he hurled a grenade in the direction of the waiting area and both opened indiscriminate fire. The time was 9:50 p.m.

As trouble broke out inside, Advocate Lakshmi Narayan Goyal was leaving the station. He was in the Mumbai High Court that day to conduct a case and had missed the Hussain Sagar Express to return to Hyderabad. Sensing something grossly amiss, he'd immediately engaged a taxi outside the station and dialled his sister-in-law Usha Chaudhari's number. He told her that he had missed the train and was coming to her house to stay the night. It was in distant Kandivali, a suburb at the northern tip of Mumbai. After a while, he informed her that the taxi had reached Dadar. His married daughter, Deeksha Kedia, lived in Walkeshwar. Around 10:45 she learned about the firing at the CST and phoned her father to enquire about his whereabouts. She wanted him to come to Walkeshwar which was much closer to the CST. Goyal said that he was already near Santacruz airport, and thereafter the call had got disconnected. Deeksha was relieved that her father was safe. She tried his number again after some time, but could not get through. Feeling that it must be a network issue, she contacted her aunt. He had not reached, said Usha and asked Deeksha not to worry. Both the women waited anxiously for Goyal to reach Kandivali or to hear from him. Like the entire city, they were riveted to television news. Suddenly a newsflash announced that a bomb had exploded in a taxi at Vile Parle on the Western Express Highway and two persons had died. In the morning when Goyal had still not returned, a desperate Deeksha requested Usha to go to the Vile Parle police station and check the identity of the deceased. The police directed Usha to Cooper hospital. Their worst fear was confirmed. Goyal had lost his life in the blast. The driver of the taxi was a Muslim, Muhammad Umar Sheikh. The blast had severed his head which was found 350 feet away in the compound of the City Swan Club. Goyal had escaped death at the CST, but it had chased him all the way to overcome him in Vile Parle. Had he gone to his daughter's house in Walkeshwar, the inquest panchanama would have featured some other mortals along with the poor driver and some other location. Which makes me wonder. The traditional Indian, across all communities and religions, avoids imposing himself or herself on married daughters and their families. We are brought up to keep a tactful and respectful distance from her husband and in-laws. The logic being that familiarity breeds contempt, and the last thing we want is to embarrass our daughters in any possible way. This self-restriction has survived all our progress and modernity. I wonder if that is what made the loving father choose a location miles away, rather than his dear daughter's house which was so close by.

Abu Soheb and Abu Umer drove to the Leopold Café in a taxi driven by Fulchand Ramkishor Bind. Soheb quickly planted the bomb under the driver's seat and they approached Leopold. One Wasim Shaikh happened to be looking for a taxi to return to Dongri, after dining at the nearby Bade Miyan – another famous eating joint. Wasim hailed Bind's taxi for Dongri and waited for the duo to pay. For the fare of thirteen rupees, Abu Umer extended a hundred rupee note to Bind. 'I don't have change, I have just started the night shift,' Bind said apologetically. 'Keep the change!' Said Umer, to the surprise of both the men. Bind was only too happy to oblige, but the young passenger's largesse did not go undiscussed on their way to Dongri.

The taxi released by Soheb and Umer at Leopold soon reached Wasim Shaikh's destination in Dongri. One of his acquaintances, Mohammad Rabiul Shaikh, came with two ladies and engaged the taxi for BIT Colony in Mazgaon. The taxi left with the two ladies as Wasim Shaikh walked home. The next morning, he learnt of the firing at Leopold and the taxi blast in Mazgaon. He began thinking of the odd-looking spendthrift youths who had got off near Leopold. Then he learned that Mohammad Rabiul's wife, Rema and mother-in-law, Zarina had died in the taxi blast in Mazgaon. He realised that not only had he had a providential escape, but he had also witnessed something terribly important – the two terrorists minutes before they had opened fire at Leopold and soon after they had planted the bomb in the taxi! He immediately rushed to the police and gave his account.

The taxi blown up in the name of Islam had killed Bind, Rema and Zarina, and injured nineteen persons!

Not just Hindus, even ordinary innocent Muslims had lost their lives in the two taxi blasts which made no sense. The only sense they made, if at all, was that all the victims were Indian nationals and that it was very difficult to segregate Indian Muslims and Indian Hindus whose day-to-day lives are weaved inextricably.

How did the attack at CST start? The hand grenade hurled by Ismail had burst with a loud deafening noise. The passengers began running helter-skelter. Some were injured and some died on the spot in the indiscriminate firing. From his cabin on the mezzanine floor, Vishnu Zende, the Railway Announcer on duty, saw the happenings and heard the firing and the grenade blasts. He immediately realised that it was a terror attack and began issuing warnings in Marathi, Hindi and English. The terrorists understood the Hindi announcements and saw the cabin from where they emanated. Kasab immediately fired a bullet in his direction, but Zende sat on the floor and continued to make his announcements. His colleague switched the lights off. The terrorists would have made it to the mezzanine and higher floors and even taken hostages as instructed by their trainers, had not Police Inspector Shashank Shinde of CST Railway Police station intervened.

His shift over, Shashank Shinde was about to leave for the day, but armed with just his revolver he instead ran to the police help counter near Platform 6 and 7 where Assistant Police Inspector Sudam Pandharkar and Constable Harshad Punju Patil of the Government Railway Police (GRP) and Constable Zillu Baddu Yadav of the Railway Police Force (RPF) were present. Pandharkar and Patil had a .303 rifle and ten rounds each, but Yadav was unarmed. Shinde and Pandharkar ran towards Platform 6 and could see Ismail. Pandharkar fired two rounds which Ismail dodged. Ismail opened rapid fire which killed Shashank Shinde instantly and injured Pandharkar severely. This was seen from Platform 1 by Constable Ambadas Ramchandra Pawar of the Security Branch of Mumbai Police's Special Branch-I. He was about to catch a train home but rushed where Pandharkar had dropped down. Pawar picked up his rifle and shot one round at Kasab which Kasab dodged. Pawar was about to fire the second round when Kasab sprayed bullets in his direction. He too died instantly. Taking the cover of the walls of the booth, Harshad Patil was trying to open fire, but his weapon had jammed. Zillu Yadav ran towards him and tried his hand at the weapon, but it refused to respond. Yadav then threw a chair at the terrorists! The terrorists opened fire at them and it was only the walls of the booth that had saved them. The heroic resistance put up by the small number of policemen forced Kasab and Ismail out of the CST or else they would have advanced to the mezzanine floor to stop the announcements, climbed higher floors and taken hostages. A standoff would have ensued as it had happened at the other three sites ending in both of them getting killed. One of the strategies that was drilled into them was to capture higher floors, become unassailable and kill the approaching policemen.

The heroic actions of Shashank Shinde, Sudam Pandharkar, Ambadas Pawar, Harshad Patil and Zillu Yadav is a fine example of unflinching commitment to duty. To their knowledge, the weapons they carried were no match for the AKs and grenades of the terrorists. Neither had they received comparable training. But they knew what they had to do. Do everything possible to take care of the commuters who depend on you for protection! Your duty is not limited by shifts and duty hours. Once a policeman, always a policeman.

Equally commendable was the commitment of announcer Zende and his colleague. They did not desert their cabin to save themselves and, thus, saved many lives.

Sebastian D'Souza of the *Mumbai Mirror* and Shriram Vernekar of the Times of India Group (TOI) – photojournalists from the TOI building which is directly opposite the CST – also displayed remarkable bravery when they clicked pictures of Kasab and Ismail which proved invaluable at the trial as did their testimonies. Vernekar not only shot pictures inside the station, he quickly returned to the TOI building and from the second-floor window clicked more pictures of the terrorists walking on the foot over-bridge. Seeing the flash, Kasab had even fired a shot at Vernekar but had missed. The pictures clicked by D'Souza captured the valiant acts of Pandharkar and Ambadas Pawar. Both the men behind the cameras were amazingly fit and agile, considering the way they jumped over the road dividers and reached the platforms and back. Had they been holding guns instead of the cameras, maybe they would have done as gallant a job as the men in uniform.

Where was the seven kg RDX bomb planted by Ismail at the CST? Obviously, it had not detonated, and Kasab was not lying. We were flummoxed. The bomb ought to be somewhere! It tormented me no end and I was after my officers to trace it. A frantic search led to its discovery! Of all the places, it was found in a room in the Railway Court, where they had kept all the unclaimed baggage which was lying scattered in the waiting area after the carnage! Prince, the canine member of the Mumbai police who had an impressive record of sniffing out RDX, was summoned. It was he who had detected it for the BDDS.

At the CST, Kasab and Ismail had killed fifty-two people which included one officer each from the Mumbai police, GRP, RPF and Home Guards. The number of injured was 108 and included four GRP, three RPF and two Home Guards.

The news of the attack on the CST had reached Cama Hospital and alerted the staff. Suddenly, they heard gunshots from the rear gate. Nurse Anjali Kulthe displayed great presence of mind. She switched off the lights in all the wards and closed the doors. With

Hira, a colleague, she began to watch the attack from a window. To their utter consternation, they saw two terrorists jump over the closed gate. A cry escaped Hira's lips prompting Kasab to fire a few shots in their direction. One injured Hira's wrist. Kulthe immediately locked the sliding door of her ward and shifted the twenty-odd women and their babies to the kitchen. She asked them to keep breastfeeding the babies to prevent them from crying. Luckily, her strategy had worked. Kasab told us later that they had found that segment of the hospital shut! Imagine the calamity and havoc if they had taken all the mothers and babies hostage!

Sadanand Date, Additional CP (Central Region), entered the Cama Hospital through its front gate on the Mahapalika Marg. He was accompanied by his wireless operator, Sachin Tilekar, Police Sub Inspector Prakash More of L.T. Marg police station, Assistant Police Inspectors Vijay Shinde and Vijay Powar from Azad Maidan police station, Head Constable Mohan Shinde and Constable Vijay Khandekar. He led the team upstairs to rescue the hostages, when a shoot-out ensued. Police Sub Inspector More and Police Constable Khandekar lost their lives and the others were injured. Date grimly held on to his position. Firing from his own revolver and the weapon of an injured policeman, he guided his injured colleagues to the exit of the building. Of them, Tilekar reported the happenings to Hemant Karkare, Ashok Kamte and Vijay Salaskar who had gathered at the rear gate with a posse of policemen. Unbeknownst to them, the terrorists had descended the stairs and run towards the front gate of the hospital where they killed Police Sub Inspector B.S. Durgude of the ATS who had just got himself dropped on the road by a two-wheeler to join Karkare and team. A band of policemen from the Azad Maidan police station was near the St. Xavier's College on the Mahapalika Marg. They opened fire on the terrorists, but without any luck. Their vehicle got damaged in the terrorists' fire, but fortunately, they did not suffer any casualties.

The Honda City with a red beacon in the Rang Bhavan lane was the official vehicle allotted to IAS officer, Bhushan Gagrani. He had to rush to the Mantralaya to attend a high-level emergency meeting to tackle the terrorist attack. His driver, Maruti Phad had been summoned with the car. Phad was driving the vehicle when the terrorist duo entered the lane from the Mahapalika Marg and opened fire. Phad began reversing, but one of the tyres of his car had burst. He received two bullet injuries. With great presence of mind, he locked the car centrally and pretended to be dead. The duo tried to open the doors, but did not succeed. Then they began walking towards the nearby Corporation Bank ATM.

Just then the Qualis of Shantilal Bhamre, ACP Pydhoni Division, entered the lane from the other end and began proceeding towards Mahapalika Marg. Salaskar was at the wheel, while Kamte sat next to him, Karkare was in the back seat and sitting right at the back were Assistant Sub Inspector Balasaheb Bhosale, Police Naik Arun Dada Jadhav and wireless operators, Yogesh Patil and Jaywant Patil. The two terrorists hid behind the thick bushes opposite the Corporation Bank ATM and opened rapid fire at the Qualis. Karkare, Kamte, Salaskar and Jadhav replied with retaliatory fire. A bullet grazed Kasab's wrists and an elbow. His AK-47 fell, but he picked it up and fired the fatal burst which killed Karkare, Kamte, Salaskar, Bhosale and Jaywant Patil. Kasab described the rest of the incident in his confessional statement:

> The firing from the car stopped. We looked inside the car. All the men were policemen and they were all dead. We tried to open the rear door but it would not open. There was a pain in my hands and I stood shaking my hands and stood with support. Ismail opened burst fire on the road behind the car. Then he pulled out the bodies of the driver and the man behind him. I pulled out the body in the front seat next to the driver and we threw them on the street. Ismail's magazine was empty so he took the policeman's Klashan. Ismail sat in the driver's seat and I sat next

to him. As we were speeding in the car, Ismail told me that he had been hit by a bullet in his groin.

Investigations revealed that twenty-nine bullets from the AK-47 had lodged inside the Qualis. Many more must have passed through the glass windows of the car. There were thirteen bullet marks on the shutter of the Corporation Bank. Maruti Phad had witnessed the entire incident from his car.

Of the four policemen lying in the rear portion of the van, Arun Jadhav was alive but his right hand and left shoulder were severely injured. Moreover, he was pinned down as the bodies of the other men in the rear portion were lying on top of him. Even Yogesh Patil was alive, but he was unable to move. Thinking all of them to be dead, Abu Ismail drove the car to Mahapalika Marg where Constable Arun Chitte was dispersing the crowd that had gathered there. Ismail opened fire at them, killing Arun Chitte instantly. Then Ismail drove to the Metro junction where a crowd had gathered. It was Kasab's turn now to open fire at them. It killed a hotel employee and injured a cameraperson from the ETV Marathi news channel. Suddenly, Yogesh Patil's cell phone rang in his pocket. To Arun Jadhav's horror, Kasab turned around and cold-bloodedly shot Yogesh, killing him instantly. Thus, in their journey from Cama Hospital to Metro junction, Kasab and Ismail had killed nine persons and injured seven. These included eight police personnel: three senior police officers, one Police Sub Inspector, one Assistant Sub Inspector, two wireless operators and a constable.

Ismail drove down Maharshi Karve Road right up to Mittal Towers near Mantralaya. En route, one of the car tyres burst and the deadly duo desperately needed to get hold of another car. Just then a Skoda car came into sight with three good Mumbaikars, perfect examples of a helpful lot, who were driving all the way from Juhu and Mahim to south Mumbai to pick up their friend, Siddharth Umashankar from Hotel Oberoi. Sharan Arsa had picked up a common friend, Sameer Ajgaonkar and his wife, Megha to rescue Siddharth who worked in a managerial position at the Oberoi. As the Skoda neared Mittal Towers, the trio saw the police Qualis with an amber beacon and heard shots being fired from it. Thinking them to be the police who were asking them to slow down, they dutifully complied. The Qualis stopped and Kasab got down. He pointed his AK at Arsa and ordered him to stop the car. Ismail also got down and pulled Arsa out of the car, at which, the Ajgaonkar couple also stepped out. Ismail asked for the car keys and Arsa pointed towards the keys which he had dropped near the wheel. Ismail asked Arsa to pick up the keys and hand them over. Arsa did as he was told. Ismail and Kasab immediately sat in the car and sped away towards Marine Drive. Did they forget to kill the trio in the anxiety to find a vehicle and get away from the spot?

Luckily Arun Dada Jadhav had managed to see the terrorists disappear in the hijacked car. Although he had mistaken it to be a Honda City, he had also managed to flash the garbled message from the wireless handset which had promptly alerted the officers on the chase. Sudhir Desai, a Control Room operator had instantaneously alerted all the wireless vans and officers about the development. Senior Police Inspector Marine Drive, Sanjay Amrute and his team soon reached the Qualis, questioned Arsa and the Ajgaonkars and conveyed the correct description of the car and the direction it had taken. The Control Room had forthwith flashed this alert to all the concerned officers and mobiles.

The D.B. Marg police station was taking no chances. Their squad at the Vinowli Chowpatty, led by Assistant Police Inspectors Hemant Bavdhankar and Sanjay Govilkar, was subjecting each and every vehicle passing the checkpoint to a thorough scrutiny. The others deployed at the junction were Sub Inspector Bhaskar Kadam, Assistant Sub Inspectors Tukaram Ombale, Sarjerao Pawar, Chandrakant Kothale, Hawaldars Shivaji Kolhe, Vikram Nikam, Ashok Shelke and Chandrakant Chavan, Police Naiks

Vijay Avhad and Mangesh Naik, Constables Ramesh Mane, Sunil Sohni, Santosh Chendwankar, wireless operator, Sanjay Patil and driver, Chandrakant Kamble.

Since Vinowli Chowpatty junction is a major entry and exit point in the area which was under attack, a four-tier checking was in progress. The first group of men asked the motorists to slow down, switch off the front lights, put on the inside lights and lower all the windows. The next set of officers checked the occupants inside and the car. The third set jotted down the description and details of the car. And the last set of officers were ready outside the van, armed with their AKs. When the alert message about the Skoda was received, the squad became vigilant. Theirs was the most likely road for the terrorists to take! And that's what happened.

The Skoda approached the nakabandi at Vinowli and abided by the first command. But at the next command, it did something totally unacceptable. Instead of switching off the front lights, Ismail switched on the headlights to blind the police party. He also began spraying the washer fluid onto the windshield. The inside of the car was not visible to the police and sensing danger, the other officers and men began advancing cautiously. Ismail swerved the car to his right, intending to cross the divider, but the car could not make it. The police advanced with their weapons and Ismail opened fire from his pistol. By then, the third tier of officers was also closing in. Assistant Police Inspector Bavdhankar and Sub Inspector Bhaskar Kadam retaliated and Ismail was killed instantly, though it was not apparent as yet. Bhaskar Kadam's shot had entered his skull. Kasab saw his buddy go limp. The police firing continued. Then Kasab opened the left door and deliberately fell out of the car. On noticing this, Tukaram Ombale moved nimbly to the door and saw Kasab lying on the ground holding his AK-47 close to his chest. Without an instant's delay, Ombale threw himself on Kasab and tried hard to snatch his gun away even as Kasab strived to throw Ombale off him. Although he did not succeed in throwing

Ombale off him, but he had managed to press the trigger. Five bullets pierced Ombale's body killing him instantly.

Kasab told us that Ombale's dead weight had made it all the more difficult for him to get up and attack the policemen which he had desperately wanted to do. The rest of the squad rushed to the left side of the Skoda and saw Kasab pinned down by Ombale who was lifeless. Just then Kasab opened fire again and a bullet pierced the left hip of Assistant Police Inspector Govilkar. The policemen pulled Kasab out and began beating him mercilessly with their batons. Kasab lost his grip on the weapon and it fell to the ground, to be immediately seized by the officers. Suddenly Sanjay Govilkar, a fine officer who had worked with me in the Crime Branch earlier, realised that he had to stop the attack on Kasab. Despite his injury, he thrust himself between his infuriated comrades and Kasab and shouted in despair, *'Arrey yala maru nakaa! Toh aplyala jiwant hawaa aahe! Tyachyakadoon mahattwachi mahiti milwaychi aahe. Toh sakshidaar aahe.'* (Don't hit him! We need him alive! We need to get important information out of him. He is an eyewitness!)

The timely action by Govilkar had averted a major mishap, or else, we would have been left holding a dead Kasab and lamenting the loss of a god-sent opportunity to get evidence out of him. The men controlled themselves and came to their senses when they saw a bleeding Govilkar hugging Kasab as if he were saving his dearest friend!

The dramatic finale of Kasab and Ismail's car ride lasted just seven minutes and wrote a glorious page in the history of Mumbai police. It was written in blood, shed by the brave and unassuming Tukaram Ombale. Armed with just a baton, he had lunged forward to grab Kasab's Kalashnikov without wasting a single thought. The page was inked with the bullets of Kadam and Bavdhankar who had fired the shots that had eliminated Ismail and paved the way for Kasab's arrest. It was written thanks to the grit displayed by the entire team of D.B. Marg police station who had braced themselves mentally to stop the Skoda, come what may and neutralise its deadly crew.

A very important role was also played by a brave young employee of the Taj. Guest Service Associate Sangeeta Sarin was about to leave for home when the attack began. Instead of bolting out, she'd notified her bosses and then headed for the telecom operators' room where she had worked before. With great presence of mind, she began calling the guests in their rooms and directed them to lock their doors and not come out. She had kept in touch with the guests until 5:00 a.m. on 27 November and, thereby, saved many lives.

K.L. Prasad had reached the Taj at 02:10 hours from the Control Room. He had just three bodyguards with SLRs and no bulletproof vests. He could not proceed towards the staircase because of the barrage of grenades and AK fire by the terrorists. Despite being unfamiliar with the topography, he had led the police to help evacuate patrons stranded in the 'Chambers' (a prestigious club for elite entrepreneurs), in the Gateway Room on the first floor and in the Zodiac Grill on the ground floor. The Security Officers at the Taj, Sunil Kudiyadi and Philip Rodrigues had also rendered invaluable support to the police and the NSG for sixty gruelling hours.

Abu Akasha and Abu Umar had walked with the GPS to Nariman House, the smallest establishment under siege where ACP Isaque Bagwan was the man who demonstrated exceptional leadership that comes with long police service at the grassroots level. He'd managed to confine the terrorists to the building until the NSG came in on the afternoon of 27 November. As a matter of fact, nobody knew that it was a Jewish establishment and a possible target for the murderous duo. Bagwan had learnt of it only on reaching the spot. The Colaba police under whose jurisdiction it fell, was busy at the Leopold and the Taj. Shortly thereafter, the MRA Mobile-1 with Assistant Sub Inspector Shinde and 2 PCs with SLRs reached the site, followed by a Striking Mobile. Bagwan cordoned off the area with their help, and evacuated at least 300 people from the surrounding buildings, deployed policemen in the neighbouring buildings and started shooting at the terrorists to pin them down. On the morning of 27 November, Sandra Samuel, the Catholic nanny, and the cook, Qazi Zakir Hussain, a Muslim, ran out with baby Moshe, the son of Rabbi Gavriel Holtzberg and his wife Rivka Holtzberg who were among those sanguinarily killed inside by the terrorists. The information that others in the building, including little Moshe's parents, were killed by the terrorists had enraged Bagwan and his men to such an extent that he called me on my cell phone.

'Sir, I have decided that I will put a wooden plank from the terrace of an adjoining building to the third floor of Nariman House and enter the building with my men. Please give me the orders?' I knew that the two-time recipient of the President's Gallantry Medal was capable of doing this even without formal orders. Thank God, he had called me to ask for orders. I had a tough time dissuading him. 'Bagwan, they have grenades!' I tried to reason with him. 'Sir, then send me grenades!' He retorted agitatedly. 'Bagwan, you know we don't have such weapons in our arsenal. And another thing, we cannot sustain any more losses,' I said. There was a pause. Then he said, 'Sir, I don't understand what you mean.' I realised that the news of the deaths of Karkare, Kamte, Salaskar and others had not reached him as yet! I explained to him what I had meant and I could sense from his tone that he was shocked and grieved. 'Bagwan, please wait, the NSG will soon reach you. Till then, please continue to do the excellent job you are doing, but don't, for heaven's sake, enter the building till then.' I said to him in as firm a voice as I could manage while addressing a veteran. After this, Bagwan ordered his men to fire tear gas shells into the building.

There was a continuous exchange of fire between the police and the terrorists until the arrival of the NSG. The toll at Nariman House was six civilian deaths and the loss of NSG Commando Havildar Gajender Singh Bisht. Two of the innocents killed by the terrorists' bullets included an elderly Muslim couple who resided in a building near Nariman House.

With such terrible details emerging out of the investigation, we began getting the hang of how the entire conspiracy was hatched and planned on the drawing board, and how it had actually translated itself into reality when combined with ground realities and with the intervention of several unforeseen, unknown and intangible factors.

Nine of the accused had died in the attack and we had arrested three – Kasab and Fahim Ansari and Sabauddin Ahmed who were lodged in Rampur Jail, UP. As per our investigations, Fahim had sketched maps of the target locations in Mumbai and Sabauddin had conveyed the same to the LeT handlers. We also found the involvement of one more accused. A US national, David Coleman Headley had played a very pivotal role in the preparations of the attack. From September 2006 he had made around seven trips to India and befriended many unsuspecting Mumbaikars including Rahul Bhatt, the son of filmmaker Mahesh Bhatt. He had stayed at the Taj and the Oberoi and done extensive reconnaissance of all the other targets and videographed them. The National Investigation Agency (NIA) which later went to the US to question Headley found that he was a key LeT operative and had shortlisted fifty-one targets all over India for terror attacks. He had later disclosed minute details of the LeT's grand design to destabilise India by causing widespread destruction through terror attacks.

Kasab's confessional statement which was recorded before a magistrate was part of the court evidence as were the five GPS sets used by the terrorists. The FBI expert had reported that one GPS had recorded fifty way-points which showed that it was used in Karachi and another fifty which showed that it was used from Pakistani waters to six nautical miles off Badhwar Park in Mumbai. The Yamaha outboard engine in the rubber dinghy was traced to have been imported from Japan into Pakistan and the Nokia cell phones of the terrorists, from China into Pakistan. The VOIP account used by the Pakistani handlers to contact the terrorists had been opened from Pakistan. The emails were sent from IP addresses in Pakistan and two of the IP addresses were also used by a couple of army officers from Rawalpindi in Pakistan! The money transferred for the VOIP connection was wired from the Karachi branch of Western Union Money Transfer. Several articles found in the Kuber had Pakistani markings. The foam sheets which were used to pack the unexploded bombs matched those used in the Azizabad LeT training camps. The hand grenades had Pakistan Ordnance Factory markings, similar to those used in the March 1993 serial blasts. US investigators secured details of the dead terrorists and also some DNA samples of their relatives which helped establish the identities of a few of the terrorists. This was the first ever case in which the FBI had testified in an Indian court via videoconferencing.

Armed with such strong evidence, a 13,350 pages charge sheet was filed within the stipulated ninety days on 25 February 2009. Additionally, a supplementary charge sheet running into 1,500 pages was filed later. The statements of 2,200 witnesses were recorded, of which thankfully only 657 had to be examined; five were examined as court witnesses. The trial commenced in the court room in Arthur Road Jail on 16 April 2009 and took 110 court working days to complete. Judge M.L. Tahaliyani (who was later elevated to the Mumbai High Court) delivered a 1,528 pages judgement on 6 May 2010 and sentenced Ajmal Amir Kasab to death. The other two accused, however, were acquitted. In February 2011, the High Court confirmed Kasab's death sentence. As regards the acquitted accused, the learned judges accepted the evidence but said that it was uncorroborated and hence could not be used to convict the accused. In August 2012, the Supreme Court upheld the judgement of the High Court. The Apex Court noted its concern about the manner in which reporting by several media outfits had aided the handlers to guide the terrorists and made the task of the security forces difficult and risky. The judges pulled up the media for its role and suggested that they should have a self-regulatory mechanism to prevent such irresponsible excesses in the future.

The Indian perspective on handling terror was bound to change after 26/11. The security apparatus now strove for better coordination, with regular meetings instead of working in silos when dealing with Intelligence. We worked out ways and means to maintain better vigil. Our wish list like CCTV cameras, bulletproof vests and weapons did not go unheeded any longer. But most importantly, we got a better understanding of a jihadi terrorist mindset. Joining a militant network gives terrorists a sense of purpose and pride, elevating their social status, providing them with the acceptability that is virtually unattainable in Pakistani society. Religious fundamentalists have indoctrinated the Pakistani masses to be in awe of bigots who are desperate to die and kill for religion, and to condone their criminal deeds and moral turpitude. We also realised that the animosity against India is so deeply ingrained in fidayeens that every Indian is their enemy and slaying our civilians is for them as good as killing Indian soldiers.

Many of the officers and men who fought the terrorists on 26/11 got their due recognition. Hemant Karkare, Ashok Kamte, Vijay Salaskar, Tukaram Ombale, NSG Commando Major Sandeep Unnikrishnan and Havildar Gajender Singh were awarded the highest peacetime award, the Ashoka Chakra posthumously for their gallantry. Sapper V. Sathish of the NSG, Police Constables Arun Chitte, Ambadas Pawar and Inspector Shashank Shinde of the Maharashtra police and Home Guard Mukesh Jadhav were awarded the Kirti Chakra.

For some heroes though, the recognition was inordinately

delayed. But for many others, it would not come at all. They were to remain the unsung heroes that they always are, working away from the limelight, quietly and doggedly. They were the drivers of our vehicles, officers and men of the BDDS and Dog Squad, policemen and policewomen who manned the hospitals and morgues, and those who worked on the investigation and prosecution. Even the men who guarded Kasab. And of course, the Control Room staff who had worked with such genuine and intense sincerity throughout the ordeal for those three days. Each one must have their own story of that day.

As for me, I was transferred out of the Crime Branch on 29 March 2010, before the trial court verdict, and was promoted as Additional Director General of the Anti-Terrorism Squad, Maharashtra. But that is cutting the long story short. The long story is the agony that 26/11 had heaped on me personally, for no fault of mine. The agony that had begun soon after the attacks, with the accusations and insinuations that I had sent my three dear colleagues to their death in the Rang Bhavan lane by failing to provide them timely help and then done a coverup to hide my tracks. The agony that had made me wish that Hasan Gafoor had ordered me to enter the Taj or the Oberoi that night, rather than put me in the Control Room. It would raise its ugly head time and again, and that too whenever I was at some critical juncture in my career! And I would wonder if this is what Mirza Ghalib had meant when he had said, *Mujhe kya bura tha marnaa, agar ek bar hota!* (Why would I consider death bad, had it but come only once!) It was like dying again and again or to be in a state of living death, without deserving it.

Strangely, there were two of us who had wished that we had died that night. Two adversaries in the same battle! One was Ajmal Amir Kasab and the other, Rakesh Harikrishan Maria, though for different reasons. He, because he wanted Paradise. Me, because I was getting hell here.

32

Uneasy Lay the Head

Saturday, 15 February 2014, began for Preeti and me even before the dawn had broken. And that too with happy tidings for a change. Quite unlike a cop's home used to shrill rings, piercing through dark nights, to announce some gloomy news. Around 4 a.m. that morning, our son, Krish burst into our bedroom, unable to contain his happiness. He had received the much-awaited email to convey that he had secured admission to the prestigious Leonard N. Stern School of Business at New York University! All his hard work had paid off. It was a delight to see his face light up with joy.

Sleep was now out of the question. A cosy chat till daybreak was followed by a hearty breakfast during which I promised that we would celebrate with a dinner that very evening at a restaurant of Krish's choice. Krish and Preeti came around 8:30 in the evening to my office in Nagpada, as planned. They waited in the antechamber for me to finish my work. Just then my cell phone rang. It was R.R. Patil, the Home Minister. *'Abhinandan!'* He said. *'Aapli CP Mumbai niyuktichi order amhi kadhli aahe. Sahebanshi boloon ghya.'* (Congratulations! We have passed the order for your appointment as CP, Mumbai. Now have a word with Saheb).

The next voice on the line was that of Chief Minister Prithviraj Chavan. He congratulated me and added in his soft, polished tone, 'We have very high expectations of you, Mr Maria! And I wish you all the very best.'

Two happy tidings in a day! It was like a dream, and a little too much to digest. A bit dazed, I thanked the Chief Minister and assured him that I would do my best. It would be an absolute lie to say that one did not harbour the dream of becoming the Mumbai Commissioner someday. Every IPS officer of the Maharashtra cadre has the cherished ambition of becoming CP Mumbai, just as every member of the Indian cricket team must be aspiring to be the Indian captain. When the day finally dawns, it is not without a sense of wonderment, as I was finding it. So coveted is the post, with many contenders feeling in right earnest that they deserve it more than anyone else! The elation also gets tinged with a fear somewhere deep inside. All of a sudden you are thrust into the limelight and under the microscope, leading a 50,000-strong Force looking up to you to lead them. And of course, a dear trusting City which puts herself under your care and with the optimism that you will not fail her.

I would have to take charge of my new office the very next day. It meant occupying the chair lying vacant in an unprecedented manner. It was nearly a fortnight from the day my predecessor had tendered his resignation, and that too, to join politics! He had entered the Bharatiya Janata Party (BJP), the diehard opposition to the ruling Congress-NCP coalition that had extended his tenure which had led to delays in the routine of transfers and promotion in the police hierarchy. All this had added spice to the usual brouhaha that brews around the appointment of the new CP and stirred up a juicy controversy to the delight of the media. Naturally, all eyes were on the new incumbent. That new incumbent would be me.

I called Krish and Preeti in and broke the glad tidings to them. They were happy, but also a little overwhelmed. I abandoned the plan of dining out and with Krish doing an admirable effort of hiding his disappointment, the three of us returned home for a quiet meal to brace ourselves for the big change that we were being propelled into.

The boy who played cricket barefoot in the gullies of Bandra, and vanished with his teammates behind trees in the gardens when the occasional policeman came patrolling down the lane, had finally made it to the portrait gallery of Police Commissioners of the city – stalwarts like S. V. Bhave, V. K. Saraf, Julio Ribeiro, D. S. Soman, S. Ramamurthy, S. K. Bapat, A. S. Samra, Satish Sahney, R. H. Mendonca, M. N. Singh, Dr P. S. Pasricha and many more before and after them! All my seniors under whom I had worked, phoned to congratulate me.

I wished my parents were alive to see this day and that was probably the only feeling of sadness when I took charge. At each new posting, Mama would counsel me that the chair given to me was only for helping people. As I sat in the CP's chair, that was the foremost thought in my mind.

The general practice for the CP was to have fixed time slots for visitors, like say from 3 p.m. to 5 p.m. I realised, however, that when an aggrieved petitioner wanted to meet the CP, he must be facing the worst times of his life and could not wait. I felt they could meet me as a matter of right as I was appointed to assist them. Time management would be a challenge, but I had to at least give it a try. I decided that whosoever wanted to meet me should be able to do so at any time during the day. So I began meeting as many people as possible, amidst my other duties. Visitors had to take their chance and they did, without grumbling if there were delays. They waited patiently if I had to rush out for some important meeting and return. They appreciated that I had other work to attend to as well. I would do my best to give each visitor as much attention as feasible and if possible, try and issue directions to alleviate their difficulties right in their presence. So the number of visitors began averaging 125 a day. After a while, we had to issue instructions at the gate to stop letting people in after 8 p.m., otherwise, there was no way I could go home. By the time I had seen the last visitor, it would be around 10 p.m.

I love detecting crimes. The greatest joy for me is when I unravel a challenging case or lead a team that lays bare an unsolved crime. As the young DCP (Detection) in the Crime Branch, I remember telling my seniors that I wouldn't mind foregoing all promotions if I were allowed to just detect crimes! My first posting in the city was in the late '80s when our topmost priority was controlling the depredations of the underworld. To this was added urban terrorism after the serial blasts of 1993. By the time I reached the post of the Commissioner, a new dimension had been added to the roster of prime concerns: women's security, and the inviolability of the safety of children and senior citizens. And with it came the need to solve crimes that afflicted these vulnerable sections of society and bring to book the scourge that preyed on them.

The serious incident referred to as the infamous Shakti Mills gang-rape case had taken place on 22 August 2013. A twenty-two-year-old girl, an intern photojournalist with a magazine, was gang-raped by five felons which included a juvenile. On an assignment with a male colleague, the victim had gone to the deserted Shakti Mills compound which is near Mahalaxmi Railway Station in south Mumbai. The accused had tied up the colleague with belts, raped the woman and clicked her photographs during the sexual assault. They had later threatened to upload her photographs on social media networks if she reported the rape. Subsequently, it came to light that an eighteen-year-old call centre employee too had been similarly gang-raped inside the deserted complex in July 2013.

The Shakti Mills case was preceded by a brutal gang-rape in the national capital which had ended in the victim's death, shaking the nation's collective conscience and bringing it to a moment of truth in its approach to women's safety. It was the Nirbhaya case – the gang-rape that had occurred on 16 December 2012 in Munirka, a neighbourhood in south Delhi. A twenty-three-year-old female physiotherapy intern was beaten, gang-raped and brutally tortured in a private bus in which she was travelling with her male friend. The six men in the bus, including the driver, had raped the hapless woman and assaulted her friend. As the victim battled for her life, the incident received extensive national and international coverage and invited wide condemnation. The nation woke up to realise that instead of paying mere lip service to its great cultural heritage of revering a woman as a goddess, it was time to act. Since our law insists on protecting the victim's identity, she was fondly named 'Nirbhaya', which means the fearless. She had put up a valiant fight against her oppressors besides giving a detailed statement to the police before her condition had worsened. Nirbhaya was airlifted to Singapore for emergency treatment, but had succumbed to her injuries, plunging the entire country into deep sorrow.

It seemed as if the anger at violence against women was waiting to be expressed and had found its voice with the ordeal of Nirbhaya. With this last straw on its back, the camel finally decided that enough was enough. The caravan of shame came to a halt and made it to front page news with a vengeance – to the headlines, to editorials, to prime time and to the internet. In popular perception, all the governments had consistently failed in providing adequate security to women. Public protests broke out and emotional picketers clashed with security forces. Nirbhaya became a symbol of the Indian woman's struggle to alter the male-dominated culture which tends to look at her as an object of lust and exploitation, and the despicable tendency of blaming the victim rather than the perpetrator of rape and molestation.

Whether the rise in sexual violence against women is a worldwide phenomenon or just an aberration at home, whether it can be blamed on progress, modernisation and loss of values, whether the upsurge in the number of registered cases merely reflects the rise in our population – these are matters for in-depth analyses and research by criminologists and sociologists. Sweeping generalisations must be avoided. It would be reasonable to assume, however, that the increase in the number of atrocities reported against women can be attributed to the growing number of women in all walks of life, to the rising levels of confidence in today's woman that comes with better education, better exposure and a more conducive social environment that surrounds her. This environment includes the formidable support from an alert media and non-governmental organisations who have gradually succeeded in sensitising our society to her plight.

When I took charge as Commissioner, the Shakti Mill gang-rape case had been taken up by a fast track court and the trial was expected to be completed soon. But an equally heinous and gut-wrenching incident had occurred, a little over a month earlier, in which a young girl had lost her life and the competence of the Mumbai police had come under severe criticism.

A twenty-three-year-old girl, full of promise, had come to the city brimming with confidence. Her name was Esther Anhuya and she was from Machilipatnam, the famous ancient city on the south-eastern coast. Esther had once confided in a friend that she considered Mumbai as one of the safest Indian cities for women, safer than even Delhi. A software engineer from the Jawaharlal Nehru Technological University in Kakinada, she had been recruited by the Tata Consultancy Services, a company known for tapping bright software engineers across the length and breadth of India. She found accommodation in the YWCA at Andheri, close to Goregaon where she worked and was happily pursuing her dreams in the free and vibrant atmosphere which is provided by Mumbai to all young people who are ready to toil hard and prove themselves.

After a pleasant Christmas and New Year break spent

in the warmth of her family home, Esther had boarded the Vishakhapatnam-LTT Mumbai Express in Vijayawada at 8 a.m. on 4 January 2014. The train had reached the Lokmanya Tilak Terminus (popularly known as the Kurla Terminus) on 5 January at 4:40 in the early hours of the morning. But Esther had disappeared!

Esther's father, Jonathan Prasad tried to phone her, but in vain. He contacted his brother, who lived in Navi Mumbai, and a frantic search began. The father was his daughter's best friend and knew it for certain that there was absolutely no reason for his precious daughter to go incommunicado. Even the happy times that she had spent in their company did nothing to suggest that she had any cause to run away from them. Esther had come with a snazzy new hairstyle and he was happy to see her enjoy her new look. She had even hosted a dinner for them and sung carols to her heart's content with the church choir. Music and singing were her passions and she liked Korean films and Japanese comics. She was even planning to go to Germany for further studies. There was therefore absolutely no reason for Esther to vanish! Unless she was in danger.

So when the family and friends could not trace her, they were worried stiff. Her uncle rushed to register a missing complaint on 5 January, but he found it easier said than done. On the matter of jurisdiction, he was turned away by two police stations – MIDC, within whose jurisdiction she resided, and Kurla Railway, under whose jurisdiction she had alighted. Shockingly, he found the police sceptical about his account, hinting that she must have eloped with some boyfriend! Esther's father had specifically instructed her to stay back on the platform until the dawn broke. Initially, he thought that she must have been kidnapped by someone. But the police let the family know that there was no evidence in the first place that Esther had even reached Mumbai, and therefore no action was possible. The family was advised that a complaint be registered in Vijayawada where she was 'last seen'. A harrowed Jonathan Prasad, therefore, filed a missing complaint in Vijayawada and then with a letter from the Vijayawada police came to the Kurla Railway police station. The latter finally registered a missing complaint on 8 January, three days after Esther had disappeared.

After realising that the police had evinced no serious interest even in their missing complaint, the family decided to keep alive the search for Esther on their own. Some good friends amongst mobile service providers helped them trace her last location, which was found to be in Bhandup (East). So they commenced a search in the area with the help of a few taxi and auto rickshaw drivers whom they had befriended. Finally one evening, they found Esther's corpse lying in the bushes and shrubs on a service road in Kanjurmarg. Her father recognised her from her clothes and her ring. They informed the police who then accompanied them to the spot. An offence had to now be registered at the local police station.

Amongst the earliest visitors that I met in my office after assuming charge as CP Mumbai, were the uncle and relatives of Esther Anuhya. The meeting was surcharged with pent-up emotions. Sadness and anguish hung in the air. I will never forget their sorrow and angst. The harrowing tale of how they had been knocking at different doors to get justice and how unsympathetically they had been treated. The anguish at having to explain that their daughter was not the 'type' to elope or was not 'responsible' for what had happened to her. The struggle to detect the possible location of the body and the shock at finding it in the condition they did. They were bitter about the Railway Police as well as the Mumbai police, and it was my job to undo the damage. The city police had probably not accorded enough interest as the initial complaint was registered with the Railway Police. For an aggrieved citizen, such distinction is meaningless, and understandably so. For them, khaki is one. I could not bring their child back. Getting to the culprits, I could and I thought I must, without wasting a single minute.

I promised the family that I would personally look into the case and immediately sent word to Joint CP (Crime) Sadanand Date, ACP Praful Bhosale and Inspector Vyankat Patil of the Ghatkopar unit of the Crime Branch. The officers met me that very evening and I took a review of the investigation. There was no breakthrough in sight. The media was already blaming the police for botching up the case and making the family run from pillar to post. The family had approached the then Union Home Minister Sushilkumar Shinde and the State Women's Commission. There were peaceful protests in Mumbai and Andhra Pradesh. Activists and NGOs were voicing their displeasure and people were disturbed. I made it known to my officers that the case had to be detected and that I wanted a daily briefing on the progress of the investigation. As a result, Bhosale and Patil began briefing me on a day-to-day basis.

The Kurla Terminus GRP had ferreted out some CCTV footage of Esther glued to her cell phone and walking out of the station with a suspicious looking man who was wheeling her trolley bag. They had linked him to one Chandrabhan Sanap, a railway porter-turned-cabbie, on the basis of photographs and suspicious movements. The suspect was even traced to a slum in Kanjurmarg, but he had given them an alibi corroborated by his mother. Satisfied by the story, they had allowed him to go.

I smelt a rat. 'Start a parallel investigation through the Crime Branch and check each and every detail, however small and innocuous it may seem,' I directed Vyankat Patil and Praful Bhosale. Both had earlier worked with me in the Crime Branch when I was DCP (Detection) and I enjoyed a good working relationship with them. They knew my style of working. Soon we formed a special squad, drawing officers of Crime Branch Units V, VI and VII, the Property Cell and the Anti-Robbery Cell. Praful Bhosale and

Vyankat Patil began a meticulous investigation which encompassed studying footage from thirty-three CCTV cameras, more than one lakh mobile call details from the Kurla area, questioning nearly 2,500 suspects who included taxi and auto rickshaw drivers, hawkers, co-passengers, coolies and railway workers!

Simultaneously, a hunt was launched for Sanap aka Chaukya and for Sahu, his close friend. Information gleaned from sources revealed that a man resembling the former lived in Kanjurmarg and had shifted to Nashik, but visited Kanjurmarg occasionally. He was involved in bag-lifting and thefts. He had been missing with his friend Sahu ever since Esther's body was discovered. Ultimately, with the help of informants and good old police legwork, the Crime Branch officers and men managed to track down both Sanap and Sahu. Sanap was picked up from Kanjurmarg on the night of 2 March. ACP Praful Bhosale had jubilantly conveyed the news of the catch to me. I asked them to bring him before me. He was and I interrogated him at length to ascertain for myself if we had the right man. He was indeed the culprit. And it was less than a fortnight since I began receiving daily reports that I could declare to the aggrieved family and the anxious city-dwellers that the transgressor was finally behind bars.

Chandrabhan Sudam Sanap was a suspended railway porter and a seasoned criminal with a record of bag-lifting and mobile theft cases which were registered at Gamdevi, Itarsi and Nashik Railway police stations. His interrogation revealed that on the day of the murder he had been drinking and came to the Kurla Terminus around 4 a.m. to commit a robbery or theft. While hunting for a target, he had spotted Esther entering the waiting room. But then in a short while, he saw her come out. She was probably not too happy with the waiting room and was toying with the idea of hailing a taxi to go home. The long train journey and the reassuring thought that Mumbai was a safe city must have perhaps lowered the unfortunate girl's defences! Sanap quickly seized the opportunity and asked her if she wanted a taxi. Esther looked apprehensive and Sanap immediately gave her his cell phone number, asking her to store it and give it to her relatives for her safety. His glib talk and the gesture of giving her the phone number convinced the poor girl to trust him.

The scoundrel then took charge of her bag and asked her to follow him. They came to the parking lot and it was then that he told her that instead of a taxi he had a bike, but he would take her safely to her destination. The bike was parked opposite the Railway Police Force office. This could have inspired some confidence in Esther and, probably, it was also too much of an inconvenience to walk back to the station to wait until daybreak. How her mind had worked is hard to guess, but she somehow fell prey to Sanap's ploy. She sat behind him and he brought her to the Western Express Highway where he stopped the bike on the pretext that it had run out of fuel. Then he dragged Esther to the shrubs and attempted to rape her. The feisty lass resisted fiercely. The rapscallion then banged her head against the ground, hit her with a stone and then strangled her with her stole. With her laptop and bag, he fled on his bike to the Sai Society slums in Kanjurmarg, only to realise that he had forgotten to take her cell phone. He then spoke to his friend Sahu. Together they returned to the scene of the crime, but could not find the phone. As the day was breaking, they were compelled to quit the search. After drawing petrol from the bike they set the body on fire and left the spot. The motive was to prevent the body from being identified. For some baffling and inexplicable reason, they did not take her gold ring. After Esther's body was found, Sahu fled to Jharkhand and Sanap to Nashik.

The Crime Branch sleuths used all their skills to dig deep into Sanap's world. We stumbled upon some very interesting evidence and found that after shifting to Nashik, Sanap had grown a beard, started wearing a *tika* on his forehead and had begun avoiding crowded places. In fact, after the murder, he had started suffering from insomnia and suddenly turned to religion. His mother was aware of the heinous crime he had committed. Soon after the crime, she had taken him to astrologers and priests to relieve his stress and to ward off the 'evil eye' from her darling son. Sanap had asked the soothsayers for 'remedies' for crimes committed against women. They had drawn his planetary charts and performed remedial rituals and rites of penance. All the fortune tellers and seers were questioned and their statements were recorded.

The charge sheet was filed and a special court headed by Judge Vrushali Joshi convicted and sentenced Sanap to death in October 2015. The testimony of the priests and astrologers proved to be an extremely important link in the circumstantial evidence collected against the accused. In March 2018, the Division Bench of the Bombay High Court confirmed the death sentence.

As regards the Shakti Mills case, on 20 March 2014, a Mumbai sessions court convicted all the five adult accused in both the cases. On 4 April 2014, the court awarded the death penalty to the three repeat offenders in the photojournalist's rape case. Of the other two accused, one was awarded life imprisonment, while the other turned approver in the case. Two minors, one in each case, were tried by the Juvenile Justice Board separately. They were convicted on 15 July 2015 and sentenced to three years (including time already spent in custody) which is the maximum punishment for a juvenile offender.

Esther's case made me extra sensitive to the precautionary security measures and systems that we needed to put in place to ensure women's safety. Like a family elder, I began going to sleep around 2 a.m., only after alerting the Control Room to confirm that Mobile vans had been sent to ensure that the Municipal Corporation Guards had locked all the subways. I also had all the police stations conduct a survey to identify the spots and pockets that could be held potentially risky or vulnerable for women, like dimly lit or deserted alleyways near tuition classes, secluded parks and beaches, approach roads to railway stations and public toilets.

Vineet Agarwal, a young and technologically savvy IPS officer was then in the DGP office. He helped the Mumbai police to tie-up with MTNL to start a dedicated helpline for women travelling alone in auto rickshaws or taxis. As soon as a woman passenger boarded a vehicle, she had to text message its number to the helpline. She would then receive an acknowledgement by a text message. The vehicle number would then get stored in our system. Therefore a woman passenger could travel in an auto rickshaw or a taxi with a sense of safety, knowing full well that the police was aware of the vehicle she was in. Correspondingly, this also acted as a deterrent for the driver. I decided that a crackdown on addicts was a must if we had to make the city safe for women. Sanap was under the influence of alcohol when he had assaulted Esther. The Shakti Mills case accused were drug addicts. So a concerted drive was started against drug peddling and a record number of cases were registered in the process.

If the earliest I could sleep was only past 2:30 a.m., 6 a.m. was the time for the 'All's well'. In any case, I would be up at 7 a.m., the time when the daily report of all the major crimes reported in the city the earlier day would land in my hands. So it would not be an exaggeration to say that as CP Mumbai, I slept only for three to four hours a day! It would take me an hour or sometimes even two, to go through the crime report. Since the time I was an Assistant Superintendent of Police, I had cultivated the habit of reading the daily crime reports meticulously and jotting my views down. I remember that in 1989 during my tenure as SP Raigad, the district police was inspected by the Special IGP, S.V. Bhave from the DGP's office who later became Commissioner of Police, Mumbai. During the inspection and subsequent discussion on the crime and detection of the district, Bhave had enquired of me the reason for the drop in crime and the increase in detection rate. I had then showed him how I used to go through the crime reports and my notes and remarks on the basis of which I made sure that the officers well understood that I was keeping tabs on crime trends at the police station level. Bhave was impressed and it was a pleasant surprise to have received a letter of appreciation land on my desk, particularly making a mention of it. It encouraged me to continue with this practice which proved very useful, as was shown in the case of the serial molester.

I think we were still in March 2014 when one day as I was going through the crime report, I felt I must go over what I had just read. I delved into it again and thought hard. Had I not read something similar just a few days back? The brain questioned the mind. Yes! Came the answer. Didn't the modus operandi sound familiar?

A little girl. A man approaches her. 'Where is your father?'

'At work,' she says.

'Come with me. I want to give you a number for him. You tell him that his friend so and so had come and given this number for you.'

The child agrees and follows him. He takes her to an under-construction building. There he threatens and molests or rapes her.

The first thing I did on entering my office that day was to ask my Reader, Inspector Sudhir Bhagwat Kalekar, and my Writer Head Constable Shashikant Janardan Naik, to compile for me a list, with brief facts, of all the cases of rape or molestation which had occurred in the city in the last two years where the victims were minor girls and the places of offence were secluded, under-construction buildings. Both the men pulled out all the stops and handed me a dossier containing two dozen cases. The cases were registered over a period of one and a half years in twelve police stations. In one case, the victim was the daughter of a police constable! Still we hadn't been able to identify and book the malefactor.

The very next day I called a meeting of the ACPs, Senior Inspectors, Inspectors (Crime), Detection Officers, Zonal DCPs and Additional CPs of the twelve police stations. I also invited the Joint CP (Law and Order), Joint CP (Crime) and the ACPs and Senior Inspectors of the Crime Branch units covering these police stations. I explained to the officers present how the observant perusal of the daily crime report had led me to locate twenty-four cases of rape and molestation of minors in their jurisdictions. 'I want you to revisit the crimes. Identify one lady Sub Inspector per police station to visit the victim and elicit from her the correct details of how the culprit had committed the offence and the description of the accused. Then commission a sketch artist to go to the girl's residence and prepare a sketch of the accused as per the description given. Remember, the sketch artists should be different. One sketch artist per victim. Also, we must have different lady officers. They must handle the victims with kid gloves and sensitivity. The girls must feel secure and confident to share the details, so the choice of the lady officers is of utmost importance. And we will meet after one week when we shall compare and match the descriptions and the sketches. I will personally see the descriptions and the sketches,' I said. The officers got involved and painstakingly and zealously put their shoulders to the wheel.

All of us met again as planned and it was a 'lo and behold!' moment. The descriptions were the same, the sketches as if of the same man, and the modus operandi was also the same!

'Abba hain kya?' (Is your daddy home?)

'Mere saath uss building ke pas chalo. Mobile number deta hoon. Woh Papa ko dena aur bolna Bambai se Irfan Bhai aye thhey,' (Come with me to that building. I will give you a mobile number. Give it to Papa and tell him that Brother Irfan had come from Bombay). (The people residing in the Mumbai suburbs often call the southern part of the city 'Bombay' or 'Mumbai'.) The poor child would trust him and follow him. After all, he was Dad's

friend, asking her to deliver an important message and note to her father! Once inside the building, he would threaten her with a knife and violate her sexually.

The descriptions were also identical:

Vay: tees tey pastees
Rangaane: kala-sawla
Dokyaavar bharpoor kes
Pote pudhe alele
Dava dola kharaab ani pandhara
Tondala daru and ammli padaarth sevanacha vaas

(Age: thirty to thirty-five
Complexion: dark
Lots of hair on the head
Stomach: protruding
Left eye damaged, white.
Mouth reeking of alcohol and narcotic substances)

Chhering Dorje, the DCP of Zone-IX, and Milind Bharambe, Additional CP (West Region) were both young, dynamic officers, eager to detect crimes. Since a majority of these offences were from the western suburbs, I entrusted them with the responsibility of expediting the investigations. They circulated the sketches to all the police stations and got cracking. The revolting thought of this horrible man continuing to molest unsuspecting little girls under our very noses kept haunting me. Needless to say, I pestered Bharambe and Dorje every day for feedback, and as I had hoped, their efforts hit the bullseye. We found crucial and definitive CCTV footage from Sion, Amboli and Santacruz. The sexual predator was wearing a pair of white chappals and had a distinct gait. Inspectors Ajay Kshirsagar and Milind Desai and staff combed the city with his pictures and soon an informant came forward with the input that the offender lived in Juhu

Galli. An officer from Malad police station recalled that he had arrested such a man before and remembered that it was in a mobile theft case in D.N. Nagar. The team fine-tooth-combed the police stations' records and ferreted out the record of his earlier offence. Soon the identity of the transgressor emerged: mobile thief Ayaz Mohammad Ali Ansari aka Firoz 'Kana'.

'Kana' is a disparaging albeit a Mumbai word (common to Hindi, Marathi and even Gujarati) for a one-eyed or cross-eyed person. Firoz Kana was a thirty-two-year-old resident of the slum Ekta Nagar which was on Wireless Road near Juhu Galli in Andheri (West). The officers located his brother and mother who had not heard from him for many days. The informants and zero numbers were activated immediately. With the help of a tip-off, Kshirsagar, Desai and staff kept a vigil near the Sacred Heart School on S.V. Road in Khar (West). After a sustained watch of two days, Firoz Kana arrived on the scene, was pointed out by an informant and arrested on 16 April 2014. He straight away confessed to fourteen cases which he could remember offhand! They were registered in Juhu, Versova, Goregaon, Nirmal Nagar, Vakola, Santacruz, Amboli, Andheri and Sion. In some jurisdictions, he had committed even more than one such offence!

For me, the joy of getting our hands on Firoz Kana was not a grain less than arresting extortionists, gangsters or terrorists. I immediately rushed to the West Region office and interrogated him at length myself. I wanted to be free from doubt that we had not made a mistake. We had not. The man matched the description and the sketches. He had damaged his eye as a young boy while playing with his friends in a wood workshop near a Juhu slum. A plywood piece had pierced the eye and he had to be treated at the nearby Cooper Municipal Hospital. He was into multiple drug abuse – cannabis, brown sugar, cocaine etc. In the course of time, he had turned into a paedophile. He was once even beaten up by his neighbour for a similar incident.

The scoundrel was extremely crafty. He used to steal four-five mobile phones every day, but took care not to use any of them so as to avoid detection. Tracing him was difficult because he did not use mobile phones. He contacted his friends and family from public call booths. He slept on streets and in places of worship, which is common amongst drug abusers. He had been previously convicted in a rape case and was out on bail in old cases registered in D.N. Nagar and Juhu. After the latest offence, he had left Mumbai and stayed at the Kamarali Darvesh Dargah near Khed Shivapur, Pune. After running out of money, he had returned to Mumbai and stolen a mobile phone. The informant alerted the police as he began trying to sell it, and that is how Kshirsagar and team had arrested him.

Firoz Kana confessed to a whopping twenty-four offences of molestation and rape! In addition, there were already eighteen offences registered against him – ten cases of molestations, two rapes, five mobile thefts, and one robbery. Some were committed on the outskirts of Mumbai in Thane and Kalyan. And despite all this, he also had a girlfriend!

To the Muslim victims, Firoz Kana would introduce himself as Irfan Bhai and to the Hindu girls as Rakesh. By a strange coincidence, in the last offence which had activated my grey cells, he had had the cheek to call himself Rakesh and this time, the forces of retribution decided that enough was enough. They set about to ensure that his vile deeds leapt into the eye of a certain real Rakesh – a pucca policewala – who would ensure that the wolf in the sheepskin was hunted down and locked away.

Several trials were and are being conducted against Firoz Kana for molestation and rape charges under the Protection of Children from Sexual Offences (POCSO) Act. In some, he has been awarded rigorous imprisonments ranging from seven to ten years. In one case, in August 2015, a court sentenced him to life imprisonment till death and in another, the court awarded him the same sentence in August 2018. The media interviews, though, indicated that the police, the prosecutors and the families of the victims had been hoping for a death sentence for the serious offences he had committed.

* * *

The dates for the 2014 General Elections were declared. They were to be held in nine phases from 7 April to 12 May 2014. The elections in Mumbai were to be held on 24 April. My 'well-wishers' got into an active mode and a whisper campaign had already begun that since I was from Mumbai city, I should be transferred out. The Maharashtra Election Commission raised questions regarding my appointment – why was I not posted outside Mumbai even after completing three years in the city; why was I made the city police chief even though I was a Mumbai resident? The State Government then sought permission from the Central Election Commission (CEC) which replied on 21 March and said that it had no objection to my appointment. Significantly enough, none of the Opposition parties wanted me transferred.

The elaborate security arrangements for elections in the sprawling and overpopulated Mumbai is always a challenge for the police. The confidence reposed in me by all the political parties was precious and I was happy that I could do justice to it. All of us worked extremely hard to ensure that the polls went off smoothly with impartial and neutral handling. It was a toughly fought election, but there were no allegations by any political party against the police machinery despite the close run. The results declared on 16 May 2014 led to the formation of the Sixteenth Lok Sabha in which the BJP came to power with a thumping majority and Narendra Modi became the Prime Minister of India. The amazing system and orderliness with which the elections achieved the peaceful transition of power, once again spoke volumes about the manner in which India had adapted to constitutional democracy which cannot happen in the absence of a basic cultural ethos of tolerance and accommodation.

Within five months, on 15 October 2014, we had elections for the Maharashtra State Legislative Assembly. Yet again the entire police machinery toiled extremely hard and the elections went off smoothly. The results were announced on 19 October and the BJP came out as winners. They were now the largest party in the Assembly. The young and dynamic Devendra Fadnavis was appointed as the Chief Minister of Maharashtra on 31 October 2014. Within a fortnight of his assuming office, I called on him to share a sincere thought. 'Sir, I have a lot of "well-wishers" in this Force who would have come and briefed you that I belong to this party or that. Sir, let me assure you that I am loyal only to my uniform and the department. But as any cricket captain would like a team of his own choice, you too might want a CP of your choice. In that case, you have to only tell me that you want a change, and I will give an application for transfer.' I said to him. Fadnavis was very magnanimous. He smiled and said, 'I have followed your career right through. I need a good officer to steer the police administration and so I need you. Please concentrate on your work and have no doubts.' I found his words very reassuring. I came out of his cabin feeling invigorated and inspired by the youthful energy he exuded. It seemed to pervade the corridors of power. I felt very hopeful for the future of the state.

On 29 September 2014, around 2:30 p.m., I was in for a surprise when a mail arrived in the inbox of my official email address. 'Frustrated of life, finishing it.' That's all said the mail and it was from one Bhushan Kharade (name changed to protect identity), who was a perfect stranger to me. I immediately called Joint CP (Crime), Sadanand Date, and asked him to make certain that the Cyber Crime Investigation Cell lost no time to get to the sender who could seriously be contemplating suicide or even committing it that very moment! Date and the Cyber Cell did a remarkable job. The email did not have any address or phone number and replying to it could have been risky, felt the Cyber Cell officers led by Senior Inspector Mukund Pawar. With the help of DCP Dhananjay Kulkarni, they contacted the Google office in the US and succeeded in convincing them of the seriousness of the situation to immediately obtain the IP address of the internet connection. It was registered under a woman's name in the eastern suburb of Bhandup. The address was traced. The officers on reaching the house, were received by the mother of the sender who had luckily not yet acted on his intentions. He was in the washroom and they informed her the reason for their visit. Then a counselling session followed and the twenty-six-year-old confided in the officers that he was depressed because his three-year-old relationship with his girlfriend had ended and he had also lost his job. He had written the mail to me so that his parents would not be questioned by the police. He did not want his parents to be bothered after his suicide! As if his suicide would not have bothered them enough! In any case, we had succeeded in saving a young life and that was a reward in itself.

The best case scenario for a CP's tenure is to be able to complete his term without any communal flare-ups and terrorist attacks. Both are like the proverbial 'Sword of Damocles' hanging over his head! If a CP can achieve a tenure sans a communal riot, it is a feather in his cap. It builds the image of the Force and is regarded not just as an achievement, but also as a blessing. It is the Holy Grail of policing amidst this melting pot of varied cultures, religions and beliefs. All of us know that communal trouble should be nipped in the bud, with a strong and firm hand. The sledgehammer policy! At the same time, we know very well how such a firm hand can also be viewed as excessive, insensitive and uncalled for, and how it is dissected in lengthy post-mortems to haul us over the coals. Tactical restraint can be viewed as protecting and encouraging aggressive mobs. Shooting them down, as identifying with the other community. So when you are the CP of Mumbai, every religious procession and every festival, when the Mumbaikars decide to worship their numerous gods and saints and let their hair down, is the time when their CP bites his nails and waits for the last reveller in the procession and the pandal to be safely home.

Luckily, a good part of the festival season had passed off uneventfully. 22 October 2014 was the second day of Diwali and I was at the Birla Matushree Auditorium in Marine Lines in the evening for a welfare function organised for police constables. Suddenly, we received information that there was communal trouble at Malad which is in the north of the city. I immediately left the function and rushed to Malad. The Shiv Sena had already started a rasta roko (road obstruction) agitation. Their grievance was against the local police, who according to them had not paid heed to several complaints lodged by the residents of a locality against a group of Muslim riff-raff, all from the same family. These criminals were now reported to have murdered a young Shiv Sena leader, Ramesh Jadhav, who was the Gat Pramukh (Group Leader) of the local party unit. Jadhav had intervened to save a neighbouring family from being attacked by the four men, one of whom was a minor who had already exhibited violent tendencies in an earlier incident in his school. Irked by Jadhav's intervention, the hoodlums had forced entry into Jadhav's house, stabbed him, and run away. Jadhav was survived by his wife, a two-year-old daughter and his mother. The wife was in a state of shock. The Jadhavs were old and respectable residents of the locality and the local residents were furious about what had befallen the family. The Shiv Sena workers had erupted in protest and hundreds of party workers had gathered outside the Dindoshi police station late in the night. Some smashed windshields of cars and of trucks parked nearby. They also blockaded the Western Express Highway.

I reached the spot and met the angry residents and workers. Tempers were running high and the general mood was unequivocally anti-khaki. I gave a patient hearing to their grievances and assured them of prompt redressal. I promised them justice and also personal supervision in the investigation and arrests. This had the desired impact and the tempers simmered down. Thus, I managed to calm the frayed nerves of the agitating crowd and as a result of which, the road blockade on the highway was lifted. I left Malad only at 6 a.m. the next day, after reviewing the police arrangements for the funeral.

The shops in the vicinity remained closed as hundreds of mourners and political leaders attended the funeral. As a mark of respect for the deceased, there were no Diwali celebrations in the area. The local police were galvanised into action and all the five accused were arrested from Mira Road in the early hours of the next day, restoring the confidence of the agitated residents to a considerable extent.

By the end of Christmas and New Year, the entire force had worked overtime, as usual, foregoing leave, rest and leisure for days together, and without a thought to their health, fitness and wellbeing. We were now on 4 January 2015, which was Eid-e-Milad – Prophet Muhammad's birth anniversary. On this day, processions are taken out in different areas of the city. All the divisions were alert and the day was passing peacefully. I was invited as Chief Guest to a function in Mulund and Preeti had accompanied me. There was a prize distribution ceremony and also the usual speeches. It ended at 9 p.m. and we sat in the car to return home. Suddenly Preeti had a bright idea. 'Why don't you take me out for dinner?' she asked. 'Out for dinner?' I said as if it was something totally outlandish. We were not used to such deviations. 'Why not?' she retorted and I wondered. 'Why not!' I said. There was no earthly reason why not! 'Come, let's go!' I said. It was amusing to watch her searching excitedly for a SoBo eatery on her phone, like a teenager, and dialling up to book a table for two.

We were on the Eastern Express Highway when suddenly on the wireless set in the car I heard the Control Room ask a Mobile van, 'What is the situation there?' The tone itself expressed trouble. I immediately intervened and enquired as to what had happened. There was tension in the Lalbaug area – sparked off by a rashly driven motorbike which had brushed against a woman! The traffic policeman had stopped the biker who, instead of accepting his mistake, had had the temerity to start arguing. The angry locals had roughed up the audacious biker. Then a mob had attacked a group of bikers who were coming from the wrong side of the road near Bharat Mata Cinema junction. This was pure unadulterated trouble, for the bikers were part of the Eid-e-Milad procession!

As soon as I got the details, I knew that the police had their task cut out for them. The situation needed immediate and deft handling. I alerted the higher echelons of the Force and initiated measures to ensure police presence on the streets. The massive Eid-e-Milad procession was still winding its way into south Mumbai. A little rumour-mongering, and the whole assemblage in that procession was prone to get incited. I asked the driver to rush to Lalbaug. With sirens blaring, the convoy came to the Takia Masjid in double quick time. I was totally oblivious to Preeti's presence in the car. My entire concentration was on mobilising manpower resources and ensuring the presence of officers and constabulary at sensitive locations. The atmosphere was tense. Traffic was blocked on both sides and a motorcycle lay burning in the middle of the road. The police had positioned themselves on the central median of the road, with a large Muslim crowd on the Takia Masjid side and Hindus on the opposite side. I had no doubts whatsoever that if a head-on confrontation began, riots would spread all over the city like a bushfire. The situation was touch-and-go!

I jumped out of the vehicle after pulling out a cane and crossed the road. Seeing me stride towards the mobs, the officers and men were relieved and emboldened. I was not in my uniform, but in a suit, aptly chosen for the prize distribution ceremony. I must have looked quite odd, dressed in a suit and walking with the lathi in my hand, accompanied by guards armed with automatic weapons.

I first went to the Hindu crowd and requested them to leave. They agreed to do so, but pointed at the Muslim crowd. 'Ask them to leave first,' they said. All right, I will, I said. Then I went to the Muslim throng. 'Please disperse, go home,' I told them. They said they were scared that the Hindus would attack them. 'Our children have to return home. They will be attacked,' they said. I explained to them that they had to first disperse. I told them that I was present at the spot to ensure that no untoward incident occurred and their children and near and dear ones had safe passage. I succeeded in pushing them back into their buildings and deployed staff to keep them inside. Then I went back to the Hindus and succeeded in pushing them back into their buildings and deploying manpower there. Both the crowds were jumpy and insecure and were bereft of any leaders who could guide them. Thankfully, both heeded my advice. Then I called the Traffic Division and made them tow away the burning motorcycle which was adding to the fears.

We had to ensure that the traffic moved smoothly so that people did not get stranded and reached their homes speedily. It must have taken me close to an hour to achieve this. As expected, rumours had started circulating amongst the Eid procession that Muslims were being attacked in Mumbai. As I was dealing with all this, it suddenly dawned on me that I had left my wife sitting in the car, virtually at Ground Zero! So I rushed back to the car and saw a teary-eyed Preeti sitting in a state of shock with a tensed driver standing outside! I had an unmarked bulletproof car without a beacon and a driver in plain clothes – which was part of my Z category security. My wireless operator and guards had naturally followed me, as was their duty. *'Inko ghar le jao,'*

(Take her home) I told the driver. 'Take care,' said Preeti and left. There was nothing more to say. The poor woman had only wished for a quiet dinner with her spouse, like an ordinary couple. As usual, it was not to be. She never made an issue out of such upsets in the past, but that day I died a thousand deaths as the car disappeared down the road. But then duty always came first. In effect, it invariably meant that you took your wife for granted! I knew she would skip dinner and wait anxiously for the trouble to clear.

The location where the trouble had erupted was an extremely sensitive area. I began patrolling up and down, on foot, like a flag march. I talked to the local residents and to the men on the bandobast to keep them alert and their morale high. I called the other senior officers like the Zonal DCP, Ashok Dudhe, and R.D. Shinde, Additional CP (Central Region). The residents were anxious and antsy. At such times, the mounting edginess provides grist to the rumour mills and precipitates more violence. A little after midnight, as I was patrolling, I noticed someone waving at me from a second-floor window. I took him to be just an enthusiastic citizen, but then he waved again and I felt that he wanted to convey something. So I called my Personal Security Officer, Vijay Kandhalgaonkar and asked him to quietly slip up to the house and ascertain what the man wanted. The officer followed my instructions and reported that the man was a Hindu. His family had provided shelter to a Muslim family of four. The latter had gotten off a bus when a mob had stopped it. We soon provided an armed escort to the shaken Muslim family and saw them safely to their home in Dongri.

The Communal Riot Scheme was in place. Police in adequate strength had been deployed at all the sensitive points of the city. Soon we learnt that a mob had gathered near Worli Koliwada (a fishermen's colony) and the situation was on the brink of escalation. I immediately rushed there. DCP Jaykumar, a very sincere, dependable and competent officer, was already on the spot as was R.D. Shinde. Again a round of talks with the mob and their leaders ensued. After much parleys, interspersed with subtle threats of stern legal action tempered with cajoling, we succeeded in dispersing the crowd. Then I went to good old Mahim to check the situation there. DCP Mahesh Patil, yet another very energetic and conscientious officer, was monitoring the situation in that location. After briefing him, I went to Dharavi and checked on the security arrangements there. These were all communally sensitive locations and needed close monitoring. I returned to Lalbaug and was there till seven in the morning. We heaved a sigh of relief as the Eid-e-Milad procession ended peacefully and the returning crowds reached their homes safely.

I received calls from leaders of various political parties. They were all worried that communal violence could escalate and spread all over the city and the state. I assured all of them that I was personally monitoring the situation, and would not allow it to get out of hand on my beat! Rumour-mongering was rife and several mendacious messages were being circulated to fan communal passions. We learned that on the very day, a fourteen-year-old Muslim boy had met with an accident and succumbed to his injuries at J.J. Hospital. Some mischief-mongers had clicked a picture of the boy and circulated it on WhatsApp to project that he had been beaten up by the other community. There were also other rabble-rousing messages inviting the members of the community to rise and react. Another picture of a damaged bike was being circulated as a motorcycle belonging to a Hindu damaged by a mob in Manish Market, a predominantly Muslim locality. Our enquiries revealed that the picture was of a bike damaged in an incident in Karnataka a couple of months ago. Maintaining peace in cyberspace was as important as maintaining peace on the ground, and the Mumbai police had to ensure that several antidotal messages were circulated to counter and quell such deadly rumours.

Many leaders, across the political spectrum, had called me to thank me for the prompt action and had specifically appreciated my efforts in the endeavour. There was an overall acknowledgement that our quick response had saved the day. Later, when I was DG (Home Guards), I'd received an envelope from the Home Department marked, *'Aavashyak Kaarwaai Karitaa'* – For Necessary Action. I opened it anxiously. Inside was a letter from an organisation called the Public Concern for Governance Trust which was formed by former Chief Secretary B.G. Deshmukh and retired Mumbai CP, Julio Ribeiro. Besides other eminent citizens from various walks of life, it also comprised ex-CPs Satish Sahney and Ronnie Mendonca. They organised initiatives like mohalla (neighbourhood) committees to promote communal harmony in Mumbai. The letter of appreciation signed by Julio Ribeiro was addressed to me and said that it was due to my personal intervention that the tension had not escalated that day. The paper pushers in the Home Department must not have even read it. Or they would not have forwarded it to me for 'necessary action' and that too after nearly a year! With the result that I could not respond to the kind and appreciative gesture of my seniors. They must have surely wondered at this gross indifference on my part.

* * *

On 25 March 2015, the Supreme Court passed an order which had far-reaching implications for the Mumbai police. It was the dismissal of the Review Petition filed by Yakub Memon, a key conspirator and accused in the serial bomb blasts of 1993. Memon had sought review of the order confirming the death sentence awarded to him.

He had been arrested by the CBI from New Delhi Railway Station in April 1994, although Yakub had claimed that he had been arrested from Kathmandu, Nepal. The trial court delivered the verdict in September 2006 and sentenced several accused under the Terrorists And Disruptive Activities (Prevention) Act (TADA). Yakub Memon was awarded capital punishment. Later he was shifted to the Nagpur Central Jail. The convicted accused had challenged the verdict in the Supreme Court, the Court of Appeal under TADA. The CBI filed appropriate proceedings for confirmation of the sentences as also appeals against acquittals. On 21 March 2013, the Supreme Court dismissed Yakub's appeal and confirmed the death sentence, relying upon and upholding several facts that had emerged from the evidence which proved that Yakub was a close deputy of his brother Tiger Memon and was actively involved in hatching as well as executing the conspiracy: officiating in the absence of Tiger, taking commands from Tiger and passing them down to the terror operatives, handling the transfer of funds through hawala, acquiring tickets for the travel for terror training.

Yakub had filed the Review Petition and sought an oral hearing, but in July 2013 the Supreme Court had rejected it and dismissed the petition by circulation. The Supreme Court was dealing with the issue of the need to grant oral hearings of review petitions in matters of the death sentence and Yakub too had challenged the dismissal of his review petition. In September 2014, the Supreme Court ordered open court hearings of review petitions involving the death sentence. Yakub Memon's review petition now qualified for 'open hearing'. It was heard and argued in the open court in March 2015 and dismissed on 9 April 2015. On 30 April, a 'Death Warrant' was issued by the Maharashtra government and stated that Yakub Memon would be executed in Nagpur on 30 July 2015.

All along, the state government and the Mumbai police had been closely keeping a track of and following the legal battle in which several renowned lawyers had accepted Yakub's brief and were making the death sentence a contentious issue. In the media, several journalists and activists were agitating for leniency for Yakub. Some even tried to present it as a case of discrimination and unfairness. With such controversies woven around the sentence, it was bound to snowball into a highly sensitive issue for the Muslims and some sections of the community were already voicing discontent. The execution of the death sentence was entirely the responsibility of the state government and its police, and within the police, the Mumbai police was obviously going to play a pivotal role. The convict on death row and his family were residents of Mumbai and the abhorrent transgressions which the malefactors had committed were far from forgotten by Mumbai.

I had already started working on the elaborate security arrangements for the funeral, working on different scenarios and possibilities with my officers. We could not leave anything to chance.

In the meanwhile, Yakub Memon filed several petitions like curative and mercy petitions to stall the death sentence. On 29 July 2015, a three-judge bench of the Supreme Court dismissed a writ petition filed by Yakub Memon and he then filed a fresh mercy petition with the President of India. The President, as per the practice, forwarded it to the Prime Minister who, upon deliberations, advised the President to reject it. Around midnight, Yakub Memon's lawyers approached the Chief Justice of India at his residence with a fresh mercy petition and sought a stay on the execution. The Registrar was called to the CJI's residence and the CJI agreed to grant an immediate hearing by the same Bench which had rejected the earlier petition the previous day. The Attorney General was also called to represent the Union Government. The petition was heard by the Bench at 3 a.m. and rejected after arguments that lasted for an hour and a half. Which meant that the execution would take place in Nagpur as planned.

I was ready with all my arrangements. Chief Minister Devendra Fadnavis also discussed the matter with me and I assured him that the Mumbai police would exercise the utmost caution and prudence, and be in battle preparedness to meet any eventuality. Just a day earlier I had received a call from Ajit Doval, the National Security

Advisor (NSA). He informed me that he had Intelligence inputs that the ISI through Dawood Ibrahim and the Muslim underworld was planning to make capital out of the hanging and create law and order issues to cause communal flare-ups. He instructed me to plan out the police arrangements accordingly. I assured him that we had factored in the possibility and would be alert and vigilant. As a matter of abundant precaution, Ajit Doval informed me that he would be camping in Mumbai on the day of the funeral. He did come down as planned, but I could not meet him as I was on the streets to supervise and monitor the bandobast.

I had planned a very elaborate and detailed security drill, taking care of even the minutest detail. Each and every lane of Mahim, the Ground Zero of the funeral proceedings, was manned by men in khakhi. Officers and men were deputed in such a manner that there was visible police presence felt, and for this we had requisitioned manpower from the State Reserve Police Force (SRPF) and the Rapid Action Force (RAF) of the CRPF.

The scene in Nagpur was handled by my batchmate, Meeran Borwankar, ADG (Prisons). Meeran was my squadmate in the Police Academy. We got along famously, despite the tiny bit of healthy competition that is the hallmark of all competitive courses like the IPS. Meeran was also close to Preeti and my sister, Poonam. We have followed each other's careers very closely and been of great support during trying times. Meeran was camping in Nagpur and we were in constant touch, updating each other vis-à-vis the rapidly evolving situation. After the Supreme Court decision, Meeran promptly spoke to me and said that post the hanging, they would conduct the post-mortem at the earliest and the body would be sent post noon to Mumbai. I, thus, got to know the schedule, and we planned the arrangements accordingly.

Intelligence sources informed us that messages were being sent out to various parts of Maharashtra, asking people to attend the funeral in large numbers as if a martyr was going to be buried. I had been camping in my office for three days prior to the hanging. The funeral prayers were supposed to be held at the Memon's residence in Mahim, but the burial was to be at the Bada Kabrastan in Charni Road. There was tension all over the city and we had identified the likely areas which could erupt in flare-ups. A meeting of all the DCPs, ACPs and Senior Inspectors was conducted and we discussed all possibilities. The local DCP was Mahesh Patil, a tough officer who knew the Mahim area well. The Additional Commissioner was R.D. Shinde, another good officer, and together they chalked out the arrangements under my watchful eye. I deputed DCP Chhering Dorje and Additional CP (West Region) Milind Bharambe to the airport to ensure that no crowds gathered there to create commotion and the body was brought to Mahim without delay. We had also carried out preventive arrests of around 750 bad characters and the social media was being monitored continuously. The officers at the police stations were also speaking to all the communities, explaining to them how peace must be maintained and the consequences if they failed to exercise restraint.

In the early hours of the morning of 30 July, I went to Mahim and met the members of the Memon family. For me personally, this was a momentous event. The clock was turning a full circle from the defining moment in Al Husseini building that night, twenty-two years ago, when my elbow had accidentally touched the key kept on the refrigerator. The key of the explosive-laden scooter had opened career avenues for a young DCP to ultimately make him the Commissioner and see the sequence through to its end – the burial of the first death row accused after his execution.

'Sir, aapne hee yeh sab bhaanda phoda tha. Waise bhi aapke upar in log ka khunnas hai. Kya aapko jana chahiye udhar? Kuchh problem hua toh?' Some junior officers asked me anxiously. (Sir, you were the one who had exposed this conspiracy. As it is, these people are antagonistic towards you. Do you *have* to go there? What if some problem arises?)

'Maine jo kiya woh mera duty thaa. Aaj bhi jo kar rahaa hoon, woh mera duty hai. Isski poori zimmedari meri hai. Agar aap logon ke upar patthar girenge toh main aapke saath patthar jheloonga.' I said to them. (Whatever I did, was my duty to do. Whatever I am doing today is also my duty. I bear its complete responsibility. If stones are going to be hurled at you, I will stand in line with you and face them.)

The mood in the Memon family was that of anger. I nevertheless made it clear to the men that if they created a problem, they will have a problem, as we were in no mood to brook any nonsense. 'It is in your interest to cooperate because we are ready to cooperate. But remember that we are fully ready to face mischief of any kind,' I told them. They listened to me intently and quietly and then said, 'Tell us what you expect of us?' I said there should be no sloganeering, no *bhaashanbazi* (speech-mongering), no procession, no rabble-rousing. The body would not be allowed to be photographed. And for anything else, you tell me what you need, the police are here to assist, I said. They appreciated what I said and agreed to cooperate. Then I walked the whole Mahim area on foot like a flag march. In policing, this plays a very important role, both for the populace and for your own young officers and men. It makes the staff alert. By ten in the morning, I had done foot patrol in each lane, asking the pickets if they knew the importance of the spot and what was expected of them. Some TV channels of their own volition declared that they would not telecast the funeral. For the others who were less inclined to do so, the DCP (Operations), Sanjay Barkund, issued a gag order to prevent them from airing a live telecast of the funeral.

Then I went to the airport and checked the arrangements there. The flight carrying the body was to arrive around one pm. Half an hour before it landed, I returned to Mahim. A huge crowd – eight to ten thousand strong – had assembled to receive the body on Veer Savarkar Marg. They had come from various areas like

Kurla, Malvani, Oshiwara, Mulund, Bhandup, Jogeshwari, Deonar and Dongri from within the city, and also from different parts of Maharashtra. The body arrived in an ambulance and was guided by volunteers to make its way to a relative's house in Bismillah Manzil. I was standing with my officers and men on the road leading from the Maqdoom Shah Baba Dargah to the Mahim police station. The streets were overflowing and all the balconies and windows were crammed with people.

As a hearse waited for the body to be carried to Bada Kabrastan on Charni Road in south Mumbai, a delegation of volunteers approached me. They said that they wanted to read the namaaz-e-janaza on the road, as the mourners had desired it. I discussed it with my officers. They expressed apprehension, and rightly so, that if during the prayers any inciteful words were uttered, people could get emotional and the situation could spiral out of control. I thought about their advise, and looked at the crowd. This was a classic dilemma that security forces often face when dealing with delicate situations in controlling emotionally-charged crowds. If I did not allow the prayer here, the crowds could feel hurt and that is what the troublemakers would love to see happen. Then an attempt to conduct the prayers forcibly would be made which would have led to a confrontation which could have spiralled into bloodshed to the delight of our adversaries. The call was entirely mine to take and there was not much time to deliberate and dissertate. As a leader, one needed to make a split-second decision that would impact not only Mumbai city but in the eventuality of something going horribly wrong, the country at large. Experience had taught me that you cannot police a crowd if you alienate them. You have to work with the assemblage, establish a dialogue so that in effect they work with you to control themselves. This is a tall order, but deliverable if your sincerity and determination is conveyed forcefully.

I said to the delegation that I would allow them to conduct the prayers there provided they were prepared to take responsibility that there would be no photography, no inflammatory speeches and no slogans. 'Sir, will you give us permission to make appropriate announcements to ensure that this is followed?' They asked me. 'Yes I will,' I agreed. 'Sir, we will need megaphones,' they said. So we allowed the use of megaphones and the volunteers made announcements, explaining the conditions and asking the crowds to cooperate with the police. They also formed a task force of volunteers comprising around fifty men and it was they who controlled the crowd. Even then, it was a nerve-racking and high-strung experience. I had assured my superiors that nothing would go wrong and it was me who had given the permission for the namaaz-e-janaza on the road! Have I done right? My subordinates had warned me but I had taken this decision with my eyes open. Fortunately for me, the mourners took the permission in the right spirit. They saw it as an indication that the police were considerate, had no animus and wanted only peace. The volunteers made sure that nothing went wrong, although in the edgy and tension-filled hour and a half, the crowds kept swelling. I stood there right in front, inspiring my men on the spot that I was there to take responsibility and not make them face it alone. The general public also realised that their Commissioner was there to protect them and would not allow the situation to get out of hand.

Now the question was, which route should the cortege be allowed to take to Charni Road? We had anticipated that the ambulance or hearse would be followed by a phalanx of motorcycles. So we had already banned the entry of motorcycles in the area at points which were at a good distance from the Memons' residence. We also did not want a procession to be formed which would wind its way to Charni Road through numerous sensitive locations which dotted the route. The police was going to pilot the hearse and it was for us to decide the route. After the prayers ended, instead of following the regular route, we piloted the hearse via the Bandra-Worli Sea Link to Haji Ali, and from there to Charni Road. This plan had not been announced earlier. So the crowds were taken totally by surprise and could not follow the hearse.

Once I was sure that the crowd in Mahim had dispersed peacefully, my convoy drove to Bada Kabrastan in Charni Road at top speed. A huge crowd had assembled there as well, and our officers and men were deployed just as meticulously as at the airport and at Mahim. Again I walked the lanes to talk to the pickets and remained there until the crowds dispersed. Alerts were also sent to ensure that no trouble erupted when the crowds returned home after the funeral. Till ten at night, we were all on very high alert. The police security arrangement was in place for forty-eight hours after the funeral to prevent any untoward incidents.

The manner in which the Mumbai police had handled the tense situation received a lot of appreciation from various quarters, but my 'well-wishers' in the Force did what they were habituated to do. Some began feeding the powers-that-be that there was no need for the CP to have been personally present for the bandobast. Some hinted that I had taken such active interest in the arrangements only to get publicity. It was like the famous Aesop's fable of the man, the boy and their donkey. The moral of the story is all that one needs to keep in mind. Please all, and you will please none. It is better to be true to your own conscience and do exactly what you feel is right. A deep sense of responsibility and obligatoriness had propelled me to check each and every detail not just on the design board, but also on the sites. That I had to personally check the strength of the foundation, the pillars and the beams. If it meant being in the streets with my officers and men, so be it. I felt I must put all my might in the effort to ensure that my city was not thrust into the abyss of communal riots once again. I did not want the enemies of the nation to succeed and cause a further rift and tear into the social fabric of the community.

But before Yakub Memon's funeral, I was sucked into the vortex of a controversy which surrounded the businessman, Lalit

Modi, the founder and first Chairman and Commissioner of the Indian Premier League (IPL) for three years until 2010. Lalit Modi had served on important cricket bodies, as the Chairman of the Champions League, Vice President of the Board of Control for Cricket in India (BCCI), Vice President of the Punjab Cricket Association and President of the Rajasthan Cricket Association. After IPL 2010, there were allegations of misconduct and irregularities against him. A BCCI committee had found him guilty and he was banned for life in 2013. He had denied the allegations and said that he was a victim of political rivalries. The Enforcement Directorate (ED) had launched an investigation against Lalit Modi, but before that, he had moved to London.

It so happened that I was in London from 12 to 18 July 2014, deputed to attend a conference on 'Securing Asia and Africa 2014'. Preeti had accompanied me. At the Conference, a foreigner had introduced himself to me as Lalit Modi's advocate and requested for an appointment with his client. He said that Lalit Modi and his family were facing grave threats from Dawood Ibrahim and his gangsters and that he was desperate to meet me. I said that there was nothing I could do in London! The advocate then said that Lalit Modi had acquainted him with the facts as to how I had helped him in the past when he was threatened by the underworld.

Now indeed there had been two instances when I had saved Lalit Modi's life. It had happened when I was in charge of the Crime Branch. The first time was sometime in April 2009. One day, a khabri had informed me that some shooters were waiting below Lalit Modi's office in Nirlon House at Worli. Their plan was to avail an opportune moment and go upstairs and shoot Lalit Modi. I rushed a team to the spot, but they could not find the shooters. Subsequently, on 5 May 2009, after acting on a tip-off, we'd arrested some men who were armed with weapons at the Sagar Hotel in Nagpada junction. During their interrogation, it was found that they were the very men Dawood Ibrahim and

Chhota Shakeel had deputed for eliminating Lalit Modi. That day at Worli, they had scooted the moment they had espied the Crime Branch team arrive on the spot. They were nabbed and an Arms Act offence was registered against them. Their other target was Varun Gandhi, the BJP leader.

Thereafter, it was learned from underworld sources that even in April 2009, Dawood Ibrahim had attempted a hit on Lalit Modi in South Africa, where he had organised the IPL, but hadn't succeeded.

Again, in January 2010, I'd played a role in saving Lalit Modi's life. I was in my office when a source had called me and said, '*Saab, aaj Lalit Modi ka game bajne walla hai,*' (Sir, today they are going to do Lalit Modi in) and had immediately hung up. I had thought that Lalit Modi was in Mumbai and contacted people who were sure to know his exact location so that we could act and he could take the necessary precaution. I did not want a shoot-out in Mumbai during my beat! The contact however said that Lalit Modi was in Phuket in Thailand. I called the informant back. He said that the shooters were waiting near the resort and would attack as soon as he stepped out of the hotel lobby. So I asked the contact to warn Lalit Modi immediately. Later I learned that thanks to the timely information, Lalit Modi and his family had managed to egress out of the resort from a back entrance without the knowledge of the shooters.

So I felt that there could be some substance in what the advocate was conveying. He told me that the threats were indeed serious and Lalit Modi was hoping that I would be able to help him. I informed the advocate that I could only act if Lalit Modi returned to Mumbai to lodge a formal complaint for us to investigate the matter. He requested my local contact number so that Lalit Modi could pass on some information to me. I gave him my number. Then I got busy with the different programmes scheduled at the Conference. I had to also make a major presentation on 'Urban Terrorism' which I had prepared with great effort. There were several interesting programmes on the agenda which also included a visit to the Scotland Yard. Overall, it was a great exchange of ideas and a welcome break from the strenuous routine of Mumbai.

The Conference concluded on the afternoon of 16 July and I received calls from Lalit Modi's advocate that evening, requesting for a meeting with Lalit Modi. When I repeated my inability to meet him, he said that Lalit Modi wanted to personally give me certain names of Mumbai-based businessmen who were allegedly working for Dawood Ibrahim in London. Losing vital information on the Mumbai underworld was not a good idea. Therefore, I told the advocate that I was scheduled to have lunch with friends the next day at a restaurant and Lalit Modi could see me after lunch.

The next day, as Preeti and I stepped out of the restaurant, I saw Lalit Modi and his advocate waiting for me outside. He said that he was receiving threats from the Mumbai underworld and disclosed certain names to me stating that those individuals were acting as frontmen for the Dawood Ibrahim gang. He kept insisting that I take some action against them. I told him that I had no locus standi in London and he should return to Mumbai and lodge a complaint. The meeting lasted barely fifteen to twenty minutes and we parted.

On my return to Mumbai on 19 July 2014, I immediately brought my meeting with Lalit Modi and the information that he had disclosed, to the knowledge of R.R. Patil, the then Home Minister. The information needed to be verified and it was decided to have the Anti-Extortion Cell of Mumbai police conduct a discreet inquiry into the matter. I issued a secret memo to the Anti-Extortion Cell stating briefly the circumstances under which I had met Lalit Modi in London and the information he had passed on to me. A similar note was also maintained in the Confidential Records at the Commissioner's office.

However, in June 2015, when a controversy had raged on about the travel documents issued to Lalit Modi, one day the press suddenly began asking me if Lalit Modi had met me in London. I answered in the affirmative and explained how the meeting had taken place. A photograph of Lalit Modi and me standing in the street outside the London restaurant began doing the rounds of prime time news. I then wrote a letter to the Additional Chief Secretary (ACS) narrating the circumstances of the meeting and stated the relevant background for my meeting Lalit Modi. The meeting was now being clubbed with Lalit Modi's flight out of India and the travel documents that he was issued. The Opposition parties demanded for the resignations of the Foreign Minister and a Chief Minister. Though there was absolutely no connection between Lalit Modi meeting me and his travel documents, I was hounded in the on-going controversy and the state government issued a letter to me, asking for a report. I complied and furnished a factual report. I highlighted that the meeting was held in broad daylight on a street and there was nothing clandestine about it; the object of the meeting on my part was not to lose vital leads that Lalit Modi wanted to give me; the meeting had lasted for barely fifteen to twenty minutes; on my return, far from suppressing it, I had informed the Home Minister about it and directed the Anti-Extortion Cell, in writing, to make confidential and discreet inquiries into the information; the Anti-Extortion Cell had made inquiries into the information and a record of the information was in the confidential records at the Commissionerate. It was, thus, absolutely clear that I had no intention or desire to keep the meeting a secret. When the media had questioned me on this issue, I had not hesitated to acknowledge the meeting and even released a press note to prevent further unwarranted speculation. I averred that nothing was dearer to me than the dignity of the office that I held and I would not do anything to undermine its prestige. My point-by-point reply was ultimately accepted, but not without causing my family and me a great deal of stress.

My term as Commissioner of Police was to end on 30 September 2015 and there was a pleasant development in the family. While studying in the US, Kunal had found his soulmate in Deeksha, a school friend and a Mumbai girl who had studied in the US and was also working there. We were overjoyed and I decided that the wedding should be scheduled after 30 September, the date that was slated for my promotion, so that I could participate without any stress. Most of the family functions that I had attended were always with some sword or the other hanging over my head, maybe an underworld feud or a terrorist threat or a sensitive investigation. I would often run out of wedding halls to answer calls from informants or talk to subordinate officers about a chase, or about clean pickups, or to brief my seniors etc. At least now, at my own son's wedding, I wanted to devote clean and unadulterated time to concentrate on my personal duties. So, sometime in early August, I made a request to K.P. Bakshi, ACS (Home) and Praveen Pardeshi, Principal Secretary to the Chief Minister, that on completion of the term I should be given a quieter non-executive posting as my son was getting married in November. Both assured me that my request would be considered favourably.

I returned home and informed Preeti that we could start planning for the wedding. All our family weddings had so far been very simple and quiet affairs. I would have only been too happy to have our usual small ceremony just for close family members, but things were a little different now. Preeti and I had attended so many weddings – weddings of the children of my school, college and other friends, children of my batchmates and colleagues, of various officials in different government departments! So should we not be reciprocating by throwing at least a reception in Mumbai? Our children too had a fairly large circle of friends who expected to be invited. Moreover, the bride was an only daughter. Her family too would have a big list of invitees. So a large gathering was inevitable. Where should the venue be? Are we too late for the bookings? We were already in August! For the first time, I would be hosting a big celebration. Not being accustomed to it, I began gearing myself up for the thought.

First of all, it meant imagining a carefree world – a world where a blast means the blast people have in parties and not a blast for which you are summoned and put in charge of the investigation! Where shooting is for a video of a ceremony and not a signal for you to drop whatever you are doing and start a chase! Where a riot is a riot of colours and not the reason for you to jump into the street and open fire to nip it in the bud and then depose before a Commission of Inquiry. Imagining a world of simple routines and not much to do. Imagining such a world was hard. Three decades of constant responsibility and anxiety cannot be shed in a jiffy. Even a snake has to make some effort to shed its skin. And this was not just skin-deep. It was much deeper. Yet, I was looking forward to entering that world and preparing myself to detach, when a case under the Arms Act was registered at the Khar Police Station on 21 August 2015.

The accused arrested was a chauffeur. He gave the police leads to his involvement in a murder committed three years back, in April 2012, which had not yet come to light! The victim was a young girl from a wealthy and influential family. Even then, not even a missing complaint had been registered anywhere for her absence! Something was seriously wrong. The conspirators had so far managed to cover their tracks brilliantly!

Justice must be done to the deceased. And it can only happen if the team investigating the crime feels strongly about it. At such times, their leader cannot be not involved. Not till he is in charge, as the head of the city's police force.

I was very much in charge, fully conscious of my duty and with no right to disengage, howsoever I may want it.

33

Hunt for the Headhunters

Who was the murdered girl? The ill-fated girl whose family had not missed her for three years? Who was responsible for her disappearance? Why was she eliminated?

The answers to these questions were shocking and ghastly. The victim was a young girl called Sheena Bora and the killer was Indrani Mukerjea, her own flesh and blood! Indrani's driver, Shyamwar Pintu Rai, in custody of the Khar police, had spilt the beans. Indrani was a high profile headhunter who had turned a TV channel promoter and executive after her marriage with media baron, Peter Mukerjea.

The three-year-old can had crossed its expiry date. As the lid lifted, the worms began to wriggle out. They would soon surprise and delight softly-lit drawing rooms, plush boardrooms and hungry newsrooms. They would reach television studios, media houses, cocktail and dinner circuits. They would slither into the homes of millions of ordinary viewers through their TV screens, tickle or revolt them into taking note, and succeed in getting them hooked like addicts to their daily fix – a concoction of a daily-soap-cum-reality show, and add spice to their quotidian fare of entertainment.

According to the driver, Sheena was strangulated in a hired car which was parked in a lane on the evening of 24 April 2012. He had driven the car in which the murder was committed and had also assisted Sheena's mother, Indrani Mukerjea to dispose the body off at a secluded spot in a forest in Raigad district. Indrani's ex-husband, Sanjeev Khanna was also very much present in the car and was an accomplice in the vile deed.

The Khar police verified the leads under the supervision and guidance of the Zonal DCP, the Additional CP (West Region) and the Joint CP (Law and Order), and apprised me of the shocking facts surrounding the murder. It was obvious that the Mukerjeas were wealthy and influential people. They would put up tremendous resistance, hire the best legal talent and could use all kinds of pressure tactics to thwart the investigation or throw it off track. In any case, the villains had managed to keep the sordid episode under wraps for three years!

Peter was a successful ex-CEO of a front ranking TV channel. He and Indrani were founders of another group of TV channels. After a while, they had sold off their media company and the loss-making channels. Subsequently, they had sold their stake in the company and resigned from their positions. Then along with the daughter, Vidhi they had obtained British citizenship and moved to Bristol, visiting India off and on.

With some of their own ilk in the dock, the media was bound to have a field day. They would milk the sensational story to its fullest and as a result the investigation could suffer under their intense gaze. I instructed the officers to exercise utmost care and register the offence only after thoroughly being satisfied with the veracity of the leads. I also asked them to keep me updated on the progress.

On 25 August 2015, the offence for the murder of Sheena Bora was registered at the Khar police station. Indrani Mukerjea was arrested on the same day. Her police custody remand was obtained and the interrogation commenced under the supervision and guidance of DCP Zone-IX, Satya Narayan Choudhary, and Additional CP (West Region), Chhering Dorje – both bright

IPS officers. On 26 August 2015, Indrani's ex-husband Sanjeev Khanna was arrested from Kolkata.

As expected, Indrani's arrest drew tremendous media attention and reporters thronged the Khar police station. Journalists started parallel investigations and 'broke news' on television and in newspapers. The 'usual suspects' and habitual participants – lawyers, ex-police officers, media celebrities and socialites began appearing on television debates, shouting out their opinions and making dramatic statements. Comparisons were drawn between the Sheena Bora case and other sensational cases. How the infamous Aarushi murder case in Noida had been botched up by the police and whether a similar fate awaited the Sheena Bora case?

Our investigating team was working under the pressure of such intense media public debate and I felt they were doing a commendable job of it. Still, I was genuinely worried and felt that in the less than five weeks that I had as CP, I must ensure that there were no slip-ups. I wanted my officers to conduct a perfect investigation and file a flawless charge sheet to secure justice for the star-crossed victim.

It was worrying and surprising that for three years, nowhere had any complaint been registered for Sheena Bora's disappearance! The charred remains of her body had been discovered in Raigad some days after the murder, but the local police had neither registered an FIR nor an Accidental Death Report. There were various aspects to be probed – scientific evidence had to be gathered, like DNA testing for identification of the charred remains of the body and digital face superimposition which would prove that the remains were that of Sheena Bora. The motive had to be established by probing into the interpersonal relationships and equations within the family. The money and property angle is always a very important factor and, therefore, the financial dealings of the persons involved had to be investigated. It meant tracing bank accounts and accounting documents in India and abroad. Several facts and circumstances had to be verified by visiting locations like Shillong, Guwahati, Kolkata, New Delhi and Bengaluru. So even in the last month of my tenure, there was a race against time to collect cogent evidence within the short remand periods. I knew how tough it was and felt that it was my bounden duty as the Commissioner to support my team and ensure that their hard work did not come to nought for lack of legal expertise which they needed right from the remand stage. They welcomed my suggestion gladly and suggested the name of an advocate Vaibhav Bagade who had recently done some good work as a prosecutor and would be able to devote sufficient time for the investigating team.

I also wanted to be absolutely certain that the officers were on the right track. Just as I had interrogated the accused in the serial molester case or the Esther Anuhya murder case, I felt I needed to interrogate the accused and question the prime witnesses. The investigating officers were aware of my penchant for and deep interest in complex and knotty cases. That was my style of functioning. Instead of wasting the officers' time by pulling them away to Crawford Market to brief me, or make them bring the accused to me, I felt it was far more effective and appropriate if I went to Khar and held meetings with them. I did not feel even for a moment that it was below my dignity to do so, or was uncalled for.

Therefore, despite my busy schedule, in order to give meaningful direction to the investigation, I paid Khar police station four visits, on the evenings of 27, 28 and 31 August, and on 7 September, and that too while attending to the routine work in my office which demanded my close attention. Addressing the grievances and concerns of the numerous visitors went on as usual. There were also the Police Establishment Board meetings at Mantralaya which I had attended. The festival season had arrived and there was an important meeting held by the Chief Minister at the

Sahyadri Guest House on 31 August to discuss the preparations for the security arrangements. The next day was the six-hour long meeting of all Senior Inspectors, Inspectors, ACPs, DCPs, Additional CPs and Joint CPs with the Brihan Mumbai Sarvajanik Ganapati Mandal Committee to ensure smooth coordination between the police and the sarvajanik mandals (associations which host public celebrations). The purpose was to chalk out the Ganapati and Govinda security plans and evolve a strategy to tackle terrorist threats. On 3 September 2015 was a meeting held by the Honourable Chief Justice to tackle the issues relating to the security of the High Court which was a serious matter. Then on 5 September 2015, the Union Home Minister visited Mumbai. This too warranted my attention and presence.

Even then, out of my anxiety to make sure that the investigation of the high profile crime did not run into trouble, I managed to visit the Khar police station. The interrogation and questioning were already underway on a daily basis, led by Choudhary and Dorje, but I sensed that my visits, especially on two consecutive days – 27 and 28 – had invigorated the team that was toiling incessantly to make the most of the short remands the court had granted them. The officers shared their difficulties with me in handling Indrani Mukerjea who came across as extremely shifty and crafty. She not only kept lying and proved a hard nut to crack, but she was also very insolent. She would put on airs and was quite good at histrionics. Based on my extensive experience in interrogating different kinds of criminals, I gave the team suggestions to tackle the three arrested accused to expose the falsehood and find chinks in their defences. I also guided them on the strategies for questioning crucial witnesses.

Vaibhav Bagade visited the Khar police station at our behest on 27 and 28 August 2015. He was briefed extensively about the status of the investigation and he agreed to represent the police in the case. Therefore on 28 August, I wrote a letter to the ACS (Home) requesting that Bagade be appointed special public prosecutor, and enclosed his consent letter. I mentioned that appointing a special public prosecutor was necessary because the crime was serious, difficult and complex; the accused who were rich and well-known figures were bound to engage top lawyers. A copy of the letter was also marked to the Chief Secretary. With this move, the investigating team felt reassured.

Whenever I interrogated the accused or questioned the witnesses, it was always in the presence of the investigating team comprising DCP Zone-IX, Additional CP (West Region), the Joint CP (Law and Order), the ACP, the Senior Inspector and other Inspectors. I recollect that I had interrogated Sanjeev Khanna and Shyamwar Rai on 28 August and questioned Rahul Mukerjea (Peter Mukerjea's son from his first marriage), and Mikhail Bora (Indrani's son from her first marriage) on the same day. I had interrogated Indrani Mukerjea on 31 August and questioned Peter Mukerjea on 7 September. All these interrogations or questionings were in the presence of and along with all the officers mentioned above.

I did not know either Peter or Indrani Mukerjea from Adam. However, for some reason, the media began reporting that I knew them very well! When I got to know this, I vehemently denied it and made it amply clear that the first time I had ever met them was in the Khar police station.

The investigating team was pursuing a number of leads but secrecy being of utmost importance for their strategy, every lead pursued, every facet of the investigation and every piece of evidence collected could not be disclosed to the media. This tactful silence was construed as sluggishness, blunders, mess-ups and even deliberate omissions! Some journalists took up the task of pursuing their own investigations and began a game of one-upmanship with the police, contacting witnesses and interviewing them. It was difficult to strike the delicate balance between the need to protect the ongoing investigation from excessive and harmful media scrutiny and meeting the demands of transparency to show that the police were doing their job sincerely. The media camping outside the police station would confront me with a barrage of questions. I would give them such details as would provide information about the case without jeopardising the investigation. The object was to quell the unnecessary speculations.

I was so swamped with my work that I had no time to sit and watch TV news. It was from family and friends that I learnt that my visits to the Khar police station were becoming a contentious issue on prime time news. There is no bar or restriction anywhere in the rule books for the CP to visit one of his police stations, nor is there any limit on the number of visits he should make! It depends on his own assessment! Even then, 'argumentative Indians' spent precious time to debate this point and infused the atmosphere with distrust and suspicion. What is the need for the CP to visit the police station to look into an ongoing investigation? No CP has done it before! What is so special about this crime? Why is he taking so much interest in this particular investigation? Is he not taking an undue interest?

It is very easy for such people to sit in the airconditioned comfort of their TV studios and make statements. They are in no way answerable to the courts for their speculative views and judgements, unlike the investigator who has to be very careful about that he says and ensure that it is backed by evidence collected by him until that point of time. The rules for increasing TRPs (Target Rating Points) and those for securing a conviction are different things altogether. One wonders if some of the TV regulars could be using the panel discussions for their own agendas, like marketing themselves or enhancing their own image in their fraternity and in the eyes of the general public. Otherwise, it is hard to explain why some advocates and ex-police officers participate in such shows who are otherwise (or rather should be) well aware of the harmful effects of media trials on an ongoing police investigation and on the trial in court.

You don't have to be a nuclear scientist to know that if a CP has to put pressure on the investigating officers, he can do it without stirring out of his office! If he has to arrange publicity for himself, he can easily become a Page 3 figure or carefully choose from the numerous invitations in his mailbox to events which are bound to get extensive media coverage. But if he has to motivate and guide the investigating team operating from a police station, he cannot afford to remain perched on his swivel chair in his office, and certainly not out of fear of baseless allegations of undue interest! In matters of sensitive and crucial investigations, there is no substitute for the superior officer's personal touch and direct interaction with the investigating team. This has been my experience as a detection officer. And my appointment as CP did not bar me from taking interest in detections.

Later it dawned on me that the footage of my visits to the Khar police station was replayed on TV channels with such high frequency levels that the viewers got an impression as if I was a permanent fixture at the Khar police station those days! This was proved by my interaction with a highly respected senior, much much later after I had taken charge as DGP (Home Guards).

When I mentioned to him that I had only paid four visits to the police station in the fourteen days that the investigation went on during my tenure, he asked me in disbelief: 'You mean to say you did not go there every day?'

'No, sir, I did not!'

'Are you serious?'

'But of course I am, sir!'

'But then why did they say you did?'

'Sir, I have no idea!'

'But that's the way they showed you on TV!'

'Sir, did you carry an impression that I visited Khar police station every day?'

'Not just me!' Came the reply, and I was aghast at the power of the electronic media. Though there is no direct similitude, it reminded me of the assessment that the repeated replay of the Babri mosque demolition footage had added fuel to the fire on 6 December 1992.

While this drama was playing itself out on the small screen and front page news, our investigation was unearthing the gory plot and its astonishing background. Sheena was the elder of Indrani's two offspring from her first marriage to one Siddhartha Das. The other was a son named Mikhail. Indrani's second husband Sanjeev Khanna lived in Kolkata and came from a well-established family of the city. They had a daughter named Vidhi. Indrani had risen in life to run her own HR agency in Kolkata and moved in the top echelons of the city's who's who. However bizarre it may sound, she had been passing Sheena and Mikhail off as her siblings! They continued to live in Guwahati with their maternal grandparents who had eventually adopted them. Fired by her blinding ambition and with the help of her influential contacts, Indrani soon moved to Mumbai and established herself, bagging contracts with top business houses. She met Peter Mukerjea who headed Star TV and, in a trice, he became her third husband. He had two sons from his first marriage, but he formally adopted Vidhi.

In the meanwhile, Indrani's family in Guwahati had started making demands on her, and Indrani had started responding. As a result, Sheena moved to Mumbai and completed her education. Indrani introduced her to Peter and his family and to the Mumbai society as her sister. Sheena also landed a job in Reliance Metro One. Even then, Indrani's relationship with Sheena and Mikhail was strained and far from a happy one. Due to a strange twist of fate, Peter's son Rahul and Sheena were struck by the Cupid's arrow and started a relationship which was strongly resented by

Indrani. And even Peter objected to the form the kinship was taking. Sheena confided in Rahul that she was Indrani's daughter and not her sister. Rahul conveyed this information to his father. He was unmoved. Indrani and Peter tried their utmost to separate Rahul and Sheena, but they were in no mood to break up. Sheena's increasing proximity to Rahul was viewed by Indrani as a potential threat to her hegemony and to Vidhi's primacy towards which Indrani was working assiduously. On the other hand, Rahul's mother Shabnam supported the young couple in their decision. They began living together in a flat in Andheri which they rented on a leave and license basis from the owners, a Mr and Mrs Machado. They told the Machados that they were married.

The bond was now forged in the kiln of love and it was not easy to set them asunder. Gradually, Sheena became more and more confident. Ultimately things reached such a pass that Indrani decided to eliminate Sheena and Mikhail. She roped in her ex-husband Sanjeev Khanna and driver Shyamwar Rai in the diabolical scheme. She also solicited the help of her employee, Kajol Sharma to arrange the logistics like hotel bookings, hiring of cars and other paperwork. Various articles were purchased for the murderous plot which included two large suitcases.

On the day of the murder, Sanjeev Khanna flew down to Mumbai and stayed at Hotel Hill Top in Worli near the Mukerjeas' flat. Indrani lured Sheena to meet her in Bandra. Rahul dropped her at the given spot where the car was waiting with Shyamwar Rai at the wheel, Indrani in the front seat and Sanjeev Khanna on the back seat. With Sheena in the car, they drove to a by-lane near R. D. National College where the trio, led by Indrani, strangulated her. The body was stuffed into a suitcase and kept in the car which was parked in the garage of the Mukerjeas' Worli flat. Early next morning, it was taken to the pre-decided location in a forest near village Gagode in Taluka Pen in Raigad district, where the accused attempted to set the body on fire to obliterate its identity.

After the murder, Indrani took all the care to make it appear to Rahul and Mikhail, the two people most affected by Sheena's disappearance, that Sheena had voluntarily chosen to disappear from their lives and did not want to keep in touch. Rahul just could not believe it and began searching for her. Indrani told him that Sheena was abroad, but he was not convinced because Sheena's passport was with him. He persisted in his enquiries when he received an SMS from Sheena's phone communicating to him that she did not want to continue their relationship. He expressed his doubts to his father that he did not believe Sheena would leave him like that, but his father Peter did not support or endorse his suspicion. Ultimately, Rahul tried lodging a missing complaint, but here too he did not get the response he deserved.

The Machados were a friendly couple. They empathised with Rahul and also found Sheena's sudden decision to leave him hard to accept. When Rahul told them that he wanted to terminate the agreement as Sheena was not going to return, they asked him several questions. They also called the estate agent for a meeting with Rahul. All of them found Rahul in a disturbed state of mind. He told them that Sheena's mother Indrani was opposed to their marriage and Sheena had left him never to come back. They were neither convinced nor were they prepared to return the deposit to Rahul alone. They asked him to give them one month's notice, bring Sheena to collect the amount or share her mother's number with them. Rahul gave them an international number on which they tried calling but failed to establish contact. He also gave them Mikhail's cell number and email id, but to no avail. Rahul vacated the flat and returned the keys. Subsequently, the Machados received a letter signed by Sheena. It sought a termination of the agreement and stated that she had no objection to the deposit being returned to Rahul. Then another letter from Sheena was hand delivered to the Machados by a person called Shyam. The Machados were still not convinced and wrote to the MIDC police station, under whose jurisdiction the flat was located, that licensee Sheena Bora had left their flat without assigning any reason and the deposit should be collected by Sheena and Rahul together by visiting them personally. All these documents were collected from them by the Khar police. The team also began to trace the financial transactions of the big wheels connected with the crime and embarked on corralling the documents from a number of banks for the purpose.

Indrani took consummate care to cover her tracks and tie up all the loose ends. She made Kajol Sharma, her executive assistant, sign Sheena's resignation letter and deliver it to Reliance Metro One. Kajol was also the one to forge the signature on the termination of the leave and license agreement of the flat Sheena and Rahul were living in. This was promptly sent to the Machados, stating that the deposit money could be returned to Rahul. Indrani made Kajol open a Hotmail account in Sheena's name and used it to send emails impersonating Sheena. Prior to the murder, she had also made Kajol open a Skype account for Shyamwar so that he could talk to Indrani from office when she was abroad and receive instructions for executing the conspiracy.

It came to light that around a month after the murder, a local resident had come across the remains of a body lying in the forest at Gagode Khurd and reported it to the Pen police. A Station Diary entry to this effect was found in their records. The Khar police had also exhumed some skeletal remains from the spot by following the necessary formalities and sent them for scientific forensic tests. The team painstakingly gathered evidence to establish the steps taken by Shyamwar and Sanjeev Khanna to help Indrani plan and execute the murder and recorded statements of material witnesses for the purpose.

The details given by Mikhail Bora revealed many more blood-curdling details of the conspiracy. It appeared that the grand plan was to eliminate even Mikhail that evening. On that evening,

Mikhail too had come to Indrani's Worli flat at her invitation. Completely unaware that his sister's dead body was hidden in the car in the garage downstairs, he accepted the alcoholic drink his mother offered him. It made him feel drowsy and he suspected foul play! Fearing for his life, he did not consume the second drink and bolted from the house at four in the morning to return to Guwahati. The purchase of two suitcases instead of one lent credence to Mikhail's account. The team also brought Sheena and Mikhail's biological father Siddhartha Das to Mumbai and began confirming the missing links in the strange story.

It was recognised that the financial dealings of the accused were of a complex nature and a special team was constituted to conduct the probe and gather relevant evidence. It comprised officers with previous work experience in the Economic Offences Wing (EOW) and to buttress their efficiency, financial auditors and tax consultants working with the EOW were also brought on board. Sanjeev Khanna confessed to the police that he had concealed some evidence in Kolkata and hence the team had to fly with him to the city to recover the articles. The police recovered his laptop from his friend in Kolkata.

The probe was thus progressing in the right direction and in right earnest. Different types of evidence was being gathered: emails, text messages, Skype conversations, Call Data Records (CDRs); bookings of cars, air tickets and hotels; birth, adoption, education and medical records of the Bora siblings; documents pertaining to financial and property arrangements like ownership and wills, if any; the financial dealings of the Mukerjeas who had been under the scanner of the special investigative agencies dealing with economic offences, and much more. A very sombre and serious issue was the way all attempts by Rahul Mukerjea to trace Sheena were thwarted. No investigative agency had taken note of his grievance and his anguish, and even his own father, inexplicably, had not taken his own son seriously.

Peter Mukerjea was summoned to the Khar police station daily and was being questioned rigorously. His version was being checked and cross-checked with the account of the other co-accused and witnesses. That he was away from India at the time of the murder did not in any way mean that he was either not complicit or could not be arrested. As soon as the team was sufficiently sure of his collusion and deceit, they would have picked him up. In such cases, it is tempting to arrest a suspect, but in the absence of sufficient evidence, such a move can backfire and provide an excellent ground for immediate release on bail. That would amount to playing into the hands of smart lawyers and falling flat on our faces.

I clearly recollect that sometime during the initial few days of the investigation, late one evening, Chief Minister Devendra Fadnavis had phoned me and enquired about the Sheena Bora case. I had explained to him in brief the facts that had come to light so far, the role of Indrani Mukerjea and the other accused arrested till then, the major evidence collected and the various steps taken by the team. I had briefed him that although Peter Mukerjea was not present during the killing and disposal of the body, his overall complicity was being probed and he was being regularly called to the police station for questioning. This was the one and only time that I had briefed the Chief Minister on the Sheena Bora case.

On the evening of 7 September 2015, I questioned Peter Mukerjea and straightaway confronted him on his inaction after his son Rahul had informed him about the sudden disappearance of Sheena.

'What is your educational qualification?' I asked Peter.

'I am from the Doon School and I have done my University education from London,' he answered.

'I don't believe it! *Tu bahot bada gadha hai!*' (You are a big donkey!) I said to him, slipping into my Hindi. I was disgusted.

'Why, sir?' Peter managed to ask me after a long silence. He was obviously shocked. No one must have ever addressed him the way I had.

'Your son comes and tells you that his fiancée – your stepdaughter or sister-in-law or daughter-in-law or whatever you call her, is missing. And you do nothing about it?' I asked him.

'No, sir. Not that I did nothing,' said Peter.

'What did you do?' I asked him.

'Sir, I had told Deven!' Peter answered looking at Deven Bharti, Joint CP (Law and Order).

I thought he had not understood my question and so I repeated it. 'You did what?' Peter answered that he and Indrani had told Deven Bharti about Sheena's disappearance after Rahul had expressed his grievance. Now there was a deafening silence in the room. The proverbial pin-dropping type. I looked at Deven with a quizzical look on my face, but he was poker-faced. And silent. I looked around the room and sensed that even the others were taken aback at Peter's disclosure. They all tried to look as if nothing of consequence had happened.

Deven Bharti was in charge of the functioning of all the police stations in Mumbai city and I thought it would be inappropriate to question him in front of all his subordinate officers. However, why had he not divulged this vital information to me, and this despite he and I meeting on a daily basis and even travelling together to the Khar police station! He had never told me that he knew Peter and Indrani! Even when I was protesting that I did not know them and the media was unnecessarily pointing accusatory fingers at me! How do I end this embarrassing situation without giving Peter an advantage, I kept thinking. In a stern voice, I told Peter, 'I do not believe you. You are telling lies. I am giving you time until tomorrow afternoon to come clean. Otherwise, the law will fall heavily on you.' He was then ushered out of the room.

Much as I wanted to ask Deven Bharti's explanation, I could not get the opportunity at the police station. When I emerged out of the police station, the media was there to seek details from me as usual. I informed them that we were probing the financial angle in the case with the assistance of forensic auditors, tax consultants and officers who had EOW working experience and that we had also requested the Central Agencies to assist us in the matter. In fact, it was under my directions that the investigating team sent a letter to the Enforcement Directorate, asking them to probe into Peter Mukerjea's financial transactions.

That night I couldn't sleep a wink. The thought uppermost in my mind was to find out the exact meaning of what Peter had told me in the evening. It meant that Peter Mukerjea knew Deven Bharti on first name terms! And I had not known this all these days! Moreover, Deven Bharti had not thought it fit to tell me even once that the Mukerjeas were close to him. On the contrary, whenever I would discuss with him the mystery of the nonregistration of the missing complaint or the accidental death report, he would keep his silence. And this from my Joint CP (L&O)? At the time of Sheena's disappearance, Deven Bharti was the Additional CP in the Crime Branch! He could have done so much then itself to look for Rahul's girlfriend! It was imperative that I get to the bottom of it all, without upsetting the investigating team that was doing a good job. I needed to do some homework and then confront Deven the very next day, as soon as I had finished the urgent matters on the agenda. If something had seriously gone wrong, I must not let it affect the investigation. If someone was guilty of grave misconduct, I must not let them get away with it.

Here the overzealous media was suspecting *me* of being friends with the Mukerjeas when I had had absolutely nothing to do with them, but the same media had not found that my Joint CP (L&O) was a very good friend of the Mukerjeas! How strange! Who was deliberately feeding them with such cock and bull stories to hide the truth? There was a definite attempt to create a smokescreen and put us off the real scent of the trail! Such subterfuge!

Sheena Bora had already been hunted down, literally, in a hunt led by a professional headhunter. Now the chase to pin down her hunters might have to take an ugly turn! And who were we exactly up against?

The morning began with these very disturbing thoughts clamouring in my head. And just as I was gearing up for the day, and contemplating how I should get to the bottom of the three long years when Sheena Bora was not missed, I was no longer the Commissioner of Police of Mumbai! The responsibility of ensuring justice to Sheena Bora and many more like her, was no longer mine. The SMS to convey this had popped up on the screen of my phone:'Hearty Congratulations! Government has promoted you to the rank of DG with immediate effect and has posted you as DG HG Regards Bakshi.'

The message was from ACS (Home). It was 11:35 a.m. on 8 September 2015, and the world out there was beckoning me, a little too early, and in a manner quite unexpected, but perhaps for my own good!

34

Thorns in the Crown

The crown was off. The thorns, however, would be difficult to shed, as I was going to discover. But then someone said that when it is rose petals all the way, we soon become drowsy, complacent; thorns are necessary to keep us awake, alert!

The Director General (Home Guards) was a perfect stepping stone to retirement, particularly for a crazy workaholic like me. I had been looking forward to such a quiet non-executive posting as an ideal drying-out facility. However, my entry twenty-two days in advance, pursuant to my unceremonious exit from the CP's office, was accompanied by a fanfare, albeit unintended. It was something the peaceful office, tucked away from the limelight in a leafy corner of Kala Ghoda, was not quite used to. Its new incumbent was not the greying public servant escaping every now and then to a lazy game of golf at the Willingdon, enjoying the sundown with his whiskey and soda at a bar, and then closing the day with Eggs Kejriwal over the latest from the corridors of Mantralaya. And he had come with baggage that was far from tranquil.

I had taken charge of my new assignment without any delay, as is expected of a disciplined officer. Yet deep down, there was a sense of hurt. It was strange that I should have received no advance communication from the state government conveying their decision to promote and transfer me before the completion of my term, leave alone give reasons for such a move. A prior intimation is the least that was expected, and a decent way of doing it. The absence of it belittled the dignity of the office of the Commissioner of Police, Mumbai and also put to nought my thirty-four years of selfless service in the IPS. Yet, the cardinal principle of government service is that postings and transfers are a prerogative of the State and I therefore kept my feelings to myself.

I was flooded with agonising queries from friends and family who wanted to know if and where I had gone wrong. It was clear that my reputation was getting sullied in their eyes, and also in the eyes of my colleagues, my seniors in the IPS and the general public. For there was a great degree of speculation on the reasons for my abrupt transfer: that I had taken undue interest in the Sheena Bora murder case and that was the reason behind my alleged daily visits to Khar police station; that I was friends with Peter Mukerjea; that I had posted officers close to me at the Khar police station and that I had shielded Peter Mukerjea by not probing the financial angle in the crime. Although the media hounded me for my answers and views, I maintained my silence as a disciplined police officer, and also in the interest of the investigation which was at a critical stage.

While all these events were unfolding, I hardly had the time to watch TV and read each newspaper and periodical carefully to see who said what and when! It is now when I sit and go through some of the old reports that I am filled with a sense of wonderment at the confusion created. I keep wondering if and how it could have been prevented. And I really have no clear answers.

Despite the suspicion created to surround my actions qua the Sheena Bora case, there were some strong voices of protest against my transfer – that it was a deliberate move to derail the investigation. Some even acknowledged that the investigating team was on its way to make a water-tight case. Not just the suddenness of the transfer in the midst of the investigation, even the swiftness with which the charge was taken over from me was being discussed. How my marching orders were issued, was described. It was reported that they had been passed hours after Chief Minister Fadnavis (also the state Home Minister) had taken off for Japan on an official visit, leaving his deputies in the ruling party and in the administration at pains to explain the reasons. This exercise of explanation was led by Bakshi, ACS (Home) and turned out to be a series of amusing 'flip-flops' for the onlookers, though an agony to me and my family.

On 8 September, Bakshi described the entire exercise as an 'administrative decision' made after 'factoring' in the law and order issues to be dealt with by the city police ahead of and during the ten-day Ganesh festival celebrations: 'It was an administrative decision and a thought-out process. We have been deliberating about the move for the past three to four weeks. The Chief Minister signed the file before he left for Japan.' So it was from the media interviews of Bakshi that I learned that the decision to promote or transfer me in this manner was not even a hurried or sudden decision as it had appeared! It was taken with a great deal of thought and was an outcome of lengthy deliberations at the highest levels. In that case, there was no reason why it should not have been communicated to me in advance! I had asked for a quiet posting. I would have gladly moved out on the given date!

Bakshi also gave an assurance that the new CP was a very competent officer and as a consequence of which the investigation would not suffer. The new CP also promised that they would be investigating the case in a professional manner and that there was a lot of scope for improvement which they were going to carry out.

Besides explaining that the sudden move was not so sudden, Bakshi also tried to scotch speculation that there was some link between the transfer and the Sheena Bora murder case. He was reported to have said, 'All investigations are important. As far as this case is concerned, most of the probe is complete and the accused are in judicial custody. We are in the process of filing of charge sheet. We cannot stop transfers and promotions for a particular case.' While it may be true that promotions and transfers cannot be halted for a particular case, who gave him to understand that most of the probe was complete was a mystery to me! I wanted the team to collect as much concrete evidence as possible so that I could demit office with the satisfaction that no effort was spared and no time was wasted.

To allay fears that the investigation would suffer on my exit, Bakshi came up with a solution. 'There is no connection between Maria's transfer and the Sheena Bora murder case probe. He will continue to monitor the probe even after his elevation to the DGP-level and transfer. We have already communicated to him that he will be heading the Sheena Bora murder case,' he told journalists! And I had received no such communication!

The Pioneer of 9 September commented as follows:

> Given that an ace investigator in Maria had gone headlong into investigating the financial trail involving key accused Indrani and her husband Peter Mukerjea, there was apprehension in certain quarters that the probe might throw up some political names of having been financial links with the once-powerful Mukerjea couple. It is no secret that the Mukerjea couple had come close to several political players when they – as co-founders of INX Media Pvt Ltd, a firm that they set up after Peter quit Star India in 2007, were preparing to launch a host of entertainment and news channels.
>
> However, in a damage control exercise undertaken in the face of media speculation that the Mumbai CP had been removed because of the apprehension that he might come up with uncomfortable truths in the investigations in the Sheena Bora murder case, the Maharashtra Government sought to allay misconceptions by going to town saying that despite his elevation and transfer, Maria would continue to head the probe in the high-profile murder case.

> The investigations by the Mumbai Police should be seen in the context of the investigations launched by Enforcement Directorate is already investigating the alleged foreign exchange violations by the INX Media Pvt Ltd, co-founded by Peter and Indrani Mukerjea in 2007. The alleged violations pertain to the investments raised by INX Media from three Mauritius-based companies.

Queries from anxious friends and family continued. The media too kept asking for explanations, but I held my silence. No state official had sounded me on any such move, but I was in a quandary. I felt that my taking up such an assignment did not augur well either for upholding the glorious tradition of my Force nor for the successful prosecution of the case. My sole objective was to ensure a thorough probe to expose all the perpetrators of the heinous crime, whatever their status in society. But how would this kind of supervisory role work? Police departments have a definite hierarchical structure and a chain of command. The CP is at the apex with all the police stations in the city and the ACPs, DCPs, Additional CPs and Joint CPs reporting to him. Creating a parallel authority to supervise and monitor an investigation conducted by a police station under the CP would damage the chain of command and undermine his authority. The government seemed to be mindful of this problem and was trying to work out some arrangement, said some media reports. For instance, a *Free Press Journal* report of 11 September said:

> Will he or won't he? Whether Former Mumbai Police Commissioner Rakesh Maria will come back and lead the team investigating Sheena Bora murder case is a question everyone wants the answer to. Minister of State for Home Ram Shankar Shinde cleared the air on Thursday evening. 'Mr Maria will have to lead the probe of Sheena Bora murder like he was doing till two days ago and there is no other option. Whether he agrees or not, he will have to do

> it,' Shinde said in an exclusive interaction with Free Press Journal. Saying that the Maharashtra government has dispatched an official order asking former CP Rakesh Maria to continue handling the probe, Shinde said: 'The state home department will ensure there is no confusion over allotment of officers for this specific case and no issues between new city Commissioner of Police, Ahmed Javed and Maria. We know how to handle it and we will do it. Priority at this hour is to ensure proper co-ordination between two top-graded senior officers helping to unravel the mystery so that the guilty are punished.

The allegation or speculation that I had posted handpicked officers at the Khar police station only for detecting the Sheena Bora case, was obviously baseless. It had emanated from the fact that two experienced officers who had worked with me in the Crime Branch, were posted at the Khar police station at the material time. However, it had no merit. There is a committee that processes these postings. Inspector Dinesh Kadam, the Investigating Officer (IO) in the Sheena Bora case, was definitely an officer I rated very highly and my long association with him was well-known. At the time of his posting at the Khar police station, however, keeping in mind his informant network and aptitude for detection, I had desired that he should be posted to the Crime Branch. I have always held a view that postings in specialised detection branches must not be tenure-based, as the expertise and informants developed over a long period of time is wasted when the officer is moved out. However, there was also a view that officers of the Crime Branch or Anti-Terrorism Squad (ATS), when posted at police stations, add value to the police station work, especially while dealing with the underworld and terror-related crimes, experienced as they are in such matters. As per the prevalent practice in Mumbai, the Joint CP (Crime) submits recommendations for officers for coming into or going out of the Crime Branch. In this case, when the Transfer Committee comprising three Joint CPs and four DCPs had convened, Dinesh Kadam's name had not figured in the list recommended by the Joint CP (Crime) for posting to the Crime Branch. It was then that the Joint CP (Law and Order) and DCP Zone-IX Satya Narayan Choudhary had requested that Dinesh Kadam be posted to Khar police station to tackle the underworld and property-related crimes in the jurisdiction. I had accepted the recommendation and Dinesh Kadam was posted to the Khar police station on 7 July 2015. The second officer, Inspector Nitin Alaknure, had been posted by the Promotion Committee to the Khar police station more than a year earlier, on 12 August 2014.

The *Free Press Journal* report of 11 September further stated that when confronted with the fear that the rest of the investigating team was also being shunted out from the Sheena Bora murder case, the Minister had denied it and said that I would get the officers I needed to expedite the probe. He was reported to have added that a legal process had already been initiated to ensure that I would have the jurisdiction to handle the case while being in charge of Civil Defence and Home Guards. The paper quoted the Minister as follows:

> We are working towards a proper legal authorisation for him so that there is no issue on why DGP (Home Guards) is probing a case under the jurisdiction of the city police chief. The process has been initiated by the State Home Department and before Ganesh Chaturthi it will be over so that Mr Maria gets all the tooth and nail he needs for the investigation to be done properly.

I shared my anxiety with some of the retired seniors and was wondering how embarrassing it would be when after a week's time, there was one more somersault! A news report in the *Hindustan Times* dated 17 September described it under the headline as, 'Maharashtra Govt Flip-flops on Maria's Role in Sheena Case Probe' and went on to state:

> The Maharashtra government has not taken any decision yet about the role of former Mumbai Commissioner of Police Rakesh Maria in the Sheena Bora murder probe and has also sought a status report, sources said on Thursday.
>
> Last week, the state government had hastily removed Maria as the Mumbai Police chief and promoted him as the Director General of Police (Home Guards) but said he could monitor the case. However, sources in the police department said Maria is not keen to continue with the investigation after his abrupt promotion and transfer.
>
> According to sources, the State Home Department has asked the Director General of Police (Maharashtra) Sanjeev Dayal to review the murder case and could ask Maria to supervise the probe if it thinks that his expertise is needed.
>
> Dayal told HT on Thursday he had received a letter from the Home Department and would be speaking to Mumbai Police Chief Ahmed Javed and send a review of the Bora case soon.
>
> Additional Chief Secretary (Home) K.P. Bakshi was not available for comment.

Whether this beating the retreat episode was due to a stiff resistance from some quarters in the police hierarchy or due to the embarrassment of a possible rejection, or because of a combination of both is anyone's guess. The ball was now sent to take a breather in the DGP's court till a safe return.

The media's interest in the Sheena Bora murder case continued unabated and so did my torment. As a general rule, people only remember the allegations and forget the explanations and denials which often appear in small paragraphs or are confined to the back pages or lost in the information overload. 'Yes, we were investigating the financial angle! The investigation had progressed sufficiently, but much more was to be dug out and linked! Yes, but we were working hard to file the charge sheet within time. Supplementary charge sheets can be filed, but the first charge sheet is extremely important! No, I had never known Peter and Indrani Mukerjea! They are not my friends! It is a myth! Complete falsehood!' Not just me, but my wife, my children, and the rest of the family and close friends too had to keep clarifying on my behalf!

Then all of a sudden on 17 September, the media began reporting that it was Ahmed Javed, the new CP who knew Peter and Indrani Mukerjea socially! The Times Now Channel began playing a clip of the phone-in that the reporter Ashish Singh had done with the CP in which the latter accepted that he had known the Mukerjeas socially. He also accepted that he had invited the couple to his Eid Iftar party at the Worli Police Officers' Mess in 2014. However, he also denied that it indicated any conflict of interest. He said that he had not received any call from Peter Mukerjea after the story had broken and also denied the unconfirmed report that he was the first person whom Peter had called.

What happened the next day, i.e. on 18 September was reflected in a PTI report which can be found on *Rediff.com* of 19 September:

> In a sudden twist, the Maharashtra government on Friday decided to transfer the Sheena Bora murder probe to CBI after days of uncertainty on the supervisory role of former Mumbai police chief Rakesh Maria who was shunted in the midst of the inquiry that he had helmed proactively.
>
> In what is seen as a snub to Mumbai's top cops, the decision for a probe free from 'prejudices' was announced at a press conference by Additional Chief Secretary (Home) K.P. Bakshi who said that financial angle of the case has also been taken into account in transferring the probe to the central investigation agency.
>
> He also said the Government was 'disturbed' by media reports that linked Maria's transfer to the investigation in the case.
>
> Stating that the government wants to 'ensure' people are convinced that the government has no interest to interfere in

the case, Bakshi said that on the other hand, it was also keen on a probe free from prejudices. The decision was taken after consulting Chief Minister Devendra Fadnavis, he said.

'In the last few days, the previous Mumbai CP (Maria) was promoted and transferred and a new officer (Ahmed Javed) was put in his place. All this while, the Sheena Bora investigation was also going on. A section of the media has put all this together and inferred that the transfers happened because of the case,' Bakshi said.

'Government was disturbed with reports that linked this case to the transfers. The CM was in Japan and then we were busy with the President's event in Nagpur and the launching of Crime and Criminal Tracking Network and System (CCTNS) then. Hence I did not get enough time to talk to the CM on the case. But now, I have spoken to the CM at length and to show we have no intention of interfering with the case, we have decided to transfer the case to the CBI,' he said.

He said that the state government had asked for a 'status report' from the Director General of Police a couple of days back and based on the contents of the report has concluded that the case is not limited to murder alone, but there are many questions on financial dealings that remain unanswered.

'After we studied the report, we concluded that the case is not limited to murder alone but many economic issues on financial dealings are still unanswered. We want the truth to come out and thus, I have spoken to officials from the Union government and the CBI and thereby transferred the case to them. It is now up to the Union government to accept our request and direct the CBI to take over the case,' he said.

Bakshi said that the government is willing to assist the CBI in all possible measures.

Sheena was murdered on April 24, 2012, and her body was burnt and disposed of in the forest in Raigad district the next day.

Apart from Sheena's mother Indrani, her former husband Sanjeev Khanna and driver Shyamvar Rai were arrested in the case and are now in judicial custody after being interrogated for 14 days by police.

Maria, who personally interrogated the accused and others including Indrani's husband Peter Mukerjea, was shunted from the post earlier this month by promoting him as DG (Home Guards) and brought in DG-rank officer Ahmed Javed in his place.

The Government, however, announced the same evening that Maria will continue to supervise the probe in the case, though it dragged on defining the actual role of the high profile officer who was reportedly unwilling to take up the responsibility. Javed was also reported to have admitted that he knew the Mukerjeas socially.

Bakshi also said that the state government did not see the Sheena Bora case as a 'high-profile murder' case. 'There is no such thing as a low or high profile murder. A murder is a murder,' he added.

On the status report submitted by DGP Sanjeev Dayal, Bakshi said that the investigation is almost completed by the local police and since all the accused are in judicial custody no further questioning of them would be possible.

'Also, for now, we feel no new arrests are warranted. The CBI will now go deep and investigate the loose threads, along with the financial angle. If the agency feels that more people need to be questioned upon preliminary investigation, they will summon whoever is required,' he said.

Bakshi said the DG's status report does not talk of 'sabotage' by any of the investigating officers of the Sheena Bora murder probe and that a decision was taken only after talking to the previous and the incumbent Mumbai CP.

Asked about the involvement of a senior Raigad police officer in allegedly botching up the case in 2012, Bakshi said, 'The officer could have been involved, but, the DG is inquiring into this as well. Once he submits a report will we be able to say for certain if there were vested interests.'

'I have taken the DG's valuable suggestion and have spoken to the CM in detail about this case. We feel that this case should not be dealt with any past or present police officer or by any state government agency. We want to send out a message that we have no intention of interfering in the case. Also since there

> are several angles involved, and to make sure the investigation is done impartially, we decided to transfer the case to the CBI,' Bakshi said.
>
> Striking a cautious note, political parties including the Congress refrained from making any immediate comment on the development, though they were taken by surprise by the decision.

I had no idea what Bakshi had meant by saying that the decision was taken only after talking to the previous and the incumbent Mumbai CP. Nobody had spoken to me about any such decision.

After my promotion and transfer on 8 September 2015, the probe remained in the hands of the Mumbai police until 29 September 2015, when the Central Bureau of Investigation (CBI) took over. There were news reports which indicated that Peter and Indrani Mukerjea had also known Deven Bharti from much before and that they had told him about Sheena Bora's disappearance right after it had happened in 2012! Such discoveries, however, did not seem to interest the angry anchors and their pugilistic panellists on prime time news who had been so livid at my non-existent friendship with the Mukerjeas.

Only fourteen days of the investigation fell in my tenure as CP (Mumbai). I had visited the Khar police station only four times during this period. I had seen Indrani and Peter, for the first time, only at the Khar police station and had never known them before. If the Chief Minister had any objection to my visits to the Khar police station or if he had felt that I had shown undue interest in the case, he had every right to ask for an explanation. And if he had found it untenable, he could have pulled me up. Just the way I had been asked to tender my explanation when Lalit Modi had met me in London. But the Chief Minister never questioned me in this regard. I had briefed him on the case only once and that too in the initial days of the investigation before I had even questioned Peter. That was the time when Peter was very much under our scanner and was regularly being called to the police station.

After my transfer, when the investigation was still with the Mumbai police for three weeks, neither the CM nor any other minister, the ACS or any other state official had called me up to discuss anything about the Sheena Bora case, nor had I contacted them.

In the meanwhile, on 20 September, *The Times of India* came out with a little analysis of its own:

> For the first time since he took over the reins of Maharashtra in October last year, chief minister Devendra Fadnavis' 'shock treatment' strategy for the police brass and high-ranking bureaucrats failed. In fact, it turned out to be counterproductive.
>
> Fadnavis had drafted a novel action plan to transfer IAS and IPS officers just before leaving on a foreign tour so that once the order was passed, there would be no scope for political interference. On five occasions, the strategy worked out well as he was unavailable to make any changes to the orders and the IPS and IAS officers were left with no option, but to accept the new assignments.
>
> A fortnight ago, when Fadnavis abruptly shifted celebrated Mumbai police commissioner Rakesh Maria to the insignificant home guards and civil defence wing on promotion, it resulted in a strong adverse reaction in the electronic and print media.
>
> Maria's unceremonious exit stunned the aam aadmi, as despite knowing that he was due for promotion on September 30, the top cop had declared that he would file a charge sheet in the Sheena Bora murder case before the step-up. Though Fadnavis was alarmed by the massive criticism, he did not cancel Maria's transfer and decided to retain him as head of the murder probe, but Maria politely declined. But during the seven days that Fadnavis was in Japan after Maria's 'promotion', there was no one to defend his decision and his high-powered media cell too maintained complete silence.

> Meanwhile, it came to light that Maria's successor Ahmed Javed socially knew Indrani Mukerjea, an accused in the murder case, and her husband Peter. Now, Fadnavis had no option but to entrust the probe to an independent agency. Sooner or later, Fadnavis will have to explain why Maria was abruptly shunted out.

It was difficult to keep pace with the numerous somersaults that the athletic Mantralaya tsars were executing one after the other. The somersaults were designed to make a digestible case for public consumption for my transfer on promotion which was unceremonious, sudden, 'a bit early' and in the midst of a sensitive investigation.

The bouquet of explanations amused those who had been there and seen it all: a CP cannot be transferred in the midst of a Ganapati festival bandobast; the new CP needed sufficient time to settle down for the festival bandobast; that night the CM was to fly to Japan, he would be away for six days and it was necessary to effect the transfer before he left; there was nothing unusual about an early transfer on promotion; there was no connection with the ongoing sensitive investigation; the investigation would not suffer as the new CP was a competent officer and he had found that there was a lot of scope for improvement in the investigation which he would carry out. Even then, a few hours later, the decision to continue me to supervise and monitor the investigation; the statement that I had been sounded out when no one had spoken to me; the assurance that there would be no confusion and the special enabling orders would be issued to govern the arrangement which were not the first of its kind! And then no action on this important decision for a long time, and then asking the DGP to submit a report of his assessment.

Along with these flip-flops, there were some other serious issues which were crying for attention. Was there a deliberate attempt to discredit the probe by spreading the falsehood that

I knew the Mukerjeas socially? I had categorically denied it, but the atmosphere of suspicion persisted. A week after my removal, it turned out that not the previous CP but the new CP knew the Mukerjeas socially and they were invitees to his Eid party! Did the CM and the ACS know about this before the new CP took charge? Knowing the Mukerjeas socially was an important issue by then! So had the new CP told the CM about his proximity with the Mukerjeas? If they knew, why did they not take the people into confidence? And if they hadn't, then did they not consider it a serious matter? How come the Mantralaya tsars did not see the danger that this could be an attempt to appoint a Mukerjea-friendly CP? In a short while, it had also come to light that Deven Bharti, Joint CP (Law and Order) was a friend of the Mukerjeas and Peter had spoken to him about Sheena's disappearance. When Rahul tried to lodge a missing complaint with the police, Deven was Additional CP in the Crime Branch. The new CP was then the Additional DG (Law and Order) in charge of all the district police stations for crime and law and order when Sheena had disappeared and the remains of a human body were found in the forest at Gagode in Raigad district. An inquiry was launched into the serious lapses on the part of the district police to ascertain if there was an attempt to destroy evidence. What happened to that inquiry?

Did all these factors point out to a possibility that the officers who had sincerely tried to bring to light the heinous crime and who were working hard to bring the culprits to book, were systematically being targeted? And on the flipside, was there an attempt to protect those who had helped the accused in covering their tracks? Did the tsars sense this danger?

It was only after the media announced the new CP's friendship with the Mukerjeas that the tsars got galvanised into action. The very next day they sent the CBI a request to take up the investigation. The ACS called one more press conference and made some announcements. The DGP's report had just come into his hands and he announced that the case was not limited to just a murder of an individual, it had a background of financial dealings! Something which I had said on 7 September itself, after questioning Peter. I had gone on record to say that the case was complex and the financial angle was being probed.

The new CP who had observed that there was a lot of scope for improvement and assured professional investigation into the case had been in charge for three weeks. The CP and the DGP had done a deep study of the investigation. And what was the conclusion of that study? That the interrogation of all the accused was over and there was no possibility of any further arrests! Which meant that with the three accused already under arrest, the Mumbai police under the changed guard was drawing curtains on the case.

The CBI accepted the case and I began settling down in my new posting. My next in command was Sanjay Pandey, a sincere, honest and hardworking IPS officer. We set about streamlining the functioning of the Home Guards and Civil Defence department. I realised that even in this office there was a lot of work one could do in matters relating to distribution of duties, weekly parades, fitness and discipline. Sanjay's posting to the Home Guards turned out to be a boon for me. I utilised his industry and application for putting the house in order and began enjoying my work.

On the family front, we began preparing for Kunal's wedding, but try as we may, it was difficult to be exuberant. Every now and then some report or the other would appear in the media about the Sheena Bora case, with the facts a little jumbled up or with some comment here or there which would leave a question mark alive against my integrity. It was so tempting to speak up, but that was not for me! The unbearable stress began to take a toll on Preeti's health as well as mine. It subdued our enthusiasm for the first ever celebration that we were planning to host in my family. By nature, I am not a gregarious person. I prefer my own company and the company of my books and music. In those trying times, they were indeed a blessing. With their help, I began rediscovering a lot of everyday miracles that I had forgotten to notice. For instance, it was not easy getting used to seeing the beautiful Mumbai sunsets after a long gap of thirty-four years. The pleasant spectacle, tantalisingly different every evening and yet reassuringly same each day in its divine splendour, never failed to soothe my aching soul. As if it was signalling at the close of each day, 'You have done your job. Don't worry. Even I am evaluating you!'

Ultimately, we decided to have only a small event for the wedding for our close friends and family. The bride's parents were most understanding and we managed to create a few happy and memorable moments despite some tense times like on the day of the Sangeet ceremony – 19 November 2016. It was on that very day when the CBI happened to arrest Peter Mukerjea. The media gathered outside the wedding venue and I began receiving calls. The CBI has arrested Peter Mukerjea! And the Mumbai police did not! What was the reason? They wanted to know.

This was enough to take my mind completely off my son's nuptials. I was back in the grave atmosphere of Khar police station where our officers and men were toiling hard to sift truth from deceit. Deceit which shrouded a twenty-four-year-old unfortunate child whose life was brutally cut short for refusing to give up the partner she had chosen for herself, for demanding her parent's attention, and perhaps even something more if we could lay our finger on it as we probed deeper!

Why had the Mumbai police not arrested Peter Mukerjea? Need they have asked this question in the first place? They could have done some basic arithmetic. After accepting the investigation, the CBI had taken fifty-two days to come to a point when they could arrest Peter. Fair enough. But then why the insistence that

I should have made my team arrest Peter in the first fourteen days? And why this insinuation that I had given him a clean chit merely because the arrest was not effected in the first fourteen days? Did they ask the CBI why it had taken them so long to arrest Peter?

They should have done some more counting. When I was kicked upstairs, we had completed just fourteen days of investigation but still covered substantial ground. All the three accused who were directly involved in the offence were in our custody. Almost all the crucial witnesses were traced and were being questioned. The financial angle was being investigated. Peter who was abroad on the day of the murder, was being called to the police station every day and confronted with what the others had to say. And no one had given him a clean chit! Quite the contrary! DCP Choudhary had given written instructions to the team on 2 September 2015 that Peter Mukerjea should be viewed as a suspect and an accused, and his role in the conspiracy should be probed; Indrani and Shyamwar should also be interrogated and the truth about Peter's complicity should be investigated. On 5 September 2015, the team was instructed that in view of the irregular financial dealings of Peter Mukerjea, his relationship with Sheena and Indrani should be investigated.

After my removal, the investigation proceeded under the changed guard of the Mumbai police for three weeks. For the answers as to why Peter was not arrested in these three weeks, they would have to confront the DGP and the ACS who had said that no new arrests were warranted! ACS Bakshi had made this statement to the press, drawing on DGP Sanjeev Dayal's report which in turn was based on the CP's assessment. Bakshi had made a slew of statements: the investigation was almost completed by the local police; all the accused were in judicial custody and, therefore, no further questioning of the accused would be possible; it was felt that no new arrests were warranted; it was the CBI who would now go deep and investigate the loose threads, along with the financial angle.

But the media clumped even those three weeks with the fourteen days under my tenure and asked, 'Why did *you* not arrest Peter when the CBI had done it!'

On 8 August 2016, I flew down to Delhi as I was called by the CBI in connection with the Sheena Bora case. During my interaction with the investigating officers, I gave them my perspective on all the facts of the case that had come to light during my tenure and also the entire chronological sequence in detail.

I returned from Delhi and got busy with my work. With the passage of time, I was trying hard to brush away the painful thoughts about the baseless aspersions cast on me. However, they were stubborn, like thorns that had refused to leave with the crown. Something was amiss. Something was not quite tallying. It was not the transfer on promotion. It was the missing phone call from the Chief Minister that I wanted to know about. I began to get a strong feeling that I had to meet the CM and ask him what it was that he had found wrong in my actions. What was the real reason? I remembered his open countenance when I had met him soon after his swearing-in. I had asked him frankly if he wanted me to vacate the post of CP for him to depute a person of his choice. And his equally frank reply, accompanied by the reassuring warmth, was something I had carried in my heart all through as I continued with my work. I must meet the CM one-on-one and before the Ganapati festivities began on 4 September 2016! I said to myself and sought an appointment. I was given the opportunity and we met. He was extremely cordial. I explained to him all that was bothering me about the allegations that I was facing in the Sheena Bora probe and how baseless they were. I asked him what he had found objectionable and he said that my transfer before completion of the term had nothing to do with the Sheena Bora case. He said that it was done solely to facilitate Ahmed Javed's posting as Mumbai CP. I understood his predicament. A great weight lifted off my chest. I did not need anything more and I appreciated his forthrightness.

We were nearing the end of October 2016. Diwali was to begin on 26 and end on 1 November. In all its sordid struggle, the city glittered with more vengeance, its residents resolutely lighting as many lamps as they could to dispel evil and darkness. I was also eager to usher in positivity back into my life. Just then some news reports appeared to say that I along with two other officers of the Mumbai police were being questioned by the CBI in the Sheena Bora case. The queries resumed all over again, from the media, friends, family, colleagues and anxious retired seniors! I was enlightening the querists to the best of my ability, least prepared for the battle of justice that I would have to wage shortly as Maharashtra celebrated Narak Chaturdashi to commemorate Lord Krishna's victory over demon Narakasura! Justice, not just for Sheena Bora but also for myself! It began when the Chief Minister's interview was telecast on a news channel that day – 29 October 2016 – which was a Saturday. The story was immediately picked up by different channels who began running it repeatedly. They hinted and implied that the CM had said that through my briefings, I had misled him for a long time, right until the probe was handed over to the CBI, and given Peter Mukerjea a clean chit! I couldn't believe my eyes and ears! I felt I had to ask the CM if this is what he had felt! I had never told him that Peter Mukerjea was not under our scanner. For the first time ever I wrote him a very long text message and poured my heart out:

> Good evening, Sir.
>
> Your interview to Times Now really shocked me. When I met you just before Ganpati, you had informed me that the reason for my transfer had nothing to do with the Sheena Bora case and was done solely to facilitate Mr. Ahmed Javed's posting as CP M'bai. But today aspersions have been cast by you on my role in the

probe, etc. After putting in close to 36 yrs of selfless service, this is grossly unfair, unjust and undeserving!! My interest as CP in Criminal investigations was never questioned in the sensational Esther Anuhya or the serial molestor cases of the western suburbs to name just a few. It is also pertinent to note that the Sheena Bora case which was undetected for 3 yrs. was unearthed by my team. If we wanted to shield them, then why would we have detected the case in the first place?! Also, I along with my team had this detection for only 12 days before I was promoted and transferred. Peter Mukerjea's role and financial transactions were being parallelly probed in the case. The CBI took 90 days to bring out Peter Mukerjea's role and then arrest him!! This is sad, unfair and unjust to me and the Mumbai Police team which detected this buried case.

I apologise for this long SMS – but Sir please try to understand my frustration, helplessness and angst at what is happening after putting in 36 yrs of dedicated and selfless service. Now I really wonder as to whether it was worth it!!

My sincere apologies again.

Regards. Happy Deepavali.
Rakesh Maria.

I am quoting verbatim the text messages the CM and I exchanged that day, and I must confess that I am doing it not without thinking a great deal about it.

First of all, I wondered if I should disclose the SMSes at all. Not just the SMSes, even the discussion in the meeting which I had sought with him to explain my position to him, and to seek his clarification. From the explanation he had given me, it seemed that he too was struggling to deal with a situation that was far from comfortable for him. By divulging these details, do I want to make it even more embarrassing for him? That had never been my intention, or I wouldn't have held my silence patiently for so long. I had been hoping that the misunderstanding would somehow be cleared and my honour redeemed, but in vain.

And now what is my remedy? Do I have to suffer this ignominy silently when it was reinforcing people's belief against me? I had to speak up, and if so, was there any other way, short of disclosing the discussion and the SMSes, to brush away the cobwebs of lies and misinformation woven around my role in the Sheena Bora murder investigation? Could I do it by paraphrasing the messages, by giving just the gist? By making some kind of veiled references which would hide the source? But then, such an exercise would raise more questions. Rewording could lend the messages shades of meaning quite unintended! I could be accused of suppressing the truth if I omitted some words. I could be accused of twisting the facts, the last thing I wanted to do. Rephrasing his messages my way could result in putting words in the CMs mouth and that could be unfair. So I decided, let our words speak for themselves! There was no other way to clear the air, however unsavoury it may seem!

The message was sent on 29 October 2016 at 06:29 p.m. I did not realise then that in my anxiety coupled with anguish, I had made a couple of mistakes in my message. Figure 12 (days) should have been 14 and 90 should have been 52. I had just shot off the message, worried that the CM may not respond at all. But he did respond on the same day at 07:32 p.m.:

> I think I have not casted any aspersions on u.. pls go through the interview and not the headline.
>
> The only thing I have said I was briefed that peter has nothing to do with this which later CBI discovered that he was also involved.
>
> I said that yes objections were raised why commissioner is taking so much of interest but mr. Maria is known to take interest in criminal investigation.
>
> I think pls go through my interview what I have said. Not how they are showing.
>
> My Diwali wishes to you.

I read and re-read the reply. I realised that I again needed to explain a few more things. I must correct what was factually wrong! I must. So I wrote back to him immediately:

> Thank you very much, Sir.
>
> Even during the 12 days that I was associated with the case, I have categorically stated that Peter's role is being probed and we are investigating all angles. I, or for that matter, the team had never given Peter a clean chit. Also, Sir, I had never briefed you that Peter is not involved!! The CBI took 90 days to fix his role and arrest Peter. Sir, do you not think that it is unfair to blame the investigating team under me which detected such a sensational and hidden case and had this investigation for only 12 days?! I had never ever met or spoken with Peter ever in my life till I questioned him in the presence of Jt CP (l&o), DCP Zone9, ACP, SrPI, other PIs, etc at PStn Khar on Sept 7th'15 night. I was transferred the next morning.
>
> My sincere apologies, Sir, for this SMS communication--but, my reputation and professionalism are being questioned. And after 36 yrs of service this is only what an officer has!!
>
> Thank you again, Sir.
>
> Regards.
> Rakesh Maria.

The CM replied to this on 30 October at 12:22 a.m.:

> Will look into it to have it properly communicated.

I was relieved and replied immediately:

> Thank you very much, Sir. This means a lot to me and I would be really obliged if the record is set straight at the earliest since the media has already started hounding me. My gratitude again. Regards. Rakesh Maria.

To which the CM replied: OK.

But then I had received one more message from the CM the next morning i.e., 30 October at 08:41 a.m., as follows:

> Also wanted to inform you one more thing which happened after yesterdays interview.
>
> If you remember you briefed me on telephone about Sheena bora investigation and you told me that it seems peter did not know all this happened. I don't question your intentions at all because It's quite possible that by that time Peter's role wasn't established so u said that and that is why after the interview Megha Prasad asked me repeatedly that who briefed you about the case I didn't tell her because I knew they will misuse it.

I was glad that he had asked me this question. Sometimes we may feel that we have communicated something well, but the recipient may labour under some impressions, gathered from various inputs, which makes him see the events in a different hue. And with the passage of time, the exact sequence is lost and just some broad distorted facts stand out. I also appreciated his anxiety to protect his officers who had briefed him, as the press does tend to take statements out of context and starts witch hunts. However, I was also facing a strange predicament and had no choice but to clarify further. So I replied again at 9:47:

> Good morning, Sir.
>
> Right through the 12 days that the investigation was on, with me as CP, I had never ever said that Peter Mukerjea was not involved or gave him a clean chit.
>
> We had spoken on the phone maybe a week or 8/9 days into the investigation. Even then I had told you that though in the killing and disposal of the body, Peter was not present, his overall complicity was being probed. That is the reason why Peter was being daily called to the P Stn. In fact, it was at my insistence

> that the Investigating Officer sent a report to the Enforcement Directorate to probe Peter and his financial transactions. The media is now stating that I misled you. Sir, you know I would never do that. During my then briefings to the Press, I have always maintained that Peter's complicity was being probed. So, Sir, where was even the thought of shielding him. As Head of the Police Department, you have justified the role of the Jt. CP (L& O) Deven Bharti giving him a clean chit, but in your interview you said that it was strange that Peter's role was not probed. This is far from the truth as it was during my questioning of Peter that he was asked pinpointed questions about his role in this sordid affair.
>
> I have never misled you as the Press is now stating. This has caused irreparable damage to my professionalism and reputation despite detecting this sensational case and collecting cogent and strong evidence to nail all the accused in the 12 days that the case was under me. Very unfair and unjust!!
>
> Regards.
> Rakesh Maria.

I waited anxiously when the CM replied on 30 October at 12:19 p.m.:

> I have just gone through press report. Nobody has spoken to me. I will speak to PTI today.

At last I had been able to present the correct position to him and he seemed to have understood. I was relieved. I replied immediately:

> Thank you and obliged, Sir.

I kept thinking hard. Was it a failure of communication? Of communication skills? On whose part? Mine or the CM's? Or the failure of the persons who were briefing him on the work of the police department – the senior officials who bridge the gap between the CM and the Police Department to make it function smoothly? I began wondering if all this could have been avoided if I had proactively kept in touch with the CM on a daily basis. I should have had a better rapport. There was no use just rushing to the streets and to police stations and doing your job if simultaneously you did not convey to the CM why you had done it and how it was the right thing to do? I should have met him more frequently, even if he did not call me. Something which I never would do, as I strictly followed protocol. I always went through the ACS or the Principal Secretary if I had to meet him. He was a busy functionary, not to be disturbed unless it was an emergency, I felt. Was I wrong? I am not a very outgoing person. Some have even told me that my reticence and shyness builds a wall around me that can easily be mistaken for snobbishness. And when I trust somebody, I get too trusting. That has been the refrain of my family and close friends all throughout and I have been able to do nothing about it. Is that what has worked against me in this matter?

The next day's newspapers and e-papers screamed that as per the CM, I had hidden Peter's involvement and misled him.

'HIDING PETER'S INVOLVEMENT LED TO MARIA'S OUSTER: CM.' This was the heading in the *Mumbai Mirror* for a report which said:

> Senior IPS Officer Rakesh Maria lost his job as the police chief of Mumbai because he misled Chief Minister Devendra Fadnavis on the role of former media honcho Peter Mukerjea in the Sheena Bora case. Responding to a question on Maria's abrupt transfer, the chief minister on Saturday told the media that the top cop initially kept telling him that the police didn't see any involvement of Peter in the murder case of 2012, which was cracked in August 2015. However, after the CBI took over the case, the CM said, the agency claimed that Peter was a part of the conspiracy. 'Questions

> were then raised as to why this was not established when Mumbai police handled the case,' said Fadnavis.

The heading in *The Times of India* was: COPS MISLED ME ON PETER MUKERJEA'S ROLE IN SHEENA MURDER: FADNAVIS. The report quoted the CM as saying:

> Fadnavis said, 'Generally Mumbai police are very efficient, but at that time I was wrongly briefed that Peter had no role to play in the case. And after the case was transferred to the CBI, they indicted Peter.'

I anxiously waited for something to appear in the papers as the CM had promised me. I trusted him and felt that he would definitely undo the damage. Apparently, he had given an interview to the PTI on 31 October, the report of which appeared on 1 November 2016. A sample of this also appeared in the *Economic Times* of 1 November 2016:

> Over a year after Rakesh Maria was removed as Mumbai police chief, reportedly for taking 'too much interest' in the Sheena Bora murder case, Chief Minister Devendra Fadnavis today said the high-profile officer was 'promoted' a bit early to 'avoid controversies'.
>
> 'There were 2-3 controversies created at that time. One was about Lalit Modi, where Maria gave a clarification and we accepted it. Secondly, when he was taking a keen interest in the Sheena Bora investigation, questions were raised why is a CP taking so much interest. But Maria is known to have a keen interest in criminal investigation. So it was quite possible that he was taking interest out of that nature of his,' Fadnavis told PTI. He said that Maria was not transferred but promoted and that there was nothing unusual in a Commissioner of Police being promoted a few weeks earlier than scheduled. 'Today, if I say that I knew that the Sheena Bora investigation was not going correctly and that is why I transferred him, it will be an afterthought. But yes,

> due to these controversies that were happening, I thought that I will promote him a little early to put an end to controversies,' he said. Fadnavis said, unexpectedly, a fresh controversy erupted after his promotion which made him give Maria the permission to 'supervise' the investigation.
>
> 'I think apart from this case, Maria had an excellent record. We should give him benefit of doubt but it is also true that till the case was transferred to CBI, I was always briefed that Peter's direct involvement (in the murder) is not seen.
>
> 'It is quite possible that by the time it (the case) was with Mumbai police they could not track it. I am not casting aspersions on anyone, but I was just surprised at the briefing that I received after Peter was arrested,' Fadnavis said.
>
> Fadnavis also said the state government has not received any official communication from the CBI about any officer's interrogation or direct or indirect connection with any accused in the case. Maria and two other senior Maharashtra police officers were recently examined by the CBI officials as they were part of the initial probe team which investigated the Sheena Bora murder case and arrested her mother Indrani Mukerjea. Besides Maria, the CBI also questioned Deven Bharti, Joint Commissioner (Law and Order) and Satya Narayan Choudhary, Deputy Commissioner of Police (Zone-X). A controversy had erupted in June last year after some TV news channels showed photographs of Maria with former IPL boss Lalit Modi in London. Modi faces charges of financial irregularities and money laundering in India. After Fadnavis demanded an explanation, Maria issued a statement saying that he had met the former IPL Commissioner at the insistence of the latter's lawyer in London in 2014.

Clearly, the CM had tried to set the record right, in his own way, but had not quite succeeded! If the news report was correct, the reason to promote me a bit early was just to put an end to 'two-three' controversies! Tainted IPL Commissioner Lalit Modi meeting me in London was one and my keen interest in Sheena Bora case was the other. For the former, my explanation had been accepted. For the latter, my explanation was not asked but my 'nature' by which I am known to take a keen interest in criminal investigations was taken as a possible reason, and sort of accepted. Which was the third controversy? The one that erupted as soon as I was promoted a bit early and in the midst of the investigation. So I could not be blamed for its eruption. In fact, the CM acknowledged that it was unexpected. Which means that neither he nor his advisors expected that there would be a big outcry! He candidly accepted that it was this unexpected controversy that led to the somersault of giving me the 'permission' to 'supervise' the investigation.

What came next in the interview hardly furthered the object of setting the record right. To say that apart from the Sheena Bora case I had an excellent record sounded like a left-handed compliment! That I should be given the benefit of the doubt also meant that there was a doubt! Then came the categorical statement that right till the case was transferred to the CBI, the CM was always briefed that Peter's direct involvement in the murder was not seen! He attributed it to the possibility that the Mumbai police had been unable to track Peter's involvement, and therefore his surprise at the CBI arresting Peter and the briefing he had received thereafter!

With all this, I was not only back to square one, one more question was added to all the unanswered questions that I had been enumerating. I had briefed the CM only once, in the early stages of the investigation, when I had told him that Peter was not present at the time of the murder, but his overall complicity was being probed and he was being called to the police station daily. I had never discussed the Sheena Bora case with the CM or any of the Mantralaya tsars thereafter. And I had never given Peter Mukerjea a clean chit. The CM, however, was categorical that all through he was being briefed that Peter was innocent. Was somebody deliberately creating this impression all throughout?

Was that somebody trying to pass it off as my assessment when I was the CP? And was that someone playing the same tune until the CM had decided to hand over the investigation to the CBI? And that is why the CM was carrying an impression that I too had given a clean chit to Peter? If so, who was or were those persons?

And how do I salvage my reputation? How do I tell people that I had not misled the CM?

I felt that I must ask for official permission to clear my reputation and sent a detailed demi-official letter to the ACS (Home), on the same day setting out how I had been completely misunderstood, how my reputation had been damaged and how I needed to take steps to clear it.

I began my letter thus:

> In the twilight of my service as a dedicated policeman, this Dipawali has brought nothing but darkness which cannot be dispelled until I speak up, as I do not feel anyone else will step in to prevent further damage to my reputation. Hence I write to you this rather unusual request letter – a request to grant me permission to speak to the Media.
>
> In the recent media reports casting scandalous and defamatory aspersions on my role in the investigation of the Sheena Bora Murder case, damning doubts have been raised on my integrity and professional competence as a police officer and a public servant. My wife and I have been flooded with queries – by calls and messages – from friends, relatives, colleagues, seniors in the Service and acquaintances from all over the world. The agony of having to give them explanations for mistakes and crimes not committed, so that my reputation does not get sullied in their eyes, cannot be expressed in words.
>
> In the best tradition of the Indian Police Service, I have always depended on the State to protect me from malicious and irresponsible Media campaigns. I have never reacted to Media reports, however provocative they may be, so as not to put my

> Government into difficulties. However, this time the Media reports have transgressed all limits and gone to the extent of insinuating that I misled the Honourable Chief Minister through my briefings vis-a-vis the role of accused Peter Mukerjea. This serious allegation is based on complete falsehood. If allowed to go unrefuted, it will not just tarnish my image, it will do injustice to the Hon. Chief Minister whose interview is being distorted and misinterpreted by the Media Reports if only to tarnish my image. The Media reports are trying to hint that for a long time, right until the probe was handed over to the CBI, I was misleading the Hon. Chief Minister through my briefings saying that Peter Mukerjea was not directly involved with the crime. They also say that the minute the CBI took up the case, the first thing they did was arrest Peter Mukerjea, which meant that I was shielding Peter and deliberately not allowing his role to get established. All these reports are malicious, unfounded and absolutely libellous. They are harming the very dignity, prestige and credibility of the office of the Commissioner of Police of Mumbai.

I then traced out the events right since the registration of the offence in the correct chronological order so that I could give a clear perspective to explain my actions and that of the investigating team. I closed the letter by sharing the suffering that my family and I had been undergoing:

> The trauma and the humiliation which I and my family are being subjected to is terrible and I cannot find words to express how outraged and hurt we feel. With these insinuations and aspersions cast on my professionalism and integrity by the Media, I feel as if the last vestige of my respectability and honour has been torn to shreds. Nothing hurts or humiliates one more than to see such malicious falsehood go unrefuted to destroy one's achievements of a lifetime in serving one's country selflessly, without a single thought to one's own security and safety.
>
> I have been a loyal officer of the Indian Police Service and I have never ever questioned the prerogative of the State

> Government to post me wherever they pleased. I have never shirked my responsibilities. Whenever called upon to take up a task in the service of the nation, I have risen to the occasion and done my best without demur. It is the first time in my 35 years of service that I am being accused of misleading my Chief Minister. This is an allegation I find hard to keep silent about, simply because I have not done it nor would I even dream of doing it. In such circumstances, I need to defend my honour and reputation and, therefore, I request you to grant me permission to address the Media on these issues to meet each and every allegation squarely, for I have nothing to hide and my conscience is clear.

However, I received no reply to the letter.

31 January 2017 was the day I would retire. Just three months to go. Was I prepared for the day? In a way, yes. I had been preparing for it much before I became the Commissioner. I knew that with all the mad passion I had for police work, I would be like a fish out of water the day I retire. Without much ado, I had been counselling myself and thinking of the things I had wanted to do and the things I had missed out on in the last thirty-six years. One of them was to 'just chill out' as my sons would say. 'Just chill, Pop!' they would say to me whenever they would find me biting my lower lip in deep contemplation and not saying a word. It was a regular feature and they knew it meant that I was planning some major moves for some detection or the other. And for that 'chilling', I just needed a quiet nook with my books and my music, a legacy I had inherited from my father and from some discerning friends and mentors who had introduced me to the different genres of Western and Hindustani classical music.

I also needed to give time to Preeti who had been waiting patiently all these years, handling everything alone so that I could do my duty unwaveringly. Sports and fitness was yet another passion which would keep me going.

Would I work again? I would give it a thought later – after I had 'chilled' to my heart's content. I would definitely like to do some good work connected with sports and youth.

And there was something more. I would write about my experiences. My story! Because I was one of the chosen few who got to do the work they want to do. By the grace of God, I was given extensive opportunity to detect challenging crimes and see the bad guys behind bars – my dream job. And to do it, I was also placed in key posts in the best police force east of Suez – the force that had legendary talent in its detection skills. Some naysayers might say that this reputation is a thing of the past. I would disagree. I still am of the firm opinion that given the constraints under which we operate and the challenges we face on a daily basis, Mumbai police is still the best police force east of Suez or for that matter, anywhere in the world!

Since childhood, a staple diet of detective stories and crime fiction was the biggest sustenance for the aspiring cop in me. In the process of gathering interesting experiences as I went about doing my job, somewhere down the line the cherished hope of telling my own story became a distinct possibility. I felt that the reader would definitely find it interesting! However, the trials and tribulations of the past few years, and particularly towards the fag end of my career made me think it over.

Like any policeman, the last thing I have ever wanted is to become controversial. That is how it is with policemen, unlike politicians or celebrities who may thrive on controversies. If I came into the limelight, it was only because I was given assignments that attracted the limelight. The limelight was not of my making. If I had attracted controversy, it was just for doing my job, and entirely unintended. Even then, at the end of my career, I was not only labelled controversial, but I was also sent packing unceremoniously from a prestigious post because of the label, as per one explanation.

Against this background, penning my memoirs wouldn't have

meant narrating just interesting whodunnits and describing nail-biting chases. It would amount to writing your version of a life about which you have kept quiet for so long. Would you do it? If you don't state your truth, it would amount to accepting other people's versions even if they are based on misconceptions, distortions, lack of understanding and even false propaganda. So it is time one said it. It is said that public memory is short, but that is no consolation to someone whose image has been tarnished with baseless allegations. In the age of the internet, search engines will not let people forget easily, nor will falsehood be allowed to die a natural death. All versions will coexist in different forms. It will be for the reader to sift facts and separate the grain from the chaff. Provided he or she cares and has the time. Otherwise, Rakesh Maria might remain the Mumbai Commissioner who had misled the Chief Minister and shielded Peter Mukerjea. A man who had taken undue interest in an ordinary murder probe and visited the police station daily which is not what Commissioners do under any circumstances! And he was the same controversial Commissioner who had walked the streets to supervise the security arrangements for Yakub Memon's funeral because he was publicity hungry!

Three months passed by in no time. With the passing of each day, the resolve to write my story got firmer and I began looking forward to the day of retirement – 31 January 2017. The press was eager to know how I was dealing with the approaching farewell and my plans for the future. I was much more relaxed now and felt there was no reason why I should not satisfy their curiosity. Of course, besides asking for my plans for the future, they also wanted to know about the 'controversial' aspect of my career and I had to take it in my stride. Do you 'regret' your handling of the Sheena Bora case? The answer came easily. The Police Commissioner's post was not a showpiece. He is not meant for cutting ribbons, inaugurations and Page 3 events. His job profile includes prevention, detection and investigation of serious crimes and maintenance of law and order. That was my understanding of it.

The day finally arrived to bid farewell to the job that I had loved so much. The phone kept ringing as some thoughtful folks made it a point to let me know that they were aware that I was moving on and that their best wishes were with me. Some close friends and colleagues called on me to convey their best wishes. Some sent flowers, others chocolates. All of it was deeply touching.

The media also wanted to capture the moment of my exit and arrived in full strength. As I was chatting with them, I realised that I was feeling unusually light and calm! Getting old is mandatory, but feeling old is optional! I quipped amidst some banter and there was laughter all around. The Sheena Bora case had to crop up. 'Transfer and postings are the prerogatives of the government. There is no ill feeling at all,' I assured them and reiterated that I did not regret the way I had handled the case. I meant every word of it. I acknowledged that the CBI had done an outstanding job and added that my only regret was that the Mumbai police had not received the appreciation they deserved for their sincere hard work. It was their work that had brought to light the serious crime – a murder suppressed for three long years by the accused who were influential people. That was the only regret I had in the Sheena Bora case, I told them.

Someone asked an interesting question. Regrets of not being able to crack any case? Offhand I remembered the Lalita Pinge murder case in Dadar, Shivaji Park, where I still felt that something more could have been done. It was not a high profile case, but it mattered to me as much as the Sheena Bora case. It had remained undetected, and for me, that was a regret. Another was the Narendra Dabholkar murder case where we were on the right trail of the Sanatan Sanstha, but the ballistic report threw us off the track!

As the day ended, I bid goodbye to the staff of the DG Home Guards and Civil Defence who had welcomed me in that office on my sudden arrival in their midst on that bizarre day in September 2015 and looked after me with warmth in preparation for this day. Farewells and partings are never easy, but I managed.

To round off the day, Preeti had planned a quiet early dinner at the Taj and we had invited Poonam, my sister, to join us. Come to think of it, it was retirement not just for me. When a cop retires, his entire family retires from the service which they have joined without their knowledge. The Maria family was retiring that day from the thankless honorary posts that they had been manning so valiantly for more than three decades! Nonstop, with no promotions and without medals, only to give me complete freedom to concentrate on my work and to give me moral support when the going was tough. A charming addition to the quiet dinner party was Deeksha, our vivacious daughter-in-law. She had threatened long ago that she would be flying down from New York to celebrate my last day in office. She had carried out the threat and filled the air with sparkling energy that only a daughter can bring.

Armed with these three precious friends, I stepped out on to the pavement, a free man. The official car was discharged for good. Soon we were at the Kala Ghoda signal and then winding our way in our own car to the Taj. To the serene ambience of the Sea Lounge, like pucca Bombayites who want to pamper themselves with a well-deserved five-star treat! And among them a Bandra Boy, who at sixty and despite a lot of 'exposure' to international cuisine, continues to get bamboozled by mysterious 'phoren' menus! He must have in them his saviours like keema-pav and bhelpuri to enjoy the melodious nostalgia drifting out of a perfectly tuned Steinbach piano.

35

This Is Not the End

The last reel hums towards its end. The credits have not yet started rolling up the screen. The audience is not yet thinking of the journey back home. It wants the answer to a pointed question.

'How would you sum it all?'

'Overall, satisfying!' I say, after a little bit of thought.

'Despite all that you have had to go through, this past couple of years?' Their eyes pierced through the darkness to get to the bottom of my heart.

'That is why I said, *overall* satisfying,' I explain.

'Go on!' They say, crushing the popcorn tubs and the empty paper bags soaked with oil from the samosas. They have a right to know.

'Let me put it this way. When I take an overall view of the last thirty-six years, I cannot complain. I had no background in the police Service, or in any administrative Service. Still, I had dared to opt for the IPS as my only choice. Not only did I get into the Service, but it also gave me opportunities to do what I liked and enjoyed doing the most – detection. I was put in the right place at the right time under super-duper seniors who spotted the spark in me. Time and again I was pulled out and put in charge of demanding and complex detections where I could rise to the challenge and lived up to expectations. Under the regimes of different political parties. And then came the most humbling moment, the crowning glory. I was made the Commissioner of Police of Mumbai city, one of the most prestigious and coveted posts for an Indian cop. I could serve my country for thirty-six years, of which almost twenty-nine years I could devote to the city that made me!'

'Don't tell us you are suddenly turning into a saint. What about those few years when you were banished to the wilderness? The inquiries? The unfair allegations? A plethora of aspersions! Smear campaigns!'

'Yes, there were those disturbing patches. But look at them from a distance as I do now, and they turn out to be just a few dark linings by and large in a silver cloud.' I assure them. 'And the biggest reward is the recognition I have received from all of you! Even now, when I am no longer in Service, I have people walking up to me, just to greet me. Some remind me how I had helped them years ago. Some are perfect strangers who just want to say hello. I have airline pilots and crew saying how happy they are to be flying me, and youngsters wanting to click pictures with me. All this adulation and love, only because of my job and my work. It is immensely humbling and satisfying!'

'If you get a chance to choose your career again what would you do?' They ask.

Would I choose something else to do? Not become a cop? I really think hard as they look at the dregs of their drinks in the plastic bottles and paper cups.

'No, I can't think of myself as anything else!' I confess.

'If you get a chance to rewind and reshoot, what would you do differently?'

'Nothing really!' I say.

'Would you still stick your neck out and walk the streets with your cane to check bandobasts and push back rioters? Interrogate the accused and visit police stations even when you don't have to?

And get snubbed for taking undue interest, and seeking publicity?'

'A ship in port is safe, but that is not what ships are built for!' I offer a quote that explains what I have to say. They are a smart audience. Not the numbskulls that some people take them to be. They even turn the tide when they want to.

'Tell us honestly, do you seek the limelight? Films have been made with you as their central character.'

'That is destiny. I am not a bonehead to believe that it was because of me. It was because of the work that I was allowed to do. If some other officer had been entrusted with those assignments, he would have been the leading figure in those films!'

'You mean there is no scope for improvement? You think you are perfect? You will not do anything differently?' They ask and I sense concern in the tone.

'You tell me how it should be! You have seen it all now,' I implore.

'Take some lessons in communication skills, maybe? Mix around. Talk more. Circulate. Not good to have such a workaholic one track mind which gets all cooped up. Shake a leg. Laugh loudly. Enjoy! Play Holi and have fun. Not just basketball and taekwondo. Have some bhel on Juhu Chowpatty. Pau bhaji in Khau Galli. Try a little beer or wine if you like. At least have some tea or coffee? Enough of that head boy stuff from St Andrew's. That makes you a pain in the neck sometimes. Ask your wife. Ask your siblings. Or your buddies,' they look at me in despair as I nod.

'Point well taken,' I agree.

'And what do you think is the biggest challenge for future detectives in the police force?' They put forth the next query. 'We know you can speak for three hours on this subject, but we don't have so much time. We have to get up early and rush to work tomorrow. Thirty seconds may be?'

'The biggest challenge? I shudder to think how our boys will conduct future probes if the media doesn't become responsible and exercise caution to protect our investigations.' That's the first thought that comes to my mind.

'What do you mean? Had it not been for the media, we would not know so many things. Even you would not have known half the things that happened to you, with all your great sleuthing skills, had it not been for those media reports.'

'True, but give me a couple of minutes to explain. The media does play a big role in unearthing the truth and taking it to the people. But when it comes to the crime beat and national security issues, investigative journalism is a dangerous game and needs some boundaries. The temptation to start a game of one-upmanship with the police and "breaking news" can be detrimental to book the crooks. There was a time when the senior-most journalists used to be put on the crime beat. They had responsible editors who used to exercise great caution. They kept a restraining hand on the shoulders of overenthusiastic colleagues to prevent them from crossing limits. Unfortunately, it is no longer so. The crime beat is left to rookies who have no understanding of the legal processes. The way investigations and criminal trials are to be conducted – how evidence is to be collected, recorded and presented before the court. When I joined the police force, we still had journalists who knew their responsibility while covering crime investigations. That species is now on its way to extinction. It makes me feel sorry for the Gen-next police detectives and the coming generations.'

'So you want to put fetters on the Fourth Estate, do you?'

'Nobody dares say, for the fear of being labelled "undemocratic" and "anti-freedom of speech". Well, the media does shape the society's acceptance of its rulers and administrators which include the judiciary and the police. They can make, mar or break any image. All that can be done is to exhort them, in the name of unfettered freedom of the press, to exercise "self-regulation".

That is why the task of modern-day police detectives is getting even more difficult. Ideally, the investigating officers can just keep mum and not utter a word, but such an approach antagonises the media and makes them suspicious. They construe your silence as suppression and in no time the police detectives get discredited. The gravest danger is that the media can easily be used or manipulated by the culprits to further their own agendas. The more influential and affluent the culprits, the more their power to inflict that damage.'

'Which one was the toughest case to crack? The most challenging and demanding?'

'Difficult to single one out. There is the famous saying: "The law is a jealous mistress." Equally true of detection of crime, when you have the passion for it! It is a very demanding mistress and every moment is challenging.'

'Any regrets?'

'The couple of cases that remained undetected. Even now I keep ruminating over what more I could have done.'

'Now what about a few acknowledgements? Don't take aeons and aeons over it! We have to take the cars out of the parking lot! We have to catch rickshaws! Buses! You don't know how difficult it is!'

'I want to thank each and every policeman who worked under me and gave me support in the most challenging of times. It was they who made me a leader. Without their contribution, I would be nothing. I am also grateful to the colleagues in my detection teams who stood by me through thick and thin, and the seniors who were always around to mentor and cheer me up when I was down in the dumps. I could not have achieved anything, had it not been for the constables, ASIs, SIs, APIs, PIs, ACPs, DCPs, Additional CPs and all the branches of the Force, right from the Special Branch to the Local Arms Division to the Control Room to ...!' I am flustered by the exercise to complete it within ten seconds. Now I know why they cry and shed tears at the Academy or Filmfare Awards when they have to do this.

'So you once again forget your spouse and the kids?'

'I know I can always take them for granted.' I say confidently.

'Don't forget to thank your detractors! In our Marathi, there is a saying by the great Tukaram, "*Nindakaache ghar asaave shejaari*!"' (Your detractors should be your neighbours!)

'Yes, I know. Even Kabir said, "*Nindak niyare rakhiye, aangan kuti chavay; Bin pani, sabun bina, nirmal kare subhay!*" My mother used to quote it. Keep your critics close to you, and you shall be cleansed without water and soap!'

'That is why the State housed you in colonies of government servants! They knew what was good for you. And that is why the wise among you want to continue in those houses forever, even after retirement.' They snigger.

'Ok. I see the point! I am grateful to all my detractors for keeping my feet planted on *terra firma* and my head way below the clouds.'

'We notice that you have not adopted the latest trend of using bloopers to run in the background for credits.'

'There is no need to. They have been retained in the film itself, all candid shots and all takes and retakes. Lots of bloopers there for all to enjoy!'

'Oh yes! True, true,' their eyes twinkle as the lights start slowly coming on and they shuffle to their feet.

'How are you going to end it, Maria? Just with "The End" or "The Beginning" or with "And they lived happily ever after…."?' The show-goers are sticklers for perfection and lovable eternal optimists. For them, all that begins well must end well.

'How do you like, *"Yeh toh sirf trailer thaa, jaani! Picture abhi baki hai!"*' (This was just the trailer, sweetheart! The film is still to come!) I ask them. They are seasoned veterans and will tell me precisely what will work.

'Oh, that sounds perfect. That is how it should be!' they laugh. 'See you soon then! And just one confirmation, please. If you take rebirth, would you want to be back in khaki, as a Mumbai cop? That's final?'

'Yes, sir, back at your service.'

And the packed audience of Mumbaikars trail out of the subconscious theatre to pour out into the streets of the City of Dreams.